# IN THE RING
## WITH
# JACK DEMPSEY

### PART I: THE MAKING OF A CHAMPION

Adam J. Pollack

**Win By KO Publications**
IOWA CITY

# In the Ring With Jack Dempsey
## Part I: The Making of a Champion

### Adam J. Pollack

(ISBN-13): 978-1-949783-01-8

(softcover: 50# acid-free alkaline paper)

Includes footnotes and index.

© 2020 by Adam J. Pollack. All Rights Reserved.

*No part of this book may be reproduced, or transmitted in any form or by any means, graphic, electronic or mechanical, including photocopying, recording, taping, or by any information storage retrieval system without the written permission of Adam J. Pollack.*

Cover design by Adam J. Pollack and Gwyn Snider ©

Front cover photo colorization by Jeremy Willett ©

Manufactured in the United States of America.

Win By KO Publications
Iowa City, Iowa
winbykopublications.com

# Contents

| | |
|---|---|
| Preface | 4 |
| 1. A Poor But Hard-Working Lad | 5 |
| 2. A Career Begins | 17 |
| 3. On the Road Again | 26 |
| 4. Improvement and Intermountain Region Recognition | 41 |
| 5. New York Tests | 63 |
| 6. Home Zone Again | 74 |
| 7. A Turn For the Worst | 89 |
| 8. West Coast Warrior | 99 |
| 9. West Coast Warrior Part II: Relationships End and a New One Begins | 118 |
| 10. West Coast Warrior Part III: The Start of Real Recognition | 146 |
| 11. Nationally Recognized Contender | 164 |
| 12. A Near Fight | 191 |
| 13. The Next Best | 207 |
| 14. Establishing Dominance | 237 |
| 15. Number One | 259 |
| 16. Needing a Man Who Can Take It | 283 |
| 17. A Glitch at the Benefit | 291 |
| 18. Dominance Re-Affirmed | 314 |
| 19. The Color Line in a New Era | 327 |
| 20. Rematches | 334 |
| 21. Sullivan-Style Exhibitions | 359 |
| 22. Championship Preparation | 382 |
| 23. The Heavyweight Championship | 473 |
| Acknowledgments | 553 |
| Index | 554 |

# Preface

To this day, many boxing fans and historians consider Jack Dempsey to be one of the greatest heavyweight champions of all time. Certainly, he was one of the most entertaining and exciting to watch. His dominance and style made him a fan favorite. His aggression, fast pace, speed, and two-fisted punching power combined with fast feet and elusive head-movement certainly have inspired awe throughout the generations. In his prime, he stood about 6'1½" and weighed around 190 pounds, but was so powerful that he could knock out much bigger men. Many years later, champion Mike Tyson compared himself with Dempsey, with good reason. Both were young heavyweights with exciting, ferocious styles, with explosive power, who injected life into the sport.

At the time, Dempsey's style often was compared with John L. Sullivan, who had made boxing a highly lucrative financial endeavor. It isn't surprising that fans were craving another champion who fought like Sullivan, who aggressively thrust himself into the fray with amazing speed and tremendous power, all while maintaining a great pace. Such a style had made boxing one of the two most popular sports in the United States (baseball being the other one). In terms of individual economic success over the course of his career, no other sports figure even came close to Dempsey.

Like Sullivan, Dempsey took boxing to new heights of popularity and financial renumeration. Dempsey inspired such awe that eventually he became the first fighter whose gates drew over one million and even two million dollars, astronomical for the 1920s, shattering all prior records. His overall financial success would not be matched for decades to come. He became a symbol of the Roaring 20s, so much so that in 1998, a U.S. postage stamp was created in his honor. He clearly was one of the most popular sports figures in the entire 20th century.

Of course, like all fighters, there is a story to be told of his rise to the championship; the trials and tribulations Dempsey endured to start, emerge, improve, and obtain top contender status and a title shot. Like many great fighters, Dempsey had to obtain experience and knowledge, to learn, grow, and be developed and marketed in order to become a champion. This is that story, in great detail, as told primarily by those who saw the fights and reported on them at the time.

As with other books in the *In the Ring* series, this book also discusses the context of the times, the color line and race in boxing and society, World War I, and how these topics affected Dempsey and the sport, in addition to how Dempsey's personal and managerial choices and issues affected his life and career.

# CHAPTER 1

# A Poor But Hard-Working Lad

On June 23 or 24, 1895 in Manassa, Colorado, future world heavyweight champion William Harrison Dempsey was born. He allegedly was named after former U.S. President William Harrison, although his grandfather on his father's side also was named William.[1]

When he started boxing in his teens, he took the name Jack, an homage to former world middleweight champion Jack Dempsey, who in the 1880s was known as the "nonpareil," or having no equal. But, for most of his youth, folks called him Harry, after his middle name. Amongst his family, he was known as Harry.

In 1900, Colorado had a population of about 539,700.

Manassa was a Mormon community in Colorado, 7,600 feet above sea level. There was a Mexican community there as well, and Jack even learned a little Spanish. Jack said there were only about 30 - 40 houses in Manassa.

Dempsey's parents, Hiram/Hyrum and Celia/Cecilia Dempsey, arrived in Manassa in the mid-to-late 1880s, coming from Logan County, West Virginia. They converted to the Church of Latter-day Saints and accepted Mormonism, though they were not strict followers, especially his father.

Hiram was a nomad who had a lot of odd jobs throughout his life, including teacher, laborer, mill attendant, and farmhand.

Hiram primarily was of Irish ancestry, with a strain of Choctaw Native American lineage. Although tall, thin, and not an athlete, his father, "Big" William Andrew Dempsey, had been a regional boxing champion in West Virginia, as well as a sheriff.

Celia, as she was known (given maiden name was Mary Smoot), was of Scotch-Irish ancestry, with a trickle of Cherokee lineage.

Dempsey was related to both the Hatfields and the McCoys, two families who were known for their bloody feud in West Virginia, which electrified the country in 1882 and cost close to 20 lives amongst Dempsey's relatives. Hiram was Anse Hatfield's nephew. Jack's mother Celia actually was related to the McCoys. There also was a cousin relationship to Henry Hatfield of West Virginia, who became that state's

---

[1] Earliest church records (1901 1903) listed his birth date as June 24, 1895. In 1920, Dempsey claimed he actually was born on June 23, 1895, rather than June 24, the generally accepted date. On his May 31, 1917 draft registration card and March 22, 1922 passport application he filled out and signed, he listed June 23 as his date of birth. During his career, the June 24 date typically was used, and his last autobiography listed June 24 as his birth date. On his signed 1941-42 World War II military draft registration card, he listed his birthdate as June 24, 1895. *Pittsburgh Daily Post*, February 29, 1920; *New York Daily News*, March 5, 1920; http://cogenweb.com/conejos/cr/bk1d1909.html.

governor in 1912. The feud may have contributed to Dempsey's parents' move West.²

"Pa" Dempsey.
(By Underwood)

The Church of Jesus Christ of Latter-day Saints church-records members-list for 1909 lists Hiram Dempsey as having been born in Logan County, West Virginia on May 4, 1857, making him 38 years old when William Harrison was born. Hiram's parents were William A. Dempsey and Hulda Blair.

Mary P. Dempsey (a.k.a. Celia or Cecilia), Jack's mother, was born on July 12, 1860, also in Logan County, making her three years younger than Hiram, and 34 years of age when William was born, just a couple weeks short of her 35th birthday. Her parents were Chas. (Charles) Smoot and Florence V. Griever.

Hiram and Celia Dempsey had eleven children total. Their oldest child, Don Bernard Dempsey (a.k.a. Bernie), was born in Logan County (just like his parents), on May 15, 1880 (when Hiram was 23 and Mary was 19), making Bernie 15 years

"Ma" Dempsey.
(By Underwood)

older than William. Following Don Bernard were Effie - born July 8, 1881; Lavlet Florence ("Florence") - April 6, 1883; and Estella ("Stella") – April 29, 1885, all born in Logan County, West Virginia. So as of 1885, the Dempseys still were in West Virginia. At the time, John L. Sullivan was the world heavyweight champion.

Alice Dempsey was the first child born in Manassa, Conejos County, Colorado, on July 19, 1887. Joseph H. Dempsey was born on August 5, 1889, making him about six years older than William. Following him were Robert – October 2, 1891 (who allegedly died before Jack was born); John ("Johnny") – April 7, 1893, ninth child William Harrison (a.k.a. Harry, a.k.a. Jack Dempsey) – June 24, 1895, Elsie – August 18, 1897, and Bruce – April 2, 1901, all born in Manassa.³

Great poverty marked the majority of Dempsey's youthful existence, for the family struggled to earn meager wages to support their quite large family. Jack was born in a one-room cabin. They lived in Manassa until he was about 9 years old. He went to Sunday school.

According to Jack, Hiram liked to drink, and had a roving spirit as well as a roving eye (an allusion to his infidelity). He did not follow the tenets of Mormonism. He had a happy-go-lucky disposition though. He rarely stuck

---

² *New York Evening World*, October 25, 1918.
³ http://cogenweb.com/conejos/cr/bk1d1909.html

with the same job for long. That caused a great deal of acrimony amongst his parents. His mother Celia was more ambitious and hardworking, cleaning and scrubbing floors, washing dishes and windows, and cooking.

Young Harry liked to swim, ride horses, and hang around the blacksmith shop. He loved the outdoors.

His much older brother Bernie Dempsey, already a grown man, taught young Harry how to box in Manassa, for Bern was a prizefighter. Boxing was a very popular pastime back then, and it could earn one a few extra dollars. Bern, who never weighed more than 165 pounds, sometimes went by the name Jack Dempsey. Brother Johnny, who was two years older than Harry, also fought, as a lightweight, and he too sometimes used the popular name Jack Dempsey.

In fact, the name was popular enough that other fighters went by the name Jack Dempsey as well, including a semi-local featherweight/lightweight, making it difficult to discern who was whom. For example, on February 26, 1900 in Pueblo, Colorado, about 140 miles from Manassa, Young Corbett of Denver knocked out a Jack Dempsey of Pueblo in the 3rd round, avenging a prior 2nd round knockout loss to Dempsey. "Corbett now holds the 126 pound championship of Colorado."[4]

Allegedly, after young Harry read John L. Sullivan's autobiography, he wanted to be a fighter as well.

In grade school, at Manassa's White House School, a fellow student gave Jack a wad of paper to throw into the school's stove. However, it was wrapped around a bullet. When Jack threw it in and it exploded, the teacher disciplined Jack, who in turn thrashed his playmate.

At about age 7, Harry Dempsey fought Fred Daniels, a fellow schoolboy, whose father during the fight encouraged Fred to bite, but Harry instead immediately knocked him out cold with a blow on the chin. Fighting was a common amusement back then. Most boys learned to use their fists. Harry said he often fought some tough and "mean" Mexican boys as well.

Harry and Elsie were the only ones who finished grammar school. Their father was not particularly a fan of school, but rather the school of life and hard knocks, observing and listening on one's own.

In later years, Hiram often drank and argued with Celia, and eventually left her for another woman in Utah, after which Jack helped take care of his mother financially.

Although allegedly he initially fought as Kid Blackie, and then Jack Dempsey, his much later nickname - Manassa Mauler, allegedly was derived from the fact that the local Manassa High mascot was the Mauler. Some said writer Damon Runyon gave him the nickname because of his style. Yet, that was not Dempsey's nickname during most of his early career.

The family left Manassa somewhere around 1904, when Harry was about 9. Having heard of a gold boom in Creede, Colorado, they moved 85 miles west, taking a wagon driven by horses.

---

[4] *Cripple Creek Star*, February 27, 1900. Featherweight seems too small for Bernie, and Johnny and Harry were mere children at the time, so it could not have been them either.

Celia opened a boardinghouse in Creede, where to earn money she fed miners and washed their clothes. Bat Masterson once had been town marshal. A local gambling parlor was quite popular. Bob Ford, who killed the outlaw Jesse James, was shot and killed in a Creede saloon called the Candle. Supposedly, 40% of the population consisted of fugitives from justice. 30 saloons were in the town with little to no law and order. It was known for its great mineral strikes. Like many gold camps, it was unsanitary and disease-ridden. Folks lived in cabins near the mines.

There is a report of a black fighter named Harry Peppers fighting a 3-round bout with a Dempsey (likely Bernie) on Tuesday May 10, 1904 at Bachelor (a "wet" town, with drinking and prostitution), just outside Creede, in a smoker for the Miners Union.[5]

Bern Dempsey kept giving Harry boxing lessons. At one point, he also introduced him to Andy Malloy, a prizefighter, who years later would fight Harry/Jack and travel with him giving exhibitions. Malloy and Bernie Dempsey fought once (likely circa 1905 - 1906).[6]

Dissatisfied with his lack of success in the mines, probably sometime from 1904 - 1906, Hiram moved the family again and headed north to Leadville, Colorado for a couple months. The mining town, nearly two miles above sea level, was lawless, mine accidents plentiful, housing deplorable, and a sewage system almost nonexistent. Violence was rampant, particularly when economic conditions began to plummet.

Celia grew ill, and took a train to Denver with Harry and younger siblings Elsie and Bruce, to obtain medical attention. She could afford only one ticket. When she could not produce a ticket for the kids, and could not afford even half-price, the conductor initially threatened to remove them from the train, but ultimately let it go. They were the only ones wearing ragged clothing and shoes stuffed with paper. Such shame and embarrassment in part made Harry motivated to earn good money one day.

After a few weeks in Denver, Celia recovered. Hiram sold the remaining good horse, wired her $75, and they rejoined him and the others in Wolcott, Colorado. They subsequently traveled to Steamboat Springs, Colorado, where all of the males worked as farmers helpers. 10-year old Harry was a wheat baler. Next was Mount Harris, a few miles west of Steamboat, for more farm work. Then Craig, Meeker, and Rifle, Colorado. The nomadic family went wherever there was manual labor work.

In Rifle, Harry was in a group fight. He liked fighting. He told Bern, "I want to be a prizefighter, just like you." Bern replied, "I'm not earning many prizes." Harry: "Well, then I will have to be better than you."

During their six months or so in northwest Colorado, the kids went to school when they could. Mostly though they worked, chopping wood, milking cows, clearing manure, and collecting eggs for the farmer on whose land they worked. Typically, kids went to school during the winter months,

---

[5] *Creede Candle*, May 14, 1904.
[6] *Leadville Herald Democrat*, July 31, 1906, claimed that Malloy had fought a "Dempsey."

when farm hands were not needed, but they worked in the spring and summer. Jack recalled that they even went skiing in Routt County.

The Dempseys next came to Delta, Colorado. Hiram worked at the Delta Brickyard. Harry went to school there and sold some newspapers. Delta was not receptive towards the dirt-poor Dempseys, feeling that they were undesirable. Concerned that the town would wind up having to take care of them, the Dempseys were asked to leave.

The family moved south to Uncompahgre, Colorado (eight miles south of Montrose), where they remained for about two years, give or take. Hiram worked as a sharecropper. Harry helped with the plowing, reaping, and sowing, and he also fished and hunted. He was a good trapper and shooter. He mowed hayfields, and cleared land for cattle, including moving huge rocks, raking, and stacking.

Harry and Bern kept boxing together as well. Bern would take fights whenever he could find them.

Harry went to a one-room schoolhouse for about five months of the year, during winter. On the weekends, he went to the dance hall.

Next the family moved slightly north from Uncompahgre to nearby Montrose, Colorado. In 1905, the Denver and Rio Grande Railroad (D&RG) had begun construction of the Gunnison Tunnel. The railroad constantly needed laborers. Eventually, the Dempsey men took the work.

In Montrose, Celia decided to open up a restaurant called the Rio Grande Eating House. Harry worked there. He waited on tables, shined shoes, mopped the floor, washed dishes, sold newspapers, and hauled coal.

Boxing was a big amusement in Montrose. The Woods family had a bunch of boys who liked to scrap, just like the Dempseys. Years later, Dempsey said Fred Woods was a school mate who always was looking for trouble, and could beat most of the kids in town. "He picked on me one day and I licked him." At one point, Jack claimed that was his first fight.[7] Another family of fighters were the Pitts, who were black. Harry fought Tommy Pitts. Harry took instruction from older brother Bernie, and sparred and trained with Johnny as well. He was small but strong, and could take it. Harry won his fights; though defense was not his specialty, but rather hard punching. Fighting was a diversion. There were no movie theaters. There were two pool halls, Saturday night dances, playing cards, gambling, drinking, and for some, fighting. Harry sometimes watched his brother Bernie in barroom fisticuffs in saloons.

On June 14, 1909, a Jack Dempsey rented a horse for one day at a cost of $2, in order to freight ore out of the Torpedo Eclipse Mine near Ouray (elevation 9,800 feet), about 43 miles south of Montrose. If it was him, Harry was 13 years old, ten days away from his 14th birthday. It more likely was his older brother Bernie, who sometimes went by the name Jack Dempsey. It can be quite difficult to discern which Dempsey was going by the name of Jack Dempsey at any given time, or even if it was one of them at all, which can cause confusion.

---

[7] *Buffalo Commercial*, April 14, 1919; *Wilmington Evening Journal*, April 30, 1919.

On September 23, 1909, the Gunnison Tunnel was completed and dedicated by U.S. President William Howard Taft. A few weeks later, the Dempseys left Montrose and made the state of Utah their new home.

Provo, 40 miles south of Salt Lake City, was the family's first Utah residence. Provo was a Mormon town, and it was reachable via railroad.

Eventually they moved to Lakeview, on a farm just on the outskirts of Provo. Harry went to the Lakeview school with about 50 kids. Naturally, William Harrison Dempsey would tussle and wrestle with all of the boys.

Harry engaged in a boxing contest with Grif Nuthall, purportedly the best boxer in the school, who was well-built and athletic. Within seconds, Dempsey knocked him out with a hard left to the chin and a pulverizing right to the stomach. This added to his confidence.

Dempsey was a much better fighter than wrestler. He was not able to outwrestle fellow schoolboy Clarence Johnson.

Harry had a strong competitive spirit. He also participated in baseball, basketball, and track and field, enjoying sprinting and high jumping.

Eventually, Dempsey graduated from the $8^{th}$ grade. He was neither large nor small for his age. But he had an abundance of strength and endurance.

Harry kept learning boxing from and training with his brothers Bernie and Johnny, and was better than all of the boys he boxed. They created a gym out of a chicken house. It had light dumbbells and a punching bag; a heavy sack full of sand and sawdust. He also skipped rope. Sometimes he would try to hit a broom as brother Johnny moved it up and down.

Young Harry Dempsey worked in a Provo barbershop for a while, shining shoes and sweeping up. He enjoyed reading the *Police Gazette*, which featured boxing prominently. He also did some fishing, trapping muskrats, horse trading, and unloading beets at a sugar beet factory. He allegedly got $2.40 a day for shoveling 50 tons of beets as part of a crew. Most of what he earned he gave to his mother.

On July 4, 1910, in Reno, Nevada (500+ miles west of Provo), in a contest promoted by Tex Rickard, black world heavyweight champion Jack Johnson defeated white former undefeated champion James J. Jeffries in the $15^{th}$ round of a fight that the entire world was discussing. The fighters made huge money, well over $100,000 each (the biggest boxing payday ever up to that point), of which a young 15-year-old Dempsey took note. Boxing, and in particular the heavyweight championship, could be quite lucrative, more lucrative than any other sports profession. Baseball players Ty Cobb and Nap Lajoie each made a league-high $9,000 annual salary that year.

In the wake of the fight, owing to its powerful symbolic racial meaning, there was nationwide race rioting, leading to many deaths and injuries throughout the country. Fearing the potential repercussions, many state and local governments banned the exhibition of the fight films. Several barred any form of interracial competition in the future.

Dempsey claimed that he lived on his own from age 15 or 16, learning to fight in various towns throughout Utah and Colorado, including Montrose. He also dug for gold, picked fruit, washed dishes, and mopped floors. From 1911 on, he traveled from one mining camp to another seeking work and informal fights. He sometimes was called Kid Blackie (owing to his dark complexion and dark hair), if not Jack Dempsey.

However, it is difficult to discern which fights were him, because often reporters and boxing folk would use the moniker Kid Blackie for anyone black or of dark complexion, and some of those fights likely were Johnny or Bernie going by Jack Dempsey. There were other boxers using the popular fighting name Jack Dempsey, as well as Kid Blackey, including an older and more experienced local featherweight/lightweight. Many of William Harrison Dempsey's fights took place in gin mills, and because most technically were illegal and informal/unofficial, the press did not necessarily report them.

At one point, Harry jumped on a train and went to Ashton, Idaho to dig ditches for $2 a day. He also went west to Yellowstone. Eventually he returned to Provo. He subsequently caught a freight train to Grand Junction, and then nearby Palisade, Colorado to pick peaches in an orchard.

Dempsey typically rode the rods or rails, meaning he traveled for free by laying on rods or struts underneath the trains, which was quite dangerous. He couldn't afford tickets. He was a hobo, or migratory worker.

In about 1911, when Harry was approximately 16 years old, Bernie got him a job as a miner in Bingham Canyon, Utah. A bully who threw dirt on Dempsey a couple times intentionally to rouse his ire found out what a mistake that was, for they fought and Harry knocked him out with a right to the jaw. Young Dempsey had beaten a grown man.

Interestingly, there is a report of a "Jack Dempsey," miner, who on Sunday March 5, 1911 in a fit of anger was alleged to have thrown a large bottle at the head of Mrs. Maggie Burns, the landlady of the Burns hotel in Upper Bingham, Utah. He was arrested and arraigned on a charge of assault with intent to do great bodily harm. Dempsey entered a not guilty plea and was committed to the Salt Lake county jail.[8] This more likely was either much older brother Bernie or two-years-older brother Johnny Dempsey, both of whom often went by the name of Jack Dempsey, well before Harry did. Years later, Johnny Dempsey would be known for having problems with alcohol and drugs, and a violent temper, including towards women.

The March 11, 1911 *Cripple Creek Times* said there would be a fight card held at the nearby Victor Opera House on Monday March 13. Among the preliminary bouts, Kid Blackie was billed to fight a much heavier opponent. "However, favorites of the 'Kid' hold that his experience and cleverness of ring generalship will more than overbalance the weight proposition and he will be awarded the decision. Blackie has fought here on a number of occasions and has been pitted against men of a much larger caliber. He is a hard nut to crack and will put up a good fight."[9]

Saying that Kid Blackie had experience and cleverness of ring generalship sounds more like a seasoned veteran rather than a young

---

[8] *Ogden Standard, Salt Lake Tribune*, March 7, 1911.
[9] *Cripple Creek Times*, March 11, 12, 1911.

fighter. If it was Harry Dempsey, he was only 15 years old. Kid Blackie's opponent, Louis Newman, was a well-known experienced lightweight/welterweight who in 1912 was listed as having fought 50 battles and only lost twice, having started his career in 1908. It would be odd for a young kid to fight a veteran of such vast experience. Plus, Harry may have been living in Bingham, Utah at the time, about 550 miles away (although he could have taken a train there). Again, there may well have been several fighters named Kid Blackie. So most likely it was not Harry Dempsey. However, Dempsey did say that for several years, he worked in the mines on and off between fights, and Bernie and he even briefly leased a mine in Cripple Creek, Colorado.[10]

On Monday March 13, 1911 in Victor, Colorado at the well-packed Opera house, in a preliminary contest, Louis Newman, the champion of Las Vegas, and Kid Blackie of Cripple Creek fought hammer and tongs from the start. At first, Kid Blackie seemed to have the better of Newman, but the more scientific Newman ducked several vicious knockout swings, and always got away clean by clever footwork. A little over two minutes into the 1st round, after Blackie worked Newman to the far side of the stage, Newman saw his chance and drove a left hook back of Blackie's right ear. The Cripple Creek boy uncovered, and Newman whipped in a stiff right jolt on the point of the jaw, and Blackie fell like a log. He was not able even to raise his head after the ten-count had been called. He was taken to his corner and his seconds revived him.

**Louis Newman**

Several days later, Newman issued a challenge to any lightweight in the state. The press said he had shown wonderful improvement, and with a little more experience, would be a strong contender for the state lightweight championship.[11]

Again, most likely this was not Harry Dempsey, who probably was living in Utah at the time, but it is possible.

Eight months later, in the social circles news of the *Provo Herald*, it was reported that the parents of Roy Stubbs held a surprise party on November 24, 1911 at Lake View, in the Provo, Utah area. In attendance were Elsie Dempsey (his sister) and Harry Dempsey (Jack's name at that time).[12]

Harry Dempsey took a lot of miscellaneous laborer jobs for about $2 a day in various cities. In Salt Lake City, he was on a steam shovel gang doing landscaping. He also worked in Ogden, Provo, and Price, Utah.

---

[10] *Albuquerque Morning Journal*, June 15, 1912, listing the record for Louis Newman.
[11] *Cripple Creek Times*, March 11, 12, 14, 17, 1911. The scheduled 20-round Kid Ross vs. Battling Jensen main event was stopped at the end of the 1st round by the police, who arrested them. The contests were considered illegal prizefights unless held under the auspices of a duly incorporated athletic club and only paying club members were admitted. *Cripple Creek Times*, March 22, 1911.
[12] *Provo Herald*, November 28, 30, 1911.

On Friday February 9, 1912 in Provo, Utah, a large crowd attended the boxing bouts held at the local opera house. One bout between two 8-year-olds was stopped when it became too vicious.

In another contest, "Because of persistent fouling, the bout between Dempsy and McAdams was stopped by the referee in the second round and the decision given to the latter." It is unclear which "Dempsy" this was that was disqualified, Bernie, Johnny, or Harry, or someone else.[13]

**George Cordosh**

Six days later, on February 15, 1912, at Provo, Utah's athletic carnival, in the main attraction scheduled for 7 rounds, George Cordosh, "the Greek lightweight," outclassed and twice knocked down a Colorado fighter named Harry Dempsey in the 1st round, but so flagrantly and obviously hit Dempsey before he rose that the referee immediately disqualified Cordosh one minute into the contest. If it was him, which cannot be confirmed, William Harrison Dempsey was just 16 years old.[14]

The February 28, 1912 *Provo Daily Herald* reported that Jack Dempsey, a young boxer formerly of Colorado, was training to box in the preliminaries the following evening.[15]

On Thursday February 29, 1912 in Provo, Utah, at the Provo opera house, there was a good exhibition of boxing and wrestling. In one bout, Jack Dempsey and Bill Allen fought to a 3-round draw. Allen decked Dempsey in the 2nd round, but Jack rose and retaliated, drawing blood from Allen in a fast and furious round.[16]

At the request of the police, Referee Roylance announced that the fans would have to be quieter, for the people on Center street were being disturbed. The announcement brought forth laughter.[17]

---

[13] *Provo Daily Herald*, February 10, 1912. The opponent likely was Verl McAdams, for the *Salt Lake Tribune* had reported that Verl McAdams was scheduled to box Gill Cox. Apparently, Dempsey had filled in for some reason. *Salt Lake Tribune*, February 8, 1912.
[14] *Salt Lake Tribune*, February 17, 1912. A couple weeks prior, on February 2, Cordosh had won a 6-round decision against Provo's Mel Cox. *Provo Daily Herald*, February 3, 1912. A George Cordish was mentioned as having won a wrestling contest on February 9 on the same card that a "Dempsy" was disqualified for fouling. *Provo Daily Herald*, February 10, 1912. The February 26, 1912 *Provo Herald* called Cordosh a well-known boxer scheduled to meet Henry Jones in an 8-round bout on the 29th.
  It is unclear whether this was William Harrison Dempsey, but the geography fits. However, he was only 16 years old at this point, so it would seem foolish for him to be fighting a seasoned pro in a scheduled 7-round main event at such an early stage of his development. Also, the contestants were lightweights, which seems a bit small even for a young Dempsey. It is possible though, for Dempsey claimed to be a lightweight early on in his informal boxing career, before his growth spurt.
[15] Dempsey was hoping to fight Peanuts St. Claire at some point in the future. The main event was a scheduled 8-round contest between Henry Jones, the lightweight wrestler (who arranged the show), and George Cordosh, the lightweight Greek boxer. *Provo Daily Herald*, February 28, 1912.
[16] This possibly was William Harrison's brother Johnny, who also fought as "Jack Dempsey." Either way, a 3-round bout would be consistent with an amateur contest. In the main event, Henry Jones knocked out "Italian lad" George Cordosh in the 4th round.
[17] *Provo Daily Herald, Salt Lake Evening Telegram*, March 1, 1912.

On Saturday March 9, 1912 at the sporting carnival held at Spanish Fork, Utah, just slightly south of Provo, before a large crowd, Jack Dempsey of Provo knocked out lightweight Dale Markham of Spanish Fork in the 3rd round. "The contest was hot and vigorous while it lasted."[18]

Dale Markham

All of these bouts just as easily could have been one of his brothers, for they all used the name Jack Dempsey at some point. There was another experienced lightweight fighter using the name Jack Dempsey as well. Dempsey did not mention any of these contests in his autobiographies. Still, it could have been him.

Regardless, William Harrison Dempsey came from a fighting family, his older brothers had boxing experience, and were able to teach their younger brother something about fighting early on, and give him some sparring experience. Young Dempsey may have taken part in many amateur and informal fights.

Dempsey said that at one time, famous lightweight Fighting Dick Hyland, who in 1909 had fought Battling Nelson for the world lightweight championship (LKOby23), used him as a sparring partner and taught him a few things. This could have been in April 1912, for Hyland fought in Salt Lake City on April 29, 1912, winning a 10-round decision over Matty Baldwin.

The April 6 and 29, 1912 *Franklin's Paper* in Denver, Colorado said, "Jack Dempsey has been indisposed this week and unable to go out on his run." Then, "Jack Dempsey, who laid off several days on account of illness, is again out on his run." This likely was the local veteran Dempsey, not Harry.

On July 4, 1912 in Las Vegas, New Mexico, world heavyweight champion Jack Johnson won a 9-round decision verdict over Fireman Jim Flynn, after the sheriff stopped the contest as a result of Flynn's incessant flagrant head-butting in response to Johnson's incessant clinching tactics.

On July 31, 1912, the United States Congress passed and President William Taft signed into law the Sims Act, which banned the transportation of prizefight films in interstate commerce, making it a federal criminal offense punishable by up to a year in prison and/or a $1,000 fine. For the next 28 years (until 1940, when President Franklin Roosevelt signed a repeal of the law), fight films only could be shown in the state where they were taken. This tremendous blow severely limited the economic value of fight films, and limited fans' ability to see fights. Many contests had generated far greater revenue from fight films than they did from the gate receipts. Underground bootlegging still allowed some folks to see fight films in private exhibitions, and sometimes even in public. Regardless, the sport of boxing had taken a very big economic hit.

---

[18] *Provo Daily Herald*, March 11, 1912. In May, 134-pound lightweight Dale Markham fought 138-pound Henry Jones in an 8-round contest. Jones had fought Cordosh.

The clear motivation of Tennessee Congressional Representative Thetus Sims' bill against the interstate transportation of fight films was to prevent folks from seeing Jack Johnson beat a white man, to prevent race riots, and to limit the earning potential of those involved with boxing, a sport which had violated the social mores of separation of the races. Sims' primary intent to was to prevent Jack Johnson's fights from being disseminated and exhibited, but boxing as a whole was being punished. It was a crushing blow economically, for lucrative fight films had generated hundreds of thousands, if not millions of dollars for boxing's participants. Right or wrong, Jack Johnson and interracial competition were blamed for hurting the sport.

From 1912 to 1914, Harry Dempsey traveled around taking various low-paying manual labor jobs, picking, digging, tossing sacks onto railroad cars, shoveling manure, and pitching circus tents. He occasionally returned to Montrose, Colorado, a fight town, and fought there. A coal-mining job in Logan, Utah paid 50 cents for each car load.

Dempsey also claimed that he and his family moved back to West Virginia for about a year, before returning to Utah. This may explain why no Dempsey was mentioned in the local papers in 1913 or for most of 1914.

Heavyweight champion Jack Johnson, following his 1913 conviction and 1-year-and-a-day prison sentence for violating the federal White Slave Traffic Act, for inducing a white woman (Belle Schreiber, a prostitute who had been Johnson's de facto girlfriend) to cross state lines for immoral sexual purposes, fled the country with his second white wife, Lucille Cameron Johnson. His previous white wife, Etta, had committed suicide. Prior to their marriage, Cameron's own mother falsely had charged Johnson with criminal abduction and her own daughter with being mentally incompetent. Many hinted that Cameron had been a prostitute as well.

As of 1913, 30 states out of the 48-state-Union (62.5%) legally prohibited interracial marriage between whites and blacks, including states in Dempsey's neck of the woods, like Colorado, Utah, California, Idaho, and Nevada. Even in those states which did not bar such marriages *by law*, there remained very strong, powerful moral opposition.

On December 19, 1913 in Paris, France, champion Jack Johnson fought black Battling Jim Johnson to a 10-round draw, the first all-black heavyweight championship contest.

On Saturday May 9, 1914 at the local opera house in in Provo, Utah, a large crowd paid from 25 cents up to 1 dollar ringside for seats at a boxing show. After one minute of fighting, a "Red" Crow of Salt Lake stopped a fighter named "Kid" Blackey with a left to the body. Most likely, this was another fighter other than 18-year-old Harry Dempsey.[19]

---

[19] Several months later there is a reference to a lightweight named Kid Blackie, and Dempsey clearly was at least a middleweight in size at this point, if not bigger. Any time a fighter was of particularly dark completion, they might call him blackie, and there may have been several kid blackies. They might call a Native American boxer "Red," "Chief," or "Geronimo," and such. One fighter was called the "Jew Kid." Red Crow fought Battling Davis a few weeks later. Referenced was the fact that Crow "sure made a hit when he put the skids under 'Kid' Blackie two weeks ago." *Provo Daily Herald*, May 11, 21, 1914.

On Tuesday August 18, 1914, about 1,000 fans attended the Ramona Athletic Club's opening event in Ramona, Colorado, a whiskey town (meaning it did not practice prohibition as the nearby Colorado Springs did at that time). In a preliminary contest, lightweights "Young" Herman and "Kid" Blackie boxed 6 fast and pretty rounds to a draw. Both lads fought hard all the way, Blackie using a stiff left to good advantage and Herman a right just as effectively. Again, this most likely was not William Harrison Dempsey, who definitely was much bigger than a lightweight at this point.[20]

**Ramona, Colorado, 1914**

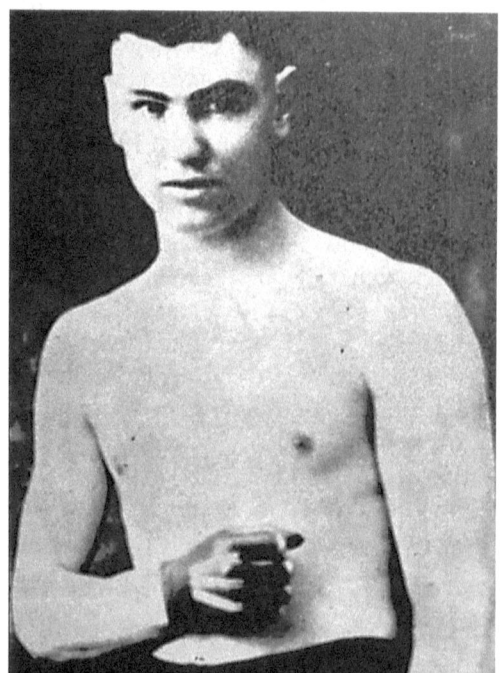

**A young William Harrison Dempsey, a.k.a. Jack Dempsey**

---

[20] *Colorado Springs Evening Telegraph*, August 19, 1914; *Colorado Springs Gazette*, August 19, 1914; *Colorado City Independent*, August 21, 1914. The fights were staged in a large tent with the raised ring at the center.

Dempsey did not mention any of these fights in his autobiographies, nor did any of the earliest records mention any of the previously mentioned bouts. It does not make sense that this was Dempsey, particularly since it was a lightweight contest, and a 19-year-old Dempsey was at least a middleweight if not light-heavyweight in size at that point. Later in 1914, in a confirmed Dempsey bout, he already was known as a heavyweight or light heavyweight.

CHAPTER 2

# A Career Begins

**Salt Lake City, Utah, 1910**

In 1914, Harry Dempsey trained at a gym in Salt Lake City, Utah, run by a very experienced veteran black fighter named Young Peter Jackson, who had fought the who's who of boxing, including Jack Johnson.

Salt Lake was another Mormon town, a cornerstone location for the Church of Latter-day Saints. The transcontinental railroad had been completed there. However, not everyone was religious, and even Salt Lake City had its own red-light district.

**Temple Square, Salt Lake City, Utah, 1912**

In early 1914, at the Garrick theatre in Salt Lake City, the Manhattan Athletic Club was hosting regular weekly 4-round boxing bouts. The Garrick became a hotbed of local boxing shows.[21]

On June 27, 1914 in Paris, France, Jack Johnson defended his world heavyweight championship with a 20-round decision over Frank Moran.

Soon thereafter, war broke out in Europe, eventually becoming known as The Great War, and later, World War I, because so many countries became involved. The U.S. did not join the war for several years.

In 1919, Dempsey claimed that his family returned to Utah in about 1913 (or 1914). His first bout was against a well-known local man named Benz, whom he beat readily in front of a huge crowd. He was paid $1.24.[22]

Heavyweight Charley Diehl told Dempsey that he could be champion one day if he worked hard enough, which encouraged him. Diehl showed him how to crouch and duck side to side. Dempsey had a number of unrecorded informal amateur type fights.

---

[21] *Salt Lake Telegram*, January 17, 1914. Dempsey may also have trained at Willard Bean's gym.
[22] *Harrisburg Telegraph*, January 17, 18, 20, 1919.

On Monday November 2, 1914 at the Garrick theatre in Salt Lake City, Utah, 19-year-old William Harrison Dempsey, fighting as Jack Dempsey, had his first truly known and definitely acknowledged fight, one that contemporary records listed as his first official contest, against Young Hancock.

The *Salt Lake Telegram* on that date advertised 36 rounds of boxing at the Garrick Theatre, the most ever locally, for 50 cents admission. There would be three all-star regular bouts and six amateur contests. One amateur fight would be a battle between "white hopes," which was "attracting all kinds of comment, as it has been many a day since the local fans have had a chance to see two big fellows in action."[23]

> **36 Rounds of Boxing for 50 Cents**
> **GARRICK THEATRE**
> TONIGHT AT 8:30
> **BIG DOUBLE BILL**
> 3 ALL-STAR BOUTS AND BIG
> "AMATEUR NIGHT"
> Seats on Sale at Stickney's Cigar Store, 229 South Main, and Ben Harman's, 50 West First South.

According to the local newspapers, Jack Dempsey made short work of "Young" Hancock. In the 1st round, Dempsey sent a jolt to the solar plexus and Hancock immediately retired, feeling that he had enough.[24]

Dempsey was called a young white hope, because at that time, Jack Johnson still was the world heavyweight champion, so any new white heavyweight was called a white hope, because boxing was hoping to develop a white heavyweight able to recover the championship for the white race. This also strongly suggests that Dempsey weighed more than 160 pounds, and probably was not the lightweight Dempsey or the Kid Blackie referenced in other 1914 reports.

Promoter and referee Hardy K. Downing, speaking in 1920, said that in about October 1914, Andy Malloy, a middleweight boxer of some fame, told him, "Hardy, I've got a fellow here, a big, punk kid, but I think he can fight. I wish you'd give him a chance. I've boxed with the boy and he looks like a fighter." Downing said the fight against Young Hancock was 19-year-old Dempsey's first real fight, except for three or four kid matches in Provo (a town 50 miles south of Salt Lake), where Senator Smoot lived and where the Dempseys had lived until Jack was about 17. Hardy said there wasn't much of a story. "It was a case of one punch and two dollars and a half. Dempsey just walked out and feinted with his left once, then drove in his right and the Hancock boy went boom. It was over in twenty seconds." So Jack Dempsey's first real payday was $2.50 for a 1st round knockout.

---

[23] *Salt Lake Telegram*, November 2, 1914.
[24] *Salt Lake Telegram*, *Salt Lake Tribune*, November 3, 1914. The *Salt Lake Tribune* reported that the fast bouts pleased the big crowd of fans. Dempsey and Hancock were called amateurs. However, on Dempsey's pro records as of 1918 and 1919, this fight against "Kid Hancock" is listed as being his first pro fight. The era's perception of the word amateur might be different than our notion of it today. It might have meant a beginner. Dempsey was paid $2.50 for the fight, which would have been the equivalent of a day's worth of his manual labor work. Interestingly, William Harrison Dempsey went by the name Jack Dempsey even at this early stage of his career.

Dempsey kept fighting for Downing in 1915 and into 1916 as a "meal-ticket" fighter. From $2.50 his pay eventually went up to $5, then $7.50, then $10, $15, and $25, all for 4-round goes.[25]

On November 26, the *Salt Lake Telegram* reported that "white hope" Jack Dempsey, who a few weeks ago had caused fans to open their eyes when he stopped another white hope with a single punch, was scheduled for a real test in four days against Bill Murphy, another hope who had been showing considerable ability in the gym.

The *Salt Lake Tribune* advertised Jack Dempsey and Bill Murphy as a pair of white hopes out to make a reputation for themselves.[26]

That same day, November 26, 1914 in Vernon, California, just south of Los Angeles, against 22-year-old black Harry Wills, top black heavyweight Sam Langford rose from four knockdowns, twice in each of the first two rounds, primarily from rights, and came back from a bad beating to knock out Wills in the 14th round, with a couple of left hooks to the jaw.[27]

On Monday November 30, 1914 in Salt Lake City, Utah, under the auspices of the Manhattan Club, at the Garrick Theatre, Jack Dempsey fought Bill Murphy. They were listed as heavyweights, and they opened the show. Club manager Hardy K. Downing lined up the card, which featured six 4-round bouts. Admission was 50 cents.

Once again, according to the *Salt Lake Telegram*, Dempsey quickly and with ease knocked out his opponent in the 1st round, outclassing Murphy. Veteran fighter Jack Downey refereed.

The *Salt Lake Tribune* reported that Murphy, who did not appear to know much, was knocked down two or three times in the 1st round, and was glad enough when Referee Jack Downey gave the honors to Dempsey, who "really is a boxer of ability."[28]

On December 16, 1914 in Teller County, Colorado, near Colorado Springs, a Jack Dempsey was arrested on a warrant charging him with petty larceny. Dempsey plead guilty and was sentenced to 30 days in jail. It is unclear whether this was William Harrison Dempsey, who appears to have been residing in Utah at the time, or one of his brothers, or another Jack Dempsey entirely, for there were others who went by that name.

---

[25] *New York Daily News*, February 27, 1920.
[26] *Salt Lake Telegram, Salt Lake Tribune*, November 26, 27, 1914.
[27] *Los Angeles Times*, November 27, 1914. Jack Kearns managed Wills in California up until the loss to Langford. "I gave up on Wills because I knew he didn't have the makings of a true champion."
[28] *Salt Lake Telegram*, November 30, 1914, December 1, 1914; *Salt Lake Tribune*, December 1, 1914. At one point during the fight card that evening, a fire started in the theater's foyer, and quickly developed into quite a blaze. The fans inside didn't entirely realize what was going on, for firemen quickly showed up and did a good job of extinguishing it. The show progressed without a hitch.

At another Salt Lake card held at the Garrick theater on January 4, 1915, former world heavyweight champion Tommy Burns was present, and he gave a speech praising the benefits of boxing.[29]

For whatever reason, there was no mention of Dempsey on any of the weekly cards for several months. It is possible that he was elsewhere, working, and possibly fighting. At that point in his career, boxing did not generate sufficient income to support him. Jack said he did mining work and various odd jobs for several years between fights.

Salt Lake City was coming to the front in the short-round boxing game. Nearly every week, fans were treated to high-class matches. Fighters such as Battling Billy Johnson and Jack Downey were experienced regulars on the Hardy Downing cards at the Garrick.[30]

On Friday February 26, 1915 in Pocatello, Idaho (164 miles north of Salt Lake City), a frequent stop by rail for those in the Salt Lake area looking work (farming, mining, etc.), at the McNichols & Wright hall, under the auspices of the Pocatello Athletic club, a preliminary bout was held between "Geronimo" and "Young Dempsey," which the *Pocatello Tribune* said went 4 fast rounds to a draw. Some have called him Chief Geronimo, and said it was an alias for a local fighter named Laverne Collier.

In the main event, the fast, classy, tough middleweight Jack Downey of Salt Lake won a close 15-round decision over Romeo Hagen.[31]

Years later, Dempsey said he got to Pocatello in the same manner he traveled everywhere in those days, deftly inserting himself under a box car of a freight train, holding on to the rods, and away he went. His draw with Young Chief Geronimo, who actually was an Italian, was a slam-fest, give and take. Jack received $4 or $5 for the fight.

Rufe Cameron, a black heavyweight (possibly 210 pounds) who was working out in Pocatello, signed Dempsey to be his sparring partner. Cameron towered over Dempsey, and gave him a lot of hard wallops, particularly with his right, but Jack liked the training and the experience.[32]

On Friday March 12, 1915 in Boise, Idaho, at Forest Park, before the biggest crowd that ever attended a local boxing show, in the main event,

---

[29] *Salt Lake Telegram*, January 5, 1915. Jack Dempsey was not mentioned on the card.
[30] *Salt Lake Telegram*, February 6, 1915.
[31] *Pocatello Tribune*, February 25, 27, 1915, March 3, 1915. Laverne Collier's record included: July 1914 D3 Kid Tyler and January 1915 KO2 Dusty Rhodes.

Dempsey likely had traveled to Pocatello from Salt Lake with Jack Downey. Dempsey said in his earliest 1940 autobiography that he sometimes went by the name of Young Dempsey. This makes sense, given that his older brothers often went by the name Jack Dempsey, so calling him Young Dempsey was a way to indicate that he was the younger brother.

Some 1918 and 1919 Dempsey records list early fights that Dempsey did not mention or discuss, and no dates are known, so they are unproven and unconfirmed, and include: KO6 Chief Gordon, KO1 Battling Johnson/Jackson, KO9 Joe Lyons/Lions, and KO6 or KO7 Johnny Pierson/Person/Berson. A fight with Battling Billy Johnson would be unlikely, given that he was a 135-pound lightweight. It may have been referencing a 1916 KO1 over Swede Johnson. *Buffalo Courier*, February 3, 1918; *Winston Salem Journal*, March 17, 1918; *Chattanooga News*, March 9, 1918; *Winston Salem Journal*, March 17, 1918; *St. Louis Star*, March 28, 1918; *Atlanta Constitution*, July 4, 1919; *Cincinnati Enquirer*, July 5, 1919.

[32] *Fairmont West Virginian*, May 19, 1921; *Cedar Rapids Gazette*, May 12, 1919. Significant bouts on Rufus Cameron's record included: 1912 L4 Walter Monahan; 1913 L4 Jack Geyer, L4 Charley Miller, LKOby13 Jeff Clark, and L4 Willie Meehan; and 1914 L15 Jeff Clark.

Rufus Cameron won a 10-round decision over Battling Brant (or Brandt). "The crowd drew the color line and made Brant the popular favorite. He was encouraged from almost the entire house all the way through, but the fans were fair to the negro at the finish, and the decision of Referee Nick Collins was well received." Cameron danced about, repeatedly landing from the most unexpected angles.

Neither local next-day newspaper mentioned Dempsey as a participant in a preliminary contest.[33]

However, in 1918, Nick Collins, who promoted and refereed the March 12, 1915 Boise, Idaho card at Forest Park, claimed that Dempsey fought at that show and scored a 2nd round knockout over a fighter named C. Hill.

> In the second round Dempsey hit Hill in the stomach, crossed to his jaw, and all was over. I told Hill to get up, but he couldn't. There was the biggest crowd at a boxing match ever held in Boise that night. Dempsey was a punk kid that came up from Salt Lake to help train Cameron. He bummed his way up from Salt Lake. He was about 19 years old then. Cameron managed him after that, and he left Cameron and had a whole string of managers afterwards.[34]

In early April 1915, the *Salt Lake Herald-Republican* advertised that Jack Dempsey, the big fellow who stopped several opponents in a round at the Manhattan club several months ago, was back in shape again and was going to be given a real tryout against Jack Downey, the classy old-timer who had a habit of stopping white hopes.

27-year-old Jack Downey was a very experienced regular local pro who fought quite often in Colorado and Utah, particularly the Salt Lake area. He had been a professional for nine years, since 1906, and had over 50 fights, perhaps even more. So he had a vast and ridiculous experience advantage over young beginner Dempsey. He typically weighed 160-165 pounds. At this stage, Dempsey probably weighed about the same or perhaps slightly more, but not much more. Downey had about 30 draws to his credit, so he was clever enough to keep it close, no matter who he fought, and regardless of the distance. One of his draws was against black fighter Young Peter Jackson (1914 D6), who had over 100 bouts of experience, including going the 12-round distance against Jack Johnson. Downey also had draws with Andy Malloy (1909 D4 twice) and Johnny Sudenberg (1913 D10). Dempsey and Downey likely saw each other box when they fought on the same February 26 card in Pocatello, where Downey won a 15-round decision over Romeo Hagen. Downey had refereed Dempsey's fight against Bill Murphy.

The local *Salt Lake Tribune* said Dempsey had cleaned up all of the local white hopes, and would get a real tryout from the local white-hope-killer. "This will be the first time that Dempsey has met a man of real class, and he

---

[33] *Idaho Statesman*, *Evening Capital News*, March 13, 1915. The only preliminary bouts mentioned were Sunshine McClure D6 Romeo Hagan (or Hagen) and Fay Rose KO2 Jimmy Thompson.
[34] *Idaho Statesman*, July 30, 1918. Dempsey did not mention having had a contest in Boise. He likely had traveled to Boise from Pocatello, about 230 miles away, mostly west but slightly north of Pocatello.

will have a chance to show whether he is made of the right kind of material or not, for Downey has a bad habit of stopping big youngsters." It would be the case of a veteran who knew every angle of the game against a strong young fellow with a powerful wallop.

The *Salt Lake Telegram* said Dempsey had stopped all of his opponents so quickly that the fans hardly had a chance to get a real line on him. He was young, big, and strong, but was meeting a man of superior boxing skill.

The *Salt Lake Herald-Republican* said Dempsey was a whirlwind in action and carried the fight to his opponents so fast that they took the count inside the 1st round, but in Downey he was meeting a past-master at the game, a mighty shifty fellow who usually stopped white hopes, for his skill could overcome strength and hitting ability. Downey figured out his foes and then dropped them with well-directed punches to the jaw. Hence, the going likely would be pretty heavy for Dempsey.

Apparently, Dempsey was not quite as green as some thought. "Although Dempsey broke in here as an amateur several months ago, it has been learned since then that he is far from being an amateur and has fought some mighty good boys around the country." Another said that those who had seen

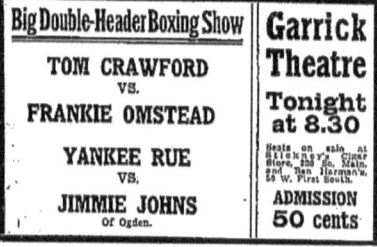

Dempsey in action were of the opinion that he was far from a novice, and it was hinted that he had fought a lot of good boys and men in Colorado and possibly elsewhere. Dempsey had the power to knock out opponents with a single blow, but Downey had real class and a punch himself, so the fight promised to be a real slugfest.[35]

On Monday April 5, 1915 in Salt Lake City, at the Garrick theater, under the auspices of Hardy Downing's Manhattan Athletic Club, 19-year-old Jack Dempsey fought 27-year-old Jack Downey in a scheduled 4-round contest.

The *Salt Lake Telegram* said there were 4 rounds of see-saw slugging in which the advantage swung back and forth, but Downey's superior class told in the end, and he had Jack looking for the bell at the fight's conclusion. Downey received a well-earned 4-round decision.

The *Salt Lake Tribune* said they fought in a slashing manner in a good scrap. Downey was aggressive all the way, piling up the points with clever boxing and heavy hitting. He made Dempsey look like a novice in the 1st round with a display of fancy boxing seldom seen. After the 2nd round, Dempsey was tired and holding on, and appeared glad to hear the bell at the end of the 4th round. Referee Hardy Downing's 4-round decision for Downey was well received.

The *Salt Lake Herald-Republican* said the old favorite Downey was too clever for big Dempsey in a fast contest. Dempsey was successful in the 1st

---

[35] *Salt Lake Herald-Republican*, April 2, 4, 5, 1915; *Salt Lake Tribune*, April 3-5, 1915; *Salt Lake Telegram*, April 4, 5, 1915. A show of 24 scheduled rounds was advertised.

round until Downey "put one under Dempsey and sent him to the floor. This was followed up by a rally of right and left hooks and Dempsey was worried for the rest of the fight."[36]

So 19-year-old Dempsey had lost a decision to a far more experienced veteran of the game. But it was good experience, and, undiscouraged, he kept learning, training, developing, and growing. At the very least it showed that Dempsey was game, entertaining, and willing to fight anyone.

Years later, Dempsey said he tore into the bald Downey, who played defense and conserved his energy, allowing Jack to spend his energy, but then came back at Dempsey cautiously but steadily, and eventually had his less experienced foe exhausted. Jack was paid $5 for the fight.

Earlier on that same date, April 5, 1915, in bigger news out of Havana, Cuba, 33-year-old (though listed as 27 at the time) 238-pound 6'6 ½" Jess Willard, who had 29 fights since turning pro in 1911, knocked out 37-year-old 227-pound 6'1 ½" Jack Johnson in the 26th round to win the world heavyweight championship.

In an entertaining, scheduled 45-round contest, Willard utilized his height and reach very well, calmly fired heavy snappy jabs and straight rights to the head and body, carefully pacing himself, moving back from Johnson's quick attacks and clinching. Johnson was ahead on points through the first 20 rounds, landing more punches, but started to tire, having done more work in order to move in and land, whereas the taller, longer, more efficient Willard

---

[36] *Salt Lake Telegram, Salt Lake Tribune, Salt Lake Herald-Republican*, April 6, 1915.

took blows well and maintained his consistent steady pace, wearing him down until he knocked out the fatiguing Johnson with a straight right to the jaw in the 26th round. Johnson earned $30,000.

The fight was scheduled to begin at 12:30 p.m. Havana time, or 11 a.m. Salt Lake time. A megaphone man stood outside the *Salt Lake Tribune* office describing the bout blow-by-blow and round-by-round.

Salt Lake Tribune, April 6, 1915

After winning the title, "redeemer of the white race" Jess Willard once again publicly re-drew the color line, which is what every heavyweight champion prior to Tommy Burns had done. "He already has announced that if he won he would not fight another negro." No black fighter was going to be allowed the chance that many believed Johnson never should have had in the first place. A photo caption for Willard in the *Los Angeles Times* stated, "The cowboy pugilist, who yesterday knocked out Jack Johnson and restored the championship to the white race." One article said "the prevailing impression was that Johnson's defeat by the big Kansan would give a stimulus to boxing and make the sport more popular all over the United States. Now that the title is held by an American..."[37] The Texas-born Johnson was not even seen as a true American. He most certainly was not going to be allowed to attempt to regain the title, regardless of economics. Johnson later claimed that he threw the fight, but few believed him, and those that did said such claims only further impugned his integrity. Johnson was utilized as a cautionary story and symbol.

Jess Willard won, so has **Genuine Pittsburgh Coal** won over the other blacks. **Pittsburgh Coal Co.**

Other top black fighters like Sam Langford, Joe Jeannette, Sam McVey, and the newly emerging Harry Wills were not going to be allowed the opportunity to fight for the title either, simply because of their race, even though they were the world's best heavyweights. Things simply went back to the way they were before Johnson won the title, with the heavyweight championship a whites-only position. In Johnson's wake, most top white heavyweight contenders drew the color line. With some rare exceptions, top black fighters primarily were relegated to fighting one another. Jack Johnson as champion was viewed as an experiment and anomaly in the heavyweight division; one that many did not want to see repeated. He was blamed for any political crackdowns on the sport, as well as the economically crushing

---

[37] *Los Angeles Daily Times*, April 6, 1915.

anti-prize-fight film transportation law; and hence, by extension, all mixed-race contests and black champions were blamed, unfair though it was.

The black-owned *Chicago Defender* wondered whether the colored boxer was gone forever. No black champions remained, and it was unclear whether any would be allowed to win another championship. "There are a few who could give Willard a go, and then some, but he is probably afraid, and the result is the old loophole, the color line."[38]

Bat Masterson said Johnson was an undesirable citizen who brought shame and humiliation to his race. "He deserves to be ostracized by both Negroes and whites because of his immorality, his flagrant and brazen defiance of decency and convention. ... Johnson has met with our unqualified condemnation for his association with white women."[39]

Although all black fighters should not have been judged by Johnson's conduct, the fact is that they were, and many whites did not want to see or even risk a repetition of such conduct, or risk having a black man as the symbol of heavyweight dominance on a national and international stage, regardless. Boxing folk thought Johnson had hurt the sport.

Meanwhile, since February 1915, D. W. Griffith's film, *The Birth of a Nation*, based on Thomas Dixon, Jr.'s popular novel and play *The Clansman*, was playing throughout the nation. Blacks vigorously protested the film; for it glorified the Ku Klux Klan as heroes and depicted blacks as having all of humanity's worst traits, advocating for separation of the races. Fearing race riots, some locations banned the film, but overall, it was a huge financial success, playing for years. Democrat U.S. President Woodrow Wilson, born in Virginia (a former New Jersey Governor and Princeton University President), screened the film at the White House. Wilson allowed the federal government to be segregated, arguing it was beneficial to both races.

The *Chicago Defender* lamented that the South, not satisfied with its persecution of the race below the Mason and Dixon line, had sent its devilish imps to broadcast race prejudice throughout the land.[40]

**Battling Jim Johnson and Sam McVey**

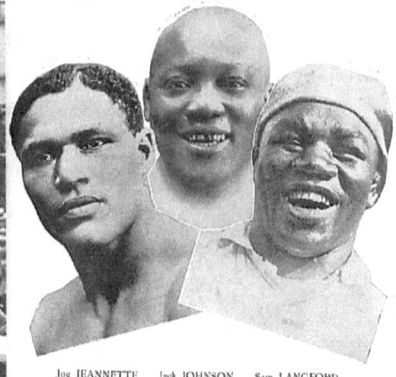

Joe JEANNETTE   Jack JOHNSON   Sam LANGFORD

---

[38] *Chicago Defender*, April 24, 1915.
[39] *Chicago Defender*, May 15, 1915. Joe Jeannette and Sam McVey had married white women as well.
[40] *Chicago Defender*, July 24, 1915.

CHAPTER 3

# On the Road Again

After the loss to Jack Downey, a still 19-year-old Jack Dempsey took a train to Reno, Nevada, over 500 miles west from Salt Lake City, to fight there a mere 21 days later. Reno was a mining town, and had been the site of the Jeffries-Johnson championship contest in 1910.

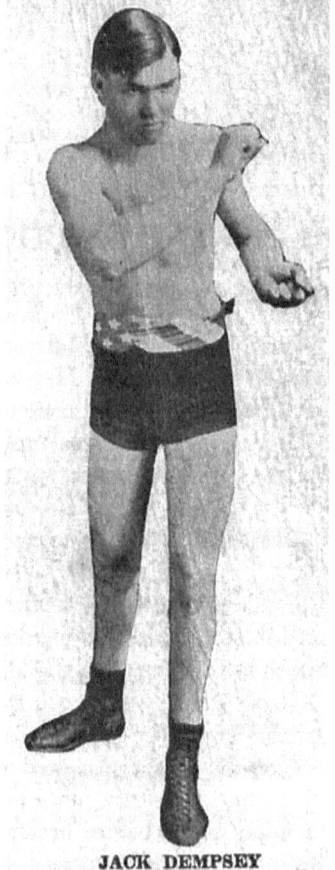

JACK DEMPSEY

The local Jockey Athletic club was hosting a boxing show at the new open-air arena on 3rd street, near Evans avenue. A preliminary bout would feature Jack Dempsey "of Butte" against Emmanuel Campbell, a black fighter out of Los Angeles, at 158 pounds. Hence, at that point, Dempsey was more of a middleweight than a heavyweight.[41]

Campbell's training showed that he was willing and game. Dempsey, who during afternoons worked out in front of a large crowd of enthusiastic admirers, was called a big untried slugger who had been unable to find any sparring partners strong enough to make him let himself out.[42]

On Monday April 26, 1915 in Reno, Nevada, according to the local *Nevada State Journal*, Jack Dempsey outfought Emanuel Campbell, his colored opponent, over the course of the three rounds that their battle lasted. In the 3rd round, following a fall to the floor by both fighters, the "colored boy" did not get up in time and Referee Roy Moore counted him out.

The *Reno Evening Gazette* said Emmanuel Campbell, a big colored fighter, took an awful beating from Jack Dempsey, and finally quit cold after running to avoid punishment. In the 4th round, after turning his back and running halfway around the ring, Campbell fell to the floor. After taking the count of eight he got off his knees, but when Dempsey made another rush at him, Campbell dropped back down. Referee Moore promptly declared Dempsey

---

[41] *Nevada State Journal* (Reno), April 17, 1915. Some called him "Anamas" or "Manues" Campbell.
[42] *Nevada State Journal*, April 25, 1915.

the winner. This writer said Dempsey showed great cleverness and aggressiveness, and "has a punch with either hand," making him a dangerous opponent for anyone.[43]

So, the two local papers had two different views of how and when matters ended, with one claiming Dempsey stopped him in the 3rd round, and the other saying it ended in the 4th round.

Years later, Dempsey claimed to have sparred a few rounds with Campbell leading up to the bout, something the latter insisted upon before deciding whether he would fight Jack. Dempsey intentionally allowed Campbell to get the better of him, so as to induce his willingness. After the fight, Campbell called Dempsey a "man-killer."

In May 1915, at the pavilion in Moana Springs, in the Reno area, lightweight Frankie Burns (101 fights), was preparing for a May 17 Moana Springs fight, training and sparring with Young Jack Dempsey.[44]

Johnny Sudenberg was matched to fight Jack Dempsey at Goldfield, a Nevada gold-mining town about 27 miles from Tonopah (said mining towns being midway between Reno and Las Vegas), on Decoration Day, in the main event, Dempsey's first main event billing. Both would weigh in at no more than 165 pounds at ringside.[45]

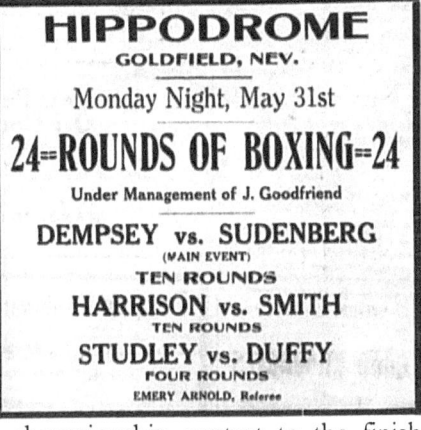

Goldfield had been the site of the famous September 3, 1906 Tex Rickard-promoted world lightweight championship contest to the finish (which was filmed) between black Joe Gans and white Battling Nelson, won by Gans via disqualification in the 42nd round.

Already a veteran of 30 pro bouts, Johnny Sudenberg was only 21 years old. He had been fighting since 1912. In 1913 in Salt Lake, Sudenberg fought Jack Downey to a 10-round draw. Ten of his fights were draws, so he knew how to keep contests close, in part because of his incessant aggressiveness. He had fought contests that lasted 10 rounds or more seven times. He had far more experience than Dempsey, who primarily had boxed in some short 4-round bouts, and was just embarking on his pro career. Sudenberg had fought in places like San Francisco and Oakland, as well as Reno, Goldfield, and Tonopah, so Nevadans were quite familiar with him.

Jack later said he had misgivings about fighting a 10-round main event against a fighter with a dangerous reputation and so much more experience, but he was offered $100 or $150, and it was too much to turn down.

---

[43] *Nevada State Journal, Reno Evening Gazette*, April 27, 1915.
[44] *Nevada State Journal*, May 14, 1915.
[45] *Reno Gazette-Journal*, May 17, 1915; *Reno Evening Gazette*, May 21, 1915; *Tonopah Daily Bonanza*, May 31, 1915.

Dempsey worked out in Tonopah, at the Big Casino. He later claimed to have sparred with both "Slick" Merrill (1912 L10 Jack Downey) and Kid Harrison to prove to promoter Jake Goodfriend that he was a worthy opponent. Kid Harrison, an old Indian fighter, was knocked out in a few punches. Jack also sparred with 50-fight veteran bantamweight Roy Moore, who had refereed Dempsey's contest with Emmanuel Campbell. Moore warned Dempsey not to slug it out with Sudenberg. Jack said Sudenberg was a heavy 10-1 favorite. Dempsey's manager at that time was Jack Gill.

In another version of the story, Dempsey said Sudenberg had been knocking out or outpointing every man they could bring into the mining camps, and had a local reputation. Jack was not eating well at the time, owing to the fact that he had little money, and he was ill from poor nourishment. Initially the promoter could not believe Dempsey was a heavyweight, and even questioned whether he was Dempsey. To test him, the promoter had him spar with a huge negro in Tonopah. The gloves began flying, Jack stepped in and out, and his confidence came to him. Soon the black man quit and said, "My lawd, that boy can hit!"

In sparring in Goldfield, Jack landed a punch high on his sparring partner's head and knocked him out. After that, he had trouble getting anyone to work with him. Yet, everyone in Goldfield was betting against him, despite the fact that he had laid out one of their tough guys in sparring.

On Monday May 31, 1915 at the Hippodrome theater in Goldfield, Nevada, before a large crowd which included 50 folks from Tonopah who traveled there by auto, Jack Dempsey "of Pueblo" and Johnny Sudenberg of South Omaha, middleweights, fought a scheduled 10-round contest. Promoter Jake Goodfriend was the announcer. Emory Arnold, a senator in the Nevada state legislature, refereed.

Johnny Sudenberg and Jack Dempsey

According to the nearby *Tonopah Daily Bonanza*, after feeling out one another for two rounds, with honors about even, Sudenberg realized that owing to the greater height, longer reach, and extra weight of his antagonist, he would have to force the fighting in order to win. Dempsey took advantage of the openings thereafter and it resulted in a good fight for the remaining 8 rounds. Referee Emory Arnold declared it a 10-round draw, though some dissatisfaction was expressed over the decision (many feeling that Dempsey had won).

The local *Goldfield Daily Tribune* said Dempsey loomed large in the scrap, for Sudenberg was unable to make headway against him. For 10 rounds, Dempsey, "who looked more like an overgrown school boy than a fighter, and who incidentally proved otherwise, met the lunges of his shorter opponent, Johnny Sudenberg, with a straight left which invariably connected with the latter's visage before Johnny could get inside the Colorado boy's guard for a slam of his own variety." For five rounds, Dempsey used his straight left, and alternated occasionally with a straight right in jabbing fashion in an effort to refrain from infighting.

However, fighting mostly on the outside was a mistake, for Dempsey eventually realized that his best bet was in close. In the 6th round, he found that he could hold Sudenberg safe in the clinches, and he opened up with a succession of right jolts, chops, and jabs to Johnny's jaw, which kept the latter's head bobbing during the rest of the fight.

Despite the description that seemed to give Dempsey the better of the 10-round contest, this writer agreed with the decision.

> Both boys were fighting strong and furiously at the bell, and under the circumstances the best decision that could have been given was the one Referee Arnold made when he called the bout a draw. Neither boy had been hurt to any extent, and although Dempsey landed the cleanest blows, this was offset by the aggressiveness of Sudenberg, who carried the fight to his rangier opponent all through the battle.

This writer noted that Dempsey showed promise of developing into a heavyweight, and though there was room for a world of improvement, with a few years of experience, he should make a formidable foe for any scrapper.

The *Reno Evening Gazette* reported that they had fought 10 fast rounds to a draw, but most experts believed that Dempsey had a slight advantage throughout, and fought like a 'comer.'[46]

Dempsey's 1919 version vastly differed from the local reports, and spun a much more exciting tale, as he often did. When the fight started, Dempsey found that he could hit him, and tore right in to win in a hurry. He scored several knockdowns in the first part of the fight. However, by the 5th and 6th rounds, a fatiguing Dempsey practically was staggering around the ring, and

---

[46] *Tonopah Daily Bonanza, Goldfield Daily Tribune, Reno Evening Gazette*, June 1, 1915.

a good blow would have finished him. He was floored, and so weak he hardly could stand, but made it through to the end.[47]

Dempsey's manager collected the purse and spent it all that night getting drunk, and then skipped town, so he had nothing to show for the 10 rounds of work and pounding. Jack was broke.

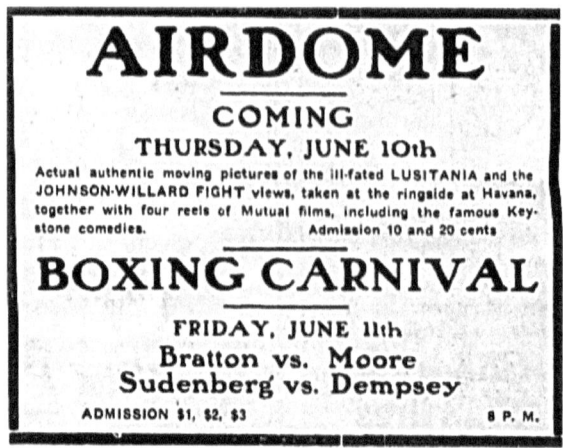

Given that many were dissatisfied with the decision, feeling that Dempsey had won, the nearby Tonopah Athletic club secured the Dempsey-Sudenberg rematch, to be held in that mining town just eleven days later. Dempsey trained at the local casino.

The two light heavyweights trained hard. Both were so confident that they made the fight winner-take-all (allegedly, though likely such a claim was made for marketing purposes). Dempsey later said he was paid $150 for the rematch.

On June 6, a large crowd at the casino saw Dempsey train. This time, Jack was the betting favorite, and they did not have to make weight.[48]

On Friday June 11, 1915 at the Airdome in Tonopah, Nevada, the Jack Dempsey vs. Johnny Sudenberg rematch took place. The show started at 8 p.m. A crowd of 1,100 paid $1, $2, and $3 for tickets. About 60 of those in attendance were from Goldfield, coming over by special train, while about eight or ten auto loads came from the gold camp.

According to the local *Tonopah Daily Bonanza*, the fighters roughed it from the tap of the gong and fought hard throughout:

1 – Dempsey's mass attacks at the start and Sudenberg's unpreparedness resulted in three floorings of Sudenberg and one slip. Jack's evident ambition was to end the battle before his antagonist could recover his defense, attacking ferociously. Jack had the superior height and reach. Johnny crouched. An uppercut to jaw rendered the local Sudenberg groggy. Jack swung and missed, but then landed a left jab and right to the face. A right to the jaw sent Sudenberg down for a count. Sudenberg rose but went down again from a right to the body and right-left-right to the jaw. Dempsey decked him yet again with two blows to the stomach. Sudenberg missed and was fought to the ropes. Johnny landed to the face at the gong.

2 – Dempsey landed a left to the face. Sudenberg took a jab and swung wildly in return, nearly going through the ropes. He took a right to the face

---

[47] *Toledo News-Bee*, June 18, 19, 1919.
[48] *Tonopah Daily Bonanza*, June 3, 4, 7, 10, 1915.

and hung on to avoid punishment. Dempsey drove in a couple rights to the face. Sudenberg returned with left and right to the stomach. They exchanged to the head. Johnny hit Jack's jaw.

3 – Jack missed swings as Johnny got under them and closed in. Dempsey fought him into a corner. Sudenberg landed two rights to the jaw but Dempsey landed one to Sudenberg's jaw. Johnny's defense had improved. Jack hit the body and John rested on his shoulder. Dempsey uppercut him on the ropes.

4 – Sudenberg hit the body. Dempsey twice hit the face. He fought in the clinches with one arm free. Short jabs were exchanged freely, but the punches were light. Dempsey landed two to the belly. They exchanged to the face. Dempsey was very tired, but money backing him still was in evidence. Both men complained of low blows.

5 – Dempsey hit the ribs, then landed right and left to the jaw, sending Sudenberg's head bouncing, but he took it well and ducked cleverly. Sudenberg landed three light ones to the jaw and missed a hard one, but then took one on the jaw, body, and then right and left to the head.

6 – Dempsey landed three on Sudenberg's head. He followed with more blows to the head and body. Johnny was solely on the defensive. He held on and took short punches in the kidneys. However, Sudenberg broke away and landed two telling blows to the neck and body, but received one on the jaw.

7 – Sudenberg landed heavily over the heart. Jabs were exchanged. Dempsey landed on the jaw, face, and body. John again wrestled. Both missed swings.

8 – Dempsey landed two rights on the jaw, but Sudenberg returned with interest. Sudenberg landed heavily on the body. Jack worked his right like a sledgehammer, and Sudenberg got quite groggy. Dempsey landed a heavy smash on Johnny's jaw.

9 – Dempsey landed two uppercuts. John hit the belly. Jack overreached and hit the face with his arm. He sent a right to John's heart, and they exchanged to the jaw. Sudenberg attacked wildly and ran into a couple blows. Both uppercut and clinched.

At the end of the round, Sudenberg suddenly showed that he had been saving himself for the finish, coming on quite strong, and there was pandemonium.

10 – Dempsey landed right and left to the head. Sudenberg hit the face and landed uppercuts to the jaw. He again landed to the jaw, but received return blows to his face. They fought on the inside, and jabbed, but without steam.

At the conclusion of the 10 rounds, Referee Jack Minnick held up both of their arms, indicating a draw, their second in a row. Some disapproval and protest was expressed at the decision, once again most of the crowd feeling that Dempsey had won, though some cheered. Dempsey supporters claimed that of the 10 rounds, 8 were Dempsey's and one was drawn. The referee based his decision on Sudenberg's recovery of strength and his taking the offensive so strongly in the 10th round.

Given the criticism, Referee Jack H. Minnick issued a statement explaining his decision. He said Dempsey spent himself in five rounds. Sudenberg recuperated rapidly, and during the 6th round and up to the finish he grew stronger. From the 7th round on, Dempsey lost ground rapidly and was a "sick man." Sudenberg found it necessary to push him away in order to break, and carried the fight from there on. In the 9th round, Dempsey suffered a hard right to the stomach and weakened. In the 10th round, Sudenberg again landed a terrific punch to the stomach which put Dempsey to his knees, and in such a condition that it was an effort for him to maintain his balance until the final gong. Sudenberg's work in the second half of the fight earned him a draw. In the referee's opinion, Jack could not have endured punishment for three more rounds if it went on to a finish.

The nearby *Goldfield Daily Tribune* reported that it had been a bully good show at the silver camp, but marred by rank decisions. Although Sudenberg had short arms, he made up for the deficiency with the sturdiness of Hercules and the courage of a Spartan. Yet, Dempsey was better.

> Dempsey knocked him down six times during the fight, five times in the first frame and once in the second. Johnny was dazed, but rose to his feet after taking a liberal number of counts and came back for more.
>
> Dempsey should have had the decision, and there is only one explanation of the draw verdict rendered by Minnick. It can be put in the form of a question: How much should be taken into consideration by the referee in rendering his verdict for a wonderful exhibition of gameness for ten rounds after being practically knocked out in the first round? There is no question but that on points Dempsey was entitled to a verdict by a big margin. Sudenberg knocked Dempsey down in the tenth round. Dempsey claims he was fouled, and the blow certainly looked low, but…Minnick was not in a position to see where it landed. The crowd always admires a game man, and Sudenberg had the crowd with him from the first round. Much of this enthusiasm for his game battle must have been communicated to the referee and influenced him in rendering the draw verdict.

The *Nevada State Journal* reported that the bouts were good but the decisions "punk" and "rank." It said the Goldfield sporting editors, who covered the Tonopah contests, claimed that Dempsey should have had the decision over Johnny Sudenberg, whom he knocked down six times during the fight and had in bad shape many times. Yet, the referee declared the bout a draw.[49]

---

[49] *Tonopah Daily Bonanza, Goldfield Daily Tribune,* June 12, 1915; *Nevada State Journal,* June 14, 1915.

In 1921, Dempsey said, "It was one of the toughest battles I have ever had. I took some mighty hard slams, but managed to knock Sudenberg down about 12 times in the early rounds. The affair was called a draw." In his 1940 autobiography, Jack changed it to 7 knockdowns, which was closer to the truth. In 1919, Dempsey said he started weakening in the 7th round from using his strength in hitting him, and Sudenberg began crowding him. Before the round was over, he decked Dempsey twice (not mentioned in the local reports). Thereafter, Sudenberg came at the fatiguing Dempsey as strong as ever. The contemporaneous reports only mentioned Dempsey going down in the 10th, which some thought was the result of a low blow. Dempsey claimed he was down in subsequent rounds, and Sudenberg was down in the 10th as well (also not supported by the local accounts). "This was really a great battle, little science entering into it at any time, but a great need for display of stamina." Dempsey said Sudenberg never received a great deal of publicity, "but my, how that fellow could fight! He never got much better than he was at the time he met me, but he was game and could punch."[50]

A couple weeks after the fight, Jack Dempsey turned 20 years old.

Sudenberg and Dempsey were scheduled to be the main attraction on Tuesday July 27 at the Jockey Athletic club in Reno, Nevada, boxing for the light heavyweight championship of the West.[51]

However, when an audience of only 150 patrons showed up on the 27th, the show was canceled, because the fighters refused to enter the ring, given that they were fighting on a percentage basis, and the gate was so small. They weren't going to fight another brutal war for a meager sum. The customers' money was returned.[52]

Years later, Dempsey said that he and Sudenberg became pals and put on a few exhibitions in Reno. They also exhibited at Mina Junction for a few rounds, passing the hat and making $4 each.

On July 31, 1915 in Temple, Texas, William Stanley, a black man arrested on a charge of murdering three children, without trial was taken from the jail at midnight and hung and burned to death in the public square in the presence of hundreds if  not thousands of men, women, boys and girls, who cheered as he went up in smoke. A lyncher's postcard of the event proudly called it a "barbecue."[53]

---

[50] *Fairmont West Virginian*, May 19, 1921; Dempsey, Jack, *Round by Round*, 1940; *Cedar Rapids Gazette*, May 19, 1919; *Toledo News-Bee*, June 18, 19, 1919.
[51] *Nevada State Journal*, July 23, 1915.
[52] *Nevada State Journal* (Reno), July 28, 1915.
[53] *Chicago Defender*, August 7, 1915.

On September 18, 1915, the *Montrose Daily Press* in Montrose, Colorado reported that Jack Dempsey and his manager had arrived in town. 20-year-old Dempsey was matched to meet Fred Woods there on Thursday September 23 at the Moose Hall. The local paper advertised Dempsey as a good, fast boy, undefeated (incorrect), and as holding the championship of the Pacific coast at 175 pounds (also incorrect). Of Woods, it said, "Our home boy needs no introduction, as he has been seen in action here before, and there should be some good, fast sparring." Some preliminary bouts were included as well. The press release was issued by Frank Wood, manager of the promotion, who perhaps was engaging in a bit of false advertising for marketing purposes.

Montrose was a regional shipping center, about 240 miles southwest of Denver, and west of Colorado Springs, with a branch railroad line that served the mineral-rich mountain region. It also was an agricultural hub.

Unfortunately, no post-fight report was issued, but in 1919, Dempsey said Montrose was a little town near where his parents lived. He learned that Fred Woods was booked to appear there. Jack had whipped him in a street fight years prior. Woods had become a pro boxer. Fred's opponent canceled, so Dempsey agreed to fill in. He was confident that he could win and earn a few stray dollars. The promoter thought he was committing suicide. Woods, the town blacksmith, was a big, burly fellow, and quite a scrapper. Dempsey replied that he could lick two like Woods in the same ring. Woods told him to keep his mouth shut or he'd rap him on the jaw. Jack took a wallop at Woods on the spot. The two were pulled apart and the promoter said they could fight it out in the ring. He agreed to pay Dempsey $10 if he won, but nothing if he lost. Jack knocked Woods out cold in the 3rd round.

In another version of the story, Jack said he and Woods fussed for months, until a grudge developed. Dempsey beat him, and Woods subsequently became one of his best boosters. "That was my beginning as a fighter. I went back to the ranch, stayed home long enough to help the old gent patch up a fence and then started out to become a fighter."[54]

In 1921, Dempsey said that he and Woods essentially were co-promoters of the venture. Woods was known as "The Fighting Blacksmith," and had a local reputation. Jack told him, "Half the folks in this town think you can lick me, and the rest of them think I can lick you. Let's stage a go and settle it. A lot of folks will pay money to see us scrap." They rented Moose Hall, put out handbills, did some ballyhooing, and advertised a dance to follow the fight. Jack was at the door on fight night selling tickets.

Dempsey knocked out Woods in the 4th round. "He slapped me pretty hard, but I slapped him a bit harder. Woods knew a lot about boxing and all I could do was slam. One of those slams went home – and the dance was

---

[54] *Buffalo Commercial*, April 14, 1919; *Wilmington Evening Journal*, April 30, 1919.

on!" He paid Woods $15 as his share. After paying expenses, he found that he had broken about even. Several early records list this as a KO4.[55]

A much later version by Dempsey said Woods was a strong and aggressive puncher, and they went at it hard. Jack decked Woods in the 2nd, but in the 3rd round, Woods doubled up Jack with a body shot. Eventually Jack recovered and tore at him with a fusillade of blows that dropped Fred. A right to the chin then knocked Woods down and out. Water was splashed over Fred to wake him up. The gate yielded $40, and after expenses were paid, they were able to split a few dollars.

On October 1, 1915 in Denver, Colorado, before a crowd of 6,000, Sam Langford and Sam McVey/McVea fought to a 20-round draw.[56]

Middleweight veteran Andy Malloy, who was much older than Jack, was at the Dempsey-Woods fight, and asked to fight Dempsey next. He was accommodated a couple weeks later.

35-year-old Andy Malloy had been boxing since 1904, and had at least 17 known fights, but most likely many more than that. He held a victory over Bernie Dempsey.[57] In 1904, he fought black Harry Peppers to a 20-round draw. Malloy twice had fought Jack Downey to 4-round draws in 1909. The most famous name on his record was Pueblo, Colorado's Fireman Jim Flynn, who twice had fought for the world heavyweight championship. In July 1915 in Pueblo, three months prior to the Dempsey contest, Flynn stopped Malloy in the 2nd round.

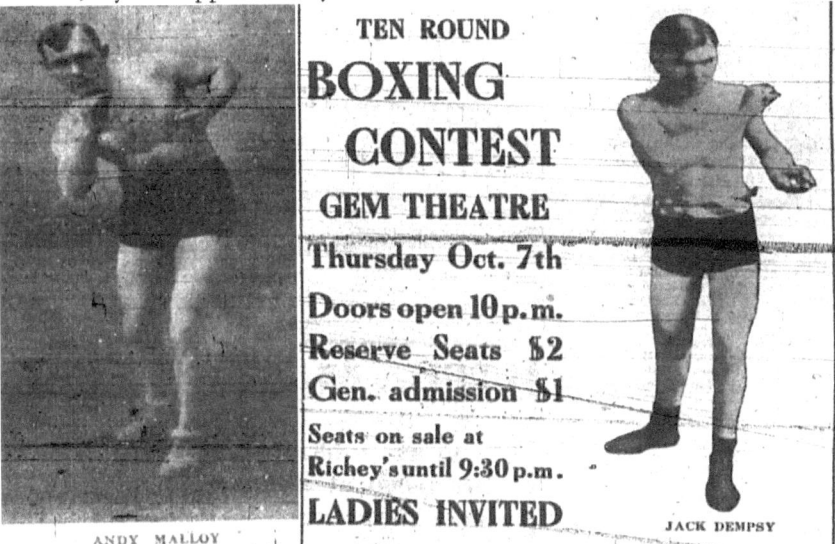

ANDY MALLOY — JACK DEMPSY

TEN ROUND
**BOXING CONTEST**
GEM THEATRE
Thursday Oct. 7th
Doors open 10 p.m.
Reserve Seats $2
Gen. admission $1
Seats on sale at Richey's until 9:30 p.m.
LADIES INVITED

On Thursday October 7, 1915 in Durango, Colorado (about 100 miles south of Montrose), another railroad mining town, at the Gem Theatre, the Jack Dempsey vs. Andy Malloy bout took place. Over 200 fight fans were on hand; paying $1 and $2 each, excited to see the main event.

---

[55] *Ogden Standard Examiner*, May 15, 1921.
[56] *Chicago Defender*, October 9, 1915.
[57] *Leadville Herald Democrat*, July 31, 1906, said Malloy had fought men such as Morgan Williams, Harry Peppers, and Dempsey (likely Bernie).

Unfortunately, before the bout took place, "Sheriff Fassbinder announced that it must be confined to a strictly boxing contest – if there was a knockout he would arrest the participants." Hence, his edict affected their performances. No one wants to get arrested and spend time in jail. Therefore, it was a 10-round no decision affair that would have to be an exhibition of skill, and they could not score a knockout, or they would incur law enforcement's wrath.

While there was no knockout over the course of the 10 rounds, the local *Durango Evening Herald* said there was some very clever boxing, and the participants showed that they had been in a mix-up. The audience declared Dempsey to be the better man. He towered over his opponent and had a longer reach. However, Malloy was game, with a clever defense, and got in some good welts too.[58] Dempsey later said he earned $35.[59]

Malloy claimed to be the champion of the Rocky Mountains, and Dempsey the light heavyweight champion of the Pacific Coast, a nice little fib for marketing purposes. Some have claimed that Malloy actually was acting as Dempsey's manager, and they were working with one another (both inside the ring and out) to earn some money.

**Jack Dempsey and Andy Malloy**

The October 16, 1915 *Montrose Daily Press* said Andy Malloy and his manager were in Montrose, Colorado to sign articles of agreement for a 10-round prize fight set to take place there at Moose hall the following Saturday, October 23, against Dempsey (though it spelled both of their names incorrectly). A subsequent notice on the 19th said, "It is expected the contest will be a fast and furious one, as both boys are in the best of trim."

---

[58] *Durango Evening Herald*, October 6-8, 1915.
[59] *Cedar Rapids Gazette*, May 5, 1919.

No post-fight report was issued for this October 23 fight, but Dempsey later said he laid Malloy low in 3 rounds. Malloy was paid $100 on the strength of his reputation and drawing power, for the hall was jammed. Dempsey didn't make much, but the result helped his reputation.[60]

In his much later autobiography, Dempsey, who often gave his foes a lot of credit (often even more credit than local newsmen gave them), claimed that Malloy hit him at will, and was the much better boxer, with a good defense. Jack took a beating and was wobbly. However, in the 3rd round, Dempsey launched a furious attack and caught Malloy, sending him down for the count. Early records also list this as a KO3 win for Dempsey.

Dempsey accepted Malloy's offer to manage him, as well as coach and teach him more about boxing. Jack said Malloy actually taught him to punch better, even though he already was a natural puncher.

Five days prior to Dempsey-Malloy II, on October 18, 1915 in Denver, Sam Langford clearly won a 15-round decision over black Battling Jim Johnson, who knocked down Langford in the 14th round for a flash, despite suffering a battering throughout.[61]

Dempsey was supposed to have a fight in Olathe, Colorado, just north of Montrose, against a local lad named Ben Parrish, but Parrish got cold feet and only wanted to wrestle. Jack was no wrestler, but was willing to do so in order to earn some money. It took Parrish 18 minutes to flop him the first time, and a lot less for the second fall. Jack earned $10, but decided he had no business or interest in the wrestling game.[62]

20-year-old Dempsey's next fight was about a month later, in November, in Cripple Creek, Colorado, another great gold mining camp, at an elevation of nearly 9,500 feet above sea level. It was just outside of Colorado Springs.

He was scheduled to fight the local heavyweight, 26-year-old George Coplen, 10 rounds in the semi-windup on a smoker card to be held at the Lyric

Jack Dempsey, of Victor, who meets George Coplen, of Cripple Creek, at the Moose Smoker, Friday evening, Nov. 19, 1915.

George Coplen, local heavyweight, who meets Jack Dempsey, of Victor, at the Moose smoker at the Lyric, Friday night

---

[60] *Fairmont West Virginian*, May 17, 1921.
[61] *Chicago Defender*, October 23, 1915.
[62] *Iowa City Press-Citizen*, May 13, 1921.

opera house, sponsored by the Moose Lodge. Jack was listed as being from Victor, Colorado.

Coplen worked out at the Roxbury gymnasium, training with local lightweight Matty Smith, who was scheduled to box Goldfield lightweight George Bauers (or Baur/Bauer) in the main event. The *Cripple Creek Times* said Coplen was showing up better than in the past and seemed to have gained some experience by his recent trip to Denver, where he fought at the National Athletic Club.

The Coplen bout was expected to be a fast and furious slugfest. Both were known as slam-bang artists, with the punch and the speed. The local paper said they were well-matched as to weight, and both had considerable experience in the slugging game. Tickets were selling rapidly. A large attendance was assured; possibly a record crowd.[63]

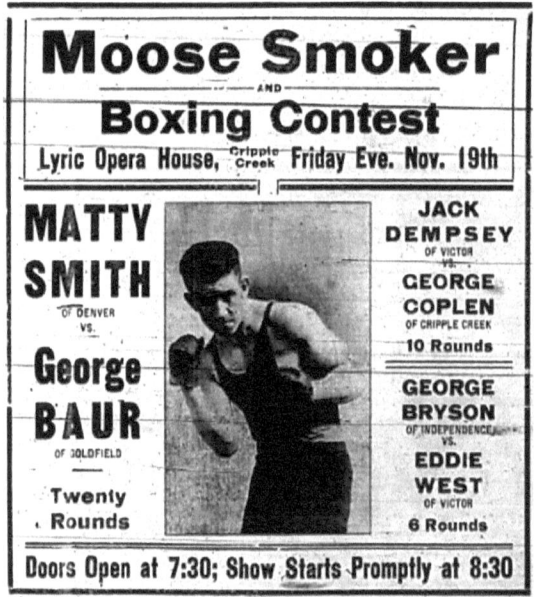

Large crowds watched George Baur train at the Mozart gymnasium, sparring with George Bryson and Jack Dempsey, both of whom would fight in preliminary bouts on the same card.

So, Smith's sparring partner Coplen would be fighting Baur's sparring partner Dempsey, and Smith and Baur were fighting in the main event.

Considerable interest was being taken in the Coplen-Dempsey battle, and there was much betting. Dempsey "of Victor" was the Victor favorite, while the local Coplen was the Cripple Creek favorite.

Both Coplen and Dempsey claimed that they would win by knockout, as was their reputation. The local paper said Coplen's record included a dozen knockout victories, while Dempsey had sent more than one ambitious fighter to the canvas for the count.[64]

Many years later, when describing his career prior to the Dempsey fight, Coplen said he had been fighting since 1908, and thought he was pretty good, having beaten most of the locals, even men weighing 200 pounds. Coplen noted that there was a 122-pound featherweight fighting in 1911 named Kid Blackey, who loaned him some trunks for a 1911 fight with Charlie Warner, whom Coplen knocked out in the 2nd round. Coplen also

---

[63] *Cripple Creek Times*, November 10, 11, 13, 14, 16, 1915.
[64] *Cripple Creek Times*, November 18, 19, 1915.

stopped a heavyweight named Jess Minium, who was knocked out so badly that three hours later, doctors still were working to revive him, and George was in jail. In the summer of 1914 at Victor, Coplen fought a heavyweight named Tommy Ryan, stopping him in the 9th round.

On Friday November 19, 1915 at the Lyric opera house in Cripple Creek, Colorado, the scheduled 10-round Dempsey-Coplen bout took place. The local *Cripple Creek Times* simply said that Victor's Jack Dempsey knocked out Cripple Creek's George Coplen in the 6th round. Dempsey had the better of the fight in nearly every round. They put up a good exhibition of boxing, though neither appeared to be in fighting form (which possibly meant that they were not in top shape, although the altitude may have had something to do with it). No further details were offered.[65]

Many years later, in his autobiography, Dempsey said he was paid $50 for the fight, and bet the money on himself to win. He decked Coplen seven times in the 1st round, and again in the 2nd, but Coplen came back strong, and by the 3rd round, Jack was fatiguing from the altitude. He was utterly exhausted in subsequent rounds, and doubted whether he could finish the fight. Brother Bernie told him that Coplen was just as tired, to rush him. Dempsey rushed in and floored him twice more until the referee stopped it (in the 6th or 7th round).

The fight hurt his confidence, because he had struggled with a good, tough fighter, but not a championship caliber one. He knew that he had to improve a great deal to make it to the top.

Dempsey alleged that afterwards, the promoter refused to pay up on the bet, claiming he had not placed the wager, but it was obvious he was angry because the Dempseys had pulled a fast one on him. He had expected Bernie Dempsey to be fighting as Jack Dempsey, wanting a softer touch for the local man, but instead got his more talented younger brother. The story does not ring true, because Dempsey had been training in Cripple Creek that week for all to see.

Coplen said Bernie "Scarface" Dempsey arranged the match between he and younger brother Harry. Coplen claimed that Dempsey weighed 184 pounds and he weighed 162. Other articles years later flipped it, claiming that "Copelin" weighed 180 and stood over six feet tall, while Dempsey was around 165 pounds. The primary source local newspaper simply said they were well matched as to weight, giving the impression that they were about the same size. Without an official weigh-in, one never knows for sure. They usually did not conduct weigh ins for heavyweight contests in those days, which was anything above middleweight, unless stipulated by contract.[66]

On December 3, 1915 in Harlem, New York, in a fast and fierce contest, 6'3" 203-pound Harry Wills won a 10-round no decision over 5'7" 195-pound Sam Langford.

---

[65] *Cripple Creek Times*, November 20, 1915. In the main event, 130-pound George Bauers and 128-pound Matty Smith fought to a 20-round draw. After the fight was over, Smith fainted and fell to the floor.
[66] *Colorado Springs Gazette-Telegraph*, May 18, 1969; Unknown *Denver Post* article published when Coplen was an elderly man and Dempsey's career was over.

Jack Dempsey, circa 1915

CHAPTER 4

# Improvement and Intermountain Region Recognition

On December 7, 1915, the *Salt Lake Telegram* announced that Jack Dempsey, the big strong young fellow who looked like a real white hope last winter, was back in town again after participating in a number of bouts in the surrounding states, and was anxious for another chance at Jack Downey, who had earned a decision over him back in April of that year. The 20-year-old Dempsey said he had learned a lot about the game since then and would beat Downey in a rematch. The fight would take place less than a month after Dempsey's victory over George Coplen.

After his 4-round decision victory over Dempsey, 28-year-old Downey had been stopped in 9 rounds by KO Brown, but avenged the loss by winning a rematch 10-round decision over him.

No stranger to the regulars, "white hope annihilator" Jack Downey was a veteran who knew every angle of the game, and had stopped or outboxed a number of aspiring young fighters. He was a local boxing instructor who worked with pupils every evening.

Jack Dempsey was called a tough proposition and promising young light heavyweight. Despite having relatively little ring experience, he was chock full of confidence. He was known for having a terrific, awful wallop in either hand, and could take a mighty hard poke as well. He "battles from the time the gong rings until the bout is over." No one ever accused him of being afraid to tear into his opponents, relying on his hard wallop to win fights, which he realized he needed to do to defeat the clever Downey. Hence, the bout promised to be a slam-bang affair from gong to gong.

On Monday, December 13, 1915 in Salt Lake City, the winter boxing season opened at the Grand theatre, under the auspices of Hardy K. Downing's Manhattan Club. The show, which consisted of six 4-round bouts, started at 8:30 p.m. Admission was 50 cents as usual.[67]

In the second preliminary, Jack Dempsey fought a rematch with Jack Downey.

---

[67] *Salt Lake Herald-Republican, Ogden Standard,* December 8, 1915; *Salt Lake Telegram,* December 9, 13, 1915; *Salt Lake Tribune,* December 12, 1915; *Salt Lake Herald-Republican,* December 13, 1915.

In the 1st round, Dempsey opened with a rush that threatened to send Downey out of the ring. They tore into each other, showing amazing speed. They gave and took more whacking blows than one might see in 10 rounds of usual heavyweight affairs. The pace was terrific. Soon Downey used his experience to good advantage, and waited. Dempsey too stood off and boxed for a bit. He showed a terrific kick, but at long-range fighting Downey had it on him, and the youngster's blows often missed by several feet. Downey's ability to duck under punches and come in close saved him often, for if Dempsey's blows had landed, they would have sent the veteran into next week.

Overall, for the first 2 rounds, Dempsey had Downey ducking and "doing the pigeon walk." Downey was cleverer by far and nicely got out of some difficult holes. The more aggressive Dempsey had a longer reach, and it looked as though his rough and tumble tactics would bring him victory.

Downey came back in the 3rd round and landed some fast, clean blows that nearly evened things up. Both tired materially, owing to the fast pace.

In the 4th round, Dempsey rushed his opponent around the ring, but Downey clinched and demonstrated some clever infighting.

At the end of 4 exciting rounds, Referee Hardy Downing (who also was the promoter) called it a draw. The *Salt Lake Telegram* said they were about even from every angle in a good 4-round draw. The *Salt Lake Herald-Republican* said the house expressed approval at the draw decision. The *Salt Lake Tribune* differed, saying half the house thought Dempsey won, and the other half was satisfied with the draw. "As a matter of fact, 'Dempsey by a shade' might have been fair enough." It had been a smashing good contest worth the admission price.[68] Dempsey later said he was paid $7.[69]

One week later, Dempsey fought again in Salt Lake. Both Dempsey and "Two-round" Gillian were called promising light-heavyweights anxious to make a name for themselves, but comparative youngsters in the game. "Dempsey started here as an amateur a little over a year ago and has only had eight or ten battles." He was well-known to local patrons, "looked upon as the makings of a mighty good man," and "the best-looking big fellow that has been seen here since the opening of the game a couple of years ago."

Undefeated Idaho native "Two-round" Gillian had fought in Idaho and Montana, going 6-0, all by knockout within 2 rounds, which got him his nickname. Gillian did not exhibit a great deal of cleverness, but had a terrific

---

[68] *Salt Lake Telegram, Salt Lake Herald-Republican, Salt Lake Tribune*, December 14, 1915.
[69] *Cedar Rapids Gazette*, May 9, 1919.

punch, and the build to absorb a heavy punch as well. Both were big powerful fellows with hard blows, so the bout likely would be slam-bang.[70]

Ticket prices were $.50, $1, and $1.50.

On Monday December 20, 1915 at the Grand theatre in Salt Lake City, under the auspices of Hardy K. Downing's Manhattan Club, Jack Dempsey fought "Two-round" Gillian.

In the 1st round, Gillian landed a couple of good punches, but Dempsey simply brushed off the blows and knocked Gillian around to all sides of the ring. Just before the halfway point of the round, off a feint which created an opening, Dempsey decked Gillian with ferocious blows to the chin. When he rose, Dempsey again feinted and then dropped Gillian.

Upon rising from the second knockdown, Gillian was helpless and practically out. Dempsey quickly rushed in to finish, but Referee Hardy Downing quickly jumped in, grabbed his drawn-back-arm, got Jack into a headlock, tackled and held him in order to save Gillian from further punishment. Harding then raised Jack's arm to declare him the winner.

The locals said it was a good stoppage, for Gillian might have been spilled all over the ring unnecessarily. Dempsey had his man at his mercy, and it would have taken but one more blow to finish him off. Gillian appeared glad that it was over. His seconds assisted him back to his corner. The man who was used to knocking out all of his foes within 2 rounds could not last even 1 round with Jack Dempsey.[71]

On January 3, 1916 in New Orleans, before a crowd of 4,000, 210-pound Harry Wills won a close but clear 20-round decision over 190-pound Sam Langford.[72]

As of January 10, 1916, Jack Dempsey still was in Salt Lake City, sparring at Young Peter Jackson's gym with lightweight Frankie Callahan (116 fights), who was preparing for a fight there scheduled for the 14th.[73]

It was announced that Dempsey, the most promising big fellow who ever boxed in Salt Lake, who always gave the fans plenty of action for their money, had been matched for a third time with Jack Downey. A little over a month ago, they gave patrons four of the greatest rounds ever seen, and fans had been clamoring for a chance to see them mix again.

They were supposed to fight on January 24, but Dempsey allegedly was sick with an attack of the grips or grippe (flu virus), so the match was delayed, for the time being.[74]

However, what really might have been going on was that as of January 20, Dempsey, the Salt Lake light heavyweight, was in Ely, Nevada, a couple hundred miles southwest of Salt Lake, just across the border, sparring with welterweight Eddie Johnson (44 fights). They were helping each other prepare for upcoming bouts to be held there at the Bijo hall (original date of

---

[70] *Salt Lake Herald-Republican*, December 18, 20, 1915; *Salt Lake Telegram*, December 19, 1915; *Salt Lake Tribune*, December 19, 20, 1915. Supposedly his real name was Jack Gillian.
[71] *Salt Lake Herald-Republican, Salt Lake Telegram, Salt Lake Tribune*, December 21, 1915.
[72] *Chicago Defender*, January 8, 1916.
[73] *Salt Lake Telegram*, January 11, 1916.
[74] *Salt Lake Telegram*, January 21, 25, 1916.

January 29, moved to February 5). Johnson wanted someone with whom he could be rough, and Dempsey fit the bill. Dempsey was scheduled to meet Danny Hayes of McGill in a 6-round bout there.

Ely, Nevada had been a stagecoach station along the Pony Express and Central Overland Route, and in 1906, when copper was found, it became a mining town.

Of Dempsey, the local Ely newspaper, the *White Pine News*, said, "This boy certainly looks true to form and appears in every way qualified to bear the great name with credit. He is a regular fighting machine. Fast and fearless, always in action and packing a punch that will drop an elephant any time it lands according to direction."[75]

On Saturday February 5, 1916 in Ely, Nevada, at the Bijo hall, in the main event, Canadian welterweight Frank Barrieau won a 10-round decision over Eddie Johnson of Pueblo, Colorado (who had sparred with Dempsey to prepare). The hall was packed full, the largest audience ever seen locally. Tom Chambers promoted.

According to the local *White Pine News*, in the preliminary, Jack Dempsey fought someone called the "Big Swede." Jack had been having difficulty finding a match. Apparently, the Hayes fight fell through. A fighter named "Argoe" was willing to fight him, but authorities prevented it because he was too small, conceding too much weight.

The "Big Swede," who finally was selected to meet Dempsey, evidently had been imbibing a little too freely when he entered the ring. He tried to amuse the audience with what he thought were funny gestures, but Dempsey took a different view. He was there to fight. He became disgusted, as did everyone else, and quickly sent him down and out in the 1st round. The Swede remained on the floor with his eyes wide open.

Dempsey was called a real prize fighter and coming man in the ring, while his opponent was called a "human crustation of the lobster variety."

The local weekly *Ely Record* said Jack Dempsey, "manifestly a fighter," was matched against a "long individual" known as the Big Swede, who seemed intoxicated. "He was in no condition for a fight and a gentle tap from Dempsey sent him to the mat to stay."[76]

Dempsey later said that he had been a sparring partner for Eddie Johnson of Pueblo, helping him to prepare for a fight in Ely. "Jack got on in a prelim bout with another Johnson. It was a one-round whirlwind in which Jack again delivered a knockout." Therefore, it makes sense that some reported that he knocked out a fighter named Big Swede Johnson, who was based out of Salt Lake City. Dempsey said he earned $25.[77]

On February 11, 1916 in New Orleans, Sam Langford knocked out Harry Wills in the 19th round, proving that he still was the world's best

---

[75] *White Pine News* (Ely, White Pine County, NV), January 23, 1916.
[76] *Pine News* (weekly mining review), February 6, 1916; *Ely Record*, February 11, 1916.
[77] *Fairmont West Virginian*, May 19, 1921. Some later erroneously called him Jim Johnson and incorrectly listed KO1 over a Battling Johnson on Dempsey's record. *Cedar Rapids Gazette*, May 21, 1919, printing Damon Runyon's story of Dempsey's life.

black heavyweight, or at least its most dangerous. A left hook to the jaw sent him down, and Wills barely beat the count. A fusillade of left and right swings sent Wills down and out for the count.[78]

On February 19, 1916, the *Ogden Standard* reported that Celia Dempsey of Salt Lake had petitioned the district court for the release of her daughter Elsie Dempsey, Jack's younger sister by two years, who was an inmate of the State industrial school. Elsie was committed to the state institution on October 1, 1915, at which time Elsie already was of the age of majority and not a minor (she was 18). She also contended that the commitment was irregular in that it was not based on a valid complaint.

Jack Dempsey returned to Salt Lake City for some unfinished business with Jack Downey. Since their last contest, a draw, Downey had won a 4-round decision over Erne Wright.

The Salt Lake City newspapers said Jack Dempsey started as an amateur about a year ago, and had defeated everyone in his class except Jack Downey. He was looked upon as a youngster of real promise, the most promising big fellow that ever broke into the game there, and if he could beat Downey, he would accomplish something that none of the rest of the white hopes had been able to do, which would show that he is improving, and with a little more experience would be a tough proposition for any of the light heavyweights. Dempsey was a hard-hitting boxer, while Downey was a past-master of the art of boxing.

The *Salt Lake Tribune* said Dempsey no doubt would become a star heavyweight in the course of a year or two if he continued to improve as he had done over the past year.

Although the Young Gilbert vs. Mickey O'Brien contest was the main event, the local press paid more attention to the Dempsey-Downey bout. The *Salt Lake Telegram* said Downey had been a prime attraction during the past three years. He had fought them all, from Young Corbett to Joe Walcott.[79]

---

[78] *Paterson Morning Call*, February 12, 1916. It was the second time that Langford had knocked out Wills (1914 KO14). However, it would be the last time that Wills lost to Langford.
[79] *Salt Lake Herald-Republican, Salt Lake Tribune, Salt Lake Telegram*, February 20, 21, 1916. On February 18, 1916, the *Salt Lake Telegram* claimed that Dempsey had stopped Johnny Sudenberg in 2 rounds in Ely, but this was incorrect, because Nevadans knew who Sudenberg was and would have named him for the promotional value at least, neither Dempsey nor Sudenberg would have taken a last minute non-main-event fight against each other, given that they knew it likely would be a war, the pay would be less, and they had refused to fight on a percentage for low pay once before, Sudenberg would not have fought as horribly, Dempsey in 1921 called the opponent Johnson, never mentioned a third fight with Sudenberg in any of his autobiographies, said he fought him in Goldfield and Tonopah but did not mention Ely, a third fight won via knockout would have been memorable and significant given that he fought him to two prior draws, the opponent "Big Swede" was called a "long individual," but Sudenberg was short and stocky, and finally, Sudenberg was from Omaha, and the February 1, 1916 *Omaha Daily Bee* said Sudenberg, a former Omaha special delivery carrier and now a promising young middleweight, had gone to St. Paul, Minnesota with his manager. He had been trying to get matches nearby, but being unsuccessful, was hoping for better luck in the Minneapolis area. Hence, Sudenberg does not appear to have been in Nevada at all, but over 1,000 miles away.

On Monday February 21, 1916 at the Manhattan Club show at the Grand Theatre in Salt Lake City, Jack Dempsey fought Jack Downey for the third time. Admission was 50 cents.

According to the local accounts, the 1st round was a hummer, with honors about even.

In the 2nd round, Dempsey rushed and carried Downey off his feet. A wicked stomach punch was the beginning of Downey's downfall. Dempsey rushed him and Downey staggered to the ropes. A one-two, followed by a varied assortment of blows, and then a hard right flush to the jaw took Downey off his feet and finished matters. Downey rose just after Referee Hardy Downing tolled off the ten-count, so it was curtains.

Against Jack Downey, Jack Dempsey had gone from a decision loss to a draw to a knockout victory, showing his improvement and progress.

The *Salt Lake Telegram* said that this time, Downey couldn't keep his chin out of the way. In the 2nd round, he took a voyage into the land of nod when Dempsey bounced a stiff right hand wallop off his chin. Dempsey, a young light heavyweight "of unusual promise," demonstrated that he was improving. He actually outboxed the clever Downey and outpunched him as well. He carried a terrific kick in either glove. Downey probably would have lost even had he not gone down.

The *Salt Lake Herald-Republican* said Downey heard the robin calling and the little birds sing when in the middle of the 2nd round, youth was served. With all his cleverness, Downey could not keep his taller opponent from scoring.

The *Salt Lake Tribune* said, "Dempsey has improved greatly since his last appearance here, and should give the best of them a busy time from now on."[80]

Dempsey said he earned $12.50 or $15 for this fight.

**Ogden, Utah rail depot, 1910**

Amazingly, Dempsey returned to the ring again just two days later, in nearby Ogden, Utah, a major railway hub about 38 miles north of Salt Lake City.

Salt Lake's Dempsey was advertised to fight a black fighter called the Boston Bear-Cat in the main event at 180 pounds for the light heavyweight championship of Utah. Admission was $.50, $1, and $1.50 for ringside seats, for a five-fight show that started at 8:30 p.m.

The local *Ogden Standard* said they were the first heavyweights to appear on a local card. Salt Lake fans considered Dempsey to be one of the most promising light-heavyweights in that part of the country. The Boston Bear Cat was a negro who was alleged to have met a number of topnotchers, including Sam Langford, Jim Flynn, and Jeff Clark.[81]

---

[80] *Salt Lake Tribune, Salt Lake Herald-Republican, Salt Lake Telegram*, February 22, 1916.
[81] *Ogden Standard*, February 21, 22, 1916; *Ogden Examiner*, February 22, 1916.

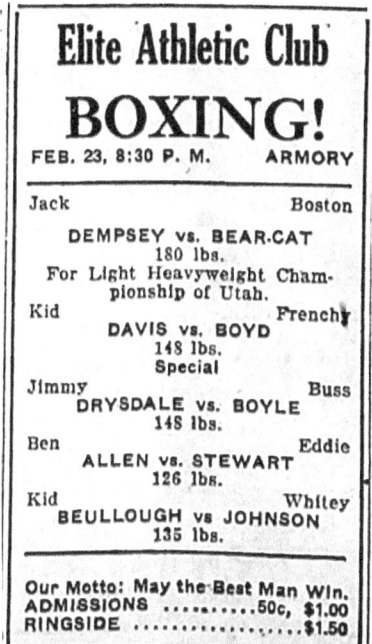

Boston Bear Cat.

On Wednesday February 23, 1916 at the Ogden Armory hall, under the auspices of the Elite Athletic Club, in a scheduled 4-round bout, before a crowd of nearly 400 fans, Jack Dempsey fought "the much heralded terror," the Boston Bear Cat.

According to the local *Ogden Standard* and *Ogden Examiner*, in the 1st round, a hard blow on the point of the negro's chin dropped him. He rose at nine in a groggy state, and before he could recover sufficiently, another blow put him down to sleep for good. The quick finish was a surprise, for the Bear-Cat appeared to be a strong and finely developed athlete, and a trifle heavier, too, than Dempsey.[82]

The *Salt Lake Telegram* said the Bear Cat claimed to have conquered Sam Langford, Sam McVey, and other "dark clouds," but his claims were doubted, given how easily he was taken out. This paper said if he ever lasted even a round with men such as Langford and McVey, Dempsey could whip all of the "black clouds" in the country in the same ring on the same night. Nevertheless, the result pleased the fans, who gave Jack an ovation.[83]

Many years later, Dempsey claimed to have earned $50 or $75. He said the Bearcat, who claimed to have gone 20 rounds with Langford, was very big and muscular at about 220 pounds (not likely). The Bear Cat's cocksure confidence made Jack nervous. But when he got into the ring, the Bear Cat said to him, "White boy, we'll just box." Jack replied, "We will, will we?" Dempsey mostly went for the body, sinking them right in, not pulling any punches, until knocking him down and out for the count.[84]

---

[82] *Ogden Standard*, *Ogden Examiner*, February 24, 1916.
[83] *Salt Lake Telegram*, February 24, 1916.
[84] *Cedar Rapids Gazette*, May 19, 1919; *Round by Round*.

A week later, the State of Utah moved to quash Miss Elsie Dempsey's petition for release. She had appealed the Salt Lake juvenile court decision committing her to the industrial school. The State alleged that the Ogden court did not have jurisdiction in the case. At the time that Miss Dempsey was brought before the juvenile court on a delinquency charge, she was a minor. However, it was said that she might be paroled at the next meeting of the trustees of the industrial school.[85]

On March 7, 1916 in Brooklyn, New York, 204 ½-pound Harry Wills won a 10-round newspaper decision over 195 ½-pound Sam Langford.

Just two weeks after the Bearcat bout, on Thursday March 9, 1916 in Provo, Utah (45 miles south of Salt Lake City), at the Mozart theatre, 175-pound Jack Dempsey fought 190-pound Cyril Cohen (or Cohn) of Havre, Montana in a scheduled 6-round contest. Both were called real contenders who had disposed of the best aspirants in their class. The 15 pounds bigger Montana champion Cohen "has a haymaker in both hands."[86]

The *Provo Daily Herald* said Dempsey demonstrated from the start that he intended to win by knockout over Cyril Cohn. It was a terrific bout, with little regard for science, for they slugged away throughout. In the 4th round, Dempsey decked him, and Cohn's seconds told promoter and referee Otto Olsen that they gave up the fight, throwing the sponge into the ring, but initially the referee failed to stop the fight. After Cohn rose to his feet, the wiry Dempsey once more attacked him. They continued, until the referee finally stopped it and declared Dempsey the winner in the 4th round.[87]

Dempsey was scheduled to fight a 15-round contest against black fighter George Christian in Price, Utah, 75 miles southeast of Provo, a mere eight days later. "Dempsey is the most promising heavy-weight in the intermountain region, has a knockout in either mitt and is game to the core." He and Christian were "the classiest pair that has been matched in Utah for a long period and the fans are all eager for the contest."[88]

Dempsey, who claimed the heavyweight championship of the Pacific coast, said he would keep training in Price, the scene of his next fight, at the Northern Bar. He was not overlooking the fact that he was going up against the hardest proposition of his career when he "meets the negro." Christian was confident that he would "call the white boy's number."[89]

George Christian, who was about 25 years old, had been fighting since 1911, a year in which he knocked out future white champion Arthur Pelkey in the 1st round. In 1912, Christian was stopped in the 8th round by Joe Jeannette, who had 95 fights and was known as one of the world's best heavyweights. Christian fought Willie Meehan, who had 78 fights, to a 1913 NC4 and 1914 D6, D10, and L4.

---

[85] *Salt Lake Herald-Republican*, March 1, 1916.
[86] *Provo Daily Herald*, March 6, 1916; *Salt Lake Telegram* March 9, 1916.
[87] *Provo Daily Herald*, March 13, 1916. The *Salt Lake Telegram*, March 10, 1916, called him Cyril Kohen.
[88] *Price News Advocate*, March 3, 1916.
[89] *Price News-Advocate*, March 10, 1916. Dempsey planned to go to Denver and the East to meet the best in his class. Dempsey later claimed to have sparred for the fight with his pal "Swede" Algreen. *Cedar Rapids Gazette*, May 21, 1919.

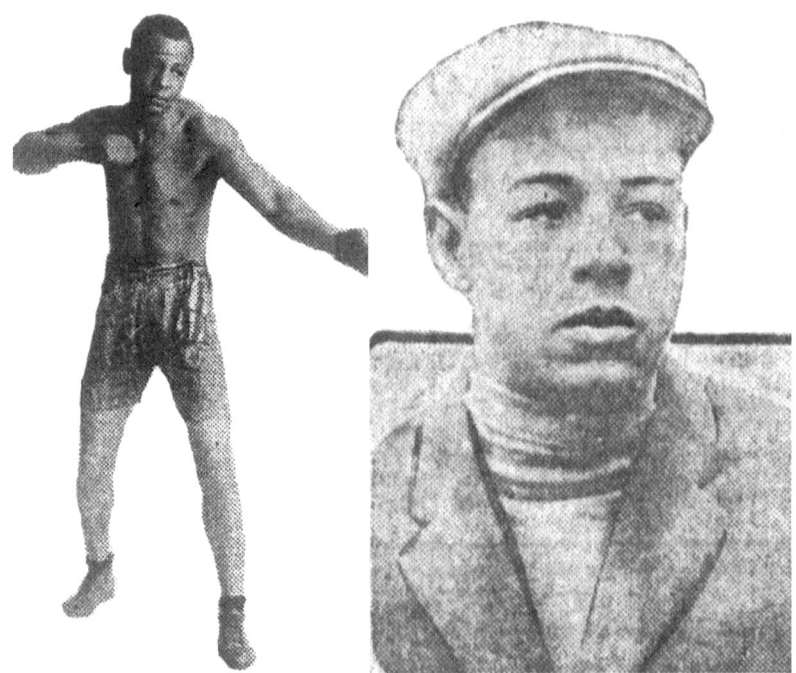

Christian was so confident of defeating Dempsey that he already was talking about fighting Young Peter Jackson next.[90]

The two were fighting for 65% and 35% of the receipts, based on winner and loser. The allegedly larger Christian was the slight favorite among local fans wagering on the contest.[91]

The local *Price News-Advocate* said both were in fine condition. The colored lad had been running 6 miles every morning and sparring the best locals every evening. Dempsey had shown class in his workouts as well. Price fans observed that even a short session in the ring with Dempsey was a big mouthful.[92]

On St. Patrick's Day, March 17, 1916 in Price, Utah, at the Eko theatre, Jack Dempsey fought George Christian of New York in a scheduled 15-round bout. The local theater was crowded to capacity. Both were in the pink of condition, having trained faithfully while in town. However, the local *Price Sun* said that despite the fact that Dempsey's weight was given as 173, he looked at least 180, while Christian, whose weight was given as 167, did not appear to weigh much more than 160. Kid Davis refereed.

Almost immediately when the fight started, Dempsey landed a terrible wallop on the jaw. This took the pep out of the colored man, and it was plainly seen that he knew he was whipped. Christian was outclassed entirely. Quite soon his jaw sagged heavily and his legs were wobbly. After a clinch, Dempsey landed a powerful uppercut to the jaw and Christian went down and out for the count, about 80 seconds into the 1st round. Christian had no

---

[90] Boxrec.com; *Salt Lake Telegram*, March 12, 1916
[91] *Salt Lake Telegram*, March 14, 1916.
[92] *Price News-Advocate*, March 17, 1916.

show whatsoever with his heavier opponent. A man who had lasted 8 rounds with world-class heavyweight Joe Jeannette could not last 1 round with the very powerful Jack Dempsey.[93]

Dempsey later claimed to have earned $260 for this fight.[94]

The *Provo Daily Herald* said Dempsey must have shown considerably more speed and punch than he exhibited at the Mozart a few days ago when he had a hard time beating down Cyril Cohn in 4 rounds.[95]

When later discussing his career, Dempsey said that over time, he learned to come in and under an opponent's blows and hit up. He learned to time punches and hit when a man was moving forward, and conversely, make sure that he was hit when moving away, pulling back, turning, or rolling with punches to take the sting out. He ducked and weaved to avoid being hit when attacking and coming in. Pivoting at the waist and using his body weight in turns generated power in his punches. He learned to move close to his own corner near the end of rounds. One time he had a bad eye, so he painted a bruise under the other eye so the opponent would not know which one to hit. He learned to vary his tactics, hitting light in one round, hard in another, box in one, attack and fight in another, which helped his efficiency. Learning all of this took time and experience.

At that time, D. W. Griffith's controversial yet financially successful film, *The Birth of a Nation*, which strongly advocated for separation of the races and portrayed members of the Ku Klux Klan as heroes and blacks as villains, was playing in Salt Lake City. The movie had been screening since early 1915, and would become the highest grossing film of all time until 1939.

On March 25, 1916 at Madison Square Garden in New York, in a contest promoted by Tex Rickard, just shy of one year after winning the title, 34-year-old Kansas cowboy (though listed as 28), 6'6 ½" 259 ½-pound Jess Willard defended his world heavyweight championship for the first time, winning a 10-round no-decision bout against 6'1" 201 ½-pound Frank Moran, who had lost a 1914 title fight 20-round decision to Jack Johnson. Since then, Moran had knocked out Bombardier Billy Wells (KO10) and Jim Coffey (TKO3, TKO9). Willard carefully but clearly outboxed Moran, using his height and reach very well, pumping in consistent jabs that were well timed, but clinching, uppercutting, and firing inside blows when Moran got close. Jess was good at rolling with, ducking, or blocking blows. Moran alternated between ferocious aggression

---

[93] *Price Sun*, March 24, 1916; *Salt Lake Herald-Republican, Salt Lake Telegram*, March 18, 1916. Dempsey later claimed that Christian was a 200-pound fighter.
[94] *Cedar Rapids Gazette*, May 21, 1919.
[95] *Provo Daily Herald*, March 23, 1916.

and moving about, but found it difficult penetrate the height and reach of the huge Willard.

After the fight, Moran, whose eye and nose were bleeding, and face bruised, said, "Willard is a powerful man. He is clever and can hit, and he took advantage of every opportunity to use his weight."

Both fighters were paid quite handsomely. For a mere 10 rounds of work, Willard earned a guaranteed $47,500, and Moran $23,750, plus $5,000 each for the motion picture rights (the films could be shown in New York state). The gate receipts, generated by a crowd of about 13,000, were $151,254. Most had called Jack Johnson greedy for demanding a $30,000 minimum payday for title defenses against legitimate challengers. Johnson had been banned from fighting in New York throughout his championship career, even to fight other black fighters like Joe Jeannette.

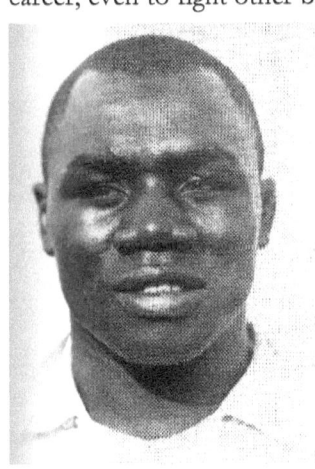

On April 7, 1916 in Syracuse, New York, before a crowd of 5,000, 202-pound Sam Langford won a 10-round no decision over 220-pound Sam McVey, winning 6-2-2.[96]

Considerable interest was taken in 20-year-old Jack Dempsey's upcoming contest with Joe Bonds, scheduled to be held in Ely, Nevada. Both had good reputations, and a fierce fight was expected. According to the *Salt Lake Telegram*, Bonds was heavier than Dempsey, and his aggressiveness would make him a favorite in the betting line. 23-year-old Bonds typically weighed 181-186 pounds. What also might have been a factor was that Bonds had far more experience, with 38 known fights on his record to that point (24-6-8), including having gone the 20-round distance in three bouts in Australia. He had been fighting since 1912.[97]

---

[96] *Chicago Defender*, April 15, 1916. Boxrec.com.
[97] *Salt Lake Telegram*, April 7, 1916; Boxrec.com. Bonds' record included: 1912 D10 and L10 Frank Farmer; 1913 D6 Farmer; 1914 D4 Farmer, D12 Tom McCarthy, LTKOby6 and W4 Al Norton; W4 Farmer; 1915 L20 Harold Hardwick, TKO12 Harry Reeve, W20 Sid Neilsen, LKOby1 Eddie McGoorty, KO10 Jack Darcy, L20 Reeve, and D4 Farmer.

The local *Ely Record* said patrons were showing keen interest in the contest. Both men worked out at Ruth on Monday for public view. Bonds was the public favorite because of his long string of victories and the good showing he made in his workouts. Bonds also was bigger by 10 or 12 pounds. However, Dempsey was no stranger to the fighting game, and it was quite possible that spectators might "receive a surprise." A big delegation from the mines was expected.[98]

On Saturday April 8, 1916 in Ely, Nevada, at the Bijo hall, before one of the biggest crowds that ever gathered for a boxing contest in that city, Jack Dempsey fought a scheduled 10-round contest with Joe Bonds. According to the local *White Pine News*, when Dempsey entered the ring, the cheers which greeted him lasted for several minutes. Still, Bonds was the betting favorite, owing to the fact that he had the reputation of being cleverer and carrying more weight, not to mention having more experience.

In the 1st round, Bonds worked all over the ring trying to find a place to land, but when the real fighting started it was Dempsey who came to the front. Jack had a shade in this round. The 2nd was even. In the 3rd, Bonds rushed, but Dempsey never broke ground. Still, it was Bonds' round. Dempsey had a shade the edge in the 4th and 5th rounds. The 6th was even. Bonds desperately tried to recover lost ground in the 7th, but it was Dempsey's round. The 8th through 10th were clear Dempsey rounds. At the end of the 10th round, Bonds claimed he had been struck low, and perhaps he had, but the referee failed to see it. The blow was accidental, and it was too late in the game to make any difference regarding public opinion as to the relative merits of the men.

Dempsey won the 10-round decision over Bonds. In the end, Dempsey clearly won at least half of the rounds, shaded some others, or they were even, and Bonds only clearly won one round. There was no question that Dempsey won and was entitled to the decision.

The *White Pine News* said it was the best battle ever witnessed in the western country. Both not only were clever, but the most willing and aggressive fighters who ever entered the prize ring. Bonds was very clever, but Dempsey was the better fighter, for he fought like a tiger from gong to gong. Yet, Bonds never stalled and was very willing. Dempsey, known to be one of the greatest fighters now before the public, proved that he should be considered as a potential future heavyweight champion and successor to Willard. He was big, strong, clever, and willing.

The local *Ely Record* said both Dempsey and Bonds were in fine condition and gave and took punishment cheerfully over the course of 10 rounds of hard and exciting fighting throughout. Bonds was thought to have the better of it at the start, but as the fight progressed, Dempsey was able to counter his foe's sledge-hammer blows and return them with interest. Referee Smoot's decision in Dempsey's favor, holding his hand

---

[98] *Ely Record*, April 7, 1916.

aloft and declaring him the victor, was met with a roar of deafening cheers.[99]

Dempsey later said he had been offered $300 for the Bonds fight, though another time he said he was offered 25% of the gate, which turned out to be $235, which was great money for him. He didn't even care who the opponent was. It was then that he took his first ride to a fight on the cushions of a train (as opposed to being a stowaway, dangerously riding the rails, underneath the train).

Without knowing one another, he and Bonds were on the same train to the fight scene. When they met, Bonds said he was making the trip to fight some sucker named Jack Dempsey before going back to the coast to meet up with his manager, Jack Kearns. Harry Dempsey did not tell him who he was. When they arrived, promoter Tom Chambers introduced them, and Jack merely grinned as they shook hands.

Jack trained in the back room of Chambers' saloon. Bonds actually hurt the gate by going around town saying it was a shame to put a fellow like Dempsey in the ring with him. Folks got the impression that Jack was going to be murdered, and they did not want to see a mismatch.

Bonds was a tough, confident man, and it was a hard fight. "I was pretty sore at him, and I went in to give him a good pasting. I knocked him down four or five times [not mentioned by the local reports] and roughed him around, and did my best to knock him out, but couldn't do it. All he did was holler foul during the fight, and he tore out of town the next day pretty well marked up."[100]

*Chicago Defender*, April 22, 1916

The *Chicago Defender*'s Henry E. Reed said the South was highly segregated by Jim Crow laws and customs. In St. Louis, black police officers were not allowed to arrest whites. Blacks always were served last at drug stores. They were called "boy" regardless of age. Blacks did all the porter work, for which they were paid $6 a week. Working on the railroad was considered a good job, earning $1 to $1.50 per day. Women working in white people's kitchens and doing the wash for a family of six earned $2 a week.

Race issues were alive in the North as well. In Wisconsin, a 21-year-old white female, who wanted to marry a black man, was

---

[99] *White Pine News* (Ely, NV), April 9, 1916; *Ely Record*, April 14, 1916. The *Salt Lake Telegram* reported that Dempsey was the aggressor all the way and had a wide edge. *Salt Lake Telegram*, April 9, 1916.
[100] *Fairmont West Virginian*, May 20, 1921; *Cedar Rapids Gazette*, May 21, 1919.

committed to a home for the feeble minded, even though physicians declared she was normal.

Fifty years after the end of slavery, blacks still had to deal with race prejudice, ostracism, lynchings, disfranchisement, segregation, Jim Crow laws, and Southern concubinage.[101]

On April 25, 1916 in St. Louis, Harry Wills won an 8-round newspaper decision over Sam Langford, decking him in the 2nd round.

Set to be held less than a month after Dempsey-Bonds, the Alhambra Theatrical company in Ogden, Utah, in conjunction with the Elite Athletic club, arranged for a first-class 10-round boxing contest between Terry Keller, "recognized light-heavyweight champion of the world," and Jack Dempsey, a top-notcher in the same weight class.

Keller was an Ogden native who allegedly had fought his way to first position among the light heavies.

20-year-old Dempsey would train in Salt Lake City until April 26, and then work out for a week at the Hermitage in Ogden canyon in preparation for the May 3 contest.[102]

26-year-old Terry Keller, who had over 50 fights of experience, far more than Dempsey, had done considerable boxing not only in the U.S., but in Australia and England as well. Keller recently had been fighting in the East, and was returning to his hometown to fight for local fans.

**TERRY KELLER**
Who Meets Jack Dempsey on May 3.

TERRY KELLER.

---

[101] *Chicago Defender*, April 29, 1916; July 22, 1916.
[102] *Ogden Standard*, April 15, 1916.

**10-Round Boxing Contest**
**ALHAMBRA Theatre**
Ogden, Utah **Wed., May 3** Ogden, Utah

Claimant of the World's Light Heavyweight Championship
**TERRY KELLER** vs. **Jack Dempsey**
OF BALTIMORE, FORMERLY OF OGDEN        OF SALT LAKE CITY, UTAH.

Greatest Sporting Events Ever Given in the Intermountain Country—Big Preliminaries.
PRICES: $1.00, $1.50, $2.00, $2.50, $3.00   GET YOUR RESERVATIONS EARLY—DON'T WAIT
EXCURSION RATES ON ALL RAILROADS.  PHONE ALHAMBRA, 207.   H. E. SKINNER, Manager.

In 1912, Keller had lost a 20-round decision to heavyweight Colin Bell in Australia, but won other 20-round bouts there. A primary source record claimed that Keller had knocked out Bell in England in the 4th round. Keller's record included such fights as: 1914 LTKOby9 Jim Coffey and LND10 Battling Levinsky; 1915 D15 Dan Porky Flynn, LND10 Tony Ross, W15, D15, and L15 Dick Gilbert, LTKOby4 Fred Fulton, and DND10 Billy Miske; and 1916 D15 Tom McMahon (who held a 1914 WND12 over Willard), all of whom were very experienced well-regarded battlers. Keller was a good fighter, but not a champion.[103]

Keller arrived in Ogden on April 23 from Baltimore. The next day, 50 fans showed up to watch him train and spar.[104]

The local paper called it the most important event of the kind staged in that section of the country in years. The spirit of the semi-local Ogden vs. Salt Lake rivalry was manifested. Salt Lake fans were with Dempsey, while Ogden fans were pulling for Keller. Still, Dempsey had become popular in Ogden as well, after his performance there against the Boston Bear Cat. Ticket prices went from $1 up to $3 in 50-cent increments.[105]

The local *Ogden Standard* said Keller was known as one of the best light heavies in the world. Sometimes he even called himself the champion, though in truth he was not. Keller's claim to the world light heavyweight championship clearly was done for marketing purposes. He had been matched to fight world light heavyweight (IBU) and European and "white world heavyweight" champion Georges Carpentier at one point, but the bout was called off owing to the war that

Georges Carpentier at left

---
[103] *Salt Lake Herald-Republican*, April 16, 1916; *Salt Lake Telegram*, April 23, 1916; Boxrec.com; *Ely Record*, October 6, 1916.
[104] *Ogden Standard*, April 24, 25, 1916.
[105] *Ogden Standard*, April 26, 1916.

had been raging in Europe since July 1914. Carpentier had joined the French military, and was a pilot in the flying service.

Jack Dempsey

TERRY KELLER.

Dempsey was listed as standing 6' tall and weighing 180 pounds. Keller weighed about the same.

The *Ogden Examiner* said the Ogden fans who saw Keller training believed he would beat Dempsey.

Keller, "The Battleship of Maryland," said, "I am in fine condition; better than I have been in a good many fights. ... I am confident of defeating Dempsey, but realize that he is a good man and a fighter from the word go."

Dempsey said, "I know I have got to fight and fight hard when I meet Keller, but I have all confidence in my ability to win. I know Terry has met some of the best of the big fellows, but that does not worry me. I have also met big fellows and won when they said I didn't stand a chance. The quicker we get together the better I will like it."

The general opinion of those who had seen both men work out was that the fight would go the full 10 rounds.[106]

The *Salt Lake Telegram* said Dempsey was the best thing in his class ever developed locally. He was taking on his most formidable foe, the cleverest and most experienced man he ever had met in his short career. Jack was only 20 years old and still could not vote, but had shown the goods in all of his mills and probably would surprise Keller. However, if the bout went 10 rounds, Keller likely would outbox his less

---

[106] *Ogden Standard, Ogden Examiner*, May 2, 3, 1916.

experienced opponent. Dempsey was a considerable boxer himself, and had a big punch. Still, Keller had plenty of experience against punchers, so Jack might find it hard to connect with a knockout blow in only 10 rounds.[107]

Fans were coming from Wyoming, Nevada, and Idaho, including towns such as Evanston, Green River, Granger, Rock Springs, Kemmerer, as well as Salt Lake, Garfield, Bingham, Logan, Preston, and others. The Alhambra theatre had a seating capacity of 2,000, and tickets were in demand. "Kellar" was the betting favorite, and Salt Lake fans would accept such wagers when they arrived in Ogden.

Kellar weighed 180 pounds and stood 6' ½". Hence, physically, he and 180-pound Dempsey were equally matched. The locals said Terry had been fighting as a pro since 1907, after having won amateur championships in previous years. He had fought in the U.S., Australia, and England.[108]

On Wednesday May 3, 1916 in Ogden, Utah at the Alhambra theatre, before a capacity crowd of 2,000, which included those from all over the state and surrounding states, Jack Dempsey fought a scheduled 10-round contest against Terry Keller. When the fighters entered the ring, Keller was the betting favorite. Jack appeared nervous, while Terry's easy attitude reassured friends.

However, within a few seconds of the fight's start, the unfavorable feeling about Dempsey ended. Dempsey began with a rush and pounded away with hard blows on Keller's already battle-mutilated features, landing at will. Terry was unable to block the punches. However, Keller was very tough and game, and fought back hard. Both took plenty of punishment in the 1st round, which was about even.

The 2nd round was nearly all Dempsey, forcing Keller to the ropes, hitting him almost at will, while Keller's swings were wild. Both were in good condition, but something seemed wrong with Terry. Either he was stalling or he was out of his class. His punching was not polished. Dempsey rocked him repeatedly with left jabs, right crosses, and uppercuts.

Keller started figuring him out, and for a moment was taking his foe's measure, but his opportunity slipped away. He allowed a couple of hard lefts to the jaw and an uppercut to land, which staggered him and sent him covering up. Terry recovered rapidly, but did not appear to be the same man for two or three rounds thereafter. Dempsey used a left hook to the jaw and a right uppercut with good effect. He also demonstrated good ring generalship. Dempsey's round.

They slowed up in the 3rd. There was much infighting, at which Dempsey showed himself superior throughout. But there was little damage done in this round, with honors about even.

In the 4th, Dempsey had things his own way, hitting the jaw at will, apparently suffering little harm from the body blows he received in return.

---

[107] *Salt Lake Telegram, Salt Lake Tribune*, May 3, 1916.
[108] *Salt Lake Herald-Republican, Salt Lake Tribune*, May 3, 1916; *Ogden Examiner*, May 2, 3, 1916.

One reporter said in this round, Dempsey opened up Keller's right eye, and from then on hammered his face at will. Clear Dempsey round.

In the 5th, Jack landed a terrific right uppercut that rocked Keller. This reporter said the blow that followed cut open Terry's right eye. Jack then trip-hammered him to the jaw. Dempsey round.

In the 6th, Terry landed a good one on the jaw, but Jack more than made up for it, and Keller appeared weak at the close. Dempsey round.

In the 7th round, Keller sent Dempsey to the floor with a terrific haymaker right swing to the stomach.

Jack took a 5-count, then rose and rallied rapidly and struggled through to the end. They fought furiously, Keller attempting in vain to follow his advantage. Keller, determined though he was, soon lost his steam and the hoped-for knockout failed to materialize. By the end of the round, Jack was strong again. Four of the five local and semi-local reporters gave this round to Keller, some saying it was the only round he won, though one reporter actually called it even.

The *Ogden Standard* said the last three rounds were fast, with both trying for a knockout. Jack completely closed both of Terry's eyes, and Keller was all but out at the final bell.

The *Ogden Examiner* said Keller was strong in the 8th and 9th rounds, but in the 10th, Dempsey came back strong. He opened an old sore over Keller's left eye, from which blood flowed freely and blinded Terry for the remainder of the round.

The *Salt Lake Herald-Republican* said the 8th through 10th rounds were all Dempsey's by a wide margin. He battered Kellar unmercifully.

The *Salt Lake Tribune* gave Dempsey the last three rounds as well. In the 10th round, he re-opened the gash from earlier in the fight. He also closed completely Terry's left eye in the final round, and the veteran was very much bewildered. At the finish, Keller was bleeding generously. Aside from a bloody nose, Dempsey did not have a mark.

Referee Tom Painter of Evanston, Wyoming, a respected official, awarded the 10-round decision to Dempsey, hoisting Jack's hand up in the air, which met with crowd approval and cheering for several minutes.

The *Ogden Standard* said that 7 of the 10 rounds went to Dempsey, one round was Keller's, and two were even (7-1-2 for Dempsey). The *Ogden Examiner* scored it 6-3-1 for Dempsey. The *Salt Lake Herald-Republican* had it 7-0-3 for Dempsey. The *Salt Lake Tribune* scored it 7-1-2 for Dempsey.

The *Ogden Standard* said Dempsey was too fast, and outclassed Keller at nearly every stage of the game, giving him the hardest beating of his career in 10 furious rounds. "Last night's fight shows that Dempsey is a comer and should now be classed with the topnotchers."

The *Ogden Examiner* said Dempsey won in 10 fast rounds, giving a fine exhibition. He demonstrated that he was a comer in the light heavyweight class, and "has a terrible punch and is able to receive an awful lot of punishment."

The *Salt Lake Herald-Republican* said Dempsey gave the older and more experienced boxer a severe drubbing. Terry won only one round. Kellar's ability to absorb terrific punches to the jaw was an outstanding feature. Dempsey appeared able to land at will, while Kellar landed few effective blows. Terry appeared awkward and showed little cleverness in blocking. Dempsey often hit the jaw with straight swings or left or right uppercuts. Kellar focused on the body, and at times hit dangerously low. Other than the knockdown he scored with a body shot in the 7th round, Kellar's blows had little effect on Dempsey.

The *Salt Lake Telegram* said Referee Tom Painter had little difficulty awarding Dempsey the decision, for he was too tough, outpunching and outboxing Kellar, which was a surprise. The best that could be said for Kellar was that he was a glutton for punishment. Jack stung him in almost every round. Conversely, Jack easily stopped Terry's lunges. It was good for Kellar that the contest wasn't longer. Aside from a bloody nose, Dempsey did not have a mark. Keller's eyes were closed and he was cut with a gash over his right eye. The *Telegram* called Dempsey a great prospect.

The *Salt Lake Tribune* said Dempsey fairly cut the veteran to ribbons. Keller, the former Ogden boy, was given a homecoming-welcome in the form of a stiff lacing. With the exception of the 7th round, which Keller won with his knockdown, the battle was all Dempsey's. After seeing the fight, ring sharps picked Dempsey as a sure-enough comer.

Dempsey later said he earned $350 for this fight.[109]

The May 4, 1916 *Muncie Morning Star* said C. W. George of Dayton was managing Jack Dempsey, a Salt Lake "middleweight," and Eddie Johnson, a Pueblo welterweight. George said he would match Dempsey with any middleweight in the country.

On May 2, 1916 in Akron, Ohio, Sam Langford fought Sam McVey to a 12-round newspaper draw.

On May 12, 1916 in Syracuse, New York, 198-pound Sam Langford knocked out 198-pound Joe Jeannette in the 7th round, avenging a 1915 12-round decision loss.[110]

On or about May 14, 1916 in Waco, Texas, a huge white mob of 15,000 to 20,000 witnessed and took part in the lynching of 18-year-old black Jesse Washington, convicted of murdering a white woman, Lucy Fryer. He was publicly tortured for two hours, hung, burned, and his fingers and toes cut off and kept as souvenirs. The sheer cruel brutality of it shocked the nation.

**Final Edition** WALL STREET CLOSING  **The Globe**  **Final Edition** WALL STREET CLOSING

## 15,000 SEE NEGRO BURNED AT STAKE IN TEXAS

A black college newspaper, the *Paul Quinn Weekly*, claimed that Fryer's husband actually committed the murder. The *Chicago Defender* asked, "Is it any wonder that members of the Race are not ashamed to speak out against

---

[109] *Ogden Standard, Ogden Examiner, Salt Lake Herald-Republican, Salt Lake Tribune*, May 4, 1916; *Salt Lake Telegram* May 7, 1916; *Fairmont West Virginian*, May 20, 1921.
[110] *Elmira Star-Gazette, Buffalo Courier*, May 13, 1916.

lynchings when it is proven that nine cases out of ten, the Race man accused is innocent." However, Fryer subsequently successfully sued the college for libel.[111]

Jack Dempsey fought again just 14 days after the Keller contest, in Provo, Utah, against Dan Ketchell or Ketchel of New York. Allegedly, he was Stanley Ketchel's cousin, and said to have a good record against topnotchers in the East. He had met Young Ahearn, Battling Levinsky, and Young Gibbons. An ad in the local *Provo Daily Herald* featured a photo of Ketchell. A classy affair was anticipated, given that

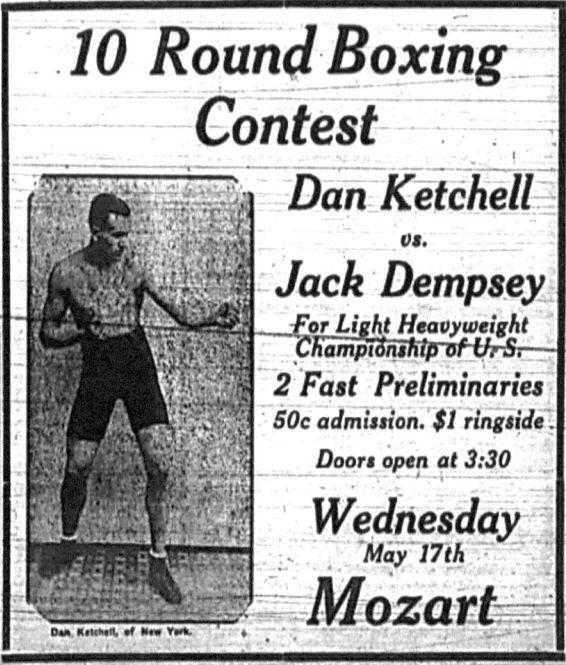

both possessed records of no mean proportions. Dempsey had defeated in a most decisive fashion many of the best in the West. The *Provo Daily Herald* said Dempsey would attract a large crowd. The fight was advertised as being for the U.S. light heavyweight championship; a bit of marketing.[112]

On Wednesday May 17, 1916 in Provo, Utah at the Mozart Pavilion, the scheduled 10-round Jack Dempsey vs. Dan Ketchell contest took place. Oddly enough, it was an afternoon show, which began at 3:30 p.m. The main event was scheduled to start at about 4:30 p.m. Tickets were $.50 general admission and $1 ringside.

The fight was one-sided. Dempsey was too classy for him, and hit Ketchell at will, having everything his own way from the start. Dempsey battered Ketchell fiercely throughout. In the 3rd round, Ketchell was so groggy and in such danger of being knocked out cold that Chief of Police Jesse Manwaring/Manwring rose from his seat and ordered Referee Dal Roberts to stop the contest, which he did. It had been a miserable one-sided beating.[113]

---

[111] *Chicago Defender*, May 20, 1916, June 10, 1916. Wikipedia.com.
[112] *Provo Daily Herald*, May 11, 14, 15, 1916; *Salt Lake Herald-Republican*, May 14, 1916.
[113] *Salt Lake Tribune, Salt Lake Telegram, Salt Lake Herald-Republican*, May 18, 1916. The *Salt Lake Herald-Republican* reported that Dempsey stopped Ketchell in the 4th round, but both the *Salt Lake Telegram* and *Salt Lake Tribune* reported it was stopped in the 3rd round. Oddly enough, the local *Provo Daily Herald* had no post-fight report.

Larney Lichtenstein, who managed Ad Wolgast, said 20-year-old Dempsey was a new 175-pound heavyweight "phenom" who was almost as fast as his namesake, the original Jack Dempsey.[114]

Jack's next fight was scheduled to be held two weeks later, on May 30 at Price, Utah. The local *Price News-Advocate* said Dempsey, the light heavyweight champion of the Pacific coast, and equal claimant to the world championship in his class, had been matched to meet 23-year-old Bob York, Colorado heavyweight champion, who weighed 190 pounds, stood 6'1", and had beaten some of the best men. Supposedly, "Colorado Demon" York had knocked out Terry Kellar in 2 rounds, as well as all comers in Colorado. His backers were strongly supporting him. (Important bouts on York's record, which began in 1913, also included 1915 D20 Eddie Johnson and 1916 L15 Young Hector.) Dempsey, who would concede about 10 pounds to York, "is a spectacular boxer, a hard hitter and has the tenacity of a bull dog."[115]

BOB YORK,

On Decoration Day (later called Memorial Day), Tuesday May 30, 1916 in Price, Utah, at the Eko theatre, Jack Dempsey fought Pueblo, Colorado's Bob York in a scheduled 10-round bout. The contest was well attended. E. M. Steuben of Price refereed the match.

In the 1st round, Dempsey allowed York to show what kind of boxer he was, practically permitting York to pummel him around the ring at will. Jack did not appear to be trying his best, taking it easy.

In the 2nd and 3rd rounds, the aggressive Dempsey waded into the game Colorado boy, and with fierce uppercuts to the head and face beat York into a near state of insensibility. York kept clinching to survive.

---

[114] *Muncie Press*, May 25, 1916.
[115] *Price News Advocate*, May 19, 26, 1916; *Salt Lake Herald-Republican*, May 21, 1916; *Salt Lake Telegram*, May 23, 1916; Boxrec.com. Jack was scheduled to leave for New York after this bout, where he expected to meet Jack Dillon in a 10-round contest.

As soon as the gong rang to start the 4th round, Dempsey was out of his corner with a bound, catching York full on the chin with a fierce uppercut. Dempsey knocked him into the ropes time after time with terrific head blows. York, though badly beaten up and staggering around the ring in a daze, gamely tried to come back, but the terrific blows rained upon him were too much. Bob's head rolled from side to side, and he staggered around under the fierce punishment.

Dempsey finally pounded him down to his knees, accomplishing the knockdown with a quick straight left to the chin followed by an even quicker right cross to the same spot.

Bob crawled along the padded floor to the ropes, where finally in a delayed reaction he sprawled out and rolled through the ropes, completely put to sleep, out for the ten-count in the 4th round.

It was ten minutes before his seconds could awaken and restore the unconscious York. The ending was most spectacular, and frightening.

The local *Price News-Advocate* called it a clean though uneven boxing match until Dempsey knocked him out in the 4th round. Jack had little trouble, practically playing with him for the first few rounds, though York gamely took the grueling punishment and put up a good exhibition of boxing up to the knockout.

The *Salt Lake Telegram* reported that Jack Dempsey, the "sensational light heavyweight of Salt Lake City," surprised boxing fans and upset the local gamblers when he beat Bob York, the man brought in with the express purpose of trimming him. Jack beat him all the way and knocked him out for the count in the 4th round. York did not have a look-in from the start until the finish.

Dempsey was expecting to leave for New York soon.[116]

Maxine Cates

According to Dempsey, sometime just before he and then-manager Jack Price left on a trip for New York, while they were at Maxim's, a saloon/cabaret on Salt Lake's Commercial Street (the red-light district), Dempsey met a woman who was playing the piano there, named Maxine Cates, from Walla Walla, Washington. She asked Jack to show her around Salt Lake. Jack said he would once he returned from his East Coast trip. Eventually he kept his word.

---

[116] *Price News Advocate*, June 2, 1916; *Salt Lake Telegram*, May 31, 1916; *Salt Lake Herald-Republican*, June 1, 1916. Fighting Dick Gilbert of Denver sent a telegram challenging the winner.

CHAPTER 5

# New York Tests

Having been a pro for only a year and a half, during which time he had about 22 contests, many against foes with far more experience, on June 5, 1916, Jack Dempsey, the man who had been toppling them over with unusual regularity during the past year, headed eastward, "to see what I've got," as he put it. Jack Price, who was managing him, took him on the trip, hoping to get one of the top light heavies to fight Dempsey. Many Salt Lake City friends would be following him with interest.[117]

Dempsey later said Jack Price was Hardy Downing's brother-in-law.

On June 18, 1916, Dempsey arrived in New York. Jack Price signed him up to meet Andre Anderson, a big, tough, Chicago-based heavyweight who had been somewhat of a sensation in New York lately, to fight 10 rounds on June 24, just six days away. The Fairmont Athletic club (in the Bronx, on the corner of 3rd Avenue and 149th Street) was staging the match, and was hoping to book the winner against Gunboat Smith.[118]

Listed as 6'4" or 6'5", 26-year-old Andre Anderson was a former wrestler turned boxer, who typically weighed anywhere from 206 to 217 pounds. He was Swedish. His manager called him astonishing and astoundingly agile. He would tower over Dempsey and have huge height, reach, and weight advantages.

Anderson's record included mixed but solid results against the best in the business, including: 1915 WND10 Marty Cutler, LKOby6 Jack Dillon, LKOby4 Fred Fulton, and KO1 Al Palzer; 1916 TKO3 Bob Devere, KO5 George Rodel, WND10 Willie Meehan, TKO6 Jim Stewart, LKOby2 Charley Weinert, and D12 Bill Brennan.[119]

ANDRE ANDERSON, (heavyweight.)

---

[117] *Salt Lake Telegram*, June 6, 1916. They would stop off in Kansas City before going to New York and possibly Boston.
[118] *Salt Lake Telegram*, June 19, 1916. Dempsey said the club was run by Billy Gibson, who later managed Gene Tunney.
[119] Boxrec.com. *Buffalo Evening News*, June 6, 1916; *Buffalo Enquirer*, June 10, 1916; *Ogden Standard*, *Buffalo Times*, June 26, 1916.

On Saturday June 24, 1916, Jack Dempsey's 21st birthday, at the Fairmont Athletic Club in the Bronx, New York, he fought Andre Anderson in a scheduled 10-round no decision contest. "Dempsey has never been seen in action around here before and it will be interesting to see how he stacks up against his elongated opponent."[120]

Several New York papers barely noticed the Bronx contest, and those that did provided only limited descriptions. There were several other boxing shows taking place in New York on that same night, at the Broadway Sporting Club and the Clermont Athletic Club, both in Brooklyn, and the Queensboro Athletic Club (likely Queens).

The *New York Evening Telegram* said the Salt Lake City heavyweight Jack Dempsey, although handicapped by 20 pounds, proved himself to be too fast and clever for Chicago's 205-pound Andre Anderson. During most of the 10 rounds, Anderson was on the receiving end. Dempsey's most effective blows were short left jabs to the face and right crosses to the jaw.

The *Brooklyn Daily Times* said a little man beat Anderson, who failed to dazzle Dempsey with his allegedly astounding agility. Anderson tipped the beam at 205 pounds, 20 pounds heavier than the 185-pound Dempsey, but failed to take advantage of his weight advantage. "Short left jabs to the face and right crosses to the jaw from Dempsey kept Anderson occupied during each of the ten rounds. He looked fat and was hardly agile or astounding. It was clearly Dempsey's fight."

The *New York Tribune* said Anderson was becoming less aggressive and less agile every day. Dempsey slowed him up considerably. James Johnston thought Andre had the makings of a champion, but no longer.

The *New York Journal* simply said Dempsey outpointed Anderson.

The national dispatch that was sent out and printed in newspapers across the nation reported that Dempsey won a decisive victory in a 10-round no decision contest, easily outpointing Andre Anderson, the reformed wrestler, who supposedly weighed 220 pounds (one said 243) and looked like a portly Swede. Anderson was no match. Dempsey showed unusual speed and clean hitting ability, hitting him with everything, and making a decided hit.[121]

Jack later said he earned only $16 for the Anderson fight.[122]

The *Salt Lake Telegram* reported that Dempsey had made such a hit with his performance against Anderson, handing him an overwhelming beating, that he was in line to be a great card. Dempsey was able to fight with both hands and was willing to tear in, which the fans loved.[123]

---

[120] *New York Morning Telegraph*, June 24, 1916.

[121] *Salt Lake Telegram, New York Evening Telegram*, June 25, 1916; *Brooklyn Daily Times, New York Tribune, New York Journal, Munster Times, Ogden Standard, Chicago Tribune*, June 26, 1916; *Buffalo Commercial*, June 27, 1916.

[122] *Fairmont West Virginian*, May 20, 1921. In his autobiography, Dempsey claimed that Anderson pounded on and decked him several times early on, until tiring, and Dempsey took over the fight, a claim not supported by any primary source report. The primary sources did not mention any knockdowns.

[123] *Salt Lake Telegram*, June 29, 1916. Also claimed was that Dempsey's manager had matched him with Gunboat Smith for a July 17 fight.

At that time, world heavyweight champion Jess Willard was exhibiting with a circus, which had him signed to a contract and would not release him to fight Fred Fulton or anyone else. The 6'4 ½" 215-pound Fulton was an emerging, impressive contender who had victories over Arthur Pelkey, Terry Kellar, Andre Anderson, Dan Porky Flynn, Fireman Jim Flynn, and Al Reich. The owner of the Sells-Floto circus said, "Willard is making us too much money; I cannot afford to release him."[124]

Next up for Dempsey was a bout with "Wild" Burt Kenny in the 10-round main event at the Fairmont, just two weeks after the Anderson contest. The hard-punching Dempsey was said to be one of the best light heavyweights in the game, having beaten the best of the big men in the Salt Lake vicinity, his home town. His recent exhibition against Andre Anderson had gained him many friends.[125]

Burt Kenny (or Bert Kenney) was a Canadian with at least 20 known fights of experience since 1914. Significant bouts on his record included: 1914 WND10 Jack "Twin" Sullivan, LND10 Battling Levinsky, and LTKOby4 George Ashe (his only stoppage loss up to that point); 1915 WND10 Frank Mantell, LND10 Leo Houck, and WND10 KO Sweeney; 1916 LND10 Willie Meehan, LND10 and DND10 Bartley Madden, and LND10 Battling Levinsky. Kenny was known for his durability. He typically weighed around 170 pounds.[126]

The *New York Morning Telegraph* said the Dempsey-Wild Burt Kenny fight was the stellar attraction of the evening at the Fairmont A. C. "Dempsey is after a match with the topnotchers among the big fellows and he intends to give Kenny a merry time of it to-night." The *New York Evening Telegram* said Dempsey recently made a great showing by defeating Anderson.[127]

On Saturday July 8, 1916 in the Bronx, New York, again at the Fairmont Athletic Club, in the main event, Jack Dempsey fought Wild Bert Kenny in a 10-round no decision contest.

The *New York Herald* said light heavy Dempsey gave Wild Bert Kenny a beating. Dempsey decked the local man on three different occasions, but the bell came to the latter's rescue and saved him from a knockout. In the

---

[124] *Salt Lake Telegram*, June 25, 1916.
[125] *New York Sun*, July 8, 1916. Dempsey reportedly had 27 knockouts to his credit, which may have been an exaggeration.
[126] Boxrec.com.
[127] *New York Morning Telegraph*, *New York Evening Telegram*, July 8, 1916. However, once again, there also were competing boxing cards taking place on the same night, at the Broadway Sporting Club and the Clermont Avenue Rink in Brooklyn.

2nd, 4th, and 10th rounds, Kenny took the count of nine, but gamely managed to weather the storm.

The *New York Evening Telegram* said although Dempsey failed to put away "Wild Bert" Kenny, he handed him a terrible beating. The bell came to Kenny's rescue several times. Kenny first went down in the 2nd round. In the 4th round he was down taking a count when the bell rang. In the 10th round, Dempsey scored three knockdowns with short left hooks to the jaw.

The *Brooklyn Daily Times* said Wild Bert Kenny was undeniably wild in his fight with Dempsey, the light heavyweight who drubbed Andre Anderson. Dempsey did all of the fighting, nearly making Kenny another knockout victim. Three times the bell came to Kenny's rescue when he was quivering tamely under Dempsey's stinging thrusts. In the 10th round, Kenny went down to the canvas thrice more, but was on his feet at the very welcome final bell.

Jack Price telegrammed the *Salt Lake Telegram*, "Dempsey wins easily, scoring knockout in the 6th round, but referee would not give it to us because Keney [sic] is a local favorite. Dempsey scored fourteen knockdowns in the ten rounds of the bout."[128]

Jack later said that Kenney was a "loose swinging fellow, whose general notion of boxing was to dash in with both hands flying in as many directions as possible." He was dangerous if the blows landed, but there was no reason why they should land on a careful man. Billy Joh refereed. "I had Kenney out in the fourth round, and heard Joh say ten, but then they dragged Kenney back to his corner, and let him revive. I had him down in every round, so I guess I won all right, although of course it was a no-decision bout, like all the New York bouts in those days. I got $3 for that fight." At another time, Dempsey said he was paid $43.[129]

JOHN LESTER JOHNSON

The *New York Times* and *New York Tribune* announced that Dempsey, a 6-footer who weighed 180 pounds and had baffled the agile Anderson, would be in a mixed-race bout and card at the Harlem Sporting Club, 135th Street and Madison Avenue, on Friday July 14, boxing 10 rounds in the main event with negro heavyweight John Lester Johnson, the "Harlem coal man." This would be just a mere six days after fighting Kenny 10 rounds![130]

---

[128] *Brooklyn Daily Times*, July 10, 1916; *New York Evening Telegram*, *New York Herald*, July 9, 1916; *Salt Lake Telegram*, July 9, 13, 1916, allegedly quoting the *New York World*. The *New York Sun* said Dempsey subdued Wild Bert Kenney in a fast 10-round affair. *New York Sun*, July 9, 1916. The *New York Evening World* said Dempsey easily defeated local heavyweight Wild Burt Kenny. July 10, 1916.
[129] *Cedar Rapids Gazette*, May 28, 1919; *Fairmont West Virginian*, May 20, 1921; *Round by Round*.
[130] *New York Times*, *New York Tribune*, July 10, 1916.

22-year-old (one month shy of 23) John Lester Johnson had about 30 known fights, many against the world's best, particularly from the black community, including: 1913 LND10 Joe Jeannette (who had over 100 fights and was considered at that time, along with Sam Langford, to be one of the world's two best title contenders) and LKOby1 Sam Langford (who had over 125 fights; Langford 185, Johnson 170); 1914 WND10 Bill Tate (Tate 6'5" 210, Johnson 175); 1915 W/DND10 Jeannette (Jeannette 194, Johnson 177), W/DND10 Bill Tate, KO10 Dave Mills, L20 Harry Wills (emerging top black fighter who weighed over 200 pounds; 22-3-4 record at that time), W10 and WND10 Mills (Johnson 182, Mills 188), and KO1 John Budinich; 1916 WDQ9 Bill Tate, TKO7 George Kid Cotton (who had scored a 1912 KO2 Harry Wills with a right uppercut, which was thrice avenged by Wills by knockout up to mid-1916), and LND10 Harry Wills (Johnson ran/moved, clinched, and fought to survive). The high quality of Johnson's opponents, going the distance with world-class big men like Wills and Jeannette twice each, some even feeling that he beat Jeannette in their second fight, as well as the sheer number of rounds of experience he had, far exceeded 21-year-old Dempsey's experience to that point.[131]

The *New York Age* called John Lester Johnson a clever colored heavyweight.

Back in Salt Lake, it was reported that Dempsey was matched for two more bouts in New York City. First he would meet John Lester Johnson, who recently boxed a 10-round draw with Joe Jeannette (one of the world's best fighters). Four days later, on the 18th, he was set to box the famous world-class Gunboat Smith.[132]

The *New York World* said Dempsey had made good in the two bouts he had engaged in thus far while in New York.

The *New York Sun* said John Lester Johnson would serve as a good trial horse for Dempsey, who had knocked out several second raters out West and came to New York well-recommended.[133]

---

[131] Boxrec.com.
[132] *New York Age*, July 13, 1916; *Salt Lake Telegram*, July 9, 1916.
[133] *New York World*, July 10, 1916. *New York Sun*, July 12, 1916.

Black Bob Armstrong, a veteran trainer, former fighter, and former sparring partner for Bob Fitzsimmons, Jim Jeffries, Tom Sharkey, Stanley Ketchel, Jack Johnson, and numerous others, took a fancy to Dempsey, who was making a hit in New York. Armstrong told the *Salt Lake Telegram*,

> Down in my heart I think Dempsey is a coming champion and, for his size, I think he is the hardest puncher in the game at the present time. I expect to see him keep right on. A man who can make Andre [Anderson] and "Wild Bert" Kenney look like selling platers, as Dempsey has done, has got to have a whole lot of class. New York has taken a liking to your Utah boy. He fights John Lester Johnson, a big colored heavy weight, at the Harlem club Friday night, and Gunboat Smith at the same club on the evening of July 18.[134]

Dempsey vs. Johnson was the first heavyweight bout between a white and colored boxer since the New York ban on mixed-race bouts had been lifted recently. Throughout Jack Johnson's reign, not only did New York state not allow mixed-race contests, but its athletic commission prohibited Johnson from boxing anyone, white or black.

The *New York Sun* said Dempsey had shown "unusual skill" in his New York bouts. Jack claimed to have won 27 of his 29 fights via knockout (a marketing fib). Although the *Sun* called John Lester Johnson a third-class colored heavyweight who had been knocked out several times (the known records do not support that assertion), many gave Johnson a good chance of dropping Dempsey. The *New York Morning Telegraph* called Johnson an "elongated ebony-hued gentleman."[135]

Once again, there were several boxing cards occurring on the same night, including at Brown's in Far Rockaway, the New Polo, Washington Park, the Freeport, and the Vanderbilt.[136]

On Friday July 14, 1916 at the Harlem Sporting Club in Harlem, New York, in the main event, Jack Dempsey fought John Lester Johnson in a 10-round no decision affair. There were a veritable varied assortment of opinions regarding this fight.

The *New York Sun* reported that 170-pound Johnson outpointed 181-pound Dempsey with ease, and the local boxer had no trouble in beating the Salt Lake City lad. Dempsey failed to live up to his reputation, and was an easy mark.

The *New York Tribune* also reported that John Lester Johnson won over Jack Dempsey in the main bout. (It further said that in another mixed contest on the card, the white race had the better of it.)

The *Brooklyn Daily Times* said 181-pound Dempsey, the much-touted boy from Salt Lake City, "failed to show any real class" against 170-pound Johnson, who "had little trouble in baffling Dempsey."

---

[134] *Salt Lake Telegram*, July 12, 1916.
[135] *New York Sun*, *New York Morning Telegraph*, July 14, 1916.
[136] *New York Evening Telegram*, July 12, 1916; *New York Evening Telegram*, July 14, 1916.

The *Brooklyn Daily Standard Union* said John Lester Johnson, "one of the dark clouds of the pugilistic sky, had an easy time defeating Jack Dempsey."

However, the *Brooklyn Daily Eagle* said Dempsey made his Manhattan debut by *winning* over John Lester Johnson, the colored heavy scrapper, in 10 rounds.

All of these newspapers were extremely brief.

The more detailed *New York Evening World* said Jack Dempsey whipped John Lester Johnson. Both men weighed 179 pounds. It was one of the most bitterly fought bouts between heavyweights seen in the city in many months, but Dempsey defeated the clever colored fighter. Dempsey was very nervous in the first few rounds, and it was learned that it was due to the news of the death of his brother (which was not true, but perhaps he was given such false news to adversely affect his performance), which he received in a telegram just before he entered the ring. However, he came on strong after the 3$^{rd}$ round, up until the end. Neither boxer ever was in danger, but at the finish, Johnson was very tired from the heavy punishment he received in the mid-section and around the head. "It was the consensus of opinion that Dempsey is one of the best white heavyweights seen here in years and should hold his own with any man in the class, barring Willard."

Conversely, the *New York Herald* and *New York Evening Telegram* both reported that Dempsey and the local Johnson fought an "uninteresting" 10-round bout to a draw. "Johnson did most of the leading, but the punches had little effect on Dempsey, who was waiting to put over the 'big punch,' but failed to deliver."

The black-owned *New York Age's* Alex Walters agreed that it was a draw. He said that in front of a large crowd at the Harlem Sporting Club on Friday night, John Lester Johnson, the colored light heavyweight of New York met Young Jack "Demsey" in the evening's star contest.

> The bout was very slow because the men seemed to be afraid of each other. The white man seemed to be the most aggressive of the two. Johnson seemed to be satisfied to be on the defensive all the time and at no time during the fight was either man in any danger. At the end of the tenth round there was little to choose between the two and if there had been a decision rendered it would have been a draw. Weight, Johnson 179, Demsey, 181.

So, 4 said Johnson, 2 said Dempsey, and 3 said it was a draw.

The mixed-race ban had been lifted recently, and in several mixed bouts that had been fought, "Up to the present time the colored fighter has more than held his own against his white opponent, much to the surprise of not only the white fight fans but many of the colored ones, too." Many colored patrons did not believe that black fighters had any chance against white boxers. The opposite could not be said of white fans, who believed in white boxers. The *Age* encouraged colored folk to show race loyalty and support, for in 18 contests since the ban's lifting, colored boxers had made good, suffering no more than 3 losses. Often the black fighter had the worst of it in terms of weight and in other ways.

Back in Salt Lake, it was reported that Dempsey had won a hard bout by a "big shade" over Johnson, one of the toughest negro boxers in New York, according to a telegram received by Dempsey's manager Jack Price, who had returned to Salt Lake owing to his mother's illness. Price claimed that Gunboat Smith had called off the match with Dempsey.[137]

In late December 1916, Damon Runyon wrote that Dempsey gave Andre Anderson a "fine pasting." He "took none the worst of it" in a tenrounder with the "gliding sliding John Lester Johnson, a grand segment of Senegambia to pick for a green 'un – if you want to get the green 'un massacred. Jack fought a listless, loggy battle that night, but none the less, he made a good showing." In March 1917, Runyon said Dempsey had bested Johnson.[138]

In a 1919 interview with Damon Runyon, Dempsey discussed the fight.

John Reisler, known as John the Barber, owned the Harlem Sporting Club. The moment the ban on mixed-race bouts was lifted, he sought the services of John Lester Johnson, but not many white fighters wanted any of his game. Jack Price advertised Dempsey's prowess and made the fight, the first mixed-race heavyweight contest in New York in many years. A few days before the fight, a telegram arrived bringing news of the death (or illness) of Jack Price's mother. He needed to leave and return to Salt Lake. Jack fought without his presence or participation.

All of John the Barber's colored customers were on hand on fight night. Quite a few caucasians were present as well, many attracted by the fact that it was a mixed-race contest. One sportswriter who had seen Johnson in several bouts and knew his ability wagered $30 to his opponent's $10 that the clever and tough Johnson would not be stopped.

Dempsey said Johnson was not rated amongst the first flight of top blacks, and yet he was a tough bird. "He is a shifty, plunging, holding type of miller; a fellow who doesn't do much to the other fellow, perhaps, but who doesn't let the other fellow do much to him."

Runyon said Dempsey "did not fight as he fought against Anderson and Kenney; he seemed slow and loggy, and there was a mighty good reason." Dempsey said, "In the second round Johnson pulled something on me I had never seen before. He just lifted my right arm up high and then soaked me in the ribs. He broke three of 'em for me. He hit me on the chin in that round, too, and I saw many a star. He knew too much for me."

For 10 rounds, Dempsey walked after Johnson wide open and swinging, but the crafty black man would slip inside the swings, smash Dempsey with his left, and then hold. Some sporting writers the next day said that Dempsey had won. "I don't think I did. I thought he licked me. I didn't know how to fight then, and Johnson did. Yes, I think he won, and he taught me more that night than I have ever dreamed of before." Dempsey

---

[137] *New York Sun, New York Tribune, Brooklyn Daily Times, Brooklyn Daily Standard Union, Brooklyn Daily Eagle, New York Evening World, New York Herald, New York Evening Telegram*, July 15, 1916; *New York Age*, July 20, 1916; *Salt Lake Tribune, Salt Lake Telegram*, July 15, 1916; *Chicago Defender*, July 22, 1916.
[138] *Salt Lake Telegram, Brooklyn Daily Times, Buffalo Evening News*, December 20, 1916; *Salt Lake Tribune*, December 29, 1916, March 11, 1917.

had a rare habit of giving far more credit to his opponents than even the fans and writers did.

Dempsey claimed that John the Barber Reisler had promised him 25% of the gate (an estimated $500 or $1,000), but gave him just $100. Reisler subsequently promised to dress him in fine clothes and diamonds.

Reisler wanted Jack to fight again soon, against Gunboat Smith, but Dempsey's ribs were smashed up, so he could not fight for a while, until they healed, and Smith had injured his hand anyhow. "I had signed a contract with 'John the Barber' for him to look after my affairs, but that contract would never have held good, because I wasn't of age." (In fact, Dempsey was of age, turning 21 on the night he fought Andre Anderson.) As a result of his reluctance to fight again until he healed up, Reisler didn't come near him or have anything to do with him, which disgusted and discouraged Dempsey, who decided to go home.

Runyon noted that John the Barber must have seen something in Dempsey, even when he was getting his pasting from Johnson, to cause him to sign Jack to a contract. The only trouble was, he did not see far enough ahead.

Runyon noted that any story Dempsey told about Reisler was from one side only. Reisler once had told Runyon that an ungrateful fist-swinger was sharper than a serpent's tooth.[139]

In 1919, the *New York Herald's* Cross Counter, who was at the fight, addressing claims that John Lester Johnson in their 1916 bout had fractured Dempsey's ribs, said probably it was only a pipe dream. He said Johnson was a foot runner, not a rib cracker. The writer had a tough time believing the claim, especially since much bigger men and much harder punchers had not been able to hurt Dempsey. "From the first to the last round Johnson sprinted with a surprising fleetness of foot. Dempsey in hot pursuit tried hard to overtake his fleet opponent." Johnson did not begin to sprint hard until he had sampled a few of Dempsey's punches. "After that he was on the dead run and never slackened his pace till the welcome bell ended the tenth and last round." Dempsey received the popular decision, and the club management berated Johnson for turning what was expected to be a fight into a foot race. "If John Lester Johnson landed a solid punch on Dempsey at any stage of the game, it escaped every one's observation." Cross Counter said Dempsey at that time was managed by John the Barber Reisler, who made the match at the Harlem Sporting Club.[140]

In 1921, Dempsey said of Johnson, "That bird was one of the toughest I have ever met. He knew all the scientific points and I knew none of them." Johnson broke his ribs, but Jack took the decision and $100.[141]

Many years later, in his 1940 autobiography, *Round by Round*, Jack said Jack Price had received a telegram saying his mother was dying. He needed money to get back to Salt Lake, so with Jack's consent, Price offered or

---

[139] *Cedar Rapids Gazette*, June 2, 3, 1919
[140] *New York Herald*, June 22, 1919.
[141] *Fairmont West Virginian*, May 20, 1921.

agreed to sell his contract to John Reisler, a.k.a. John the Barber. Reisler had arranged or would arrange the Johnson match.

If Reisler simply had purchased the contract that Price had, and Price had signed the contract with Dempsey before Jack turned age 21, then Dempsey might have had a point about the contract being invalid, if it was a mere assignment. However, if Dempsey signed a new contract, or affirmed the assignment in writing after he was 21, then the contract would be valid.

Dempsey said few boxers were willing to fight the crafty and dangerous Johnson, and he saw why. Johnson nearly ended his career, hitting very hard, like a pile-driver. Jack was not yet experienced enough to go up against such stiff competition. In about the 2nd round, a hard body blow cracked two of his ribs. The effects lasted throughout the fight and for weeks afterwards. Jack said it felt like he was breathing fire. He doubled over for a few rounds, though he kept fighting and landed some solid blows. He was tougher than Johnson, and even had the better of it at the end of the fight. Some said Johnson won, some said Dempsey won, particularly because of his strong showing at the end, while others said it was a draw. But Jack was hurt, and his confidence had taken a blow.

Four days after the fight, the *New York Tribune* announced that John Reisler, known as John the Barber, was Dempsey's new manager, having signed him up for three years. Reisler immediately sent forth a defi to challenge any light-heavyweight in the world.[142]

However, Dempsey was due to return to Salt Lake on the 18th, four days after the Johnson fight. The Harlem Club (meaning Reisler) tried to induce him to remain for a meeting with Jack Dillon (who had accepted a $5,000 guarantee), but Jack believed that a summer of rest and recovery and then working out with a wise old bird like Bob Armstrong would be the wiser course. Dempsey was homesick and wanted to see his mother. Many said Jack was making the correct decision, for in the fall he would be in demand for even bigger money at Madison Square Garden.[143]

Indeed, Dempsey did not fight again for over two months. Perhaps his ribs actually were healing. Yet, there was a report as of August 9 in Salt Lake City that he was sparring, less than a month after the Johnson fight.

Years later, Jack said that after informing Reisler that he needed time for his ribs to heal, Reisler was disgusted with him, and told him to come back when he was ready to fight again. Already Reisler wanted to match him with some of the toughest fighters in the game, and didn't care at all about Dempsey or his injury. Dempsey got the feeling that Reisler simply wanted to make as much money as possible off of him as quickly as possible, only thinking about the short term, and didn't care who he matched him with, when, or what condition he was in. What was worse, the Johnson fight was packed, yet Jack only received $100, which he thought was low given the large attendance and fact that he was supposed to earn 25% of the gate. So, things between he and John 'the Barber' Reisler got off to a rocky start.

---

[142] *New York Tribune*, July 18, 1916.
[143] *Salt Lake Telegram*, July 18, 1916.

Questions remain. Did Jack Dempsey leave New York for financial reasons, or because he needed time to recover, or for personal reasons, or a combination of factors? Was he claiming injury as a means to get away from Reisler and not fight for him, given that he thought he was not being treated fairly financially? Were his financial claims made later on as a way to break the contract, given that he did not seem to like Reisler? Did Dempsey feel that Reisler was trying to overmatch him too soon in his young career? Clearly Dempsey was not satisfied with his New York pay, perhaps having anticipated much greater financial remuneration in the nation's most populous city. He had made no more than, and actually less than he recently had been earning in the much less populated intermountain region, despite being matched tough.

During 1916, U.S. President Woodrow Wilson signed an executive order designating "The Star-Spangled Banner" by Francis Scott Key as the national anthem. Key's song, based on his experiences in the War of 1812, included a verse criticizing the British for promising freedom to slaves who rebelled against the U.S. and fought on its side. Key, a slave-owner, gleefully taunted that even the tactical use of mercenaries and rebellious slaves was not enough to secure victory over the United States. The lyrics included:

> And where is that band who so vauntingly swore,
> That the havoc of war and the battle's confusion
> A home and a Country should leave us no more?
> Their blood has wash'd out their foul footstep's pollution.
> No refuge could save the hireling and slave
> From the terror of flight or the gloom of the grave,
> And the star-spangled banner in triumph doth wave
> O'er the land of the free and the home of the brave.

Hence, even in 1916, the U.S. president supported a national anthem that was written pre-emancipation and contained such a verse, although typically it was omitted from public performances. It further highlights the inherent American contradiction - a country which supported slavery and then legalized mandatory segregation (or de-facto via custom or contract) while proudly claiming to be a land of freedom, willing to engage in violence and warfare to support its freedom.

Like the country at large, the sport of boxing vacillated and oscillated regarding the issue of segregation.

CHAPTER 6

# Home Zone Again

When 21-year-old Jack Dempsey returned to Salt Lake City in late July 1916, he went back to the same saloon where he had met Maxine Cates, and saw her again. They began dating. Dempsey claimed she was 15 years older than him and an experienced woman, though she denied it. Cates claimed that she was one year younger than Dempsey, which probably was correct. Many even have said or suggested that she was a prostitute. He said that soon after they started seeing one another, she wanted to get married. He wasn't sure why, because he was not making much money back then.

In late July, the *Salt Lake Telegram* reported that Dempsey made such a hit in defeating John Lester Johnson that John Reisler had signed him to a five-year contract. Jack allegedly had to return home because of his mother's illness. Nothing was mentioned about any injury.[144]

In early August, Jack Price announced that Dempsey would start training for a Pacific Coast campaign in San Francisco, and had offers for fights in New York as well. So, apparently, Price still was acting as his manager.[145]

As of August 8, Jack was sparring with Young K.O. Brown.[146]

Dempsey refereed the August 17, 1916 Eddie Palmer vs. Rex Morris bout in Salt Lake City, calling it a 6-round draw, though the local *Salt Lake Telegram* opined that the colored boxer, Palmer, deserved the decision.[147]

On August 22, 1916, Jack Dempsey signed a 5-year boxer-manager contract with A. J. Auerbach. Auerbach was to be paid 25% of Dempsey's fight purses. So, it seems that three different men allegedly simultaneously had managerial contracts with him: Price, Reisler, and Auerbach. The local *Telegram* later cautioned Dempsey against signing with too many managers, or he might get himself barred in New York.[148]

Years later, Dempsey said Al Auerbach, owner of a Salt Lake City beauty shop where one of Jack's sisters worked for a while, had managed Dan Ketchel. After Dempsey knocked out Ketchel with ease, Auerbach gave up on Ketchel, and eventually began arranging matches for Dempsey. Auerbach later said that he had been advancing Dempsey money and helping to arrange his matches even before they signed a contract.

In September, Fred Winsor was in the city hoping to sign Dempsey to fight Young Hector, his Colorado light heavyweight, whom he spoke of highly and believed would be a great card with Jack.[149]

---

[144] *Salt Lake Telegram*, July 30, 1916.
[145] *Salt Lake Telegram*, August 7, 1916.
[146] *Salt Lake Herald-Republican*, August 9, 1916.
[147] *Salt Lake Telegram*, August 16, 18, 1916.
[148] *Salt Lake Tribune*, August 24, 1916; *Salt Lake Telegram*, September 25, 1916.
[149] *Salt Lake Telegram*, September 10, 1916.

Con Gallagher, a Murray, Utah promoter, was trying to arrange a fight for Dempsey there on September 28 as a benefit for the Murray fire department. He reached out to Jim Flynn, Gunboat Smith, Dick Gibson, and Young Hector of Denver as potential Dempsey opponents.[150]

Manager A. J. Auerbach with Dempsey

Gallagher eventually signed Denver's Young Hector to fight Dempsey on September 28 at Murray, Utah for a 15-round bout. Dempsey's manager A. J. Auerbach agreed. The press said Dempsey had been working out in Salt Lake ever since returning from New York, where he defeated three foes in a row.

The local papers said 23-year-old Young Hector had won the AAU Rocky Mountain championship two years ago, before turning pro. He held Jim Flynn (D10), big Jack Barry (D20), and Jack Burns (D20) to draws, and knocked out Bob York in 4 rounds.

Secondary sources say 29-year-old Young Hector Conrew (or Curnow), a.k.a. Battling Hector, had been boxing as a pro since 1911. His record included: 1912 LKOby2 Fireman Harris; 1915 KO4 Jim McMahon; 1915 TKO1 Salinas Jack Burns; and 1916 W15 Bob York and LKOby6 Dick Gilbert. There are primary source references to Hector having had over 40 fights even as of 1912.

Both young heavyweights were considered comers. It would be the first time that the popular local boxer Dempsey would be seen in action since his return from his "victorious New York trip." The *Salt Lake Telegram* claimed that Dempsey had gained a national reputation by defeating the best they had in New York. Colorado fans predicted a bright future for Young Hector. However, Dempsey and his manager A. J. Auerbach considered Hector to be another stepping stone.

---

[150] *Salt Lake Tribune*, September 14, 1916.

The bout would be held in Murray, Utah at the Trocadero hall, which could accommodate up to 1,600 people.[151]

Young Hector's manager Fred Winsor said his man was classy and clever, the cleverest big fellow Dempsey ever had met. "Dempsey is a tough boy, but he is going to meet a big fellow who is more clever than he and who can also hit." Hector was sparring with Jack Downey, who could give him insight, having fought Dempsey three times.

**Manager Fred Winsor with Young Hector**

Dempsey was boxing every day at Cox's gymnasium with anybody and everybody who was willing to put on the gloves with him, including lightweight/welterweight Kid Irish.[152]

Locals considered Dempsey to be one of the most rugged and dangerous light heavies in the game.

Hector was known as a great athlete in Colorado. He was a boxing instructor at the Denver Y.M.C.A. Colorado Governor George Carlson and his two sons were amongst Hector's former pupils.

Hector tipped the beam at 198 pounds with his clothes on. His manager Winsor predicted that he would outpoint Dempsey at the very least. Dempsey's manager Auerbach was sure that Jack would win by knockout.[153]

---

[151] *Salt Lake Telegram*, *Salt Lake Herald-Republican*, *Salt Lake Tribune*, September 17, 1916; *Salt Lake Herald-Republican*, September 20, 1916; *Salt Lake Telegram*, September 22, 1916. The October 18, 1912 *Trinidad Chronicle-News* claimed that 187-pound Young Hector already had more than 40 fights.
[152] *Salt Lake Tribune*, September 24, 26, 1916. Jim Flynn wrote that he would like to meet Dempsey. Carl Morris also wanted to meet the winner.

THE BOYS WHO WILL FURNISH THE FEATURE.
On the left is Jack Dempsey and on the right Young Hector. The picture was snapped yesterday, just after the two boxers had placed their names to the final articles of agreement. Notice how evenly they are matched as to size and build.

**FIGHTERS' MEASUREMENTS.**

| HECTOR. | | DEMPSEY. |
|---|---|---|
| 23 years | Age | 21 years |
| 5 ft. 11 in. | Height | 5 ft. 11½ in. |
| 190 pounds | Weight | 187 pounds |
| 7 inches | Ankle | 8 inches |
| 15 inches | Calf | 14¼ inches |
| 23 inches | Thigh | 22½ inches |
| 33 inches | Waist | 32 inches |
| 40 inches | Chest Normal | 41 inches |
| 44 in. | Chest Expanded | 43½ in. |
| 13 inches | Forearm | 12 inches |
| 14 inches | Biceps | 13½ inches |
| 16 inches | Neck | 16 inches |
| 78 inches | Reach | 76 inches |

The *Salt Lake Herald-Republican* said it was an even matchup for the championship of Utah and Colorado. The local papers said they were matched evenly physically, though Hector was half an inch shorter and inclined to be a little squattier. They had records that were on par as well. Bob York was their only common foe, both stopping him in 4 rounds. Hector also had a 20-round draw with big Jimmy Barry and a decision over Tom McMahon to his credit. Hector allegedly was 23 years old, 190 pounds, and 5'11", while Dempsey was 21, 5'11 ½", and 187 pounds.

Young Hector predicted that once it was over, Dempsey would say it was the toughest match he ever had.

Dempsey said, "I hardly know what I want to say. I am going to win. Say that if you want to. I have enough confidence in myself to think I can beat anybody I can land on, and I haven't yet met the man, when the match went long enough, on whom I couldn't land." Dempsey and his manager were so sure of victory that they already were signing up for other matches in the vicinity.

Fans liked Dempsey because he always gave them everything he had.[154]

On Thursday September 28, 1916 in Murray, Utah, a south Salt Lake City suburb just 8 miles south of the heart of Salt Lake City, at Trocadero Hall, Jack Dempsey fought Young Hector of Salida in a scheduled 15-round bout. Hardy Downing refereed. Dempsey was a 3 to 1 favorite, and a lot of betting was made at 2 to 1 that Hector would not stay 5 rounds.

---

[153] *Salt Lake Telegram, Salt Lake Herald-Republican*, September 24, 1916.
[154] *Salt Lake Tribune, Salt Lake Herald-Republican*, September 27, 28, 1916.

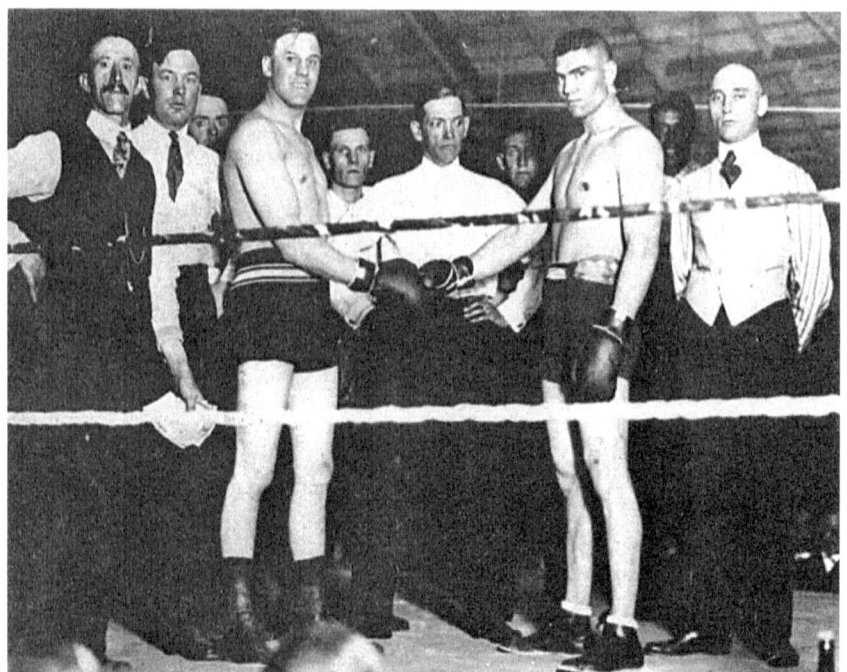

The 1st round was more of a feel-out, for they started off cautiously. Hector mostly used a dainty left which was like a flea bite to Jack, who was satisfied to watch and occasionally slip over a light left on his moving target. Hector's style of taps did not appear as if they would be a match for the sturdy panther-like Dempsey, who moved with the cool-headedness of a world's champion and had the kick of a mule from either glove. Hector gave the impression of a gymnasium boxer more than a fighter. However, Dempsey bided his time, seeming to devote the 1st round to finding out if his antagonist had anything to offer. Most already believed that he would have a cinch on his hands.

In the 2nd round, Hector continued his fancy footwork and dainty left jabs, while Dempsey decided that an uppercut would finish the show, and began playing on the Denverite's jaw. The finish began as early as the middle of the round, when Jack opened up more. A four-inch left uppercut broke open Hector's mouth.

Late in the round, while coming out of a clinch, another left uppercut dropped Hector flat on his back, though he was up in a flash and the bell saved him from any follow-up.

In the 3rd round, Dempsey went in to win. Hector led, but Jack was not there. A left uppercut and swinging right uppercut to the jaw as Hector stepped back sent him to the floor. He was up quickly.

Jack went right after him, trying to finish. Hector shelled up but took a powerful right uppercut that decked him nevertheless.

Hector rose slowly from his hands and knees and covered up. Another uppercut square on the chin sent him down for the third time in the round, the fourth time in the fight. This time Hector was out of it.

However, Hardy Downing counted up to nine, when the bell rang, saving him from an official knockout at that point. Hector was on the mat waving his hands and acting as if he had gone "cookoo" for keeps. Saved by the bell, his seconds carried him to his corner, but he fell out of his chair.

There were some vagaries regarding whether Hector retired in the corner between rounds, or simply was not able to continue when the 4th round bell rang. On one hand, the *Telegram* said Jack Dempsey stopped Colorado's Young Hector in the 3rd round. It suggested he retired in the corner, saying it was for the best. However, it also said that the ringing of the bell for the 4th round found Hector unable to return. Either way, Hector was not able to continue when the time came, he retired, and it was a technical knockout.

The *Tribune* said Hector was dragged to his corner, propped up in a chair, and efforts were made to revive him, but they were unavailing, so the 4th round never opened.

The *Herald-Republican* said Hector was unable to continue when the gong rang, and Dempsey was the winner.

If the bell rang to start the 4th round, it would be considered a 4th round TKO, but if Hector or his corner retired him before the bell rang, it was a 3rd round TKO. Most said Hector went out in the 3rd round. The number of reported knockdowns in the 3rd round varied from two up to four.

When his attendants assisted him from the building, Hector still was not fully recovered.

The *Salt Lake Telegram* said Dempsey had too much class and was too rough for Hector, who could not stand the "gaff." Dempsey stopped him without much apparent effort. He hardly had gotten under way, mostly using lefts. Dempsey once again demonstrated that when he connected, it usually was curtains for the other gent. Jack had improved. He did not tear after his opponent, but saved himself and his punches until the right time came. He clearly had the goods.

The *Salt Lake Tribune* said in baseball terms, Dempsey hit him with a single, a double, and a triple, and was an easy winner.[155]

Dempsey later said he earned $300 for the Hector fight.[156]

Jack's next bout was scheduled already – a rematch against Terry Keller at Ely, Nevada on October 7, just nine days from the Hector bout. Promoter Tom Chambers arranged the contest at Bijo hall in Ely to determine who was the "light heavyweight champion of the world."

According to the local paper, Keller had an enviable world-wide reputation, with a long list of knockout victories. In early May, Dempsey got a 10-round decision verdict over Keller in Ogden. Keller was eager for an opportunity to redeem himself, claiming that he was not at his best the first time, and was in better condition this time.

---

[155] *Salt Lake Telegram, Salt Lake Tribune, Salt Lake Herald-Republican, Reno Evening Gazette*, September 29, 1916.
[156] *Cedar Rapids Gazette*, June 3, 1919.

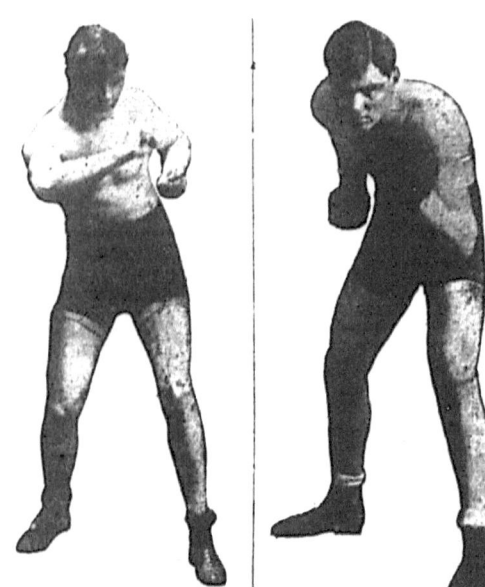

In fact, since losing a decision to Dempsey, 182-pound Keller had lost a 15-round decision to Tom McMahon and lost a 10-round no decision to highly-regarded 192-pound Bill Brennan.

The local *White Pine News* hyped it as the biggest fight since Joe Gans vs. Battling Nelson. Dempsey had fought the Big Swede and Joe Bonds locally, and talk about the Bonds bout made Jack a walking advertisement. "Jack Dempsey is undoubtedly the Bob Fitzsimmons of today. He is not only clever, but is a fighting demon. He is a glutton for punishment and the more is administered to him the faster he comes on."

The *Ely Record* said the eyes of the sporting world were focused on Ely. Keller had fought in Europe, Australia, and America, and was of championship caliber. Dempsey was recognized as the most scientific man of his class in the country. This paper echoed that he needed no introduction to the locals. Tom Chambers was promoting the event.[157]

Although advertised as fighting to determine who was the "light heavyweight champion of the world," in truth, it was not a championship fight, nor was either one technically a light heavyweight, but boxing folk always have been good at marketing.

On Saturday October 7, 1916 in Ely, Nevada, at the Bijo hall (one local said the fight was held at the Knights of Pythias hall, which possibly was the same thing), Jack Dempsey fought a rematch with Ogden's Terry Keller.

Dempsey was first to enter the ring, and he was cheered loudly. Keller followed, and also received an ovation.

According to the local *White Pine News*, the first two rounds were not replete with action. Neither accomplished much. They were feeling each other out. Dempsey picked up the attack in the 3rd round and landed a fusillade of uppercuts which gave him a clear advantage. The 4th was even. The 5th round bustled with activity. Keller devoted his energies almost entirely to the jaw and face, and earned the round. Honors were even in the 6th. In the 7th round, Keller had fire in his eye, and had the crowd cheering for him. He also had all the better of the 8th, connecting with the jaw on numerous occasions, but he could not drop his sturdy opponent. The 9th

---

[157] *White Pine News*, October 1, 1916; Boxrec.com; *Ely Record*, October 6, 1916.

round was Dempsey's, for he showered right and left hooks to the head, which slowed up Keller. Dempsey also was strong in the 10th, and forced the fighting. Keller was on the defensive for most of the round.

Referee C. W. Hicks of Ruth raised Dempsey's glove, signifying that he had won the 10-round decision. However, Keller's fans vociferously protested the decision, which they felt should have been a draw. This local paper scored it 3-3-4, feeling that it was an even fight. "Only a large congregation of devotees of the ring game didn't blush when they heard the verdict of the ring arbiter." Of course, if the referee felt that Dempsey had shaded one or more of the 4 rounds that the local writer scored even, then one can understand the decision.

The local *Ely Record* was not as detailed. It said the contest at the Bijo had a large attendance, but on the whole the fight was not what the patrons had expected. Neither man appeared to be in good form, and both were cautious, each one fearful that he had been overmatched. Hence, they sparred for time, and seemed anxious to avoid a real slugging match. Dempsey performed much better in his prior Ely engagements. Keller had a world-wide reputation, but lost the decision, "which a considerable number of those present resented vociferously."

In Utah, it was reported that Dempsey had defeated Keller by a narrow margin on a hair-line decision. Another said the decision met with the approval of the large crowd. The fight was good, but not as vicious as expected. However, the Salt Lake man handled himself in great style throughout.

Dempsey later said he was paid $225 for the fight. He won another 10-round decision over Keller, who performed better than he did the first time they fought.[158]

Just two days after the Keller fight, on Monday October 9, 1916 in Farmington, Utah (just north of Salt Lake), Davis county, 21-year-old William Harrison Dempsey of Salt Lake City married 20-year-old Maxine Cates of Salt Lake City, whom he had met in the spring of 1916 before he left for New York, but had been dating for only two months since his return. A justice of the peace performed the ceremony.[159]

In his autobiography, Dempsey claimed she was 15 years older than him, but this is different than their sworn affidavits in support of a marriage license application and their marriage license, which said he was 21 and she was 20 years of age.[160]

Dempsey said Cates was sweet and friendly at the time they married, but it didn't last long. Her moods were changing constantly and her friendliness turned to hostility once the honeymoon (in a tacky hotel room) was over. She was okay with the fact that they might be separated for months at a time, given his profession. His family was not happy about his marriage,

---

[158] *White Pine News*, October 8, 1916; *Ely Record*, October 13, 1916; *Ogden Standard*, October 9, 1916; *Salt Lake Telegram, Salt Lake Tribune*, October 7, 9, 1916; *Cedar Rapids Gazette*, May 23, 1919.
[159] Marriage license application and license; *Davis County Clipper*, Bountiful, Utah, October 22, 1916.
[160] Ages of 20 and 21 seem consistent with other documents. *Salt Lake Telegram*, January 26, 1920.

disapproving of his choice of partner. Between fights, Dempsey claimed that he lumberjacked and worked in some mines.

Hardy K. Downing announced that Dempsey's next contest would be 10 rounds against Louisville, Kentucky's Fighting Dick Gilbert at the Salt Lake theatre, sponsored by Downing's Manhattan club, on October 16, which would be just nine days after the 10-round Keller rematch, and seven days after Jack got married.[161]

According to secondary sources, 27-year-old Dick Gilbert had over 50 fights of experience, likely many more, going all the way back to 1907. He had fought multiple fights that went 15 and 20 rounds. Significant bouts on his record included: 1912 LND10 Tommy Sullivan, L15, L20, and L25 Battling Levinsky, ND15 Tom McMahon, and L20 Joe Borrell; 1913 WND6 and LDN10 Tom McMahon, LND6 Leo Houck, LND10 George Chip, W15 and TKO14 Mike Schreck; 1914 LND10 and L15 Jack Dillon, W15 Jack Geyer, and L12 Tom McMahon; 1915 KO7 Bob Devere, L20 KO Sweeney, LND12 Gunboat Smith, LND15 Tom McMahon, L15, D15, and W15 Terry Keller; and 1916 L15 Billy Miske, LND10 Bob Moha, and KO6 Young Hector.[162]

The local press said Dempsey was the local light heavy champ and one of the most talked of youngsters in the boxing game, who had a rapid rise to the top since he fought his first bout in Salt Lake as an amateur at Downing's Manhattan club a little over two years ago. He was the most popular man ever developed locally. Most local folk were of the opinion that in a couple of years he would be heavyweight champion of the world.

Gilbert was said to be one of the toughest propositions in the light heavyweight division. Boxing as a pro for eight years, despite being only 27 years old, he had met nearly 100 of the best in the country, and none ever

---

[161] *Ogden Standard*, October 10, 1916.
[162] Boxrec.com. *Salt Lake Herald-Republican*, October 11, 1916.

had knocked him down for the count. He weighed around 175-180 pounds. He was known for his experience, durability, and toughness.

Fighting Dick Gilbert, Who Meets Dempsey Monday Night

The locals alleged (perhaps with varying degrees of accuracy) that Gilbert had boxed Gunboat Smith 12 or 15 rounds to a draw, and Jack Dillon to a 10-round draw, two of the best in the division. He beat top light heavy Battling Levinsky four times, twice in 15 rounds, in 20 rounds, and once over the 25-round route. He also beat Terry Kellar in 15 rounds, stopped Mike Schreck twice, beat Sailor Petrosky in 20 rounds, and also had fought the likes of Bob Moha, George Chip, Al Norton, Billy Miske, Jack Herrick, Sailor Carroll, and Tom McMahon. Gilbert claimed to have never been knocked off his feet, and said it took a real champion to beat him.[163]

Gilbert's sparring with Jack Downey impressed locals, for he showed that he could take a punch and give one, and was quite aggressive. Gilbert was scarcely 5'7" tall, but he said height did not bother him at all. He had a good defense, as his unmarked face proved. In fact, many of those who saw Gilbert in training said Dempsey had made a bad matchup for himself, for

THE TWO BOXERS AND PROMOTER HARDY DOWNING.
On the left is "Fighting Dick" Gilbert, in the center Promoter Downing, and on the right is Salt Lake's likely young champion, Jack Dempsey.

Gilbert was too experienced, formidable, tough, dangerous, and rugged. The more that fans watched Gilbert work, the less certain they were that Dempsey would win. They hoped that Jack had not made a mistake.

---

[163] *Salt Lake Herald-Republican, Salt Lake Tribune, Salt Lake Telegram,* October 11, 1916; *Box Elder News,* October 13, 1916. The *Salt Lake Tribune* said Dempsey was awarded newspaper decisions over two of the boxers he met in New York and drew with the other.

Dempsey was sparring with recent foe Terry Keller, who had fought Gilbert three times and Dempsey twice. Keller later claimed that Dempsey's manager had hired him to spar with and teach Dempsey about the finer points of the game. Certainly, he could give him some Gilbert insight.

Dempsey looked bigger and better than ever, appearing to weigh around 190 pounds. Local fans were convinced that he would be the next champion of the world unless he was taken to the front too rapidly, a concern given that he had chosen a mighty tough proposition in Gilbert.[164]

Gilbert said, "I had to fight big fellows all my life. ... They all look alike to me. Anyhow, Dempsey can't be any tougher than Jack Dillon or Gunboat Smith. I'd like to fight the Gunboat every night."

The *Salt Lake Telegram* and *Salt Lake Herald-Republican* said Dempsey had a real test and tough job on his hands. He had to be careful and survive the body punching he was very apt to receive. Gilbert was tough, not much of a boxer, but carried a good powerful right to the body and head. Still, they expected Dempsey to win, because although he might not stop Gilbert, he figured to outpunch and outbox his more experienced but much shorter foe. Considerable action was expected.

Dempsey had shown that he was clever for a big fellow and had a terrific wallop in either hand. He would have to prove that he could take punishment as well, for the strong Gilbert not only could take it, but could dish out hard blows too. Gilbert's sparring with Jack Downey showed how rugged he was.[165]

On Monday October 16, 1916 at the Salt Lake theatre in Salt Lake City, Utah, Jack Dempsey fought Dick Gilbert in a scheduled 10-round contest. Gilbert entered the ring looking like a slightly enlarged edition of a Kewpie, whereas Dempsey looked like an Adonis, towering over his pudgy opponent.

1 - They sparred a bit. Gilbert went into a clinch at every opportunity and tried to do a little infighting.
2 - More of the same. When Dempsey led they clinched, with Dick boring in quite close.
3 - The pattern remained, with Dick attempting to hit the body and clinching, while absorbing Jack's punches like a sponge.
4 - Same again, with lots of clinching and infighting.
5 - Dempsey slowly was solving Gilbert's style, but as usual most of the time they were head to head, with no appreciable damage done.
6 - It was the same old story, but both woke up in the middle of the round and swapped some blows. Jack was plugging away as Dick came in.
7 - They again swapped some punches, and Dempsey was doing better, having made some adjustments, punching as Dick was advancing, and moving back a little to use his range and prevent Gilbert from getting close and grabbing so easily.

---

[164] *Salt Lake Herald-Republican*, October 12-14, 1916; *Salt Lake Telegram*, October 13, 14, 1916.
[165] *Salt Lake Telegram*, October 15, 1916; *Salt Lake Herald-Republican*, October 15, 16, 1916.

8 - During a mix-up, Dempsey slipped in a blow that crimsoned Dick's nose. This caused Jack to liven up and he got busy with lefts to the head followed by right hooks which sometimes landed.

9 - Dempsey kept using the same improved tactics, maintaining his range. At one point, he got Gilbert into a corner and fired away.

10 - There was more of a real fight in this round, with both trying harder. Jack kept away better and landed many good wallops, which seemed to worry Dick slightly, but Gilbert kept coming right in and landing some good body blows in the clinches.

Referee Hardy Downing's decision for Dempsey met with approval from both the crowd and the press.

The *Salt Lake Herald-Republican* said not even the most delicate could have found anything offensive in the bout between Dick Gilbert of Louisville, Kentucky and Jack Dempsey, the local light heavy. From the looks of it, the contest could have gone on for 10 rounds more without any damage done. Until the 6th round, it was a tame wrestling match. From then on, things brightened up a bit, and the fans saw a little going in the last three rounds, but nothing to get excited over, although there was enough fighting that the referee legitimately could give Dempsey the decision.

Dempsey towered over his pudgy opponent. Still, it could be seen how and why no one had stopped Gilbert. He clinched continuously.

The *Salt Lake Telegram* said it took Dempsey six rounds to figure out how to beat Gilbert, but then it proved to be easy. He won a clear-cut victory. The first six rounds were slow, but the last three were good enough for Dempsey to pull out a victory. Gilbert was tough and hard to hit. Dempsey did as well as he could, given Gilbert's infighting style, which puzzled him for a while. They would lead and clinch, several seconds of tugging and wrestling would follow, and then a repetition of the same - lead, clinch, wrestle.

Up to the start of the 7th round, honors were even. Gilbert occasionally landed a roundabout right hook to the body, his favorite punch. Dempsey learned to watch for that blow, and started defending it. Jack only had a small degree of success in the first six rounds.

In the latter half of the 6th and at the start of the 7th round, Dempsey tried a new system, and it worked. He resorted to boxing and stepping back with each punch to prevent Gilbert from reaching for a clinch, the only style to beat a such a man. Jack jumped in and out with a straight left and an occasional right counter. In that manner he often caught Gilbert stooped over in his effort to get a hold for a clinch, and Jack could shoot in a whole armful of lefts and rights to the head. Using such tactics, Dempsey piled up a good shade, and just was getting well-started on giving the visitor a good licking when the last gong ended it.

The last three rounds were fast enough to make up for the somewhat dilatory scrapping of the first five rounds. The ultimate conclusion was that it takes two to make an entertaining fight, which Gilbert was unwilling to do.

The *Salt Lake Tribune* said the first six rounds were a case of slam-bang, wrestle, back away, and then repeat. In the 7th round, Dempsey showed his superiority and soon had the Louisville terror floundering about the ring, which continued until the end. Dick's best was at infighting. Although he landed quite a few in the stomach, the local boy never backed up from the punches, and at the end was the fresher of the two. Referee Hardy Downing's decision met with everyone's approval.

The *Price Sun* reported that for 6 rounds the battlers stalled for the most part, clinching and sparring in monotonous fashion. In the 7th, Dempsey demonstrated his superior strength and began pounding Gilbert around the ring sufficiently until the end of the fight such that the crowd applauded the referee's decision. Gilbert could do little with Dempsey during the infighting, as he found him too tough for short-arm blows. That broke down Dick's major offensive tactics.[166]

In 1920, promoter Hardy Downing claimed that Dempsey earned $500 for the Dick Gilbert fight, the first time he was paid real money. The most he had been paid before then (at least by him) had been $25.

Downing said Dempsey had no education, but was a big, good-natured kid who helped out his family with any money he earned. He drank, but not too much. Dempsey's favorite amusement was cabarets (somewhat of a nightclub with women singing and dancing). "He fooled around them." It was claimed that Jack had made it through the eighth or ninth grade. Downing replied to such assertion, "Maybe, but I went as far as that, and I know that Jack and I don't spell the same way."

Downing said Dempsey "never had the benefits of environment. No home life in the real sense."

Responding to a story that Jack used to shine shoes in Salt Lake, Downing replied, "Never did a day's work in Salt Lake that I know of. Certainly when I wanted him for fights nobody ever told me: 'O, he's working.'" Dempsey may have stolen train rides when he was younger, but after he went East (in mid-1916) he never rode over or under; always on the cushions thereafter.[167]

In late October, A. J. Auerbach filed suit against Harry Dempsey, known as Jack Dempsey, to recover $320 which he claimed he had advanced to the fighter, for which he never had been reimbursed.[168]

As of early November 1916, 21-year-old Jack Dempsey had been a professional boxer for 2 years. He already had at least 28 fights. His only official loss had been a mere 4-round decision to the far more experienced Jack Downey very early on in his career, which he avenged by knockout.

Dempsey's next bout was scheduled for Thanksgiving eve, November 29, in Salida, Colorado, just west of Colorado Springs, southwest of Denver,

---

[166] *Salt Lake Herald-Republican, Salt Lake Telegram, Salt Lake Tribune, Ogden Standard*, October 17, 1916; *Price Sun*, October 20, 1916. In an undercard bout, Swede Johnson and Young Maloney fought hard, in exciting fashion. Referee Jack Price gave the bout to Maloney, but the fans howled in derision, feeling that Johnson earned no worse than a draw. This likely was the "Big Swede" that Dempsey had fought.
[167] *New York Daily News*, February 27, 1920.
[168] *Salt Lake Herald-Republican*, October 26, 1916.

in a 10-round rematch with local fighter Young Hector (Conrew) of Salida. The Salida Business Men's association was promoting the bout. Hector was well known to fans throughout Colorado. Dempsey was looked upon as one of the most promising young heavyweights in the country. The fight would be staged at the Salida rink, which had a capacity of 2,000.

Hector blamed his prior performance against Dempsey (LTKOby3) two months ago upon a broken hand, which he suffered a few days before the fight. He thought he could do better in a rematch, now that his hand had healed. They both would train at the City hall gym.[169]

The local *Salida Mail* said, "Both boys are in the pink of condition and a rattling good bout is expected. Much interest is shown throughout the surrounding towns by the heavy advance sale of tickets and one of the largest houses that ever turned out is expected. ... This will be worth seeing. All seats reserved. Ladies cordially invited."[170]

On Wednesday November 29, 1916 in Salida, Colorado, inside the local Rink, Jack Dempsey fought a scheduled 10-round rematch against Young Hector. The event drew a large crowd from Salida and adjoining towns.

The *Salida Mail* said Dempsey stalled during the 1st round, permitting Hector to hit him a few times and then pretending he was about all in. Hector was game and did all the leading.

In the 2nd round, Dempsey awaited his first opportunity, and, after a clinch, when Hector lost his balance, the chance came. A solar plexus punch, followed by two other body blows sent Hector through the ropes to the floor, where he alighted on his head and shoulders for the full ten-count. Just like that, the fight was over in the 2nd round.

This time, Hector was stopped one round sooner than in their first fight. The *Salida Mail* said the local boxer was outclassed clearly by the Salt Lake visitor, who was one of the best light heavyweights in the country.[171]

Dempsey later claimed he received only $90 for the Young Hector rematch.[172]

Throughout 1916, 5'7" 190-200-pound Sam Langford had been competing with 6'3" 205-210-pound Harry Wills for the title of best black heavyweight. The old guard of 30- or 31-year-old Sam Langford, 37-year-old 5'10" 195-pound Joe Jeannette, and 32-year-old 5'10 ½" 220-pound Sam McVey/McVea were aging, but still effective and dangerous (and avoided by most top white fighters), and the younger 24-year-old Wills was emerging and improving. Although in 1916 Langford lost a 20-round decision to Wills (over whom Sam had scored KO14 in 1914, but had lost a 1915 ND10), in their subsequent 1916 contest, Langford knocked out Wills in the 19th round. Still, in two more fights thereafter, Wills won 10- and 8-round newspaper decisions over Langford. Also in 1916, Langford had a WND10 (twice) over Sam McVey, as well as a DND12 and D20 with

---

[169] *Leadville Herald Democrat*, November 15, 1916; *Salida Mail*, November 21, 1916.
[170] *Salida Mail*, November 28, 1916.
[171] *Salida Mail, Salida Record*, December 1, 1916.
[172] *Cedar Rapids Gazette*, June 3, 1919.

McVey. Wills had won a most recent 1915 12-round decision over McVey (though McVey had twice beaten Wills via decision previously, 1914 W20 and 1915 WND10). Langford also knocked out Joe Jeannette in the 7th round in 1916, avenging a 1915 12-round decision loss to Jeannette. Wills and Jeannette had fought to two 10-round draws in 1913 and 1914. Langford also knocked out the very durable black Battling Jim Johnson in the 12th round, and then won a 12-round decision over him. Langford fought Bill Tate to a DND10, but then lost a 12-round decision to Tate in early 1917 (which he would avenge with a 6th round knockout).

Other than the LKOby19 to Langford, Harry Wills had won all of his 1916 fights, including W20 Langford, then WND10 and WND8 Langford after the knockout loss to Sam, WND10 John Lester Johnson (before Johnson fought Dempsey), W20 Jeff Clark, and WND10 Bill Tate. However, in February 1917, Battling Jim Johnson would stop Wills in the 2nd round, when Harry retired owing to a broken wrist, which loss Wills would avenge in June 1917 via WND10. Wills would not lose another fight again until 1922, and even then it would be via disqualification for knocking down Bill Tate on a break. No one would beat him on the merits for the next decade, doing no worse than a draw in any contest.[173]

*Chicago Defender*, October 7, 1916

None of these fighters were going to be given or even considered for a title shot, and very few in the white press or public advocated for them at that time, content with and accepting of Jess Willard's drawing of the color line in the wake of Jack Johnson's reign.

Langford's challenge to Willard was ignored. Sam's manager Joe Woodman said Langford could beat Willard, and could have beaten Jack Johnson. "It is an absurd and untenable position for a world's champion to draw the color line, especially when he was enabled to gain professional honor and distinction by a victory over a somewhat debilitated champion, a Colored man."[174]

---

[173] Boxrec.com.
[174] *Chicago Defender*, November 4, 1916.

CHAPTER 7

# A Turn For the Worst

In early December 1916, Jack Dempsey went back to the East coast, seeking fights in Philadelphia or New York. He trained and sparred with highly respected very experienced light heavy Jack Dillon, who had nearly 200 fights.[175] On December 19, 1916 in New York, Jack Dillon fought Billy Miske in a close 10-round no decision contest. The *Brooklyn Daily Times* and *Buffalo Evening News* reported that Miske squeezed out a win by a shade.

In late December, Damon Runyon wrote that Old John the Barber Reisler, "volatile soul that he is, claims he has acquired the eastern rights to what, in our opinion, is about as promising a prospect as has been seen in these parts in a long time." Utah's Jack Dempsey stood 6'1", weighed 190 pounds, and mostly won by knockout. "He walks right into the folks, pasting away with both hands, and...we predict that Jack Dempsey will go a long way in the heavyweight division."[176]

Yet, at end of December, the *Salt Lake Telegram* said Dempsey had more managers than opportunities to fight. He was on his way home, for he had not found a match.[177]

Dempsey had been in New York with Manager "Liz" Fisher, and Barber John Reisler again tried to "steal" him away. Fisher sold Reisler a phony contract he claimed he had with Dempsey. Reisler purchased suits, coats, shoes, hats, and shirts for Dempsey and Fisher. But then Dempsey left. However, the locals had no sympathy for Reisler, calling him a parasite who always was trying to steal fighters.

Reisler later claimed to have signed Dempsey to a 3-year contract on or about December 16 or 18, 1916. Yet, Dempsey did not fight for him.

Dempsey arrived back in Salt Lake on or about January 4, 1917, after spending less than a month in the East.[178]

In his first autobiography, *Round by Round*, Dempsey claimed that when he went back to New York, Reisler made it clear that if he wanted to fight, Dempsey would have to fight whomever he said to fight, or he would not fight at all, for he had him under contract. Reisler wanted him to fight guys like Gunboat Smith (who held a win over Willard) and Frank Moran (who had just fought Willard), top world-class heavies, whom Dempsey believed had too much experience for him at that point in his development. He had

---

[175] *Salt Lake Telegram*, December 20, 1916. Jack Dillon had victories over fighters such as Battling Levinsky, Dick Gilbert, Al Norton, Fireman Jim Flynn, Charley Weinert, Porky Dan Flynn, Tom McCarty, Gunboat Smith, Andre Anderson, Tom Cowler, Billy Miske, Bob Devere, and Frank Moran.
[176] *Salt Lake Telegram, Brooklyn Daily Times, Buffalo Evening News*, December 20, 1916; *Salt Lake Tribune*, December 29, 1916.
[177] *Salt Lake Telegram*, December 31, 1916.
[178] *Salt Lake Telegram*, January 2, 4, 1917.

been boxing as a pro for only 2 years. Jack refused, feeling that Reisler was willing to sacrifice him for one or two paydays. Reisler became furious, saying that he was through with Jack and he should leave town, for Reisler would make it impossible for him to fight anyone. So he left. New York was closed off to him.

Dempsey went to Philadelphia to try to get a fight there, but found no success; which he believed was due to Reisler.

Then he stopped off in Kansas City, where he had heard that Frank Moran was going to fight Carl Morris. He asked Moran's camp if they wanted to hire him as a sparring partner, but they were not interested.

So he went to Morris's camp and made the same offer, and they accepted. Morris stood 6'4" and weighed around 235 pounds. Dempsey would be paid 75 cents a day to spar with Morris. Jack said Morris was very fast and a good fighter. Jack had been at the camp for three or four days when the fight was called off. Neither Moran nor Morris wanted to risk a loss to one another, so they agreed not to fight.

Actually, there is primary source evidence that Morris had a fight scheduled with *Charley Weinert* (not Moran), set to take place in Kansas City on January 1, but on December 24, Morris canceled the match.[179]

Dempsey said Morris was obnoxious, had money and liked to show it off, and teased the hungry Dempsey about his lack of funds, humiliating him. Making things worse, when camp was closed and everything got lost in the moving process, including Jack's suitcase, a Morris handler told him that things got misplaced all the time, to leave a forwarding address, and he would send the suitcase when it was found. He did, but cash on delivery, and Jack didn't have the money, so he had to borrow.

He returned home to Maxine empty-handed. She wanted money, more of it than he could give her at that point. She was changing towards him. If he could not provide her with sufficient funds, she was content to be separated from him and not see him. Regardless, whether it was lust or love, Dempsey wanted to make her happy. His folks wanted no part of her, feeling that she was sexually immoral. They said anyone who worked in the Tenderloin district couldn't be any good (perhaps an allusion to her potential prostitution).

It was reported that while training in Salt Lake City on January 18, 1917, Dempsey strained his shoulder and injured his hand.

Dempsey said he got in a mix-up with a gym apparatus; the nail was torn from the little finger of his left hand, and he suffered a slight shoulder strain. He would resume training within a week.[180]

Jack was booked to meet Carl Morris at Murray, Utah on February 6. The 6'4" Morris was a giant who outweighed Dempsey by 40 pounds. No one mentioned that they had sparred recently.[181]

---

[179] *St. Louis Post-Dispatch*, December 25, 1916.
[180] *Salt Lake Tribune*, January 19, 20, 1917.
[181] Carl Morris had defeated Jim Coffey, Al Norton, Porky Flynn, Tom McMahon, Arthur Pelkey, Gunboat Smith, Dan Daly, and Battling Levinsky. In 1913, Morris lost a 10-round no decision to Jess Willard. *Salt Lake Tribune*, January 21, 1917; Boxrec.com.

However, promoter Fred Winsor then reported that Morris had disappointed him and was not going to fight Dempsey, due to alleged illness, though some said it was because he wanted softer matches. Therefore Winsor was compelled to find another opponent, and was talking with Gunboat Smith, Jim Flynn, and the Greek Knockout Brown.[182]

On January 30, it was announced that "Fireman" Jim Flynn would meet Jack Dempsey at Murray, Utah on Wednesday February 14, 1917, just two weeks away, in a scheduled 15-round bout at Trocadero hall to benefit the Murray fire department. Flynn's manager Jack Curley had agreed to the fight. Within a few days, the bout date was changed to the 13th so as not to compete with another show scheduled for the 14th.

JACK DEMPSEY,
Salt Lake light heavy weight, who is to be pitted against a man of class next month at Murray.

When asked whether he was willing to meet the tough battler Flynn, Dempsey had okayed the match. "I will meet anybody, except Willard, right now. I might as well start now and lick somebody besides young Hectors, Bob Yorks and such kind, so bring him on." He felt that he had gotten to the point where he might as well take a whirl at some of the top-notchers.

Promoter Fred Winsor said, "Dempsey is naturally a card here, and we have every reason to believe that he will do his best. We have never seen him against a man who might carry the fight to him like Flynn surely will, so his showing will go a long way toward proving whether or not he is the future champion he thinks he is." Winsor noted that everyone knew that Flynn was one of the most dangerous fighters in the game. He had fought the likes of Jack Johnson and Sam Langford and held his own (with one 10-round victory over the great Langford). He had a kill- or be-killed attitude. He had been beaten, but only by world-class men. "He is a savage miller and if Dempsey can take his aggressiveness, and perhaps outbox him or knock him out, Jack's reputation will have been made."[183]

Pueblo, Colorado's Jim Flynn had met them all. His record read like the who's who of boxing. He had been fighting since the 1890s, when Dempsey was a mere child. He had a reputation for being able to assimilate punishment and dish out vicious blows as well, having beaten much larger men with his aggression, pace, and power.[184]

---

[182] *Salt Lake Telegram,* January 28, 1917.
[183] *Salt Lake Tribune,* February 4, 1917.
[184] *Salt Lake Tribune, St. Joseph Gazette,* January 30, 1917; *Salt Lake Tribune,* February 4, 1917.

JIM FLYNN.

The vastly more experienced 37-year-old Fireman Jim Flynn had about 125 known fights on his resume. In 1906, he had fought Tommy Burns for the world heavyweight championship, getting stopped in the 15th round in a grueling and entertaining bout that actually raised Flynn's stock. Significant results followed, including: 1907 W20 Jack "Twin" Sullivan, KO18 George Gardner, KO7 Dave Barry, WDQ18 Tony Ross, LKOby11 future champion Jack Johnson, and KO6 Bill Squires; 1908 D10 and LND10 Jim Barry, LKOby9 Al Kaufman, and LKOby1 Sam Langford; 1910 WND10 and LKOby8 Langford; and 1911 KO10 Al Kaufman and WND10 Carl Morris.

His victories over the 205-pound Kaufman and 232-pound Morris catapulted Flynn into a title shot against Jack Johnson in 1912. In that championship fight, the 192-pound Flynn ferociously and quickly attacked in consistent nonstop fashion with heavy blows, but the careful and defensive 214-pound Johnson peppered and uppercut him and clinched constantly. Flynn's frustration with Johnson's incessant holding, and his inability to land often or meaningfully despite his best efforts, caused Flynn to start headbutting flagrantly and often, which ultimately led to the sheriff stopping the fight in the 9th round, and Johnson won the contest via a points decision.

Subsequent significant Flynn results included: 1912 TKO15 Charley Miller and LTKOby16 Luther McCarty; 1913 LND6 McCarty, DND10 Jim Coffey, LTKOby5 Gunboat Smith, LND10 Battling Levinsky, and LND10 George Rodel; 1914 D10 and L10 Jack Dillon, LKOby4 Coffey, KO6 Al Norton, LND10 Levinsky, LDQ9 and L10 Carl Morris, and KO7 George Davis; 1915 LND10 Tony Ross, LND10 Gunboat Smith, LKOby9 Jim Coffey, KO2 Andy Malloy, TKO14 Morgan Williams, WND10 and D10 Al Reich, LND10 Jack Dillon, and LND10 Levinsky; and 1916 LND10 Dillon, LKOby2 Fred Fulton, LKOby4 Dillon, and WDQ3 Texas Tate.

The question arises, if Dempsey was not willing to fight far more experienced fighters like Smith or Moran for John Reisler recently in New York, why then was he willing to fight vastly more experienced men such as Morris, Smith, or Flynn in Utah just a couple months later? Economic necessity may have had something to do with it. Jack was broke, had not fought in two months, and his wife was pressuring him for money. Perhaps Dempsey's sparring with Dillon and Morris had boosted his confidence; for they had beaten Flynn. Also, Flynn was 37 years of age, had not fought since late July 1916, and had lost most of his fights over the past couple of years; apparently on the down slide. Still, Flynn only lost to top world-class fighters, and usually was competitive, known for giving it everything he had.

The local press said Flynn typically won by a mile, by knockout, or was beaten decisively himself. He was one of the hardest marks that could have been chosen for Dempsey. Some believed that 21-year-old Dempsey was stepping up just a little too fast.[185]

Flynn looked good physically, and was taking the bout in an unconcerned, nonchalant attitude. He had no fear of Dempsey's reputation as a puncher. Flynn said he had been training all winter and weighed slightly more than 180 pounds (though he usually weighed around 190+ at this point in his career). Dempsey tipped the scales at about 190 in the gym. Both men were working out impressively.[186]

On February 7, Dempsey sparred Jack Downey for 3 rounds and then 2 more with Johnny Dunn.

Flynn was tireless in sparring 3 rounds with Young Peter Jackson and 3 more with Martin Davis. 10 cents admission was charged to watch the work at Jackson's gym at 48 East Second South, but the place was packed.

Flynn said there was an important reason for his recent hard training and change in habits, no longer seeking the night life when he should be sleeping. He recently became a father to a baby girl, and this motivated him. Those who saw him working out noticed the change and improvement.

In another training session, Flynn skipped rope, punched the bag, and sparred three opponents 3 rounds each, for a total of 9 rounds, against Swede Johnson, Jack Davis (or Martin Davis), and Young Peter Jackson.

Dempsey ran 7 miles and worked 2 hours in the gym. He boxed Joe Hennessey, Johnny Dunn, and an unknown middleweight. He looked faster than a cat.[187]

Flynn was a past-master at infighting. He was so confident that he was wagering considerable money on himself to win.[188]

Flynn was so rough that he had a tough time finding sparring partners willing to go with him on a consistent daily basis. He asked the crowd whether anyone was willing to step into the ring with him for a few rounds. Promoter Fred Winsor surprised him when he put on the gloves for 2 rounds. Flynn asked, "Where do you get that stuff? I never knew you could box."

---

[185] *Salt Lake Telegram*, February 3, 4, 1917.
[186] *Ogden Standard*, February 6, 1917; *Salt Lake Tribune*, *Salt Lake Telegram*, February 7, 1917.
[187] *Salt Lake Tribune*, February 8, 9, 1917; *Salt Lake Telegram*, February 8, 1917.
[188] *Salt Lake Tribune*, *Salt Lake Telegram*, February 10, 1917.

Here we have Fred Winsor and the light heavy weights who are slated to furnish what looks like a classy card at Murray next Tuesday evening. Jack Dempsey is on the left; Promoter Winsor in the center, and Jim Flynn on the right.

Billy Roche, Flynn's manager, and A. J. Auerbach, Dempsey's manager, agreed upon Frank Armstrong to referee the bout.[189]

Though on the down swing and not the same as he was four or five years ago, Flynn was one of the toughest fighters in the business. He still was dangerous, especially to a young fellow without nearly the same experience. And he appeared to be in great shape, given how he performed in sparring.

Dempsey had shown that he could hit, and was far better than the average big fellow as a boxer and clean hitter. But it was the first time he was going up against a man of such vast, quality, high-level experience.

On the day of the fight, both fighters were confident. Flynn said, "I wish I could be as positive of everything else in the future as I am that I am going to win this battle."

Dempsey believed he was faster than Flynn and had the better punch. He noted that he had stood up to sluggers like Wild Bert Kenney, John Lester Johnson, and others, and therefore was not worried about Flynn's powerful attack. "Stepping stones, that's what you call them, isn't it? Well, that's what this bout is going to be for me tonight."

Young Peter Jackson, who had trained with both, predicted a great battle, and advised Flynn not to take Dempsey too lightly. He liked Dempsey's chances. A lot would depend on how good Flynn was on the day of the fight and how much punishment Dempsey could stand, because Flynn was likely to hand it out.

Dempsey was quoted by the *Ogden Standard* as saying, "I want to win badly, and I think I am going to win. We all have to learn, but there is no better way to learn than to take a chance. I don't think Flynn is so much better than the big fellows I have already met, and none of the others ever made me run. Jim will have a better opinion of me when he leaves here."

Supposedly, Dempsey was a few pounds bigger than Flynn.[190]

---

[189] *Salt Lake Telegram*, February 11, 12, 1917.
[190] *Salt Lake Telegram, Salt Lake Tribune, Ogden Standard,* February 13, 1917.

On Tuesday February 13, 1917 in Murray, Utah, the Salt Lake City suburb, inside the Trocadero hall, in a scheduled 15-round bout, Jack Dempsey fought Fireman Jim Flynn. Frank Armstrong refereed (though some called him Ralph Armstrong). Fans paid from $2 up to $5 for seats.

The *Salt Lake Telegram* reported that the fight did not get started until close to midnight, rather than the 9 p.m. advertised time, much to the discomfiture of the audience and the fighters. Promoter Fred Winsor later explained the excessive delay, saying that it was due to a wrangle between one of the fighters and his manager.

The *Salt Lake Tribune* said patrons waited 45 minutes for the main event. The delay was due to financial arguments in the box office. A couple firemen gave a 3-round exhibition to fill the time.

The local *Deseret Evening News* said the gate receipts amounted to about $5,000. It was called a benefit for the Murray fire department, but the promoters only gave them their $250 guarantee. The gate receipts were split after considerable wrangling, but those connected with the affair would not say who got the big end. It was understood, however, that Flynn's demands were met.

According to the *Salt Lake Telegram*, as he entered the ring, Dempsey appeared very nervous and scared out of his wits. He shook like a leaf as his seconds put on his gloves. Flynn seemed to realize it too.

At the bell, Dempsey forgot to shake hands, but Flynn insisted on the formality, which took about five seconds. Flynn then rushed at Dempsey as if he had the last car to catch. Jack bent over and covered up. Flynn rushed again, tearing in, pushed him into position with one hand and then laced him with the other. Dempsey stepped back, though apparently not in great distress. He bent over and walked toward Flynn with both forearms and gloves covering his face, and at the same time, Flynn rushed in again, gave Jack's head a quick shove toward his right (using his left hook) and sent a short right-hand hook through his guard and onto the point of the chin. Dempsey immediately went down face first in his gloves. It was all done in a flash. Those who saw the blow and the knockdown knew it was over. Jim Flynn had knocked out Jack Dempsey in the 1st round. It was one of the fastest bouts ever seen. It was all over in 25 seconds.

The *Telegram* said Dempsey forgot to duck. A right hook square on the chin sent him to the place where the birdies sing, and it was curtains. Flynn used a trick that he had learned from Langford. Dempsey usually stalled at the start, but such tactics didn't work this time, for it gave Flynn an opportunity to nail him. The locals believed Dempsey would learn something from the experience.

The *Salt Lake Tribune* version also said Flynn flattened Dempsey in 25 seconds. The local man was unprepared for the onslaught. During those 25 seconds, Flynn punched Dempsey twice on the right side of the head, twice on the left side, broke down Jack's guard with his right and put the finishing touches on with a steaming wallop with his left to the jaw. (So, one writer said a right was the final blow, and one said a left, though likely it was both.)

Dempsey was out for about a half minute. When he began to regain consciousness, he evidently thought he still was in a fight, for he put up a battle with those who were trying to bring him around.

Although Dempsey knew that it was Flynn's way to start fast, hurling himself into the fray with all of his speed and strength, he did not prepare properly for that first onslaught. He looked dazed by the swiftness with which things moved, and he was as helpless before Flynn's two rushes as though he were but a child.

Those who had seen Dempsey fight always had admired his ability to take punishment, but usually it came over the course of a battle, rather than all at once like a bolt of lightning, which was too much. He was hopeless against the tornado which caught him right at the start. During the few seconds that the fight lasted, Flynn made two attacks. He bent his head downward and bore in, whaling away with both hands. There was a wee bit of a lull, during which time the referee tried to do some separating, and then came the onslaught with its two-blow finish.

The crowd was disappointed by the speedy termination, but none doubted that Flynn's whirlwind tactics gave the veteran an easy victory.

These sources likely were not including the time it took to count to ten. Often back then, the ten-second count was not included in the time of the fight. They meant it was 25 seconds of fighting until the fighter went down.

The *Deseret Evening News*, based in Salt Lake City, said Dempsey appeared ready to do battle at the opening gong, and rushed in with all his speed, but Flynn's hammer punches ended his aspirations. Flynn cut loose for a knockout from the start.

After shaking hands, Dempsey was hit twice on the side of the head. He appeared dazed, and was helpless against the final rain of blows. He was hit twice more on the other side, and then Flynn landed a terrific finishing left to the jaw after 25 seconds of fierce fighting, knocking Dempsey out. Dempsey was insensible for several minutes, and when brought back from the land of nod, he evidently thought he still was in the fight, and attempted to slug his own seconds.

The *Ogden Daily Standard* said a "one-two" to the jaw was about all there was to the much-advertised battle. It was one of the shortest bouts in history. The contest lasted 20 seconds, and in that time, Dempsey never laid a glove on Flynn. They shook hands, Flynn put his head down and bore in. He landed a left to the face and had the local boy covering up. As Jack dropped his guard from his chin to peek out, Jim landed a right swing to the jaw, followed quickly with a right to the same spot, Dempsey went down, and Referee Ralph Armstrong counted ten. It was all over except hauling the local pride to his corner.

It was Jack Dempsey's first knockout loss as a professional.

Interestingly enough, the result was so shocking, unexpected, and upsetting that in another next-day article, the *Ogden Daily Standard* said that Utah fights were to be condemned. Following Dempsey's defeat, "and the condemning of the whole affair as the worst prize fight fiasco in the history of the state, a movement was on foot today to persuade the legislature, which is now in session, to bar all professional boxing matches." Why such an incredibly harsh reaction? Why would this fight garner a movement to ban boxing? Did they suspect or believe the bout had been fixed? Why else would a fast knockout cause folks to want to ban boxing altogether and condemn it as the worse fiasco ever? Certainly the paper was alluding to strong suspicions of a fix. Perhaps these folks simply could not believe that Dempsey could be stopped legitimately in only 20 or 25 seconds.[191]

A few days later, the *Salt Lake Telegram* harshly said, "Jack Dempsey's development, we are sorry to note, is all confined to the region below the ears."[192] Meaning great body; not much brains. Ouch. Talk about harsh.

The question is whether they meant he was not an intelligent boxer, or that he was dumb enough to throw a fight. Perhaps he simply got caught by a very experienced, fast-starting, powerful fighter. Such things do occur. Or, perhaps Dempsey indeed threw the fight because he was feeling pressure to earn more money to satisfy his wife Maxine, and the quickest way to make more money would be to accept inducements to throw a contest. Word on the street may have been that he had taken a dive.

Still, the way both seemed to train hard, the fact that Dempsey was nervous before the fight, and the fact that he woke up and tried to fight his own cornermen, he was so out of it, indicates that it was a legitimate result, or at the very least that it was a legitimate knockout. Some later wondered whether he intentionally allowed Flynn to nail him hard and knock him out, especially since it was his first knockout loss as a pro, and Dempsey never again was stopped in his entire career. So it stood out as an odd anomaly. Folks may have been speculating, because the result so defied expectations. But boxing sometimes can be like that. Yet, it is interesting that Flynn before the fight said he wished he could be as positive of everything in the future as he was that he would win this fight. It could have been typical confidence, but the statement resonates differently in light of the debate.

Although perhaps there are several reasons, it is interesting to note that Dempsey never again fought in Utah.

The following month, in March 1917, Damon Runyon wrote that Flynn was an example of an athlete who defied years.

Runyon said Dempsey had been seen in New York, when he "bested Andre Anderson and John Lester Johnson in 10-round bouts." (So Runyon believed Dempsey had beaten Johnson).

> Andre wasn't much, but John Lester Johnson is that slippery, slashing Harlem black that few heavyweights care to tackle. He is the Levinsky of the colored brigade. John the Barber thought so well of Dempsey that he signed him to a contract, which Dempsey promptly broke, returning to his old Utah home. He came on here again, and made up with John the Barber, just a few weeks back, only to once more do a

---

[191] *Salt Lake Telegram, Salt Lake Tribune, Deseret Evening News, Ogden Standard,* February 14, 1917.
[192] *Salt Lake Telegram,* February 18, 1917.

lammister after John had dressed him up like a horse and buggy and ironed the wrinkles out of his stomach.[193]

In 1919, Runyon, in speaking of the Flynn fight, said, "There now befell an incident which I am inclined to think Jack Dempsey has often regretted." Runyon said there was something "queer" about the Jim Flynn contest. He had heard several versions of it, but none from Dempsey, who talked little about it, "and he has reason for reticence on the subject. It does not reflect much credit on him, whatever the circumstances."

The rumor was that Dempsey had thrown the fight. Dempsey later testified that he had made $1,500 for the first Flynn fight, the most he ever had made for a fight up to that point, very good money in those days. He was hit on the chin and went down like a log to be counted out.[194]

In his autobiographies, Dempsey denied throwing the fight, arguing that money meant a lot, but not enough to make him blow a fight, particularly since losing would and did hurt his reputation a great deal. It was a stunning setback to his career. Jack claimed that after the fight, Maxine spent the night with him, took the money he earned, and was gone the next morning.

Around the time of the fight, Dempsey blamed the loss on being hit when he reached out to touch gloves at the bell. He later said he had failed to warm up properly. Either way, he was crushed, and thought his chance to become champion had slipped away. He later claimed that his brother had thrown in the towel, and Jack was angry at him for doing so, but none of the local reports supported such an assertion. Dempsey was out cold and counted out.

Still, the rumors, hints, and strong suggestions that the Flynn fight was fixed persisted over the years. The question was whether he in fact threw it, or whether some preferred to have folks believe he took a dive rather than have to admit vulnerability and a legitimate loss. However, if Dempsey indeed took a dive, that would affect adversely the perception of his honesty and integrity, which could be worse.

Following the Flynn fight, Dempsey and his manager A. J. Auerbach split up, at Auerbach's suggestion. The question was whether Auerbach broke things off between them as a result of believing that Dempsey had thrown the fight, or because he believed that Dempsey had lost legitimately and simply did not have what it took, or for other reasons.

The fight's result garnered little discussion at the time, because Dempsey still was a relative unknown nationally. However, more would be revealed or claimed a couple months later, in April 1917, which affected the perception about this fight, and again alluded to and revealed both before he became champion and after. More than a few folks with intimate knowledge believed that Dempsey had thrown the fight, and such was said or alluded to directly or indirectly over the years, including by Hardy Downing, A. J. Auerbach, and even Dempsey's wife. To be continued.[195]

---

[193] *Salt Lake Tribune*, March 11, 1917.
[194] *Cedar Rapids Gazette*, June 6, 9, 1919. *San Francisco Examiner*, June 15, 1920.
[195] *New York Daily News*, February 27, 1920, March 1, 3, 1920. *Enid Daily Eagle*, February 8, 1920.

CHAPTER 8

# West Coast Warrior

Jack Dempsey had a new manager – Fred Winsor, who had managed Young Hector and promoted the Jim Flynn fight. In March 1917, Winsor asked Dempsey to come out to the West Coast, in the San Francisco/Oakland area, where boxing was quite popular. Dempsey agreed. Much to his surprise, his wife Maxine decided to go with him. Jack said she usually did not travel with him.

Fred Winsor

Winsor signed Dempsey to box in Oakland, California against Al Norton in a 4-round bout, the longest distance allowed in that state at that time.

The approximately 25-year-old Al Norton's career began in 1913. His record included: 1914 L10 Jack Dillon, DND10 Bob Moha, TKO6 Joe Bonds (who would last the 10-round distance with Dempsey in 1916), LKOby6 Jim Flynn, and L4 Bonds; 1915 W10 Tom McMahon (who held a 1914 WND10 over Jess Willard), L10 Carl Morris, LKOby2 Al Reich, KO2 Joe Cox (who held a 1911 TKO5 retirement victory over Willard in Jess's eighth pro bout), KO7 Jack Moran, and LTKOby4 Jack Dillon; 1916 L4 Bob McAllister, W4 Charley Miller (who fought Willard to a 1913 D4), W4 Terry Keller, and L4, D4, and D4 Willie Meehan.[196]

AL NORTON

The local *Oakland Tribune* said Norton was in wonderful shape, weighing just a fraction under 175, and his good showing against the very experienced, crafty, clever, rough, tough, and awkward Willie Meehan gave him confidence. (That same paper on Feb. 21 listed Norton as weighing 187 pounds to Meehan's 220.)[197]

The *Tribune* said Oakland and San Francisco observers were impressed with Dempsey's appearance in training at the Association Club in San Francisco and more recently the West Oakland Club gym (which was sponsoring the contest), saying he was the fastest man seen there since Harry Wills. They had woken up to the fact that a real fighter was in town. Dempsey was no great gym performer at rope skipping, shadow boxing, or bag punching, but when it came to actual boxing, he had all the ear-marks

---

[196] Boxrec.com. Most believed that Norton had beaten Meehan in their third match.
[197] *Oakland Tribune*, March 11, 1917.

of a man who knew his business thoroughly and loved it. He had speed and power. The *Oakland Enquirer* said, "We have it from good judges of boxers that Dempsey is the regular goods and figures to hold his own with any heavyweight in the country. ... He has a left hand as fast as Bob McAllister's and knows when to shoot the right. He is as quick as a lightweight on his feet and he can deal a K.O. punch with either hand." Dempsey was listed as standing 6' tall and weighing 178 pounds. He still was only 21 years of age, and his pro career was just over 2 years old.

Jack Dempsey of Salt Lake

Dempsey explained his recent loss to Jim Flynn by saying that when he came to ring center for the 1st round, he put out both gloves to touch his opponent's mitts as is customary, but Flynn took advantage of the moment by whipping over a right haymaker to his jaw. "Press accounts bear out Dempsey's story and say that the young Utah fighter really was the victim of an unprofessional act on the part of the tricky veteran."[198]

Dempsey also was quoted as saying, "We shook hands, and then walked to our corners, when we walked out again at the sound of the bell. I put out my hands to touch gloves, as is customary, and Flynn instead of touching gloves let go a punch and copped me. I suppose it was my fault, but Flynn, you know, is an old bird at the game and takes advantage of what he has learned. They'll never get me again with that trick."[199]

Many were predicting that Dempsey would beat Norton, and said that he should be no worse than even money against George Sharkey's scrapper, even in the face of Dempsey's one-punch loss to Flynn. "Dempsey claims that Flynn's

---

[198] *Oakland Tribune*, March 16, 1917; *Oakland Enquirer*, March 17, 1917.
[199] *Salt Lake Telegram*, March 19, 1917.

victory was a fluke." Ringside critics agreed. Allegedly, even Flynn himself admitted that it was a lucky punch. Dempsey "looks up like a mighty shifty heavyweight in his gymnasium work." The press said he had a good record too, with victories over men like Terry Keller, Andre Anderson, Wild Bert Kenny, Joe Bonds, and John Lester Johnson.

On the afternoon of March 18, Dempsey entertained a big crowd at the West Oakland club's gym, displaying fine pugilistic wares in his bouts with Dick Trounce and black Young Jack Johnson. The *Oakland Enquirer*, edited by Bob Shand, wrote, "Dempsey has a very fast left hand and he is light as a bantamweight on his feet. He is the possessor of a dandy left hook and a right cross and he is always boring in." One expert, Moose Taussig, believed him to be the best heavyweight prospect at present.

Norton was in fine condition too, and his performances against Meehan showed that he would not be an easy man to beat.[200]

Dempsey and Norton were matched evenly physically, and practically were mirror images of one another in every way in terms of height, weight (around 180 pounds), reach, and general appearance. Dempsey looked a lot like Jack Dillon, some saying he was a dead ringer for him.

Dempsey was drawing crowds to see him train and spar. Old timers' critical eyes were praising the young man. They said he had the movements of someone who had learned the game well. Although he was the favorite to beat Norton, many predicted that Norton would give him a tough time.

The *Oakland Tribune* said Dempsey vs. Norton was the best heavyweight match carded there in three years. Norton was the first really promising heavyweight developed in California in years, since the exit of the old game. "True, we have had Willie Meehan, but the latter's extremely weird style in the ring makes it hard to judge his opponent's performances." Critics said the Utah man was better than anyone Norton ever had faced. This fight would give both Norton and Dempsey a chance to prove themselves. Both were hard hitters, though Jack seemed a bit faster.[201]

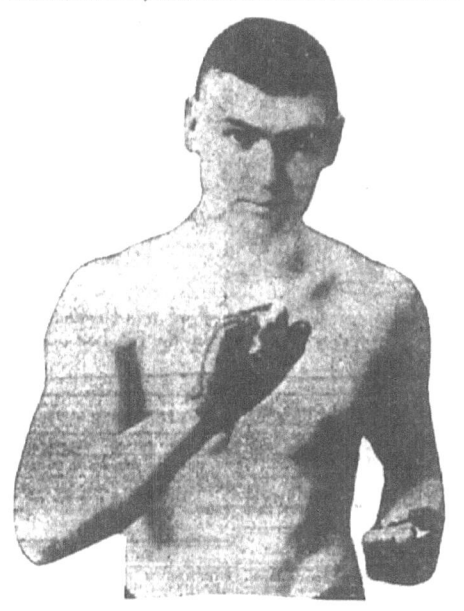

**JACK DEMPSEY**
A likely looking heavyweight from Salt Lake who meets Al Norton at the West Oakland club tomorrow night. "Dempsey has a long K. O. record and will be matched with Willie Meehan should he trim big Al.

---

[200] *Oakland Enquirer*, March 19, 1917.
[201] *Oakland Tribune*, March 17-21, 1917; *San Francisco Call*, *Salt Lake Telegram*, March 18, 1917.

The *Oakland Enquirer* said the winner would meet Meehan for the Pacific coast title. The California-based Norton likely would have the toughest battle of his career. Dempsey had shown championship form in training, boxing 4 to 8 rounds each day with Young Jack Johnson and Dick Trounce. "He has a left hand that shoots out like a piston rod, hitting its mark almost every time he starts it." His sparring partners said he also had a mean right hand, liable to score a knockout with it as well.

This writer believed Norton had beaten Meehan clearly, but the judges only gave him a draw. "Norton has boxed Meehan three times, losing the first match, getting an even break in the second and was robbed out of the third." Al had stopped men that others, including Meehan, had failed to knock out. It looked like Dempsey-Norton was an even matchup.[202]

> **BOXING**
> **Tomorrow Night**
> **Al Norton**
> vs.
> **Jack Dempsey**
> 6 Other Bouts
> **West Oakland Athletic Club, Oakland**

The *San Francisco Bulletin* said Norton likely would have a tough time with the newcomer. A knockout was a possibility, for both men were hard hitters.[203]

The day of the fight, the *San Francisco Call and Post* said Norton, from Los Angeles, was a 10 to 7 favorite over the "Mormon white hope." "There is no doubt that Norton is the very best hope in the four round ranks. He has had plenty of experience and he can box as well as he can hit. His last stand against Willie Meehan convinced all who saw the battle that big Al can mingle in fast company." Dempsey had a good reputation, having beaten Bonds and Gilbert, who had been considered candidates for big fights. "The Salt Laker looks like a fast boxer and a fair sort of a puncher, but of course, he must convince the Oaklanders."[204]

Norton's manager George Sharkey predicted that Al would win by knockout, declaring that his fighter was hitting harder than ever.

The *Oakland Enquirer* said Dempsey had "shown an abundance of class," and if he could take a punch, would give Norton all kinds of trouble. "Dempsey can box, can hit, has a cool head and is mighty fast for a big fellow. The only unknown quantity is his ability to stand the gaff. We will know all about that after tonight's battle as Norton is easily the hardest hitting man in the west at the present time."

Spider Kelly and George Sharkey would handle Norton, while Fred Winsor would be Dempsey's chief adviser.

Bob Shand, the *Oakland Enquirer's* sporting editor, would referee.[205]

On Wednesday March 21, 1917 at the West Oakland club in Oakland, California, in the main event of a card promoted by Tommy Simpson, Jack Dempsey had his first fight in California, against Al Norton. The crowd which packed the pavilion was one of the largest seen there in some time.

---

[202] *Oakland Enquirer*, March 20, 1917.
[203] *San Francisco Bulletin*, March 20, 21, 1917.
[204] *San Francisco Call and Post*, March 21, 1917.
[205] *Oakland Enquirer*, March 21, 1917.

1 - They sparred, and each worked a left lead and right cross. Dempsey seemed a bit slow at the start, but managed to get out of the way of Norton's wild rights. Jack shot in several stiff lefts that made Norton stop his rushing tactics. Dempsey drove a hard right to the head, while Norton crossed him with a right to the chin. Dempsey was fairly fast and landed another right to the head and left to the body. Norton clinched. Coming out of the clinch, Norton landed a right to the jaw and left hook to the head.

Dempsey landed a left hook to the head that brought blood from Norton's eye. Norton shifted and landed a hard right to the head which brought a little claret from Jack's optic.

Like a wounded lion, Dempsey fought back hard, landing several hard rights and lefts. Jack hooked a hard left to the body and sent Norton against the ropes. Jack was using a left lead and right cross. He missed a swing and went down as a result of losing his balance. After Jack rose, Al hooked a left and right to the head, but Dempsey landed two body blows which forced Norton to clinch. Dempsey kept attacking, his left hook working fine and landing almost every time. He had Norton backing away.

The *Oakland Tribune* said it was Dempsey's round.

Summarizing, the *Oakland Enquirer* said they tore after each other from the start, each trying to land a knockout blow. Norton's judgment of distance was not as good as usual, missing several chances to land telling blows. On the other hand, Dempsey uncorked a left hook that inflicted much damage. Both were cut above their eyes and bleeding.

2 - Norton shot two lefts to the face and head, one of which shook the Salt Lake boy. Dempsey shot his best punch, the left hook, to the head. Norton was anxious to land a right cross, and managed to land one on the chin, but without damage. Dempsey was there when it came to taking punishment.

Dempsey shifted neatly, and before Norton knew what was happening, Jack shot out three rights to the head and a left to the body. One of the rights opened up Norton's other eye. Norton countered with a stiff uppercut, and also landed a left to the body and another to the head. Dempsey's left hooks to the body forced Norton to clinch again.

Dempsey rushed the fight again and landed a left to the head and right to the chin. Norton was backing up at the bell, with Dempsey on top of him landing lefts and rights.

The *Oakland Tribune* said it was Dempsey's round by a shade. The *Enquirer* seemed to agree that Dempsey had won the round.

3 - Norton came out with a rush, trying to overcome the "small lead" that Dempsey held over him. He landed a terrific right to the chin that shook Jack. He followed it up to the head with right, left hook, and right, followed by an uppercut. Both fought wildly, swinging several times. Norton was trying to win by knockout. Dempsey landed two lefts to the head. Jack also landed a right uppercut to the head and shot a left to the body. They traded uppercuts. Another Dempsey right to the body and left to the head caused Norton to back away.

Dempsey followed closely and shot in two of the hardest left hooks seen there in many a day. Both landed on Norton's jaw and sent him reeling backwards against the ropes and nearly over them. If it had not been for the ropes catching him, Norton would have been knocked clean off his feet. The fans were on their feet yelling for a knockdown.

Dempsey tore in to finish him, landed six lefts to the head and a right uppercut. Norton was cut badly about the face and bleeding freely. Dempsey kept coming, landing two more lefts to the head. Norton retaliated with a right to the jaw. Off a Norton missed left, Dempsey stepped in and landed a short right cross to the jaw. At the bell, Norton was groggy and returned to his corner in pretty bad shape. The *Tribune* said it was another Dempsey round, and the *Enquirer* seemed to agree.

4 - Dempsey hooked a left to the head. They swapped rights. Norton slowed up Dempsey with right chops and uppercuts. Dempsey suddenly blew up and seemed on the verge of utter exhaustion. Norton took advantage and slipped in several rights to the jaw. Dempsey mostly stalled for the balance of the round with Norton on the aggressive, though unable to do any particular damage.

Dempsey landed a right to the mouth that hurt. Al landed two lefts to the body which caused Dempsey to clinch. Coming out, both landed hard rights to the jaw. Norton forced the fighting, landing several hard rights. Dempsey came across with a left to the head and right uppercut to the body. At the bell, both were fighting hard.

The *Tribune* said it was Norton's round. The *Enquirer* said that much to the crowd's surprise, Norton had staged a pretty comeback.

Judge Joe Cabral thought Norton had won, but judges Jack Murphy and Jack Brown both called it a draw. Hence, it was a majority draw.

The *Oakland Tribune* reported that even the most rabid fans got their fill of fighting in the 4 rounds. Dempsey tired after winning, so it resulted in a 4-round draw. It was what was known as a "re-match decision," the judges preferring to see the men in action again before giving the palm to either one.

> To the average man it looked as though Jack Dempsey, after having a clear lead in the first three rounds, blew up in the fourth from sheer exhaustion. The very evident weakness he displayed in the last few minutes undoubtedly influenced the judges in withholding the decision from him, for based on his work in the first, second, and third rounds there was nothing to it but the Salt Lake scrapper.

Dempsey's condition was poor because he had suffered an attack of tonsilitis. Yet, he showed all that was expected of him. He outboxed and outfought Norton, cut open both of his eyes, nearly knocked him over the ropes, and had him clinching repeatedly. Norton depended almost entirely on an overhand right chop, which usually fell short.

The *Oakland Enquirer* said Dempsey was suffering from tonsillitis, and Norton was stale from too much training. Nevertheless, they staged one of the greatest heavyweight battles ever seen there. This writer believed the draw verdict was correct. Some fans insisted that Dempsey was entitled to the decision. He possibly would have won had he attacked during the last round as he had in the 3rd round, but he was short of wind, probably due to the tonsillitis. Dempsey's punches did not travel far, but carried plenty of steam. "He had Norton worried on several occasions."

George Sharkey said Norton would have knocked him out had he not been overtrained and stale. "The decision was O.K."

Fred Winsor said, "Jack was a sick boy. He had tonsillitis and was visited by the doctor yesterday. He would have stopped Norton had he been right. The decision was satisfactory."

The San Francisco newspapers thought Dempsey had won.

The *San Francisco Examiner* said Dempsey won all the way.

The *San Francisco Chronicle* said Dempsey had a shade over Norton in the main event of the West Oakland Club fights, but got a draw verdict. He looked to be a good boy and was unscathed. Though neither was hurt/seriously damaged, Norton was cut badly about the face.

The *San Francisco Call and Post* reported that Dempsey outfought Norton, and earned "the right to the decision on his aggressiveness and cleaner punching, but the best he got was a draw. Dempsey showed a lot of boxing ability and knowledge of the defensive game, coming out of the battle without a mark. His punch marred Norton's complexion a little, though the latter was not badly cut."

The *San Francisco Bulletin* said Dempsey came mighty close to copping the decision, and many thought he should have had the decision, but it was a close fight with plenty of work in each round. Dempsey was outweighed by several pounds, "and his work of shading Norton, who hits like a mule kicking, is therefore worthy of special attention."

The Salt Lake press reported that it was a fast bout, and Dempsey made himself a favorite from the start with his aggressive tactics, winning by a shade but only getting a draw.[206]

In his autobiography, Dempsey said he had a fever and 102-degree temperature going into the fight. The arena was tobacco-smoke-filled and mostly attended by colored folk, who had paid 25 to 75 cents apiece. Norton, the local favorite, was tall, a good ring general, and a hard puncher. Still, Jack did his best, earned a draw, and won the crowd's approval.

Impressed with his performance, Dempsey was invited to fight in the Oakland area again just one week later. Those who thought that he would pass up the crafty and puzzling Willie Meehan were very much mistaken. Just as soon as the "local fat boy" issued his challenge, Jack accepted it. Possibly he did not realize what he was getting himself into, underestimating Meehan as a result of his body type.

They would fight the following Wednesday evening at the new Emeryville arena/open-air pavilion for the Emeryville Athletic Club, just

---

[206] *Oakland Tribune, Oakland Enquirer, San Francisco Examiner, San Francisco Chronicle, San Francisco Call and Post, San Francisco Bulletin, Salt Lake Tribune*, March 22, 1917.

north of and adjacent to West Oakland, across the bay from San Francisco. Once again, the event was being promoted by Tommy Simpson. The press reported that Dempsey had made himself such a magnet by his sensational showing against Al Norton that the West Oakland pavilion would not be large enough to accommodate all of the fans who wanted to see him. Hence, the fight was taking place in nearby Emeryville, on Hollis street.

The *Oakland Enquirer* said Dempsey, "who gave Al Norton an artistic trimming," would be fighting Meehan for the heavyweight championship of the coast and middle-west. "Meehan holds the title for the coast honors, while Dempsey is hailed as the champion of the middle section of the states."

JACK DEMPSEY, the Salt Lake sensation, in fighting pose; WILLIE MEEHAN, his opponent, and MEXICAN KID CARTER, who appears in the special event.

Jack was training at Freddie Bogan's place on the beach in San Francisco, and was packing the house, for folks enjoyed watching him spar with George Benson, Battling Rector, and Mexican Kid Carter, 2 or 3 rounds each. On March 25, four days after the Norton contest, Jack had them rush him like Meehan so he could step aside and counter. He was not a showy performer, but meant business from the start, giving his partners rough usage. Jack said he had recovered from his illness.

Meehan trained at the Association club. He was doing plenty of road work, and sparring the biggest men available, preparing to guard against Dempsey's deadly left. On the 25th, he ran 10 miles and sparred 6 rounds.

The *San Francisco Call and Post* said,

> Dempsey looks like the very best big fighter imported since the days when twenty-round battles were in vogue. His great showing against

Al Norton last week won for him many strong boosters on both sides of the bay. Big Jack is a cleaner and a faster puncher than Meehan, but the latter knows the ins and outs of the game, and that peculiar awkward style of his may puzzle Dempsey. Anyway, Jack appears to be perfectly willing to take his chance, and he's confident of winning.

The local Oakland and San Francisco press said if Dempsey made as good a showing against Meehan as he did against Norton, he would be rematched with Norton. Dempsey's performance against Norton had made him a sensation on both sides of the bay.

Jack's throat was healed from the tonsillitis attack. Still, the wise ones were picking Meehan to beat Dempsey, for Meehan usually won his first encounters with most everyone, for his style was quite puzzling, baffling, and difficult to solve. It required some study to figure out how to fight him.

The *Oakland Tribune* said Meehan made Norton look like a boob the first time they met, but Norton improved and showed to advantage in subsequent encounters, one saying Norton clearly won their last contest, despite the draw decision. Dempsey did not look like the type of boxer who would be fooled by Meehan's wild behavior. Jack was fast on his feet, possessed a lightning left, and was not at all awkward. His fast left hook was powerful. Still, many called San Francisco's Meehan invincible, particularly in a short bout. Meehan's style was "peculiar" and tough to overcome. The question was whether Dempsey's wonderful left hand would offset Meehan's cleverness, roundhouse swings, and bass drum wallop.

San Francisco native 23-year-old Willie Meehan had the far superior experience; 121 fights since turning pro in 1910, with a 76-11-33 record,

**TO DEFEND CROWN**

WILLIE MEEHAN, Coast heavyweight champion, who will defend his title against Jack Dempsey, middleweight champion, at Emeryville tonight. Meehan is peeved at Dempsey, because the latter laughed at him for being so fat when they met, and says he is going to play havoc with the features of the newcomer.

making him an active seasoned veteran. His record included: 1913 W4 Rufe Cameron; 1914 D6, D10, and W4 George Christian (whom Dempsey stopped in the 1st round in 1916), L4 Harry Wills, and W4 Charley Miller; 1915 WTKO3 Young Jack Johnson; 1916 TKO3 Lewis Fink, WND10 Bert Kenny, LND10 Andre Anderson (whom Dempsey beat), WND6 Homer Smith, WND6 Sailor Jack Carroll, WND6 Larry Williams, W4 (twice) and KO3 Charley Miller, D4 Bob McAllister, TKO2 Kid Carter ("a giant negro"), W4 Frank Farmer, and W4 Al Norton; and 1917 W4 Soldier Elder and D4 (twice) Al Norton.

Meehan was confident that he could lick anyone, and didn't need to see them beforehand to do it. Meehan laughed at Dempsey's threat to knock him out. "I don't know where Dempsey gets all his talk and chatter. ... Yes, I'm in good shape, and I think that I should win by a knockout in two or three rounds." Meehan treated all of his foes as jokes, believing himself to be as good as Willard. Willie likely weighed over 200 pounds.

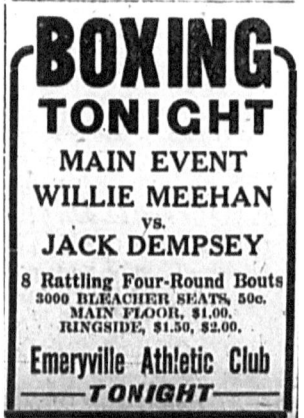

The *Oakland Enquirer* called it the best heavyweight battle arranged by a local club in many a month, the kind of fight the fans were willing to lay down their money to witness. Dempsey made a profound impression a week ago. He was one of the best two-handed boxers seen in a long time, an exceptionally hard hitter with very short blows that only needed to travel a foot to sting. "He had Norton groggy from right and left hand uppercuts which seemed to have no punishing force behind them, but when they landed they almost tore the southern heavyweight's head off. Personally we would just as soon monkey around the business end of a mule as fool with this Dempsey boy's fists when he is set for action."

Dempsey was going up against a mighty tough opponent in Meehan, and was liable to be bewildered by his peculiar, unique style that was all his own. Willie could cut lose with round-house and loop-the-loop punches, and few had been able to figure him out on their first attempt.

The *San Francisco Bulletin* said Young Jack Dempsey made a great showing and a decided hit with the fans "when he outpointed Al Norton" but only received a draw. The upcoming fight likely would be one of the best, hardest-fought heavyweight contests seen in the past year. Meehan was in good condition and promised to make Dempsey travel at top speed to beat him. They were "two of the best heavyweights in this neck of the woods." Meehan had trained hard, figuring that he would have his hands full in subduing the hard-hitting tough youngster.

The *San Francisco Call and Post* said Dempsey looked like a far better boxer and cleaner puncher than Meehan. His bout against Norton convinced spectators that he was every inch the great fighter that his boosters claimed for him. They all felt that Jack had beaten Norton.

Dempsey said, "I came out here to show the fans that I can fight and I think I'm on my way to make good." He looked like a perfect athletic specimen. He stood 6'1" and weighed 185 pounds. "Aside from being a hard puncher he can box and step around as fast as the ordinary welterweight." Still, Meehan said Dempsey would prove to be a soft mark. The fans believed that the former newsboy was in for a tough battle.[207]

The day of the fight, the *Oakland Tribune* said the wise ones thought Meehan's style would baffle Dempsey, and Willie would win a decision. This paper looked for Dempsey to secure a draw with his great left and improvement in physical condition.

The promoter told the judges to give a verdict one way or the other, that they should not give draws with the idea of a return match. In that case, the local writer predicted a shade to the local fighter, Meehan.[208]

On Wednesday March 28, 1917, in Tommy Simpson's new open-air Emeryville arena at Hollis and Park avenue, just one week after the Norton contest, in a 4-round main event contest sponsored by the Emeryville Athletic Club, Jack Dempsey was back in action again to fight Willie Meehan. *Oakland Enquirer* editor Bob Shand refereed.

Tickets were $.50 for the 3,000 bleacher seats, $1 for the main floor, and $1.50 and $2 ringside. The open-air show was a big success. The weather was comfortable, lighting excellent, train and car service efficient and convenient. There was a good attendance, and everyone went home satisfied with the 8-bout card. The local *Oakland Tribune* and *Oakland Enquirer* had round-by-round accounts of the main event, though their accounts differed from the San Francisco newspapers' versions.

1 - They went to close quarters and attacked the body. From the start, Meehan got his bass-drum left-hook body-punch working, and then tried to land on Dempsey's bad right eye. Willie succeeded in landing several hard rights, but without inflicting damage. Meehan made Dempsey miss, and attacked his stomach. Dempsey landed a right uppercut to the chin, and they traded rights to the stomach. Meehan hooked his left to the head repeatedly, while Jack sought an opening. Dempsey hooked his left to the head and followed with a right uppercut to the body. A stiff right to the chin made Meehan back up a little. Meehan slipped in a left hook to the body and then right cross to the head. Jack landed a hard right uppercut to the body, and Meehan retaliated with right and left to the body in return. Both landed hard left hooks at the same time to the body. Meehan ducked some blows. After ducking, Meehan landed a left to the body that could be heard all over the building. Dempsey came back with lefts and rights, forcing Meehan to the ropes. The *Tribune* said the small cut over Dempsey's left eye (suffered the previous week) had been opened. It said it was an even round. The *Enquirer* did not mention a cut.

---

[207] *Oakland Tribune*, March 23-27, 1917; *San Francisco Bulletin*, March 24, 27, 28, 1917; *San Francisco Call and Post*, March 26-28, 1917; *Oakland Enquirer*, March 23-27, 1917.
[208] *Oakland Tribune*, March 28, 1917.

2 - Meehan rushed and landed three left hooks to the body in succession. They indulged in a furious rally, with honors even. Meehan showed a disposition to trade wallops. Dempsey landed left and right to the body, then shifted the same blows to the head, forcing Meehan to cover. Dempsey landed a right to the chin and Meehan went to the ropes. Meehan ducked away and then landed another left hook to the body that could be heard from far away. The punches did not seem to bother Dempsey much. A Dempsey left hook to the head shook Meehan, who brought a right to the body. Dempsey rallied and landed three lefts to the head without return. Meehan blocked a right. Meehan rallied, landing lefts to the stomach a few times. Willie also shot in four left hooks at long range, each sounding like a rifle shot. He had Dempsey backing away at the bell. The *Tribune* said it was Meehan's round.

3 - The *Tribune* said Meehan once again worked his left to the stomach very well and often, occasionally varying with a right cross to the jaw or left hook to the head. Dempsey tried but could not connect, for Meehan slipped by all of his punches. Clear Meehan round.

The *Enquirer* version said they went right to work, slugging at long range for 15 to 20 seconds, bringing the fans to their feet. Meehan had a little better of the going as he landed more punches, though Dempsey's blows were harder. After the slugging bee, Meehan shot a left to the head. Dempsey missed some uppercuts and finally landed a left hook to the head and right uppercut to the body. Meehan played his bass drum punch to the body. Dempsey shot right and left to the head. Willie covered up. Meehan shot a left to the body and right to the head. Both men landed stiff lefts. Meehan landed two more left hooks to the body and then shifted and landed on the face. Dempsey was trying hard and finally landed a right to the body and left to the chin.

4 - The *Tribune* said they came to close quarters and indulged in a furious rally, each swinging to the jaw. Dempsey tried in vain to land a haymaker, but could not hit the shifty man. Meehan pounded away at the stomach and ducked away from the returns. Meehan had a clear lead at the bell.

The *Enquirer* said they went in for another slugging bee in which Meehan came out the best. They let go many punches that would have stopped ordinary boxers. They also missed several that might have proved fatal. Meehan was coming fast, while Dempsey's punches seemed to lack steam. Meehan played his bass drum punch to the body and ducked out of the way of several hard right uppercuts. Dempsey hooked his left to the body and right to the head. He repeated the combination. Meehan was taking things easy. Dempsey landed another right to the head and left to the body in combination. Then Meehan came on again, shooting the deadly left hook to the body that made the fans groan every time he landed. It did not hurt so much, but scored many points and made loud sounds. At the bell, Meehan was boxing fast, with Dempsey backing away.

The judges were Jack Murphy, Jack Brown, and Dick Adams. The *Enquirer* said, "One of the judges called it a draw, but the other two gave it to Meehan." The *Tribune* suggested that Brown and Adams had awarded the 4-round decision to Meehan. It was Jack Dempsey's third loss, two of the losses by mere 4-round decisions to men with far more experience.

The local *Oakland Tribune* said Meehan still was the marvel and riddle of the ring. He showed up the Salt Lake boxer so thoroughly that there was no room for argument. Dempsey was as helpless as a man with both hands tied. Meehan was in great shape, for he had lost 20 pounds, and was not as paunchy as usual. He was confident, and discarded all his clownish tactics for the first two rounds, carrying the fight to his opponent and actually outfighting him. Then Willie began pulling some of his circus stuff, but Dempsey still could not land. Meehan won from here to next week.

The *Oakland Enquirer* agreed, though not as vociferously, saying that champion fat fighter Meehan proved to be a close-call winner to retain his coast heavyweight title. Meehan's bass drum left hook to the body, which landed often, won it for him. Many ringsiders thought Dempsey was entitled to a draw, but the *Enquirer* believed Meehan had a clear enough lead at the finish to win. "Willie simply bass-drummed himself into the decision. His body hooks were working to perfection and although there was no force behind the blows he landed often enough to keep Dempsey busy. Also Willie made Jack miss repeatedly. Dempsey fought a decidedly clever fight, but none of them can lick Meehan in the first attempt." With the knowledge he gained, Dempsey would be even money in a rematch. Even Fred Winsor, Jack's manager, said the decision was okay.

Meehan fought the same way against Norton the first time they met. When he got in a tight hole, he resorted to ducking tactics and had Dempsey missing. He also kept his right close to his jaw, protecting against Dempsey's hard left hook. He kept his hands up well and was able to block punches in addition to ducking. He was in good shape and had perfect wind. His judgment of distance was good, especially when he was on the ropes. His bass drum punch worked throughout, and landed so often that it was hard to keep track of the punches. It was this punch that won him the fight. The fans applauded the decision. Still, Dempsey also received applause as he left the ring. They appreciated him too.

The *San Francisco Call and Post* vehemently disagreed, saying Meehan was handed a controversial shade verdict over Dempsey, who held his own. "That the battle should have been declared a draw was the opinion of at least three-fourths of the spectators who figured that the clean punches landed by the visitor held him even with Meehan's ring generalship." This newspaper agreed with the judge who scored it a draw.

Dempsey started out as the aggressor, showing a willingness to wade in and take a chance at every opportunity. He used a left jab to the head with good effect and several times in the first two rounds made Meehan run for cover and hold on. Meehan used all of his old-time tricks and pulled some of his comedy. He needed his experience to stop Dempsey's rushes, for

Jack kept on leading and trying all the time. The fat boy saw that he would have to get busy, so in the 3rd round he cut loose with a burst of speed. He hurt Dempsey several times with a left rip to the body, though Dempsey gamely kept coming. The 4th round was all in Dempsey's favor, and his dash should have netted him a draw. Meehan slowed down and held on. Had Dempsey a bit more experience and knowledge, he would have outpointed him clearly, but Meehan managed to weather the storm without suffering serious damage.

Likewise, the *San Francisco Bulletin* said although Meehan was awarded the contest, "The decision, however, was on the closest kind of shade, and many of the fans left the building thinking that a draw would have been much better." The local fat boy was lucky that the fight was not a long one. Meehan's peculiar style puzzled Dempsey at first, as it did with all others, and as a result, the first 2 rounds went to Meehan, his bass-drum stomach blows landing with considerable regularity. Dempsey got going in the 3rd, and if the fight had been longer, "Meehan might have found himself in serious trouble, for Dempsey was hitting hard, and Willie was tired at the finish and doing a lot of grinning that he didn't mean and which was intended to fool the crowd into believing that he was taking things easy, when, as a matter of fact, he was hoping and praying that the final bell would ring."[209]

So, just as convinced that the local Oakland *Tribune* and *Enquirer* were that Meehan had won, the San Francisco *Call and Post* and *Bulletin* were certain that Dempsey had earned a draw and was coming on strong.

Back home, the *Salt Lake Telegram* reported that Meehan won a shade decision over Dempsey. Fight experts said a draw would have been a better decision. The first two rounds were fairly even. Meehan was leading by a nose in the third, while Dempsey came along in the 4th. Meehan did a lot of stalling. His only good punch was a left to the stomach. Dempsey landed the cleaner blows, while Meehan's punches lacked pep.[210]

In 1919, Damon Runyon wrote, "Meehan may be a better fighter than most fistic experts are willing to admit." He had a bizarre style that at first gave the impression of clowning more than anything else, but it was that style that made him hard to beat. "He runs, falls, gets behind a man, slaps and generally cavorts about in a most astonishing manner, but all the time he seems to be scoring points." Those in the East said he had no class, but nonetheless he was very good at winning 4-round points decisions. Although some appreciated Meehan's style and tactics, others were disgusted by his ways.[211]

Years later, speaking about the fight, Dempsey said "Slapper Meehan" and "Fat Willy," despite being a town clown and wonderful kidder, and in spite of his fat, was a fast, adroit boxer, able to keep out of harm's way, while he scored from time to time with a fair punch. Meehan lacked a

---

[209] *Oakland Tribune, Oakland Enquirer, San Francisco Call and Post, San Francisco Bulletin*, March 29, 1917.
[210] *Salt Lake Telegram*, March 29, 1917
[211] *Cedar Rapids Gazette*, June 9, 1919.

knockout blow, but was too good at defending and keeping out of reach, so the bout was a disappointing one to watch.

When speaking about Fred Fulton, tagged as the man who might be able to dethrone Jess Willard, boxing manager Jack Kearns said 218-pound Fulton hit as cleanly and sharply as Harry Wills did, but with much more force. "There isn't a man in the world that Fulton can't whip."[212]

On April 6, 1917, the U.S. under President Woodrow Wilson formally entered the war in Europe (later known as World War I), joining Great Britain, France, Russia, Italy, Japan, Serbia, Romania, and others to fight against Germany, Austria-Hungary, the Ottoman Empire, Bulgaria, and others. Germany had been sinking passenger ships with Americans on board for the past several years. All U.S. men from ages 21 to 31 were required to register for the draft. Over the next year and a half, more than two million American soldiers would serve on the battlefields of Western Europe, 53,402 of them would lose their lives in combat, another 63,114 more would die from other causes related to the war like disease, and over 200,000 would be wounded or badly maimed. And yet, the American casualties were relatively small compared with European nations, which had been ravaged by "The Great War" for the past three years before the U.S. entry into the brutal conflict, suffering casualties in the millions. It subsequently was called the first modern war, because for the first time, war saw the use of machine guns, tanks, submarines, airplanes, and poison gas.

*Chicago Defender*, March 31, 1917

Blacks were drafted and allowed to enlist in the U.S. military, but were placed in entirely segregated units. Many white supremacist politicians like James Vardaman and Benjamin Tillman opposed their military training and participation in combat roles, fearing that they might eventually demand equality of rights and try to obtain it by employing their military training. Blacks could not serve in the Marines, and eventually only were allowed limited, menial positions in the Navy and Coast Guard. The Army was far more progressive, allowing combat participation, but in segregated units.

Fred Winsor next scheduled Jack Dempsey to meet Al Norton in a return bout in Oakland, to be held on April 11, just two weeks after the Meehan match. Fans and promoters wanted to see them in action again.

Norton trained at Freddie Bogan's place on the beach with Seattle Frankie Burns and Jack Downey. Dempsey worked at the San Francisco Parkside club, sparring with welterweight Rex Morris.[213]

---

[212] *San Francisco Bulletin*, March 28, 1917.
[213] *Oakland Enquirer*, April 7, 1917.

Tommy Simpson once again was promoting, this time at the West Oakland Club. The *Call and Post* said they fought a few weeks ago, and despite it being ruled a draw, Dempsey had a shade. Dempsey really wanted a rematch with Meehan, "who was given a questionable decision over him," and Promoter Simpson guaranteed him a return bout provided he held Norton to at least a draw. Jack said he was somewhat baffled by Meehan's peculiar tactics, but felt that he could defeat him in another meeting.

Fred Winsor claimed that Tommy Simpson had an awful time getting Norton to sign for a rematch, likely because he remembered how roughly Dempsey treated him in their last encounter.

The *Oakland Enquirer* called their last fight a heavyweight classic. Norton and Dempsey had the speed of lightweights and the punch of heavyweights. It was called a good draw, and probably was, but most opined that Dempsey was entitled to the decision. Before Dempsey came to town, Norton had been a fan favorite. However, Dempsey's showing against Norton had won over half of them. The fans wanted a rematch.[214]

For whatever reason, despite most feeling that Dempsey won the first time, the oddsmakers had Norton a shade the favorite heading into the rematch. Both were fast movers with a kick in their fists with either hand. Their prior bout had action every minute. Norton claimed that he was in much better shape this time, and planned to attack right away and not wait until the last round as he had in their first fight (when most thought Dempsey won the first three rounds before tiring in the last round as Al came on with a rush and forced the fighting).

The *Enquirer* said that despite losing to Meehan, the fans still picked Dempsey as the one lad who could put both Norton and Meehan out of the running. In their prior fight, the Norton side claimed he was stale and overtrained. The Dempsey side said he was suffering from illness for four days before the fight. Yet, they still put up one of the fastest contests seen for a long time. Hence, a hard and entertaining fight was expected.

The *San Francisco Bulletin* said the fight promised thrills. Both were in great shape, game, and possessors of knockout punches. Neither had an abundance of science, but knew enough to avoid the haymakers. In their first contest, the "majority of the fans" thought Dempsey "had the shade over Norton." The preliminary bouts would begin at 8:30 p.m.[215]

On Wednesday April 11, 1917 at the West Oakland Club, in the main event, Jack Dempsey and California's Al Norton staged a sensational thriller rematch. Bob Shand refereed. Once again, there were some different perspectives regarding this one.

---

[214] *San Francisco Call and Post, Oakland Enquirer, San Francisco Bulletin*, April 9, 1917.
[215] *Ogden Standard*, April 5, 1917; *Oakland Tribune, Oakland Enquirer*, April 10, 11, 1917; *San Francisco Call and Post*, April 10, 1917; *San Francisco Bulletin*, April 10, 11, 1917.

According to the *Oakland Enquirer*, in the 1st round, both were cautious during the first minute of the fight, feeling out one another. Norton landed first. He was boxing, shooting out his straight left jab to the head. He landed twice before Dempsey got down to business. A Norton right cross to the body shook Dempsey. Then Jack landed a left to the body, right to the head, another left to the body, and right cross to the chin, all of which landed, but without sufficient force to do harm. After Norton missed a left swing, Dempsey shot in a right to the face. Norton kept trying to outbox him, tapping Jack with several light lefts to the head. Dempsey landed a right to the chin and Norton missed right uppercut. At the end of the round, Norton was getting his range and landed three hard blows; a right to the chest followed by another to the belly and left to the chin. The *Enquirer* felt that Norton had a shade the better of the 1st round.

According to the *Oakland Tribune*, in the 1st round, Norton started to make the same mistake as last time – allowing Dempsey to bring the fight to him. This writer believed that Dempsey had a shade on the round for his leading, although Norton met him effectively all the time with a left jab.

The *Enquirer* said that for most of the 2nd round, Norton played for the body, and was very effective with his body blows. He also swung wildly at times. On several occasions, they stood toe-to-toe and slugged.

At the end of the round, Norton had Dempsey going, and slipped over a right to the jaw that looked like the end of the bout. But just then the gong sounded. Dempsey walked back to his corner in a wobbly condition. This writer gave Norton the round.

However, the *Tribune* said the 2nd round practically was even, for Norton had changed tactics and met Dempsey halfway when it came to aggressiveness. At the close of the round, Norton landed some stinging stomach blows that slowed up Dempsey a bit.

As for the 3rd round, the *Enquirer* said Dempsey performed a little better. He landed four straight lefts to the head. They mixed it freely in the round. Dempsey backed Norton to the ropes, where Al took blow after blow. Norton was content to let Dempsey swing, and after the melee, he actually seemed to be in better shape than Jack. Both rushed the fight in an effort to land a telling blow. Their swings were hard, but fell short of the mark most of the time. Dempsey held Norton even in this round.

The *Tribune* said that all through the 3rd round, Norton landed solid body blows that had an impact, but the round still was practically even.

In the 4th round, according to the *Enquirer*, Norton tried hard to land a knockout punch. He kept sticking out his left to the face all the time and then tried to drive home his famous right. Dempsey was trying all the time as well. He kept pumping lefts and rights into Norton's body, tiring him out. Both missed some hard rights. Norton uncorked a right cross that grazed the chin. At the bell they were fighting as best they could, but both were tired. This writer said Dempsey may have had the edge in the round.

The *Tribune* said that in the 4th round, the pace began to tell, but both had the strength to last it through. First Norton appeared ready to drop, and just as Dempsey would square away for a finishing blow, Norton would come to life with one that would rock Dempsey. Thus, things swung back and forth in that last round for a finish seldom seen. The crowd was yelling for Dempsey to finish Norton, but most were with Dempsey from the start, and those doing the yelling were too biased to see that Dempsey himself was just about as worn out and nearly as ready to drop as was Norton. The *Tribune* said the last round was another even round.

The judges split the decision, one voting for Dempsey, one for Norton, and one a draw. So it was another 4-round draw.

The *Oakland Tribune* said that other than the 1st round, in which Dempsey had a shade, it was a close and primarily even fight throughout. Overall, the pace grew faster all the way, and by the last round, both had thrown boxing to the winds and were slugging away with blows in all directions. For 4 full rounds, with the possible exception of a minute in the 2nd round, they were rushing and slugging away at each other. It was one of the fastest local bouts ever seen, and both had reason to be ready to drop.

The *Tribune* said the draw decision was the only one that could have been given in fairness to both. Promoters already were laying plans for a third bout.

The *Oakland Enquirer* said Dempsey manager Fred Winsor was wrong and unsportsmanlike by hollering robbery over a just decision. He either was blind or too biased. "The truth of the matter is that if there was any shade at all last night it belonged to Norton. Al had the first two rounds and held his own in the third. The fourth was a mushy session, and to give Dempsey all the better of it we will say he won the round. Both boys were tired in the last period and did little work." Near the end of the 2nd round, Norton had Dempsey in a bad way, although Jack fought evenly or slightly better in the 3rd and 4th rounds.

This version said the fight was slower and less interesting than their first contest. Both had much respect for the other's punch, and stayed away from it most of the time. Not many hard blows were landed by either, and those that did land did not do much damage. Their roundhouse wallops made plenty of noise, but inflicted little or no damage.

The *San Francisco Bulletin* said they put up a hard fight, each trying to win by knockout every minute of the entire 4 rounds. Dempsey "had a little shade over Al Norton in the main event." Yet, although some thought Dempsey should have been awarded the decision, "it was a very slight shade he had and the draw declared by the judges was about right."

Once again, the *San Francisco Call and Post* had a totally different perspective, and criticized the decision. It said the judges overlooked Dempsey, who yet again was a victim of a "funny decision." "Despite that Jack gave Al Norton a fine lacing and should have been declared a winner by all of a city block, the judges handed him a draw. The decision was a most unpopular one and was loudly hooted by nine-tenths of the crowd."

Dempsey showed better hitting powers, better footwork, and did far more clean work than Norton.[216]

Essentially, the *Call and Post* felt that Dempsey had been robbed in three consecutive bouts. It felt that he should have won both fights with Norton, but only got draws, and that he had earned a draw with Meehan, but was handed a loss.

After the show, it was announced that Dempsey would box Meehan again, 10 rounds at Goldfield, Nevada, in one month, on May 10.

A couple days later, the *San Francisco Bulletin's* Marion T. Salazar said if Dempsey and Norton fought again, young boxers should get ringside seats and watch closely, for they were the only two men who had boxed in the vicinity for the past two years who really knew how to hit. Other so-called punchers whanged away blindly and trusted to luck. Dempsey and Norton picked their punches and spots well, and fighters could learn a few things by watching them.[217]

Despite what the official record might say, a lot of folks believed that Jack Dempsey had won several of the draws he had throughout his career, and some believed he had earned a draw in his loss to the local Meehan (which might have been ruled a draw had the promoter not insisted that the judges rule one way or the other). Often back then, officials were more likely to score closer fights a draw.

From the start of his career, and continuing in California, Jack Dempsey quite often had been fighting tough boxers with far more experience; fights which today some might call ridiculous, and some commissions might not even sanction. He was not a protected fighter, but took tough fights to earn what he could, against fighters who were expected to beat him, often in their hometown/region/state, fighting as often as possible, and learning on the job to a certain degree. Nevertheless, many observers of talent were impressed with the young fighter, and saw his potential. Except for style and race, in many ways, young Jack Dempsey was a lot like a young Jack Johnson.

---

[216] *Oakland Tribune, Oakland Enquirer, San Francisco Call and Post, San Francisco Bulletin*, April 12, 1917.
[217] *San Francisco Bulletin*, April 13, 1917.

CHAPTER 9

# West Coast Warrior Part II: Relationships End and a New One Begins

In his last four bouts, 21-year-old Jack Dempsey had gone 0-2-2. He had lost to Flynn and Meehan, and had two draws with Norton. A fighter easily could have his confidence shaken by such results, and possibly that happened to Dempsey. But that didn't tell the entire story. He had fought well and ferociously in entertaining contests in his West Coast bouts, against well-respected men; the state's best. Some thought he deserved to win the Norton fights. It was acknowledged that Meehan always did well against everyone in their first fight with him, particularly in short 4-round bouts, and some thought Dempsey had earned a draw with him. Plus, Dempsey had a hard-punching, entertaining style that promoters liked and fans enjoyed, and he showed promise and potential, so he remained in demand.

However, perhaps discouraged or disheartened by his mixed results of late, or for other more personal or financial reasons, Dempsey left his manager and wife and disappeared. Did he feel he did not have what it took to be champion, having a crisis of confidence? Was he homesick? Was his marriage rocky? Did he have a financial dispute with Fred Winsor, feeling that he was not being paid well enough? For whatever reason, shortly following his April 11, 1917 4-round draw with Al Norton, Dempsey left and returned home to Salt Lake City. However, he left his wife Maxine behind, didn't tell her that he was leaving, where he was going, when he was returning, or if he was going to return at all. He just disappeared.

On April 19, 1917, the *San Francisco Bulletin's* Marion T. Salazar wrote,

> Jack Dempsey, by running out on his manager, Fred Winsor, is not showing a new trait. He has run out on a couple of other managers, so it is said, one of them being John Reisler, "The Barber." Dempsey has been located at Salt Lake City, and so far as the Coast promoters are concerned, will remain there. When he left San Francisco Dempsey forgot to take his wife along, leaving her here with $30 to pay gas and other bills. A fine bird is Jack.

But there was more. A lot more. A headline in the same newspaper that day revealed a bombshell, explaining why the writer speculated or hoped that local promoters would not want Dempsey to return:

**MRS. JACK DEMPSEY STATES THAT HER HUSBAND RECEIVED $500 TO FAKE FIGHT WITH JIM FLYNN**

Angry and humiliated by her apparent abandonment, four days after he disappeared, Mrs. Maxine Dempsey, "a snappy-eyed, pretty brunette," went to the *San Francisco Bulletin* office with a story about her husband. She said that Jack had taken a dive/flopped/faked/laid down against Jim Flynn two months ago, on February 13, 1917, for $500, explaining his unexpected defeat by the old-timer. At that time, Dempsey was looked upon as a prospective heavyweight champion, but foolishly intentionally took a punch on the chin and went down for the ten-count. Mrs. Dempsey said,

> And for doing that, Jack received $500. That money came from the pocket of Flynn. In addition to the $500, Jack received from the club enough money as his share of the purse to net him $1,100.
>
> I knew it was wrong, but, of course, couldn't say anything. The money was handed to Jack by Flynn before the fight.
>
> It was a dirty mess all the way through. Jack was so unprincipled about it that he permitted his own brother, a working man, to bet $150 on him, and lose – wouldn't tell him the fight was a fake. Jack's father, I believe, bet money on him too, and, of course, lost it.
>
> I saw the money that Flynn gave Jack. It was hidden under the bath tub in our room, and when Jack came in and showed it to me I asked what it was for.
>
> He laughed and said it had been given to him by Flynn, that he was to lose the fight, that Flynn was getting old, and he thought it was worth $500 to let the news be sent out over the wires that he had whipped a young husky like Jack Dempsey.
>
> After the fight, Jack came home laughing and told how he stuck out his chin and let Flynn hit it.
>
> Then Jack's brother came in, very downcast, and, when he saw me smiling, he wondered at it, and remarked that I didn't seem to feel very badly over Jack's defeat.
>
> How could I feel badly? I knew Jack was to be whipped, and he seemed to be feeling so happy over the extra $500 he made.

Mrs. Dempsey also said she did not want to see another prize-fighter as long as she lived. "They're all the same. My advice to young girls is never to look at a man who has anything to do with boxing gloves. When I married Jack I thought he was a fine fellow. Now I know that I was fooled in the man." She said Dempsey had left her with only $30 and a number of unpaid bills, and also took her diamond rings.

> That he didn't leave me any money to speak of, doesn't worry me much, because I have relatives who will look after me. But I wish he would send me my three diamond rings. He asked me for them just before he left for good last Saturday [the 14th]. Said he was going to the bank. That's the last I saw of him. If boxing, as they say, is a

sport, I hope what I am telling about my husband will do it some good. I am glad to be rid of Jack. He is a faker, and a cheap faker at that. He had the brightest prospects as a fighter, all the experts rated him as a 'comer,' and he threw away all his chances for $500.[218]

Fred Winsor actually came to Dempsey's defense. He explained that Jack's claim to have thrown the fight merely was "alibi stuff," needing an excuse for losing in order to save face with his wife. Winsor had promoted the fight. He said if it was framed, he didn't know a thing about it. "I am not saying that Dempsey didn't tell his wife that the fight was a fake, but I think if he did tell her that, it was to alibi himself for his defeat." (Plus it wouldn't make sense for Dempsey to allow his own brother and father to lose money wagering on him if he knew he was going to take a dive.)

In response, Mrs. Dempsey agreed that Winsor might not have known about the frame-up, but insisted that she knew the day before the fight that her husband was to lose. She further said,

> There are some incidents in connection with the fake that are still making me laugh. The day after the fight Jack and I went to dinner at the Alton Hotel in Salt Lake City with 'Curley' Rodberg, trainer of Jack, and with Joe Anderson, a detective. We all ordered chicken, and Jack, who was supposed to have a very sore jaw as the result of the $500 punch Flynn gave him on the chin, began breaking the chicken bones with his teeth. Suddenly he stopped and grabbed the side of his face. 'Gee,' he said, 'but my jaw is sore.' Can you imagine a man with a sore jaw chewing chicken bones?

Winsor's explanation for the defeat was that Dempsey was in no condition to fight, and he had been living the night-life.

> Dempsey had been running around cafés, and when he entered the ring to fight Flynn his hands were shaking, not because he was afraid, but because he had been dissipating and was nervous. Anyhow, Dempsey didn't figure to whip an old campaigner like Flynn. The fact that he didn't win decisively over Al Norton and Willie Meehan in Oakland shows that Dempsey is no great fighter.

So Dempsey had a wife calling him a faker with no integrity, and a manager (or ex-manager) saying he wasn't a faker, but lost legitimately because he really wasn't that good and didn't take his preparation seriously. Ouch. Talk about a one-two punch combination those two made.

Mrs. Dempsey said she wanted nothing more to do with Dempsey, and would not have him again even if he were studded with diamonds, though she would like him to return her rings. "I'd like to get my jewelry as soon as possible, because Jack is such a stupid that it won't be long before he'll be 'soaking' whatever he has to keep himself in coffee and doughnuts."

The *San Francisco Bulletin* said boxing was better off without fighters such as Dempsey and Flynn, who should be banished, and that promoters who

---

[218] *San Francisco Bulletin*, April 19, 1917.

gave them matches would be putting themselves in a class with fakers, and should be looked upon with suspicion. The writer harshly said that Flynn never was anything more than a third-rater, and Dempsey was not even a third-rater, but rather "one of those low-browed dubs who come to a certain level and then sink back into mediocrity – the ham-and-egg class, it's called, because its members are lucky if they earn enough money in the ring to keep them in ham and eggs and are too lazy and shiftless to work." Wow.

Salazar noted that when Dempsey deserted his wife and manager and left for Salt Lake City, he threw up a 10-round go with Willie Meehan in Nevada set for May 10.[219]

Back on March 20, 1917 in New York, in his only fight since defeating Dempsey, 182-pound Jim Flynn had lost a 10-round no decision to 198-pound Bob Devere, who outboxed him.[220]

In late April, the *Tacoma Times* reported,

> Jack Dempsey is in bad in San Francisco – awfully bad. It seems that Jack took $500 to be knocked off the boards by Jim Flynn at Murray, Utah, in February.
>
> Mrs. Dempsey spilled the beans the other day after friend husband had hopped an east-bound rattler, taking with him all the family cash and diamonds, and leaving her with $30 and a lot of unpaid bills.[221]

By the end of April, Jack returned to San Francisco from Salt Lake. Dempsey told Salazar, "All there is to the story that I faked with Jim Flynn, is that my wife thought I wasn't coming back and she wanted to get even on me. It's the same old story of a woman scorned, only my wife wasn't scorned, merely thought she was." Dempsey claimed that he and his wife had made up. Salazar said Dempsey never again would leave his wife without first telling her where he was going and when he expected to return. But questions remain. Were her claims the truth or not? Why did he leave?

The next day, Salazar reported that Dempsey was not likely to make up with Fred Winsor. "Dempsey blames Winsor for all his recent troubles."[222] What exactly was meant by that is unclear. Perhaps it was financial. Regardless, Dempsey would go from fighting all the time locally to not being seen on the fight scene for months, quite a while for a previously very active fighter. Perhaps he was doing intermittent manual labor work to earn.

A few years later, Salazar claimed that when Jack returned to San Francisco, he asked Maxine to disavow the story that she had told, but she refused to do so, insisting that it was true. Hence, no retraction ever was printed in the newspaper.

Marion Salazar believed that the Great War might be a boon for boxing and re-establish it. The military encouraged boxing. Soldiers and sailors were not likely to be deprived of a sport they enjoyed and which was

---

[219] *San Francisco Bulletin*, April 20, 21, 1917.
[220] *Brooklyn Daily Times, New York Sun, Buffalo Enquirer*, March 21, 1917.
[221] *Tacoma Times*, April 27, 1917.
[222] *San Francisco Bulletin*, April 27, 28, 1917.

sanctioned by their officers. It would not be surprising if legal limitations might be loosened, and longer bouts with decisions could return. It would be ironic and inconsistent to object to boxing at a time when men were being asked to fight for their country. "And if boxing is good sport in time of war, if it has official sanction of the military authorities, why should it be put under the ban in times of peace by the civil authorities? The truth is that boxing, whether in peace or war, is good sport. Show us the American who refuses to read the account of a world's championship match."[223]

Alex Greggains, a local promoter who as a referee in 1905 awarded Marvin Hart a highly controversial 20-round decision over Jack Johnson in San Francisco, a decision which many believed was racially biased, gave a statement regarding how to whip a black fighter. "A negro can't fight when you crowd him. That applies to all negroes. The mind of the black man doesn't work very rapidly. When he has to think quickly he can't do a thing." He also said that any fast-thinking black fighters were part white.[224]

On May 22, 1917, there was a boxing card at the Dreamland Rink in San Francisco. Near the main entrance, Fred Winsor said something about Harry Foley, who was promoting the show, being a "cheap guy." Foley refused to admit some of Winsor's friends for free. Foley took exception to the remark and swung a right hook to Winsor's mouth. After bystanders intervened and separated them, and Winsor was wiping off the blood, along came Jack Dempsey, who recently had broken off from Winsor's management, and said, "Well, you finally got yours." Winsor glared at Jack and responded, "Yes, I got mine, maybe, but you didn't give it to me." Winsor then fired a blow to Dempsey's chin, almost flabbergasting him with surprise. Just as Dempsey was about to respond in kind, bystanders interfered, as they had in the case of Winsor-Foley a few moments previous. Dempsey was dragged away, vowing that he would get Winsor's goat sooner or later. "Thus the matter stands. Everybody got something. Foley got satisfaction from Winsor. Winsor got satisfaction from Dempsey. And Dempsey got a punch on the chin."

Winsor subsequently claimed that he wasn't trying to get his friends in for free, but just himself, for he had done favors for Foley, and thought that as a fellow promoter he should not have made him pay. Conversely, Foley insisted that Winsor became ugly when refused several passes for friends.

Winsor also claimed that when he was wiping the blood off his face, Dempsey took a punch at him, attempting to hit him first, and that he ducked the punch and landed on Dempsey's chin.[225]

On May 31, 1917, William Harrison Dempsey submitted his draft registration card. He listed his date of birth as June 23, 1895 (rather than June 24), born in Manassa, Colorado, current address as 116 Mason Street, San Francisco, California, eyes brown, hair black, race Caucasian, tall, with a medium build (physical characteristics listed on page 2). He listed his

---

[223] *San Francisco Bulletin*, May 12, 1917.
[224] *San Francisco Bulletin*, May 17, 1917.
[225] *San Francisco Bulletin*, May 23, 25, 1917.

present trade/occupation as "Carpenter," but "Not employed now." In answer to the question regarding whether a parent, wife, child under 12, or sibling under 12 was solely dependent upon him for support, he answered, "Wife and Mother." When asked, "Do you claim exemption from draft (specify grounds)?" he answered, "Wife and Mother dependent."

On June 9, 1917, the *Sacramento Star* reported that to make up for a month without a local boxing exhibition, matchmakers had arranged a local show for the following Friday night (June 15) at the L-street arena for the Hoffman club. Willie Meehan was matched to fight "Salt Lake terror" Dempsey again. "These two heavyweights fought the most sensational draw in Oakland seen in years. Both are hard hitters." Although Dempsey technically lost, clearly this writer believed it was a draw. However, for whatever reason, the fight did not take place.

The June 12, 1917 *Ogden Standard* quoted the *San Francisco Bulletin* as asking what had become of Dempsey. He was supposed to box Meehan in Sacramento on June 15, but some said he would not show up (and possibly had gone south to box Sailor Petrosky 25 rounds at Mexicali in three or four weeks – though on June 24 it was reported that Petrosky had enlisted in the marines in San Diego the previous day).

The June 14 *Sacramento Star* said no trace had been found of Dempsey, who disappeared after agreeing to fight Meehan. That same day, the *Sacramento Bee* said efforts to locate Dempsey or Jack Kearns, his (new) manager, proved unsuccessful.

The June 15 *San Francisco Chronicle* claimed that Dempsey was in Calexico, California, on the Mexican border. Others said he was in Los Angeles.

On June 18, Marion Salazar, reporting for the *Bulletin*, said Dempsey had been located in Seattle, Washington. He allegedly had a match in the north, and might not return to San Francisco for three or four weeks.

On June 21, the *Examiner* announced that Dempsey had been found not down south, but up north in Seattle, Washington, where he had troubles of the "domestic variety." No surprise there. His wife was from Washington.

Dempsey's "absence caused considerable worry to the promoters and managers recently." They wanted him on the local cards, for the fans enjoyed watching him fight.

At that time, the *Examiner* reported that Jack Kearns had signed (or agreed) to manage Dempsey. The *Bulletin* said Dempsey had written to Jack Kearns from Seattle. "Dempsey says that he is working in a shipyard, that he has turned over a new leaf, and that if Kearns will get him some matches he'll show that he can really fight. Kearns will look around, and if he can't get Dempsey started again in California he may take him East."[226] What did Dempsey mean by he had turned over a new leaf?

Several years later, Dempsey said that he and manager Fred Winsor had a disagreement and parted company. Dempsey found employment in a Seattle shipbuilding plant. Jack Kearns, who had managed Joe Bonds, a fighter Kearns thought of highly, whom Dempsey had beaten, saw Jack's potential, and reached out to him, offering to become his manager. Kearns told him, "Crude as you might be now, you can be turned into a champion, if you're properly trained." Jack asked, "Will you train me?" Kearns replied, "You're on." Dempsey trained hard under Kearns' tutelage.[227]

In his final autobiography, *Dempsey*, Dempsey alleged that while in San Francisco, wife Maxine flew out of control for no obvious reason. She became hysterical, throwing things around, screaming. A neighbor called the police. When they showed up, Maxine claimed that Jack had belted her, which he said was a lie. The police told them to keep it down and left.

Things subsided, but then sometime thereafter (likely in early June 1917), Maxine disappeared. Neighbors said she had gone to Yakima, Washington to see her mother. He went up there to see her, but it turned out that she and Dempsey essentially and functionally were through as a couple (though it is possible that they might have had a limited, on-again off-again relationship thereafter). He got a job at the Tacoma (or Seattle) Shipyards, helping to build ships for the war effort. While there, he got into a big bar brawl.

---

[226] *San Francisco Examiner, San Francisco Bulletin*, June 21, 1917.
[227] *Fairmont West Virginian*, May 20, 1921.

In his autobiographies, Dempsey neglected to mention that he had disappeared on Maxine or that she had informed the *San Francisco Bulletin* that he had thrown the Flynn fight. Sometime after he went up north to Washington, whether it was Tacoma or Seattle, really bad news came.

Less than a week after it was reported that Dempsey was located up north in Seattle, Washington dealing with domestic matters and working in a shipyard, on June 26, 1917 in Salt Lake City, 16-year-old Bruce Dempsey, Jack Dempsey's younger brother, was murdered by 31-year-old Pete Turloupis, who stabbed him in the abdomen with a stiletto. Bruce Dempsey was listed as the son of Hyrum Dempsey, a workingman living at 156 West Seventh South street in Salt Lake City. Police were hunting for Turloupis.

On June 27, a posse captured Turloupis in a farmhouse at Layton. In his possession was a knife that had congealed blood. He had stabbed young Dempsey in a quarrel. At first he denied the act, but then confessed and said he was sorry. He later claimed self-defense and of being under the influence of liquor. He claimed that Dempsey was one among a group of four that tried to start trouble, and Bruce had tried to strike him.[228]

Jack had to return to Salt Lake City briefly for the funeral (which he later claimed to have missed by several hours). Eventually, Jack Kearns sent him money for a train ticket to return to San Francisco.

In his posthumously published autobiography, *The Million Dollar Gate*, Kearns said he approached Dempsey about managing him. Initially, Dempsey said, "No, I'm sick of it. I made a trip East and didn't do any good. Then I went back to my folks in Salt Lake City and got married last year. Now all I want is a decent job." Dempsey admitted that recently he had an argument with his wife in San Francisco. He was down in the dumps. Clearly this was a potential turning point in his life.

Kearns asked Eddie Kane what he thought of Dempsey. Kane responded, "Well, I saw him box Al Norton or somebody in Oakland, and he looked like he might be a helluva fighter. He wasn't in shape and he got tired. But he looked like he might be all right. I hear he got flattened in one round in Salt Lake City by Jim Flynn, but it was supposed to be one of those things." Kearns said he interpreted Kane's words to mean that Dempsey had thrown the Flynn fight. "Kane's wink told me that Dempsey might have taken a dive in the interest of a quick payday. What I learned later certainly seemed to substantiate this theory."

Kearns said Dempsey had gotten a job as a Salt Lake saloon bouncer, and married the saloon piano player Maxine Cates. The romance hit a rocky road, for they were poor, and Maxine warned Jack that if he did not come up with some money quickly, she was "going back to work, one way or another." (Was she threatening to return to prostitution?) So Jack took the Flynn bout (and threw it for the extra money). After that, he was unable to get another match there, and migrated to the coast. He only got a few minor matches, didn't make much money, and was ready to give up on boxing.

---

[228] *Salt Lake Tribune*, June 27-30, 1917; *Salt Lake Telegram*, June 29, 1917.

Dempsey told Kearns that he had another go-round with his wife. Jack wanted to go to Seattle to work in a shipyard, and asked Kearns to loan him money to travel there, which Kearns did. A friend told Kearns that he heard that Dempsey had belted his old lady, and the cops were looking for him. Dempsey eventually wrote Kearns a letter from Seattle, saying that he was doing well. After Dempsey's brother died, Kearns sent him money to return to San Francisco, and they started working together.

On July 16, 1917, the *San Francisco Bulletin* reported that Dempsey had written Kearns from Salt Lake, saying he was called home suddenly as a result of his 16-year-old brother's murder. Dempsey said he would arrive in San Francisco in a few days and put himself under Kearns' management. Kearns also would be managing 18-year-old welterweight Marty Farrell. "With Dempsey and Farrell there will be three scrappers in the Kearns stable, other being Red Watson."[229]

Promoter Tommy Simpson signed a Dempsey vs. Meehan rematch to take place on July 25 at Emeryville, for the Emeryville Athletic club. The local press said both liked to fight and tried all the time, so the fans would get their money's worth.[230]

A younger, thinner Meehan

The *Oakland Enquirer's* Bob Shand said the Meehan-Dempsey fight loomed up as one of the most attractive heavyweight scraps on the calendar. "Dempsey has placed himself under the management of Jack Kearns and wants to show his new boss, and incidentally his former manager, Fred Winsor, that he is still a regular fighter. Meehan is a hard guy to beat in four rounds and Dempsey should have his troubles."

Meehan was called the fattest heavyweight in captivity, the inventor of the bass drum punch, the loop-the-loop, and other blows. The fight was attracting widespread attention. "Willie thinks he can stop Dempsey and is going to tear right in from the jump." Though never credited with possessing a stiff punch, Meehan believed otherwise.

The *Examiner* said Dempsey, who now was in Jack Kearns' stable, had shown that he could box if he chose to do so.[231]

The *Oakland Tribune* predicted that Meehan's wild, weird, peculiar, windmill style, "if you want to call it a style," always on the move and able to hit from any direction or angle, would keep Dempsey guessing. "Meehan looks due to force the fighting all the way and figures to be the winner."

---

[229] *San Francisco Bulletin*, July 16, 1917. Kearns claimed Dempsey sparred with Farrell and Watson.
[230] *San Francisco Chronicle, Oakland Tribune*, July 18, 1917.
[231] *Oakland Enquirer*, July 20, 21, 1917; *San Francisco Examiner*, July 21, 1917.

On July 22, Dempsey sparred 4 rounds with Young Peter Jackson, appearing to be in better shape than when seen last. The *Oakland Enquirer* said, "The big fellow has a mighty stiff punch and he is confident he can land it. Dempsey figures that Meehan can not hurt him, so he will step in and tear right from the start. Meehan, however, is a peculiar guy and hard to fight." Willie could throw from any angle, and although not a puncher, generally racked up enough points to garner the decision.[232]

**BOXING TONIGHT**
MAIN EVENT
Willie Meehan
vs.
Jack Dempsey
8 Rattling Four-Round Bouts
Bleachers 50c
Reserved Seats $1.00, $1.50
Ringside, $2.00
**Emeryville Athletic Club**
EMERYVILLE
*TONIGHT*

Since his W4 over Dempsey, Meehan had lost a 4-round decision to Chet McIntyre, won a 4-rounder over KO Kruvosky, and won a clear 10-round decision over Al Norton at Goldfield (after Norton's D4 with Dempsey). Meehan's own manager Moose Taussig was surprised at his wonderful showing. Taussig said if Meehan could go as fast as he did against Norton, he was a cinch to beat Dempsey.

Dempsey fans insisted the worst that Jack should have received in their first fight was a draw.

Dempsey declared that he was going to leap to the top of his division in one great bound. His new manager, Jack Kearns, said, "Just watch his smoke."

Bob Shand, who would referee the contest, said the fatter that Meehan looked, the better he fought, and he was none too slim. "Willie admits that his bass drum punch, while a good point scorer, is not very effective, and he is going to close his hands tonight when he hits." He often slapped.

The *Bulletin* said Meehan appeared to be at his best, having trained hard.

The *Oakland Tribune* said Meehan was the favorite to win a decision. Tommy Simpson was promoting. The show would start at 8:30 p.m.[233]

On Wednesday July 25, 1917 in Emeryville, California, a now 22-year-old Jack Dempsey fought a 4-round main event rematch with Willie Meehan. One said the attendance was less than expected, possibly as a result of the unexpectedly cold weather. Another said a very nice crowd of 3,500 people were on hand, half of which came over the bay from San Francisco.

The local *Oakland Enquirer* said Dempsey clearly won the 1st and 2nd rounds, fighting like a champion, crossing the "fat boy" quite a few times with hard rights to the chin. He worked faster and seemed able to solve Meehan's style better than the last time they fought. Meehan kept using the old left hook to the body and occasionally shot a right for the head, but Dempsey merely took them and fought back hard.

The *San Francisco Chronicle* agreed that Dempsey had a huge lead after the first two rounds.

---

[232] *Oakland Enquirer*, July 23, 1917; *Oakland Tribune*, July 22, 1917.
[233] *Oakland Tribune*, July 24, 25, 1917; *San Francisco Examiner*, July 24, 1917; *Oakland Enquirer*, July 24, 25, 1917; *San Francisco Bulletin*, July 24, 25, 1917; *San Francisco Call and Post*, July 25, 1917.

The *Oakland Tribune* said Meehan, with rolls of fat over his belt, was a disappointment. He took a lot of punishment, but always gamely came back for more. In the 2nd and 3rd rounds, Dempsey had Meehan just about to the groggy stage, but each time, Meehan pulled himself together, rallied, and finished the round with a strong attack. But he was too fat, and not in condition to make his old-time whirlwind attack. Only once or twice did he tear loose and bore in with a two-handed windmill attack, and each time he did, he had the big fellow all but sewed up. But Meehan did not have the strength or wind to keep it up.

The *Enquirer* said the 3rd round belonged to Meehan, for he made his best showing in that round. He chased Dempsey about the ring, landing many times with left hooks and right uppercuts. Many of the blows sounded all over the ring.

The *Chronicle* said Meehan came on strong in the 3rd and had a shade.

The *Enquirer* said the 4th round was about even. Meehan was not able to keep up the pace, and Dempsey held him even, slowing up Meehan with stiff lefts and right uppercuts.

The *Chronicle* agreed that the 4th round was about even.

This time, Jack Dempsey won a 4-round decision over Meehan. All of the local reporters agreed with the decision, as did the crowd. "The decision in favor of Dempsey was well received."

The *Enquirer* said Meehan was unable to duck as he used to do, and instead of ducking out of the way, he ducked into the punches each time.

The *Tribune* said although Meehan was game, after the first two rounds, he did not have the punch to do any damage. If the fight had gone two or three rounds longer, Dempsey would have had Meehan at his mercy. Dempsey looked like an improved fighter over prior local appearances.

The *Chronicle* said Dempsey reversed the tables, piling up such a lead in the first two rounds that it entitled him to the verdict, even though Meehan had a shade in the 3rd and the 4th was even. The *Enquirer* had the exact same score. Meehan was boxing as usual in his wild style, but could not land any effective punches. Dempsey showed to fairly good advantage.

The *San Francisco Examiner* simply reported that the contest was rather uninteresting, and Meehan lost (for he could not land effectively).

The *Call and Post's* Bert Lowry said the bout was nothing to enthuse over. "Willie was fat and flabby and has evidently lost his punch. Dempsey was but little better and when the contest ended no one was really sorry."

The *Bulletin* simply said, "Dempsey's hard and consistent punching throughout the contest gave him the decision. Meehan fought in his usual slam-bang style; but he fought seriously, cutting out his usual clownish tactics, and, though he lost, nobody could accuse him at the finish of not fighting the best he knew how."[234]

An impressed Jack Kearns was trying to obtain major fights for Dempsey, including against top contenders Fred Fulton or Carl Morris.

---

[234] *Oakland Enquirer, Oakland Tribune, San Francisco Chronicle, San Francisco Examiner, San Francisco Call and Post, San Francisco Bulletin, Santa Ana Register,* July 26, 1917.

Back on June 19, 1917 in Boston, the 6'4 ½" 210-215-pound Fred Fulton had scored a major victory, punishing Sam Langford, decking him for a nine-count with a left hook to the jaw in the 2nd round, often nailing him with lefts, hurting him with rights and right uppercuts to the jaw, nearly decking him on other occasions, and closing his eye, until Langford retired after the end of the 6th round. What few blows Langford had landed, Fulton did not seem to mind. It was the first time since 1906 that any boxer had stopped Langford. The impressive victory over the man considered to be the world's best black fighter helped solidify Fulton as the top contender to Jess Willard's crown, particularly since Willard drew the color line. A white man finally had knocked off the great Sam Langford.[235]

THE EAST ST. LOUIS HORROR

BESMIRCHING THE FLAG

The country's race relations remained troubling and problematic. The East St. Louis, Illinois race riots (a.k.a. the East St. Louis massacres), which started with some attacks on blacks in late May and throughout June, culminated into four days of full-blown riot, from July 2-5, 1917, causing between 40 and 200 deaths (mostly black; clubbed, shot, and burned to death) and extensive property damage, amongst the worst riots and worst cases of labor/race-related violence in U.S. history. Many blacks had migrated from the South to the North, fleeing prejudice and taking advantage of the job opportunities northern industries offered (particularly since European immigration had waned as a result of the war). However, the increased labor competition caused increased racial tensions in the North. White unions, which had excluded black workers, were angered by industry owners utilizing blacks as replacements, resenting the competition. This led to white union workers

---

[235] *San Francisco Examiner*, July 31, 1917; *Salt Lake Telegram*, August 1, 1917; *Boston Globe*, June 20, 1917. Langford was coming off a May 1917 LND6 Harry Wills. After Langford was stopped by Fulton, Wills would score a September 1917 WND10 Langford, and November DND12 Langford.

attacking blacks and burning down their neighborhood, leaving thousands homeless. Many chanted, "We don't want the nigger." Even the North was not immune to such rioting, including Pennsylvania and Ohio, which also had minor riots, at least relative to the massive one in Illinois.

The *Chicago Defender* bemoaned the fact that homes were laid to waste by the lawless mob which found no interference from the police or soldiers until the Second Regiment of Chicago arrived. Some even said national guard members attacked blacks rather than stopping the riot.

***Chicago Defender*, September 2, 1916**

Women had been stripped of their clothing, and children and men had been killed while the Sixth Illinois looked on and laughed. "If this is the way they intend to represent the government, Germany has already won the war."

Ultimately, over 400 people were arrested. Even East St. Louis mayor Fred Mollman, a Democrat, would be indicted by a grand jury for neglect of duty and malfeasance. His personal secretary was indicted for conspiracy, for the mayor used him to muzzle the cameras and to order destroyed all photographs relative to the riots. The charges against the mayor later were dismissed. Many police officers who participated in the riots either did not lose their jobs or eventually got them reinstated.

The *Defender* noted, "What is happening in the way of Negro migration in southern Illinois is happening in smaller degree throughout the north. Not a city but has remarked the increase in Negro population and has been troubled by it." Northern racial tensions and prejudices were increasing.

A race riot in segregated Houston, Texas on August 23, 1917 followed, which involved an all-black infantry regiment known as the 24th, local black citizens, white civilians, and local police. 11 civilians, 5 policemen, and 4 soldiers died. In general, segregated white communities did not appreciate the presence of armed black soldiers in their midst, and antagonism, hostility, and abuse by the general public and local police eventually led to violence, followed by retaliation and revenge by the soldiers. A year later, 19 black soldiers would be executed for mutiny. 41 were sentenced to life imprisonment. President Woodrow Wilson approved their sentences.

Later that year, the *Defender* further lamented that whenever any black person broke the laws, the rest of the country was advised of the matter in a manner designed to increase prejudice and race hatred.

Jack Johnson was a prize fighter, and, as far as we were concerned, he remained in that class. When he committed an 'overt act' he was heralded as the leader of our Race. Regrets were expressed, by ignorant whites, that his actions retarded the Race fifty years; then to make their statement good they proceeded to pass miscegenation and 'Jim Crow' laws in order to keep the superior white race SUPERIOR.[236]

Jack Kearns scheduled Jack Dempsey for a third match with Al Norton at Emeryville, to be held just one week after Jack defeated Willie Meehan.

The *Oakland Enquirer's* Bob Shand said Dempsey had made a fine impression in his prior fight against Al Norton, which was called a draw, "with Dempsey having what edge there was."

Both men knew how to deliver a punch, and because it was "the boys with the big wallop that the fans fall for," and there always was a chance for a knockout blow when these two were in the ring, the bout was attractive to ringsiders. "It takes a mighty good man to whip Willie Meehan, but Dempsey turned the trick last week and he won by quite a margin." Jack "gave Meehan a good lacing in the first pair of rounds, took a little the worst of it in the third and broke even, or maybe had a shade, in the fourth and last session."

AL NORTON,
Who will box Jack Dempsey four rounds at the Emeryville arena tomorrow night.

Dempsey appeared to be in even better shape than the week prior, and his manager Jack Kearns was willing to bet everything that Dempsey would win this time. Norton manager George Sharkey was just as confident in his man. Both had "ten-second wallops," hard enough that one solid connection could mean a knockout.[237]

Kearns told the *San Francisco Bulletin* that Dempsey was a "comer," and Norton would take the count. The way Jack was training proved that "he will from now on tread the 'straight and narrow' path in his efforts to top the division in which he boxes." Jack had changed. Kearns said, "This fellow Dempsey looks like the goods to me, and I think it will only be a question of a few months that I will have him boxing fellows like Fulton and Morris. I have seen them in action and am certain that Dempsey will give either a tussle."

Norton was training hard as well, and was in great shape. "One thing is certain: If either of these heavyweights connect properly, one of them is going to take the count."[238]

---

[236] *Chicago Defender*, July 7, 14, 21, 1917, September 15, 29, 1917, February 16, 1918.
[237] *Oakland Enquirer*, July 28, 30, 31, 1917.
[238] *San Francisco Bulletin*, July 31, 1917.

Both Dempsey and Norton were credited as having a victory and a loss to Willie Meehan. Norton most recently had lost a 10-round decision to Meehan in Goldfield, Nevada. Dempsey and Norton had fought each other to two 4-round draws. Some agreed with the draw decisions, while others believed Dempsey had won both times, particularly their first contest. The second fight was closer.

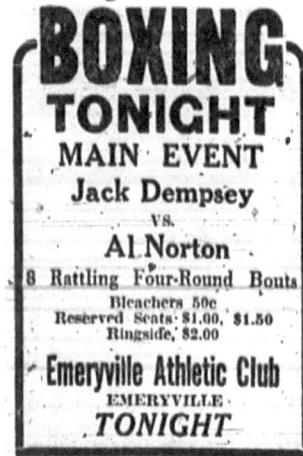

The day of the fight, the *Bulletin* said Dempsey looked to be about the best prospect in the heavyweight division on the Pacific Coast. Dempsey, Norton, and Meehan were the three best heavyweights on the coast. If Dempsey beat Norton, he would be the clear coast champion. No gamer or harder-hitting fighters than Dempsey and Norton could be found locally.

The *Examiner* and *Enquirer* said the red-headed Tommy Simpson had arranged the best card of the season at the open-air arena. "Simpson has a genius for signing up lads who forget how to stall, but who tear right in and deliver the best they have right from the jump, and tonight's card will be no exception." Heavyweights always were popular with local fans, and Dempsey and Norton were "the hardest hitters now performing in California." Norton had a right that meant business, and when it landed it was good night. Both of their managers said they were ready, and would have no excuses to offer if beaten. The show would start at 8:30 p.m.[239]

On Wednesday August 1, 1917 in Emeryville, in the main event, Jack Dempsey fought Al Norton for the third time. Bob Shand refereed.[240]

The *Oakland Tribune* said the fight was quite good while it lasted, but after only a minute of combat, Norton tried to side-step out of a corner and was caught off his balance by a Dempsey left hook and went down.

Though apparently not badly hurt, Norton took a nine-count and arose with caution. They went at it, and Dempsey started his rushing tactics again. After getting Norton into a corner, Jack planted a left on the face and followed with a right hook that caught Norton squarely on the chin, putting him down for the 10-count in the 1st round. The knockout brought the crowd to its feet.

The *San Francisco Chronicle* said that soon after the fight began, Dempsey connected with a right to the jaw and Norton went down for an eight-count. Dempsey backed him into his own corner and swung another right that sent him down again. This time Norton elected to stay down and take the full count. However, Dempsey suffered a slight cut over his eye.

---

[239] *San Francisco Bulletin, San Francisco Examiner, Oakland Enquirer*, August 1, 1917.
[240] The following account is taken from the *Oakland Tribune, Enquirer, San Francisco Examiner, Chronicle, Call and Post, Bulletin*, August 2, 1917; *Salt Lake Tribune*, August 4, 1917. The crowd was somewhat poor in size relative to the class of card offered.

The *San Francisco Examiner* believed that Norton quit, feigning unconsciousness. After the second knockdown, he crawled to the ropes and then stretched out flat. Perhaps this writer simply did not understand the delayed reaction. The writer said that once again, Dempsey demonstrated that he can fight when it pleases him to do so, whatever that means. Perhaps the writer was alluding to the fact that the Meehan fight was criticized as uninteresting, although that may have had more to do with Meehan than Dempsey.

The *San Francisco Call and Post* said Al Norton, the heavyweight that George Sharkey thought was the coming world champion, quit in the 1st round. Dempsey fought better than he ever had since his arrival in northern California. In the middle of the 1st round, he planted a short left hook and Norton went down on his back, rolled over, then got to his knee and took a nine-count. When he rose, Dempsey waded right in after him, and in a few seconds landed on the chin and Norton went down in his own corner with his head resting on the top rope. While Referee Bob Shand was counting, Norton reached up, took the rope away from under his head and stretched out flat on the floor. This writer took this as an indication that he quit.

Writing for the *San Francisco Bulletin*, Warren W. Brown said Dempsey clipped Norton on the chin with a right-hand swing early in the 1st round, decking him, and then finished him with one more clout; Norton finding a resting place in the corner. The fight essentially was over from the first right. He might possibly have been able to rise from the second knockdown, but if he had, he would have been sent flying out of the ring. Norton also had a badly cut optic. Dempsey's nose was glove-slashed.

Referee Bob Shand, writing for the *Oakland Enquirer*, said that a half-minute into the fight, Dempsey looked like a 1 to 10 favorite. Norton lacked pep. Dempsey hooked his left to the point and Big Al went down for eight. A right hook dropped Norton for the count.

Shand disagreed with those who said Norton quit. "There are those who say that Norton deliberately quit, but Big Al was badly stung." When he went down the second time, his eyes were glassy and his mouth wide open, snuggling under the ropes. He wasn't out cold, but was so groggy that he could not continue. Norton was cut as well. When he finally rose, he still was wobbly and had to be assisted to his chair. Even an hour later, he remained dazed and groggy and had to be helped to the train.

Norton said he had inadequate sparring owing to being cut by Young Jack Johnson in training, so he had to back off to allow it to heal. Yet, he also announced that he was retiring.

Shand was very high on Dempsey:

> Dempsey showed more class last night than he has displayed in any previous bout in this vicinity. He was in prime condition and worked like a champion while the bout lasted. His hitting was hard and accurate and it will take a mighty good man to beat him over the four-round route. Dempsey suffered a bad cut over his left eye when

Norton's head bumped him in the clinch, and it was necessary to take three stitches in the wound immediately after the scrap.

JACK DEMPSEY

Jack Kearns started calling Dempsey the "submarine destroyer." Kearns was the only local manager who seemed perfectly at ease when he came to see sportswriter Marion Salazar. "Handsome" Kearns liked to wear $8 shirts. He manicured his hands, and wore a snow white golf cap. He said Dempsey was the coming heavyweight champion of the world. He wanted to match him with Willard. Salazar responded that before matching him with Willard he had better whip guys like Fred Fulton and Carl Morris. Kearns responded that they would be nothing but suckers for Dempsey, and "if we said anything different in the paper we'd only be making ourselves ridiculous." Confident Kearns certainly believed in his fighter.[241]

Dempsey's performances had been good enough such that the larger town, nearby San Francisco across the bay, wanted to see him in action there. Just nine days after knocking out Al Norton in the 1st round, Dempsey had his first fight in San Francisco, a third fight with local Willie Meehan. They were 1-1 against one another.

The *Examiner* predicted that Kearns' protégé was due to meet with a reversal when he went up against Meehan. "Roly-Poly" Willie said he was determined to prove that his downfall before Dempsey's onslaught sixteen days prior was a fluke. He had worked out hard and shed excess poundage.

The *Bulletin* said Meehan never had worked harder. On August 8, after working out for an hour, sparring with Joe Coughlin and Joe Welsh, he stepped on the scales at 190 pounds.

Dempsey was training at Wixson's in Oakland. It seemed that since Kearns had taken over, Dempsey was leading the simple life, training hard, and "will observe training rules from now on. Dempsey weighs over the 200-pound mark at present, and with no superfluous flesh to speak of is a mighty trim built fellow." It appeared to be an even matchup, "and there is more than an even chance of it ending in a draw."[242]

---

[241] *San Francisco Call and Post*, August 7, 8, 1917.
[242] *San Francisco Examiner, San Francisco Bulletin*, August 9, 10, 1917.

On Friday August 10, 1917 at the Dreamland rink in San Francisco, Jack Dempsey and Willie Meehan fought their third 4-round contest.

According to the *Bulletin's* Warren W. Brown, Dempsey led in the 1st round by a shade. Although Willie's weird wallops had Jack bewildered most of the time, Dempsey managed to be just inside or just outside the bass drum and other sweeping clouts that Meehan spread around.

In the 2nd round, Meehan fired a couple of pivot punches, copping Dempsey with a back-hand swipe, twirling around on one foot after he missed the third one. Dempsey actually was shaken by the second of these woozy punches.

The 3rd and 4th rounds saw more wild milling, with Dempsey doing the clean punching, and Meehan landing every so often with an open-handed bang that made a lot of noise (or a slap in today's parlance).

Referee William Snailham, the bout's sole arbiter, declared it a draw.

Brown, who actually thought Dempsey had won, noted that before the fight, "Em" Kammerling had announced, "This contest will conclude the evening's entertainment." In terms of entertainment, Willie was there. Brown humorously asked,

> Didn't Willie with his wild swings, his pivot punches, and his front porch that wobbled just like the jelly that ma used to make, contribute his share of the evening's entertainment? What did it matter if Dempsey did all the solid punching? Wasn't it fifty-fifty on the entertainment thing? ... Snailham's decision was right as far as we're concerned. But it's all 'Em's fault. If he hadn't told us we were there to be entertained we'd have gone away thinking that Dempsey should have had the decision. As it was Willie surely entertained us, and he certainly kept us cool with his pivot punch, his flip flops and his hippopotamus hopping.

The *Chronicle* said fat fellow Meehan was like a whirling dervish having a fit, and nearly hit the fans too. Willie fought like no man living or dead, and pounding his soft-looking stomach was about as profitable as slamming at a rubber mattress. Willie used the pivot blow; the dipsy-dew, and every other punch at his disposal. Sometimes he hit Dempsey and at other times it looked as if he was aiming at the boys in the dollar seats. Spider Kelly, who was in Dempsey's corner, said he had seen every worthwhile fighter in the last 30 years, but never looked upon the likes of Meehan.

The *Examiner* said Meehan had the edge but got a draw, being robbed of a perfectly good victory. He had the best of the last three rounds, and, although he took some punishing blows, he gave a goodly percentage more than he took. But Referee Billy Snailham saw it as a draw and awarded it accordingly. Likely the referee believed that Dempsey's more powerful blows offset or balanced out Meehan's greater volume.

The *Call and Post* said Meehan won, but Referee Billy Snailham called the fight a draw. Although Meehan didn't beat him up, and Dempsey was the fresher of the two at the end, still, Meehan had fooled him time and again into leaving openings through which he could slam his freakish punches, which, coming one after another in the last few rounds, kept Dempsey so busy that he had no time to try his own blows.

In the middle of the 2nd round, coming out of a clinch, Willie whirled on the ball of his foot and at close quarters landed a back-hand slap on the side of Jack's face. The unexpectedness of it and the crowd's laughter seemed to rattle Dempsey. Although never in trouble, Jack was unable to gather and set himself to make his fight. Meehan used his bass drum and other unique punches and kept in front. This writer said Referee Snailham's eyes were full of cobwebs.

The *Oakland Enquirer* said Willie tried to box cleverly in the 1st round, but upon Moose Taussig's advice, "Willie pulled the Charlie Chaplin stuff after the first and Chaplined himself into a draw with Jack Dempsey."[243]

A few days later, the *Examiner* said Jack Kearns was causing amusement by writing that Dempsey was robbed of victory with the draw decision, for the opposite was true. "It's great stuff, this writing letters to the papers after your man has been beaten, claiming that he was robbed of the decision. But it has been pulled off before."[244]

J. B. Dempsey, Jack's brother, said Jack was born in Conejos county, Colorado, on June 24, 1895. His real name was Harry, and he assumed the name Jack for fighting purposes.[245]

At that time, the *Oakland Tribune* was running a weekly feature on and by Frenchman and European Light Heavyweight and Heavyweight Champion Georges Carpentier, in which he wrote about his experiences in boxing as well as in the military, fighting as an aviator in the war. Such press made him even more popular.[246]

Great at boosting his fighter, the savvy marketer Jack Kearns was sending out press releases throughout the country, telling everyone that Jack Dempsey was the coming champion. High-class championship referees Eddie Graney and Jack Welsh/Welch both agreed that Dempsey had real ability.

**Georges Carpentier in the military. Is that a cigarette in his hand?!**

---

[243] *San Francisco Bulletin, Chronicle, Examiner, Call and Post, Oakland Enquirer*, August 11, 1917. Chaplin was a film star who often utilized physical comedy, and humorously survived dangerous situations.
[244] *San Francisco Examiner*, August 14, 1917.
[245] *Salt Lake Telegram*, August 15, 1917.
[246] *Oakland Tribune*, August 10, 1917.

Kearns wrote:

> It is the truth when I tell you that I have the most sensational heavyweight fighter in the country.... To my mind, Jack Dempsey is the coming heavyweight champion. ... He is only 22 years of age and stands six feet one inch and weighs 202 pounds in condition. Spike Kelly, who has been training him and knows a fighter when he sees one, thinks that Dempsey is the greatest piece of fighting machinery he has seen or handled since the days of Jim Corbett, Bob Fitzsimmons and Stanley Ketchel.
>
> Dempsey is not the mauling, bruising kind of boxer like Carl Morris and others. He is a ring master of the Benny Leonard type and knows how to box as well as fight. ... I am ready to match him with any heavyweight in the world and do not draw the color line. I hope to take him east during the coming season and it will be my aim to match him up with Fred Fulton, whom I consider the best heavyweight in the country today; Carl Morris, Frank Moran, etc. I say this because I do not think any of them can stop Dempsey and we are willing to take a chance over any distance.[247]

Dempsey's next contest was a fourth bout with Willie Meehan, set to be held about a month after their last fight. Four days before the fight, on September 3, Meehan won a 4-round decision over Charley Miller.

Kearns said Dempsey would put up a different battle this time, and he would not be the least bit surprised if he won via knockout. Kearns called Dempsey the greatest boxer he ever managed. The *Bulletin* humorously responded, "since the last one." The *Bulletin* agreed though that there was not a boxer on the coast who could beat either Meehan or Dempsey.

The *Bulletin's* Warren W. Brown said, "The last time the mountainous Willie dragged his bass drum punch into the ring, he was given the benefit of a draw with Dempsey, though Jack did most of the boxing, and what little clean hitting there was spread over the four rounds of wild walloping." Brown thought Dempsey had won. Both fighters believed they had won. Kearns vehemently disagreed with the draw decision.[248]

On Friday September 7, 1917 in San Francisco, at the Dreamland rink, in the main event, the fourth Dempsey-Meehan bout took place. Toby Irwin refereed all of the contests on the card.

The *San Francisco Bulletin's* Warren W. Brown said Fat Meehan, with his large front porch, started off very slowly, and could not locate Dempsey at all. Dempsey hit his body for 2 rounds. In the 3rd round, Meehan got going and looked good. He continued his good work in the 4th round, and for half the round had Dempsey bewildered and all at sea. Towards the close of the round, Dempsey steadied his course and did better, but then the bell rang.

Referee Toby Irwin called it a 4-round draw, their second in a row.

---

[247] *Salt Lake Tribune*, September 2, 1917.
[248] *San Francisco Bulletin*, September 5-7, 1917. Scoring the Dempsey-Meehan contests seemed to be more about what one liked, cleaner, harder punches, or ring generalship and volume, with less power.

Brown said that once again, supremacy was left undecided. "Toby Irwin's decision that the cruel struggle was a draw, was undoubtedly the best ruling that could have been made." This author believed that Meehan's showing in the 3rd and 4th rounds entitled him to a draw, even though Dempsey looked by long odds the better of the two in the first two rounds.

The *San Francisco Chronicle* said Dempsey worked a good uppercut in the first two rounds to take a shade, but Meehan rallied with belated rushes and wild swings at the close to even up the bout and secure a draw for himself. It was a good decision and a slow match.

Marion T. Salazar, now writing for the *San Francisco Call and Post*, said it was a 50-50 draw encounter. It was half wrestling and half fighting. In the first 2 rounds, they mostly braced themselves against one another's shoulders and shoved and tugged this way and that. From the start of the 3rd round on, they let go and began slamming in plenty of loud, though ineffective punches. The slamming noise put the crowd in good humor and caused it to forget the first two bum rounds, and even applaud when Referee Toby Irwin held up both men's arms, signifying the draw decision.

The *Oakland Tribune* said it was a draw, but nobody took enough interest in it to care whether the decision was right or not. All the Kearns talk about Dempsey's great prowess was not seen. Jack took a lead in the first two rounds, but could not even hold Meehan even in the last two rounds, which led to the draw.

The *Oakland Enquirer* said they boxed a slow draw. "Dempsey kept in close and uppercut himself into a lead in the first two rounds. Meehan bass-drummed himself into a draw in the last pair of cantos."

The *San Francisco Examiner* briefly reported that Willie was the aggressor, but said nothing more.[249]

Clearly, something about Willie Meehan's style prevented Dempsey from showing his best stuff, and threw him off, but clearly also, something about Dempsey offset Meehan as well. It was their second 4-round draw in a row. They were 1-1-2 against one another.

Dempsey next was matched by Tommy Simpson, matchmaker for the Emeryville shows, to box Big Charley Miller, the motorman, just twelve days after the Meehan contest. There also was talk of Dempsey meeting Bob McAllister soon, as well as the world-renowned Gunboat Smith in early October. Kearns was hard at work making matches for his man.[250]

The approximately 32-year-old Charley Miller, who typically weighed around 220 pounds, had nearly 60 known fights of experience, having been boxing since 1908. His record included: 1910 D4 and W4 Victor McLaglen; 1911 L4 Dave Mills, W4, LTKOby1, and D4 Gunboat Smith, WTKO3 Ed Dunkhorst, D4 Jim Barry, and D10 Jack Geyer; 1912 W4 Al Kaufman, LTKOby15 Jim Flynn, and D4 Frank Moran; 1913 W4 Rufe Cameron, D4

---

[249] *San Francisco Bulletin, San Francisco Chronicle, San Francisco Examiner, Oakland Tribune, Oakland Enquirer*, September 8, 1917; *San Francisco Call and Post*, September 7, 8, 1917.
[250] *San Francisco Chronicle, San Francisco Examiner*, September 14, 16, 1917; *Oakland Enquirer*, September 18, 1917.

Jess Willard (*Examiner* - Willard more effective but Miller gamer/more aggressive), WND10 Al Palzer, LDQ3 Tony Ross, and LKOby3 Gunboat Smith; 1914 D4 Tom McMahon, LKOby1 Harry Wills, and L4 Willie Meehan; 1916 L4 (twice) and LKOby3 Meehan, and L4 Al Norton; and 1917 L4 Meehan. The fact that at various points in time he could hold his own and draw with Gunboat Smith, Jim Barry, Frank Moran, and future champ Jess Willard, and defeat Gunboat Smith, Al Kaufman, and Al Palzer, all world-class heavyweights, showed that Miller was a competitive threat. He was bigger (by about 30 pounds) and more experienced than Dempsey.

The *Chronicle* said Charley Miller had long been noted for his gameness and ability to step around and give his opponent much trouble, so the bout should be interesting. The *Bulletin* said Miller might give Dempsey a tougher argument than the fans realized. However, the *Call and Post* harshly said, "Neither man is of much consequence in the heavyweight division, but still each is a willing fighter and possessed of a punch, and fans might see either man bring over the haymaker."

Bob Shand said Dempsey would have to whip Charlie Miller in decisive style if he expected to be a card with Gunboat Smith. "Manager Jack Kearns has been press-agenting Dempsey so strong that nothing less than a K.O. will satisfy the fans tonight." Miller was a big fellow with a clumsy, awkward style, but that actually made him a hard man to fight. "However, Dempsey has been making so many claims of late that it is strictly up to him to dispose of the big motorman in jig time." Fair or not, the greater the hype, the greater the expectations.[251]

On Wednesday September 19, 1917 at Tommy Simpson's Emeryville arena, near the Hollis Street station via the Key Route boats, in the Oakland area, Jack Dempsey fought Charley Miller. This time it was the semi-final bout and not the main event.

They advanced quickly. Miller fiddled about. Within 10 or 15 seconds of the start of the fight, with his second punch, Dempsey shot a hard left to the chin and Miller hit the floor. He rose in a couple of seconds. Miller attempted to cover up and defend. About half a minute later, Dempsey stood away, measured, fired a short but heavy right to the jaw and Miller fell through the ropes, hitting the ring floor with a thud. He was half in the ring and half out. Miller was so dazed that he crawled out of the ring instead of back into it. One said Referee Bob Shand stopped the bout. Another said Miller was down and out for the long count. Either way, he was in no condition to continue.

The *Oakland Tribune* said the fight had not lasted a full minute. "Perhaps we have seen the last of Charley Miller." Referee Bob Shand, who wrote for the *Oakland Enquirer*, said Charlie Miller lasted about half a minute.

---

[251] Boxrec.com; *San Francisco Chronicle, San Francisco Bulletin, San Francisco Call and Post, Oakland Enquirer,* September 19, 1917.

After being completely out of it for a couple of minutes, upon regaining consciousness, the big San Francisco motorman Miller asked, "What time is it?" After being taken back to his corner, still dazed, Charlie tried to ascertain when the fight was going to start, and how the street-car strike was getting along. Another said he asked, "What round is this coming up?" When Dempsey was in his dressing room, Miller still was sitting in his corner asking what had happened. Yet another said he was so out of it that when he left the ring, Miller offered to fight an innocent newspaper man half his size, evidently believing him to be Dempsey.

Jack Dempsey proved that he had the power to knock out a much heavier man. Jack Kearns likely would be sending a letter to sportswriters, telling how Dempsey "stopped the man who made Jess Willard run."

Marion Salazar said "Handsome Jack" Kearns actually had been "Fighting Jack" at one point. Private sources said that Kearns, of "manicure fame," once fought for the Canadian lightweight championship back in 1908, but was knocked out.[252]

Gunboat Smith, who recently defeated Frank Moran in New York, arrived in San Francisco to prepare for a meeting with Dempsey in a contest promoted by Jimmy Coffroth. Kearns had been issuing press releases throughout the nation calling Dempsey a world beater, which helped get the fight made. The Gunner would train at Billy Shannon's. He said, "If I can't whip this Dempsey, I may as well go back to New York and go into business."

But first, Dempsey vs. Bob McAllister was scheduled for Emeryville, set to occur just seven days after the Miller bout.[253]

25-year-old Bob McAllister had a known 25-3-7 record, which included: 1913 W10 Willie Meehan; 1914 WND10 Battling Levinsky, LKOby7 Mike Gibbons, and D12 Tom McCarty; 1915 WND10 Tom McMahon; 1916 D4 Meehan and W4 Al Norton; 1917 WND10 Bert Kenny, WND10 Mike McTigue, DND10 Battling Levinsky, DND10 Gunboat Smith, LKOby3 Tom McMahon, WND10 Joe Bonds, and LND10 Clay Turner. Victories over Meehan, Levinsky, Norton, Kenny, McTigue, and Bonds, as well as a draw with Gunboat Smith, certainly showed that McAllister posed a competitive threat to Dempsey. Still, he typically weighed in the 160-168-pound range, so Dempsey would have the weight advantage.[254]

Bob Shand said McAllister was working like a Trojan getting ready. On September 21, he sparred 4 torrid, exciting rounds with Battling Ortega.

Dempsey was training at Cliff Wixson's gym in Oakland's Watts tract, and had Kearns-managed middleweight Marty Farrell as his sparring partner. They staged some lively gym battles. Farrell was a tall, rangy fellow who knew what he was doing in the ring.

---

[252] *Oakland Tribune, Oakland Enquirer, San Francisco Chronicle, San Francisco Examiner, San Francisco Bulletin*, September 20, 1917; *San Francisco Call and Post*, September 19-21, 1917.
[253] *Salt Lake Tribune*, September 20, 1917; *San Francisco Chronicle*, September 22, 1917; *San Francisco Call and Post*, September 24, 1917.
[254] Boxrec.com.

Jack said his knockout of Miller was no fluke, and expected to hang the ten-second wallop on McAllister's chin as well. "Dempsey has been reading some of the letters Jack Kearns has been writing about him and he has read himself into believing that he is destined to wrest the heavyweight crown from the massive forehead of Jess Willard."[255]

On the 23rd, before an admiring throng at the West Oakland club, McAllister boxed 8 rounds, appearing to be in fine shape, going 2 rounds each with Battling Ortega, Len Rowlands, and John Tholmer, and another 2 with Rowlands.

McAllister showed signs of improved punching power, as well as all of his old-time skill, shiftiness, and speed. "Bob's left hand still works like a piston rod, and he should give Dempsey all kinds of trouble." McAllister always had been a fan favorite.

That same day at Cliff Wixson's gym, before a big crowd, Dempsey and Farrell boxed 4 rounds. Farrell made a fine showing, for he knew how to handle himself. "He is a better boxer than Dempsey," and though outweighed, more than held his own.

The *San Francisco Call and Post* said McAllister was one of the best boxers ever produced by the Olympic Club, which was saying a lot, given that James J. Corbett was an Olympic Club veteran. McAllister would be in the best of condition. The fans who watched him spar Battling Ortega "claim that Dempsey will find it difficult to even lay a glove on the local boy."[256]

Bob Shand said Dempsey would have the clear weight advantage at about 192 pounds, but McAllister had the well-known class, so Dempsey was not a top-heavy favorite. Despite weighing only about 160 pounds, McAllister had defeated a lot of high-class heavyweights.

Shand said Kearns liked to go around telling tall tales, claiming that Dempsey had scored eight or ten straight knockouts, but those in the know locally knew he was kidding only himself. His letters were designed for eastern consumption. Dempsey had managed only draws with Meehan recently, though Shand admitted, "you can't judge a boxer's class by his fights with Bad Bill."

Dempsey not only had a weight advantage, but he indeed had a knockout punch. "Dempsey can probably hit twice as hard as Lanky Bob and should he connect solidly there is no question about what will happen to McAllister." Still, McAllister "must be considered a much superior boxer" to Dempsey. He could box rings around most fighters, perhaps with

---

[255] *Oakland Enquirer*, September 22, 1917. Kearns later claimed that Farrell taught Dempsey a lot.
[256] *Oakland Tribune*, September 23, 1917; *Oakland Enquirer, San Francisco Chronicle, San Francisco Call and Post*, September 24, 1917. Bob Shand recently resigned as referee, owing to criticism of his decisions.

the exception of the Gibbons boys and Harry Greb. He had exceptionally long arms and a great deal of class. "Maybe a good big man can whip a good little man, but the good big man has an awful time turning the trick when the good little man knows as much about boxing as does Bob McAllister."[257]

The *Chronicle* said if McAllister outpointed Dempsey, it could seriously imperil the upcoming Gunboat Smith contest.

James J. Corbett with Bob McAllister

The day of the fight, many expected McAllister to outbox Dempsey, given that it was only a 4-round contest.

The *Chronicle* wrote, "It is thought McAllister will rule favorite against Dempsey because of his cleverness."

The *Enquirer* said, "McAllister's science is expected to carry him through a winner. Bob should box rings around the slow-moving Dempsey, and he is clever enough to keep away from the knock-out punches which Jack has in stock all the time."

The *Call and Post* said McAllister was a clean-cut, fast-moving boxer with a fair punch. Dempsey was a big, strong fighter, "with little or no knowledge of the boxing end of the game." The question would be whether the quick-moving boxer could

offset the rushes and punches of the lumbering fighter, but many were wagering on McAllister.

---

[257] *Oakland Enquirer*, September 25, 1917.

The *Bulletin's* Warren W. Brown said Dempsey was getting his first real tryout. "In McAllister, Dempsey will find an opponent vastly different from the wild swingers that he has met so far along the line." This was the first truly clever boxer he had met, and the majority of fans were inclined to reserve judgment on Dempsey's ability as a ring prospect until they saw what happened against McAllister. A loss could cause a slump in the "submarine destroyer's" stock, while victory would give Jack Kearns "ground for a couple of letters of even longer length than his former efforts in the writing line."[258]

On Wednesday September 26, 1917 at the Emeryville open air arena, just outside Oakland, in a contest promoted by Tommy Simpson, in the main event, Jack Dempsey fought a scheduled 4-round bout against Bob McAllister. Eddie Hanlon refereed. Two judges rendered the decisions, with the referee acting as a tiebreaker only if necessary. The show, which started at 8:30 p.m., was well attended. Fans paid $2, $1.50, and $1 for seats, and $.50 for the bleachers.

In the 1st round, a high left hook from Dempsey sent McAllister staggering, and a right cross almost sent him down. Thereafter, lanky Bob engaged in safety-first tactics, apparently being satisfied to try to last the 4 rounds.

In the 2nd round, McAllister used his left hand to good advantage, and while he failed to hurt Jack, he annoyed him by shoving his fist into his features. Dempsey did all the leading, and had McAllister backing up all the time. Time and again Jack had him all but helpless, but could not finish him. Towards the end of the round, McAllister rained in five or six straight lefts to the chin, but those were the only clean blows he landed during the entire bout. This turned out to be Bob's best round.

In the 3rd round, a couple of right hooks to McAllister's chin had him in a bad way, but Jack backed away and gave Bob a chance to pull himself together. McAllister did not show the punch, speed, or shiftiness that he had in shown training, and generally missed his jab. Dempsey rushed him all around the ring, and McAllister seemed awkward.

In the 4th round, Dempsey came on strong and rocked McAllister several times with left hooks and right crosses. McAllister survived to the end of the round, but that was all he did. He was very tired at the end. It was Dempsey's round by a wide margin.

Dempsey had dominated from the start, being too strong for the former Olympic Club man, mauling him around the ring, outboxing and outfighting him throughout. McAllister was far outclassed at all stages, and frequently hung on to escape punishment. Only McAllister's experience, crafty skill, footwork, and clinching, combined with the fact that it was contest of only a short distance, kept him from being stopped.

The judges, Dick Adams and Jack Murphy, were unanimous that the verdict went to Dempsey. Therefore, referee Eddie Hanlon's tiebreaking

---

[258] *San Francisco Chronicle, Call and Post, Bulletin, Oakland Enquirer*, September 26, 1917.

vote was not necessary, though he would have voted for Dempsey nevertheless.

The *Oakland Tribune* said McAllister showed nothing, and the bout was a fizzle. He lost the decision by as wide a margin as a man could lose a decision. Bob was through as a main eventer.

Bob Shand for the *Oakland Enquirer* said Dempsey won handily, with no trouble at all, for McAllister made a sorry showing. McAllister did not appear to have any confidence in himself, and was backing up continually and at the same time overlooking many openings for his left. Outside of a flash in the 2$^{nd}$ round, he might as well have left his left at home. McAllister's tactics got him nowhere except into the bad graces of the paying customers and promoters. Dempsey fought a "nice, heady battle."

The *San Francisco Bulletin's* Warren W. Brown said Dempsey outclassed McAllister in every minute of their engagement. Bob refused to outbox Dempsey, but instead gracefully ran his chin into every sort of punch sent his way. McCallister could not hit, and his defense was full of holes. The hard-swatting Dempsey maneuvered him around at will and cracked him about as often as he desired. Often it seemed as if Jack would score a knockout, but Robert assimilated the punishment and showed that he was thoroughly game. McCallister did not land a solid punch. Once, he began jabbing away and halted the destroyer for a second or two, but it was just a flash, and immediately Bob relapsed into a state of helplessness. His poor showing helped make Dempsey look like a champion.

The *San Francisco Chronicle* and *San Francisco Examiner* agreed that Jack Kearns' scrapper won handily, with ease.

The *San Francisco Call and Post's* Marion T. Salazar believed Dempsey intentionally carried McAllister and allowed him to "stick." He chased and tapped him all over the ring. He permitted him to last, but "did it so clumsily, so inartistically, that the only persons present who were fooled were those who didn't know anything about boxing – the women and so forth." Wow. Skeptical Salazar was an agitator.

Salazar believed Dempsey could have stopped him in the very 1$^{st}$ round had he wanted to do so, and he came near doing it, too. Two or three wallops to the chin started Bob wobbling, and Dempsey had an awful time holding back during the remainder of the round - to hold back and still not appear to be doing so, while McAllister recuperated. After that round, Dempsey was very careful not to let fly too hard at long range or to hit him too hard in the clinches.

Before they entered the ring, some of the wise ones were commenting freely that there was an arrangement between the two. Dempsey had jollied McAllister into the match by agreeing to allow him to "stick." Dempsey's work bore out exactly what the wise ones said. "Funny, isn't it, how Dempsey fooled us – fooled us just like he did the people of the Middle West when he flopped to Fireman Jim Flynn."[259]

---

[259] *Oakland Tribune, Enquirer, San Francisco Bulletin, Chronicle, Examiner, Call and Post, Salt Lake Telegram*, September 27, 1917. On the undercard, welterweight Marty Farrell fought a draw with Len Rowland.

Doubling down, the next day, Salazar said Dempsey and his manager Kearns might as well know that San Francisco and Oakland "will not stand for fakers." Salazar insisted that Dempsey faked with McAllister. Some even hinted that Charley Miller took a dive for him. "Dempsey, as everybody knows, faked with Fireman Jim Flynn before he came to San Francisco."

However, Kearns told Salazar that he was doing an injustice to his fighter, that Dempsey had been wearing big 10-ounce gloves, and McAllister was a hard man to stop in only 4 rounds. "Who has stopped him in the last year aside from Tom McMahon?" Nevertheless, Salazar was not convinced. He believed that Dempsey had pulled his punches and held back. That is what his eyes showed him.

> McAllister has been a hard man to stop in four rounds, we'll admit, but when he was hard to stop it was only because the other fellow couldn't hit him one-tenth as many times as Dempsey did nor one-twentieth as many times as he could have hit him. And as for the gloves Dempsey and McAllister used being ten-ounce ones, Sol Levinson, who made the gloves, says they were eight-ounce gloves, the same size that Dempsey used in the supposed knockout of Charley Miller.[260]

Dempsey's problem was that sometimes when he knocked out someone quickly and with ease, some writers would suspect the fighter took a dive, perhaps failing to realize that Dempsey was that powerful and good; and sometimes when he didn't knock out a foe, some writers claimed Dempsey carried them, failing to realize it was not always easy to knock out everyone, especially in only 4 rounds. Perhaps Dempsey, cognizant of the fact that he had a very big, important fight coming up soon, did not want to take too many risks of injury to his face or hands, and was content to coast to a clear and easy victory. Plus, it can be challenging to stop a clever man who is fighting very cautiously and defensively, refusing to open up and take risks, moving quickly and grabbing often. However, Maxine Dempsey's accusations, true or not, had caused writers like Salazar to be more likely to suspect something nefarious whenever it came to Dempsey.

A month later, McAllister claimed he fooled Dempsey into believing that he wasn't hurt, playing on his inexperience. "Jack had the chance of his life to knock me out in the third round…but I talked him out of it." Bob was out on his feet, but got close in and told Jack that he was going to take the Gunboat Smith match away from him and box Smith himself. Dempsey did not realize how hurt he was. "If he had more ring experience he would have paid no attention to my chatter, but would have finished me up right there, after I was out on my feet." McAllister was a talker, who perhaps tricked Dempsey into being more cautious than he needed to be, convincing him that he was not hurt.[261]

---

[260] *San Francisco Call and Post*, September 28, 1917.
[261] *San Francisco Bulletin*, October 27, 1917.

CHAPTER 10

# West Coast Warrior Part III: The Start of Real Recognition

22-year-old Jack Dempsey's next fight, against Ed "Gunboat" Smith, also called the "gunner," "gooner," or "goner," was quite significant, the most significant fight of Dempsey's career to that point. Jack was going to have a chance to show his talent against a world-class fighter. It was scheduled to be held only six days after the Bob McAllister contest. Harry Sullivan was promoting the show at Recreation Park in San Francisco.[262]

GUNBOAT SMITH

Gunboat Smith leisurely toying with the medicine ball at Billy Shannon's

The Gunner still wears his old smile and he promises his friends that he will still be smiling after he meets Jack Dempsey

30-year-old Gunboat Smith had over 100 fights of experience, and had been fighting the world's best for years, starting his career in 1909. He had been a Navy champion, and a sparring partner for Jack Johnson (purportedly even dropping him). His record included victories over the likes of Jess Willard, two-time title challenger Frank Moran, Sam Langford (a huge upset when Langford was considered the top contender to the crown), Arthur Pelkey (for the white world heavyweight championship), two-time title challenger Fireman Jim Flynn, Carl Morris, Battling Levinsky, Young Peter Jackson, Jim Stewart, Tom McMahon, Bombardier Billy Wells, Jim Coffey, former title challenger Tony Ross, Dick Gilbert, Joe Cox, Charley Miller, Bill Tate, and many other well-regarded fighters.[263]

---

[262] *San Francisco Examiner*, September 28, 1917.
[263] Gunboat Smith's record, 74-26-8, included: 1909 LND4 Denver Ed Martin and W10 Young Peter Jackson; 1910 LKOby9 Jim Barry and W10 Jack Geyer; 1911 KO4 Walter Monahan, L6 Jim Barry, L4,

Gunboat Smith W20 Jess Willard, 1913

Smith was coming off his most recent significant victory over Frank Moran (WND10), whom Smith had beaten three times. The Gunner was known for being able to box and punch, particularly with his very powerful overhand right. He had far more experience than Dempsey.

The *Oakland Enquirer's* Bob Shand said Gunboat Smith had a meteoric career since he came ashore from a warship in San Francisco bay about nine years ago "and knocked a big negro cold at the West Oakland club," which "made a big hit with the fans." He soon became a ring idol, and kept on flattening the big fellows. Jim Buckley signed him up, saying that anyone who could hit like that was good enough to fight under his management. Smith scored a series of important victories (including over Willard, Langford, and Moran) and became one of the world's best fighters.[264]

---

TKO1 and D4 Charley Miller, KO2 Mexican Pete Everett, and LKOby9 Jack Geyer; 1912 L10 Geyer, LND12 and WTKO7 Jim Stewart, LND10 Dan Flynn, WND10 Tom McMahon, WND6 Al Kubiak, KO3 Jim Savage, DND10 Jack Twin Sullivan, and W20 Frank Moran (Smith 186, Moran 206 pounds); 1913 KO2 Bombardier Billy Wells, WND10 and TKO3 George Rodel, W20 Jess Willard (Smith 180, Willard 230 pounds)(most believed it should have been ruled a draw), TKO5 Jim Flynn, WDQ5 Carl Morris, KO10 Tony Ross, KO3 Charley Miller, and W12 Sam Langford; 1914 TKO15 Arthur Pelkey (180 vs. 205, for the white world heavyweight championship), LDQ6 Georges Carpentier (loses white championship), LND10 Battling Levinsky, LKOby3 Sam Langford, WND10 Jim Coffey, and TKO4 Tom McCarty; 1915 D12 and W20 Battling Levinsky, WND10 Jim Flynn, LND10 Jack Dillon, WND10 and LND10 Charley Weinert, W12 McCarty, WND12 Dick Gilbert, WND10 Tom Cowler, WND10 Jack Hemple, WND10 Sailor Jack Carroll, WND10 Al Reich, L10 Colin Bell, WND8 Joe Cox, and LKOby4 Jim Coffey; 1916 LND10 Jack Dillon, LND10 Porky Flynn, L10 Carl Morris, WND10 Bob Devere, LND6 and L12 Battling Levinsky, W8 Arthur Pelkey, WND10 Tom McMahon, WND6 Jim Coffey, WND10 and LND10 Tom Cowler, WND10 Joe Cox, and WND10 Frank Moran (186 vs. 197 ½); 1917 LND10 Levinsky, D12 Jack Moran, L20 Jack Dillon, DND10 Bob McAllister, D/LND10 and LND10 Kid Norfolk, WND10 Bill Tate, and WND10 Frank Moran (180 vs. 198 pounds). Boxrec.com
[264] *Oakland Enquirer*, September 18, 1917.

The San Francisco native Smith was weighing about 181 pounds, and expected to weigh around 178 for the fight, while Dempsey probably would be about 190. Smith's manager Jim Buckley said his man would knock out Dempsey without turning a hair. He did not think much of Kearns' alleged "logical successor to the heavyweight crown."[265]

The *Examiner* said Dempsey's clear and easy victory over Bob McAllister had lifted the big boxer substantially in local estimation. McAllister was regarded as one of the cleverest men in the ring, and few believed that Dempsey would make any sort of showing against him. McAllister had been meeting the best men in the East and holding his own. The opinion was growing that at present, the best boxers in the country were in the West.[266]

Smith, trained by Moose Taussig, was working out at Billy Shannon's gym in San Rafael to the tunes of a brass band. He sparred with K.O. Kruvosky and Young Jack Johnson. Those who saw him train said he was the same old Gunboat in action, ever ready to deliver the knockout punch with his right.

Gunboat Smith and Jack Dempsey Meet Tomorrow

GUNBOAT SMITH

The *Call and Post* said it was a crossroads fight for Dempsey. If he won, he might be heard from among the "higher ups" of the ring, but if he lost, "he is not going to be with us very long."[267]

Kearns indeed was calling Dempsey "the logical successor to the world's heavyweight laurels," trying to garner publicity for his man however he could. His boosting helped get Dempsey the fight with Smith. But Dempsey had to win in order to show and prove to the press and public what Kearns saw in him.

Dempsey had been training at Wixson's in Oakland, working with Len Rowlands and Kearns' fighter Marty Farrell, "and reports say that he has learned some clever stuff lately." Kearns pronounced Dempsey to be in the best form he had been in for any local bout. Dempsey's easy victory over McAllister, who fought evenly with and possibly even beat Smith, gave him an abundance of confidence.

Still, the locals were predicting that the Gunboat would defeat Dempsey, who most felt still had a lot to learn before he could beat the very best in the business. Smith was the betting favorite. If Dempsey won, it would force the boxing world to take notice.

Bob Shand said if Smith was as good as he was the night he walloped Frank Moran a month ago, he should beat Dempsey. Smith's manager Jim

---

[265] *San Francisco Examiner, Salt Lake Telegram*, September 25, 1917.
[266] *San Francisco Examiner*, September 30, 1917.
[267] *San Francisco Call and Post*, October 1, 1917.

Buckley saw Dempsey beat Bob McAllister, but did not think much of him, saying he was a fair second-rater. Buckley believed that Smith was the best heavyweight in the world, and claimed that Willard was afraid of him.

Shand said Kearns had been over-selling and over-touting Dempsey. As a result, fans incorrectly believed it was a 50-50 fight, and even money was being offered amongst them.

Buckley and Kearns wrangled vigorously over who would referee and decide the contest.

The *Call and Post* said both men had trained well and were in good condition. They promised to go in and fight from the start. Hence, a torrid contest was anticipated. The winner would be in line to box other top big fellows, "while the loser will drift back into the preliminary class." Both men were confident. "In fact, the Salt Lake man does not like the slams about his faking with Bob McAllister and Jim Flynn, and says he will prove to the fans that he is much better than rated."[268]

On Tuesday October 2, 1917 at Henry Berry's Recreation Park in San Francisco, at 15th and Valencia streets, under the auspices of the Recreation club, Jack Dempsey fought Gunboat Smith in a scheduled 4-round bout. The show was promoted by Harry Sullivan and Joe Watts.

A large crowd showed up to the open air ball park. The weather was ideal. The ring was erected over home plate, and 1,500 chairs were placed on the infield. To save the turf, a canvas was stretched over the grass. Fans could purchase higher priced infield seats, or cheaper grandstand seats. Tickets were $.50, $1, $1.50, and $2. Close to $2,100 was taken in.

The show started at 8:30 p.m. Toby Irwin refereed, and would be the bout's sole arbiter. Dempsey and Smith were meeting for what was heralded as the heavyweight championship of the Pacific Coast.

Spider Kelly seconded Dempsey. When he entered the ring, Jim Buckley asked for a stool for Smith, and Kelly confidently responded, "What do you want of a stool? Why don't you go get a stretcher?"

In the 1st round, Dempsey landed a left and right cross that sent Smith back against the ropes. Thereafter, Jack hooked his man repeatedly. Dempsey dodged Smith's terrific right swings with ease and agility, winning the round by quite a margin.

---

[268] *San Francisco Bulletin*, October 1-2, 1917; *San Francisco Examiner, San Francisco Call and Post, Oakland Tribune, Oakland Enquirer, Salt Lake Telegram*, October 2, 1917.

In the 2nd round, Smith came to life, crossed over his powerful right flush on Dempsey's chin, and the fight came close to being over right there. Dempsey was staggered, his knees sagged, and he almost fell, but remained upright and fell into a clinch. It was the same heavy right swing that Smith had used to deck and knock out so many men over the years. One reporter said Jack did not go down, but was so dazed that he could do little but cover up thereafter to weather the round. The *Examiner* said Dempsey recovered and actually managed to finish the round strong. The *Chronicle* and Bob Shand differed from that account, saying that it took Jack that entire round and a part or half of the 3rd before his head cleared. All agreed that Smith clearly won the 2nd round due to that terrific swing.

In the 3rd round, Dempsey gradually recovered and forged ahead, looking good again, winning it, some saying by a shade, others saying by a clear margin.

In the 4th round, Dempsey had Smith missing by a city block, while Jack was landing. The crowd was urging on Dempsey, for he was chasing Smith all around the ring. The round clearly was Dempsey's.

Referee Toby Irwin awarded Dempsey the 4-round decision. The local press and fans all agreed with the decision.

The *Examiner* said that overall, Smith received a beating. Dempsey dodged all but one right swing. The one that landed early in the 2nd round came close to ending the fight, but that was the only round Smith won.

The *Chronicle* said Smith had lost his youth, judgment of distance, and stamina. He never hit Dempsey hard save the one blow in the 2nd round. Dempsey hit him with an onslaught and had the superior judgment of distance. Smith was lacking in everything save the spirit to try. Three of the four rounds belonged to Dempsey by a wide margin. Dempsey won it, and won handily. The decision could not have been otherwise.

The *Bulletin*'s Warren W. Brown said Smith put up a sorry showing against the submarine, who batted him all over the park in three of the innings. Smith had a hard punch, particularly his right, but he did not use it often enough. He "landed one, count 'em, one punch on the classic mug of J. Dempsey, sometime submarine destroyer, and in exchange Mr. Smith accepted gracefully, and otherwise, a collection of singles, doubles, triples, bunts, and sacrifices, and departed from the ring with a beating – nothing more." Dempsey hit him as he pleased. At one point, Jack nailed him with a left, and if the ropes and post hadn't been in the way, Smith might have crashed into the bleachers. Dempsey took the one big punch Smith landed and proved he could bear it. But that was all that Smith landed. There was no room for argument about the decision.

The *Oakland Tribune* agreed that Dempsey earned a decisive victory. Gunboat won only one round, and the only reason was because he happened to land a big swing that staggered Dempsey. In the other rounds, Dempsey had so far the better of the argument that Smith's followers did not have a chance to holler for a draw. Dempsey left no room for debate. By the time the bout was over, Dempsey was chasing Smith all over the ring, landing punches almost at will, while Smith was swinging wildly. In another two rounds, Dempsey probably would have finished him with ease. Referee Toby Irwin did not need to worry when he gave Dempsey the decision, for no other ruling was possible.

The *Oakland Enquirer's* Bob Shand said the old round-house swing was Smith's sole asset, and he connected solidly just once. He made a miserable showing, and no one kicked at Referee Toby Irwin's decision. Overall, save for the one big blow, Dempsey made Smith look foolish.

Dempsey's showing was impressive. He stepped inside most of Smith's wild swings and countered and blocked like a veteran. The most pleasing feature was that Jack also proved his ability to "take 'em." He never before received such an acid test, and he showed himself to be thoroughly game. "On his showing last night Dempsey is some considerable heavyweight and he should show improvement in future bouts, as he is still a youngster." Folks were starting to see what Jack Kearns saw.

Marion Salazar said the offices of "Handsome Jack Kearns" would be busy typing and sending letters to sporting editors telling how Dempsey was the real heavyweight champion of the world. Dempsey had stopped Charley Miller in a couple of punches. Miller fought Jess Willard to a draw. Gunboat Smith won a close 20-round decision over Willard, but Dempsey earned a clear decision over Smith.

Salazar agreed that Dempsey's clear victory over Smith left no room for argument. The only time the Gunner seemed to have a chance to win was in the 2nd round, when he swung his roundhouse right to the chin and caused Jack to stop dead still, then wobble, and almost fall. But both prior to that and from then on, Dempsey had everything his own way. He outshoved the Gunner in the clinches, beat him at infighting, and on one occasion made Smith turn and run at full speed to the ropes to avoid powerful straight punches.

Salazar said the Gunner was not the same fighter that he was a few years ago when he whipped Pelkey. All he did was temporarily wobble Dempsey. Still, Salazar admitted that Dempsey now was a big card, while Smith was in the discard.[269]

Smith later claimed that he had hurt hands, but the fans who saw the mill said he didn't have much chance to use his hands, he was beaten so badly. Shand said the fans did not accept the excuse. The Gunner hit Dempsey hard with his right in the 2nd round, and tried to hit him with the same punch many times before and after, but failed. No one with a hurt hand would have swung as hard as he did.

Shand said most believed that Smith had no stomach for the aggressive style of the hard-hitting Dempsey. Smith almost ran through the ropes on one occasion trying to get away, and had the ropes been weak, he would have gone into the laps of those occupying front-row seats.

After hitting Dempsey with his best punch, which would have decked most heavyweights, and Dempsey showed his gameness in standing up

---

[269] *San Francisco Bulletin, Examiner, Chronicle, Call and Post, Oakland Tribune, Enquirer,* October 3, 1917.

under punishment like a champ, fighting back just as soon as his head cleared, Smith realized he was beaten. Shand also said Smith failed to try hard enough to finish Dempsey when he had him hurt, perhaps astonished that he did not fall. He failed to seize his opportunity adequately. While he was wondering, Dempsey's head cleared, and the next thing the Gunner knew, a very ferocious young man was hammering away at his stomach.

Warren Brown said a friend claimed that Dempsey was the fastest war vessel afloat. He had to be in order to catch up with the Gunboat, who had taken to sprinting around to avoid blows. Smith had planned to have three more local fights, but now that he had fallen from grace, his future was unclear. Fans were not partial to marathon running inside the roped square. They could go watch a track meet instead for much less money.

Conversely, Dempsey was "the big noise in the heavyweight circles just now." "Dempsey has shown conclusively that he can beat all the second rate heavies in the world." Fans now knew he had the goods.

Marion Salazar said the total receipts actually were $1,890. $750 was taken in on the 50-cent tickets. 420 tickets were sold at $1. Given that it was the first boxing show held at the ball park, and most fans were not accustomed to Tuesday boxing shows, and considering the street-car strike situation, it was a good attendance.[270]

In 1919, Dempsey said Smith landed a long looping overhand right on his chin, the hardest smash that ever hit him. "I was plumb out, standing up. I don't know yet how I managed to keep on going. My, what a wallop!" Kearns said Jack just fought on instinct thereafter.

In his first autobiography, Dempsey said he was groggy in that $2^{nd}$ round, but hung on and kept fighting. Smith didn't find another opening. Jack was strong again in the $3^{rd}$, and they told him he held his own. He attacked so viciously in the last round that he had Smith covering up and clinching to avoid punishment.

Afterwards, Dempsey apologized to Kearns for losing, feeling that just about washed him up. Kearns replied, "But you won! What's the matter with you? You won, I tell you!" Jack said he could not remember anything about the fight after the time that blow landed in the $2^{nd}$ round, so he assumed that he had been knocked out. Instead, the victory had catapulted his career, making him a valuable property.

Jack Dempsey had fought four times in the span of one month (Sep. 7, 19, and 26, and Oct. 2 – Meehan, Miller, McAllister, and Smith, all experienced well-respected ring veterans).

Kearns kept mailing out clippings about Dempsey's prowess as a fighter, constantly touting him. He advertised that it was getting to be quite difficult to find opponents willing to fight him.

Another world-class fighter, Carl Morris, agreed to box Dempsey next. They would fight one month after Dempsey's victory over Gunboat Smith.

"Sapulpa engineer" Carl Morris was the biggest boxer seen since Jess Willard. The locals said if mere physical strength was any indication,

---

[270] *San Bernardino News, Oakland Enquirer, San Francisco Bulletin, Call and Post*, October 4, 1917.

Dempsey was due to lose. Morris stood 6'4" and weighed around 235 pounds, though he expected to train down a bit. He had an 80-inch reach. Dempsey would be 40 pounds the smaller man at least, more than two inches shorter, and outreached by a couple inches as well.

33-year-old Morris had a 47-12-1 known record, and had been boxing since 1910, after Johnson beat Jeffries and the world was scouring the Earth for white hopes. Morris had been a soldier who fought in the Philippines in the 1898 war. In 1910, the 235-pounder made former champion 212-pound Marvin Hart retire after the 3rd round. It was Hart's last fight. Morris also held victories over Fred Fulton, Frank Moran, Gunboat Smith, Jim Flynn, Arthur Pelkey, Battling Levinsky, Al Norton, Bob Devere, Tony Ross, Joe Bonds, Andre Anderson, and Mike Schreck. Such significant victories showed that the huge Morris was a dangerous man and a threat to the world's best. In 1913, 234 ¼-pound Morris lost a 10-round no decision to 235 ¾-pound Jess Willard in what was mostly a dull wrestling match.[271]

Morris wanted to blot out the memory of the semi-recent Fred Fulton fiasco, in which he was disqualified for excessive fouling (head butts). He admitted to fighting hard and rough, but claimed that Fulton was equally so. He said Fulton was responsible for the rap in the mouth sustained by the referee, which was deserved. He let Billy Miske outpoint him the following week, for fear of being accused of using rough tactics.[272]

---

[271] Carl Morris's record included: 1910 KO3 Marvin Hart; 1911 KO6 Mike Schreck and LND10 Jim Flynn; 1912 LKOby6 Luther McCarty (Morris's only stoppage loss); 1913 LDQ5 Gunboat Smith and LND10 Jess Willard; 1914 WDQ6 Fred Fulton, WDQ9 Jim Flynn, KO6 Fred Fulton, and W10 Jim Flynn; 1915 W10 Al Norton, LND10 Jim Coffey, TKO8 Bob Devere, and TKO4 Tony Ross; 1916 TKO4 Arthur Pelkey, W10 Gunboat Smith, and W15 Battling Levinsky; 1917 W8 Joe Bonds, WDQ5 Fred Fulton, KO3 Andre Anderson (who went 10 with Dempsey), LND10 Jim Coffey, WND10 Frank Moran, LDQ6 Fred Fulton, LND10 Billy Miske, and TKO3 Joe Bonds (who went 10 with Dempsey).
[272] *San Francisco Examiner*, October 21, 1917.

On October 22, 1917, former world middleweight, heavyweight, and light-heavyweight champion Bob Fitzsimmons died, after battling pneumonia for five days. He was 54 years old.[273]

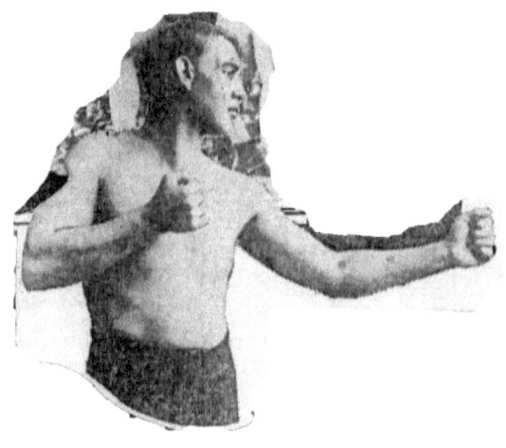

Although Carl Morris had the reputation for being a rough and foul fighter, when the locals saw him train, they were surprised. He wasn't at all the wild man he was made out to be. He made a favorable impression.

Morris said no one could beat Willard over 10 or 20 rounds, including Fulton, who was fast and clever, but had no heart. Speaking about himself, Morris admitted that he wasn't too fast. Kidding, he said, "There are two kinds of boxers, slow, and slower. I'm just below the second division." However, if he was put in the ring with anyone, and allowed to stay in there long enough, "I'll walk out, and the other fellow will be helped out." Morris said he had enlisted in the military when he was 14 years old, and was so big they never bothered to question him about his age. Despite his reputation as a foul fighter, "I've been disqualified just twice for fouling." He disagreed that he fouled Gunboat Smith (low blows). Against Fulton, "I still believe that the referee acted as he did because he was hit in the jaw with a wild swing. The worst part of it is that I wasn't the guy who hit him, the more's the pity." He said he did not head butt intentionally. Warren Brown said the "man mountain" Carlo was likeable, not a boaster or knocker, and had a sense of humor.

The Morris-Dempsey fight was supposed to happen on the 26th, but it was delayed for one week. Kearns said Morris was afraid of Dempsey, just like everyone else, and wanted more time to train and bolster his courage.[274]

Dempsey trained at Wixson's in Emeryville, sparring with former foe Al Norton (who lost a 1915 10-round decision to Morris) and Kid George.[275]

Some claimed that Morris and Dempsey were friends, and were going to box to a draw, but there was nothing to substantiate such a charge. Morris said he once had met Dempsey in Kansas City and shook his hand, but that was it. He had no dealings with him. He met him again recently in San Francisco and they just passed the time of day. However, some thought that they were too chummy, which made folks think there was an arrangement. Morris said there was no foundation for such a belief, because a victory over Dempsey could put him in line for a title shot with Willard.[276]

---

[273] *San Francisco Examiner*, October 22, 1917.
[274] *San Francisco Chronicle, Bulletin,* October 23, 1917.
[275] *San Francisco Call and Post*, October 25, 1917.
[276] *San Francisco Chronicle*, October 25, 1917; *San Francisco Examiner*, October 26, 1917.

On October 25 at the Parkside Club, Morris sparred 3 fast rounds with local Joe Welch. A large crowd was on hand, and Morris surprised them with his knowledge of the game's fine points, stepping around well. He was not a lumbering, hit-at-anything type, and banished the idea that he was nothing but a mauler. "If his work in the gymnasium is to be taken as a criterion of what he can do in actual combat, Jack Dempsey…is in for the hardest battle of his career."

An upset Morris got in sportswriter Marion Salazar's face and prodded him multiple times with his index finger, informing him that he and Dempsey were not chums or friends, and he did not appreciate the insinuation or suggestion of such by local reporters.

Salazar said either they would give the best they had or they would be marched straight from the ring to the jail for faking. Both men strenuously denied that they would fake. Still, many believed that he and Dempsey had more than just a speaking acquaintance. Regardless, "Morris is rather leary about this jail business." Such might motivate him to fight on the level, even if there was any funny business.

Dempsey told Salazar that he and Morris were not friends, and never had seen each other except in street clothes. "I admit that I have done some things that were not exactly right, but for the last several months I've been going straight," said Dempsey. Salazar disagreed. "Let's see; has it been several months since Jack's little affair with Bob McAllister?" What "things" had Jack done that were "not exactly right," prior to "going straight"?

Many years later, Dempsey admitted that he had sparred with Morris for a few days back in late 1916. But they were not friends. In fact, Dempsey said he did not particularly like Carl.

Morris was rough with his sparring partners, but not foul. On October 27, Morris hit colored "Pinkey" Lewis a wallop in the stomach which caused him to roll his eyes and say, "Oh, Lawd!" On October 28, Morris knocked out Charley Miller in the 1st round with a short right to the chin.[277]

Morris was looking good in his gym sparring, boxing several men one after another. He demonstrated that he could cover up and move away, doing some lively stepping, and be genuinely clever when such was required. He quickly was gaining admirers. If he could box as well in the fight as he did in the gym, a great contest could be expected. The *Examiner* often called Morris "Carlo" and Dempsey the "submarine destroyer."

Dempsey's ability was well known to local fans. "He appears a champion in the making." A decisive victory could give him a "just claim to a chance at Jess Willard and the championship title."[278]

Marion Salazar said the reason he suspected there might be or have been an agreement between the fighters was that he received a letter from someone who ought to know saying that Morris and Dempsey had been gym chums in Kansas City, and Morris had asked Dempsey to fix things so they could box a draw at Salt Lake. All parties involved denied it.

---

[277] *San Francisco Call and Post*, October 26, 29, 1917.
[278] *San Francisco Examiner*, October 28, 29, 1917; *San Francisco Call and Post*, October 30, 1917.

Salazar had shown the letter to Dan O'Brien, San Francisco captain of police, who had charge of boxing there. O'Brien said he thought Dempsey had "pulled" in a fight with Meehan, meaning he was fighting under wraps, or faking, not giving it his best. He said he would watch the Dempsey-Morris contest, and if they tried to bunk the public he would see to it that they spent time in the county jail.[279]

The *Bulletin* said Dempsey was in the best shape of his career, and looked like a champion in the gymnasium. He would give the lumbering giant Sapulpa engineer the time of his life. True, he was boxing only with "mediocre boxers" like Kid George and Al Norton, "but the way he mauls them around gives the fans a good line on his ability. He could have stowed either away at any time after the trainer gave the word 'go' had he so desired." Marty Farrell absolutely refused to don the gloves with him, saying he was much too rough and hard-punching. Jack had been training for two or three weeks, and allegedly weighed around 195 or 200 pounds.

Jack's sparring partner and former foe Al Norton predicted that Dempsey would defeat Morris. "I fought this fellow Morris on February 1, 1915, back in Kansas City. The bout lasted ten rounds and I gave him a good argument. ... My last bout with Dempsey...lasted but half a round, Dempsey stopping me. And, mind you, he has only been at the game a short time and is practically a youngster yet." However, Morris had stopped Anderson and Bonds, who had gone the distance with Dempsey.[280]

While watching Dempsey train, "Handsome" Jack Kearns said to Warren Brown, "Look at him, will you? Greater than Corbett! More wonderful than Fitz! A thousand times more rugged than Jeff at his best! Why, Dempsey is a marvel! He's the wonder of the twentieth century!" Kearns certainly was the talking champion. Continuing, he said, "When he finishes up with Morris, Fulton'll be a joke for him." Kearns said Dempsey's right was a piledriver, and his left, "Wow!" "Didya see him step inside that one?" "It wouldn't surprise me any day to learn that Jess Willard has left the country. Right now I feel sorry for Carl Morris. The poor chap came a long way to get what Jack will give him next Friday evening. ... Dempsey is such a wonderful ring performer that some day Carl will be glad to tell people he once boxed with him."

Apparently, sparring partner Pinky Lewis was the first black man that Morris ever had boxed. Previously, Morris had drawn the color line even in training. The lack of sparring partners made it necessary to cross the line.

Spider Kelly, considered the world's greatest ring second, was working with Dempsey. The Spider said, "This fellow Morris is a strong hitter and the type that keeps fighting all the time. Such a man is made to order for Dempsey. With his speed and snappy left hand Jack should be able to peck Carl to ribbons."[281]

---

[279] *San Francisco Call and Post*, October 30, 1917.
[280] *San Francisco Bulletin*, October 30, 1917; *San Francisco Examiner*, October 31, 1917.
[281] *San Francisco Call and Post, San Francisco Bulletin*, October 31, 1917.

The police forbade the fighters from wearing hand bandages of any sort, including tape bandages. However, some said Kearns had tricky ways, and did not always follow the rules. The theory was that Dempsey would appear with his hands exposed, and the tape would be concealed beneath a towel. After the gloves were chosen, the ready-made hand-tapes would be inserted into the gloves, and then Dempsey could slide his hands into them. Everyone knew that a fighter with tape bandages could hit a lot harder than one without. However, Morris's manager said he would be watching out for any such tricks. He was willing to allow soft surgical bandages though. They just wanted it to be fair; with both using the same thing.[282]

The *Call and Post* said not since the days of 20-round fights had heavyweights attracted so much attention in San Francisco. Such a large attendance was expected that the promoters installed a new bleacher seating section at the Dreamland Rink.

CARL MORRIS, heavy - weight, who is to meet Jack Dempsey tonight in a four-round bout.

Morris, who had been training hard, said, "I have always wanted to perform before the San Francisco public, and now that I have been granted the opportunity I will give them the best that is in me. I have no fear of the result." He also said, "I am ready. No fancy, long-range boxing for me. I tear in and keep going. Look for Dempsey to fall."

Dempsey was just as confident. "I realize that Morris is a big, strong fellow, but I am certain my speed and superior boxing knowledge will offset his punch and ruggedness and that I will be returned the winner." Jack also was quoted as saying, "Where is Jess Willard living? I will want to know after laying Carlo low. You will see me champion of the world. Jack Kearns is too handsome a man not to have a great fighter." Kearns said that after Dempsey beat Morris, they would be chasing after Fulton and Willard.

The *San Francisco Examiner* said Morris was weighing about 230 pounds, so he would have a 35-pound weight advantage (or more). Carlo was trained to the minute. An exciting fight was anticipated.[283]

The day of the fight, the *San Francisco Chronicle* said Morris was easy to hit, but very rough and tough, known for being a foul fighter, willing to butt or do anything to win.

> Now, Dempsey isn't any fiver. He is some boxer, can punish his opponent, and what is more, can stand a punch now and then. For a

---

[282] *San Francisco Chronicle*, November 1, 1917.
[283] *San Francisco Call and Post*, November 1, 1917; *San Francisco Examiner*, November 1, 2, 1917.

big fellow Dempsey is remarkably fast. He proved in the Gunboat Smith fight that he can weather a hard punch and come back to win. He's going to be a tough nut to crack this night at Dreamland Rink, and when Morris finishes up he will know he's been in something of a session.

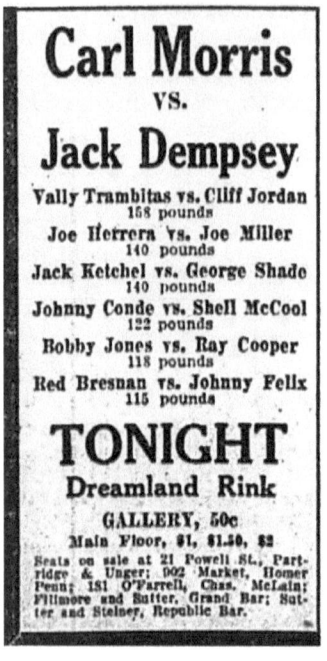

Ticket purchasers would be hit with a 10% war tax, so $2 tickets would cost $2.20, $1 tickets $1.10, $1.50 would go to $1.65, and the 50-cent tickets would be 55 cents. All boxing shows to follow would be taxed in the same manner.[284]

The *Call and Post* said the fans would learn just how good a boxer Jack Dempsey really was. The "Oklahoma Giant" was a real acid test. "Morris in his preparatory work has shown himself to be a fighter of the rip-tearing sort, the kind that is happiest when the fighting is hottest." "Dempsey appears a future champion. He has speed, cleverness and a great left hook, and if he can decisively defeat Morris tonight all fandom must put on him the stamp of approval." Alex Greggains would advise Morris, while Spider Kelly would work with Dempsey.

Marion Salazar said Morris would get his chance either to make or kill himself in San Francisco. "Morris in his workouts has performed like a fighter – there is no question as to that." It remained to be seen whether he would perform as well in the actual fight. Carl was known as a foul fighter who often leaned on his opponent and stalled. Dempsey was strongly suspected of faking in several bouts. If either one faked in this fight, it could spell doom for their careers, as well as jail.

Warren W. Brown said the boxing game and the fighters were on trial. It was the most talked of match since the game came back. This writer said Morris had engaged in over 90 fights. Except for one 1912 knockout loss early in his career, a LKOby6 to Luther McCarty, Morris had finished every fight on his feet. He essentially was a fighter, not a boxer. Morris said, "If Dempsey comes to me I'll stop him, and if he should happen to wallop me he can go out and tell the world he's been in a battle."[285]

On Friday November 2, 1917 at the Dreamland Rink in San Francisco, Jack Dempsey fought a scheduled 4-round bout against Carl Morris. There was a good-sized crowd. One said it was the largest audience at Dreamland since the game "came back." Yet, Promoter Schuler announced that the

---

[284] *San Francisco Chronicle, San Francisco Examiner*, November 2, 1917.
[285] *San Francisco Call and Post, San Francisco Bulletin*, November 2, 1917.

receipts were only $2,200, which seemed a bit low in view of the apparently large crowd. The 10% war tax was $220.[286] Dempsey was a 10 to 6 favorite.

The 1st round mostly was a feel-out. Dempsey was very cautious, some saying timid, ascertaining how best to fight his huge 6'4" 230-pound foe, who dwarfed him by comparison. He stayed away, apparently afraid of the bulk. Morris led and countered a bit, and grabbed and uppercut. There was a fair amount of clinching and wrestling by both. Morris did more of the leading, landing some uppercuts.

In the 2nd round, Dempsey bounced from his corner and surprised Morris, slamming in good stiff rights and left hooks, then moving away, with Morris following him and taking it. Dempsey worked around Morris as a cooper does around a barrel, peppering constantly with right and left jabs. Morris floundered after him, getting outboxed.

In the 3rd round, Dempsey connected with both hands to the head and body, violently rocking Carlo aplenty. When Morris reeled a bit, some thought it meant he was about to fall and bring down the building. Dempsey rocked Morris with a right cross to the head and stiff stomach punches. Carl was hanging on often, and accomplished nothing.

In the 4th round, Dempsey, now full of confidence, stepped around his man and measured him, sending in lefts and rights that confused and bewildered Morris. He kept pounding on Carlo and moving around. The crowd lustily called upon Dempsey to finish him off. At the bell, Morris went to his corner badly mussed up.

Referee Toby Irwin awarded Dempsey the clear 4-round decision. Morris simply smiled. Dempsey had shown his class, handling Morris like a punching bag throughout.

The *Examiner* believed if the fight had been longer, Morris eventually would have been knocked out, perhaps in a couple more rounds.

The *Chronicle* said had Dempsey been a bit faster and had more experience, he could have won by knockout.

The *Examiner*'s Fred A. Purner harshly called Morris a big joke who made a sorry showing. Dempsey easily won the decision. Morris lumbered around, and when he did extend his massive arms it was to hold, cuff and paw. Dempsey, small in comparison to his bulky 230-pound opponent, found no difficulty whatsoever in peppering in rights and lefts during the last two rounds, and had Carlo rocking to and fro, such that the crowd believed a knockout was imminent.

Only in the 1st round did Morris show even a semblance of boxing skill. But mostly he grabbed and pawed around. He had a little uppercut that landed on occasion, but that was all. When Dempsey broke away from his affectionate but uncomfortable rival, Morris was all at sea, with the compass apparently lost. Purner harshly said the only reason Morris did not look so bad in the 1st round was because Dempsey took his time, ascertaining just

---

[286] Sometimes promoters reported lower numbers so as to minimize their tax bill, or, if the fighters were working on percentage, the amount they would have to pay them.

how big a joke he really was. It was surprising that a fellow who had called for so much attention, Morris, could be so woefully lacking in boxing skill.

Likewise, the *Chronicle* cruelly said Morris could not fight a lick, was a joke, knew nothing about boxing, and was the worst fighter ever seen. He depended upon his height and weight to win fights, but his natural advantages availed him nothing against Dempsey, who might have lost the 1st round as a result of his caution or stage fright, but Jack clearly won the 2nd through 4th rounds. Morris could neither box nor punch. He simply depended upon getting close in, with the idea of tiring out his man with his weight. His method did not work on Dempsey, who stood away and worked around Morris. Carlo was all at sea, floundering through the last three rounds in tiresome style. He was hissed as he left the ring. He did not foul, but he didn't fight either.

The *San Francisco Bulletin's* Warren W. Brown said Morris left his speed in the gym, and Dempsey had little trouble taking the decision, for he was too fast for Morris, who tried, but didn't get anywhere. Morris could not solve Dempsey. Still, he fought cleanly and did his best. Unlike Gunboat Smith, Morris never ran away.

Dempsey opened up in rather timid fashion, and didn't start making life miserable for Morris until the 2nd round. He came along faster and faster as the fight progressed, and had a large lead at the end. Still, "the main event was not calculated to drive anybody insane from the excitement."

The *Oakland Tribune* said the elephantine Oklahoman was an even bigger disappointment than expected. Dempsey had killed off another easterner who came west. Morris tried to use his weight by hanging on and leaning in. About all he did was hug up to Dempsey and try to shoot in an occasional uppercut that rarely landed, and there was not much on the blows he did land.

After Dempsey used the 1st round to become accustomed to Morris and his elephant tactics, from the 2nd round on, Dempsey stood away and poked in about everything that he wanted. He showed improvement over his former fights, and demonstrated that in time there may be something to Jack Kearns' claims that Dempsey is as good as any of the boys who think they have a right to meet Jess Willard. "But just at present Dempsey is a bit too inexperienced to go aiming too high." It was laughable that just a short time ago Morris was touting himself as the logical man to meet Willard. He looked like a fourth-rater.

The *Oakland Enquirer's* Bob Shand said that as a boxer, Morris was worse than Willard. Shand's harsh report had a comical tone. Morris laid all over the 40-pounds-lighter Dempsey, but had not hit him yet. Morris landed two blows in the entire fight, and Referee Toby Irwin stopped both of them. The first punch caught Irwin on the nose, and the second between the waist and the knees. "While Morris was aiming at Dempsey and hitting Irwin, Kearns' fighter was stepping around the huge hulk in front of him and landing repeatedly with left hooks to the head. It was an awful fight." Morris' boxing skills and footwork were criticized, and he was said to be as graceful as a sea-sick elephant. He could not hit hard enough to hurt even the referee, and was the greatest lean-on guy in the world. His plan was to lay on top of Dempsey, force him to the ropes, and then try to cut his back with the hempen strands. It got him nothing. "You must hit the other fellow at least a couple of times to win a fight hereabouts, and Morris only won a decision over Referee Irwin."

Marion Salazar called Morris the poorest scrapper he had seen in a long time. He was 226 pounds of beef going against a 195-pound man, and not only did Morris lose the decision, but had the fight been 10 or even 6 rounds, he would have been knocked out. "One thing can be said for Morris. He tried to fight." He did the best he could, but didn't seem to know what to do.

> He was just like a big Newfoundland dog pitted against a bull terrier. When he stood away and tried to box, Dempsey cracked him on the chin, and cracked him hard, and when he didn't crack him on the chin Dempsey sank his gloves into the stomach, so Carl had to do something to protect himself, and what he did was just what any dub fighter does when punches are coming at him too fast – he ran in and hugged.

For Morris, the fight was one hug after another.

Whatever damage Morris did was in the clinches. He half-struck, half-scraped Dempsey's face with his wrist and back of his glove. Most of it was done in the 1st round and early part of the 2nd, before Dempsey had overcome his nervousness. Thereafter, Morris mostly wrestled. "Harry Wills, when he was fighting in San Francisco, would have put him out in a round or two."[287]

Jack Kearns noted that Gunboat Smith once had defeated Willard, and Carl Morris went 10 rounds with Willard in a slow, dull contest. By comparison, Dempsey had done better than Willard in his performances against these same men. Kearns continued touting his man.

Morris was surprised by the fact that Dempsey had hit and moved. He had not expected that style. His ring adviser, Alex Greggains, said Carl had to follow Jack, which always makes a big fellow look bad. Continuing, Morris said, "I am not a four-round fighter. It takes longer than that to feel out a man." He said he had misjudged Dempsey, and would improve in a longer rematch.

The *Bulletin* subsequently reported that Dempsey could have asked for a postponement of the fight, for during the close of his training, he had an attack of ptomaine (food) poisoning, and after that he injured his hand, so he really wasn't at his best. Yet, he performed quite well.

The *Bulletin's* Leon Meyer said Dempsey was every bit as entitled to consideration as a title challenger as any of the eastern heavyweights. If he was turned loose in the East, he might halt the championship aspirations of

---

[287] *San Francisco Examiner, San Francisco Chronicle, San Francisco Call and Post, San Francisco Bulletin, Oakland Tribune, Oakland Enquirer, Salt Lake Telegram,* November 3, 1917.

aspiring contenders like Fred Fulton, Bill Brennan, Billy Miske, and black Kid Norfolk of Panama. Interestingly, Norfolk's manager had announced that his fighter was drawing the color line, and would box only whites, not blacks like Langford, Jeannette, or Wills. There were so many white heavyweights that he did not need to box blacks. (However, that edict did not hold for long, and Norfolk fought other black fighters too.)[288]

Marion Salazar said the Morris fight proved that there were no good heavyweights in the East. Most of the eastern writers had seen dub heavyweights for so long that they had forgotten what a real fighter is. They had boosted and touted Morris as one of the best in the business. His performance made Salazar wonder whether Fred Fulton might be overrated too. What was most remarkable was the difference between Morris's performances in the gym versus in the fight. "The Tulsan worked like a champion in the gymnasium."

Perhaps Dempsey's ability had something to do with Morris' performance. The local press, even Salazar, finally was embracing the idea that 22-year-old Dempsey might be something special.

> This young chap, Jack Dempsey, has a better chance of winning the world's heavyweight championship than most persons think. Dempsey weighs almost 200 pounds, is just big enough not to be too big, and he has a punch, weight, speed, ability to take a punch; he has, in fact, everything a champion needs, including, apparently, deep remorse for whatever misdeeds he may have been guilty of in the period of his early pugilistic career. Dempsey can hit too hard and too accurately for any fighter smaller than he. And we've already seen what he can do with a big beef like Carl Morris. Fred Winsor may yet live to regret, much more than he does now, the move that separated him and Dempsey and put the latter in the hands of Jack Kearns.[289]

Famous referee Jack Welch/Welsh urged careful handling of Dempsey, telling Kearns to go slow and take his time in matching him with Willard, who was too big for him, and much better than folks realized. Welch didn't want to see him rushed in too fast, without the proper experience. Many a good fighter had been ruined by such methods.

> Dempsey has the makings of a good man if he is properly handled. But for the present Kearns should forget about wanting to meet Willard. The champion is too big and rangy for the present crop of heavyweights. Jess is underrated. While I was refereeing the Johnson-Willard bout in Havana the big fellow showed me that he possesses a lot of class, and if he does not go back too fast he will be the title-holder for some little time to come.
>
> What Dempsey needs is to learn how to use his left hand better. He has everything – speed, punching power and the physique – but he

---

[288] *San Francisco Examiner, San Francisco Chronicle, San Francisco Bulletin*, November 4, 1917.
[289] *San Francisco Call and Post*, November 5, 1917.

lacks confidence. If he could learn to hook better with his left and shoot out the straight left harder he would be a 50 per cent more proficient fighter. He knows how to handle his right, and in course of time I look for him to develop into a champion, but Kearns should go slow with him. Let him show what really poor excuses of fighters the Carl Morrises are, and when he improves, as he figures, then will be the time to go after Willard.[290]

Dempsey left town to head back to Salt Lake City to visit his mother, who was ill.[291]

By the end of 1917, Jack Dempsey had been a professional for three years. Although early 1917 had mixed results, perhaps leaving him with some career doubts, nevertheless, he had obtained quality experience against far more experienced veterans, and became a fan favorite. Since his partnership with Jack Kearns began, Dempsey had gone 6-0-2 and had won the two biggest fights of his life, quickly catapulting his career and changing its trajectory. He appears to have buckled down, was training harder, living more cleanly, taking his career more seriously, and gaining confidence. His overall known/confirmed record to that point was 29-3-9, with 18 KOs.

The *Chicago Defender*'s Henry Davis said that since the U. S. government had been recognizing boxing as having value, the game was being treated better. This likely was a result of the war.

On November 5, 1917, in the case of *Buchanan v. Warley*, 245 U.S. 60 (1917), the United States Supreme Court held that a Louisville, Kentucky city ordinance prohibiting the sale of real property to blacks in white-majority neighborhoods or building areas and vice versa violated the 14th Amendment's protections for freedom of contract.

However, for years to come, many folks either via custom or via racial covenants in their deeds continued to agree not to sell property to blacks. The court simply held that the city itself could not prohibit such transactions. Still, it was the first civil rights victory in the Supreme Court in a very long time. The general rule, that state laws mandating separation of races where separate but equal accommodations existed, decided in the 1896 case of *Plessy v. Ferguson*, still remained the law of the land. However, this was one rare exception, and gave civil rights advocates a glimmer of hope.[292]

*Chicago Defender*, January 5, 1918

---

[290] *San Francisco Examiner*, November 6, 1917.
[291] *San Francisco Examiner*, November 7, 1917.
[292] *Chicago Defender*, December 29, 1917.

CHAPTER 11

# Nationally Recognized Contender

Following Jack Dempsey's two biggest victories, against recognized world-class fighters Gunboat Smith and Carl Morris, Jack Kearns planned to take Dempsey east to the Midwest, East Coast, and the South in 1918, letting the rest of the country see him, with the hopes of an eventual match with Fred Fulton, and then to force a Willard fight. Having him travel around and fight folks all over the country would help market him, gain him further experience, and develop real momentum for a title challenge.[293]

The *Examiner* reported/claimed that before the John Lester Johnson fight, someone handed Dempsey a telegram containing news of the death of his brother (which turned out not to be true), and the best he could do was to "shade the shifty, plunging Lester."

John the Barber took him on, fed him, bought him clothes and jewels, but then Jack disappeared. Subsequently he lost to Flynn, and folks lost interest in him. He was not really heard from again on a national level until he beat Gunboat Smith, which put his name back on the map.[294]

On November 27, 1917 in Minneapolis, Minnesota, Fred Fulton stopped Gunboat Smith in the 7th round.[295]

In December, Harry Smith of the *San Francisco Chronicle* said Dempsey wanted to work his way up the fistic ladder and fight Fulton, for beating him was the best way to force a fight with Willard. Jack was big, but not too big or bulky. There were many huge heavyweights, but they mostly relied on their bulk. Dempsey was big enough to hold his own with big ones, but not so large that he was lacking in speed.[296]

Jack Kearns said that given Dempsey's victories over Gunboat Smith and Charlie Miller, both of whom had done better with Willard, he believed that Dempsey was better than the champ. Jack Welsh (who refereed Johnson-Willard), Jim Coffroth, Eddie Graney, and Spider Kelly all said 22-year-old Dempsey had a good chance to defeat Willard.[297]

Dempsey and Kearns were headed to the Midwest for fights in that region, and to chase after, challenge, and talk business with Willard, who primarily was a circus performer, allegedly weighing in the neighborhood of 300 pounds. Jess only boxed in short exhibitions.

---

[293] *Salt Lake Telegram*, November 9, 1917.
[294] *San Francisco Examiner*, November 10, 1917
[295] *Minneapolis Tribune, Oakland Tribune*, November 28, 1917. No weights were taken or announced, but estimates were 220 Fulton vs. 185-187 Smith.
[296] *San Francisco Chronicle*, December 21, 1917.
[297] *La Crosse Tribune*, January 12, 1918. It was noted that Dempsey was married.

While in Chicago, Willard suggested an elimination bout between Dempsey and Fulton for the right to fight him.[298]

The *Milwaukee Sentinel* said Willard had only Fulton to dodge, for the big champion would have an easy time beating all others. The Midwest was not yet familiar with Dempsey.[299]

Kearns' latest sensation was scheduled to fight Homer Smith in Racine, Wisconsin, about 25 miles south of Milwaukee, on January 25.

22-year-old Homer Smith was a "young giant" from Benton Harbor, Michigan. He had a 19-5-2 record, which included: 1916 LND6 Willie Meehan, KO2 Mike Schreck, LND6 Bill Brennan, WTKO4 Sandy Ferguson, and LTKOby7 Tom Cowler (his only stoppage loss); and 1917 WND10 Terry Keller and LND10 Bill Brennan.

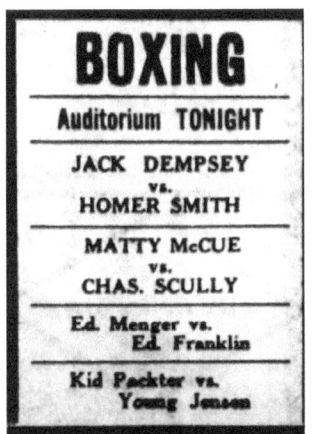

The *Post-Crescent*, based in Appleton, Wisconsin, said Dempsey was refreshing. He was willing to fight anyone in his path to prove he deserved a chance at Willard, including top fighters like Fred Fulton or Bill Brennan.[300]

Eddie Geiger of the *Milwaukee Free Press* reported that Dempsey might get a try at the heavyweight title. In Chicago, Willard had promised him a match if he could satisfy the general public that he was worthy of a clash. Merely mentioning Dempsey put a stamp of interest upon him. How good he was would be demonstrated against Homer Smith. "Smith isn't a Jess Willard, but he is a giant in size, and a fitting opponent for a man like Dempsey who will be on trial."[301]

The local *Racine Journal Times* described both boys as young, hard, and fast. Both fighters claimed that they would win by knockout. Smith had fought the hard-punching Bill Brennan at a fast clip throughout the entire fight. Some later said Smith had never before been dropped. He had been training with Sam Langford.

Willard's manager would be on hand to look them over.[302]

On Friday January 25, 1918 at the Lakeside Auditorium in Racine, Wisconsin, in his first Midwest bout, coast idol Jack Dempsey fought Benton Harbor giant Homer Smith in a scheduled 10-round contest. Johnny Wagner's club staged the bouts.

At the bell, both came out of their corners looking fit. Smith poked across a long blow that slapped Dempsey on the nose. It aroused Dempsey, and he swung a hard one that Smith tried to escape but didn't, and he

---

[298] *Post-Crescent*, January 16, 1918.
[299] *Milwaukee Sentinel*, January 20, 1918.
[300] *Post-Crescent*, January 18, 22, 1918; *La Crosse Tribune*, January 23, 1918; *Milwaukee Journal*, January 25, 1918; Boxrec.com.
[301] *Milwaukee Free Press*, Friday January 25, 1918. Smith generally reportedly weighed 190-200 pounds, height unknown, so it is unclear why they called him a giant.
[302] *Racine Journal Times*, January 25, 1918.

flopped to the floor. Smith crawled back up to his feet at eight. Dempsey promptly put him back on the mat for the second time. Homer rose at nine, but Referee Harry Stout stepped in and prevented a wholesale slaughter, giving the fight to Dempsey via 1st round technical knockout. There had been only one minute fifteen seconds of fighting.

The local *Racine Journal-News* said Dempsey had all the ear-marks of a real fighter, and appeared to be a likely contender for Willard's crown. He looked a little light for big company, yet was only 22 and filling out rapidly. The way he handled Smith left no doubt in the minds of observers as to his ability. Dempsey's first appearance in the Midwest had been impressive.

The promoter said he would try to match him with Bill Brennan, who had the world's kayo record. They were well-matched physically, and both were clever and hard-hitting mixers with fast feet. Dempsey showed he had real kick in both hands, so it would be some fight.[303]

The semi-local *Milwaukee Sentinel* and *Milwaukee Free Press* reported that Dempsey decked Smith three times before Referee Stout said that was enough. Chet Koeppel timed the fight at one minute fifty-five seconds.[304]

Billy Birch, writing for the *Chicago Herald*, said Smith never even got acquainted with his foe. He ran into a couple of terrific wallops that sprawled him on the mat before the 1st round was half over.

The *Streator Times* said Dempsey had to be given credit for knocking out Homer Smith, who never before had been knocked off his feet, and several top heavyweights, including the hard-punching Bill Brennan (twice), had undertaken the job to do it and failed.[305]

Ed Smith, sporting editor for the *Chicago American*, also saw Dempsey knock out Homer Smith. This was his impression:

> Dempsey is something new and fresh and different in heavyweights. He is an overgrown middleweight with the speed of a Ketchel, the skill of a Gans and the wallop of a Jeffries. He is as loose as a busted sack of oats. There is nothing tied up about him. He lets fly from the jump, there is aim and direction to his work and effectiveness in the extreme. No wonder Jack Kearns wouldn't trade him for Fred Fulton. Verily this will be bad news for the Fultons and the Brennans and the rest of them. Dempsey weighed 194 and Smith 190 ½ pounds.[306]

Kearns next scheduled Dempsey to face Carl Morris in a 10-round rematch at Charley Murray's Queensberry club in Buffalo, New York on February 4, just ten days after the Homer Smith fight. Morris had insisted that he would do better in a rematch, with more rounds, and Easterners wanted to see for themselves whether Dempsey really was better than Morris, whom they highly regarded.[307]

---

[303] *Racine Journal-News, Eau Claire Leader-Telegram, Milwaukee Journal*, January 26, 1918.
[304] *Milwaukee Sentinel, Milwaukee Free Press*, January 26, 1918.
[305] *Chicago Herald*, January 26, 1918; *Streator Times*, February 11, 1918.
[306] *Rochester Democrat and Chronicle*, February 1, 1918.
[307] *Racine Journal News*, January 29, 1918.

Dempsey was not one of the elephantine class of boxers of late. He was not a big man, but instead of being big, slow moving, or clumsy, he was quick like Corbett, but husky enough to take on big men, minus unnecessary bulk. There was a mistaken belief that a boxer capable of licking Willard, Morris, or Fulton had to be a huge man. This writer noted that Billy Miske had outpointed both Morris and Gunboat Smith. A very good little man often walloped a fairly good big man.

Kearns was hoping to match Dempsey with Willard on July 4, 1918. Some Wyoming oil men allegedly were offering a $100,000 purse.

The boxing world had its eyes on the Dempsey-Morris bout, because both wanted a shot at the title.

The *New York Tribune* claimed that Dempsey had been promised a match with Willard if he did not run into a sleep punch in the next few months. For most fighters that would mean steering clear of tests and only taking on second- and third-raters. Not so with Dempsey. He was matched with Morris, who was a tough test.[308]

Ed Gunboat Smith, who had fought both, said Morris was much bigger, but Dempsey was much faster and cleverer.

Morris had been sparring in New York with Joe Jeannette. Carl was called the Giant Sapulpa engineer, being from Sapulpa, Oklahoma.

Dempsey had been training in Chicago, and even was making money in a theatrical engagement at the Englewood Theatre, training before audiences and sparring 4 rounds with former opponent Andre Anderson.[309]

Kearns, who was calling Dempsey the greatest heavyweight sensation seen in the last 15 years, was so confident that he already matched Dempsey for a rematch with Jim Flynn, the Pueblo fireman, to be held at Fort Sheridan, Illinois on February 14. Dempsey wanted to avenge his only knockout loss.

On February 2, 1918 in Abington, Massachusetts, former world heavyweight champion John L. Sullivan died of heart failure at age 59. James J. Corbett said, "In his day he could have bested any man. Even though I won the championship from John L. I could never have won nor no man could have won had I faced him in his prime."[310]

Local Buffalo fans were impressed with Carl Morris's appearance, staring and gasping in awe and wonderment at the 6'4" 220-pound man who

---

[308] *Buffalo Commercial, New York Tribune*, February 1, 1918.
[309] *Buffalo Commercial, Buffalo Evening News, Middletown Times-Press*, February 2, 1918
[310] *Rochester Democrat and Chronicle, Buffalo Courier*, February 3, 1918.

looked trim and fit. Morris sparred 6 rounds with black heavyweight Tom Goodman, showing good footwork and lots of hand speed.[311]

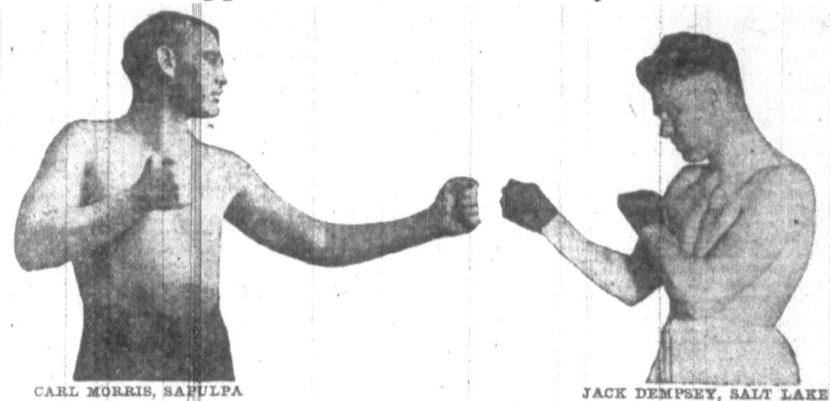

CARL MORRIS, SAPULPA                    JACK DEMPSEY, SALT LAKE

The *Buffalo Courier* said the 6'6" Morris was impressive in every way. "We'll say this for Morris. He's as big and strong as any man that ever stepped into the ring and those who say he doesn't know much about boxing are uninformed or misinformed. He knows enough to be champion."

Morris said he felt good enough to beat Willard. "I don't imagine I'm going to have any cinch with this fellow Dempsey Monday night, for I have fought him before and I know how he's gaited." Morris admitted that Dempsey beat him last time, but didn't think he could do it in a long fight:

> He beat me in every round of the four and he beat me worse in the fourth than he did in the first. I'll give him that. I never expected to see such speed, but he had that four-round thing down pat. Lord, he came at me with all cylinders working and he pecked me and licked me to a fare-thee-well. He didn't exactly hurt me, and when I got ready to start the bout was over. Oh, it was great – for Dempsey, but there is a world of difference between four rounds and ten rounds. Dempsey is good, but I don't think he can last ten rounds with me in my present condition.[312]

The *Buffalo Times* called the Dempsey-Morris contest the most important ring engagement in a long time. Jack was hoping to defeat Morris decisively, so he could get a chance at Willard. Dempsey was listed as 6', 200 pounds to Morris's 6'4" 220 pounds. According to the law, those who wanted admission had to join the Queensberry Athletic Club.

Morris's sparring partner said Carl was in top condition. Morris said, "Don't let them tell you I'm a foul fighter. All I want is a fair test with this fellow and I'll be satisfied."

Dempsey was as hard as nails all over. He was a dead spit image of John L. Sullivan. He had the fighting face, the speed, and the shoulders. He was confident, but not a boaster. When someone said something about Morris

---

[311] *Buffalo Times*, February 3, 1918.
[312] *Buffalo Courier*, February 3, 1918.

being too big for him, Dempsey responded, "I like them big. Somehow or other the bigger they are the better luck I have with them." The local writer said of Dempsey, "He is as fine a tempered fellow as the old Jack and he answered all questions good naturedly."

Al Spink of the *Chicago Times* reported that Sam Langford had told him that Dempsey "was the best fighter in the world."

Jack Kearns said they were willing to fight Willard, Fulton, or any big fellow. They were not asking for guarantees either. Dempsey would weigh 190 pounds in the ring. He was a whirlwind, surprising observers with his great speed.

Allegedly, twenty Wyoming wool growers, or oilmen, who were millionaires, were willing to put up $5,000 apiece to finance a July 4 fight between Willard and Dempsey, for a $100,000 purse.[313]

Morris told the *Buffalo Commercial*,

> All I want is a fair chance. Out in 'Frisco I was a victim of the native son stuff. They let Dempsey get away with murder. I'll show the Queensberry members that I am not a foul boxer. Willard gave me that reputation for personal reasons. He doesn't want my game. Jess says I'm too rough. Well, it's a rough game. Willard makes me laugh. Willard and Fulton are a couple of frightened birds when my name is mentioned.[314]

Kearns told the *Buffalo Enquirer*, "Jack gave Morris a merry pasting in that Frisco bout, and unless Carl cuts up in the ring he'll do it again. But I think the big fellow will box it out fairly. That's all we want."[315]

Kearns said of Dempsey,

> He's fast and he can punch. He's not only a fighter but a student. He learns more rapidly than any man I've known in the game. ... He's also the easiest boxer to handle I've ever known. He wants to be fighting all the time and never asks who he is matched with or where. Willard is his goal and I honestly think he'll be the first to meet the champion.

Dempsey told the *Buffalo Courier*, "This bout means a lot to me. In fact it means a lot to both of us." Jack had tried to get a Fulton fight, but Fulton said he was looking for Willard after his upcoming contest with Moran.

> Now if I can beat Morris, I will insist on meeting the winner of the Fulton-Moran bout at New Orleans and if successful in that meeting, I will challenge Willard. ... I believe the people will be back of a man who fights his way to the chance, and that's what I expect to do. I figure Morris a tougher man than Fulton. ... Morris can take it. Many people doubt whether Fulton can.[316]

---

[313] *Buffalo Times*, February 4, 1918.
[314] *Buffalo Commercial*, February 4, 1918.
[315] *Buffalo Enquirer*, February 4, 1918.
[316] *Buffalo Courier*, February 4, 1918.

The hype and coverage surrounding this contest showed that Kearns' marketing had been working, and that the bout was meaningful to the Eastern writers, who were familiar with Morris.

On Monday February 4, 1918, at the Broadway auditorium in Buffalo, New York, under the auspices of the Queensberry Athletic Club, Jack Dempsey fought a rematch with Carl Morris in a scheduled 10-round no decision contest. Fans were anxious to see the latest ring sensation, and it was the Queensberry Club's largest crowd yet. Dempsey allegedly weighed 198 pounds to Morris's 226 pounds, though one local paper said Morris was 236 pounds.

There was a pre-fight wrangle over the bandages. Dempsey appeared with surgical adhesive tape across his knuckles. After a long dispute with Jack Curley, Dempsey agreed to substitute gauze instead. The club only permitted gauze or linen bandages. It didn't matter.

From the start of the 1st round, Dempsey showed his supremacy. He leapt from his corner like a lightweight, landing a straight left, doing so four times and following with a right to the body. Morris clinched and bore Jack to the ropes. In every clinch, Morris leaned on him, forced Jack against the ropes and pumped in dangerously low blows to the body. Some thought Morris' sheer bulk might win in the long run by wearing

Dempsey down, but as matters progressed, Dempsey brilliantly proved able to meet the lumbering head-down rushes, and straightened him up with stinging uppercuts and right and left smashes to the face, alternating with some mighty bothersome tummy punches. Dempsey electrified the crowd with his snappy, accurate blows. He damaged Carl's nose, tearing skin from it and making it bleed freely. Carl's face reddened quickly and his body showed the effects of Jack's straight left. Carl wrestled him to the ropes and bent him over with rough tactics, trying to use his weight on him.

In the 2nd round, Dempsey forced the issue, and was so eager that he was cautioned for hitting in the breakaway. Dempsey let go with all he had, and it was a wonderful assortment. He stabbed away with his left, then registered three corking rights beneath the heart, the last bringing an audible grunt from Morris. Carl ripped in a left hook and followed with a clinch, when he committed his first overt act of hitting low, which brought a warning from the referee, who pried them apart. Just before the bell rang, Dempsey slashed a right to the jaw which sounded like slapping a wall with a shingle. The punch jolted Morris down to his shoes.

In the 3rd round, Dempsey gave a wonderful exhibition of all-around fighting. He opened up with a fusillade of punishment all over that stung Morris. He danced like a lightweight, feinted Morris into a groping lead, then whirled with a shift just like Ketchel and banged both hands to the head. The left landed on the nose, and a trickle of crimson showed. The crowd cheered, and Dempsey pressed his advantage, stinging Morris with sharp, short, vicious clouts at close range, but with full power and purpose, each one hurtful. It was a splendid exhibition of clean and accurate punching. Jack never missed. Morris was unsteady and bore in wildly, but Jack stepped back and sent Carl's head up to the ceiling with a right uppercut. At the close of the round, Morris landed a couple of desperate lunges for the head and punished Jack somewhat while leaning his weight on him against the ropes.

In the 4th round, Morris came out slowly, showing signs of the wear. He crouched, showing his dislike for the body punishment. He held his long left far in advance. Jack wheeled forward and under and shot Carl's head back with a left and then hammered him twice with the right on the sore ribs. Infuriated, Carl rushed and pinned Jack in a corner, where two punches were palpably low. Morris was fighting wildly. Jack smiled and merely looked at the referee, who quickly acted by issuing a warning. Returning, Morris landed a solid left hook on the side of the head that bent Jack over and made him take a step to keep his balance. Before Morris could follow up Jack charged back in, bringing more crimson from the distressed Morris. Carl's nose had been battered ruddy, and he was losing confidence as a result of Dempsey's alert and stinging aggressiveness, carrying the fight to him.

In the 5th round, Dempsey sailed into him, bouncing his gloves off Carl's head and body. Morris tried with everything he had, but Jack checked his every punch, knocked them down in transit and in close handled Morris easily, shoving him back by the crooks of his elbows and shifting his head with every swing or hook. Morris simply couldn't find him, while Jack countered with both hands, landing frequently and solidly. In a furious mix on the ropes, Dempsey landed on both sides of the chin with right and left, powerful punches, and as Carl tottered forward to clinch, a ringing right uppercut almost ended the bout. Morris was groggy. Referee (Dick) Nugent warned Morris for hitting low. Dazed, his punches had lost all sense of direction. Carl apologized. Dempsey had him in a bad way, and it could be foreseen that it was just a matter of time before he inevitably would be knocked out. Morris virtually was beaten when he went to his corner at the bell. The crowd was cheering frantically for Dempsey.

The well-beaten Morris answered the call for the 6th round, delaying matters to take a long last drink of water even as Jack was advancing. Dempsey, full of fight, continued his whirlwind attack, determined to win quickly. He fired whipping rights to the face that jolted Carl's head back. Heavy drives to the body sapped the steam from the elephantine man. There was wicked purpose to Jack's every move. Dempsey was boxing masterfully, raining blows on the bewildered Morris, who fought back as best he could in his own clumsy way. Dempsey flashed in and out and had Morris very unsteady and confused. A right to the body was followed up by a battering to Carl's head. Morris was bleeding freely, and his mouth was open. Swiftly Dempsey flung two rights to the chin and buried his left into the tummy as Morris clinched.

Referee Nugent urged Morris to raise his blows when they were in the clinches, for they were straying low. Jack was boxing fast and furiously, just a wee bit overanxious. In another clinch, Morris received another warning for low blows.

A moment later, from a crouching position, Morris threw a low left and then a right swing from the floor, and both landed so palpably low that it brought an instant yell from the crowd. Referee Nugent leapt between them, stopped the fight and disqualified Morris, awarding the contest to Dempsey by raising his glove, an action which suited the assemblage.

Some believed Morris had fouled intentionally to get himself disqualified and save himself from a knockout, or at least to slow Dempsey down. Others did not believe the fouling was intentional, but the product of being so far gone and nearly out on his feet that he did not know where he was throwing.

The crowd booed Morris when he left. He had not won a round, though one local reporter said the 1st and 3rd were fairly even. Still, he had been outboxed and outgeneraled badly.

The *Buffalo Enquirer* reported that Morris fouled out in the 6th round when a knockout loomed. Morris took a severe drubbing from Dempsey, who showed amazing speed and was as fast as a lightweight on his feet, whipping Morris with plenty to spare. Referee Nugent warned Morris for low blows a few times. Each time Morris mumbled an apology. In the 6th round, as Morris was coming in with head and body bent forward, Dempsey whipped over a terrific left hook that caught the giant right over the left eye, splitting the skin and causing Morris to reel and stagger. The house was in a frenzy of excitement. Enraged and blinded by the blow, Morris hurled himself at Dempsey, got him on the ropes and committed additional low blow fouling. Referee Nugent, exasperated, separated them and announced the disqualification. Morris protested between bloody lips and swollen eyes, but most believed the fact that he failed to control himself after several warnings meant he was willing to be disqualified, given the beating he was taking. Dempsey had him on the verge of a knockout.

There had been 5 ½ rounds of red-hot sizzling battling, and the crowd had enjoyed it while it lasted. The impression was if Morris had not been disqualified, and Dempsey ever got him in bad shape again, Morris would hit out blindly, caring not where he landed. His acts appeared to be deliberate though.

Dempsey clearly had the speed necessary to be champion. He danced and pranced like a kid. He was not the slow, shifting, body-twisting sort who made punches miss by a hair so he could counter. He did not have the craft and tricks of old-timers. But certainly he had speed, strength, youth, and confidence. His ability to take a punch was proven, for he took a lot of stomach blows from Morris and never winced. Rather, he came back and gave Carl more than he received. Early in the fight, Morris landed a vicious right cross nearly flush, but never fazed Dempsey. Jack kept pumping away, and in the clinches was able to smother the infighting of the more experienced Morris. At long range he had Morris whipped too.

Dempsey was the fastest two-handed heavy seen in a while. He might not yet be ready for Willard, but he would be some day, unless careless. He was rather open to a right-hand punch, and would have to watch out for that. A long left jab like Fulton's might bother him, but it would not dishearten him, for he had plenty of pluck.

In another article in the same newspaper, Edward Tranter said it was the consensus of opinion that Dempsey was the best, most promising raw material of championship possibility at present before the public. He did not have the same ring experience as some of the leading contenders. He was not a seasoned veteran, nor possessor of sufficient ring-craft to be stamped as a wonder. But he possessed what the others lacked, including Morris, Fulton, and Gunboat Smith. He was exceedingly fast for a heavyweight. He was as quick as a lightweight and as nimble on his feet as a bantam. He hit a terrific punch. He had an awkward fighter before him, one who had ring generalship, hulk, strength, and superior experience battling top men for years. Despite all of that, Morris was ineffective against the swiftness of the Dempsey attack. It was the steady, unceasing, disheartening method of attack by the comet that wore Morris down. If the referee had not stopped it, the much larger Morris would have been knocked out by his younger and stronger foe. The disqualification was timely and beyond criticism.

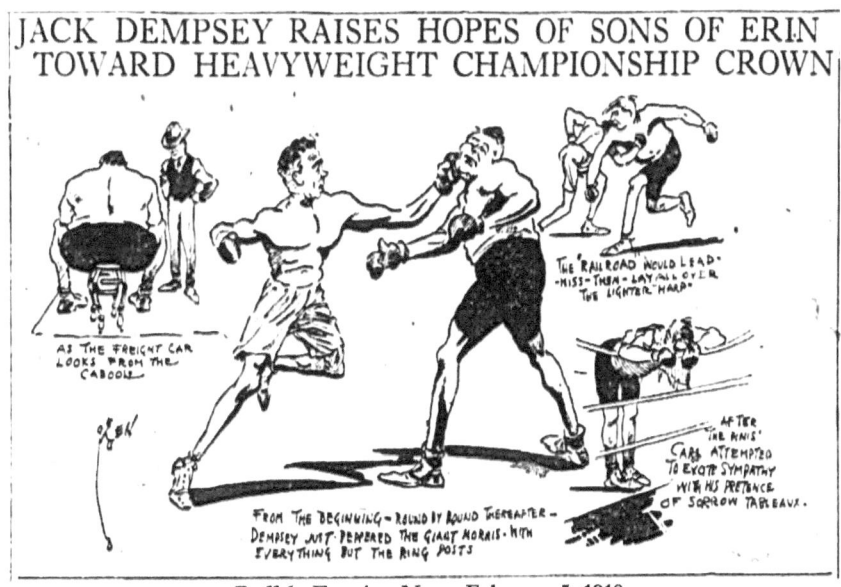

*Buffalo Evening News*, February 5, 1918

The *Buffalo Evening News* said Dempsey was much better than Morris. The Oklahoma giant fouled out when he was in a bad way from Dempsey's pummeling. Dempsey battered the lumbering, clumsy bulk all over the ring. Referee Nugent stopped it when Morris was obviously but blindly looking for a way out. He fouled so palpably that it could not be overlooked. The fans did not like Carl's tactics. He was slow and stumbled clumsily about, using his weight and roughing it with his head down. Dempsey looked like a lightweight next to the huge Morris, but as fast as a flash in comparison.

The *Buffalo Commercial* writer called Irish lad Dempsey a successor to Corbett. His family ancestry was of County Cork, Ireland. He allegedly was born in West Virginia (which some claimed, even Dempsey at various times, oddly enough).

Dempsey was a swift-moving, clever, game, aggressive, two-handed scrapper. He gave Morris a thorough and artistic lambasting, outclassing his lumbering foe. Halfway through the 6$^{th}$ round, with Morris tottering and rapidly degenerating into a helpless condition, out on his feet, he hit low and Dempsey was awarded the honors on a foul. Had matters been allowed to progress, within a round or two Morris would have been knocked clean out. Jack won by a mile, systematically beating him, master of the situation from start to finish.

Dempsey never complained about the low blows, wanting to win in decisive fashion. He was made of the right stuff, game to the core and not looking to steal the decision on a technicality. He actually was disappointed it was stopped, wanting to win with a clean knockout. Even Carl's own manager surprisingly admitted defeat, saying that he was about to toss in the towel. There was no criticism of the referee. He could not overlook so many fouls. Plus, in a way it was an act of kindness, for he saved Morris from additional hard whacks.

Dempsey was all that had been said of him, a wonderfully clever boxer, fast as Corbett was, he could punch, and knew how to protect himself. He slipped around the ring with the skill of a dancing master, dodging and ducking and either getting under the other fellow's guard or slipping blows over the guard. He stood 6'1" and weighed 198 pounds. Scribes said he had Jeffries' punch, Ketchel's speed, and Gans' skill. This writer said he hit hard, but not quite as hard as Jeffries. Dempsey weighed 28 pounds less than the 226-pound Morris, but his speed, cleverness, coolness, and defense offset Morris' edges in weight, height, reach, and strength. Dempsey knew how to guard, both at long range and in close. He feinted out openings, and was as quick as a cat in countering. He was able to slip away from many bull rushes, or stopped the lumbering giant with short snappy drives. Morris, like all giants, appeared to be less clever than he really was. He was an extraordinarily strong man who used every opportunity to use his weight to advantage. He mauled Dempsey now and then and roughly pressed him to the ropes, but Dempsey's cleverness offset much of the roughhouse stuff. "The man who whips Dempsey will win the title from Willard."

The *Buffalo Courier* said that rather than take a knockout, Morris intentionally fouled out. Dempsey punished Morris severely, giving him a sound licking despite the weight disparity, showing championship class. Morris was almost out when Dick Nugent disqualified him after repeated warnings. "At last, a heavyweight fighter!" He beat the huge Morris to a frazzle. Morris was dizzy and drunk from the accurate pile-driving punches of the newest western marvel. Morris would have crumpled in a round or two more at the most. He was dazed for a minute even after the bout was over, practically out on his feet.

It was a marvelous whirlwind battle while it lasted, even though it was one-sided. In most mixes, Dempsey made him look clumsy and slow, but Carl actually fought a fast fight for so big a man, and showed remarkable agility afoot. He was at his best.

Morris had received three warnings before fouling out to avoid taking the count. He struck Jack low in the 2$^{nd}$ round, the 4$^{th}$, landing two low blows at that time, and again in the 5$^{th}$ round. Referee Nugent gave warnings each time, and in the 5$^{th}$ stopped matters to give him a heart-to-heart talk, with Morris putting his hands on the referee's shoulders and apologizing, stating that his acts were not intentional. Dempsey shook his hand and they went at it again. The final act in the 6$^{th}$ round left the referee with no alternative.

Dempsey made good on every advance report of his prowess. He was as light as a featherweight on his feet, stripped like a greyhound, but with wonderful shoulders and legs. He hit hard with both hands, jabbed fast and sharp, and had a shift like Ketchel's. He was cool and collected, and quick to take advantage of openings. He tied up Morris in the clinches so effectively that Morris could not get free. He was a smart fighter.

Dempsey said,

> I didn't want to win that way. I don't want to say Morris meant to foul. He just loses his head and doesn't know what he is doing. He did the same thing in our Frisco bout, and I carry the marks yet. He's just hotheaded and irresponsible when he's stung. I wanted to stop him, knock him out, so that Fulton and Willard could not put my challenges aside. I'm ready for them both now.

Jack Curley admitted that he had no excuses for his man:

> He was licked, and by the best young heavyweight I've seen in years. Morris was fit and at his best. Just say for me Dempsey is the best-looking fighter of the day. My, how he can fight. He's the Stanley Ketchel of the heavyweights and [will] beat 'em all. I don't think Morris meant to foul. I rather think the referee was influenced more by a desire to stop further punishment. God knows, Morris took enough of it.

The *Buffalo Times* said for 6 rounds Morris took a thrashing, then deliberately fouled out. Morris looked big enough to sweep Dempsey from the ring with one punch, but from the start, Dempsey began a systematic hit and get away attack, and soon had his enormous foe staggering from well-timed blows to the head and body. Dempsey actually was the harder puncher. In the 2nd and 3rd rounds, Morris was warned for striking low, and frequently up to the 6th round hit low. A hard left to the groin forced the halt. There was little doubt he would have been knocked out. He was beaten badly in every round, and practically out on his feet when it ended.[317]

Frank Menke, who had a press-box seat for the Johnson-Willard fight, said Willard was a "cheese champion" and overrated. He was beaten by much smaller men such as Tom McMahon and Gunboat Smith, the latter being 50 pounds lighter and six inches shorter. He was in great shape for Johnson, and proved he could take a punch, but he won not because he was a better boxer than Johnson, but because Johnson was old, fat, and weary from beating on him for 20 rounds. Menke claimed that Johnson quit, and knew he was all-in well before the finish, because he sent his wife away from the ringside two rounds before the fight ended. After the 23rd round, Harry Frazee, now owner of the Red Sox, and the bout's financier, climbed up to Johnson's corner and held a whispered conference with him. Immediately after, a message was flashed to Johnson's manager Tom Flanagan, who was sitting with Johnson's wife. The message was, "Get Mrs. Johnson away from the ringside." She left. Jack knew he was tired and could not knock out Willard, and the end was near, and did not want her to see him get stopped (which he was in the 26th round).

Menke said 259-pound Willard had fought only once since 1915, in 1916 against 204-pound Frank Moran. 170-pound light heavyweight Jack Dillon just a few months later beat Moran with greater ease. Jess had avoided the ring since then, and now was claiming that because Fred Fulton recently had managed only a draw with Billy Miske; the showing was so disappointing that he could not regard Fulton as a formidable foe, and the match was off. He was finding any excuse not to fight.[318]

The *Buffalo Courier* said fans agreed that Dempsey was a real fighter, his artistic trimming of big Morris having left a wonderful impression, but still were divided on his chances to beat Fulton or Willard. Yet, they agreed that with another year of development and experience, he would be ready for anyone.

It had been a long while since such an impressive-looking youngster had been seen. Most highly-touted newcomers had proven to be busts, but Dempsey's performance against Morris proved that he was for real, and the one bright exception. He was only 22 years old, and had not fought over 40 fights. He had significant victories over strong men like Morris, Gunboat Smith, and Homer Smith. "Dempsey is fast, clever, has a good head, is shifty on his feet and can hit."

What he would do against men like Fred Fulton, Billy Miske, or Battling Levinsky, men who knew how to feint and use finesse and ring tricks, remained to be seen.

---

[317] *Buffalo Enquirer, Buffalo Evening News, Buffalo Commercial, Buffalo Courier, Buffalo Times*, February 5, 1918.
[318] *Buffalo Times*, February 5, 1918.

Dempsey clearly was learning rapidly. The way he handled Morris in the clinches, tying up his arms and preventing all of Carl's infighting efforts, showed he had learned a few things about ring-craft. And he could hit. His punches went right to the mark, solid and true, and he knew how to put his weight behind them. Jack Curley said Dempsey had Morris hurt, whereas Fulton never jarred Morris. "I would have tossed in the towel had it gone another round."

According to the *Buffalo Commercial*, Buffalo fans said Dempsey looked like the best heavyweight in the country. He promised to secure the adulation of a John L. Sullivan.

Carl Morris said Dempsey was better than Fred Fulton. "I'd admit I was groggy in the sixth round, but so help me I didn't mean to hit low. ... Dempsey is a great boy. ... He will lick Fulton, if they ever meet."

Jack returned to Chicago to fulfill a week-long theatrical engagement.

Leo P. Flynn, manager of black heavyweight Kid Norfolk, claimed that Norfolk could beat Dempsey and make him look foolish. Dempsey was more of a fighter, but Flynn insisted that a negro could box much better, and his left jab would make him feel sick. "Of course, you know that Sam Langford, Harry Wills and Joe Jeannette can whip Norfolk, but none of the white heavyweights can do it by any means. If Norfolk meets Dempsey go bet your last quarter, raise all the nickels you can, and bet on the coon to whip him." Norfolk was built like Dempsey, not quite as heavy, but almost as fast and probably as clever. He had fast feet. He had losses to Jeff Clark (L20)(avenged - W20) and Langford, who knocked him out in the 2rd round in late 1917. Norfolk had fought Gunboat Smith twice in 10-round no decisions in 1917, the first fight being quite close (two gave it to 183-pound Norfolk by a shade, one gave it to 178-pound Smith 4-2-4, and another said it was a draw), but most said Norfolk clearly won the rematch. Norfolk also had a W12 Billy Miske and KO13 (twice) Arthur Pelkey.

Dempsey was scheduled to box the highly regarded Bill Brennan in Milwaukee in the near future. Leo Flynn, who managed him, also said that Brennan would give Dempsey a nifty pasting as well.[319]

The Wyoming oil men who were willing to pay $100,000 for a July 4 Dempsey-Willard fight said they would do so as long as they had the consent of the war department (which could be tricky as long as the world war was ongoing).

Dempsey said, "That's all I want to do – meet Mr. Willard. I think he is serious about wanting to fight and defend his title. He said a couple of months ago he would give me a chance just as soon as I had shown something. Later Mr. Willard, through Walter Monahan, congratulated me on the showing in some of my fights."[320]

Willard said he was ready to meet the winner of a Dempsey-Fulton contest.[321]

---

[319] *Buffalo Courier, Buffalo Commercial, Buffalo Enquirer*, February 6, 1918.
[320] *Milwaukee Sentinel*, February 13, 1918.
[321] *Decatur Herald*, February 14, 1918.

Robert Edgren said Willard's record did not compare favorably with Fred Fulton's record. Fulton had knocked out Gunner Smith and Tom McMahon, both of whom had decisioned Willard. Fulton also knocked out Langford, much faster than Willard did Johnson, and there "wasn't much to choose between the two black fighters." Willard went 10 rounds with Morris, while "Fulton punched Morris's head off in their last fight and might have knocked him out if Morris hadn't taken to persistent fouling, apparently preferring to lose that way." Fulton showed class in every fight, and "looks more like a heavyweight champion than any other fighter we've seen in a long time."[322]

Next up for Dempsey was a rematch with Pueblo, Colorado's 38-year-old Jim Flynn, the only man to have stopped him. It had been exactly one year since that 1st round knockout loss, which some believed was a fix.

A 182-pound Flynn had fought only once since his victory over Dempsey, a late March 1917 10-round no decision loss to 198-pound Bob Devere.[323] Flynn typically weighed around 190 pounds, sometimes more, sometimes less.

The *Chicago Tribune's* Ray Pearson said Dempsey had made wonderful strides over the course of the past year, now being reckoned as a championship possibility, and did not think Flynn would be able to repeat. Flynn would be the long-shot in any betting.

The show would be held at Fort Sheridan, Illinois, where the Fortieth infantry was encamped. The show's profits would go to the camp. Special trains would take folks there from Chicago, for Fort Sheridan was just 30 miles north. Tickets were being sold for $1, $2, and $3. Confident Kearns said he was discussing terms for a potential bout with Fred Fulton.

The *Chicago Examiner's* Sam P. Hall said Dempsey was battling a ring relic in a rematch, aiming to square accounts with Pueblo's Jim Flynn. The bout was scheduled for 10 rounds to a decision. No one anticipated a Flynn victory over the rugged, hard-clouting young heavy. The ancient one was credited with a knockout over Dempsey, "but most folks seem to think that was either an accident or a fake." One thing that had to be said for Flynn was he was there to do his best and fought to the last gasp. His heart never had been questioned. He appeared to be in fairly good trim.[324]

---

[322] *Milwaukee Sentinel*, February 15, 1918.
[323] *Buffalo Enquirer*, March 21, 1917.
[324] *Chicago Tribune, Chicago Examiner*, February 14, 1918.

On Thursday February 14, 1918 in Fort Sheridan, Illinois, just ten days after the Morris contest, Jack Dempsey fought a scheduled 10-round rematch with "Fireman" Jim Flynn. Despite stormy conditions, a good crowd was on hand, with soldiers prominent. Officers occupied choice seats on the stage. Women were in the balcony. The 40th infantry band played before the fights and between them. The gate receipts were about $1,400.

All week the old fireman said he was ready for a tough fight. His manager predicted that Jim would go the distance. However, Flynn did not appear to be fit for a long walk. He had a big roll of fat around his stomach, making him look like a valentine on Valentine's Day. He was heavy.

From the start, Dempsey showed confidence, as if he had had nothing to fear, demonstrated by his demeanor when they started, forcing the fight right away. He was too fast for Flynn. Jack used a corking left hook from the outset, alternating it with an occasional straight right, and soon had Jim's head rocking. A series of lefts and rights to the head drove Flynn to the ropes.

Flynn tried to keep in close to avoid punishment, but Jack was too shifty for him. Less than a minute into the fight, either a dazzling left hook to the chin or a terrific right to the jaw (or perhaps both; local sources differed) crumpled Flynn down to the canvas on his back.

Flynn took a good long nine-count and staggered up to his wobbly pins. Dempsey was on him like a flash, attacking like an enraged bull. He propelled both left and right with terrific speed, hitting the head, and did not pay any attention to the fireman's efforts. A powerful left hook shot Flynn through the ropes and down to a sitting position. Flynn was in such a helpless state that he finished on his haunches outside the ropes. (Non-local reports said he was knocked into the crowd).

One said that at the solicitation of Referee Smith, Flynn's manager Tom Jones consented to defeat as soon as Flynn went down. His seconds came to Flynn's assistance and the referee stopped the fight. It was however a complete knockout, for it took nearly a minute for Flynn to realize where he was.

Some said the fight had lasted 1 minute 10 seconds, another said 1 minute 30 seconds, and another 1 minute 32 seconds. It was a 1st round knockout, Flynn having gone down twice.

The *Chicago Tribune*'s Ray Pearson said Dempsey squared accounts so quickly that Flynn scarcely knew he was in a fight. Jack had turned the tables and done to Jim what he previously had done to him. Flynn was through as a fighter, for he was too old.

The *Chicago Examiner's* Sam P. Hall said Dempsey flattened Flynn in the 1st round in one of the most one-sided matches ever perpetrated. Jim never had the ghost of a chance, and gave a pitiful exhibition. He was a fat mass of ancient, helpless humanity. Tom Jones had been predicting loudly for days that Flynn would stick the limit, which turned out to be a ridiculous prognostication.

The *Chicago Herald's* Billy Birch said the old man Flynn was pitiful, and the fight was a joke, just as he predicted. Flynn had seen his best days, and went up against one of the leading contenders for the title.

The *Moline Dispatch* said Flynn may have laced Dempsey once, but never could do it again.

Champion Jess Willard confirmed that he was ready to meet the winner of a bout between Dempsey and Fulton.[325]

Although the press did not seem to want to give Dempsey a great deal of credit for beating Flynn, certainly the bout was of some significance, for he had avenged his only knockout loss in the same manner.

The *La Crosse Tribune* said Dempsey was an unusual young man in that he offered no alibi or excuse for his prior loss to Flynn. All he said was, "I don't know how it happened, but it came off all right. I stepped out and got mine." This time, Flynn got his.

Some said Billy Miske might give Dempsey more trouble than Fulton, because of his speed and cleverness.[326]

On February 17, 1918 in Panama City, Panama, Harry Wills knocked out Sam McVey in the 5th round. McVey's claim of foul was not recognized.

Next up for Dempsey was another significant fight, a 10-round bout against Bill Brennan in Milwaukee, Wisconsin in late February, his fourth fight in the span of one month (H. Smith, Morris, Flynn, and Brennan).

At age 24, 195-pound "Knockout" Bill Brennan already had about 50 fights to his credit, possibly more (with a known 39-6-4 record), including: 1916 KO7 and TKO3 George Rodel, WND10 Larry Williams, KO3 George Davis, KO8 Tony Ross, D12 Andre Anderson, WND10 Terry Keller, KO8 Soldier Kearns, LDQ7 and WND10 Joe Cox, LND10 Tom Cowler (twice), and WND6 Homer Smith; 1917 WND10 Joe Cox, LND10 Tom Cowler, WND10 and KO2 Joe Bonds, WND10 Bob Devere (twice), KO3 Joe Cox, WND10 Bartley Madden (twice), D12, W12, and L12 Battling Levinsky, WND10 Tom McMahon, DND10 Jim Coffey, and WND10 Homer Smith; and 1918 D12 Battling Levinsky.[327]

---

[325] *Chicago Tribune, Chicago Examiner, Chicago Herald,* February 15, 1918; *Decatur Herald, Rock Island Argus, Moline Dispatch, Milwaukee Daily News, Milwaukee Free Press,* February 15, 1918.
[326] *La Crosse Tribune,* February 18, 1918. Jack used to be called the Submarine Destroyer because of his terrific body punching.
[327] Boxrec.com.

On Friday afternoon, February 22 at Morgenroth's in Milwaukee, a large crowd watched Dempsey work out, sparring 3 action-filled rounds with Andre Anderson. They hammered and lunged at each other with great force, as if it was a real fight. Some wondered what those punches might do to Brennan, who also had a wonderful wallop. The local paper credited KO Bill with having 41 knockouts. The *Milwaukee Daily News* said the betting was about even, though few were wagering on Brennan.[328]

*Milwaukee Sentinel*, February 24, 1918

Dempsey's sparring with Andre Anderson on the 23rd made such an excellent impression that the fans made him a 2 to 1 favorite "over a fighter who has a much better record than he." The local *Milwaukee Sentinel*'s J. J. Delany believed the fans were being irrational. Brennan had a string of knockouts and impressive performances over better men than Dempsey had fought, which stamped him as a "heady, shifty boxer as well as a hard hitter." Brennan combined the footwork of a middleweight with the punch of a heavyweight. He also had proven ability to take a punch, for never had he been stopped. "There is no understanding the fickleness of fight fans." Still, the writer understood, "Dempsey looks like a fighter and he fights like one. ... Monday night's bout will demonstrate Dempsey's worth. If he can get by Brennan, we are willing to concede him a contender..."[329]

The *Milwaukee Daily News* said Dempsey looked like a champion. He was tall enough, as lithe as a panther, had the speed of a bantam, deep black eyes, and correct body poise. He was efficient, intelligent, and well developed.

The "elimination" bout was attracting unusual attention and interest even in Chicago, on account of the fact that one of the combatants might potentially fight Willard. More than 500 folks from the Windy City had ticket reservations. The winner would be seeking a meeting with the victor of the upcoming Fred Fulton vs. Frank Moran contest.[330]

The *Milwaukee Free Press* said Dempsey was the new John L. Sullivan, scoring knockouts in sensational manner.

---

[328] *Milwaukee Daily News*, February 23, 1918.
[329] *Milwaukee Sentinel*, February 24, 1918.
[330] *Milwaukee Daily News*, February 25, 1918.

Jack Kearns said, "I believe that I have the next heavyweight champion of the world in Jack Dempsey. He is fast for a big fellow and can hit like a pile driver."

22-year-old Dempsey said, "They say Brennan is a big tough fellow who has a great string of knockout victories, but I don't think he can add my name to the list, for I intend to put over the haymaker."

Brennan's manager Leo Flynn said talk of Dempsey stopping Brennan made him laugh. "Brennan is an experienced boxer who has met the best in the game and who holds the best K.O. record of any heavyweight that ever lived." No one could stop him, and no one had.

"K.O." Brennan simply said, "I think I will win." Bill was peeved by the fact that he was the underdog, saying that he had a much better record than Dempsey.

This writer noted, "Brennan is a shifty boxer, possessing a good left hand. He has a tough jaw that can take a solid punch as shown when he fought Homer Smith in Racine. The Benton Harbor giant stung Brennan good and plenty, but Brennan always came back for more." Brennan did not score a knockout, but said he had a bad hand. Dempsey had stopped Smith in less than a round with some crushing punches back of the ear. He usually went out to win in a hurry, battering down his opponents. Walter Houlihan would referee, and he was just as big as the battlers, so he could pry them apart.

*Milwaukee Free Press*, February 25, 1918

Burdette Kirkham of the *Milwaukee Free Press* said about 700 Chicago fans were in town, and they were split on the likely winner. Brennan had many friends, but Dempsey also had a lot of admirers as a result of his hard punch with either hand. Dempsey was the 10 to 6 odds favorite, and it was not clear whether the odds would shift as a result of the arrival of Brennan's Chicago admirers. "Many figure that [Dempsey's] aggressive style will batter down Brennan's defense and then the old right hand will go over and if it does it means a long count. … Dempsey will weigh about 196 pounds while Brennan will scale around 198 pounds."

That same night, in New Orleans, 210-pound Fred Fulton was scheduled to fight former two-time title challenger 196-pound Frank Moran in a scheduled 20-round bout. The winner of that contest likely would fight the winner of Dempsey-Brennan, with the winner to meet Willard.

Billy Miske was another man who had to be considered in the title mix. He made a good impression in his recent bout with Fulton, which many considered a draw. "Fulton has got to win from Miske before he can claim a bout for the title."

Still, Fulton had knocked out several of the best, including Sam Langford, Gunboat Smith, Al Reich, Charley Weinert, and Tom Cowler. "He is a scientific fighter, speedy and can hit with knockout steam."

Also fighting that evening, in St. Paul, Harry Greb was taking on world middleweight champion Mike O'Dowd in a title fight.

J. J. Delany of the *Milwaukee Sentinel* said fans were going to see a real fight, with the winner having a chance to battle Willard. "Bill Brennan, Chicago knockout artist, who has a list of knockouts as long as the list of German defeats will be, clashes with Jack Dempsey. If you don't know who Jack Dempsey is, you have not been reading the newspapers. According to his record, he is the original knock 'em dead kid." Big crowds had turned up to see Dempsey's local workouts, and the fans liked what they saw.

The *Milwaukee Journal* said Dempsey was a product of the rough school, and had been in the ring game for about three years.[331]

On Monday February 25, 1918 in Milwaukee, Wisconsin, at the Elite Rink, under the auspices of the South Side Athletic Club, just ten days after the Dempsey-Flynn bout, in a scheduled 10-round affair, Jack Dempsey fought Bill Brennan.

It was a capacity, sold-out house. The Elite rink resembled a sardine box, the humanity jammed into every seat available. About 300 of the 3,500 fans present had to view the bouts on foot.

The *Milwaukee Daily News* said America was the greatest fight-loving country in existence, and Milwaukee turned out the most enthusiastic boxing fans. Slathers of fans from Chicago turned up as well. South Side Athletic Club matchmaker Joe Ornstein was quite happy. The immense crowd was splendidly handled. The seating arrangement had been improved from prior shows. Many ladies were noticed, attired in "natty" tailor-made and semi-evening toilettes.

Special trains both by steam and electric to and from Chicago and other cities were put on the tracks to convey the fans to the fight and back to their various points of destination.

The main event fighters entered the ring at 9:45 p.m. In Dempsey's corner were Eddie McGoorty (who previously had been sparring with Brennan in Chicago in preparation for the fight. Did Kearns pay him for his insights?), sparring partner Andre Anderson, and manager Jack Kearns. K.O. Brennan had Leo Flynn and Barney Fluhry.

---

[331] *Milwaukee Free Press, Milwaukee Sentinel, Milwaukee Journal*, February 25, 1918.

Bill Brennan's weight was announced as 196 pounds. The Chicago crowd gave him a big hand. Jack Dempsey was announced as 188 ¼ or ½ pounds, depending on the version. They had weighed in officially at 3 p.m. that day. Hence, prior reports of Dempsey's weight had been a bit inflated. Walter Houlihan (some called him Houlehen) refereed. After a discussion of the rules, the fellows squared away.

1 – The *Milwaukee Free Press* said they clinched, and Dempsey scored at will at infighting. Outside, Brennan jabbed away, and appeared to be very nervous. Bill then fired a neat one-two to the back of Jack's ear. Jack came back with two lefts and Bill again resorted to jabbing and boxing. This version said Brennan earned a shade in the round, having dodged the haymakers.

The *Milwaukee Journal* said Dempsey did not tear after him in the opening round, which was pretty even, with fairly hefty blows exchanged.

The *Milwaukee Daily News* said the 1st round was Dempsey's.

The *Milwaukee Sentinel's* J. J. Delany presented a totally different perspective from the other local papers (perhaps erroneously). He said that after 30 seconds of fiddling, Dempsey started playing a tattoo on Bill's jaw with his right, and hammered him to the floor. It was not a single punch, but a succession of short, snappy pile drivers that took the sap out of the rugged Brennan, and he wilted. He was weak when he rose, but clinched and managed to last out the round. Dempsey tried to shake him off, but Bill's eight-pound weight advantage helped him.

2 – The *Free Press* said Dempsey wasted no time in sparring, but started showering punches to Brennan's face at long range, and when he came in close, he clubbed his blows to the head and half shoved and half knocked Brennan to the canvas.

Bill appeared amazed, and after rising, for the next 30 seconds fought back viciously. Dempsey tore through Brennan's defense, and with a succession of head blows knocked him down again for a nine-count.

Brennan gamely rose, but was weak and wobbling. Another attack followed and Brennan went to the floor for the third time in the round, but the bell rang before Referee Houlihan had passed three on the count.

The *Journal* said the cyclone decked Brennan three times in the 2nd round, and the bell rang at the count of four for the last knockdown.

The *Daily News* said for the first two knockdowns, Brennan took eight-counts, and the third time he took a nine-count. Brennan's nose was broken. It was a clear Dempsey round.

The *Sentinel's* Delany said the round was a massacre, during which time Eddie McGoorty, in Dempsey's corner, pleaded with the referee to stop it. Brennan hit the floor a few times, from both rights and lefts. Dempsey hit hard enough to deck him with either hand, and with any punch, straight rights and lefts, or hooks. The crowd went mad, standing up and cheering. As Referee Houlehen counted while close to Brennan, Dempsey strode up and down the ropes on the other side of the ring, like a caged lion. When Brennan rose, Dempsey was on top of him in an instant. He belted him this way and that, and just when Bill was about to sink again, the welcome toll of the bell sounded.

3 – The *Free Press* said Dempsey tore in furiously and drew blood. His rights and lefts hit the face, and Bill tried to hold on. Dempsey pounded, hammered, and battered Brennan throughout the round, but the gritty Chicagoan refused to go down, and when the bell rang the big throng gave him an ovation for his gameness.

The *Journal* description said Dempsey tore in, and Brennan remained on the defensive.

The *Daily News* also said the round was Dempsey's.

The *Sentinel's* Delany said when the round began, amazingly Brennan was himself again, and brought forth applause by landing several wicked lefts on the jaw, though only one of them tossed back Jack's head. Dempsey did not seem to mind. He fought with both hands down, without any guard, but worked both rights and lefts to the face. Brennan grew weak again, but by clinching and punching managed to last.

4 – The *Free Press* said Dempsey rushed him and landed a back-handed blow, which drew a caution from the referee. They shook hands. Dempsey sunk a hard right to the stomach which hurt. Brennan reached the jaw with a light right. Dempsey appeared to be playing for the body. At the bell, as Bill returned to his corner, he was reeling badly.

The *Journal* version differed slightly, saying Brennan did well in the round, particularly early, starting out at top speed, but by the end of the round he was leaning on Dempsey for support.

The *Daily News* said Dempsey began using illegal tactics, and the referee reprimanded him. Still, it was Dempsey's round.

The *Sentinel's* Delany said once again the fight nearly was over when Dempsey landed a short cracking right to the jaw. Bill sagged, but kept his feet, fought off the wicked bull, and blocked other punches.

5 – The *Free Press* said Brennan surprised everyone by electing to slug. They exchanged punches at mid-ring, and Dempsey won the exchange, for he was very fast in firing both hands to the mark. Jack shot a hard left to the stomach that crimped Brennan, but Bill sent a feeble right to the jaw. Bill barely was able to hold up his hands, but he remained determined, and the bell came to his rescue.

The *Journal* said Dempsey rested in the round, backing off a bit.

The *Daily News* said both men were groggy in the round. Brennan showed great recuperative powers. Even round.

The *Sentinel* said it almost was a repetition of the prior round, with Brennan the chief receiver of the blows.

6 – The *Free Press* said when the bell rang, Brennan seemed out of it, and waited for a second before responding. He then walked out to "meet the man who had already battered him into a state of coma." They came together at ring center. After three exchanges, Dempsey shot a right flush to the jaw that sent Brennan up against the ropes and down to the canvas.

Brennan was a pitiable sight when he arose at nine, and the crowd was yelling to save the game battler from further punishment. Referee Houlihen waved Dempsey back, awarding him a technical knockout victory. As he stood at ring center, bleeding from the nose and mouth, Brennan was unable to understand the stoppage, half protesting to the referee. He was willing to continue to the bitter end.

The crowd left with heaps of praise for Dempsey, as well as the very game man he had defeated.

The *Journal's* version of the 6th round said Dempsey again resumed his fast work and sent his opponent to the canvas. Bill winked and smiled while down.

Upon rising at nine, Brennan was weak. Still, he was game to the core, willing to continue. The furious Dempsey, displaying a tigerish rage, pounced upon him, hitting Brennan's jaw with pile-driving blows. Brennan was dizzy, and the referee proved to be a humanitarian by stepping between them and stopping the contest.

It had been a good fight. It was the first time that anyone had stopped Brennan. He had assimilated plenty of punishment, but had shown no white feather, so he was astonished by the stoppage. He asked, "What's the matter?" He was out of wind and said nothing more. The bout had been halted in order to avert brutality.

The *Sentinel's* Delany said in the 6th round, Brennan was weary, and Dempsey wanted to finish him. Jack leapt out of his chair and met Bill almost before he had time to get out of his chair. Dempsey banged him often. He shot a right to the stomach and followed with a left to the jaw. That was the beginning of the end. Dempsey shot a terrific right to the jaw and Brennan fell through the ropes in the corner.

He took a nine-count, and gamely rose. Dempsey whaled away at the helpless Brennan until Jack got him to the opposite corner. Unable to protect himself, Brennan was resting upon the ropes with one arm hanging over, and with the other trying unsuccessfully to ward off the storm of wallops. Dempsey crashed rights and lefts to the temple. Referee Houlehen stepped in and humanely put a stop to the slaughter.

The *Daily News* simply said Dempsey sent Brennan down and practically out.

The majority of the local reporters agreed that Dempsey had decked Brennan four times total, three times in the 2nd round and once more in the 6th round.

Burdette Kirkham of the *Milwaukee Free Press* said Dempsey's 6th round stoppage of Brennan had earned him a bout with Fred Fulton. After the 1st round, Dempsey had things his own way, outclassing Brennan. It was a bitterly contested battle, with Dempsey holding the whip from the start. His terrific attack floored the Chicagoan thrice in the 2nd and once more from a solid right smash in the 6th, before Referee Walter Houlihan stopped the unequal combat, even though Brennan gamely rose and was willing to continue.

Fans were calling for a Dempsey-Fulton contest, with the winner to fight Willard for the championship.

Dempsey looked like a champion, cool at all times. The way he lashed in wicked rights to the face and body would have chased many heavyweights out of the ring. He carried the fight at all times, and when he connected, the blows either knocked Brennan down or sent him reeling.

Brennan made the mistake of playing it safe and attempting to keep out of harm's way, but it was futile. Bill dodged the haymakers in the 1st round and was entitled to a shade on the round, but Dempsey opened fire in the 2nd, and from then on it was only a question of how long the game Brennan would be able to stand the gaff. By the time he realized that he could not stave off the rushes, Brennan was too badly punished to land an effective blow. He stayed in close when he could, but Dempsey proved to be a terrific infighter and scored many damaging punches at close quarters. Dempsey was faster than Brennan, and although eight pounds lighter, carried a knockout blow in either hand. He showed the Ketchel shift, and all in all was licensed to carry the moniker of the old Jack Dempsey, 'the nonpareil.'

The *Milwaukee Journal's* Sam Levy said Dempsey, the western "submarine," had converted Milwaukeeans. Referee Walter Houlehen had counted over Brennan four times. Bill was too weak to continue, so Houlehen called a halt. Dempsey emerged without a mark. He had displayed real class, and was too much for Brennan. He proved that a good smaller man can beat a good larger man, for Jack was about eight pounds smaller.

The *Milwaukee Daily News* also said the coast submarine destroyer started the slaughter in the 2nd round before stopping him in the 6th round. There was no similarity in their styles. Dempsey's condition was much superior to Brennan's. He exhibited speed equal to a bantamweight. He showed little liking for open fighting, meaning the outside. Four-fifths of his blows were of the in-fighting variety. Brennan was game but too slow.

The locals were hoping that Dempsey vs. Fulton would be held there, for a very large crowd would come to see it.

The *Milwaukee Sentinel's* J. J. Delany said the terrible fighter from the West battered the Chicagoan into submission. Bill was knocked down four times before the referee called a halt to matters in the 6th round. It was one of the best scraps the writer ever had seen. Brennan was not easily trimmed. He knew how to fight, and had no quit in him. He tried to box, and failed. He tried to slug, but Dempsey made him back up to the ropes. "After two years of unparalleled success among the heavies, Brennan finally found his master." Brennan was a great fighter who stood up with courage and went out with guns firing, but he was up against a superior fighting fiend. It was his first stoppage loss.

Other semi-local reports were high on Dempsey as well. The *Racine Journal-News* said it had been one of the best scraps ever seen. Brennan was not easily trimmed. He was of Irish ancestry, and knew how to fight, and did not know how to quit. He was beaten early in the contest, but was tough, stood in there and "tried to box this terrible kid." He failed to box him effectively, so he tried to slug as well, but Dempsey made him back up to the ropes and pounded away at him there as well.

The *Oshkosh Northwestern* said Dempsey gave the Chicago Irishman a most terrific beating.

The *Wisconsin State Journal* said Brennan showed strength and landed some telling blows, but Dempsey outpunched him at every turn.

The *Sheboygan Press* said there was little doubt about Dempsey's class. He propelled terrific right and left crosses, administering punishment that would have stopped many opponents much sooner. Referee Houlihan stopped the fight with Brennan almost out on his feet, blood streaming from his nose and mouth, and his eyes glassy, with a complete knockout inevitable. There was no way to stall off the onrushing Dempsey, who shifted from one side to the other. His blows were as accurate as a sharpshooter, and thrown with terrific force. Brennan's frame weakened from the terrific bombardment. He tried to keep going, but the stoppage was for the best. Brennan was a beaten man, wobbly upon rising from the last knockdown, and the referee was wise to stop it.

The *Leader-Telegram* said Dempsey had the advantage from start to finish. He had a shift that puzzled Brennan. Jack was equally clever with both hands and landed at will with lightning rapidity, mystifying the Chicagoan. Brennan was game, but when the referee saw that his case was hopeless and he was on the verge of a true knockout, he stopped the contest.[332]

On the same evening, in New Orleans, 216-pound Fred Fulton knocked out 197-pound Frank Moran in the 3rd round. Fulton cut Moran's right eye and bloodied him in the 1st round, and in the 3rd round landed repeated left and right uppercuts and jabs to the chin and body, finally decking him with a hard right-cross to the jaw. Moran's seconds tossed in the sponge.

The *La Crosse Tribune* said Fulton had whipped every top heavyweight en route to his title challenges, including Sam Langford, Frank Moran, Charlie

---

[332] *Milwaukee Free Press, Milwaukee Journal, Milwaukee Daily News, Milwaukee Sentinel, Racine Journal-News, Oshkosh Northwestern, Wisconsin State Journal* (Madison, WI), *Sheboygan Press, Leader-Telegram* (Eau Claire, WI), *Capital Times* (Madison), all February 26, 1918.

Weinert, Al Reich, Andre Anderson, and Billy Miske. Fulton could box and fight. He barred no one.

Fred Fulton.

The *Milwaukee Sentinel's* J. J. Delany said Fulton's knockout of Moran made him one of the contenders for Willard's crown, but "there is another." Dempsey was "a fighting piece of machinery" and "the best collection of heavyweight mechanism seen around these parts in the last decade. Jack Dempsey is a fighter, if ever there was one. Shades of Stanley Ketchel, but this kid from the Golden Gate can fight."

Delany said Dempsey-Fulton would be worth traveling thousands of miles to see. "They stand at the head of their class, and if Jess Willard refuses to meet the winner of such a scrap, he ought to be tossed into the ash barrel with the other refuse."

In St. Paul, Minnesota, world middleweight champion Mike O'Dowd narrowly retained his title in a furious but close 10-round no decision against Harry Greb. One reported that O'Dowd clearly won 4 rounds, with the rest being even. O'Dowd was better at the infighting and landed the cleaner blows, though Greb never was in distress. Three local newspapers had it for O'Dowd, two for Greb, while one scored it a draw but at the same time said strictly speaking Greb had a shade on points. Hence, many perceived it as a draw. Most dispatches said O'Dowd had won.[333]

Bill Brennan subsequently claimed that he had broken his ankle in one of the falls in the 2nd round, which hampered his performance thereafter. About a month after the fight, Brennan said,

> I wouldn't call Dempsey a one-punch man. Jack is a great fighter, all right, but he's the type that wears a man out. Jack grabs you by the back of your neck with one mit and wallops with the other, giving a fellow no chance to escape. He sort of drags you forward into his punch. ... I believe it was Dempsey's system of jerking my head forward that smashed my ankle. I thought it was just turned a little, though it hurt. If I had known it was broken, I'd have quit right then – taken no chances.[334]

Folks were calling for a Dempsey-Fulton title eliminator, arguing that the victor would be the man most entitled to fight Willard. The *Milwaukee*

---

[333] *Milwaukee Free Press, Milwaukee Daily News, Milwaukee Sentinel, La Crosse Tribune*, February 26, 1918. Boxrec.com, citing *St. Paul Dispatch, St. Paul Pioneer Press, Minneapolis Journal, Minneapolis Daily News*, and *Minneapolis Tribune*, and *St. Paul Daily News*.

Harry Greb's career to that point included: 1915 DND6 Billy Miske and LND10 Tommy Gibbons; 1916 LND10 George Chip, WND10 Bob Moha, and WND6 Joe Borrell; 1917 LND6 Mike Gibbons, WND10 Al McCoy, D20 Jackie Clark, WND10 (twice) Jeff Smith, WND10 and W10 George Chip, WND10 Jack Dillon, WND10 Battling Levinsky, WND10, W8, and W12 Gus Christie, WND10 Len Rowlands, LND10 Soldier Bartfield, and WND6 Willie Meehan; and 1918 WND10 Terry Keller, W20 Augie Ratner, and W10 Moha.

[334] *Atlanta Constitution*, March 17, 1918.

*Sentinel's* J. J. Delany said a Fulton-Dempsey bout "must come," for the fans would not be satisfied until they saw the two mix. If the fight happened, a great deal of Milwaukee money would back Dempsey. "In the opinion of many who saw the Dempsey-Brennan fight, Jack is unbeatable." They believed that Dempsey's aggressiveness and gameness would overcome Fulton's or Willard's superior size and weight. "Dempsey will strike terror into the hearts of any fighter he faces." Jack was the new sensation, the "biggest pugilistic attraction in the country today," who had no fear, and his only interest was to end the fight as soon as he could. He was a larger version of Stanley Ketchel.

Jack said, "I'm out to finish every bout I start just as quickly as I can."[335]

Allan Markley of the *Milwaukee Free Press* said Fulton had vindicated his sorry showing against Miske with his brilliant performance against Moran. Dempsey, who had been termed a second edition of John L. Sullivan since his spectacular rise, would be Fulton's final test. Willard could not avoid a clash with the winner. Fulton appeared to have the advantages over Dempsey, but the ease with which Dempsey had won his victories could not be underestimated. Fulton had the experience advantage, as well as height, reach, and weight advantages. Dempsey was a relative newcomer by comparison. "Dempsey is not a scientific fighter. He hits straight from the shoulder in much the same manner that characterized the ring career of the veteran John L."

Billy Miske, who gained a newspaper draw with Fulton, also was in the title mix, and could register a justified claim for a bout with Dempsey.

The press described Dempsey as a rushing, tearing fighter, always aggressive. He was a quick hitter, and his blows carried terrific force.

Fulton was a careful, deliberate fighter who methodically sparred for an opening and then shot over a powerful blow with lightning speed and perfect accuracy. He knew how to use his physical advantages.

The question was whether Willard would fight one or the other, or wait until they fought each other. There were alleged offers of a $100,000 purse for Willard to fight Fulton, as well as Dempsey. The club where Fulton beat Moran offered Jess $100,000 to fight Fulton 20 rounds there, the purse to be divided however the two principals agreed.[336]

---

[335] *Milwaukee Sentinel, La Crosse Tribune, Oshkosh Northwestern*, February 27, 1918.
[336] *Milwaukee Free Press, Milwaukee Sentinel*, February 27, 1918.

CHAPTER 12

# A Near Fight

**Fred Fulton and Tom Cowler**

On March 11, 1918 in St. Louis, Missouri, the approximately 215-pound left-handed "Minnesota plasterer" Fred Fulton (who could fight out of the orthodox or southpaw stances), fought an exciting war with the approximately 210-pound "Cumberland Colossus" Tom Cowler, whom Fred had knocked out in the 1st round previously. This time, Cowler put up a much better performance, in the 1st round hurting Fulton with a right, and then decking Fulton with another right for a nine-count. Cowler tried hard to finish him, dazing Fulton, but Fred survived.

In the 2nd round, the powerful "gladiator-gorilla" Cowler hurt Fulton again, but Fulton landed three lefts and a right that decked Cowler, who rose quickly and sparred.

In the 3rd and 4th rounds, Cowler kept attacking successfully, his punch like the kick of a mule. Tom clearly was ahead on points, though he was spitting blood.

In the 5th round, Fulton recovered and hammered the tiring Cowler terrifically, finally nailing Cowler with right chop to the jaw that put him down. Cowler rose fairly quickly. Fulton landed a lightning left and smashing right cross, and the bruised and bleeding Englishman staggered around. Fulton drove in a succession of powerful blows, battering and smashing him with every punch. A hard right caused Cowler to put his gloves to the floor. As soon as he removed his hands from the floor, Fulton attacked immediately and hit him again, and he collapsed in his corner, out for the count. It had been an exciting war.

Fulton said he had been ill for the last few days and probably should not have fought. "Cowler clipped me on the jaw in the opening round and I went down for the second time in my career. I was dazed for three rounds and did not get going good until the fifth. Cowler is greatly improved since I fought him a year ago."

Cowler claimed that a long count in the 1st round had saved Fulton. He believed that Fred had been down for 13 seconds.

Some said the fight lowered Fulton's stock, for they were not sure whether he could handle a man with the height, reach, size, and power of Jess Willard. Others said the performance proved that Fulton had heart, gameness, condition, and power, coming back from being hurt to score a knockout.[337]

Fred Fulton            Fred Fulton            Arthur Pelkey

By mid-March 1918, word was that Jess Willard had agreed to fight Fred Fulton on July 4, 1918. The 26-year-old Fulton stood 6'4 ½" and weighed around 220 pounds. His 84 ½" reach was even longer than Willard's. He was naturally left handed, and was a remarkably fast and clever boxer with power in both hands. He allegedly decked Willard in a 1914 exhibition. Some called him a super-sized Fitzsimmons.[338]

Fulton was very well respected, for he had not been beaten on the merits since 1914 (only a couple of disqualification losses since then), his record including: WND10 and KO5 Arthur Pelkey (former white heavyweight champion), TKO4 Terry Keller, KO4 and KO1 Andre

---

[337] *St. Louis Star, St. Louis Post-Dispatch*, March 12, 1918.
[338] *St. Louis Star and Times*, March 16, 1918; *Kansas City Post*, March 25, 1918.

Anderson, W20 and KO2 Porky Flynn, KO2 Jim Flynn, KO1 Tom Cowler, KO2 Charlie Weinert, LDQ5 and WDQ6 Carl Morris, TKO7 Sam Langford, TKO7 Gunboat Smith, DND10 Billy Miske, TKO4 Tom McMahon, TKO3 Frank Moran, and KO5 Tom Cowler. Most considered him to be the number one contender.

Some said Willard had been hounded into the match. He was dubbed a pacifist champion and derided because he had been content to earn easy money appearing in the circus rather than defending his crown.[339]

Jack Dempsey had impressed those in the Intermountain region, the West coast, the East, and the Midwest. Kearns next took him to the South.

On Saturday March 16, 1918 in Memphis, Tennessee, before a fair-sized crowd at the reopening of the Phoenix Athletic Club (after 6 months of idleness), Jack Dempsey fought a fighter purported to be Jack Smith of Chicago. However, Smith's identity was somewhat of a mystery. He actually was believed to be Bull Soddy or Satty of Milwaukee, camouflaging under the ring de plume of Jack Smith. Manager Larney Litchenstein of Chicago accompanied him, but said he was doing so at the request of "a friend." When Litchenstein was asked before the fight if Smith's real name was Bull Satty, he admitted that it was, and added that he had changed his name for personal reasons.

It later was learned that Bull Satty had been working around gyms in Milwaukee as a sparring partner, and was there when Dempsey fought Brennan. Some subsequently reported that Satty/Soddy had been a Dempsey sparring partner for the Brennan fight. Jack Kearns claimed to have no knowledge of Smith. When asked if he was not Satty, and if he had known him in Milwaukee, Kearns coyly replied that he did not know whether his name was Smith, Satty, Satinsky, Bolsheviki, or what.

---

[339] *Denver Times*, March 16, 1918.

Referee and promoter Billy Haack disclaimed any knowledge of Smith other than what he had learned in a telegram from Litchenstein. He had wired a dozen managers in an effort to secure an opponent for Dempsey. Litchenstein had told him that Smith was from Montana and had been fighting in Canada.

Herbert Caldwell, writing for the local *Memphis Commercial Appeal*, said Dempsey, heralded as an heir to the heavyweight throne, showed himself for the first time before a local audience (or any audience in the South). He wore white trunks encircled by a green ribbon sash.

Less than a minute into the fight, Dempsey maneuvered the fat-looking Smith/Soddy into a corner and floored him with a semi-left uppercut to the face.

Smith rose at nine, then made two or three awkward swings that missed by feet. Dempsey backed him to the ropes, and sent Smith to the canvas again with a blow similar to the one that decked him the first time.

He rose at nine with an expression of fear, and his lips quivering as if attempting to mutter something to Dempsey. Jack rushed him again. Smith floundered around the ropes to another corner. Hardly had he anchored in the corner when Dempsey chopped him on the chin with a short right, and Smith sank to the floor, coiled up in a knot, and Referee Billy Haack counted to 10, a needless formality. The fight lasted 1 minute 30 seconds.

Non-local sources said Jack Smith (who actually was "Bull" Satty) had been knocked out in the 1st round of a scheduled 8 rounder, having been floored three times, twice with lefts to the face and a third time with a right chop to the chin, and counted out in a dazed condition.[340]

Ultimately, the feeling was that Kearns had pulled a fast one, trying to fool the public, for he had set up the situation where Dempsey would fight and earn money under false pretenses, getting an easy knockout over a man he recently had been using as a sparring partner, whom he knew would be an easy mark.

The *Denver Times* (likely sports-editor Ed Lyons or writer Eddie Day) said Dempsey's recent knockout was wonderful only from the standpoint that the police allowed Dempsey and his manager to get away with it. They were traveling around taking on set-ups. Smith really was Saddy, only a gym performer, on the job to collect a loser's end. They were trying to bilk the public, and "it is high time that the perpetrators be put out of business." Such antics hurt the sport. This writer said Kearns/Dempsey actually were shy to take on tough challenges, despite their claims.

Another alluded to Dempsey's marital issues: "Jack Dempsey appears to be wild to meet about anyone in the world except his wife who says she wants her diamonds back."

John Reisler filed suit in Chicago for breach of contract, and was seeking an injunction to restrain Dempsey from fighting under any other management. Dempsey declared that Reisler had no just claims against him.

---

[340] *Memphis Commercial Appeal, Boston Globe, Louisville Courier-Journal, Chicago Tribune, St. Louis Post-Dispatch,* March 17, 1918. Some later records list him as "Bull Sadee."

Al Spink said upsets were numerous in the ring game. Folks thought Flynn would give Dempsey a test the other night, but he did not. Then they expected Bill Brennan to give him a lacing, but Dempsey put it all over him. This writer said Brennan was the first real fighter that Dempsey had beaten.

The *Denver Times* reported that the Memphis police were on Dempsey's trail, the Wisconsin boxing commission ready to bar him, and the press and public wise to his game. He had been mixed up in too many shady deals, beginning with "his deliberate 'flop' to Jim Flynn," when even his own brother had bet on him to win. Knocking out his own sparring partner and having him use a fake name branded him as a faker. Warrants were issued for the participants, but they had left town. They dared not return to Memphis.

Supposedly they had planned to duplicate the stunt with a certain Jack McCarty or McCarthy in Milwaukee, but the commission discovered that McCarty was Jack Heenan, a dub of the Saddy type, and refused to permit the affair. Dempsey also had been scheduled to box Frank Miller in Denver, who really was Marty Cutler, ex-wrestler and "would-be fighter" (though Cutler had been a Jack Johnson sparring partner and had gone the distance with Tom McMahon, Bill Brennan, and Andre Anderson). The feeling was that Kearns only wanted to match Jack with set-ups and dubs, and was giving the sport a black eye. "This bunking the public is old stuff."[341]

Word was that a Minneapolis club had offered $125,000 for the right to host the Willard-Fulton fight. Some said Willard might start as the odds favorite against Fulton, but the odds might close quickly. "Fulton has whipped every good heavyweight now before the fistic public."

Some speculated that the Cowler bout had won Fulton the Willard fight, for Jess had been afraid to fight him, but now that Fred had shown some vulnerability, Willard had become agreeable. Others said it was a matter of business, that Willard wanted whatever fight was going to pay him the most.

In New York, it was reported that John the Barber Reisler had obtained an injunction restraining Jack Dempsey from fighting in any formal bouts in that state unless he did so under Reisler's management.[342]

Just over a week after the Satty contest, Jack Dempsey was in Joplin, Missouri to fight there against Tom Riley. Dempsey was called a contender for the heavyweight crown and a fan favorite. Kearns said Riley would take the count at an early stage. "We'll treat Riley just the way we have treated all the rest of 'em. That is, knock him out as quickly as possible." Nevertheless, a record-breaking local crowd was anticipated. Nearly 300 enthusiastic fans watched the two work out on March 23, greater than the crowd size at several recent battles.

Dempsey was a crowd pleaser, playing with his sparring partners in every conceivable way that could give spectators a laugh, and they got plenty of them. Jack was as playful as a kitten, and worked with the enthusiasm of a colt just turned out to pasture.

---

[341] *Denver Times*, March 19-21, 1918.
[342] *Memphis Commercial Appeal*, March 17, 1918; *St. Louis Star*, March 21, 1918.

Lou Goldman, Riley's manager, said, "Just stick around and watch us upset the dope. You know what Cowler almost did to Fulton? Well, we'll do a lot more than that to Dempsey." Riley appeared to be in good condition, strong and husky. He did a lot of hard road work. He made no pretense about being a clever boxer, but carried a kick in either hand. Goldman said Riley had great fighting heart, and would surprise folks. Still, it would be mighty challenging to convince anyone who had seen Dempsey work that Riley had a chance.[343]

In Denver, they said that Dempsey was going up against another unknown who appeared to be the biggest mark of them all, the alleged Canadian champion, whom no one had heard of before.

Some reported that in the gym, Riley showed tremendous hitting power with both hands.

Dempsey was the fastest big man ever seen locally. He was a combination of Stanley Ketchel and John L. Sullivan, with speed, shiftiness, and aggressiveness. He weighed around 200 pounds, with a reach of 78 inches, and stood 6'1 ½". He was only 22 years old and growing rapidly.

Dempsey said he heard Riley was a hard boy to beat and had big power. Riley said, "This is one star that I am going to knock out of the sky."[344]

Apparently, Dempsey was a replacement for Fred Fulton, who after struggling recently against Tom Cowler, did not want to ruin his chances at Willard, so Fred called off the Riley fight. Others said that once Fulton agreed to fight Willard, he called off the Riley contest. Dempsey immediately accepted instead.

Nine days after the Smith/Satty bout, on Monday March 25, 1918 in Joplin, Missouri, before the Southwest Athletic Club, Jack Dempsey took on Toronto's Tom Riley, allegedly the champion of Canada, in a scheduled 12-round contest (though some said 15). Supposedly, less than a year ago Riley had scored a knockout victory over Tom Cowler, who recently had put up a remarkable fight against Fulton (though the claim is unverified).

Dempsey's weight was announced as 195 pounds, while the larger Riley weighed 210 pounds.

According to the local *Joplin Globe*, Riley swung like a windmill, landing only one blow to the face, which Jack took with a smile, his head not even rocking, and he kept going right into Riley. After their preliminary skirmish, Dempsey waded in with an assortment of jabs and swings that left no doubt that it would be over soon.

Dempsey proceeded to floor Riley eight times in less than three minutes. Dempsey refused to allow Riley to fall into clinches or get any rest, decking him over and over again. Riley made one despairing grab around Jack's neck, but referee/promoter Jimmie Bronson pried him off. Following that clinch, Dempsey released the punch that ended the affair in the 1st round. After Referee Bronson tolled the fatal ten, Riley was so badly out cold that

---

[343] *Joplin Globe*, March 24, 1918.
[344] *Denver Times*, March 23, 1918; *St. Louis Star*, March 25, 1918.

it took rigorous treatment for more than ten minutes to bring him back to consciousness.

The locals were very impressed. The *Joplin Globe* said,

> That Dempsey will eventually be champion of the world in his division there is no doubt. He has everything a champion needs and he is so fast and so clever that he showed most of his stuff in the few seconds the fight last night lasted. He is fast as a lightweight, can hit harder than any man that ever appeared in a Joplin ring and can see and avoid blows easier than any boxer that ever showed anywhere.[345]

Other semi-local papers, such as the *Kansas City Post* and *St. Louis Post-Dispatch*, reported that Dempsey went after Canadian Tom Riley from the sound of the gong, wading into him viciously, landing repeated lefts and rights to the head and jaw that either knocked him down against the ropes or turned him around. Dempsey decked him seven or eight times, until Referee Jimmy Bronson counted him out in the 1st round. Riley was game to weather the fusillade as long as he did. He landed only one blow, a right to the head, but it only caused the "submarine" to grin. It took a physician 10 minutes to resuscitate and awaken him from slumber-land. Dempsey startled the crowd with his cleverness and marvelous speed. He had pretty footwork, and his blows carried a terrific kick.

The *St. Louis Star* said Thomas Riley lasted less than 2 minutes. Riley scored the first blow, a right cross, but failed to hurt Dempsey. Jack shot over his right to the chin, sending Riley to the mat. Tom rose hastily, and rushed into a clinch, landing one or two body blows. He seemed dazed, and when caught flush on the chin with a left uppercut, went down again. He was not badly hurt, and rose immediately. Rushing in for more, Tom landed a left to the stomach. Dempsey was not stopped in the least, but shot over his right cross for the third knockdown. A solid right sent Riley down for the final count. Hence, this version claimed four knockdowns.

Dempsey impressed spectators as having more power than Fulton, with the ability to hit from any position. He was a whirlwind, and did not spend time boxing, but hit all the time. Riley was a big powerful fellow, and gave his best, but was overwhelmed by the cyclone.[346]

The same day as Dempsey-Riley, in Chicago, Jess Willard and Fred Fulton met to sign formal articles of agreement to fight on July 4, 1918. A Fort Wayne, Indiana club allegedly bid $140,000 for the contest. Some said Willard would earn 75% of the net receipts after expenses were paid. Fulton would receive a flat sum of $20,000. Colonel J. C. Miller was promoting. Each fighter deposited $1,000 forfeits guaranteeing their performances. Willard appeared to weigh about 265 pounds. It would be a battle of giants.

---

[345] *Joplin Globe*, March 26, 1918.
[346] *Kansas City Post, St. Louis Post-Dispatch, St. Louis Star*, March 26, 1918. Dempsey was scheduled to open a one-week engagement at the Standard theater in St. Louis. He also was scheduled to fight Billy Miske in St. Paul in about a month for promoter Jack Reddy of the Capital A.C.

WILLARD and Fulton signing fight articles yesterday in Chicago. In the front row, reading from left to right, are: Ed W. Cochrane, stakeholder; Willard, Col. Miller and Fred Fulton. Directly back of Miller is Ed W. Smith, famous referee. Between Miller and Fulton, standing, is Otto Floto. At the extreme right, standing, is Al Spink, former well known St. Louisan.

Sam Langford was upset that he never had been granted a title fight.

How come dat dis Willard person if he is a real champean, don't give de liddle Boston Tar Baby a chanct – jest one liddle chanct. Dis big cornhusker ain't got no right to pull dis cullud bizness on me. If it hadn't been for a big sick shine he wouldn't be struttin' roun' like a peacock now an' callin' hisself champean. ... How come big Jess champean? By whippin' a pore sick an' wore out cullud man named Jonsing. ... Dat alibi stuff about not fightin' a culled man don't go wid me.

When asked what he thought of Dempsey, Langford replied, "Say, man, thar's one rooster dat looks awfully good to me. Don't laff – but say, he looks pretty near as good to me as I was when I was at my bes'. He ain't one of dem pretty boys. He's jest a plain, ordinary fightah wid a kick in each han'." When asked if Dempsey was big enough to hook up with Willard, Langford said, "Foolish question. He's big enough to hook up with any man's fightah. He might even whip me, an' I'll give him a chanct if he wants it. But dis Dempsey got a hard punch, no use talkin', a very hard punch. He treat Mr. Brennan shamefully, an' he's liable to muss up big Jess if he don't bar him like he did me."

Langford also was high on Fulton, who beat him. "Some fightah, dis Fulton man – some fightah, believe me. A slam in each han' jest like Dempsey. It won't be no Sunday school meet when dey hook up."[347]

The *Chicago Defender* lamented that in spite of the existing world war, in which black folk were participating in the American war effort, lynchings in the South had not ceased.

> It would seem that the lust for gore could now be amply satisfied if those who believe in such methods would appear upon the battlefields of France and assist those who are now engaged in the patriotic work of slaughtering Germans. The Germans are reputed to be cruel and inhuman in their treatment of their enemies, while the southern lynchers are equally cruel and inhuman in their treatment of their friends, provided said friends have a dark skin.

WHERE THE COLOR LINE BEGINS TO FADE

This writer argued that at this particular time, when the country was engaged in war, folks should be focused on the enemy abroad, and the pastime of lynching discontinued. Before Americans could put up a united front to the enemy, there should be changes at home. "A country that preaches democracy and practices something else doesn't inspire the confidence of other countries."[348]

---

[347] *Denver Times*, March 23, 1918.
[348] *Chicago Defender*, March 30, April 6, 1918.

The *Denver Times* received letters from readers who felt that it had criticized Colorado native Dempsey unjustly. For the benefit of doubters, the paper reprinted Mrs. Jack Dempsey's statements which appeared in the *San Francisco Bulletin* on April 19, 1917, claiming that Dempsey deliberately faked the February 13, 1917 Flynn fight and laid down.

United Press staff correspondent H. C. Hamilton of New York said a Fulton-Dempsey bout would be challenging to make, for neither one would be too eager to face the other, even though it would be a great fight. Dempsey likely would be a tough nut to crack, and if Fulton failed to stop him, his match with Willard would be imperiled. On the other hand, Dempsey would be going up against the toughest proposition he ever tackled, one of the hardest-hitting heavyweights ever seen, as well as one of the cleverest. Fulton was more experienced, too. A loss to him would set Jack way back. "Many a good young fighter has been pushed along too fast. It isn't at all improbable that just this thing is happening to Dempsey."[349]

The *St. Louis Star* described Dempsey as imperious and chockful of confidence, strutting around with the dignity of a king.

Dempsey manager Jack Kearns, former manager of Les Darcy, said Fulton had ducked Dempsey, and Willard only signed to fight Fulton after "Ferocious Freddy" struggled with Tom Cowler. Willard selected the lesser of two evils and picked Fulton over Dempsey, who would have been the tougher foe. He did not blame him, saying it was the wise business decision, but Kearns was wise to his game. "Dempsey has fared better in bouts with Morris and Smith than Willard ever did." He said the public would not take Fulton seriously until he defeated Dempsey. Their fight was a way to sidetrack Dempsey. "He is plenty big enough, can hit as hard as any of them, and best of all, he is a thoroughbred and a game boy. What more could be asked?" Jack's greatest handicap was relative inexperience. A lot of his fights were limited by law to only 4 rounds.

Kearns said Dempsey's system simply was "beating 'em to it." Dempsey was the greatest puncher since the days of Sullivan, and he was as shifty as Ketchel. He was not a boxer, but a fighter. Unlike Willard, who was a businessman, he fought because he liked fighting. He fought for honor more than the money, and would fight anybody at any time. He was game and hit all the time, never taking a backward step. He was so game that when Morris resorted to fouling when he was being pummeled, Dempsey did not claim a foul, but instead begged the referee not to interfere, saying, "If any one's going to stop this bird, I'll stop him."

According to Kearns, Dempsey had whipped Morris (in sparring) in Kansas City almost a year before he met him in the ring. When they were introduced while there, Dempsey said, "Gee, you are a big slob, ain't you?" He then placed his fist against Morris's stomach and remarked that it was a great place to bury the good old right. "Dempsey got Morris' goat at that time." Kearns claimed that Dempsey received some training in a northwest lumber camp in Seattle.

---

[349] *Denver Times*, March 25, 26, 1918.

Dempsey said, "I changed my name to Jack because of the Nonpareil. He was one of the greatest of them all, and like old John L., was always on the dead level. I hope I will be like him all my life."

Jack said he had no fear of Fulton's long rangy left, for he had fast feet and always got in close. Brennan had a good left, but nevertheless he got in on him. "Besides that, in fighting a tall man, I would crouch more and make him hit down at me." Jack would step in and smash the ribs. "That's where I live. I am a body puncher, first, last, and all the time."

Speaking of his shiftiness and style, Jack said, "They talk about a certain shift I have. It isn't a shift at all. If I miss with my right hand, my right foot goes forward in front of my left, and in that position I hook or curve my left to head or body, as the target is presented." He always was hitting, and was told that he fought like John L. "I am not afraid to work into instead of away from an opponent's left hand. I seldom stand directly in front of a man, but sway with his blows from side to side." But his main system of defense was cracking away at a man as fast as possible, beating him to it and keeping him on the defense. He buried his chin down well, and didn't mind taking blows on top of the head, and then slammed away wherever he saw flesh. "I find that I will do something that few fighters care to do. I'll take a chance." He wasn't reckless, but presented what looked like an opening to his opponent in order to get in a fair shot himself. "The so-called experts find fault with my style and say that I am easy to hit. They used to say John L. couldn't box." Jack managed to make his foes miss often enough, and he hit them aplenty. He had good balance, and even when he missed, he found a way to launch a good blow with the other hand. "I will meet them all, first come, first served. You will not catch me bending the hinges of my knees to any man as Fulton did to me."

Kearns said Dempsey, like Sullivan, picked up boxing by watching others, and weighed 196 pounds, just like John L. in his prime.[350]

A New York court held that Dempsey had to box for John Reisler, granting an injunction. Reisler had a contract signed by Dempsey. The fighter appeared in 1916 under the management of townsman Ed Price, who had sold his business to take over Dempsey's management. Reisler paid Price enough money to get home. Apparently, Price and Dempsey had no contract, and Reisler signed Jack after seeing him box Andre Anderson. Reisler advanced him certain sums of money. He fought John Lester Johnson. Dempsey alleged that his brother had died, and then disappeared and was not seen for nine months. He re-appeared with a George Fisher of Indianapolis. Dempsey alleged that he was under age when he signed the first contract. In a second contract that he signed, he swore before a notary and witnesses that he was more than 21 years of age. Reisler gave him more money, but Dempsey disappeared again. Reisler alleged that Dempsey had laid down to Flynn.[351]

The *Montrose Daily Press* said his real name was William Harrison Dempsey. The 22-year-old clever heavyweight was married, and his home town was Salt Lake City. His wife (allegedly) lived at the Dempsey home in Salt Lake City with his parents. Jack was born in Manassa, Colorado and began boxing in Salt Lake in 1915 (actually 1914).[352]

H. C. Hamilton believed that the Willard-Fulton fight was a lucky break for Dempsey, because it saved him from fighting and losing to either one. "Fulton would have given him a licking at his present stage of development," as would Willard. Dempsey was progressing in a "nice, easy fashion," getting himself ready for a championship which would mean a lot more to him in the future.[353]

Six days after the Riley contest, on March 31, 1918 at the Standard Theater in St. Louis, Dempsey began exhibiting in a week-long theatrical engagement. He sparred with black fighters Jack Mitchell and Scotty Wilson, and alleged Canadian heavyweight champion Al Williams (1913 LTKOby8 Jess Willard; 1916 LTKOby6 Bill Brennan). Fans enjoyed watching Jack work. Dempsey was a grim, determined scrapper, using the same ferocious, rushing, tearing style as Sullivan.

Tom Riley's manager, Lou Goldman, complimented Dempsey, saying he reminded him of Sullivan in every way. He had a harder punch than Willard or Fulton, and Jack fought and thought faster than both of them.

> Riley can beat most of these big fellows in a punch, but he couldn't get by the Dempsey hurdle. This tough Irishman is the greatest heavyweight of them all since Johnson was in his prime. He's another Sullivan, and I pity the man who makes him extend himself to the

---

[350] *St. Louis Star*, March 28, 1918. Kearns at various times also had managed Kid Scaler, Dick Hyland, Mysterious Billy Smith, Billy Murray, Red Watson, Eddie McGoorty, Jimmy Clabby, Joe Bonds, and Harry Wills.
[351] *Denver Times*, March 28, 1918.
[352] *Montrose Daily Press*, March 29, 1918.
[353] *Denver Times*, March 29, 1918.

limit. Personally, Dempsey is no friend of mine, but I believe in giving credit where it is due. ... He is the fastest big man on his feet I have ever seen. ... Watch his short, quick, snappy moves with his feet. He gets around as fast as Attell once did. Mark my words, Dempsey is the next coming heavyweight champion of the world. Those who see him will not soon gaze on his like again.[354]

It was believed that Willard-Fulton would have a very big gate. Willard-Moran had the second largest gate ever at $140,000, second only to Johnson-Jeffries at $270,775. Third was Johnson-Burns at $97,000. Such figures did not include the immense sums derived from motion pictures.

A movement to lift the ban on fight pictures traveling in interstate commerce in the U.S. was started. Some argued that in war times, a repeal of the federal law could increase revenue which could be taxed.

The *Denver Times* harshly said that Dempsey was a newspaper-made fighter who, except for the Brennan victory, had built his reputation mostly on nobodies or has-beens, and had been involved in a fake knockout to Flynn, which he avenged with ease. Kearns tried to get Willard to fight Dempsey instead of the more-deserving Fulton, touting him as the meteor and cyclone. However, the publicity syndicate could not fool the public. Dempsey had to earn his title shot.

The *Denver Times* writer also criticized Kearns for being tough and demanding in negotiations, asking for more than Dempsey was worth. He generated only $1,200 for the Flynn bout, $1,400 each for the Homer Smith and Carl Morris contests, and $4,000 for the Brennan fight. Kearns was asking for $2,500 guarantees with a privilege of 40% of the gate receipts if larger, plus round-trip tickets from Chicago, with all expenses paid.[355]

John Reisler, also known as John the Barber, filed for an injunction in St. Louis, preventing Dempsey from completing his contract there. Jack was supposed to have his final performance in St. Louis on April 6, but the Reisler temporary restraining order obtained on the 5th prevented it. Reisler claimed that Dempsey signed a 1916 contract for him to manage him, but since then, Dempsey had not permitted him to do so. He estimated losses at $10,000, but would be satisfied if Dempsey returned to his management hereafter. Reisler had been granted an injunction in New York, but it was good only in that state.

When asked about the suit, Jack Kearns replied, "Dempsey declares he was not of age when he signed the contract with Reisler and because of this fact, the latter cannot prove his claim in court." However, the truth was that in December 1916, Dempsey was 21 years old, which was the age of majority/ability to contract. Kearns knew this, saying,

> Dempsey was barely 21 when he went East in 1916. He was ignorant as a wild ass. He fell into Reisler's hands. Reisler is a barber in New York who dabbles in the fight game. He puts on a contract the name

---

[354] *St. Louis Star*, April 1, 1918.
[355] *Denver Times*, April 1, 3, 1918.

of every likely looking pugilist that crosses his trail, in the hope that some day some one of them will come to life and be a meal ticket for him. He gets them for nothing and does little for them. He made three matches for Dempsey in New York, I'm told – with Wild Burt [Kenny], Andre Anderson, and John Lester Johnson. For the three fights Dempsey was paid a total of $156, in one of which he suffered a broken rib. He was so little cared for by Reisler that he had to hock his clothing before the Johnson fight, in order to get something to eat. Reisler did nothing to develop him, to bring him out or to put him on the map in any way. Dempsey was an unknown working in Seattle ship yards when I found him. Now that he's a title possibility this Reisler wants to step in and pick the kale.

Jim Flynn was in town, and wanted a third fight with Dempsey. Speaking of his recent contest with Jack, Flynn said, "Well, what if he did stop me in one round? I just forgot to duck and he caught me. The same thing happened to him ... I stopped him in less than one round when he forgot to lowbridge in time." Flynn said he weighed 187 pounds. However, there was no demand for a third contest between them.[356]

On April 8, 1918 in Chicago, Jess Willard surprised everyone in the Arcade gymnasium by sparring 5 rounds without difficulty against Tony Melchoir and Carl Miller.

Al Spink picked Willard to beat Fulton, saying the time had not yet come for him to lose his title, for he was in better shape than many believed. Others noted that Fulton knocked out Moran, something Willard had not done. Still, Willard had more of a cautious style, with better defense, knew how to use his height and reach, and was sturdy and strong, with a wonderful ability to absorb blows.[357]

On April 12, 1918, Dempsey won his St. Louis court battle with Reisler. Circuit Judge Garesche denied the injunction and dissolved the temporary restraining order against Dempsey which had been granted on April 5. The judge ruled that prizefighting was illegal, entitled to no protection from the court, and hence the contract was and is against the law and public policy of the state, and therefore not valid or enforceable in Missouri.[358]

On April 14, 1918 in Panama City, Panama, Harry Wills knocked out Sam Langford in the 6th round.

Early on, the Willard-Fulton promotion was having difficulties of the political variety. There was a wave of objections to the fight, and the governors of several states were supportive of the objections. The argument was that these men were profiteers who were fighting for money and self-benefit while a war was ongoing and Americans were risking their lives and dying for the country, which was unpatriotic and a slap at Americanism. In newspaper polls, readers allegedly overwhelmingly voted 87,562 to 435 that the two should be fighting in the trenches in France, not in the ring.

---

[356] *St. Louis Post-Dispatch*, April 6, 1918.
[357] *Denver Times*, April 8, 9, 1918.
[358] *St. Louis Star*, April 12, 1918.

It soon appeared that no heavyweight championship fight would be allowed while the war was ongoing. The *Buffalo Enquirer's* Edward Tranter wrote, "But to promote and foster a boxing contest at high prices, just to provide a huge purse for these men, at a time when the country is calling upon the inhabitants to buy Liberty Bonds, Thrift stamps, and contribute to Red Cross and other war funds, and make personal sacrifices, is more than the patriot can stand for." Governors of Colorado, New Mexico, and Nevada immediately wired that they would not allow the fight during the war. It appeared that others agreed. "The fight cannot be pulled off in any state in the Union, according to present indications. The governors of the so-called fight states, which permit decision boxing contests, will refuse to let Willard and Fulton stage this prize fight."

**Wisconsin State Journal, April 21, 1918**

The promoters tried to salvage the promotion by offering to donate the profits or a portion of the profits from the venture to the war effort, but once the anti-fight campaign got started, the momentum was too great to overcome. Others claimed or implied, perhaps erroneously, that Willard was greedy and did not like the idea of giving up a large portion of the proceeds to the government. For a brief time it appeared that the Minnesota boxing commission would sanction it, until Governor Burnquist reversed course and said that under no circumstances would he permit the championship fight to be held in Minnesota, which drew applause from the press, the same press that often supported and reported on boxing and had urged Willard to defend his crown. Now they were criticizing him for attempting to do so.[359]

Of course, there was more than a little hypocrisy and irrational anti-boxing-bias to it all, for there were plenty of businesses and businessmen making a great deal of money during the war, but heavyweight championship boxing had powerful public political (and racial) symbolism, and as such was subject to expedient political whims and pyrotechnics. As

---

[359] *Knoxville Sentinel*, April 13, 1918; *Wisconsin State Journal*, April 21, 1918; *Buffalo Enquirer*, April 22, 1918; *Denver Times*, April 23, 24, 1918; *Princeton Union*, May 2, 1918; *Kansas City Post*, May 5, 1918.

Tex Rickard once said, no heavyweight championship fight ever could be brought to fruition unless one got himself right with the politicians first. The promoters had failed to get right with the politicians. So Willard-Fulton appeared to be off.

To combat the bad press for his failure to join the military, Willard subsequently admitted that he was older than previously represented, over the draft age limit at that time of 31. He actually was 36 years of age. Hence, he never had registered, because he was not legally required to do so.

*Denver Post*, May 5, 1918

Otto Floto said many wanted to see Fulton and Dempsey fight first, and the winner to fight Willard.[360]

John the Barber Reisler said that when he first met Dempsey, he was a very rough-looking customer, down on his luck, needing clothes, a bath, a shave, and other life necessities. They struck a bargain quickly. Pursuant to their management agreement, he paid for these things, including new underwear and a new suit of clothes, but instead of living up to his contract, Dempsey flew the coop.

Dempsey admitted signing an agreement, but said, "John did me dirt. He got a chunk out of my fight with [John Lester] Johnson. I should have had half. But all John gave was a hand-me-down suit of clothes, which he bought on Baxter street, and which couldn't have cost more than $1.98 in real money."[361]

---

[360] *Denver Post*, May 1, 1918.
[361] *Denver Times*, April 22, 1918.

CHAPTER 13

# The Next Best

Next up for "Submarine Destroyer" Dempsey was a fight with Billy Miske, the "St. Paul Thunderbolt," also known as the "Minnesota Wildcat," one of the best young contenders in the sport, in a fight to be held in Miske's home state of Minnesota. Dempsey did not need to worry about a potential hometown decision, because the contest was a 10-round no decision bout, all that the law allowed in Minnesota at that time.

Although Fulton and Willard were not immediately available, Dempsey was willing to fight top fighters, taking a real risk to further prove himself and keep the momentum going for an eventual title shot. Miske was considered the next best man to Fulton and Willard, other than Dempsey.

At that time, Minnesota was a hotbed of boxing in the Midwest. The state had produced formidable fighters like Billy Miske, brothers Tom and Mike Gibbons, Fred Fulton, and Mike O'Dowd.

At 24 years of age, Billy Miske was only slightly older than Dempsey, but already had a tremendous amount of quality experience, with at least 57 known bouts to that point, losing only 6 decisions or newspaper decisions. His record included: 1914 LND10 Tommy Gibbons; 1915 DND6 Harry Greb, WND10 Mike O'Dowd, LND10 Tommy Gibbons, KO2 Jack Lester, and DND10 Terry Keller; 1916 WND10, LND10, and WND10 Jack Dillon (who had 146 victories), W15 Dick Gilbert, WND10 (twice) Battling Levinsky (who had 125 victories), WND10 Bob Moha, and WND6 Larry Williams; 1917 WND10 (twice) Charley Weinert, WND10 (twice) Jack Dillon, LND10 Battling Levinsky, KO1 Joe Bonds (who had gone the 10-round distance with Dempsey), WND10 and TKO5 Bert Kenny (who had

BILLY MISKE.

gone 10 with Dempsey), WND10 Carl Morris, WND10 Charley Weinert, and L12 Kid Norfolk; and 1918 DND10 Fred Fulton (Miske 186, Fulton 218 pounds), WND10 Gus Christie, TKO7 Tom Cowler (the strong 210-pounder), and W10 Gunboat Smith.[362]

---

[362] Boxrec.com. The United Press called the Miske-Fulton fight a draw. The *St. Paul Daily News* gave it to Miske. The *St. Paul Pioneer Press* called it a draw. The *Minneapolis Tribune* said Fulton won by a shade. *Bemidji Pioneer, Minneapolis Tribune*, January 19, 1918.

Miske's victories over Dillon, Levinsky, Morris, and Smith, as well as having fought a recent no decision draw with Fulton, made him a highly regarded contender. He was respected for his well-rounded skills and ability. He was quick, clever, crafty, aggressive, and tough, able to fight on the inside and mix it with the best. Not only had he never been knocked out, he never even had been knocked down.

Newswriters said that after Willard-Fulton, Miske-Dempsey was the hottest fight on tap. One writer actually said, "Compared to the Willard-Fulton scrap this meeting between Dempsey and Miske looks like the more attractive prospect of the two by a whole lot, and it should be worth going miles to see." Miske carried the fight to Fulton in their draw, proved he could take it against a big powerful man, and Dempsey was known for his rushing, tearing style.

Another writer said Dempsey had been meeting a lot of set-ups and knocking them out cold in 1 round; having fought former sparring partners on at least two occasions. In Miske, he was meeting a true world-class fighter who could hold his own with anyone, and was a much cleverer boxer than Dempsey.[363]

The *Duluth News Tribune* reported that Miske admirers were fearful of the result. For the first time in years, Twin Cities (St. Paul/Minneapolis) fight fans were alarmed and afraid for their hometown favorite, for "Dempsey has made a tremendous impression on fans who know the real thing when they see it." However, "Miske is the more experienced of the two, is a better ring general and possesses more ring craft than his opponent." A great fight was expected. It was the most important battle in both of their careers, and likely would be fought toe to toe. In their local workouts, Dempsey liked to attack the head and jaw, while Miske liked to play for the body. Both had great left hands, but Dempsey's left appeared to be the better of the two.[364]

The *St. Paul Daily News* said the Minnesota plasterer Fred Fulton might box the winner. The Willard-Fulton bout appeared to have fizzled out completely. Many expressed the opinion that neither Dempsey nor Miske could beat Fulton. However, after Miske fought Fulton at the St. Paul Auditorium several months ago, the *Daily News* gave Miske the verdict, and hundreds of fans agreed.

Miske was training at the Nonpareil gym in St. Paul, while Dempsey was working out at Potts' in nearby Minneapolis. Throngs were expected to flock to the two gyms in the afternoon to take a look at the two battlers. Both men had been battering their sparring partners about the ring.

Miske had trained down to about 182 pounds, while Dempsey still was over 190 pounds.

Ticket orders had been received from Eau Claire, Mankato, Chicago, Milwaukee, La Crosse, and dozens of other places.

---

[363] *Fort Wayne News and Sentinel*, April 20, 1918; *Lima Daily News*, April 22, 1918.
[364] *Duluth News Tribune*, May 1, 1928.

Dempsey had been a 10 to 7 favorite the prior week, but Miske's good form in training brought the odds to even.[365]

Jack Veiock reported that Dempsey said his fighting ability was an inborn natural talent and instinct. Without that talent, one had no chance to make a real reputation. Continuing, Dempsey said,

> You've got to have the fighting heart. And if you don't like to fight you can make a bet with yourself that you haven't got it. Learning some of the fine points about fighting may be all right, because you have to know a few things to keep within the rules. But when you get into the ring with a stranger it's up to you to make your own fight and you've got to do it as you go along. Trying to get the low down on the other fellow in advance doesn't do you a whole lot of good, for you may go in there figuring on fighting along certain lines and then change it all after you get started. Take it from me, fighting instinct is with you when you are born.

Dempsey had his ups and downs, and many young chaps might have quit early on when he endured struggles and some mixed results. But the natural old fighting instinct kept spurring him on. Otherwise he would be working in a Seattle shipyard today instead of trailing Willard or Fulton. He was crestfallen when Flynn sent him out with a hard right swing to the jaw. "But he realized that he wasn't in condition when he met Flynn and that he had taken a bout with one of the toughest old-timers in the business on short notice. So he didn't exactly give up hope." Dempsey figured that you could not keep a real fighting man down. Furthermore, good management by Kearns had helped bring the Colorado Demon to the front.[366]

Abe Attell said the Dempsey whirlwind was the greatest fighter of the age. He noted that Dempsey had not been battered up by his opponents. The *Denver Times* harshly responded, "Perhaps Abie hasn't seen the scars on Dempsey's back caused by his taking the flop to Jim Flynn in their now famous battle at Murray, near Salt Lake City."[367]

John "the Barber" Reisler of New York, who alleged that he had certain managerial rights to Dempsey via a three-year contract entered into on December 16 or 18, 1916, wanted to settle his interest. Reisler claimed that he was to receive 30 percent of the net proceeds of all of Dempsey's contests. He alleged that Dempsey had earned more than $25,000 since the contract was signed. Reisler claimed that had Dempsey been under his management, his earnings would have been more than $50,000, and Reisler's share would have been more than $15,000. Reisler also alleged that under the contract, he was guaranteed at least $2,500 per year, and if the 30% did not meet that amount, then Dempsey was required to make up the balance (which some found to be laughable).

---

[365] *St. Paul Daily News, St. Paul Pioneer Press*, May 1, 1918.
[366] *Denver Post*, May 1, 1918.
[367] *Denver Times*, May 2, 1918.

Reisler's attorney had applied for injunctions to restrain Dempsey from boxing, but five different Minnesota judges in Minneapolis and St. Paul denied the request. He even tried to get the State Athletic commission to help him, but his request went ignored. One local judge said Reisler had waited too long, and that enjoining the fight now would prejudice too many people, including the Capital City club, Miske, and the Twin Cities fans. Still, Reisler planned to keep pressing his claim.

The *Denver Post* said Reisler's claim appeared to be of the shakedown variety. In St. Louis, Kearns had obtained a $2,000 judgment against Reisler for his interference, and would further sue him for malicious interference.

Dempsey was a 5 to 4 favorite in the upcoming contest. A large Chicago contingent would arrive, and the odds likely would shift to 10 to 6.[368]

The *Duluth Herald*'s Larry Moore picked the sensational Dempsey to defeat the phenom Miske by a slight shade. The gladiators were pretty evenly matched, but Dempsey had some advantages. Still, it was expected to be a great and close battle. Dempsey was 22 to Miske's 24. They were listed as 6'2" 192 pounds for Dempsey to 6'1" 184 pounds for Miske. Jack had a couple inches reach advantage. Dempsey was an Irish-American, and Miske a German-American.

### HOW THEY COMPARE.

| DEMPSEY. | | MISKE. |
|---|---|---|
| Irish-American. | Nationality. | German-American. |
| 22 | Age | 24 |
| 192 pounds | Weight | 184 pounds |
| 6 ft. 2 in. | Height | 6 ft. 1 in. |
| 78½ in. | Reach | 76 in. |
| 42 in. | Chest (normal) | 42 in. |
| 46½ in. | Chest (expansion) | 45 in. |
| 17½ in. | Neck | 16½ in. |
| 32½ in. | Waist | 33 in. |
| 8½ in. | Wrist | 8½ in. |
| 23 in. | Thigh | 22 in. |
| 13½ in. | Biceps | 12½ in. |
| 15 in. | Calf | 15 in. |
| 9 in. | Ankle | 8½ in. |

It was one of the most important ring battles of recent years. Many believed that the winner would have a good chance to defeat the winner of Fulton-Willard, should the latter bout be permitted.

Miske had improved wonderfully in the past year. He had grown heavier, and was boxing more aggressively. He was working on his power, for he was not known as a knockout boxer. He mostly had won bouts on points. Dempsey was a puncher, but in Miske he would encounter a man much tougher than usual, one with the ability to take it. Miske had fought better men. Still, many were impressed with Dempsey's fighting ability. Local fan and expert opinion appeared to be about evenly divided.[369]

Tickets were selling like hotcakes. Each man had flocks of backers. Both were well-respected and declared themselves to be in top condition.

On a coin flip, George Barton of Minneapolis was chosen to referee. Kearns wanted a Minneapolis man, while Jack Reddy, for Miske, wanted a St. Paul referee. Miske was from St. Paul, where the fight was being held. However, one local reporter later said referee George Barton actually lived in St. Paul, but so often had been used as the third man in the ring for Minneapolis shows, he was perceived as a Minneapolis referee.[370]

---

[368] *St. Paul Dispatch, Minneapolis Morning Tribune, St. Louis Star, Denver Post*, May 2, 1918.
[369] *Duluth Herald*, May 2, 1918.
[370] *Minneapolis Morning Tribune*, May 2, 1918; *St. Paul Daily News*, May 4, 1918.

"Empty" Caine of the *St. Paul Daily News* predicted that Dempsey would have the edge over Miske and win on points. He had advantages in weight, height, reach, speed, punching power, and boxing ability. Nevertheless, a sensational affair was anticipated, and it would not be easy by any means. Miske was one of the world's greatest battlers. But Dempsey was the best-looking heavy that had appeared in St. Paul since boxing was legalized in Minnesota three years ago.

Miske's one big advantage was experience. Billy started his career three years before Dempsey, and had fought better men, including Tommy Gibbons twice, Harry Greb, Al McCoy, Jack Dillon five times, Bob Moha, Battling Levinsky three times, Charley Weinert twice, Joe Bonds, Carl Morris, and Kid Norfolk. Miske knocked out Bonds, stopped Wild Bert Kenney/Kenny, and annihilated Carl Morris. He was outboxed by Gibbons in their two bouts, and outpointed by Levinsky, though he avenged the loss in a rematch. His showing against Fulton was particularly creditable.

This writer said none of the men Dempsey had beaten, with the exception of Bill Brennan, could be classed as first raters at the time he beat them, but his frequent "kayoes" proved he packed a deadly punch, which he also demonstrated in his local gym workouts. Jack's reach was 1.5 inches longer. He was one-inch taller, and 8 pounds heavier. He was faster on his feet, a clever dodger, and both hands had mule-like kicks. Miske always displayed bulldog tenacity and could be relied upon to give everything he had all the time. Still, this writer felt that Dempsey's greater speed, more powerful punch, and better boxing ability would gain him an advantage in total points. However, it would be the first real test for Dempsey with a world-class young fighter. Miske would force him every minute, and it would be no experiment for him, for he had been tested and proven himself many times before. Both were hard hitters, willing mixers, tough and rugged, and they liked infighting.[371]

Otto Floto, sporting editor for the *Kansas City Post* and *Denver Post,* said much interest was manifested in the year's biggest fistic contest. "It is and has been recognized as the best bout scheduled in years between two high class men." It was an even matchup between two elite heavyweights. Miske had "never been knocked off his feet in 74 encounters in which he has engaged." Dempsey was a big puncher who was "deemed by many experts as the logical candidate to meet Willard for the title."

Spider Kelly and former world middleweight champion Eddie McGoorty were training Dempsey. Kelly was known as one of the best cornermen in the business, having worked with Jimmy Britt, Stanley Ketchel, and Tom Sharkey. McGoorty told Floto, "I have seen a lot of big men, but never one with the speed and driving power of this fellow, Dempsey. ... Add to this the fact he possesses powers of assimilation beyond the ordinary mortal and you'll have an idea what Billy Miske is up against tomorrow night."[372]

---

[371] *St. Paul Daily News*, May 2, 1918.
[372] *Kansas City Post*, May 2, 1918. Johnny Reddy was promoting.

The day of the fight, the *Duluth Herald* said Dempsey was the slight favorite, but Miske had a strong following. Dempsey had "knocked out so many sparring partners that his manager found it difficult to obtain boxers to work out with him."

The *Minneapolis Journal*'s John Ritchie said wagering was even in St. Paul, but Dempsey was the 10 to 8 odds favorite in Minneapolis. The fight would settle the argument regarding who was going to whip Fulton or Willard for the championship. The fans favored Dempsey because he was slightly bigger and had a known wallop. Miske was the home favorite on sentimental grounds. The fans believed Billy was a shade the better boxer, but he was not a knockout artist. He had scored technical knockouts and made men quit, though. Dempsey boxed well enough that he wasn't just a slugger. There would be about 5 pounds difference between the two.

Advance seat sales were reported to have reached the $10,000 mark.

Empty Caine said it would be a case of a clever boxer against a tough mixer who knew no fear and liked to bore in and assimilate punishment to send over a haymaker. The show started at 8:15 p.m.

E. R. Hosking of the *St. Paul Dispatch* believed that the local St. Paul lad should win, for his experience and ring generalship probably would prove to be the deciding factors. Because it was such an even matchup, prospects for a vast crowd were bright. Thousands wanted to find out which one was most entitled to challenge for the championship.

Hosking said Dempsey seemed to have every qualification for a coming champion except experience, which he was acquiring rapidly, but at this point, Miske's superior knowledge of ring tactics should prove sufficient to counterbalance Dempsey's superior hitting power. The only area Dempsey appeared to be clearly superior was strength and punching power. "Dempsey is a free hitter and has tremendous power in his wallops. He can hit hard from any angle, and in this respect undoubtedly is superior to Miske. His footwork also compares favorably with that of Miske." Dempsey had a deceptive shift as well.

However, "In ring-craft Miske is Dempsey's master. He knows what to do and how to do it. He is more expert in going into and coming out of clinches, and at infighting he should more than hold his own tonight." Though Dempsey was stronger, he was no more rugged. Miske had faced the fire of Fulton's dreaded left for 10 rounds without being knocked down or seriously in distress at any time. A prime Dillon could not knock him down either, nor could Tommy Gibbons, Charlie Weinert, Gunboat Smith, Tom Cowler, Carl Morris, or Kid Norfolk. "Dempsey has never met a boxer of Miske's ruggedness or high class, and it remains to be seen whether or not his attack can stand up under the fire he will be subjected to tonight. If, with the limited experience he has had, Dempsey can beat Miske tonight, he will stand out as a coming champion." Even if beaten, it would be no shame, and Dempsey would not necessarily be eliminated from contention for long, for he was young and still growing and developing.[373]

---

[373] *Duluth Herald, Minneapolis Journal, St. Paul Daily News, St. Paul Dispatch,* May 3, 1918.

The *St. Paul Pioneer Press* said fans were divided on the likely outcome, but all agreed that it should be a hummer. Mike Collins, Fred Fulton's manager, wagered $1,000 against $250 that Miske would be on his feet at the end of 10 rounds. Miske was favored to last the full 10 rounds.

Both men had looked great in their training. The only doubtful point raised about Dempsey was whether he could take punishment. He had stopped his foes so quickly that few had seen him go through 10 rounds of grueling fighting, the kind that Miske was likely to give him. Jack Kearns said Dempsey could take just as much as he could deliver. He pointed out the fights Dempsey had early in his career when he was a rank novice only weighing 165 pounds, but still fighting as a heavyweight, often against heavier and more experienced veterans.

No one questioned Miske's ability to take punishment, or his courage under fire. The locals had seen him in several hard bouts. He took on all comers, and did not look for setups. Billy had improved greatly, as shown in his recent bouts with Fulton, Gunboat Smith, and Cowler, which "proved very conclusively that there are very few boxers in the game today who have any business in the same ring with him."

Fred Coburn for the *Minneapolis Morning Tribune* said if Dempsey lived up to his form in the gym he should win, but if he did not, he would lose. Miske was one of the finest defensive fighters in the game. He never had been upset and had met practically every good big man in the country. Previous criticism was that he was not a puncher. But recently Miske had shown improvement in power, for he scored a knockout over Cowler, and sent Smith down for a count, although it wasn't a knockout. Miske's followers did not believe any man living could best him by any wide margin. He had the ability to give and take and keep boring in every minute, showing fistic grit, as shown by his bout with Fulton.

Dempsey was willing to rough it with anybody, could hit hard with either hand, and had stamina and courage galore. Hence, on paper, it was a great matchup. A $20,000 house was predicted.

The *Chicago Herald and Examiner* said Dempsey was the 5 to 4 odds favorite. A big Chicago delegation was heading to Minnesota to attend the event.

The *Kansas City Post* said Dempsey's gym-showing installed him as a favorite with the fans. "They have doped Miske as perhaps the better boxer and very fast, but Dempsey is a hard hitter and by no means slow."[374]

Boxing writer and former referee Abe Pollock of Denver's *Rocky Mountain News* predicted that Miske would beat Dempsey. The fight would be followed with keen interest all over the country. It was an acid test for Dempsey, who had been boosted sky high. "Dempsey was unknown a few months ago in ring circles, but thru the notoriety he has received he has come to the front faster than any fighter now before the public." His most important bout to date was with Brennan, a well-known tough mixer. Most of Dempsey's other fights were "setups," against unknowns, gym trial

---

[374] *St. Paul Pioneer Press, Minneapolis Tribune, Chicago Herald and Examiner, Kansas City Post*, May 3, 1918.

horses, and men who were past it or out of shape. The 6'1" Dempsey was about 195 pounds, fairly clever, with a good kick in both mitts. He was meeting a shifty, young, first-class man, an all-round two-handed boxer and fighter who knew all the fine points of the game, who was next to Fred Fulton in point of record. He stood about the same height as Dempsey and weighed around 185 pounds. He had been fighting since 1913 and was able to secure a newspaper draw against Fulton, who outweighed him by 30 pounds and had height and reach advantages. Pollock said that outside of Willard and Fulton, Miske looked like the best scrapper in the country. "In my opinion Miske is too clever and knows too much about the boxing game for Dempsey, and I look for Billy to get the newspaper decision in tonight's bout."

On the East Coast, H. C. Hamilton wondered why Dempsey was the favorite even though his record was not as impressive as Miske's. It appeared to be because of his superior punch. The fight would prove whether Dempsey was a "fluke pretender" or really had the goods. This writer believed Miske would win on points, or do no worse than a draw, for he was the best man Dempsey ever had met.

The *Denver Times'* Eddie Day said Dempsey would receive an acid test, and his fighting ability put on trial. Miske was one of the best in the business, and had much greater experience against top men. "I look for Miske to win. ... If Dempsey wins in clean-cut fashion he will be entitled to a great deal of credit."

Dempsey had been knocking out his sparring partners. On three consecutive days during the past week he knocked out Bill Moore on Monday, black Rough House Ware on Tuesday, and Al Henning on Wednesday.[375]

On Friday May 3, 1918 in St. Paul, Minnesota, at the St. Paul Auditorium, under the auspices of the Capitol City Athletic Club, Jack Dempsey fought a scheduled 10-round no decision contest with Billy Miske. George Barton refereed. At 3 p.m. that day, Dempsey weighed 187 ½ pounds stripped, which was a surprise, for most had expected Dempsey not to go below 190. Miske weighed 182 pounds in his street clothes.

It was a good-sized crowd, one of the largest houses ever to see a fight in the city. Yet, one said it was not quite as large as hoped/expected, with some bare spots here and there throughout the building; hence a bit disappointing given the pre-fight hype and quality of the competitors. Otto Floto reported that it was *the* largest house ever to gather in the city to witness a boxing bout. There were 5,035 admissions, including 380 complimentary tickets/passes that were given out. Tickets went from $1 up to $5, in one-dollar increments. Locals said the official gate receipts were $13,400 or $13,536.80. The state would receive a 10% tax for the state anti-

---

[375] *Rocky Mountain News, Evening State Journal and Lincoln Daily News, Denver Times*, May 3, 1918. Rough House Ware's record included: 1912 D10 Young Jack Johnson; 1913 L8 Jeff Clark, D10 Dave Mills, and LKOby6 George Kid Cotton; 1914 LKOby10 Harry Wills and LTKOby5 Sam Langford; 1915 L25 Kid Norfolk, DND15, LKOby15, and LTKOby11 Clark; and 1916 L25 Kid Norfolk and LTKOby5 Cotton.

tuberculosis fund. Another said a $1,524.60 tax was owed, which meant the receipts were $15,460. Others said the gross receipts were estimated at around $16,000 or $19,000 (and the real numbers were under-reported).

Dempsey earned $4,000 or $5,000, depending on the source. One said Dempsey was working on a 33 1/3% basis or a guarantee of $4,000 (likely whichever was greater). The actual amount he was paid was not known, for he sold his purse to Jack Flynn of St. Paul for a flat sum.

Dempsey likely sold his share in advance as a way to thwart any John Reisler efforts to attach his purse. Reisler had filed a $50,000 suit in St. Paul against Dempsey for money due him under his managerial contract, and was attempting to attach and garnish any money owed to Dempsey.

Miske, playing on percentage (25%), received a sum a trifle less than Dempsey's minimum guarantee, with one saying Billy earned $3,384.20.

Given the cost of the purses, preliminaries, taxes, and other expenses, the promoters, Hilton and Reddy (who also was Miske's manager), probably would be able to show only a small profit, though the amount was unclear.

Ed Smith said that at ringside, Dempsey was the 7 to 10 favorite.

Dempsey entered the ring first, at 9:55 p.m. Miske followed a minute later. Dempsey was seconded by Spider Kelly, Jack Kearns, Arthur LaForest, and Rough House Ware. Miske had brothers Ed and Jack Reddy, the latter his manager, Billy McCarney, and Sap McKenna. They posed for a photo at ring center, received instructions from the referee, and went at it shortly after 10 p.m.

The following round-by-round accounting is based on reports from newspapers which had reporters at the fight.

1st round

The reporters generally agreed that the round was fairly tame and even, with both sparring and fiddling around very cautiously, feeling out one another. Nervous and tense, neither really wanted to lead. They fired, led, and countered, to the body and head, but few blows landed, and even fewer landed solidly. Mostly they landed taps, not really attempting hard blows. They clinched and ducked quite often. There was little action. They were quite careful, boxing evenly both at close and long range.

Seven ringside reporters scored it even, while only one said Miske won by a slight shade:

*Minneapolis Morning Tribune* (MMT)(by Fred Coburn) - Tame even round.
*Minneapolis Journal* (MJ)(by John Ritchie) - Honors even.
*St. Paul Daily News* (SPDN)(by Empty Caine) - Not a solid blow was struck. Round even, with any possible shade to Miske. Miske may have landed one more blow but Dempsey was the aggressor.
*St. Paul Pioneer Press* (SPPP)(by E. R. Hosking) - Tame feel-out round. Dempsey led more often, but his leads were blocked easily. Even round.
*Duluth Herald* (DH)(by Larry Moore) - They sparred. Dempsey impressed the crowd with his clever footwork. Dempsey landed the first real blow of the fight when he smacked his left up against Miske's chin. Round a draw, with Dempsey having a hairline, if any.
*Duluth News Tribune* (DNT)(by Louis Gollop) - Miske by a slight shade. He landed a few telling blows and did most of the forcing.
*Chicago American* (Smith)(by Ed W. Smith, sports-editor) - Even feel-out round.
*Kansas City Post/Denver Post* (Floto)(by Otto Floto) - Even round, with feinting and feeling out.

2nd round

The reporters generally agreed that they picked it up a bit in this round, both landing some good blows, but Dempsey seemed to have Miske a bit puzzled. Jack used his shifting to good effect, landing some solid hooks and body blows with both hands, causing Miske to hang on. Jack drove him to the ropes. Miske was clinching often, as Jack was attacking primarily to the head, forcing the pace more, while Miske was hitting the body.

Seven of the ringside reporters agreed that Dempsey won the round, while one was a bit ambiguous, perhaps implying that it was even.

MMT - Dempsey took the round by a good margin.
MJ - Miske not boxing cleverly at all in this round and seemingly was puzzled by Jack's tactics. Dempsey round.
SPDN - Dempsey landed with both hands to the jaw, driving Miske to the ropes. Billy clinched. Dempsey scored several right and left hooks to the jaw. Dempsey's round.
SPPP - Dempsey started forcing the pace and hooked two lefts to the chin, but Miske landed a hard right to the face. There were some even exchanges,

and as the round ended, Jack landed a stiff right to the face and followed it with a left to the chin that gave him the edge. Dempsey round.

DH - The fight really got started and the crowd roared. Dempsey had the best of a melee; swinging right and left, though connecting only partially. Dempsey, hitting unpardonably low at times, is jeered by the crowd. Dempsey works lightning shift with good effect and lands one or two with his great left. Dempsey's round.

DNT - Another feel-out round. Toward the end, Dempsey evened it up with a solid left and repeat to the head. Dempsey used his famous shift to much advantage, and during the early part of the fight had Miske puzzled.

Smith - Dempsey's round.

Floto - Dempsey shook up Miske considerably with a right to the jaw and forced Miske around the ring, earning the round by a shade.

3rd round

Dempsey seemed to be landing harder and more often, having more impact with his blows, though Miske made a comeback at the end of the round to make it closer.

Six of eight on-scene reporters said it was Dempsey's round, five of them saying by a slight shade margin, and one saying it was Dempsey's round clearly. One reporter seemed to indicate it was even, and another said it was a clear Miske round.

MMT - Miske was fighting better, running in with both hands, but missing, for Dempsey was able to back away and was very clever at ducking and sidestepping. Dempsey caught him with a hard left and Miske slightly staggered. Billy displayed his rallying power, however, and landed what proved to be almost if not his very best punch of the evening, a right to the jaw. It was high, and did not slow up Dempsey. The rally was not sufficient to prevent Dempsey from gaining a shade in the round.

MJ - Dempsey again started as the aggressor. His left was worrying Miske, and he also landed a hard right to the body. Miske replied with two low lefts and Dempsey shot a wicked one to the stomach and followed with a right to the head. Dempsey rocked Miske's head with hard left and right and flashed a second right to the head. He was making Miske look very bad. Miske reached the head, and Dempsey returned with a stiff straight left to the head and right to the body. Miske jabbed Dempsey twice at the bell. Dempsey's round.

SPDN - Close in, Dempsey landed three rights to the jaw, and followed with another left and right to the jaw. His left landed again and they clinched. A hard right shook Miske and they clinched. Dempsey shot four lefts and rights to the face and Billy clinched. Dempsey sent two lefts and one right to the jaw, and Miske planted a left to the stomach. Miske sent left and right to the head. Close in, Dempsey sent a hard left to the stomach. Miske ended the round with two solid left uppercuts and a right to the jaw, helping to overcome any big lead Dempsey had. Dempsey's round by a slight margin.

SPPP - The round was comparatively tame, starting as usual with Dempsey doing the leading and Billy making him miss. No damage was done.
DH - Dempsey's left still was making itself felt. Miske staved off a bad beating by making strenuous efforts to come back towards the end of the round. Dempsey's round by a shade.
DNT - Miske took the round by a wide margin, staggering Dempsey with a hard jolt to the jaw.
Smith - They started fast but then clinched. They mixed it up. A Dempsey left to the jaw staggered Miske. Billy landed three to the face but it was not enough to even the round. Dempsey's round by a shade.
Floto - Round went to Dempsey on his aggressiveness alone.

4th round

Miske got busier and more aggressive in this round, though there still was a lot of clinching and wrestling, without many effective blows being landed by either. It was a close round, though all but one of the on-scene reporters agreed that Miske had the edge, particularly coming on strong late in the round with clever attacking and infighting. The lone dissenter had it even.

MMT - Miske attacked like a wild man, and Dempsey met him toe-to-toe for some of the fight's best battling, though they missed their hardest wallops by a hair. Miske came on strong at the finish, outslugging Dempsey momentarily and winning his first round.
MJ - Miske rushed Dempsey to the ropes and they clinched and infought, with Miske having the better of it. They exchanged low pokes but neither complained. Miske landed two rights to the head. He poked a hard right to the jaw and a left to the solar plexus. Miske again rushed him to the ropes and landed heavily to the stomach and jaw. Miske's round.
SPDN - They exchanged, clinched, punched, and wrestled, mostly in close, fairly evenly. Dempsey shot two hard lefts to the jaw and went in and landed two more lefts to the jaw. Dempsey hit a low right to the body and was booed. Billy got the best of a session of close-in work, and was out and in again, landing two rights and two lefts to the stomach, earning Miske the round.
SPPP - The pace quickened in this round, with Miske coming to life and doing more than half the leading. He drove Dempsey across the ring and landed a hard right swing that put Jack against the ropes. Dempsey hit one low punch, for which he apologized.
DH - Miske leapt into the center of the ring and lead off with a right to the jaw. Dempsey returned with a left to the face. Dempsey's blows were hard and swift, but Miske was blocking a lot of them. Miske got a slight shade on the round with his clever in-fighting.
DNT - Miske.
Smith - Miske started to get aggressive, but neither did much but wrestle. Miske landed a right hook to the neck but took a left to the same place. Jack

was cautioned for a low punch. Dempsey landed a right to the face. Miske made him cover up with rights and lefts to the jaw. Miske round.

Floto - Dempsey started as though the end was in sight, but Miske finished strongly enough to be given an even break.

5th round

Miske rushed and attacked again, but Dempsey landed a vicious right. They fired rapid blows, fighting about evenly on the inside, though some said Miske did the better work on the inside. Dempsey landed less often, but he landed harder with his right, hooks, and uppercut. Still, Miske had some spurts of hard and effective punches as well. They also engaged in their usual clinching. Dempsey's shift was not as effective, as Miske seemed to have solved it.

The aggregate mix of reporters saw this as a pretty even round. Three gave it to Miske, two gave it to Dempsey, and three saw it as even.

MMT - Miske began carrying the fight to Dempsey, but suddenly was checked when Dempsey landed a vicious right to the side of the jaw. It was the best punch up to that point, and was followed by some others, then rapid-fire work by both men, and some clinching which marked every round. Dempsey won this round.

MJ - Dempsey opened with a stiff left to the face and Miske started rushing again, forcing Dempsey to the ropes, where they scored evenly in the infighting. Dempsey landed a hard crack to Miske's jaw, and Billy went in close for a clinch, then scored right and left hooks to Dempsey's head, and they exchanged rights and lefts. Dempsey scored a left to the stomach. Miske landed a light left and they bulled into a clinch. Honors even.

SPDN - Dempsey led with his left to the face. Miske came back with two lefts and a right. At in-fighting, Miske had the best of it. Dempsey crashed a terrific right to the jaw, and when close-in, sent two lefts to the head. They clinched. Miske again got the best of the infighting, but no damage was done. Miske sent a left to the face. Miske backed Dempsey into a corner, where they clinched. Dempsey landed his left to the face and they clinched. Dempsey took a left to the jaw at close range, and they clinched again. They were rushing at the bell. Round even.

SPPP - There was some more lively work. Billy seemed to have gotten his bearings and landed his left to Dempsey's jaw and scored repeatedly in the infighting. Dempsey came back with a hard right to the jaw and several straight lefts to the face that evened the score. Dempsey tried his shift repeatedly in this round, but got nowhere with it. The round ended with a lot of harmless fiddling.

DH - Miske cleverly ducked Dempsey's swings. Miske seemed to have solved Jack's shift for the first time. Miske's round.

DNT - Miske.

Smith - They mixed fiercely, with Miske having a shade in the initial exchange, rocking Dempsey twice. Dempsey landed a terrific left to the face, making Miske clinch. Dempsey uppercut him. Miske looked a trifle tired. Billy landed a hard left to the face. They mixed it. Miske landed a left at the bell which straightened Jack up. Dempsey's round.

Floto - Miske's round by a clean margin, for Dempsey seemed tired.

6th round

They were cautious, and wrestled around a bit. Miske landed several punches, but one said his blows had no effect. Jack landed a hard left to the mouth that drew a little blood. Miske finished strong, landing several blows in succession. A wonderful right from Miske landed cleanly. Dempsey backed and danced away. Miske forced him back to the ropes at one point. Except for one who called it even, the other reporters unanimously agreed that it was Miske's round.

MMT - The round started slowly. Miske landed right, left, and right, but had no effect on the sturdy Irishman. Jack landed a hard left to the mouth which cut Bill a little and drew some blood. It was the only gore-producing punch of the bout. Miske, though stung, fought better. He came on strong at the finish, as he did in several other rounds. Miske round.

MJ - Dempsey fired a left to the stomach and light right to the head. Then he landed a right to the stomach. Miske tore in with blows, and they exchanged lefts. Miske fired right and left. He followed with two more. Dempsey landed a right to the head and a left to the jaw. Coming out of a clinch, Miske shot right and left to the head and followed with fusillade of rights and lefts that Dempsey could not stop. Just before the bell, Miske went on another rampage and scored two rights to the face and a left to the body, followed by two more lefts to the body. Miske's round.

SPDN - They were cautious and bullied each other around. They clinched. They exchanged lefts and rights. Dempsey sent a left to the face and rushed in with a left to the body. Miske shot a right to the jaw and they clinched. Dempsey sent in an easy left and right to the head. Dempsey danced around and they clinched. Miske drove in two lefts and a right to the body and followed with two lefts to the head with no return. Dempsey smeared Miske with a solid left to the mouth and they clinched. Miske dashed in and sent a fusillade of nine lefts and rights into the midsection without return. He backed Dempsey to the ropes. At in-fighting, honors were even, with no damage. They were slashing when the bell sounded. Miske's round.

SPPP - After some harmless sparring, Billy opened up and scored four clean blows with right and left to the face without return. Dempsey backed away, but came back with a left hook to Miske's jaw. Dempsey missed a heavy right swing and Billy got in quickly and shot a hard right followed by heavy left to Dempsey's jaw. He rushed Jack to the ropes. Dempsey broke ground repeatedly in this round. The round was Miske's, his best showing yet. He took a clear lead in this round.

DH - Dempsey led with his left to the stomach. The crowd soon realized that Jack was playing for a knockout in the vicinity of the solar plexus. Miske landed a wonderful right to the jaw, with the crowd cheering wildly. Dempsey fired a right into Miske's midsection, following with a left to the

jaw. Miske earned a slight shade in the round by returning with rights to the jaw.
DNT - Miske clearly, for he had Dempsey groggy.
Smith - Dempsey's shift was not finding much success. Miske landed his left to the face. Dempsey uppercut the jaw. They exchanged hard blows with both hands to the face and body. Miske took a hard left to the jaw. Billy hit Jack's face seven times without return. They clinched at the bell. Miske round.
Floto - Even round, for many punches were exchanged from start to finish.

7th round

Dempsey badly hurt and nearly decked Miske in this round, hurting him more than anyone ever had, starting with a right uppercut. He landed the most effective blows of the fight in this round. However, Miske held on and survived, and even rallied a bit near the end. All of the reporters agreed that Dempsey won this round, in what would be the clearest and most dominant round of the entire fight.

MMT - Dempsey almost knocked Miske off his feet, something which no one ever has done. After breaking from a clinch, Miske stood still for a second with his hands down. Dempsey took advantage of the momentary lapse and landed a crashing right uppercut to the chin. Bill went in the air and fell back against the ropes. Dempsey was on top of him, firing left and right, landing, but without finishing force. Miske managed to clinch and cover up. Dempsey landed two more rights to the chin, and Miske was fighting desperately, showing courage, but when the round ended, he was groggy, weak, and glassy-eyed. It was the first time someone really was hurt and on the verge of going down. This round was so much in Dempsey's favor that it would help earn him a clear shade in any decision.

MJ - Miske came out aggressively and confidently, but Dempsey shot a left to the head, right to the body, and repeated his left to the face. He followed up with a right to Miske's body. Miske landed a light left to the face and right and left to the head. Dempsey stepped in with a hard right to the stomach, left to the head, and wicked right to the jaw, and Miske was hurt. Billy jumped in and clinched and hung on until his head cleared, but following a break, Miske could not dodge a hard left to the jaw. Dempsey went after him with a right to the jaw. Miske suddenly made a remarkable rally and started trying to carry the fight to Dempsey. Jack met him with right and left to the face and two to the stomach at the bell. The clear Dempsey round had come close to being the end for Miske.

SPDN - They danced around carefully. Dempsey started with two lefts to the face and another left to the head, but did no harm. Miske came back with two rights to the head. Dempsey drove an easy left to the head and they clinched. They danced and went into a clinch again; with no damage done. They were out and in again, and wrestled.

Dempsey drove a powerful right uppercut to the jaw and shot left and right to the chops, driving Miske to the ropes. The first right was the hardest blow of the fight and Miske seemed dazed. He hung on and clinched until his head cleared. Dempsey followed with a hard left to the jaw and again Miske held on. After breaking, Dempsey tried hard for the knockout, but was wild. They stood toe-to-toe and slammed away, each landing four blows of about equal power. They broke from a clinch and rushed together again. Dempsey was the aggressor. He missed a hard right and shot a right to the stomach. They clinched, and as they broke, the bell ended the round. Dempsey's round.

SPPP - Dempsey recovered lost ground. He started this round with two harmless rights that landed on top of the head. They fiddled, and Jack suddenly worked his shift and shot a hard right to the stomach that made Billy wince. His knees bent a little and he backed away. Dempsey rushed him to the ropes and planted a hard left swing to the jaw. These probably were the most damaging blows landed during the entire fight. Billy rallied quickly and was holding his own as the bell rang, but it was Jack's round by a mile.

DH - Dempsey had his best round by slashing furiously into Miske, swinging rights and lefts to the jaw, and rushing his opponent into the ropes. Miske was groggy for a moment, but soon awakened, and apparently enraged, returned the compliment and rushed Jack back into the opposite hempen lines, slipping in four beauties. Dempsey backed his man to ring center and had the best of the exchanges. Dempsey's round.

DNT - They fought their best. Miske was staggered in the early part, but toward the end sent eight fast uppercuts to the jaw. Dempsey took the round by a slight shade.

Smith - Miske rushed him to the ropes and landed to the body. Jack did considerable dancing, trying to get in his shift. He landed an awful uppercut to Miske's jaw, making him hold on. Dempsey landed a left to the face and they clinched. They slugged, with Dempsey having the best of it. Dempsey's round clearly.

Floto - It looked like curtains for Billy. An uppercut to Miske's chin caused his knees to sag, and as he began to sink he held on fast. Dempsey pushed him off and tried to finish him, but Miske clinched well. Dempsey again jolted him, shaking him up until the bell rang.

8th round

Miske gradually recuperated in this round. Dempsey rushed him to the ropes and landed hard to the body, but Miske fought back well. They clinched often, and Dempsey showed his strength. Later in the round, Dempsey nailed him with several body and head shots, and Miske was hanging on. Still, Miske did some good infighting. He had an uncanny ability to recover and recuperate well from hard blows, and showed his gameness by firing back soon after being hit.

Six reporters gave this round to Dempsey, four of whom said he won it by a shade, while two others called it even.

MMT - Miske recuperated rapidly, until eventually he was the same old Miske. Dempsey rushed him to the ropes, but Miske fought back with everything he had, landing hard but too high with a right. Miske was hanging on in the latter part of the round. Dempsey had the round.

MJ - They danced and feinted. Dempsey landed two to the face and Miske came back with a right to the jaw. Dempsey rushed Miske to the ropes and landed two hard rights to the body. Miske cracked two lefts to the body. Dempsey shifted and shot a right to the stomach. He followed with a right to the head and whipped his right to the body. Miske landed a right to Dempsey's ribs and Dempsey rocked Miske with right and left to his face. Jack was working on Billy's body, and they swapped lefts at the bell. Dempsey's round.

SPDN - They danced about for a bit. Dempsey fired right and left to the face. Miske landed a right to the head. They rushed to a clinch, broke out, and Dempsey lifted his left to the chin and rushed Miske to the ropes. They clinched, exchanged lefts, and clinched again; then wrestled. Miske drove a left to the face, but took left and right to the same place. They swung, dodged, and clinched. Close in, Dempsey dodged and sought an opening. He played for the stomach. Miske crossed a right to the head and they clinched. Dempsey's strength showed in the clinches. They exchanged lefts and Dempsey landed a right to the head. They clinched and broke several times. Dempsey sent a right to the body and left to the head as the round ended. Dempsey's round by a shade.

SPPP - Dempsey had a slight lead in the round.

DH - They exchanged wallops, Dempsey landing the best blow, a left to the chin. Jack's left was worrying Miske a lot. Billy did some excellent infighting. Round is a draw.

DNT - Even round.

Smith - Miske came up fresh. They mixed it furiously, Miske landing a hard right to the head. Dempsey rushed him to the ropes. Miske landed left and right to the head. They clinched. Dempsey landed a right to the body and they clinched. Dempsey landed a hard right to the jaw and a left to the head. Dempsey's round by a shade.

Floto - Dempsey again sent in stiff blows, shaking up Miske a bit, but doing no other material damage.

9th round

This round featured a fair amount of clinching. Both fighters had slowed up their pace, though they still were fighting hard, exchanging back and forth. Nevertheless, few solid or effective blows were landed. The round was about even. Three writers called it even, three gave it to Dempsey, and two gave it to Miske.

MMT - Dempsey appeared tired, for he loafed a bit. Miske came on strong enough to keep the round even. Few solid lands by either one, with a fair amount of clinching. Even round.

MJ - Dempsey again started with a lead left to the body. Miske crossed a hard left to the face. Dempsey found Miske's ribs with a right. Miske sent a right to the head, then followed with a left hook to the face and right to the ear. They were showing signs of the travel, but fighting hard. They clinched. On the break, Miske scored a right and left to the stomach. At this stage, Dempsey was boxing more wildly that at any time, and Miske was taking advantage of it to drive. Dempsey rallied slightly at the bell with several light body punches, but not enough to take the honors. Miske round.

SPDN - They started carefully. Miske landed two light lefts but took one in return. Dempsey landed a left to the head and they clinched. Dempsey led with a straight left and followed with a right to the body. Miske responded with a right to the head and left to the body. He followed with two rights to the head. They rushed in close. Miske sent a right cross to the head. Dempsey repaid him with a hard left. They clinched and wrestled. Dempsey landed a right hook to the jaw and they clinched. Close in, Miske drove in three light body blows and Dempsey sent two to the head. Close infighting was even. Dempsey blocked a hard right and sank two lefts and rights to the stomach at the end. Round even.

SPPP - Miske by a shade.

DH - Dempsey did all the leading, but few telling blows were delivered. Dempsey's round by a shade.

DNT - Dempsey.

Smith - They mixed furiously. Miske was a trifle weak, but landed a hard left to the face. They clinched. Dempsey uppercut him. They slugged at a fast pace, toe to toe. Miske took a hard left to the jaw, but landed a right in return. Dempsey landed a hard right to the stomach. Round even.

Floto - Dempsey was the aggressor throughout, carrying the fight to him all the way.

10th round

They kept exchanging and fighting hard, but both were a bit fatigued, and still clinching a fair amount as well. The crowd was disappointed that they did not have a whirlwind finish, feeling that they should have opened up more. Some said Dempsey attacked more, others said Miske, while others said they both fought hard and had their moments. Miske met Dempsey's powerful blows with clever guarding, though some got through. Miske did some good infighting.

Overall, it was another even round. Four local reporters said the round was even, two said it was Miske's round, and two said it was Dempsey's round.

MMT - The final two rounds were similar. The bout ended tamely, with hardly a sold blow landed, and the crowd was upset by the lack of real fighting ambition by both men in these rounds. There was too much clinching. Even round.

MJ - Dempsey billeted right and left to the body. He also registered a right to the jaw and followed with a second to the same spot. Dempsey landed a left to the head and they clinched. On the break, Miske put a right to the head and Dempsey fired a left to the body. Miske scored right and left to the head. Dempsey started rushing hard and landed a right to the head and left to the body. Miske scored the same in the exchange and then grabbed and hung on. Miske was tiring, but hit right and left to the head, and they exchanged rights. Dempsey shot another right to the jaw and came back with right and left to same spot. Miske jabbed the stomach. Dempsey's round and fight.

SPDN - They rushed to a clinch and wrestled. Dempsey missed right and left and they clinched. Dempsey swung his left, but took a left and they clinched and wrestled. Close in, Miske reached the head with his right, and Dempsey repaid him in kind. Miske landed a hard right to the head and they clinched and wrestled. Miske sent two rights to the head, and when close in, landed two light ones to the body, but ran into one of Dempsey's terrific uppercuts. They clinched, and both swung wildly. They exchanged lefts and rights and clinched. Dempsey sent in left and right to the head and followed with a crashing right to the jaw. Miske came back with two light lefts and a right to the head. Round even.

SPPP - Even.

DH - Dempsey was determined to lay Miske low with his left. Miske met the attack with clever guarding. Both were fighting hard, but did not open up as much as the crowd had expected. Miske's in-fighting earned him a very slight shade in the round.

DNT - Even.

Smith - Miske took a hard left to his face, and they mixed furiously. Dempsey seemed tired. Miske landed a right to the head but took a hard left to his head. Both swung hard. Miske tapped repeatedly and then landed three stinging swings to the face. They clinched. Miske did the leading, landing left and right to the head, and again to the jaw. Dempsey held. Miske landed a hard left. They slugged. Miske's round, but Dempsey's fight by a shade.

Floto - Dempsey's consistent aggressiveness, carrying the fight, earned him the final two rounds and the fight. "This entitled him to the decision beyond a doubt."

If one were to score each round based on the majority view of the reporters for that round, the fight would be scored 4 rounds Dempsey, 2 Miske, and 4 even (4-2-4), for Dempsey's fight: 1 – E, 2 – D, 3 – D, 4 – M, 5 – E, 6 – M, 7 – D, 8 – D, 9 – E, 10 – E.

The majority view of the individual reporters was Dempsey by a shade, though there were plenty who thought it was a draw. Only one believed Miske had won. Combining the votes of the on-scene reporters and the referee, they had it 5 for Dempsey, 1 for Miske, and 3 for a draw, or if one includes the I.N.S., U.P, and A.P., it would be 7 votes for Dempsey, 1 for Miske, and 4 for a draw.

Individual reporters and participants rendered their verdicts as follows:

*Minneapolis Morning Tribune*, by Fred Coburn: Dempsey (5-2-3)
*Minneapolis Journal*, by John Ritchie: Dempsey (5-3-2)
*St. Paul Daily News*, by Empty Caine: Dempsey (4-2-4)
*Chicago American*, by Ed Smith: Dempsey (5-3-2)
*Kansas City Post/Denver Post*, by Otto Floto: Dempsey (6-1-3)
United Press (U.P.): Dempsey (5-2-3)
International News Service (I.N.S.): Dempsey
*St. Paul Pioneer Press/St. Paul Dispatch*, by E. R. Hosking: Draw (3-3-4)
*Duluth Herald*, by Larry Moore: Draw (4-4-2)
George Barton, referee for the fight: Draw
Associated Press (A.P.): Draw
*Duluth News Tribune*, by Louis Gollop: Miske (5-2-3)

The *Minneapolis Morning Tribune*'s Fred R. Coburn was at the fight. He reported that Dempsey obtained a shade verdict over Miske in a relatively tame bout. A near knockout wallop in the 7$^{th}$ round, which nearly ended matters, the most damaging punch of the fight, and superior aggressiveness gave Dempsey the edge. Billy's superb courage was a big asset. Neither man was damaged excessively. Dempsey was not even troubled. Although in many respects it was a tame affair, there were moments when the crowd was thrilled by the battlers' earnest efforts. Towards the end, both were hooted for their continual clinching.

In the 7$^{th}$ round, after breaking away from a clinch, Dempsey landed a big right uppercut flush on the point of the chin, and Miske went reeling back against the ropes. The wicked blow nearly decked Miske, but he kept his feet. He covered quickly, and managed to make sure that follow-up blows were only glancing. He clinched often for dear life until he recovered. Despite taking a bad beating in the 7$^{th}$, Miske was strong and good again in the next round.

Miske was the worst offender in the holding tactics, which kept the referee busy prying them apart, especially in the later rounds.

Dempsey showed great speed, splendid aggressiveness, and an occasional dangerous punch with either hand. His major wallop in the 7$^{th}$, plus several of a more minor character, and his determined aggressiveness entitled him to the shade verdict.

Miske was courageous under fire, and kept trying. He fought the 8$^{th}$ round with more determination than ever. He seemed to be the stronger of the two at the final bell. But he never was able to hurt Dempsey, who was unmarked and never seemed to fear Miske's most vicious swings and jabs.

Dempsey did not make the showing of which he was capable. Both seemed over-anxious and nervous for the first few rounds, missing continually. Dempsey's shift bothered Miske at first, but he solved it with some success later on. The majority felt that Dempsey would have to improve a great deal or he would lose to Fulton. Miske appeared to be the better conditioned one. However, Dempsey was very fast.

Coburn scored it 5-2-3 for Dempsey: 1 – E, 2 – D, 3 – D, 4 – M, 5 – D, 6 – M, 7 – D, 8 – D, 9 – E, 10 – E.

John Ritchie for the *Minneapolis Journal* said Dempsey had the clear edge on Miske in a fast but featureless battle. He made a good showing against a man capable of testing his worth. Miske failed to analyze and solve his foe, and could not work up the steam to win. Dempsey's margin was not great, but it was clean and conclusive nevertheless.

There was not a suggestion of a knockdown or drop of blood, but they stepped fast throughout. Miske found an opponent whose offensive tactics bothered him, and who had a rather effective style of blocking or slipping his punches. Miske found most big men to be slow, and he was able to be aggressive with them. Dempsey met him a little more than half-way in that respect and Miske never thoroughly solved the problem of how best to meet his style of battle.

Dempsey started a dancing fight in the 1$^{st}$ round, and kept it up. He never allowed his rival to get firmly set, and Miske does not shine as a deliverer of punishment until he can assume his usual "spraddle" stance. Dempsey kept him well out of this throughout the fight.

Miske tried in every round, but at long range and at shorts Dempsey was beating him to it just a trifle, but piling up those trifles to a lead that while not wide enough to be called a mortifying Waterloo by any means, was convincingly clear as to the class of the men at the finish. Dempsey never was in trouble. Conversely, in the 7$^{th}$ round it looked like it might be over for Miske. A hard right to Miske's stomach followed by a strong left to the head and two fast rights to the jaw and Miske went owl-eyed and wobbly at the knees. Dempsey tore after him, but could not finish him. Miske recuperated very quickly and clinched, and by holding and wrestling for a few seconds he weathered the gale, and made a dash to retrieve lost ground before the round ended, but was tired at the bell. The 8$^{th}$ was slower, with both tiring, but toward the close, Miske seemed recuperated and picked up strength rapidly.

Dempsey proved himself every whit as clever a boxer as Miske, and able to hit harder. Miske never was able to faze Dempsey. Dempsey's victory over Miske was much cleaner-cut than the one Fulton scored a few weeks ago, though Fulton had a clear shade on points. Dempsey inflicted much more punishment and in a more workmanlike style than did Fulton in winning his points edge over Miske.

Dempsey showed class both at fighting at long range and when they mixed it close in. Miske was clever with both ends as well, but Dempsey had the call seemingly most of the time.

Dempsey's right was better than his left. It was a short snappy right cross, which landed repeatedly to the head, under the heart, and to the stomach. But only once, in the 7$^{th}$ round, did he have Miske in anything like apparent distress. Hence, some wondered exactly how hard he punched. Or perhaps Miske simply took it well, or defended, clinched, and recovered well.

Particularly early on, Miske did not show his usual form of aggressiveness. He was more cautious than usual. He was content to stay away and fence. He did not tear in, and his boxing seemed to suffer by it. In the 3rd round, Miske seemed confused and baffled by Dempsey's dancing in and out and side rocking. At this juncture, Dempsey's left jabs were doing the business for him, but later, when Miske started closing in for action, Dempsey called the right into play and showed its effectiveness. Miske throughout did not box as cleverly as he did against Fulton, though possibly Dempsey was responsible for it.

Ritchie scored it 5-3-2 for Dempsey: 1 – E, 2 – D, 3 – D, 4 – M, 5 – E, 6 – M, 7 – D, 8 – D, 9 – M, 10 – D.

"Empty" Caine, writing for the *St. Paul Daily News*, said Dempsey got a slight shade victory over the local St. Paul boy Miske. Dempsey's slight margin was due mainly to his more powerful blows, two of which shook Miske badly, necessitating his hanging on to recover his equilibrium in the 7th round. It was a battle well worth seeing, though there was much clinching and wrestling, due to the fact that both packed such stinging wallops that they did not care to take too many chances. Dempsey proved that he could hit and take them. He landed several blows that would have knocked out nine out of ten men. He took everything that Miske could give him without wincing, though he appeared to be somewhat slowed up in the 6th round, Miske's best.

Dempsey did most of his work with his left, though when he brought the pile-driving right into play, it could be heard all over the house, and when he connected with Miske's jaw in the 7th it looked like curtains, but Billy held on wisely until he cleared his head. Then he came back in splendid shape, giving another demonstration of his great fighting heart.

Caine said he cast aside personal and sentimental feelings, and forgot the hometown bias for the local man. Viewing the bout without bias and as neutrally as possible, Dempsey won, and "we cannot see the affair in any other way, though we want to say right here that Miske deserves all kinds of credit and his 'comeback' after apparently being on the way to slumberland was great." To all appearances the bout was fairly even, but a close examination of the score sheet revealed that Dempsey was entitled to the edge because he was aggressive, his wallops were tremendously solid, he rocked Miske two or three times and had him on the verge of a knockout. Still, Miske was the greatest battler Dempsey ever had met, and he would have to travel far to meet another as tough.

## THE POINTS BY ROUNDS

|         | 1  | 2  | 3  | 4  | 5  | 6  | 7   | 8  | 9  | 10 | Total |
|---------|----|----|----|----|----|----|----|----|----|----|-------|
| Miske   | 6  | 5  | 8  | 12 | 10 | 18 | 6  | 6  | 10 | 10 | 91    |
| Dempsey | 5* | 14 | 15 | 8  | 10 | 8  | 13*| 8* | 10 | 10 | 101   |

The score:

|         | 1 | 2 | 3 | 4 | 5 | 6 | 7 | 8 | 9 | 10 |
|---------|---|---|---|---|---|---|---|---|---|----|
| Miske   | E | O | O | X | E | X | O | O | E | E  |
| Dempsey | E | X | S | O | E | O | X | S | E | E  |

Note—E, round even; X, clear margin; S, shade; *, aggressor.

Caine scored the fight 4-2-4 for Dempsey, which was spot on with how the majority scored each round: 1 – E, 2 – D, 3 – D by a shade/scant margin, 4 – M, 5 – E, 6 – M, 7 – D, 8 – D by a shade, 9 – E, 10 – E.

Caine noted that men were not the only ones interested in boxing. Women attended fights, and even wagered on them, looking to the local writer to settle their wagers. Caine admitted that most of the local St. Paul fans polled thought it was an even draw bout.

E. R. Hosking, reporting for the *St. Paul Pioneer Press*, said it was a draw. Dempsey landed the harder and cleaner punches, and was more aggressive, but Miske was the better boxer, outboxing him. "Fifty-fifty is the fairest verdict that can be rendered in summarizing the ten-round Miske-Dempsey bout at the Auditorium last night. Miske outboxed his young rival, made him miss a lot, but Dempsey evened count by his superior aggressiveness and the fact that he landed harder when he did connect."

Neither boxer was in distress at any time, except for a moment in the 7th when Dempsey, after taking a shower of punches directed at his head and chin, suddenly shifted and whipped a hard right into Miske's stomach. Billy's knees seemed to sag a little. He backed to the ropes, where Jack shot a hard left to the jaw. Miske rallied quickly, however, and held his own during the remainder of that round.

The 7th round marked high tide for Dempsey, while Miske's best work was in the 6th, when he had Dempsey puzzled and at sea. Dempsey's lead in the 7th round offset Miske's advantage in the 6th, and there was little to choose between them in the other rounds.

As was expected, Dempsey proved the harder hitter of the two and he also showed better footwork throughout. He led more often than Miske, but the home boy furnished a superior brand of boxing. Billy's blocking was beautiful and he was quick to take advantage of openings. But his old fault was in evidence - that of lacking steam in his punches.

Dempsey depended on his left hook most of the time, but it was blocked so frequently that Jack began to use his right more often, and he had better success with it.

Miske used both hands in his attack, although he did more damage with his left.

Viewed as a whole, the battle was disappointing. It had been expected to bristle with action throughout, but it did not. Both seemingly had a lot of respect for the other, and there was a lot of clinching and pulling.

Miske started slowly, and seemed to find it hard to get warmed up. Dempsey, too, was careful in the opening stanzas, and there was little real fighting before the middle of the 4th round.

They got busy in the 5th, and from that point up to the end of the 7th round the fight was what had been anticipated, but the last three rounds were devoid of excitement.

They were all even when the 10th round started. The fans expected a hurricane finish, but were disappointed. There was a lot of clinching, with spasmodic rallies by both. No harm was done by either one and it was an even round, with Dempsey a trifle the more aggressive of the two, but missing most of his well-intentioned efforts.

To the extent that Dempsey fully held his own with a more experienced opponent, one who ranked higher than any boxer he ever had met before, the bout yielded him more honors than it did Miske. But considering it as a boxing match pure and simple, it was about as even an affair as any fan could desire, though a majority of the outside critics appeared to consider that Dempsey's one big round, the 7th, was sufficient to give him a shade in the whole ten.

Summarized by rounds, Miske had a commanding lead in the 6th round and he also took the 4th and 9th. Dempsey's big round was the 7th, and he had a shade in the 2nd and the 8th. All the other rounds were even. Hence, this writer scored it 3-3-4.

Jack Reddy, Miske's manager, and promoter of the fight, pronounced it to be a darn good draw.

Referee George Barton said he would have called it a draw had he been allowed to render a decision. He said both boys had their good rounds, and both were shaken up at different stages. When Barton told Dempsey that he considered it to be about even, Dempsey replied, "That suits me." Hence, a draw was an equitable verdict.

Hosking also wrote a report for the *St. Paul Dispatch*. He said the general verdict seemed to be that a draw was a fair result. The fight did not come up to expectations, for they had too much respect for each other most of the time to cut loose. Some of the later rounds, beginning with the 6th, were full of action, but throughout there was much more clinching than had been anticipated. Miske was slow in getting started, or he could have had a clear lead at the end. It was not until the 4th round that he realized that he was the better boxer. Dempsey was more aggressive, his footwork was better, and he landed the harder cleaner punches when his wallops landed. Miske's blocking was beautiful, and not many of Dempsey's left hooks connected with anything but elbows or gloves. Dempsey did his greatest execution with his right, with which he landed the majority of his blows.

Larry Moore, writing for the *Duluth Herald*, said he drove 200 miles to see Dempsey and Miske fight to a subdued draw. Two fistic greats put up a somewhat disappointing battle. A hairline decision could be given to either participant. Shades either way, and a draw, were the opinions of those at the fight.

Writers from other cities agreed with the Twin City contingent that the contest was not decisive enough to bring a clean-cut decision to either fighter.

The Chicago writers agreed on a shade for Dempsey and a draw, it was understood. Dempsey and Miske both declared that a draw decision "was about right."

There were those at ringside inclined to believe that the dynamo blonde Miske had earned a shade, but in full view and cognizance of every fact, the bout had to be called a draw. Dempsey himself had good reason to claim a shade, and many critics awarded it to him.

All in all, the bout was spiritless. Between rounds, Miske spat a few shots of pinkish saliva from between his teeth, while Dempsey let go one or two drops of blood from his nose, but that was about all the blood that flowed. Neither man had a scratch on his body. The reason that the showing was insipid was that both were fighting carefully. Each respected the other sufficiently that they preferred to take a draw rather than chance a knockout, so they spent considerable time feeling out one another, always taking care that no opening was left for a fatal blow.

At times, however, they opened up with vim, and then the going was enough to bring consolation. Miske deserved credit for being the only lad Dempsey recently failed to knock out. Jack never was close to stopping him.

Moore was impressed by Dempsey's lightning-fast speed for a heavyweight. He had a wicked left. More than once he had Billy guessing with his shift – first the left foot advanced, then the right, then two wicked hooks with both wings. "And that left – O-o-o-o-h! At times it shot out like an unpremeditated bolt of lightning from a maelstrom of rain clouds." Invariably Dempsey advanced his onslaught with that left. He was no clumsy heavyweight. He danced and ducked and waltzed around with the agility of a lightweight. Miske often missed his haymakers, bewildered by the head movement, low ducking, and weaving.

Many of Miske's local fans thought he shaded the fight. But that likely was influenced by enthusiasm instilled by the fact that their home pride valiantly met everything the famous invader had to offer.

Miske was careful not to take any chances with such a big puncher. But he also fought his usual rugged, energetic scrap, boring in and always coming back for more. Billy still lacked some power behind his blows, and could not be said to be a knockout king. But he was fast and his infighting excellent.

Moore said that round summaries collected by the writers gave four rounds to Miske, four to Dempsey, and two even, 4-4-2, with Dempsey having the advantage, if there must be some, in the most indefinite innings. Hence, some had it 6-4 for Dempsey. But Moore thought it was even.

Louis Gollop, writing for the *Duluth News Tribune*, said Miske won by a hairline over Dempsey. "If one should call it a draw he would not be doing either any injustice. Miske can be given the decision because of his cleaner fighting and forcing ability." It was one of the fastest and most furious seen there for some time. Yet the same author contradicted himself a bit by also calling the bout tame and a love affair in terms of damage done.

Miske plainly was worried in the 7th round, but held his own the rest of the way. The fight was without spectacular feature. Miske continually resorted to infighting and managed to get inside of most of Dempsey's blows.

Miske landed only one hard blow in the fight, a right cross in the 3rd round. Dempsey scored in the 2nd, 3rd, and 7th rounds, and his Chicago supporters seemingly were inclined to give him a shade for this work. On the other hand, the writers who gave Miske a shade based their verdicts on the fact that he made Dempsey miss many blows.

Gollop had it for Miske, 5-2-3: 1 – M, 2 – E, 3 – M, 4 – M, 5 – M, 6 – M, 7 – D, 8 – E, 9 – D, 10 – E.

In another article published a day after his first article, Gollop said fans were disappointed with Dempsey, calling him a "paper champion." The men he had beaten were setups, and he finally bumped into a real fighter and was held up. The fight proved that 10 rounds were not enough to decide a contest between Dempsey and Miske. Still, Gollop admitted that Dempsey "is one of the cleverest heavyweights in the ring today. He made Miske miss several punches, which if landed, might have meant a trip to dreamland." He was clever in the early part of the fight, but after Miske played for the body, Dempsey became slower in every round.

The 7th was a great round. Dempsey nearly had Miske out. Billy was staggering around the ring. But suddenly he came to life and rushed his man to the ropes, sending in a volley of uppercuts that stopped Dempsey for a while at least. "It was hard to pick a winner but that Miske had a slight edge of the fighting there was little doubt." Still, more rounds were necessary for a truly decisive victory.

Ed W. Smith, *Chicago American* editor and famous fight referee, who was present, said Dempsey had just a shade on Miske, but clearly enough such that there could be no dispute that he won. It was a wild, hard battle. "At the finish the decision would have to be given to Dempsey though he didn't have any big shade." Dempsey could not land effectively very often. He occasionally staggered the local lad, but Miske held on and weathered the storm, particularly in the 7th round. Dempsey's famous shift did not work as well as it had in other fights. Miske had a good defense, and a style and speed that baffled Jack. However, in speed and cleverness Dempsey had a shade, and his punching was far in excess of Miske's. Both were holding on at the end, "but Dempsey unquestionably had the shade as they finished." Miske was spent and all in, while Dempsey still was fighting as hard as he could and banging in punches. Dempsey inflicted more punishment than Fulton did upon Miske.

Both were nervous at first, but Dempsey was steadier, and in a fast, clever opening round had quite the margin on the local favorite. He landed a couple of stiff rights, but Miske was shifting and switching his head well. In the 2nd, Dempsey staggered Miske with a sold right, but despite flopping around, Miske was game and stood up to a desperate fire. Grand exchanges of swats took place in the 3rd and 4th rounds, and the battle was waged evenly up to the 7th, in which round Dempsey landed a heavy uppercut to the chin, Miske's knees sagged, and he was all but out. But Dempsey was too tired to follow up his great advantage. From then on, Dempsey had a big shade in the scoring, though Miske put up a surprisingly good battle, and fought nearly evenly in the last few rounds.

Smith had it scored 5-3-2 in rounds for Dempsey: 1 – E, 2 – D, 3 – D, 4 – M, 5 – D, 6 – M, 7 – D, 8 – D, 9 – E, 10 – M.

Otto Floto, sporting editor for the *Kansas City Post* and *Denver Post*, who also was there, said Dempsey clearly beat and mastered Miske. Floto was the highest on Dempsey, believing that an educated boxing eye could tell that he was the superior fighter. It was the first time since a prime Fitzsimmons that there was such a thorough fighter, boxer, and puncher. Dempsey had a masterful shift. Few fighters other than Miske could have weathered the 7th round after that fearful uppercut to the jaw. His gameness and the bell saved his record of never having been knocked down.

Dempsey had earned the right to be the logical contender for the crown. He handled Miske easily during every round. Miske was one of the toughest men in the game, but Jack never was in any danger. True, Miske did some great work and earned the 5th by a shade, but this was the only round in which Dempsey suffered by comparison. In all others, Dempsey held his game and willing foe even or shaded him.

When it came to effective punching, delivering blows with steam, which counted the most in the final totals, there was nothing to it but Dempsey from start to finish.

Furthermore, Dempsey repudiated claims that he was just a newspaper-made champion. It was a very fast battle, and showed Dempsey to be a more wonderful man than rated previously. He proved conclusively that he could give and take. He demonstrated straight punching, hooks, and shifts, with excellent balance and footwork, against a man with a great reputation, who had battled the best in the game. Yet, Dempsey was master of the affair at all stages. No Miske punch ever shook him even once, and when aggressiveness was considered, Dempsey won by miles.

Floto scored it 6-1-3 for Dempsey: 1 – E, 2 – D, 3 – D, 4 – E, 5 – M, 6 – E, 7 – D, 8 – D, 9 – D, 10 – D.

Lambert G. Sullivan, writing for the *Chicago Daily News*, said Dempsey had a decided shade the better of the milling, and won the popular verdict. He claimed, "The California boxer was hailed as winner by virtually every newspaper expert at the bout as well as by the majority of the crowd which saw the contest. Dempsey's victory, however, was not of a nature which permits him to demand a bout with Willard or Fulton." His points victory was a surprise, because most had believed that if it went the limit, Miske's cleverness would give him a shade. Dempsey showed as much skillful boxing as the St. Paul man, and had a much harder punch. Furthermore, "Dempsey's peculiar style had Miske handcuffed much of the time and the home fighter was unable to get over any punishing blows or even to score often enough to pile up points." Jack delivered the only really hard punch of the fight, in the 7th, when his right to the jaw had Miske groggy and shaking at the knees. Miske clinched and weathered the round, the only time either one came anywhere near a knockout. Many of Dempsey's fans actually lost money, because they had bet on him to win by knockout.

A day later, the *Chicago Tribune* said either man, the "Minnesota Wildcat" or the "Submarine Destroyer," would give Willard a tough fight, but Dempsey was considered to be a bit better and had won the popular verdict. This report said the house was packed. The federal government made money on a war tax, and the state got 10% on a tuberculosis tax. Minnesota was seeking $1,524, ruling that the fund should realize on complimentary tickets, estimated to be worth $1,700.[376]

Eddie Day said the cyclone turned out to be only a gentle dancing master. Even his own partisans admitted that Dempsey adopted an elusive style with Miske and refused to swap punches.

Chicago's Ray Pearson said Dempsey's dancing tactics prevented Miske from getting set, and thereby prevented him from doing his most effective work. Still, Dempsey outpointed him. Some criticized Dempsey for boxing, while others gave him credit for showing versatility.

Allegedly, the receipts were only $13,536.80, as opposed to the advance claims of $25,000. Dempsey received a $4,000 guarantee.

The *Denver Times* reported that out of eight critics seated at ringside, 4 said Dempsey won, 3 said draw, and 1 had it for Miske. Some discredited Dempsey because he failed to win by knockout. Others said the performance was excellent given his relative lack of experience, but he took criticism because the syndicate behind him had hyped him up so much that he did not live up to expectations. Otherwise, his performance would have been hailed as a great feat and caused a sensation.[377]

On or about May 6, three days after the fight, Dempsey's attorney had John Reisler served with a federal-court restraining-order, preventing him from further interfering with Jack Dempsey's boxing career. Reisler said he intended to fight the case.[378]

Otto Floto called attention to the fact that not one twin city paper gave the fight to Miske, and local papers quite often were biased for the local man. It was no tame draw as some said. Miske was on the verge of being knocked out in the 3rd and 7th rounds. The *Minneapolis Journal, Morning Tribune,* and *Evening Tribune* all said Dempsey won. The *Minneapolis News* version written by George Barton, the referee, called it a draw, with perhaps Dempsey having a slight shade. The *St. Paul News* said Dempsey won, while the *St. Paul Dispatch* and *Pioneer Press* both called it a draw. No local paper gave it to Miske. "Do you know what that means in Miske's own home town?" All of the Chicago papers awarded the verdict to Dempsey, with the exception of one, which called it a draw.

---

[376] *Minneapolis Morning Tribune, Minneapolis Journal, St. Paul Daily News, St. Paul Pioneer Press, St. Paul Dispatch, St. Paul Pioneer Press, Duluth Herald, Duluth News Tribune, Kansas City Post, Denver Post, San Francisco Examiner, St. Louis Star, Pittsburgh Daily Post, La Crosse Tribune, Chicago Daily News,* all May 4, 1918; *Chicago Tribune,* May 5, 1918.
[377] *Denver Times,* May 6, 7, 1918.
[378] *Denver Post,* May 8, 1918; *Twin Falls Daily Times,* May 8, 1918.

Floto wanted his readers to remember his prediction, that Dempsey would be the next heavyweight champion of the world "without a single doubt." Dempsey was a master in action, with dazzling speed, great hitting power, clever shift, correct position of his feet, and splendid thinking faculties, a combination rarely found. Plus he could take them, and was gameness personified. "Regardless of the injustice done Dempsey by the press reports, his own work will make all his detractors eat their own words – remember this prediction, too." It was "only a question of a short time when he'll be the greatest heavyweight champion America has ever had."

Miske subsequently said he wanted to fight Dempsey 15 or 20 rounds, feeling that he could win in a longer contest.

Dempsey challenged Willard or Fulton. "Having disposed of Billy Miske, I am ready for Jess Willard, or his perpetual challenger, Fulton. I'll fight either man any time or place, my share to go to the Red Cross" or any other war fund.

Dempsey claimed he failed to knock out Miske because he had a bad hand. He also claimed that Reisler's constant pestering was a distraction. The federal injunction against Reisler would make a difference in his fighting. "A man can't do his best and have writs put under his eyes continually." Jack said he only needed 4 rounds to stop Fulton, and if he failed to do so, he would add another $500 donation to whatever war charity benefit for which they would be fighting.[379]

Floto said the sporting community was laughing at John the Barber's shakedown attempts. He was paying more in lawyer's fees than he ever would recover. Dempsey said, "I'll go back to Colorado and work in the mines with a pick and shovel again before I allow John the Barber to manage me."

Speaking of the fight again, Floto said that whenever Miske and Dempsey got into a clinch, the referee ordered them to break immediately, much too quickly, which eliminated infighting. They primarily fought at long range as a result.[380]

Col. J. C. Miller, Willard's manager, having attempted to promote the contest, said that given the public sentiment in opposition to the Willard-Fulton fight owing to the war, he had called off the match.

Willard said he had been under the impression that the public demanded that he defend his title, but given that the public did not want him to fight during the war, he would not. "I will be ready to fight at any time that public sentiment indicates there should be a championship match."[381]

Tom S. Andrews wrote that the Dempsey-Miske superiority remained undecided. "Reports of the contest varied, some giving Dempsey the shade, others claiming he won easily, while others called it a draw and one critic even thought Mr. Miske won on points." Andrews said Dempsey had a shade on the local St. Paul man, but nothing to brag about. It was a hard

---

[379] *Denver Post*, May 8, 1918; *Minneapolis Morning Tribune*, May 9, 1918.
[380] *Denver Post*, May 9, 1918.
[381] *Denver Post*, May 11, 1918.

battle and still room for argument as to who was the better man. Only once did Dempsey put over what looked like a knockout blow, in the 7th, but Miske shook his head and covered for a moment to protect himself. Dempsey made a big hit with the fans on account of his clean-cut work, and if they met again, he would be the favorite in the wagering.[382]

In his autobiography, Kearns said although he figured that Miske's puzzling defensive style would make it a "clinker of a match" and neither man would shine, he thought Dempsey would win and gain valuable experience. Plus, he thought the fight's result might induce Fulton to fight Dempsey, which it did.

An attempt to stage a rematch between Dempsey and Miske in Milwaukee, Wisconsin was prevented by John "the Barber" Reisler. The boxing commission would not allow Dempsey to box in Wisconsin unless he could prove that he was not legally bound to Reisler.[383]

Former heavyweight champion Tommy Burns enlisted in a Canadian regiment, to do his part for the war effort.[384]

On May 19, 1918 in Panama City, Panama, Harry Wills forced Sam Langford to retire in the corner after the 7th round.

---

[382] *Minneapolis Tribune*, May 12, 1918.
[383] *St. Louis Post-Dispatch*, May 22, 1918.
[384] *Denver Post*, May 16, 1918.

CHAPTER 14

# Establishing Dominance

Given that Fulton vs. Willard was not going to be allowed to happen while the war was ongoing, there was talk of a potential Dempsey vs. Fulton bout to be held in July 1918. In the meantime, Kearns kept Dempsey busy.

On Wednesday May 22, 1918 at Excelsior Springs, Missouri, about 30 miles northeast of Kansas City, just 19 days after the Miske contest, before a crowd of 1,500, in a scheduled 10-round benefit bout in which the entire proceeds would be donated to the Red Cross, Jack Dempsey fought a rematch with Dan Ketchel/Ketchell. Dempsey had stopped Ketchel two years before, in May 1916, in the 3rd round. Since then, Ketchel's results included 1916 L6 Jack Downey and LKOby5 Jack Moran.

This time, Dempsey knocked out Ketchel with a right cross to the jaw in the 2nd round. He was out cold.[385]

John the Barber Reisler still was on Dempsey's trail. He and his attorney were gathering up affidavits for his case against Dempsey, seeking an injunction in Wisconsin. Reisler said,

> Dempsey has made some statements that are plainly false. If he testifies to them under oath he will be perjuring himself and we will ask that he be punished for it. He says he fought three fights under my management. He never fought once. Every contract for every fight he had in New York is on file with the boxing commission and is a matter of indisputable record. He can't get away from them.[386]

Kearns said he had little trouble booking fights for Dempsey, for he was receiving more offers than he could accept. Everyone wanted to see him. Plus, he was likeable. All who came into contact with him liked him from that moment on.

Dempsey said, "If I can get Willard in the ring I'll be the champion, you can go bet on that." He would turn over part of the proceeds from any such engagement to a war fund.[387]

Jack was scheduled to box a 15-round bout against Arthur Pelkey at the Stock Yards Stadium in Denver, Colorado, just one week after knocking out Ketchel.[388]

At one point, 210-pound Canadian Arthur Pelkey had been known as the white heavyweight champion of the world, in 1912 having knocked out

---

[385] *Santa Cruz Evening News, St. Louis Post-Dispatch, St. Louis Daily Globe-Democrat, Munster Times*, May 23, 1918; Boxrec.com.
[386] *Rocky Mountain News*, May 23, 1918.
[387] *Kansas City Post, Denver Post*, May 23, 1918.
[388] *Munster Times*, May 20, 1918; *Oregon Daily Journal* (Portland), May 24, 1918.

in the 1st round then white heavyweight champion and top contender to Jack Johnson's crown, 200-pound Luther McCarty, unfortunately killing him in the process. The powerful McCarty had beaten Frank Moran, Jim Flynn, Al Palzer, Al Kaufman, and Jim Barry, and drawn with future champion Jess Willard in an exciting and hard-hitting 10-round no decision contest (though some said Willard had beaten McCarty[389]). Hence, Pelkey's knockout victory over McCarty was quite significant, and a huge upset. Pelkey had the wallop to hurt and win unexpectedly.

Prior to winning the white championship, Pelkey's record, which began in 1910, included: 1912 LND10 Jess Willard (Jess won primarily with his jab and right uppercut in a dull contest); 1913 LKOby2 Jim Coffey and DND6 former champion Tommy Burns (Pelkey down in rounds 2 and 5, Burns down in round 4). He was a big strong man with a punch, and had shown durability in going the distance with Willard and Burns.

Subsequent to winning the white championship, Pelkey lost more significant fights than he won, including: 1914 LTKOby15 Gunboat Smith, LTKOby19 Bill Lang, and LKOby4 Sam McVey; 1915 LTKOby2 Jim Coffey, LTKOby3 Al Reich, LTKOby8 Joe Jeannette, LKOby7 Battling Jim Johnson, LKOby9 Joe Cox, LND10 and LTKOby5 Fred Fulton; 1916 LKOby5 Carl Morris, L8 Gunboat Smith, and LKOby13 Kid Norfolk; and 1917 LKOby13 Norfolk yet again.

Certainly, the 33-year-old Pelkey (some claimed he was 37) was on the downward slide, and expected to lose, but he did have a great deal of experience against the world's best, having fought at least 55 fights.

---

[389] Regarding the August 19, 1912 Luther McCarty vs. Jess Willard contest held in New York's Madison Square Garden, the next-day August 20, 1912 *Brooklyn Standard Union, New York Sun, New York Tribune, Brooklyn Daily Eagle*, and *Binghamton Press* all called it a draw. The *New York Times* said Willard won by a shade with accurate jabs and terrific right uppercuts. The *Brooklyn Citizen* said, "Willard won by a big margin, and with good handling looks to be of championship caliber. He is strong, game, fast and naturally clever..." The general accounting was that McCarty was the aggressor throughout, and made the fight. However, Willard landed more cleanly and accurately, meeting McCarty's rushes by landing a hard left jab full in the face, and a powerful right and right uppercut on the attacking McCarty. He also was unexpectedly clever at blocking. Both proved their ability to absorb hard blows without flinching. Willard's judgment of distance was better, and he was cool and never lost his head. McCarty was more of a fighter, but Willard boxed nicely and scored frequently. Jess made an "excellent showing." "Very few novice boxers have such an astonishingly good eye for distance as Willard displayed last night." Weights: Willard 224, McCarty 203 ¼ or 208 ¼ pounds, depending on the source.

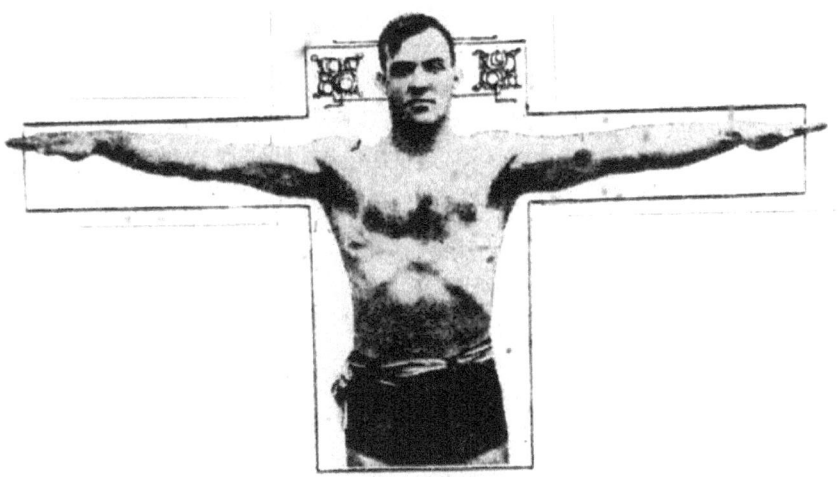

The *Denver Post* (likely Otto Floto) said the Colorado Tornado Dempsey was the most phenomenal boxer seen in a decade. He was going to show the people of his own home state just why he now was the ring's most feared man. He would train for four days at the local Empress theater, where patrons could pay to see him exhibit prior to the fight.

Dempsey was the "active champion of the world." His relatively recent rise had been meteoric, and "his unquestionable fighting prowess has stamped a record that shall be remembered as long as the annals of boxing remain." Many were saying he was the best fighter since Jim Jeffries. Pelkey was a one-time champion himself, and one of the ring's toughest gladiators.[390]

"DEMON" JACK DEMPSEY.

Kearns and Dempsey were described as happy, good-natured, congenial fellows. Kearns didn't even mind any adverse publicity or criticism, because controversy made Dempsey the most talked of boxer in the world. Kearns said he had no fear of John Reisler starting a suit in Denver, for a federal court injunction restrained him from interfering with Dempsey.

H. C. Hamilton predicted that the recent 'Fight or Work' order issued by the provost marshal general would kill the boxing game. The order that all men of draft age either had to fight or work at some useful occupation that helped the war effort in some way by no later than July 1 gave those in professional sports, as well as the theatrical world, some real concern.[391]

---

[390] *Denver Post*, May 22, 23, 1918.
[391] *Denver Times*, May 24, 1918.

Each day, local writer Otto Floto wrote about his admiration for Dempsey. He said the Colorado Submarine's showing against Miske proved that he had plenty of class. Bob Edgren agreed. Floto believed that Dempsey was destined to become one of the greatest champions ever. Dempsey's offer to fight for the Red Cross was another move which would gain him great popularity. He was willing to donate his services to raise money for war funds (hence, making his boxing a useful occupation).

Demon Dempsey arrived in Denver on May 23. Nearly a thousand admirers of the man whom the sport popularly had termed the active king thronged the platform to meet him. Rick Ricketson said Dempsey stood nearly 6'2" and appeared to be physically perfect. "Dempsey has little to say of his success in the ring. He is quiet, the last man you would pick as a boxer. He was glad to be back in Colorado among his friends, and that was all." Kearns deserved great credit for his rapid rise. His careful, shrewd management sent him from the 4-round game on the coast to the active championship. Lately, Jack had been exhibiting to benefit the Red Cross.[392]

**DENVER EXTENDS THE RIGHT MITTEN OF WELCOME TO JACK DEMPSEY**

Rick Ricketson of the *Denver Post* sports department, Jack Kearns, matchmaker Jack Kanner, Jack Dempsey, promoter James Hamill, Leslie Whitaker, and Louis Levand.

---

[392] *Denver Post*, May 24, 1918.

Eddie Day for the *Denver Times* said that personally, Dempsey was known as a "prince of good fellows." He was not a rowdy or an egotist.[393]

Otto Floto said not since the days of Corbett had a heavyweight shown such marvelous speed, and not since the days of Fitzsimmons had a heavyweight demonstrated such tremendous driving power in his punches. Never had a heavyweight possessed such an efficient shift. He was courageous too. He had all the earmarks of a great champion. Jack weighed 196 pounds.

Jack Kearns said of the upcoming contest,

> Pelkey is a tough bird. I will not hesitate to give him his due. He would have been a far greater fighter than he is if his managers had ever given him the correct training and matched him properly. In Pelkey, Dempsey is meeting a fellow who is a genuine fighter and a pretty fair boxer. He comes in at all times and we expect rough going. Personally, I have no doubt as to the result, for Jack is toppling them over, no matter who they are. He would do the same thing to Fulton, Willard, or any of them.

Kearns noted that Pelkey had met the era's best men – Jess Willard, Carl Morris, Gunboat Smith, and Luther McCarty. He never dogged it and was an audience pleaser. Dempsey was only 22 years old, but had class that had not been seen for decades.[394]

Floto said the combination of brains plus an unusual kick in either wing gave Dempsey a royal chance to rule. He did not need to depend on weight or size to carry him to success, like many heavyweights in recent years. Many big men liked to lead, clinch, lean in and bear their weight down on foes, wrestling and mauling smaller men. Dempsey was a reversion to the time when champions were skilled in all departments and knew how to deliver effective blows. Floto insisted that Dempsey was all that ever had been said about and claimed for him.

When seen at the Empress theater, the large crowd was pleased with Dempsey's remarkable speed and ability to work the shift at will. He was having difficulty obtaining sparring partners. Even though he promised to be careful, every now and then he landed a blow that was not pleasant for the receiver, even with heavy gloves, and few wanted to box him.

---

[393] *Denver Times*, May 25, 1918.
[394] *Denver Post*, May 25, 1918. Pelkey worked out at the Glenarm gym.

On May 25, Dempsey sold newspapers at the fire and police athletic carnival at Broadway park for the benefit of the Red Cross.

Jack Veiock said Dempsey was a better heavyweight prospect than Miske. Dempsey was more of an aggressor, with the harder punch. Miske did a lot of clinching to save himself and prevent Jack from hitting him.

Arthur Pelkey said, "I truly believe that I will spoil all [of] Dempsey's chances for the championship when I meet him Wednesday night. I don't want to brag, but I have met them all, and I have been a tough bird for them to subdue. Dempsey will be no exception, as I have been training for the last three weeks and think I am in fine condition to take the fight to him." Pelkey said he was weighing close to 235 pounds. Given that Dempsey was about 196 (or less), Pelkey would have a 40-pound weight advantage.[395]

Matchmaker Jack Kanner, Arthur Pelkey, promoter James Hamill

The next day, Pelkey said a lot of folks wanted to see him beat Dempsey, but deep in their hearts "feel that I am doomed. This fellow Dempsey is a wonder, no doubt of that. And the public in general go to see him stow away his opponents in a round." Pelkey said a big surprise was in store. He was not in the habit of being stopped quickly. He did not have a paper chin, and his body could take a few stiff ones too. He would carry the fight to Kearns's phenom and give him the roughest sledding of his career. He gave Willard the roughest battle he had, and went the distance. "Yes, he wasn't so old in the game then, but he was good at that. And he was young and full of pepper. But along the seventh round he was not so full of the hot seasoning as he was in the first." Although Dempsey was regarded as a whirlwind, he sometimes was a trifle slow in getting started. Jack actually showed to better advantage as the fight progressed. Hence, Pelkey intended to start fast right away, before Dempsey could get warmed up, and nail him good and hard. "I don't care how good they are, a properly placed punch

---

[395] *Denver Post*, May 26, 1918.

will rock anyone's tank. ... I have the advantage in height, weight, and reach." It would be no love match. Pelkey felt at home in the ring, had met the best of them, and no one ever said he dogged it or quit. "Even Kearns admits that I am a tough customer to whip, and Kearns is so wrapped up in Dempsey that he seldom admits anyone has a chance with Jack."

Otto Floto noted that all the great colored fighters of a decade ago were slipping, and their best days past them. "Harry Wills is about the only real good colored fighter we have. ... Incidentally, all the blame for the elimination of the colored biffer can be laid at the doors of a man of their own race – Jack Johnson, who by his action made it almost impossible to tolerate him." After Johnson, black fighters were limited to fighting each other. During 1918, Wills had scored a KO6 Sam McVey, and KO6 and TKO7 (towel/sponge thrown in after the round) Sam Langford.

At the Empress theater, Dempsey was offering to donate $500 to charity in the event that he failed to stop any exhibition opponent within 4 rounds. Anyone could come box him on the stage.[396]

ARTHUR PELKEY HOLDING BRAMER.

Arthur Pelkey of Canada

[396] *Denver Post*, May 27, 1918.

To show his strength, Arthur Pelkey picked up Harry Bramer and whirled him over his head fifteen times. In the gym, Pelkey made a good impression, demonstrating a short and powerful right cross.

Spider Kelly was very high on Dempsey, whom he said had class and was one of the greatest fighters ever, as shown by his performance against Miske. "Jack will be the next champion if they give him the chance to fight for it. He is a natural distance battler and in 20 rounds there isn't a man in the world who has a chance with him, and this takes in all of them, irrespective."

Kearns admitted that Pelkey could hit like a mule. "Jack will have to sail right in and watch for the right hand attack while he does so." Dempsey was not worried about the altitude affecting him. "No chance of this altitude getting me, for I used to work on the old farm all day and never finished with more than a healthful sweat."

Immediately after the fight, Dempsey planned to return to the Pacific coast, where he would appear in a Red Cross benefit show for James Coffroth. He would appear in several such entertainments within the next six months across the country. He would pay his own expenses, and wanted the Red Cross to receive the entire gate receipts. He was doing his part for the war effort.

The *Denver Post* said a great deal of Dempsey's success was due to his ripping, tearing, battering tactics, sending well-directed punches to the body and head. He sometimes assumed a half crouch, shifting with bewildering speed.[397]

The local *Rocky Mountain News* harshly called Pelkey a has-been and a set-up for Dempsey. Hence, there was no wagering on the contest. The *Denver Times* agreed.[398]

The day of the fight, the kindlier *Denver Post* (likely Floto) said the whirlwind Colorado Submarine, the state's greatest boxing machine, would display to the citizens of his own state his wares and ability to dominate. Pelkey exceeded him in weight, height, and reach, and he had met the toughest men in the division during the last decade. He was a tough one, and beating him was not child's play. If Dempsey polished him off it would mean he had that rare championship skill to battle against odds of physical nature and win on his merits as a fistic phenomenon. "Dempsey has weathered the reaps and malicious insults of several men who pose as writers. But he has won a warm place in the hearts of thousands of fans and admirers." He was ever ready to help national and patriotic movements.[399]

On Wednesday May 29, 1918 at the Stockyards Stadium in Denver, Colorado, Dempsey's birth state, in a card promoted by Jim Hammill, just one week after the Ketchell contest, and less than a month after the Miske fight, Jack Dempsey took on Arthur Pelkey in a scheduled 15-round bout. Fred Fulton and his manager Mike Collins were in attendance to scout Dempsey and negotiate a bout between them. Fulton had knocked out Pelkey in 5 rounds a few years ago. Less than 1,200 were at ringside, and 200 of them were "deadheads." It was a good-sized crowd, but smaller than anticipated.

Otto Floto, writing for the *Denver Post*, said Dempsey was first to arrive. He looked cheerful and fresh. He was attended by his manager and chief second, Jack Kearns. He received a great ovation. Pelkey followed him. Promoter J. P. Mulvihill, the Danbury, Connecticut promoter, who was offering $25,000 for a Fulton-Dempsey contest over 20 rounds in his city on July 4, was introduced, and made a short speech, which was well received. Mike Collins and Fred Fulton also were introduced.

At the gong, Dempsey glided from his corner like a panther. Pelkey tried to ward him off. Following a lightning-quick feint, Dempsey sent a lead left hook to the jaw and Pelkey skidded to the resin for a short count. He rose, received a right cross to the chin, and Pelkey went down again. Arthur struggled to rise at six. His eyes were glazed and his pins were wobbling. Dempsey shifted and planted a right to the back of the ear and Pelkey went down for the third time, laying there outstretched, out cold. Referee Johnny Kenney counted to ten. Dempsey picked him up like a child. It was five

---

[397] *Kansas City Post, Denver Post*, May 28, 1918.
[398] *Rocky Mountain News*, May 29, 1918; *Denver Times, Cincinnati Enquirer*, May 27, 1918.
[399] *Denver Post*, May 29, 1918.

minutes before Arthur was able to leave the ring. The end came at 32 seconds of the 1st round.

Other versions printed throughout the country said that from the start, Dempsey rushed in savagely on his toes and fired a right. Pelkey either tripped, stumbled and fell to the floor without being struck, or the right landed on the jaw and sent him down (sources varied).

Pelkey rose quickly at the count of two and clinched. Dempsey landed a right or right uppercut on the chin and Pelkey went down again.

Pelkey rose at the count of six. Dempsey landed a left to the jaw (some saying a short jab), and Pelkey went down for the full 10-count, plus remained on the canvas for another 30 seconds. Some speculated or believed he could have risen had he wanted to do so.

The fighting had lasted only about 33 or 34 seconds.

Many thought it was a practical set-up to put a 22-year-old against a much older has-been who had been knocked out a dozen times in the last few years; saying the contest did the fight game no good. The public was tired of uneven matches. Dempsey's blows did not appear to be all that powerful, yet they had their effect.

Still, the speed which Dempsey accomplished the task was impressive. No one had stopped Pelkey so quickly. Few fighters stood any chance with the powerful Dempsey, who carried heavy artillery sufficient to batter most men into submission. Dempsey had been touted as the greatest battler in the country, and he was true to form.[400]

The *Denver Times* said the fans had been bunked and the fight was a farce. The toothless old man from Canada lasted less than a minute and was knocked out by a draft. The game received another black eye. With a wild swing that many declared missed, Dempsey knocked down Pelkey in the first ten seconds. Pelkey rose twice, only to be flopped to the canvas again each time. When he was counted out, only 45 seconds had expired.

The only redeeming feature was that fewer local fans fell for the game than had been anticipated. Notwithstanding that the contest had been skyrocketed for weeks by local publicity, it did not draw very well. The fans did not want to pay real money to see a paper-made champion fight an old man. However, many would "take advantage of the fact that three or four years ago Pelkey stayed ten rounds with Fulton as evidence that Dempsey's victory last night was a great feat." However, Fulton had stopped him the next time they fought, and had improved since then.

The knockout occurred when Kearns was shouting to Dempsey to stay away from him. The plan was to stay away for a few rounds and be cautious. Kearns feared Pelkey's power. Instead, Dempsey launched right at him, obviously feeling that the faster he took him out, the less chance or time Pelkey would have to land a big one himself.

---

[400] *Denver Post, Rocky Mountain News, St. Louis Post-Dispatch, Kansas City Post, Des Moines Tribune Tacoma Times San Francisco Chronicle, Nebraska State Journal, Chicago Tribune, Oregon Daily Journal, Salt Lake Herald-Republican, Salt Lake Telegram,* via International News Service, *Leadville Herald Democrat,* all May 30, 1918; *Montrose Daily Press,* May 31, 1918.

Otto Floto said the unbeatable phenomenon Dempsey was just too much for Pelkey. A right to the back of the ear was the finishing touch. The envious tongues of a world of knockers would wag as they may. One fact could not be denied. Dempsey's quick victories, scored artistically and decidedly, made them all look like suckers.

True, Pelkey was not the world's greatest fighter. But few others would last much longer with Dempsey, and no one else could stop Pelkey as quickly. The great Fred Fulton appeared to be the only active fighter to have a chance against him.

It was not Dempsey's fault that his terrific right-hand blows, well-timed and steamed, were too much for Pelkey. He did not want to hippodrome and carry him. He knew just one thing – to fight and put everything into his blows, which is what he did. Floto said the fact was that Dempsey had genuine class, and was the gloved wonder of the day. It was not his fault that opponents could not stand the gaff.

So, folks had the balance of the *Denver Times* typically tending to be hard on Dempsey/Kearns, with the *Denver Post's* Otto Floto being high on them.

Fulton and Dempsey met up at the *Denver Post* offices the next day, on May 30, to sign with promoter Joe Mulvihill to fight 20 rounds at Danbury, Connecticut on July 4 for a $25,000 purse. Otto Floto said a battle between Fulton and Dempsey would decide once and for all who was entitled to succeed Jess Willard as champion, now that Jess appeared to be retired. Dempsey told Floto that he was ready and willing to fight Fulton, and/or to fight and work for Uncle Sam if put on the job. Mulvihill said he would give 10% of the gross receipts from the contest to charity.

Jess Willard insisted that he was not retired, and would fight again when allowed to do so. "I have always felt, and feel now, that I can whip any man living." He always was the biggest, strongest, and fastest, even as a young boy. He had been active, always doing something outdoors to remain healthy and in vigorous condition at all times.[401]

According to the *Denver Times*, Kearns left the Pelkey fight with $700, and took the street car to save taxi fare. This paper doubted whether the Fulton fight would be held, for the government's 'work or fight' order went into effect as of July 1.[402]

John the Barber Reisler was suing Dempsey in Wisconsin and Minnesota for a total of $50,000, and trying to restrain him from boxing.

In early June, Dempsey returned to the San Francisco area, arriving in the "role of hero." Those in Utah and Colorado claimed he was from there, where he got his start, but San Franciscans maintained that their city was where Dempsey truly took his first steps up the ladder of fame. The *San Francisco Examiner* had to admit that Kearns was right or nearly right about Dempsey; that he was the coming champion. "After that Jim Flynn episode was expunged from the records there was never any doubt on the score that

---

[401] *Kansas City Post, Denver Times, Denver Post,* May 30, 1918. As a result of the Dempsey-Fulton dealings, Jack was not able to make the May 31 Red Cross charity show in San Francisco.
[402] *Denver Times,* May 31, 1918.

Dempsey could fight." Jack had gained a bit of weight since he last was in San Francisco, but still was trimly built.[403]

It appears that Billy Miske and Dempsey had struck up somewhat of a friendship outside the ring, perhaps borne of mutual respect. Photos were taken of them together at Neptune Beach, Alameda, California, on the shore of San Francisco Bay, enjoying the company of women. Both were wearing Neptune Beach shirts. Was it an advertisement for the park, which had opened in 1917? Clearly at that point, both were considered world-class, and more than just the ordinary pugilist.[404]

The *San Francisco Examiner* opined that when Dempsey headed East again, there would be a lot of grief around Neptune Beach, for he had been knocking 'em dead thereabouts. Apparently, he was popular with the ladies.[405]

Dempsey and Kearns left San Francisco on June 15. But before leaving, Dempsey paid his local draft board a visit, and despite a "temporary scare," being informed that he was classed A1, investigation ultimately proved that he was entitled to class A4, "which gives him a new lease of life." He was exempt from the draft (as a result of having dependents).

Dempsey was due to appear in Milwaukee on June 22 for an examination by John Reisler's attorney. Eventually an agreement was worked out wherein Reisler would not attempt to prevent Dempsey from fighting Fulton, which fight was postponed until July 13 (or later) after

---

[403] *San Francisco Examiner*, June 4, 1918.
[404] *Richmond Palladium and Sun-Telegram*, July 22, 1918; *San Francisco Chronicle*, June 13, 14, 1918. On May 31, 1918 in San Francisco at the Red Cross benefit show, Billy Miske stopped Henry Hendricks in the 2nd round. On June 7, 1918 in Los Angeles, Billy Miske and Willie Meehan fought to a 4-round draw. On June 14, 1918 in San Francisco, Miske won a 4-round decision over KO Kruvosky.
[405] *San Francisco Examiner*, June 11, 1918.

Connecticut Governor Marcus Holcomb said the Dempsey-Fulton fight would not be allowed in his state. Hence, a new location had to be found.[406]

In the meantime, Kearns kept Dempsey active. A month after the Pelkey contest, a now 23-year-old Jack Dempsey traveled to Tulsa, Oklahoma to take on Tom McCarthy, who had been boxing since 1911, and whose record included: 1914 W12 Jack Lester (twice), D12 Bob McAllister, D12 Joe Bonds, WND10 Jim Savage, WND10 Battling Levinsky, WND10 Terry Keller, and LKOby4 Gunboat Smith; 1915 WND10 Terry Keller, DND10 Porky Flynn, LND10 Charley Weinert, LND10 and D10 Jack Dillon, LND10 Battling Levinsky (twice), WND10 George Rodel, WND10 Colin Bell, L12 Gunboat Smith, and LKOby3 Tom Cowler; and 1917 LND6 Victor Dahl. McCarthy had been fairly inactive for the last two and a half years, but he had high quality experience and solid performances against some of the world's best fighters. He typically weighed 180-190 pounds.[407]

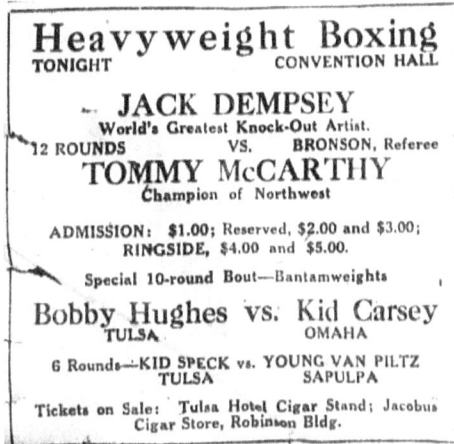

Locals who saw Dempsey making preparations had nothing but praise for him. Jack ran 3 miles and did wind sprints without showing any fatigue. He never dissipated, working out daily, never permitting himself to get out of good condition.

Jack said, "Right now I am in the best shape of my whole career. The way I feel right now I would agree to take on both Jess Willard and Fred Fulton inside one week." Jack said he was not stuck on himself, but knew those big fellows, and knew what he could do to them. They knew just as well as he did, which is why they were shunting him off. He said he would knock out Fulton and create such demand that Willard would have to fight him. He would donate his end of the purse to the war fund.

Jack never took anyone for granted, lest some unknown might upset him. "They ain't going to catch me sleeping. I train my hardest for the less important fights." He liked to get to work quickly, so his opponents did not have a chance to get started. He had knocked out many fighters in the 1st round. The ones who lasted longer could take it. "That's the way to lick them, hop right on them and give it to them fast and plenty. That's my style."

McCarthy and Dempsey appeared to be similar in size. McCarthy said he was ready to slug with the more famous man. The *Tulsa Daily World* called Dempsey the "probable next world's champion."[408]

---

[406] *San Francisco Chronicle*, June 14, 16, 18, 1918; *San Francisco Examiner*, June 23, 1918.
[407] Boxrec.com.
[408] *Tulsa Daily World*, July 1, 1918.

On Monday July 1, 1918 in Tulsa, Oklahoma, at the Convention Hall, under the auspices of the Mid-Continent A.C., Jack Dempsey took on Seattle's Tom McCarthy, heavyweight champion of the northwest, in a scheduled 12-round bout. 1,500 patrons attended, paying from $1 up to $5 for seats. A fellow named Bronson refereed (likely Jimmy Bronson).

The local *Tulsa Daily World* reported that after 30 seconds of foot-racing by McCarthy, Dempsey got him into a corner and fired away, landing his sleep producers, and the pride of the north fell over amongst the spectators, the first and only knockdown required. The promoters called the ambulance.

The crowd was amazed by how quick and skillful Dempsey was, demonstrating a masterful style, stopping with such ease a man who had solid experience. He showed up wonderfully, and had all the earmarks of a champion. Local Tulsans had nothing but praise for him, and were pulling for Dempsey to get a crack at Willard.

Non-local accounts reported that Dempsey sized up McCarthy for a moment, then rushed him, swung a terrific blow at the solar plexus which just grazed the body, and then followed with a left swing to the jaw and McCarthy went down for the count under the ropes, 20 seconds into the fight. McCarthy had not struck a blow.[409]

Kid Norfolk had been on the trail of Fulton and Dempsey, but both had dodged the issue of fighting the ebony-colored fighter. Edward Tranter wrote, "A black man will never be as popular a heavyweight champion as a white man, but that is neither here nor there when it comes to comparing pugilistic merits of professional boxers and title claimants."

Kearns had not yet matched Dempsey with any black fighter. At that time, Dempsey and Fulton were scheduled to clash with each other in either Jersey City or Newark, New Jersey in mid-to-late July (details were in a state of flux), and Dempsey already had two other matches scheduled in the interim.[410]

On the witness stand in Milwaukee, John "the Razor" Reisler ran into an unexpected barrier in his effort to prevent Jack Dempsey from appearing under any other management. A few months back, Reisler went through bankruptcy proceedings. At that time, he failed to list the Dempsey contract as an asset. Since then, he swore at St. Paul that Dempsey's contract was worth $75,000. If true, then the contract belonged to his creditors, not Reisler. So, either he committed perjury in the New York courts by swearing he possessed no other assets of value, or there was no contract, for it had been rescinded, as Dempsey claimed.

The *Kansas City Post* said Dempsey was dropping his opponents as fast as they could bring them up. It didn't matter whether they were good or bad, experienced or not, the result was all the same. He had his foes hitting the floor hardly before they could put up their hands.[411]

---

[409] *Tulsa Daily World*, July 2, 1918; *Salt Lake Herald-Republican, Kansas City Post*, July 2, 1918.
[410] *Buffalo Enquirer*, July 2, 1918; *Kansas City Post*, July 2, 4, 1918.
[411] *Kansas City Post*, July 4, 1918.

Dempsey was back in the ring again a mere three days after the McCarthy contest, in Joplin, Missouri, against 23- or 24-year-old Bob Devere. Devere's record included over 40 fights: 1915 LKOby7 Dick Gilbert, DND15 Jack Lester, LTKOby8 Carl Morris, and KO4 Charley Miller; 1916 KO2 George Davis, LTKOby3 Andre Anderson, LND10 Battling Levinsky, LND10 Gunboat Smith, LND10 Jack Dillon, D20 and L10 Sam McVey, KO3 Heriberto Rojas, and LND10 Sam Langford; and 1917 LND10 Jim Coffey, KO5 Larry Williams, WND10 Jim Flynn (one month after Flynn stopped Dempsey in 1 round), LND10 Sam Langford, LND10 Bill Brennan (twice), LTKOby5 Fred Fulton, and WDQ2 Terry Keller. He generally weighed about 190-195 pounds.[412]

The *St. Louis Post-Dispatch* said Devere was no set-up. The semi-local Kansas City heavyweight had survived encounters with hard-punching blacks Sam Langford (twice going the 10-round distance) and Sam McVey (D20 and L10), and also went the full route with top whites Jack Dillon, Jim Coffey, Jim Flynn, Gunboat Smith, and Bill Brennan. The durable Devere was a husky 200 pounds. Though the same height, Dempsey was smaller than Devere, weighing less than 190 pounds. Hence, the "Salt Lake meteor" had a real fight on his hands.

Of the men Dempsey had been beating, "None of the dangerous black dynasty was included in the lot." Although most of his victims lacked class, the manner and method Dempsey used to defeat them was impressive. Miske was the only one who recently was able to last the distance.

Noted was the fact that boxing was not undergoing the same level of attack from government agents recently as it once had, for the government appreciated the war utility of such athletics, with the U.S. having entered the great world war.

The *St. Louis Star* described Devere as a tough, rugged boxer, capable of furnishing a stiff test for the best heavyweights. He left a machine shop to become a boxer. He was game, had a punch, and could take punishment. He had been a pro for nearly four years. He was a plodder, but clever enough to outpoint some well-known men, and game enough to give them a hard fight. He was a hard enough hitter to be dangerous for anyone. He still was young, a crafty general, and a tearing and smashing type of mauler, like Dempsey. He had a fair defense, and a nearly top-notch left hand. His best punch was his straight right cross. He also was apt to shift to an uppercut. He knew how to set himself and put weight into his blows. He would take a lot of punishment before accepting defeat. Outside the ring, he was likable and well educated.

The local *Joplin Globe* said Dempsey, the "Human Submarine" and "coming heavyweight champion of the world," expected a hard battle. Jack was as brown as a coffee berry from weeks of work in the sun. Those who saw him train were amazed. "His almost unbelievable quickness with his hands and on his feet would be amazing in a bantam or a featherweight and in a man of his bulk it has to be seen to be appreciated." This paper said he

---
[412] Boxrec.com.

weighed 195 pounds stripped, with no fat, but all muscle set on steel springs.

Kearns said Dempsey ordinarily did not fight "for blood," but Devere was the only man in the world other than John the Barber Reisler whom he really disliked. Devere had agreed to fight Dempsey on two other occasions, but pulled out both times, grasping for more money, causing Jack a lot of inconvenience and loss of revenue. "Believe me, Dempsey is going to 'get even' with Devere."

Kearns said Dempsey was in the best condition of his life. "He is so full of 'life' that he can't sit or stand still a moment."

Speaking about his recent bout with Tommy McCarthy, Dempsey said, "Aw, he is a good boy, and I hated to do it, but I've gotta box someone or starve and it isn't my fault that these other birds aren't able to put up a real scrap. Sure, I know what they are after. They figure maybe, if they're lucky, they'll get a chance to knock my block off like Tom Cowler did to Fulton – but, believe me, none of 'em are going to be lucky."

Regarding his next foe, Dempsey said, "As for Devere, he's different. Bob isn't a coward. I don't believe he 'ran out' because he was afraid of me, but he did 'run out' and I'm going to get him for it. It ought to furnish you fellows a lot of fun, too, for Devere is about the toughest bird I've met so far, with the exception of Morris and Brennan."

Devere denied running out of fights with Dempsey, and claimed that his record was better than Jack's record.

The day before the fight, the confident Kearns announced that Dempsey would be fighting Porky Flynn in two days in Atlanta, and then Dempsey and Fulton would fight on July 20, 8 rounds at Jersey City, New Jersey, the longest distance allowed in that state, using 8-ounce gloves, as required there. Kearns said there was no possibility of Fulton or anyone else beating Dempsey. "I'll send Jack in there just like we were out on the coast, boxing one of those little four-round affairs where nothing but fight goes, and Fulton won't be able to stand it." He said Jack could do 8 rounds at just as fast a pace as 4 rounds, "and believe me, Fulton or no other man in America can stand that pace with Dempsey." Kearns essentially was presuming victory for Dempsey in all of his upcoming fights, as well as lack of injury that could derail any of them. At that pace, Dempsey would fight four times in one month.

On Thursday July 4, 1918 in Joplin, Missouri, outdoors at Miners park (also called the Joplin baseball park or the Western League ball park), under the auspices of Jimmy Bronson's Southwest Athletic Club, and governed by the Joplin Boxing Commission, in a scheduled 12-round contest, Jack Dempsey fought Bob Devere. Ticket prices were $2 up to $5. Edward W. Cochrane or Cochran, sports editor for the *Kansas City Journal*, refereed. The ring was 20-feet-square. The show started at 4 p.m. The crowd was fairly small, which disappointed promoter Bronson.[413]

---

[413] *St. Louis Post-Dispatch, St. Louis Star, Joplin Globe*, July 3, 4, 1918; *St. Louis Star*, March 27, 1918.

The local *Joplin Globe* reported that Devere looked fat and soft, and it was apparent from the opening gong of the 1st round that it would be only a matter of moments until Dempsey would land the knockout blow. At one point, they engaged in a hard exchange in which Devere received the worst of it, and then he fell into a clinch.

Just as they were separating from the clinch, Dempsey landed a short left hook to the point of the jaw and Devere went down for the ten-count, less than two minutes into the 1st round. "Devere was really out, too, for the blow that Dempsey landed was one of the kind that paralyzes. The big Kansas Citian made desperate efforts to rise to his feet but was unable to do so." (Fighters were supposed to protect themselves at all times, including coming out of clinches.)

The "California Submarine" did not break a sweat, fighting coolly and carefully during the short time the bout lasted. He treated all of his opponents alike, regardless of experience or ability.

The man who had lasted 10 rounds twice with Sam Langford and Bill Brennan, 10 and 20 rounds with Sam McVey, and beat Jim Flynn, could not get out of the 1st round with Jack Dempsey.[414]

The *St. Louis Post-Dispatch* version by John E. Wray was more detailed. The house drew about $1,260, which included 500 men and women at the baseball park. The low attendance was due to the fans' unwillingness to pay $5 to see Dempsey score what they believed would be a quick knockout, despite Devere's solid record. The ring was 16-feet square, pitched over home plate. It was white-hot under the blazing sun. Devere appeared flabby and not in top condition. He weighed at least 200 pounds, if not more.

When the gong rang, Dempsey shook hands and then moved around to get the sun out of his eyes. He cautiously felt him out, given the 15-pound weight difference. Dempsey led with a tentative left and right. Devere ducked one blow and leaned back out of reach of another, then stepped forward with a left hook that reached Dempsey's face. Dempsey then began speeding up, and soon had Devere pawing. Jack stepped around his foe in a bewildering way, yet without haste, landing stinging blows. Bob twice clinched, and in close handled himself well, like an experienced fighter.

As they stepped out of the second clinch, Dempsey suddenly lunged forward and clipped Devere on the jaw, dazing him. A feint lured Devere into a lead, and almost at the same time Dempsey countered on the chin with a blow that did not travel more than a foot. Devere straightened up, and another short chop angled to the jaw sent him down face first as if his legs had been shot off. He rolled over on the floor onto his back, giving a spasmodic twitch, but oblivious to the referee's count. At ten he still was on his back.

Another description of the knockout said a right to the chin and another blow to the angle of the jaw sent the 200-pound Devere down, curled up like a singed caterpillar.

---

[414] *Joplin Globe*, July 5, 1918. *Kansas City Times*, July 5, 1918. The *Kansas City Times* reported that after they had separated from a clinch, a left hook sent Devere down for the count.

His seconds dragged Devere to his chair like a slaughtered pig – inert if not totally unconscious. When he tried to climb out of the ring five minutes later, he all but fell to the ground.

Dempsey had stopped Bob Devere in 1 minute 15 seconds, lending color to the prevailing opinion that he was the hardest hitter in the country and a great fighter, in fact the world's most remarkable fighter. He was the man who put hurry into hurricane.

The *St. Louis Star* agreed that Devere lasted only 75 seconds. In the opening seconds, it looked like he would make a good showing. His work to the body in the initial clinch raised hopes that Devere would weather the storm and put up a good fight. However, Dempsey sailed into him, and a left smash to the ribs staggered Devere. In the second clinch, both worked earnestly, with Devere showing well at inside work. In the breakaway, however, Dempsey landed a short jolt to the jaw and Devere was rendered groggy. A second and third jolt followed in quick succession. Devere tried to steady himself, but Dempsey landed a stinging hook to the left jaw and followed with a smash on the point of the chin. Bob lunged forward to clinch, but Jack backed away and Bob went to the floor. He tried to rise, but fell flat on his face and was counted out.

Newswriters said that although Dempsey's punch was impressive, he still needed to prove himself against capable, conditioned fighters, for in all of his recent bouts except two he had been opposed to has-beens or foes of the second-rate caliber. Still, the newswriters noted that Dempsey was knocking them out quickly, for the most part: Homer Smith, 50 seconds, Jim Flynn, 30 seconds, Jack Smith, 60 seconds, Tom Riley, 1 minute 50 seconds, Arthur Pelkey, 30 seconds, Tom McCarthy, 20 seconds, Bob Devere, 75 seconds, as well as several others. Only Morris (6), Brennan (6), and Miske (10) had lasted rounds with him recently.

Just two days after the Devere contest, in Atlanta, Georgia, Dempsey would fight Dan "Porky" Flynn, his third fight in the span of just six days (McCarthy, Devere, Flynn), an amazing pace of activity. At the end of the month, he would fight Fred Fulton (for an alleged $7,500 each).

Some New York promoters requested Dempsey's presence at an army benefit at Madison Square Garden on July 15, and to meet black Kid Norfolk, who had won a 1917 12-round decision over Miske. Kearns sent a telegram to the promoters saying, "Have just matched Dempsey with Fulton, July 20. This is Dempsey's great championship opportunity, and therefore would prefer to appear at some later benefit, if possible. If not, will be glad to have Dempsey oppose any white heavyweight, no negroes."

Kearns explained that his reason for barring negroes was that they were not gate draws. Also, "He contended that if he consented to the Norfolk match he would have Langford, Wills, McVey and other representatives of the dark dynasty hounding him for matches." Kearns drew the color line.

One writer noted that it was the eight-year anniversary of Jack Johnson defeating Jim Jeffries, when he "turned daylight into darkness," a "sad day indeed 'fo de white folks,' but they have managed to live it down and have since witnessed the dethronement of this same Jack Johnson by another pale faced fighter and the championship restored to the Caucasian race."[415]

*St. Louis Post-Dispatch* sports editor/columnist John Wray said debate was torrid regarding whether Dempsey was real championship material or just cleverly built-up camouflage. Some said his record was padded with worn-out has-beens and men who were out of condition. Others countered that even an out-of-shape veteran usually could last a few rounds with anyone, but condition was not a factor, for Dempsey was taking them out quickly. He stopped Brennan, doing what no one else had done, and beat Miske too; and both were young, vibrant, top men. Dempsey said he was 188 pounds in top shape. He would concede a lot of weight, height, and reach to the best men, a concern for some. Still, he seemed to have the right stuff, with confidence, a love of fighting, and a very powerful wallop.

Wray said suspicions regarding the genuineness of his knockouts were unfounded. He carried no one, dropping them all as fast as he could, despite the fact that allowing fights to last longer might help the gates and satisfy the fans more. In answer to those who said Dempsey was matched with "cheese champions," promoters responded, "We can't get anybody to fight him. And if we could, State executives are stopping all fights of importance unless the boxers are enlisted men." The McCarthy bout in Tulsa only drew $1,500. The Devere contest only drew $1,200. "In these times of thrift and war work, fans are thinking twice before they give the price of a war-saving stamp to see a farcical boxing show."[416]

PORKY FLYNN.

Boston's 30-year-old 200-pound Dan "Porky" Flynn had been fighting since 1907, and had nearly 100 fights, his results including significant victories over Jim Barry, Jack Twin Sullivan, Jewey Smith, Gunboat Smith, Tom McMahon, Battling Jim Johnson (who drew with Jack Johnson), and Colin Bell. Even in losses, Flynn had proven his durability in going the distance with men like Joe Jeannette (twice), Fred Fulton (L20 and LND10, but subsequent LKOby4 and LKOby2), Jack Dillon, Carl Morris, Tom Cowler, John Lester Johnson, and Kid Norfolk. He even had fought a few draws with Battling Levinsky. Sam Langford had stopped Flynn in 14 rounds and 4 rounds.[417]

---

[415] *St. Louis Post-Dispatch, St. Louis Star*, July 5, 1918; *Kansas City Post*, July 4, 1918.
[416] *St. Louis Post Dispatch*, July 6, 1918.
[417] Dan Flynn's record included: 1909 W12 Sailor Burke, L12 Jack Twin Sullivan, and L12 Frank Klaus; 1910 W8 and W12 Morris Harris, LKOby3 Stanley Ketchel, WND6 (twice) and WND12 Billy Dunning, W12 Jim Barry, and W12 Jack Twin Sullivan; 1911 D12 Sandy Ferguson, L20 Bombardier Billy Wells, WDQ4 Gunner Moir, DND10 Jack Twin Sullivan, WND10 Jewey Smith, WND10 Jim Barry, and LND10 Joe Jeannette; 1912 W20 (twice) Jim Barry, LKOby14 Sam Langford, W12 Barry, and WND10 Gunboat Smith; 1913 DND10 Battling Levinsky and LKOby4 Sam Langford; 1914 LND10 (twice) and DND10 Battling Levinsky, KO4 George Rodel, WND10 Soldier Kearns, WND10 Tom McMahon, and W12 Battling Jim Johnson; 1915 LND10 (twice) Jack Dillon, DND10 Tom McCarthy, D15 Terry Keller, LND10 Charley Weinert, LND6 Carl Morris, NC8 Sam Langford, WND10 and TKO2 Colin Bell, LND10 Battling Levinsky (thrice), WND10 Tom McMahon, and LND10 Tom Cowler; 1916 L8

Dempsey was called the western flash, and Flynn the Boston battler. The local *Atlanta Constitution* said, "Dempsey is reputed to be the hardest hitter in the game, while any man that can drop Fred Fulton twice, which is one of Flynn's accomplishments, can also hit some." Flynn had decked Fulton twice in their first fight, though Fulton won the 20-round decision.

> **DIVISION OF HOUSE**—All ringside and stage seats and the left-hand side of the boxes, dress circle and gallery for white patrons. The right-hand section of the boxes, dress circle and gallery reserved for colored patrons.
>
> **MAIN BOUT**—Jack Dempsey, of Salt Lake City, vs. Dan ("Porky") Flynn, of Boston, 10 rounds.

Ticket prices were $3.30 ringside, $2.20 for boxes, dress circle, and stage, and $1.10 general admission. All men in uniform would be admitted for half price. Patrons also would have to pay a war tax, $1.80, $1.20, and 60 cents. The arena would be segregated by race. Certain sections were for whites, and certain sections were for blacks.

Joe Woodman, who managed him, said, "Flynn is in great shape and Dempsey is going to have a real battle on his hands." "Dempsey is in for the hardest battle of his career. I have never seen Flynn in better shape, and the meteoric career of that young westerner is liable to be stopped right short unless he is considerably better than I give him credit for being." Dempsey was a good man, but Flynn was not going to back up, and there would be considerable punch swapping, given Dempsey's reputation for carrying the bout to his foe. The local press agreed that Flynn appeared to be in great condition. They said he was about 28 years of age.[418]

The night before the fight, Flynn sparred 3 rounds with middleweight Tommy Gavigan in front of 5,000 soldiers who applauded his work. The local writer called Porky Flynn the game's best trial horse, a battler who, with the exception of but a few, had taken on all of the big fellows.

> **BOXING TONIGHT**
> **AUDITORIUM-ARMORY**
> 10 ROUNDS—
>   PORKY FLYNN vs JACK DEMPSEY
> 6 ROUNDS—
>   "Spike" Wilson vs. Young Jackson.
>   Joe Slaughter vs. Charlie Stinson.
> **Big Battle Royal—11 Participants**
> Special Section Reserved for Colored Fans
> General Admission $1.10; Boxes and Dress Circle $2.20

Jack Kearns said, "We expect a tough battle." He called Flynn a tough bird, the toughest in the game. Flynn had lost a 20-round decision to Fulton, but many believed that Flynn had won or at least drawn, with his knockdowns of Fulton in the 4th and 12th rounds. (Fulton scored two subsequent early knockouts of Flynn in rematches).

Joe Woodman said if Dempsey could beat Flynn, then he certainly was entitled to a bout for the championship. Woodman called them two of the hardest hitters in the business, so someone likely was going to hit the canvas. They were about the same height and weight, with Flynn perhaps a bit bigger (he typically weighed around 195-200 pounds).[419]

---

Dillon, L20 and LND10 Fred Fulton, WND10 Gunboat Smith, D8 Levinsky, LND10 Joe Jeannette, and LND10 John Lester Johnson; 1917 LKOby4 and LKOby2 Fred Fulton; and 1918 L12 Kid Norfolk.
[418] *Atlanta Constitution*, July 3-5, 1918.
[419] *Atlanta Constitution*, *Atlanta Independent*, July 6, 1918.

On Saturday July 6, 1918 in Atlanta, Georgia, at the Auditorium Armory, in a scheduled 10-round contest, Jack Dempsey fought Dan "Porky" Flynn.

According to the local *Atlanta Constitution*, Flynn presented himself confidently, like a great fighter. Although the announcement was made from the ring that Flynn weighed six pounds less than Dempsey, who was said to weigh 196 pounds, Flynn appeared to weigh six pounds more, so the announcement likely was in error and the weights reversed.

At the start, they fiddled momentarily, but then they slugged away for about a minute. Dempsey caught Porky with a left smash just below the ribs. It slowed down the Boston man, and he used all the tactics at his command to save himself. But it was to no avail, because Dempsey kept boring in and driving him from corner to corner. He just wouldn't stop.

Finally, like a flash, Dempsey caught Flynn again with his smashing left into the pit of the stomach and quickly followed with a terrific right cross to the chin, and Flynn reeled, sagged, and crumpled down backwards; laying stretched out at full length on his back in his own corner. Referee Dick Jemison tolled the fatal ten. Flynn was asleep for several seconds longer, knocked out cold. The contest had lasted less than 2 minutes.

Dempsey did not give Flynn a chance to show much, for Jack was on top of him from the tap of the gong until it went down as the shortest fight local fans had witnessed since the start of the city's pugilistic renaissance.

Flynn had been added to Dempsey's long list of 1st round knockouts, his fourth 1st round knockout in a row, three of which were over the course of just one week, on July 1, 4, and 6. A man who had gone the distance or lasted rounds with several top men, including Gunboat Smith (W10 twice), Joe Jeannette (LND10 twice), Sam Langford ( LKOby 14 and 4, and NC8), Battling Jim Johnson (W12), and Fred Fulton (L20, LND10, LKOby 4 and 2), and many more, could not get out of the 1st round with Jack Dempsey.

Jack was scheduled to fight again that same month, against top contender Fred Fulton.[420]

A day later, Dick Jemison, who refereed Flynn-Dempsey, said although he would have liked to have seen him for a longer period of time, "Jack Dempsey showed me enough in the one minute and fifty-eight seconds of battling for me to record myself as believing that Atlanta boxing fans saw the next heavyweight champion of the world in action Saturday night."

Jemison said Dempsey's only obstacle was Miske, the Minnesota bearcat. Their styles were similar, on par in aggressiveness, with a slight shade in Dempsey's favor in ring generalship, although in hitting power and weight, Dempsey had the strong edge. Jemison said he would referee such a fight for free; it was destined to be so good.

Dempsey was of a likable disposition outside the ring, only 23 years old, 6'1" in height, and 196 pounds.

---

[420] *Atlanta Constitution*, July 7, 1918. Amongst the preliminaries earlier that evening, there was a battle royal between nine young negroes. The remaining fighter after 3 rounds, Oscar Bridges, spent five minutes gathering coins from the canvas.

He is a splendid ring general, quick of eye, uses splendid judgment in picking his openings, a two-handed fighter who shoots his punches from any angle without having to be set. ... A good offense is a good defense. ... Dempsey's defense then is superb, for he packs the most wicked offensive I have ever had the pleasure of watching. But Dempsey's best asset is his ability to time his punches. He hits cleanly, sharply and quickly. ... I have never seen any cleaner, quicker or more decisive hitting than that displayed by Dempsey Saturday night.

Before the bell, Jemison heard Kearns tell Dempsey, "Let him stay awhile, Jack, we've got a nice house and I'd like to give the fans a run for their money." Dempsey nodded his assent, but still couldn't help but stop him quickly. Flynn made the mistake of trying to stand up and fight. He saw an opening and clipped Jack on the chin with a sharp right hook, and out went Kearns' instructions. Dempsey grew furious and rushed in to attack. He feinted a right and shot his left straight to the pit of the stomach. It did not travel more than eight inches, but landed with Jack's full body weight behind it, and Porky grunted. Quicker than the eye could follow he crossed the right to the chin and "one-twoed" with the left and Porky crumpled. Jemison counted off the fatal ten, but Porky did not hear him.[421]

Dempsey was supposed to meet Billy Miske at Madison Square Garden on July 16 in a benefit bout, but Jack sprained an ankle in training and called it off. Miske had a hurt hand from his victory over Bartley Madden on the 15th anyway, so it appeared that both men were fine with the cancellation.

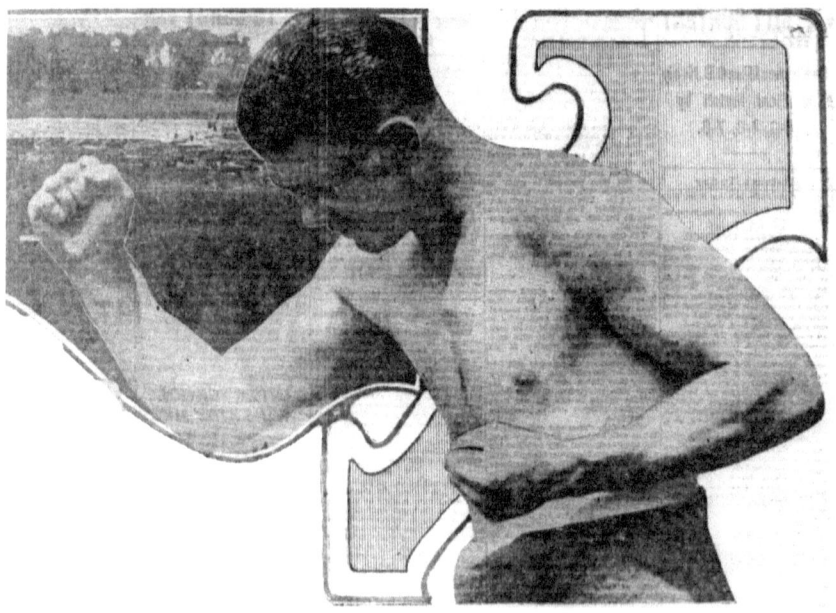

[421] *Atlanta Constitution,* July 8, 1918.

CHAPTER 15

# Number One

Next up for Dempsey was the most important fight of his career up to that point, against Fred Fulton, the Rochester Plasterer, the man who for some time fans and writers were saying should be Willard's next challenger.

27-year-old Fred Fulton had a 41-6-1 record. He was big and tall, at 6'4 ½" and around 215 pounds. He was known for being fast, skillful, and powerful. His major results included: 1914 LKOby4 Al Palzer, and LDQ6 and LKOby6 Carl Morris; 1915 KO5 Jack Moran, TKO6 Frank Farmer, WND10 and TKO5 Arthur Pelkey, TKO4 Terry Keller, and KO4 Andre Anderson; 1916 W20 and WND10 Dan Porky Flynn, KO2 Fireman Jim Flynn, TKO9 Al Reich, and KO1 Andre Anderson; 1917 KO1 Tom Cowler, KO2 Charley Weinert, LDQ5 and WDQ6 Carl Morris, TKO7 Sam Langford, KO4 and KO2 Porky Flynn, TKO3 Jack Moran, TKO5 Bob Devere, and TKO7 Gunboat Smith; and 1918 DND10 Billy Miske, TKO4 Tom McMahon, TKO3 Frank Moran, and KO5 Tom Cowler.

Fred Fulton.    FRED FULTON.

Dempsey-Fulton had been scheduled for July 20 in Newark, New Jersey, but local politicians got in the way, which meant the location and date had to be changed yet again.[422]

Dempsey trained at Jimmy De Forest's gym in Long Branch, New Jersey, at the Broadway Theatre building. De Forest was a diminutive elderly-looking gentleman who was known for his boxing knowledge.

Jack was in the audience at a boxing card on July 12 at the Ocean Park Casino, and after being introduced, was compelled to enter the ring to acknowledge the fans before the clapping would cease. He left at 10 p.m., believing in going to sleep early and rising with the sun.[423]

---

[422] *Trenton Evening Times*, July 12, 1918.
[423] *Long Branch Daily Record*, July 13, 1918. Spellings also included De Forrest, DeForrest, or DeForest.

The *Long Branch Daily Record* said knockout artist Dempsey stood out as the probable next heavyweight champion. He was one of the most sensational fighters in a generation.[424]

After a lot of uncertainty regarding when or where the Dempsey-Fulton bout would take place, on the 16th it was announced that they would meet on July 27 at the Harrison, New Jersey Federal League Park, a baseball park, with enough seating for 20,000 spectators. Harrison was just outside of Newark, on the east side of the Passaic River. It was within 10-12 miles of New York, close enough for fans from that state to come to the show. The bout was scheduled for 8 rounds, the longest distance allowed in New Jersey. After a special session at Trenton, the New Jersey state boxing commission approved the promoters' request for a license. Jack Curley was managing the new club, the Hudson County Sportsmen's Club of Harrison, and promoting the contest.[425]

The *Trenton Evening Times* said Fulton likely would be the favorite.

New Jersey law required larger 8-ounce gloves (rather than the usual 5-ounce), but promoters usually got around the point by loading three ounces at the wrists or sleeves of the gloves, so that punches still were effective and knockouts just as frequent.[426]

Fulton had a pair of excellent sparring partners: 184-pound Bartley Madden and 205-pound Harry Wills. Madden had proven durability, going the distance with Bill Brennan, Jim Coffey, and Battling Levinsky, and he just went 8 rounds with Billy Miske on the 15th. Harry Wills had emerged as the world's best black heavyweight, with a 1918 record that included KO6 Sam McVey, KO6 and TKO7 Sam Langford, and W20 McVey. He was a top contender in his own right, but the color line which Willard had drawn, and most accepted, firmly prevented him from being granted a title shot.

On July 19 at Grupp's in New York, Fulton sparred with Madden and Wills, 3 rounds apiece.

While training in Long Branch at the De Forest gym, Dempsey was wearing an ankle brace, recently having sprained it slightly.[427]

The *New York Evening World's* Robert Edgren humorously wrote that Dempsey and Fulton were battling for the privilege of having to wait until Willard was too old to fight. Most felt that either Dempsey or Fulton were Willard's logical successors.[428]

Dempsey was like Stanley Ketchel, but bigger and better. Though only 190 pounds, he had knocked out men 10 to 50 pounds larger than himself. His career had been relatively short at only three and a half years, and he had been stopped only once, which loss was avenged. Dempsey had been known as the "Bull Miner" to all of his fellow Colorado miners who gave him a licking before he grew and learned how to clean them up.

---

[424] *Long Branch Daily Record*, July 15, 1918.
[425] *Plainfield Courier-News*, Bridgewater, N.J., July 16, 1918; *Long Branch Daily Record*, *Trenton Evening Times*, *Newark Evening News*, July 17, 1918.
[426] *Trenton Evening Times*, July 18, 1918.
[427] *Plainfield Courier-News*, July 19, 1918; *Daily Home News* (New Brunswick, N.J.), July 20, 1918.
[428] *New York World*, July 19, 1918.

Jack said he expected Fred to last about 5 rounds.

Fulton said he was pleased to hear the match really was on. He expected to weigh in the neighborhood of 215 pounds in the ring. He too was confident of stopping Dempsey within 5 rounds.

The press and promoters liked that Dempsey was a fighter who enjoyed fighting, fought often, and was not unreasonable with promoters.

The *New York Herald's* boxing writer, known as Cross Counter, said the fight likely would end via a knockout, for both could punch, and a decisive win for either one could compel a Willard fight. "Dempsey's aggressiveness, dynamic punching and thorough gameness are the three qualities that should enable him to win. He may not box quite so skillfully as the plasterer, but he is a bulldog for fighting."[429]

The *Buffalo Enquirer* said both men carried a terrific punch. Fulton was cleverer, but not as rugged. Fred likely would use his long fast left. Jack would use his terrific body smashes. Dempsey was not awkward, but very fast for a big man and not deterred by jabbing. He was a tearing fighter and his body punches could spell curtains for anyone.

According to the *Newark Evening News*, in training at Jimmy De Forest's Long Branch Broadway Gym, Dempsey impressed fans as a real old-fashioned fighter, possessing an abundance of ability, remarkable aggressiveness, and an equally hard knockout wallop with both hands, making him a real sensation. He was a hard man to figure out because of his peculiar style of attack. For a man standing 6'1 ½" and weighing around 195 pounds, he was remarkably light on his feet, and his hitting ability was not limited to any particular kind of punch. "Every punch is a knockout punch with Dempsey." Although not a boxer, he had defense, for he was able to avoid many punches. He fought his way in close, boring in with swings, getting in quickly before his foe could set himself, and it behooved one to cover up once he got going. He had no marks. Kearns explained that Dempsey smothered an opponent's attack so quickly by his aggressiveness that the other fellow was prevented from landing any hard or clean blows. He fought with head down, eyes at his foe's waist, and hands carried about level with his hips, neither one extended to any degree.

Conversely, Fulton stood with his long left extended, and was more cautious, although hard-punching as well. It would be a case of a natural swinging fighter in Dempsey against a scientific mechanical fighter in Fulton.

Some believed that the long-armed Fulton would not have much difficulty in landing on Dempsey. However, watching Jack in action would chase away any such thoughts. He had a system of rolling his head sideways, frontward and backward, like Mike Gibbons, and was adept at it. He never stood perfectly still for more than a moment, so that a fellow did not have a stationary target to shoot at, which explained his unmarked face. He was like a much larger Stanley Ketchel, with the same fighting qualities and instincts. He had the head and pompadour of Jack Dillon, with longer arms.

---

[429] *Daily Home News, Buffalo Courier*, July 20, 1918; *New York Herald*, July 21, 1918.

Dempsey hit harder than Miske, and was very much faster, which was saying something for a fellow scaling close to 200 pounds.

On July 21, Dempsey sparred 3 fast rounds with light-heavyweight "Big Chief" Clay Turner (who was said to be an Indian but looked a bit like a mix of races, or a light-skinned black man. Some blacks tried to pass for other races, thinking or hoping it would get them more fights.) Turner held victories over Johnny Sudenberg, Bob McAllister, Joe Bonds, Jamaica Kid, and Gunboat Smith.[430]

Dempsey hit Clay Turner so hard in their 3 rounds that by the end, Turner was all in, and even with big gloves, Dempsey had cut Turner's left eye and his ear. "Like all natural fighters he finds it impossible to hold back, even in the gymnasium, and for that reason has difficulty in finding sparring partners."

Jack said it was a good omen that the fight was in Harrison, for that was his middle name: William Harrison Dempsey. When he started boxing, he took the name of Jack, because it sounded more like a fighter than Bill. He said his father was of Irish descent and his mother three-quarter Scotch and one-quarter Cherokee. "That makes me an Irish-Scotch-Indian." His parents were born in Virginia, but he was born in Colorado.

He claimed to have weighed only 165 pounds when he came to New York the first time in 1916, but fought full-fledged heavyweights. He had been a true full-fledged heavyweight for only a year. He was happy with his current weight, and did not want to get any bigger, fearing it might slow up both his punching and his considerable footwork.[431]

Jack Kearns said he had been involved in boxing for 20 years, and never had seen Dempsey's equal in the game. Even old timers were saying he was the greatest heavyweight seen in the last 30 years. "He can hit any one in the world. And no one can hit him hard enough to stop him. I'll bet on that. Just for the fun of the thing I'll bet $50 now that if there is a knockdown Dempsey scores it." Fulton's manager Mike Collins took him up on the bet, feeling that if there was a knockdown, Fulton would be the one scoring it.[432]

Potential issues threatened to derail the contest. Fulton and Dempsey were under investigation by the draft board. It was to be decided whether they came under the Work or Fight order, as interpreted by the Secretary of War. If men of draft age did not fight, they were expected to work in an industry or profession that was deemed valuable or essential to the war effort, or contributed to the effort in some way. The alleged failure of the two to give their services gratis/for free for boxing tournaments to raise money for war benefits had a great deal to do with the attitude of those who appealed to the draft board and state athletic commission to prevent

---

[430] Clay Turner had such results as: 1916 KO10 Johnny Sudenberg; 1917 WND10 Bob McAllister, WND10 Joe Bonds, and WND10 Jamaica Kid; and 1918 LND10 (twice) Tommy Gibbons, WND10 Gunboat Smith, LND6 Leo Houck, WDQ15 George Chip, LND15 Harry Greb, TKO9 George Robinson, and LND10 Bartley Madden.

[431] *Long Branch Daily Record*, July 22, 23, 1918; *Newark Evening News*, *New York Tribune*, *Buffalo Enquirer*, July 22, 1918.

[432] *Buffalo Commercial*, *Buffalo Times*, July 22, 1918. The *Buffalo Times* reported that they would be splitting $20,000 evenly, 50/50%, an amount which Jack Curley guaranteed.

the contest. Some folks were upset that these men were battling for a $20,000 purse while thousands of men were getting paid far less for military service, risking their lives battling the "Hun."

To counteract the bad publicity regarding his failure to enlist in the war, Jack Kearns said Dempsey indeed had helped raise over $60,000 for war funds in boxing benefit performances, and no boxer in the country had done more in benefit work for war funds than him. Dempsey would star in a $100,000 benefit fund show sponsored by Jim Coffroth in San Francisco, after which he would return to his trade as a shipbuilder. "He has boxed in San Francisco, Joplin, Oakland and Chicago, where he engaged in ten benefits. I picked him up in the Oakland shipyards, where he was not earning enough to support his invalid wife and two children, his aged mother and father and a widowed sister with three children." (Actually, Dempsey had no children.) Dempsey signed up with Kearns in order to earn enough money to help his family. Therefore, given that his family needed him, he had been classed 4A, or exempt from service.[433]

The *New York Tribune*'s Fred Hawthorne called them "Ferocious Freddy" and "Demon Dempsey."[434]

Needing a man who could handle hard blows, Jack Kearns hired a new sparring partner for Dempsey. 30-year-old Battling Jim Johnson, known for his rugged strength and durability, having been stopped only three times in about 80 fights, was an experienced 225-pound black fighter who had been fighting since 1909 and had fought all of the best black heavyweights and held his own, including against then champion Jack Johnson (1913 D10), Sam Langford (LND6, D12, L15, LKOby12, L12, L10), Joe Jeannette (WND6, LND10, LDQ15, D12, LND10), and Sam McVey (D15, LKOby21, LND10 twice, L20, L25), having fought draws with all of them at one point, and Harry Wills (LND10, TKO2, and LND10).[435]

On July 23, Dempsey and Battling Jim Johnson sparred for the first time. First, Jack used the pulley weights and hit the bag. In the sparring, Dempsey alternated between Clay Turner and Battling Jim Johnson, each sparring partner going a round and then taking a round of rest (each round being 2 minutes) while the other entered and worked, while Dempsey remained inside the ring throughout without taking any break whatsoever.

---

[433] *Trenton Evening Times*, July 22, 1918; *Buffalo Commercial*, *Brooklyn Citizen*, July 23, 1918.
[434] *New York Tribune*, July 23, 1918.
[435] Battling Jim Johnson's record included: 1910 DND6 Tony Ross, LND6 Sam Langford, D15 and LKOby21 Sam McVey; 1911 TKO11 Jewey Smith; 1912 W15 Tom Cowler, WND6 and LND10 Joe Jeannette, and KO2 Bill Tate; 1913 LND10 and LDQ15 Jeannette, and D10 Jack Johnson; 1914 LND10 (twice) and D12 Langford, L12 Porky Flynn, LND10 (thrice) and D12 Jeannette, and LND10 McVey; 1915 L20 and LND10 McVey, LND10 (twice) and L15 Langford, KO7 Arthur Pelkey, LND10 Jeannette, and LND10 Harry Wills; 1916 L10 Joe Bonds and LKOby12 Langford; 1917 L12 Langford, WTKO2 and LND10 Wills, L20 and L25 McVey; and 1918 L10 Langford and LND4 Kid Norfolk.

In the 1st round, Dempsey tore into Johnson like a bearcat and twice floored him. Clay Turner was up next, and endured rough usage as well. In their 2nd round (Dempsey's third), Johnson attacked this time, but found that Jack was just as plucky and versatile as he was. Dempsey was cool under fire, and after 45 seconds of the roughest milling, Dempsey sent Johnson through the ropes, flat onto his back. The fact that the burly and tough Johnson weighed 35 pounds more than Dempsey and had many more years of quality ring experience against the world's best did not matter. After this, the third knockdown of the sparring session, Johnson had enough. Johnson's carrying of the fight to Dempsey had been to Jack's liking. Clay Turner went one more round with Dempsey, and was well used up at the end.

Dempsey looked better than ever, having both men worn out after their 2 rounds, despite giving each a round of rest in between, while Dempsey was fresh and strong after his 4 rounds without rest, breathing easily.

Afterwards, Johnson said, "Some bearcat. That boy can hit like a mule can kick, and he keeps 'em a goin' a mile a minute all the time. He sure is bad."[436]

The *Brooklyn Daily Eagle* said Dempsey had been in New York back when he still was relatively inexperienced and unknown, and he boxed twice at the Fairmont A.C. and once at the New Polo Club, neither of which were among the big New York clubs, and as a result, only the dyed-in-the-wool boxing fan saw the bouts or knew much about his worth. He was just a kid at the time, and did not create much of a ripple.

Today things were different. Dempsey was touted as the next champion. He was a natural born fighter who liked to fight. According to him, he was born in a small hamlet in Colorado. He had a brother in the service, one rejected from service, and he was waiting to receive his call. He also had two sisters. He said his family moved to Colorado from West Virginia, and his father was Irish and mother of Scotch and Indian blood. Dempsey looked more Italian or Greek than anything. Although he had a surly appearance, he was a good social mixer, and not nervous about the upcoming bout.

Dempsey was pleased to spar with big Battling Jim Johnson, the colored boxer, for he wanted someone big enough with whom he could really hit. Jack said most sparring partners wanted to hold him.

Observing their sparring, the *Eagle* said that in the 1st round, Dempsey dropped Johnson with a left hook to the chin. He staggered to his feet, and Dempsey was on top of him quickly, hitting him with two or three more punches, and down went Johnson again. Jim looked as if he had been knocked cold. Kearns begged Dempsey to let up, or he would lose yet another sparring partner. "Don't hit him so hard. He is the only one I can get." Dempsey grinned and let up for the remainder of the round. After the round concluded, Johnson said, "That boy is certainly some tough baby."

---

[436] *Long Branch Daily Record*, July 24, 1918. Some misidentified Johnson as Fulton's sparring partner Wills.

Joe Humphreys said, "Dempsey is an enlarged Terry McGovern. I never saw a big man who was quite so fast on his feet. He certainly would make a popular champion." The one critique was his defense. He seemed to be open to a fighter willing to take a blow to give one back. Both Jim Johnson and Clay Turner hit him a fair amount, though Dempsey usually stepped in to meet a blow and let it slide by with a movement of his head.[437]

One writer said that Turner, although considered a good heavyweight, was a poor match for Dempsey, for he could not stand Jack's punches, even though Dempsey was wearing large gloves. Turner mostly stalled and hung on for 3 or 4 rounds each day. Dempsey also had worked with a Frenchman, but he quit.[438]

Australian bookmaker Jackie Morris said Dempsey was like Les Darcy. Morris claimed to have seen Fulton box Joe Bonds in an exhibition, and was not overly impressed. He wanted to bet $10,000 on Dempsey, whom he had seen spar in Chicago, and concluded was a real star. However, others said Fulton was an in-and-outer, fighting to the level of his competition. He often rose to the occasion, putting forth his most impressive performances against his toughest foes.[439]

On the 23rd, Fulton sparred 4 rounds with Jack Espen and 4 more with the Jamaica Kid, a black fighter, demonstrating excellent condition. After his workout, he stepped on the scales and tipped the beam at 208 pounds.

Apparently, the draft board had not summoned Fulton; hence the bout seemed to be assured. Fred said, "I have not been hailed before any draft board under the work or fight law. I am under the jurisdiction of a draft board in Minnesota, and have been placed in Class 4A because I have a wife and two children dependent upon me."[440]

A couple days later, reports were that Fulton was participating in a nonessential profession and the Minnesota draft board was requesting his arrest for failure to appear for a physical exam.

Fulton was the 10 to 7 betting favorite, but many members of the press seemed to favor Dempsey. Old-timers said they had not seen such a puncher since Bob Fitzsimmons. Like Fitz, Dempsey was powerful with both wings and very accurate, with good timing and position, and could land from any angle.[441]

On the 25th, only two days before the fight, many came to watch Dempsey work. Jack was like a ferocious beast. He knocked Battling Jim Johnson down, yet still had much more to offer. Jack said, "It is too close to the fight for real, hard work." The experts laughed.

Dempsey was a ripping fighter, and the underdog at 7 to 5 odds. If one preferred the clever careful man with a terrible punch, they went with the

---

[437] *Brooklyn Daily Eagle*, July 24, 1918.
[438] *Newark Evening News*, July 24, 1918.
[439] *Buffalo Commercial*, July 24, 1918. Fulton and Bonds boxed a charity exhibition at Madison Square Garden on June 20, 1918. The next-day *Brooklyn Daily Eagle* said Bonds, who claimed to be the Navy's heavyweight champion, "was no match for the challenger of Jess Willard." The *Brooklyn Daily Times* agreed that Bonds "was no match for the plasterer."
[440] *Trenton Evening Times*, July 24, 1918.
[441] *New York Herald, Plainfield Courier-News, Buffalo Commercial*, July 25, 1918.

favorite Fulton. However, Dempsey appeared to be a wonderful fighter, and he received the stamp of approval from those who saw him in action. He was not the most skilled, but he knew how to fight and had a certain cleverness. He knew what he was doing. When he feinted with his left he followed with a vicious right. He always was working his way in and never gave ground. He hit the body and head and was tireless. He was the best two-handed fighter seen in many years.

Battling Jim Johnson, who was treated roughly in their sparring bout that day, said, "I would rather fight any man in the world than box Dempsey just in fun." This was coming from a man who had gone the distance in fights with Wills, Langford, McVey, Jeannette, and Jack Johnson. Clay Turner, with whom Dempsey simply toyed, said, "Jack is a tiger. I ought to know, and I don't want any further proof."

Dempsey said he had not intended to spar so close to the fight, but so many newsmen and boxing commissioners had shown up that he did not want to disappoint them. In that respect, he was like Jack Johnson.

> Since the first time I started boxing I have always thought I would some day be champion of the world. ... I am a fighter, not a boxer. Perhaps some of the experts who have been doping this fight think Fulton will beat me on points. ... I am a better fighter than Fulton. I will admit that he is a better boxer than I am but no one wants to be fooled into thinking I'll box with him. I'll permit Mr. Fulton to do all the fancy work and confine myself to just plain fighting. I have been winning all my fights in short order and on this occasion I think the shorter I can make the fight the better. I don't expect to win without getting hit or hurt. I realize that Fulton swings a wonderful left. He'll realize that I have got two good hands. I have knocked some opponents out with my right hand and have knocked others out with my left.

Jack understood that easterners did not know him as well as they did Fulton, so it was natural that Fred should be regarded so highly. However, he was confident that when the fight was over, folks would realize that he was a worthy title challenger. "It may be that I am over-confident but I believe I will whip Fulton in a few rounds. I'll certainly try."[442]

The *Brooklyn Daily Eagle* opined that Fulton's mighty long left may be Dempsey's undoing. He had stopped men like Charlie Weinert in 2, Tom McMahon in 4 (McMahon once outpointed Willard over 12), Gunboat Smith in 7 (who also had a win over Willard), Bob Devere in 5, Sam Langford in 6, Frank Moran in 3 rounds (who went the distance with Johnson and Willard), and Tom Cowler twice (1 and 5 rounds). Dempsey had more of a chance to win by knockout than to win a decision. Fulton was the better boxer, but he was not a soft tapper; he could punch too. Fulton had advantages in height, reach, and weight. The majority of boxing followers favored Fulton, the man who had pulverized Langford. Dempsey

---

[442] *Long Branch Daily Record*, July 26, 1918.

would have to break through his guard and hit the body, and overcome the physical handicaps with his speed and power.[443]

| PHYSICAL COMPARISON OF FIGHTERS | |
|---|---|
| FULTON | DEMPSEY |
| 27 years ............Age............ | 23 years |
| 6 ft. 5½ inches........Height........ | 6 ft. 1" inches |
| 84½ inches........Reach........ | 81½ inches |
| 42 inches........Chest (normal)........ | 43 inches |
| 49 inches........Chest (expanded)........ | 49 inches |
| 18¼ inches........Neck........ | 18 inches |
| 35 inches........Waist........ | 37 inches |
| 15½ inches........Calf........ | 16 inches |
| 12 inches........Ankle........ | 11 inches |
| 14 inches........Biceps........ | 14½ inches |
| 8½ inches........Wrist........ | 9 inches |
| 210 pounds........Weight........ | 195 pounds |

Fulton declared, "My left hand has never failed me and that trusty right uppercut has often answered the call, and I cannot see any reason why Dempsey should escape me when most of the others have failed. I am certain of stopping Dempsey in five rounds, with all due respect to his ability."

The *Newark Evening News* said Fulton actually hit harder than Dempsey. He had a more powerful right, and his left was far more educated than Dempsey's. He had much greater one-punch power, whereas Dempsey usually beat his man down with a steady attack that didn't necessarily last that long. Fulton could stop men with a single blow. However, Dempsey was a quick finisher, usually found a way to land a series of blows that spelled doom, and seldom could a man escape him. But Fulton was without peer as a boxer. He could outjab anyone. He had beaten a higher caliber of boxer than Dempsey, stopping Langford and Moran, two of the world's strongest and most rugged heavyweights. Fulton was the favorite, but plenty of men were wagering on Dempsey, who was a larger version of Jack Dillon, with more height, reach, and weight, and a better defense. If he could take a punching, he had an even chance.

**Jimmy De Forest and Jack Dempsey**

Fulton had convinced the local draft board that the draft notices sent to him were defective. Hence, the request for his arrest was withdrawn.[444]

The *Trenton Evening Times* said Dempsey was 23 years old, 6'1 ½", and 186 pounds (some said 195), while Fulton was listed as age 27, 6'5 ½", and 210 pounds. Only one man had gone more than 7 rounds with Fulton in the last year, in more than fifteen fights. Dempsey too had been scoring mostly early knockouts in 1918. Miske went 10 rounds with both men.[445]

---

[443] *Brooklyn Daily Eagle*, July 26, 1918.
[444] *Newark Evening News*, July 25, 26, 1918; *Daily Home News*, New Brunswick, NJ, July 26, 1918.
[445] *Trenton Evening Times*, July 27, 1918.

Dempsey finished his training by posing and exhibiting for moving picture films. The training footage would be shown to soldiers in France for their entertainment. He was done with sparring though.[446]

---

[446] *Long Branch Daily Record,* July 27, 1918.

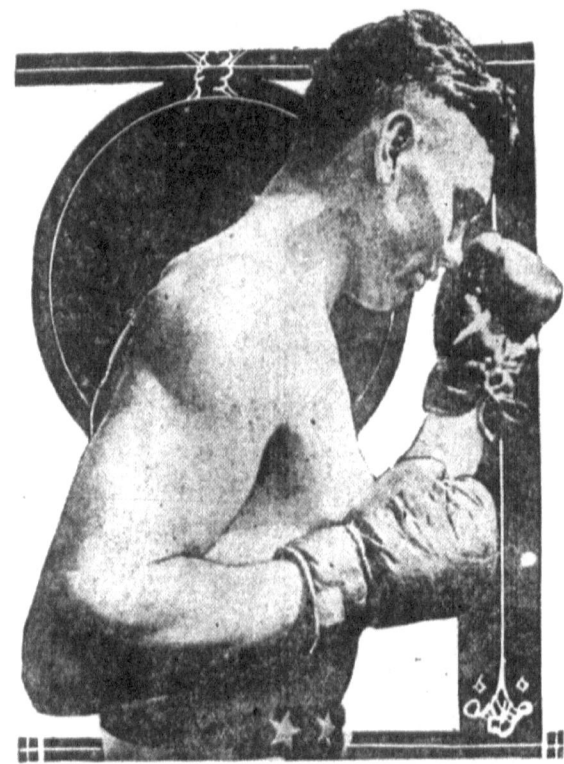

On the 26th at the Ocean Park Casino, Dempsey sparring partner Clay Turner outpointed/shaded Joe Bonds over 8 rounds.[447]

The *New York Herald* noted that Fulton was the favorite owing to his experience, height, reach, weight, skill, and heavy hitting. He had Corbett's jab and Fitz's uppercut. He was called the perfect pugilist. The only question was his ability to stand the gaff under punishment.

Despite his underdog status, Dempsey had plenty of supporters, for he was the kind who administered punishment with the tenacity of a bull terrier.

Moving pictures of their fight would be taken, which would be turned over to the authorities, with the proceeds devoted to war funds. Hence, they were doing their part for the war effort.[448]

Robert Edgren said they were different fistic types, but both knockout artists. The two were considered the best in the business outside of Willard. Fulton had the physical advantages, but Dempsey seemed to be more of an iron man and steadier. Fulton's reach was about 84 inches, while Dempsey's was about 10 inches less. Fulton had wonderful recuperative powers, but he could be knocked down, and had been dazed in several fights. He usually rose and won though. Tom Cowler decked Fulton twice, but Fred came back to win by knockout. Dempsey was stopped only once, when he was a novice, but later avenged the defeat with ease. He had fought much bigger men, but they never hurt him. Dempsey could take a hard punch without showing effects, and had plenty of strength. Jack believed that superior speed would overcome Fred's bulk and strength.

Dempsey had no marks, despite his aggressive style. He was so aggressive that his foes usually were busy trying to do little else but avoid being knocked out. Jack couldn't keep sparring partners, because he knocked them out so often.

---

[447] *Long Branch Daily Record*, July 27, 1918.
[448] *New York Herald*, July 27, 1918.

Fulton was of a more excitable nature. When Morris fouled Dempsey, he wasn't affected at all, and kept his head. When Morris fouled Fulton, butting and cutting him, and hitting him low, Fulton retaliated by intentionally striking Morris low.

Fulton had more experience, looking like a master in badly beating Sam Langford and Frank Moran, who were better than anyone Dempsey had faced. Fulton had done better with Moran than either Jack Johnson or Jess Willard. In stopping Langford, the man whom most were afraid to fight, Fulton really made a name for himself.

Billy Miske, who had fought both, predicted that Dempsey would stop Fulton in 2 rounds. He said Dempsey had him so hurt that he didn't know where he was for the remainder of their contest.[449]

Jack's camp reported that he was weighing 189 pounds.

The day of the fight, Dempsey said, "I think I am the best heavyweight in the ring today. I will try to prove it tonight."

> I am ready to set a pace with Fulton that will make him go to the limit to hold his own. I will start the fight in my usual tear in fashion, to win or lose through rushing the bout from the start. I intend to keep right after the big fellow from start to finish. I don't think the affair will go eight rounds. ... I fully realize that Fulton is a powerful and experienced opponent, but he will have to do better than he ever has before to beat me.[450]

---

[449] *New York Evening World*, July 27, 1918.
[450] *Long Branch Daily Record*, July 27, 1918.

Jack also said he would hit the taller man's stomach and hammer away at any weak spots he could find.

The *Brooklyn Citizen* said a knockout was expected, for both delivered effective blows. "While Fulton is the public choice to win, many of Dempsey's supporters are willing to wager even money on their favorite."[451]

Allan Markley said both were in excellent condition for the match which might decide the title. The fight would be held in accordance with the new Hurley law, which legalized boxing in New Jersey. Fulton was the betting favorite. Both had spent ten days training locally, after completing a tour of the country boxing for different war charities and the Red Cross.[452]

On Saturday July 27, 1918 in Harrison, New Jersey, the Jack Dempsey vs. Fred Fulton fight took place. The fighters were paid at 10 a.m. that day, each receiving an alleged $12,500, $10,000, $9,000, or $7,500 or less. Dempsey was the whirlwind, and Fulton the Minnesota plasterer, regarded as the most logical successor to Willard's title.

At 3 p.m., Fulton tipped the scales at 208 pounds. At 5 p.m., Dempsey, who arrived later, weighed in at 188 pounds, 20 pounds less than Fred.

General View and Close-Up of Ring at Harrison Field

The fight was staged at the old Federal League baseball grounds, a few minutes ride from the heart of Newark, and within easy access of New York, Jersey City, and nearby cities. One said Harrison really was a suburb of Newark. Promoting the fight was the West Hudson Sporting Club, with Jack Curley acting as manager and shouldering 25% of the financial end.

Seats were $10 for ringside box seats, $7 or $7.50 in the reserved grand stand section, $5 brigade, $3 for the field stand at the extreme flanks, and $2 for bleacher seats in faraway center field.

The evening was hot and the sun bright.

It was a mixed crowd, representing all walks of life, from highbrows of political, financial, and industrial ranks, as well as the stage and sports, all the way to newsboys. Stage comedian Eddie Foy was there. Former champs Jimmy Britt and Freddie Welsh were in attendance, shaking hands with entertainer/actor/songwriter George M. Cohan. There was a fair sprinkling of men in service uniform. Women were present in scant numbers. New Jersey Governor Walter Edge was present.

---

[451] *Brooklyn Citizen*, July 27, 1918.
[452] *Kansas City Post*, July 27, 1918.

Attendance reports varied. One said the fight was a financial failure, with attendance a little under 6,000 and receipts only $17,654.50 (with paid attendance at 4,460), as announced by the state inspectors who took a 10% tax on the gross receipts. These numbers normally would be very good, but not in this instance, for the total gate was less than the $25,000 allegedly guaranteed to the two main event fighters (one-half to each, win or lose). Considering the purse, and the expenses of renting the ball grounds, erecting the ring, and temporary arena seats, paying the many attendants and other incidental expenses, the promoters lost heavily on the bout. Promoter Jack Curley confirmed that he would suffer a loss on the promotion. Other total attendance reports included: no more than 8,000, no more than 7,000, and less than 7,000. The arena could have seated 25,000.

Some thought the adverse publicity surrounding the bout affected the attendance. Fulton had been threatened with arrest as a delinquent for failing to comply with the government's "work or fight" order. Allegedly Dempsey was a shipbuilder, and announced that he would go back to his trade after the contest. Others said that had nothing to do with it, but the ticket prices were too high at $10 ringside, and even those seats which were close enough to see the fight well were fairly expensive at $7. The bulk of the ticket sales were in the $2 to $5 sections, with very few sales in the higher priced sections. Some said it was a mistake not to hold the fight later in the evening, which would have attracted a larger crowd, including the racetrack crowd, but the ballpark did not have electric lights.

Photographers and moving picture men were present taking pictures. The moving pictures would be shown at army and navy camps throughout the country, and possibly Europe. Apparently, the federal law prohibiting the interstate transportation of fight films was not going to be deemed applicable to the armed forces.

The preliminary bouts began at 5:45 p.m. The show started 15 minutes late because the crowd was slow to gather. Assemblyman Joseph Hurley, father of the boxing bill, who now was in uniform for the U.S. Navy, was introduced, as well as other notables, including a navy recruiter who delivered a stirring address.

The ring had massive brass posts and natty-green plush-covered ropes. It was erected over what once was a baseball field.

Most of the high-priced seats were empty, and by the time the main event was about to get started, when it became evident that they were not purchased seats, there was a big rush of folks from the cheaper bleacher seats into those unoccupied seats. They leapt the barrier and streamed across the field. The police and home guards were powerless to stop them, and unable to get them to return to their proper seats. One said the lack of proper police control led to a general stampede for the high-priced seats. Jack Curley punched one man who was trying to get a better seat in the rush, but he was but a straw in a whirlpool. Curley threatened to stop the show, but was hissed and hooted. There were too many seat crashers, the stampede too great, and the police were loath to shoot so many people.

It was 7:07 p.m. when 23-year-old Dempsey appeared, wearing white trunks. He climbed through the ropes, assisted by a number of sailors. He sat down on a stool inside the ring in a corner. Fulton entered at about the same time, taking the opposite corner, wearing green trunks with American colors interlacing the belt.

Fulton was much heavier and taller, with longer arms. The 6'5 ½" Fulton was announced at 208 pounds to 6'1 ½" Dempsey's 188 pounds. Some said 27-year-old Fulton had an 84 ½" reach. Neither carried any superfluous flesh at all. Fulton was huge, but Dempsey looked like a gladiator.

Dempsey was handled by Jack Kearns (who was wearing a beret/cap, dark tie, and striped long sleeve shirt), Jimmy De Forest, and Clay Turner (wearing a tank top). Fulton had Mike Collins, Fred Sears, and Dan Hickey.

They would box 8 rounds with 8-ounce gloves, pursuant to New Jersey state law, with no formal decision if there was no knockout. The state athletic commission selected Johnny Eckhardt of Atlantic City to referee. At 7:17 p.m., the parties received the referee's final instructions at ring center. The fight began at twilight.

According to several New Jersey newspapers, including nearby Newark, at the gong, they feinted for a second or so, but Dempsey, with head bent forward, wasted little time in sparring, and assumed the aggressive. Fulton led with a light pawing left (and perhaps right) and Dempsey closed in on his towering opponent. They entered a half clinch. Jack landed a left hook to the jaw and whipped a right under the heart immediately followed by a left to the body. Fulton flinched/winced and drew away. Trying to stave off the hurricane onslaught, the distressed giant Fulton brought forth his rangy left as though to push him away. Quick as a flash Dempsey leapt at him like a pouncing lion, sending his right over in a short downward chop that crossed Fred's extended left arm and glanced off the point of his chin, and Fulton dropped down backwards to the canvas with a thud, his right arm crooked beneath him and his head and shoulders hanging over the lower rope. It happened in the blink of an eye.

The surprised crowd was in a tumult. Referee Johnny Eckhardt tolled off the ten-count very slowly, in dramatic tones, some saying he took 14 seconds to count to 10. Fulton's body quivered. He made a slight move, but his mind appeared to be blank, and he could not rise. All the prostrate pugilist could do was roll over on his right side, hanging over the ropes. Others said Fulton turned over on his face, very slowly, and was on his hands and knees when the referee reached 10.

The referee and a squad of seconds all carried Fulton to his corner. Dempsey stood off, looking surprised. He then turned on his heel in a nonchalant manner and stepped out of the ring to be engulfed by the surrounding throng. Others said Dempsey rushed over to assist Fulton to his feet and helped carry him to his corner. After Dempsey removed the gloves he went back to Fulton, who still was seated on his stool, his head in his hands and his elbows resting on his knees. They shook hands, though Fulton remained on his stool. As Jack left the ring, the spectators cheered him. He returned to his dressing room, accompanied by manager Jack Kearns and trainer Jimmy De Forest.

Most reports said Fulton had hit the canvas just 18 3/5 seconds after the fight began. The *New York Sun*'s "Daniel," *New York Tribune*'s Fred Hawthorne, *Brooklyn Daily Eagle*'s Rice, United Press's H. C. Hamilton, and Damon Runyon all said the fight lasted 23 seconds. The official timekeepers were New York's Billy Considine for Dempsey, Tom Andrews, veteran Milwaukee sporting authority, for Fulton, and New York's Dr. George H. Muth for the club promoting the fight. Two of the three official timers, Consadine (for Dempsey) and Muth (for the club), agreed that it lasted 18

3/5 or 18 ¾ seconds. Andrews (for Fulton) maintained that the fight went 25 seconds. Counting from the tap of the gong until the moment Fulton went down, the figures of 18 3-5 seconds generally were accepted. Unofficial timers, including Bob Edgren of New York, agreed on that point.

Plus, there also were the ten seconds required to count out Fulton, so technically it lasted at least 28-29 seconds total, if one included the count. Since many said the referee actually took about 14 seconds to count up to 10, the fight actually might have lasted 32-33 seconds. But back then, the time of the knockout was when the man went down for the final time, without including the count.

Just like that, in a shocking flash, the man who had beaten Langford and Moran with ease, as well as several other top fighters, was down and out.

*New York Sun* sportswriter "Daniel," who was present, said Fulton was first to lead, sending a light left to the head. Dempsey immediately rushed to close quarters and landed a heavy left to the stomach. Fulton backed away and sparred at long range. Dempsey made another furious rush and landed a right and left to the face, sending Fulton halfway across the ring. Fulton attempted to cover, lifting both gloves up to his jaw as Dempsey rushed in for further vigorous attack.

Into the pit of the stomach Jack sent a short left hook. Up again it swished to the jaw, accompanied by an overhand right, and Fulton crumpled like a struck ox as he fell on his back close to his own corner, with his head resting on the lower ring rope.

Fulton's seconds sprayed him with water from sponges, and he rolled back and forth against the ring rope, trying to rise, but was unable to do so. The referee stood over him waving his arm up and down indicating the fateful seconds, "ten, and out," before Fulton had even raised his head from the hemp pillow on which it rested.

Instantly the ring was overrun with joyous Dempsey adherents.

The *New York Tribune*'s Fred Hawthorne said the round began with Dempsey rushing from his corner and going to close quarters at once. The giant tried to keep him away by sticking out his long left arm, but he only pawed at Dempsey, who bore in, chasing him around the ring. He came in wide open, but his rush carried Fulton backwards until his back came up against the ropes. Jack fired the left for the body, and as Fulton dropped his arms to ward off the punch, Dempsey fired a terrific right to the ribs. Fred turned his body sideways with a sheepish grin, but just for a second. Dempsey suddenly shifted his attack to the head and landed crushing right and left hooks to either side of the jaw. Fulton crumpled and toppled backward, crashing to the floor. He lay on his back on the lower rope, swaying up and down with the motion of the rope, threatening to fall out of the ring, the sun beating down on his face.

Referee Eckhardt counted, raising and lowering his hand, while Dempsey flitted about behind him, ready to pounce the moment Fulton might rise. But when it became evident that was not going to happen, Jack stepped away further and waited.

Some implored and begged Fulton to rise, some shrieked, one threatened him, and another showered him with water from a sponge. But Fulton was deaf to it all. At the count of seven, he finally rolled over onto his stomach, making vain efforts to raise his head and rise. He got his right foot underneath him at eight, but a moment later fell back again, his head resting sideways on the floor, and it was over.

When the count concluded, Dempsey, who had been standing a few feet away, helped Eckhardt carry Fulton to his corner and onto his chair. Then Jack raised his own right hand above his head and shook his gloved fist in acknowledgement of the wild shrieks from those hailing the victor.

Jack seemed anxious to get to his dressing room. Kearns put a bathrobe around him and tried to keep the fans back. But despite the efforts of the home guard and the Newark police, Jack was tossed about the ring for five minutes before order was restored. Fulton sat on his chair, head bowed down. He kept shaking his head. He received no sympathy.

Scarcely ten blows had been struck. The crowd was stunned.

The *Brooklyn Daily Eagle's* "Rice" said they shook hands at 7:06 p.m., just as the rays of the sun were fast descending. Dempsey immediately rushed Fulton and got him to the ropes. He swung for the jaw, and followed to the body. Fulton lightly poked at Dempsey, mostly just trying to keep him away. Dempsey was pressing all the time, swinging high and low. Fulton fired a left jab, but Jack ducked to one side and swung a terrific left to the body so quickly one hardly could follow the movement. He then whipped a right to the jaw over the guard and Fulton went down and rolled half out of the ropes, nine-tenths unconscious. It was a clean knockout.

H. C. Hamilton, United Press staff correspondent, said at the gong, Dempsey dashed in. Fulton led first by firing a light left and Dempsey countered immediately with a rapid right to the middle of the body. They clinched, stepped back, and Fulton vainly tried three times to reach Dempsey with his rapid left. Jack suddenly shifted and smashed over the right and the fight was over. Fulton did not rise until three seconds after the count was over, and even then it was with assistance. "That Dempsey is one of the greatest fighters the world has ever seen is undoubted."

Damon Runyon's version said Fulton walked out of his corner extending his long left in a light jab at his shorter, dark-skinned, beetle-browed opponent. Dempsey rushed in and winged his right for the body. Then he ripped his left to the same mark. They broke. Fulton feinted his right. Dempsey threw his left (and right) in an overhand fashion and landed on the tip of the chin and down went Fulton. His legs caved under him with startling suddenness. He fell into the ropes and hung there an instant before sagging down slowly and limply to the floor. The final blow was so fast that some did not even see it.

Runyon said Dempsey stopped Fulton with only three punches. The Minnesota plasterer was overwhelmed by the sudden wicked onslaught. Two punches to the body, and then a right hook to the jaw flattened him without having landed a single blow in return. There was one brisk flurry of brown gloves, and it was over. Dempsey simply had marched right at the giant swinging both hands without any apparent idea of direction, but in a very cold-blooded methodical fashion.

The *New York Times* version said Fulton, smiling and confident, tried to jam Dempsey with his long left arm, but Jack cracked him with a hard right over the heart. Fulton seemed hurt, and Dempsey went tearing after him. A left hook to the jaw tottered Fred a bit, and after Jack had rushed him over near the ropes, Dempsey's right arm swung high and came down with a terrific crash on the jaw. The kangaroo-like Fulton crumpled and sagged to the floor, his head falling over the lower rope. His eyes closed, and there was a look of pain over his pale face.

Dempsey had a cold, sneering look of the primitive man. He was the conqueror, his teeth set and fists clinched, ready to spring again, but it was not necessary. Fulton tried to get up, but could not move his giant frame more than an inch or so from the floor, and then sank back. His manager Mike Collins implored him to get up, but he was out cold.

Dempsey fought like a larger version of Terry McGovern. At the bell, he had rushed in, determined to make a fight of it, whereas Fulton tried to box and hold him off so he could get a line on him. But Dempsey did not give him any time to think.

Jack Kearns said the fight was won with three punches. Jack walked right into him, hit him with a stiff left hook to the body that caused Fred to bend over a little. Jack ripped his left to the jaw, staggering Fulton back to the ropes. Dempsey followed, and as Fred rebounded off the ropes, Jack hit him with a right swing to the point of the jaw, which finished the job. He went down like a man struck with a club, hitting the lower rope when he fell. The referee gave him a good long count, but he was completely out. Five minutes later, Fulton still didn't know what had happened. Fred never landed a blow. A left jab just brushed Jack's cheek.

The *Newark Sunday Call* said the fight scarcely was underway when Dempsey sent Fulton to the floor with a sharp right to the jaw. Dempsey hit Fulton and Fulton hit the floor was the story. Such was the start, middle, and finish of the fight. It was all over in 18 3/5 seconds, the most disappointing and yet most remarkable fight ever waged between two top contenders for the crown. The throng was stupefied by the quick ending, leaving the victor the new heavyweight champion of the world by default, given that Willard seemed unwilling or unable to fight. It took a year to bring them together for a $25,000 purse and all the fame that goes with it. Yet it was settled in a little more than a quarter of a minute.

No marks were visible on Fulton as he sat in his corner. His hair scarcely was mussed. Yet, he seemed dazed. "I can't understand it, I can't understand," he muttered repeatedly. He left a minute later.

It was the shortest big fight on record. In 1899, Terry McGovern knocked out Pedlar Palmer in 30 seconds (meaning he went down at the 30 second mark). Bob Fitzsimmons knocked out Peter Maher in 1 round.

James J. Jeffries took out Jack Finnegan in just under a minute. John L. Sullivan had stopped many men in the 1st round, often in mere seconds.

Dempsey did not want to say much. "Let the fight tell the tale," was all he said as he hurried away into a waiting automobile. Before the fight, he freely made the prediction that he would win by a knockout in short order.

Fulton, when asked how it happened, replied, "It was just a knockout. I'll say he's a wonder, that bird." When asked how and where he was hit, Fulton replied, "I can't understand it myself. All I remember is that I tried to break clean as he closed in on me in that first rush. As I recall it, I tried to grab him by the elbows, figuring Dempsey would step away. Then bing – he caught me on the chin and it was all over. He must have crossed over my left arm with his right." Fulton said he was fit for the fight of his life, feeling great and boxing fine. He had no excuses to offer on that score. "He simply caught me with a lucky one right off the reel."

Fulton's one excuse was that Dempsey did not break clean. "I was intent on breaking clean in the clinches, as the referee instructed us. Dempsey did not live up to that agreement. Consequently, I was off my guard when he slipped me that right hand punch to the chin. But I'm not attempting to camouflage my defeat. Dempsey won, as you saw. That's all there is to it, and he's entitled to all the credit."

When asked whether he had prepared for Dempsey's attack, Fulton replied that he was not entirely surprised by Dempsey's rushing, boring-in tactics. "I saw him box once. That was in Denver, with Arthur Pelkey. ... Dempsey dropped him in about thirty seconds." So, he knew what to expect. Fred wanted a rematch. "Surely I can outbox Dempsey." However, many opined that Fulton was through as a top attraction.

Upon learning of the result, from Lawrence, Kansas, Jess Willard said, "I'll fight Dempsey after the war." "I'm not surprised at the result. All you have to do is hit Fulton to have him down." Jess believed that there would be no more major boxing events allowed until after the war. "Just as soon as the war is over I am going to take on Dempsey, or any other claimant. I have not retired from the ring, and I have no intention of doing anything of the sort." He also said, "Dempsey has a rough road between him and the championship. He is not going to win the championship in eighteen, nor in an hour and eighteen seconds."

The *Daily Home News*, out of New Brunswick, New Jersey, said Fulton was knocked out in the twinkling of an eye. Only four blows were struck. Fulton tried to cover up after the solar plexus blows were struck, but Dempsey landed the knockout blow easily. It was done so quickly, with such short, lightning-fast blows that few saw the punch that sent the Minnesota plasterer's large frame sprawling, and few were absolutely sure what blow did the trick. "In fact I wouldn't want to have to swear that it was a solar plexus blow that sent the favorite to the mat."

It was very unexpected. Fulton was the odds favorite, but Dempsey was too quick for him from the start, and landed the type of chance blow that ends a bout in a hurry. Some called it a fluke. Still, Dempsey clearly had the drop on him, and had been landing those chance knockout blows quite quickly and often lately. It was his fifth 1st round knockout in a row. Dempsey had fought four times in the month of July alone.

Jack had earned a reported $12,500 for a mere 18 seconds of work.

Referee Eckhardt praised Dempsey's skill, calling him a "genuine fistic marvel," the greatest since the days of Corbett, Choynski, and Jeffries. Eckhardt said it was two punches that earned Dempsey the right to meet Willard – a left to the stomach and a follow-up right to the jaw. The second blow crushed Fred and shook the foundations of the ring.

The *Perth Amboy Evening News* said it ended between 18 and 25 seconds, authorities disagreeing on the exact time. Many had no idea how it happened, it was so fast. Fred said afterwards, "We broke clean and then Bing! So long!" Fully 20 autos from Perth Amboy were at the fight, as well as those who went via train and trolley.

The *New York Sun* said Dempsey was as quick as a flash, and landed his blows with the accuracy of a sharpshooter. He had excellent judgment of distance and timing of punches. He was a fast, rushing tornado, with such speed and battering-ram power that no one could avoid him for long, and he could crush all obstacles in his way.

Daniel said the actual fighting only occupied 23 seconds, making it one of the shortest bouts between notable heavyweights in history, if not the shortest. Fulton made better than $363 a second, counting his ten seconds on the ground, the highest average yet.

Dempsey said Willard, the circus man, had to fight him, or he should resign the title and retire.

Fred Hawthorne said Dempsey never had to take a real punch. He was fierce, but wide open. He was like Stanley Ketchel. He rushed in and never gave Fulton a chance to use his deadly left jab. And he was so far superior on the inside that there was no comparison.

The *Brooklyn Standard Union* said Dempsey was the hero of the pugilistic world. He shot over a right cross to the jaw and the Minnesota plasterer went to sleep. To bring him back to life, Fulton's seconds threw water on him and the referee slapped him.

Fulton had height, reach, weight, and cleverness in his favor, but Dempsey was so fast and hit so hard that there was not much chance to size up either one. It was the shortest battle between big men of such prominence ever staged.

Dempsey's attack was all that had been said of it. He wasted not a second. Fulton never had a chance to show what he could do. "That Dempsey is one of the greatest fighters the world has ever seen is undoubted." As a result of the performance, Dempsey would be known as the best fighter in the world, if not the champion. Some said he was the real champion, given Willard's reluctance to fight.

The *Brooklyn Daily Eagle's* "Rice" said the fight was over in 33 seconds: 23 seconds of fighting and 10 seconds of counting. A left to the body and right to the jaw did the trick. The victor showed excellent judgment. He was up against a first-class boxer with a deadly left, who had at least 20 pounds weight advantage, and several inches of height and reach, yet Dempsey overcame it all. Given that Willard refused to fight, the championship seemed to be between American champion Dempsey and European champion Georges Carpentier.

Jack Kearns said he was certain that Dempsey could dispose of Willard within 8 rounds. He also claimed that Dempsey would engage in shipbuilding to assist with the war effort.

The *New York Evening World*'s John Pollock said Dempsey fired a right and Fulton forgot to duck told the whole tale.

Robert Edgren timed the fight at 18 3/5 seconds, plus Fulton was on the floor for 14 seconds (for a long count). Dempsey lifted him up four seconds after being counted out.

Fulton claimed it was a lucky punch, and wanted a rematch. He simply forgot to duck. He admitted that Dempsey was a great fighter and looked like a champion. Fred had to start all over again.

All who saw the bout were unanimous in the opinion that Dempsey was one of the greatest fighters since John L. Sullivan was in his prime.

Jack Curley, promoter of the fight, said of Dempsey: "He would have beaten Jack Johnson at his best. I have seen many a good fighter in my time, but he is the best I ever looked at. … Sam Langford couldn't last three minutes with him." He said his opinion was totally objective, for he had no financial interest in Dempsey. "There's a suspicion that I have an interest in him. I wish I had. I'd give $25,000 for part of him any time." Curley later claimed to have lost $13,000 on the promotion.

JACK DEMPSEY

Kearns claimed that Jack now was the world champion, given Willard's refusal or reluctance to fight. Some even advertised the Fulton bout as being for the championship. However, the general rank-and-file members of the public and press didn't take the claim seriously. They felt that Willard needed to be defeated in the ring, or he needed to retire definitively, before Dempsey could be recognized as the champion.[453]

Needing an excuse to save face, his reputation badly damaged, Fulton later pushed his claim that Dempsey broke the agreement to break clean from clinches, and hit him on a break. Dempsey replied that straight Queensberry rules governed the contest, which meant they were required to

---

[453] *Long Branch Daily Record, Newark Sunday Call, Daily Home News* (within 30 miles), *Passaic Herald-News*, July 28, 29, 1918; *New York Tribune, New Brunswick Sunday Times*, also known as the *Daily Home News*, July 28, 29, 1918; *New York Sun, Buffalo Times, Buffalo Courier, New York Times, Brooklyn Standard Union, Brooklyn Daily Eagle*, July 28, 1918; *Buffalo Commercial, Paterson Morning Call, Bridgewater Courier-News* (about 35 miles away), *Perth Amboy Evening News* (about 25 miles away), *New York Evening World*, July 29, 1918; *Elmira Star Gazette*, July 31, 1918; *Buffalo Times*, August 1, 1918.

protect themselves at all times, and furthermore, there never was a clinch, and never once did the referee tell them to break.[454]

Battling Levinsky, who won the world light-heavyweight championship in 1916 with a victory over Jack Dillon, issued a challenge to Dempsey. He said Dempsey was a great fighter, but Bat thought he could beat him, having beaten all of the swinging punchers in the country, as well as having fought every top heavyweight in the game except Fulton and Willard. Levinsky was 5'11 ½" and weighed 175 pounds, not much less than Dempsey. Levinsky had stayed the full 15 rounds with 240-pound Carl Morris, so size did not bother him. Levinsky said he beat Miske, who stayed 10 rounds with Dempsey in what many said was a draw.

Starting on July 26, 1918, the day before Dempsey vs. Fulton, Philadelphia was the scene of another Northern race riot. Two days after a black woman, Adella Bond, moved into a primarily white area, a large crowd of unhappy whites gathered outside of her home. Someone threw a rock through her window. With her pistol, Bond allegedly fired a warning shot, but the bullet hit one of the men outside in the leg. During the next four days, the city's mounting racial tensions ignited and led to rioting and clashes between thousands of whites and blacks all over the city. Three whites were killed (including a member of law enforcement) and one black man was killed by police officers who shot him in the back while in their custody (though the officers would be acquitted of murder charges). Those same officers badly beat another black man that same day. Many were wounded and beaten badly in the rioting. Property was damaged, and homes burned. 60 blacks were arrested, but only 3 whites. The military had to be called in to quell the riotous behavior.

---

[454] *Dayton Daily News*, August 25, 1918.

CHAPTER 16

# Needing a Man Who Can Take It

Georges Carpentier, European heavyweight champion, still was in the French military, often giving boxing exhibitions. He had been in the habit of boxing with aspiring U.S. Army heavyweights, and had demonstrated marked superiority over all comers.

Carpentier occasionally was mentioned as a man who could give Dempsey an interesting contest once the war was over. Despite being in the military, or in part because of his military service, the talented Carpentier remained on the minds of sportswriters. He was doing his part for the war, and was treated like a hero. He was one of the first top athletes to put aside his aspirations to the heavyweight crown and take up arms in defense of his country. He even had been wounded in action. He still found time to give exhibitions for his comrades or for a war fund.[455]

Consistent with the propaganda of the day, given that the U.S. was in a war with Germany, famous sportswriter Tad Dorgan noted that in the history of the prize ring, there was not one fighter of German birth who was looked up to as a model of fearlessness. There were good German fighters like Ruhlin, Wolgast, Papke, Klaus, and Houck, but they never drew the thrill that fighters like Sullivan, Fitzsimmons, Dempsey, and Ketchel did. Tad called the German a frontrunner, a wildcat while the going was in his favor, but unable to stand the gaff when things turned, and a bit of a quitter. "Our boys in France will prove it, too, again and again."

Jack Kearns said Jack Dempsey would appear at the Knights of Columbus War Fund bouts at Ebbets Field on August 20.[456]

The *San Francisco Examiner* said membership in the "I Knew Him When" Club had taken a big hop in the last few days. It wasn't long ago that Dempsey had come to San Francisco from Salt Lake City (in early 1917) and was spoken of as a big bum.

> That was just after the fight in Salt Lake with Jim Flynn, wherein it is said on good authority that the gent who now seems to be champion of the world did a most apparent flop. In fact, Dempsey never made any strenuous denial of the accusation. He was young and badly advised, that's all. Also he was broke.
>
> But now that is forgotten. Dempsey has redeemed himself in grand style since, and San Francisco is doing its best to claim him as a local product. He isn't, although he is sufficiently fond of the city to call it home.

---

[455] *Newark Evening News*, July 18, 1918; *Dayton Daily News*, August 9, 1918.
[456] *Kansas City Post*, July 28, 1918; *Brooklyn Citizen*, July 31, 1918.

As to Dempsey himself, he is a big, affable, uneducated fellow, who likes everybody and wants everybody to like him. He might have been a bum once, but after he got started on the right track he took good care of himself and his money and won a lot of respect from those who had knocked him hardest. And incidentally he did a lot to rehabilitate Jack Kearns in the good graces of the populace. Kearns dubbed around as a half-portion manager for a long time, and there wasn't anything too mean for some persons to say about him. He wore silk shirts and perfumery and it's difficult to overlook such offenses. But now Kearns is being extolled as a young man of great wisdom and foresight. He recognized in Dempsey a coming champion, and therefore what Dempsey is, Kearns made him. And it has been many a week since mention has been made of Kearns' silk shirts or fancy perfumery.

Kearns is expected to bring Dempsey here for a boxing match on Labor Day for a big war benefit. The populace will turn out to meet them both, to greet them with the hand that only too short while ago was lifted to grip the nostrils when they were mentioned.

But neither Kearns nor Dempsey is thick skinned. They'll clasp every extended hand and announce that they are glad to be back home.

It's a funny old world, isn't it?[457]

The *Brooklyn Daily Eagle* said the fight-or-work order was hitting the boxing world. Professional athletics was not deemed to be an essential occupation. Hence, if they did not want to enlist, many athletes had to find another or additional job. Some were trying to prove their value by volunteering their services for war fund exhibitions. Dempsey even said he would fight Willard for free, with the money to go to a war fund.

"Indian" Clay Turner agreed to box Dempsey at the upcoming war fund exhibition. He said Dempsey would not have such an easy time with him. He had boxed him 4 rounds nearly every day in training camp, and, "Everyone knows that Jack fights just as hard in his training quarters as he does in the ring." Those who saw their sparring sessions said they were better than some ring fights. Turner took everything that Jack could dish out and never was on the floor. "He dropped Battling Jim Johnson…but he

---

[457] *San Francisco Examiner*, July 31, 1918. Was the *Examiner* hinting or subtly suggesting that Jack Kearns might have been effeminate? It isn't clear. Born as John McKernan, in March 1909, Kearns was convicted of contributing to the delinquency of a minor when as the bartender in a Spokane bar owned by Kid Scaler (whom he managed), he served a 15-year-old girl (a juvenile delinquent) alcohol which her of-legal-age brother purchased. Both Kearns and Scaler were fined $100.
    In May 1909, matchmaker Kearns was accused of engaging in fight fixing in Calgary, Canada, arranging Kid Scaler to box Billy Lauder to a 15-round draw, and then to have a rematch (which never took place). Scaler and Lauder had fought a 15-round draw in September 1907.
    In February 1913 in Vancouver, Kearns was accused of procuring a "girl" from the U.S. for immoral purposes, which charge was dismissed when boxing promoter Kearns testified, and the "girl" corroborated, that she had been a Spokane dance-room employee, and he simply told her that he was going to Vancouver, and asked her to look him up if she ever got over that way. Kearns also had been accused of fraud/forgery (acquitted by judge) and embezzlement/theft (charge dismissed). *Spokane Spokesman-Review*, March 21, 1909; *Spokane Chronicle*, March 20, 1909, May 13, 1909, February 27, 1913.

never dropped me." Clay said he knew Dempsey's style down pat, knew where his defense was weak, and could make him work for 4 rounds.[458]

John Reisler had Dempsey served with a lawsuit in Long Branch to collect what he claimed was his share of the Fulton fight purse.[459]

Dempsey arrived in Chicago on August 5.[460]

WILLARD'S NEMESIS HOT ON HIS TRAIL

JACK DEMPSEY

The conqueror of Fred Fulton says he will not stop until he gets Jess Willard into the ring. Fulton lasted 23 seconds with him.

Former champion James J. Corbett said Dempsey's victory over Fulton stamped him as the most sensational heavyweight since Jim Jeffries' time, and ranked him among the greatest since the mitt game began. Fulton had proven himself, being the first to stop Langford at heavyweight, and also Moran, whom neither Jack Johnson nor Jess Willard had been able to knock out. Touted as Willard's most dangerous prospective foe, Fulton was bigger than Dempsey in every way. Not once had someone of Fulton's status been put out with such ease and speed.[461]

Promoters wanted to match Dempsey with boxers who appeared to have a chance to go rounds with him. Terry Keller/Kellar (both spellings were used), who twice had gone the 10-round distance with Dempsey in close and competitive contests in 1916, was willing to fight him again, and lobbied for a match. Terry said, "I have boxed Dempsey twice within the last two years. The first time I lost the decision to him after he had hit me with everything but the stool and all he did to me was to open up a cut over my eye which I received in a 15-round go with Tom McMahon at Baltimore a short time before." The bout was at an altitude of 6,000 feet. "I was taking the rounds at the end of the go and dropped Dempsey for the count of nine in the eighth round. However, Dempsey's points in the early rounds got him the verdict." That was in Ogden.

In their second bout, at Ely, Nevada, "I chopped his face to ribbons without taking a good punch in return. I trimmed him so easily that his manager at that time, a Mr. Auerbach [sic - Auerbach] of Salt Lake, made me such a good offer to travel with Jack and teach him something about the game that I accepted and we were stable mates for about four months." Kellar had fought Billy Miske as well, and thought that Miske was better than Dempsey. Miske had bull-dog grit, could stand punishment, was cleverer, and could hit just about as hard.

Also challenging Dempsey were Battling Levinsky, "Boston Tar Baby" Sam Langford, and "Oklahoma Hypnotist" Jack Thompson. Langford said, "I'm an old fellow, so they claim, but no man living can stop me in 23 seconds." Levinsky said, "I am ready to take on Dempsey for any distance

---

[458] *Brooklyn Daily Eagle*, August 7, 1918. On August 9, 1918 in Jersey City, Clay Turner lost an 8-round no decision to Harry Greb.
[459] *Buffalo Commercial*, August 5, 1918.
[460] *San Francisco Chronicle*, August 11, 1918.
[461] *San Francisco Examiner*, August 7, 1918.

suitable to him, and in addition, I'll bet on myself that I can defeat him." Tom Gibbons said he would fight Dempsey as well. Basically, everyone wanted to fight him, now that he had attained top contender status.[462]

Writers were saying that Dempsey had the punch, speed, heart, youth, stamina, and good judgment of distance, as well as a speedy, quick-footed attack that did not allow foes to set themselves. Plus he loved to fight.[463]

The Dayton Gymnastic Club of Ohio signed Dempsey to fight there on August 24 in a 15-round contest. Dempsey agreed to fight any fighter they selected. They were trying to arrange a meeting with either Keller, Gibbons, Levinsky, McMahon, or Miske.[464]

A few days later, on August 12, the Dayton Gymnastic Club announced that Dempsey would fight Terry Kellar on August 24, just under a month after the Fulton fight. Kellar's manager claimed that Terry earned draws in both of their prior contests (although Dempsey won 10-round decisions both times).

Those prior fights are what got Keller the fight. He had performed somewhat poorly against Bob Devere, whom Dempsey stopped in 1 round. Yet Kellar had proven to be durable, given that he went the distance with Dempsey twice, as well as Brennan, Miske, Greb, Levinsky, and McMahon. Keller wanted the Dempsey fight to be 15 rounds, for he felt that he would do better the longer it went.[465]

Leo Flynn and the black fighter he managed, 175-pound Kid Norfolk, said Dempsey was afraid of him. They offered to wager $2,500 on the outcome of a match between them. Flynn noted that Norfolk outboxed Miske clearly in their 12-round bout, whereas Dempsey only managed a draw with Miske. He said Dempsey could not claim to be the best heavyweight in the world in one breath and draw the color line in another.

On the 14th, Kearns said Dempsey had been with him at the Springs in Benton Harbor, Michigan, training there for upcoming contests. They would be in Brooklyn in two days for the Knights of Columbus War Fund benefit at Ebbets Field.[466]

On Friday August 16, 1918 at Ebbets Field, Brooklyn, New York, more than two score pugilists volunteered their services and participated in a boxing carnival for the benefit of the Knights of Columbus war fund. 17,000, 20,000, or 25,000 spectators were present, generating for the war fund at least $15,000, some saying $25,000. In one bout, Battling Levinsky went 4 rounds to a draw with Billy Miske. Jim Coffey won a 4-round bout against Joe Bonds.

---

[462] *Dayton Daily News*, August 4, 5, 1918; *Lima News*, August 6, 1918.
[463] *East Liverpool Evening Review*, August 5, 1918.
[464] *Dayton Herald*, August 9, 1918.
[465] *Dayton Herald*, August 12, 1918; *Dayton Daily News*, August 1, 12, 1918.
[466] *San Francisco Chronicle, Brooklyn Standard Union*, August 14, 1918.

Jack Dempsey boxed 4 exhibition rounds with "Indian Chief" Clay Turner, his sparring partner. The *New York Herald* wrote, "Though it was an exhibition pure and simple, Turner stopped a few hard ones. Dempsey had trouble chaining his punches and despite the fact he tried to pull them, some went home with a force that shook Turner. Jack also showed considerable boxing skill."

The *Brooklyn Daily Times* said Dempsey was the fastest heavyweight since Jim Corbett's time. He moved around like John L. Sullivan, catlike and fast, in and out, with a good right and left hook, a neat straight left, and corking shift. He stood with his legs spread apart and crouching like Jeffries, but not as pronounced or as often. "There is no question that he is a rattling boxer and good hitter and he should get along in the fistic world." His exhibition with Turner was not particularly exciting, though they hit each other hard enough to draw some blood.

The *Brooklyn Daily Standard Union* said although it was just an exhibition, it was a lively scrap, for at the opening, Dempsey uncorked his famous shift and landed his left swing to the jaw, which nearly decked Turner. In the 4th round, a stiff right to the body almost curled Turner up. Overall though, Dempsey refrained from landing heavily on him, and even took a few now and then. Dempsey was bleeding from the nose and mouth, while Turner bled from the left ear, nose, and mouth.

The *Brooklyn Citizen* said Dempsey looked more like a light-heavyweight than the big men the local fans had been accustomed to seeing. "There is no class to his style of boxing, but that he can hit, and hit hard with either hand, was made evident on the few occasions he turned loose last night."

The *New York Tribune* said that in the 3rd round, Turner brought blood from Dempsey's nose with a stiff left jab. Dempsey returned the blow with interest, having Turner bleeding from the mouth and nose before the round was over. Dempsey opened the 4th round as though he was trying for the knockout, but after landing a few stiff jabs, cooled down.

When various items were auctioned off for the cause, Dempsey paid from $25 to $35 for copies of songs and silk flags.

Some said that Dempsey was supposed to box Levinsky at the benefit show, but Jack was sick with a fever, so he declined; only willing to box his regular sparring partner. Others said Kearns was afraid that Jack might get outboxed in a short bout. Still others said Turner was the opponent all along. Kearns said they never had consented to box Levinsky. Still, several writers criticized Dempsey for not boxing Levinsky.[467]

---

[467] *New York Herald, Brooklyn Daily Times, Brooklyn Daily Standard Union, New York Times, Brooklyn Citizen, Buffalo Times, New York Tribune*, August 17, 1918.

John Reisler, the Barber, filed a lawsuit in New York asking for $100,000 in damages, alleging that on December 18, 1916, he made a 3-year contract with Dempsey in which 70% of the proceeds of Jack's battles and theatrical appearances were to be paid over to him.[468]

In his local workouts in Dayton, Ohio, Terry Keller showed conclusively that he had the punch and could absorb wallops as well. He said he would be in better shape for the Dempsey fight than any other in the past year.[469]

> **CHAMPIONSHIP BOUT**
> 15 Rounds
> Jack Dempsey vs. Terry Keller
> 10 Rounds
> Dick Loadman vs. Joe Haley
> 6 Rounds
> Micky Dunleavy vs. Young Webb
> **WESTWOOD PARK**
> SATURDAY EVE., AUGUST 24th

The question being asked was whether Dempsey was one of the greatest battlers ever, or simply the best of an ordinary crop of heavyweights. There was considerable difference of opinion.

The locals who saw Dempsey since he arrived from New York said he sure looked like he could scrap.

Dempsey said he expected to stop Keller inside the 15-round route. He also thought he could do the same with Willard. He and Keller fought nearly two years ago, and although he admitted that Terry was a rough, tough bird, "I think I have improved enough to take care of him."

The *Dayton Daily News* said Kellar had put up good fights against Greb (1918 LND10), Miske (1915 DND10), McMahon (1916 D15 and L15), and others (1916 LND10 Brennan).

Since losing a close and controversial 10-round decision to Dempsey in 1916, which many thought should have been a draw, Terry Keller's record included: 1916 L4 Al Norton; 1917 LRTD3 Jim Coffey, LND10 Homer Smith, LTKOby5 Al Reich, and LDQ2 Bob Devere; and 1918 LND10 Harry Greb and D20 Jim Downing.

The confident Kellar was not worried at all. "Why, I have fought him 10 rounds on two occasions, and I can truthfully say he never hurt me with that wonderful punch they talk about." Kellar claimed to be in the best shape of his life. He also said he never had been knocked out, and did not believe Dempsey "the giant killer" could do it. Kellar had fouled Bob Devere and was disqualified, the fight having taken place the previous winter, which soured him to local fans, but he claimed that he was not in shape for that one. Those at the Dayton gym were pleased with Kellar's hard work and appearance. Regardless, Dempsey had improved a great deal over the past two years.[470]

On Saturday August 24, 1918 in Dayton, Ohio, at Westwood Field, under the auspices of the Dayton Gymnastic Club, in the presence of 2,500 fans, Jack Dempsey fought Terry Keller for the third time. The main event was scheduled to start at around 9:30 p.m. Jack Kearns cornered Dempsey,

---

[468] *New York Tribune*, August 18, 1918.
[469] *Dayton Daily News*, August 17, 1918.
[470] *Dayton Daily News*, August 22-24, 1918; *Dayton Herald*, August 24, 1918.

while Keller's brother, Frankie Mantell, and Al Reich looked after Terry. Lou Bauman refereed.

**They're Ready to Face Each Other in Ring at Westwood**

Terry Kellar

Jack Dempsey

In the 1st round, Dempsey tore into Kellar from the start and forced him to cover up. In the middle of the round, Dempsey caught him with a hard blow to the jaw and Kellar went down.

The wallop would have caused most to retire, but Terry rose at nine and came back as best he could. When the round ended, Kellar looked tired as he went to his corner.

In the 2nd round, Kellar came back looking stronger. However, Dempsey opened a cut under Terry's right eye, and kept pounding on him.

In the 3rd round, there was not as much action, but Kellar continued to be the receiver, though he landed a few in return. His mouth was cut in this round.

In the 4th round, Kellar gradually was growing weaker, but gamely kept taking his medicine as Dempsey pounded away at him.

Throughout the 5th round, Dempsey slammed and rained blows to all parts of Kellar's head and body, at a high frequency. Terry was bleeding profusely from cuts over the eye and around his mouth. He had been beaten badly, was helpless, and in such dire straits that eventually Referee Lou Bauman was compelled to stop it. The fans applauded the referee's action in stopping the fight. Dempsey was the winner all the way.

Local *Dayton Daily News* writer "Jerry" said Dempsey demonstrated why he was regarded as the best heavyweight in years. Kellar twice had lasted 10 rounds with him, but had a hard time lasting to the 5th round with this version of Dempsey. The tough Kellar was decked in the 1st round for a nine-count, and gamely absorbed 4 2/3 rounds of severe punishment, as severe as any man ever had absorbed. He never quit, but never really was in the fight either. Dempsey was admired for his prowess, and Kellar for his staying qualities.

That it took so many punches and so long to end Kellar did not mean that Dempsey could not punch, but that Kellar could absorb punishment. He certainly was a tough nut to crack. At times during the contest, Kellar looked almost helpless and about to go down, but he would recover quickly and stage little rallies which drew applause. Terry never landed a hard wallop, but he tried all the time. It simply was the case of Dempsey being too good. The game local battler absorbed punishment throughout.

Dempsey was a hit. He made good on the advance notices about him. He looked like a champion, and the general opinion was that he would beat Willard. He was fast and powerful enough to hurt anyone.

The *Dayton Herald's* "Collins" said that in the 1st round, Kellar took a half dozen blows that would have knocked out any ordinary scrapper, and then was knocked to the floor by a sledge hammer blow for a nine-count. He came back for more of the same in each round. Dempsey made a chopping block of him, cut his face in many places, blackened his eyes, and opened an old cut over his eye. Kellar was game to the end, even breaking his right hand. Terry's valiant exhibition of toughness vindicated him in the eyes of local fandom. Wonderful gameness was all that held him up.

Afterwards, Kellar said, "Every blow Dempsey struck Saturday night cut me, but he never dazed me." However, Kellar granted that Dempsey was the hardest hitter he ever faced, and said he did not believe anyone could defeat Jack. This local writer agreed that Dempsey was the coming champion.[471]

---

[471] *Dayton Daily News*, August 25, 1918; *Dayton Herald.*, August 26, 1918.

CHAPTER 17

# A Glitch at the Benefit

Following his dominant victory over Terry Kellar in 5 rounds, stopping him for the first time in their three meetings, Jack Dempsey headed to San Francisco to box Willie Meehan again in the 4-round main event of a war benefit boxing show arranged by Jimmy Coffroth, which would take place just three weeks after the Keller contest. Dempsey was donating his services to benefit the war fund, something he had done several times already.

On Monday September 2, 1918 at Neptune Beach, the athletes of the Oakland Y.M.C.A. staged a field day. Bill Larue/LaRue had been coaching a school of young boxers who gave an exhibition. Dempsey appears to have attended as a guest, for a photo was taken of him joining Larue in a blackberry pie eating contest with some of the kids.[472]

Jack Kearns said if Dempsey did not knock out Jess Willard within 10 rounds, he would be willing to forfeit $5,000 to him.

Willie Meehan had joined the military, and was a seaman second class. Despite being only 24 years old, Meehan had over 140 fights of experience. His prior history with Dempsey included 1917 W4, L4, D4, and D4. Since

---

[472] *San Francisco Chronicle*, September 1, 1918; *San Francisco Examiner*, September 3, 1918. Dempsey allegedly was weighing 205 pounds.

then, Meehan's record included: 1917 D4 Willie Webb, WND6 Jack Dillon, DorLND6 Leo Houck, D12 Tom Cowler, and LND6 Harry Greb; and 1918 W4 Ed Petroskey, D4, W4, and L4 KO Kruvosky, W4 KO Brown, W4 (thrice) Kid Kenneth, and D4 Billy Miske. He fought often, particularly in 4-round California bouts, at which he was quite adept. He was known for his chin, durability, and awkward, hard-to-figure-out style.[473]

Dempsey trained at Cliff Wixson's place in Oakland's Watts tract. Meehan was at Billy Shannon's San Rafael camp, trained by Moose Taussig. One sportswriter humorously wrote, "If Willie wants to be at his best the less training he does the better." Both men were seeking sparring partners. Dempsey promised not to hurt whomever helped him.

Calling him the "champion," some debated whether Dempsey could put "Phat Boy" Meehan to the mat. He had not done so in four prior contests. Opinion was about equally divided.[474]

Confident Meehan laughed at claims that Dempsey was the coming champion and would knock his head off.

> You didn't see that bird knock my head off in any of our four fights, did ya? You saw me beat 'im a mile once, didn't yer? ... And you saw a referee rob me once, didn't yer? ... Well, he won't knock my block off this time, neither. That bird Miske gave him plenty in that ten-round go in the East. ... I took the same Miske on in Los Angeles and I gave him a licking.[475]

On September 10, 1918 at the San Francisco Olympic Club, Dempsey exhibited and sparred with "Red" Roak, Young Peter Jackson, and Jim Barry. Jack hit Roak a couple of left wallops, and when a right hook landed, Red went down and out. Dempsey lifted him up to his corner, but he was too out of it to continue. Then veteran black fighter Young Peter Jackson (148 fights) alternated rounds with 200-pound veteran Jim Barry (76 fights) in boxing 4 more rounds with Dempsey.

---

[473] *San Francisco Chronicle*, September 3, 1918; *San Francisco Examiner*, September 5, 1918; Boxrec.com.
[474] *Oakland Enquirer*, September 7, 10, 1918.
[475] *San Francisco Examiner*, September 8, 1918. Actually, Miske held Meehan to a 4-round draw.

Neither had much fun. Dempsey was not one to take it easy, slamming in with both hands. Another reporter said he treated them as gently as he could. Jack was fast, too, skipping in and out with the speed of a lightweight. He seemed to leave himself open, but with his style of stooping and moving his head back and forth, he was harder to hit than one might think.

Dempsey was scheduled to box 10 rounds in Reno the very next night after the Meehan benefit exhibition bout, against Jack Moran.[476]

Meehan said he had no fear of Dempsey, and was supremely confident that he would hold his own. He looked good in training. He stepped around as nimbly as a kitten and had all of his punches at his disposal, including the bass-drum and loop-the-loop blows. Meehan said Dempsey had hit him with everything he had, and he just laughed at him. "[H]e never saw the day when he could put me away." Of course, they only boxed in 4-rounders.

Dempsey was showing all of his old-time pep, but was handicapped by a lack of sparring partners. Few would work with him on a consistent basis. Some tried to get black Pinky Lewis to spar him, but Pinky refused, saying, "Say, man, what ya think I am – crazy? Dat guy hit me so hard one time that I couldn't eat fo' a week, and Ah had lots o' dough at the time. No, say, none o' dat Dempsey man fo' lil Pinky!"[477]

The proceeds of the Meehan contest and all other bouts on the card would go towards aiding soldiers and sailors. The boxers were fighting for trophies instead of money, volunteering their services. Ticket prices were $1, $2, $3, and $5. Women would be admitted.

The locals said Meehan likely would give Dempsey a hard tussle.

According to the *Examiner*, in his workouts, Dempsey had shown improvement both in science and knowledge of how to hit.[478]

Jack Kearns issued a direct challenge to and attack upon Jess Willard, whom he called a cheese champion and cheese patriot. He said Dempsey was the real champion, one who was willing to fight, unlike Willard, who was just a commercialized financial champion. Willard never had done anything for the war effort, never boxing for war charities, unlike Dempsey, who never passed up a chance to aid any patriotic cause. Kearns questioned Willard's sportsmanship, manhood, and patriotism. "Trusting that this letter will have some effect on Willard, and arouse his blood, if he has any…"

---

[476] *San Francisco Examiner, Oakland Enquirer, San Francisco Chronicle*, September 11, 1918.
[477] *Oakland Enquirer*, September 12, 1918.
[478] *San Francisco Examiner*, September 13, 1918.

Bob Shand, who refereed the first Dempsey-Meehan fight, and who wrote for the *Oakland Enquirer*, said Meehan clearly won their first contest. "Willie had an honest-to-goodness edge at the finish." Dempsey won a decision in the rematch, followed by a pair of draws. The upcoming fight was even money. Dempsey had been knocking them stiff, and "his record is probably the most formidable of any heavyweight champion in the history of the game." Still, there was no reason to believe he could knock out Meehan in a mere 4 rounds, for he had not even decked him in four prior contests. The local Meehan was popular because he was different from any heavyweight who ever lived. He was born and raised in San Francisco, started boxing as a flyweight and grew into a heavyweight. He was fat, but it did not matter. He had a very baffling style, with an assortment of blows. It was hard to look good against him. He was, in modern-day parlance, a spoiler.

Dempsey was as modest as ever, saying, "Willie is a hard guy to fight, and I ought to know, for I boxed him four times. But I don't care, he was the most suitable opponent and I wanted to fight the man who would draw the most money for the soldiers and sailors. Maybe I won't knock him out, but he is not going to hurt me, so I should worry. I have been handicapped through not having sparring partners, but you can see for yourself that I am in the 'pink.'"

Dempsey had another handicap going into the fight – a literal handicap, with an injured left hand. When the reporter noticed his badly swollen left hand, which Dempsey had not even mentioned, and asked what was the matter with it, Jack replied, "Oh, that don't amount to much. I broke it a couple of months ago when I boxed Terry Keller back east and the bone has not knit." Actually, he had fought Keller less than a month ago, on August 24, only three weeks prior. Fighting and/or sparring with a broken hand was foolish, but

HERE'S DEMPSEY! MEET HIM TONIGHT
LATEST likeness of the chap who claims the heavy-weight championship, and boxes Meehan at the Coffroth patriotic show tonight

Dempsey seemed determined to box for the charity show no matter what.

Shand said Dempsey differed from other top-notchers, not trying to create an alibi before the fight. Most fighters with a sore hand would let the world know about it in advance, but he had not. He never would have mentioned it unless the reporter had called attention to its swollen appearance. "The large bone on the outside of the hand shows plainly where it had been broken and the swelling indicates that it overlapped instead of knitting. But Dempsey is not complaining. He is out to help the soldiers and sailors… and would just as soon fight with one hand if it would help the boys in khaki." Many fighters would have called it off altogether.[479]

The *San Francisco Bulletin's* Leon Meyer said both were in condition. The "sailor boy" had been training and residing at the San Pedro Naval Training Station, and recently at Shannon's in San Rafael. "Never did the 'Phat' boy look better." Dempsey, who was "now looked on as the world's champion," was in shape too. "Since his rapid advance to the top he has been taught that it pays to be in condition at all times, and he has followed orders, with the result that he is in better shape right now than at any time in his career."

Meyer noted, "The contest will be but a four-round affair, generally too short a route for men of their ability to decide who is the better man." Such short bouts had limited meaning, but regrettably, that was all that was allowed. It was the biggest bout that could be staged on the Pacific Coast, other than one with Willard.

Dempsey admitted that he would have trouble putting Meehan to sleep. Meyer did not think Dempsey could stop Meehan in such a short bout. In 1914, Harry Wills had decked Meehan in the 1st round, but Willie was there fighting gamely at the final bell. However, if there was any knockout or knockdown, Dempsey would be the one to score it. "That's a certainty." Jack was known for having a record of 1st round knockouts. "Meehan has never been looked on as a hard hitter."

Meyer also noted that Kearns had several offers that would have made them thousands of dollars if they had passed up this show, but instead were

---

[479] *Oakland Enquirer*, September 13, 1918.

volunteering their services and honoring their word to benefit the Army and Navy. The first bout of the ten-fight card would start at 8:15 p.m. sharp. George Harting would be the timekeeper. Jim Coffroth was promoting.[480]

Another writer said Navy seaman Meehan had worked hard to get into condition for his fight "with the champion," and promised to surprise the boys who thought he would not last much longer than Fred Fulton did.

On Friday September 13, 1918 at the Civic/Exposition Auditorium in San Francisco, California, Jack Dempsey fought Willie Meehan for the fifth time in a 4-round bout. 9,000 or 10,000 people were present, contributing $17,082 to the fund set up for soldiers and sailors. Before the fight, famous film actress Mary Pickford sent Meehan a telegram from Los Angeles, which said, "Mr. Willie Meehan: Good luck. MARY PICKFORD."

## GET MEEHAN'S LOOK OF DISDAIN

WHEN Jack Dempsey (left) and Willie Meehan posed for The Chronicle photographer, Sailor Willie stepped across the ring to shake hands with Dempsey. But he did so in an indifferent way.

Meehan climbed through the ropes nonchalantly, and looked at Dempsey with a comical smile. He was introduced as the Pride of the Navy. Dempsey was introduced as the fighting champion, although most acknowledged that Willard was the actual champion, even though he was inactive.

Referee Eddie Graney noticed the fair amount of bandages on Dempsey's left hand, asked him about it, and Dempsey replied that his hand was in bad shape. Graney replied, "Then don't have a decision rendered." Dempsey and Kearns replied in unison, "No, no. You give a decision to the man who wins the fight. That is the agreement we have and we are willing to take a chance."

Once again for a Dempsey bout in the San Francisco area, there would be differing perspectives and opinions.[481]

---

[480] *San Francisco Bulletin*, September 13, 1918.

1st round

The *Examiner's* Fred Purner said that from the start, Wee Will bounded from his corner and attacked, landing repeatedly on Dempsey's stomach. Jack was cool and collected, but not landing anything effective. It looked as if he was laying back. Meehan did what leading and landing there was.

The *Examiner's* Al Joy said it was Meehan's round. There was not much kick to his blows, but he landed them, and came out of every clinch with overhand swings that landed somewhere every time.

The *Chronicle's* Harry Smith said the round was a trifle slow, though the next three made up for it. He offered no score for the round.

The *Bulletin's* Leon Meyer found the round to be so uneventful that he did not even discuss it.

The *Oakland Tribune's* Eddie Murphy said not much was done in the round, but Dempsey had the edge.

The *Oakland Enquirer's* Bob Shand said the round was fairly even. Meehan went on the aggressive from the start, and had Dempsey ducking out of danger in a neutral corner. Jack even grabbed the rope to get out of the way. Several long swings landed on Dempsey's ears, although they did not cause any damage. Dempsey got in some good work to the body; two right smashes making Meehan double up. In a mix-up, Meehan was shoved down.

So, two reporters from the same newspaper had it for Meehan, one reporter scored it for Dempsey, and one (possibly three) called it even.

2nd round

Fred Purner said Dempsey cut loose with a deadly right to the chin that hurt "Phat Willie," who covered up. Dempsey stepped around quickly and pounded on him with rights and lefts for about two minutes. Eventually, as Meehan was backing up, Dempsey struck him with a right, and Meehan lost his balance and went down in his corner in a sitting position.

Meehan rose quickly, and protected himself well. At the end of the round, Willie fought back, but was pounded up a bit. No blood was drawn, but Meehan had suffered a battering in the round.

Al Joy said Dempsey won the round by a considerable margin.

Harry Smith said Dempsey half pushed/half knocked Meehan down with left and right. Jack also gave Meehan a bad left eye in the round.

Leon Meyer said Dempsey almost knocked out Meehan, for he decked him with a left hook to the jaw and landed several pile-driving punches to the head and body. At the bell, Meehan was wobbly.

The *Call and Post's* Marion T. Salazar said Dempsey "hit Meehan so hard on the chin in the second round that he broke the straps of the supporter around Meehan's waist. The punch knocked Meehan down and came very near ending the fight."

---

[481] The previous and following descriptions and analysis are from the *San Francisco Examiner*, September 14, 17, 1918; *San Francisco Chronicle*, September 14, 15, 1918; *Oakland Tribune*, *Oakland Enquirer*, September 14, 1918; *San Francisco Bulletin*, *San Francisco Call and Post*, September 14, 1918.

Eddie Murphy said Dempsey unquestionably won the round by a large margin, as he hammered Meehan all around the ring. "Maybe because Meehan is a San Francisco boy that no one wants to give Dempsey credit for knocking him down, but that is just what he did in the second round, although it is said that Meehan slipped." Regarding the knockdown, Meehan rushed in, ran into a straight right, and went down to the mat for a one count from the timekeeper. He rose before the timekeeper got to two, but he had been knocked down by a punch nevertheless.

Referee Eddie Graney allowed Meehan to clinch often, and rarely broke them, or did so too late. Meehan was allowed to clinch all through the 2$^{nd}$ round to survive. Still, Dempsey gave him a merry beating in the round.

Bob Shand's version said Meehan rushed to ring center and jumped high in the air as he missed an uppercut. Dempsey came back with a short right to the stomach that sent Willie into his own corner, and Dempsey followed him. As Meehan missed with his right, Jack shot a light left and a hard right that followed, both blows landing on the chin, and Meehan went down.

Meehan rose, and Dempsey forced him to the ropes on the other side of the ring. Meehan looked beaten and ready for a trip to slumberland. Had Jack's left hand been in good shape, he might have finished him, but with only his right in working order, Jack could not get over the big finishing wallop. Meehan finally lashed away at the body, but a stiff right to the face closed his left eye and slowed him up. Willie took a lot of punishment in the mid-section in this round, and appeared to be in bad shape as he returned to his corner. It was a clear Dempsey round.

Hence, all of the reporters not only agreed that Dempsey won the round, but won it big, clearly dominating, doing damage, and decking Meehan.

3$^{rd}$ round

Purner said Meehan was back at his man again. His "bass drum" body blow was his favorite, hitting the stomach. Jack seemed unable to block it. They would clinch, and Meehan would pull his arms free and hammer away. He landed some hefty blows that seemed to hurt Dempsey. Jack tried to land his right, but could not, for Meehan covered his jaw well with both arms.

Al Joy said the round was Willie's by so much that the fans were cheering madly for "the fat boy," perhaps surprised by the local man's comeback after his poor prior round.

Harry Smith said Meehan was revived, and swung away, landing. Yet he did not open up when Dempsey wanted him to do so.

Leon Meyer said the round found Meehan fully recuperated, and he fairly tore at Dempsey, swinging his arms from every angle. He forced Jack back to the ropes. When Meehan again rushed, Dempsey landed a left swing that staggered Meehan. However, Jack then dropped his arm in pain, and afterwards it was discovered that his left hand was in a badly swollen condition. Jack acted as if in pain, and didn't fight back as hard as he might have done. Meehan took the lead and kept it to the end of the round. Still,

Willie's punches usually missed, and even though his rushes forced Dempsey back, the punches had little or no effect. Those who thought Dempsey was affected by the blows were wrong.

Marion Salazar said Meehan jumped in the air to try to puzzle Dempsey, but when Willie landed, Jack crashed another right on his chin. However, Dempsey made a mistake by not remaining outside and landing his straight punches, which Meehan seemed unable to avoid, and instead played Meehan's inside game. Once in close, Meehan swung his arms and landed occasional open-hand wallops that sounded more loudly than they hurt, but brought the fans to their feet.

Eddie Murphy said Meehan came out with a vengeance. Dempsey had the best of the early part of the round, using his right wallop and peppering the body with his left. But in the second half of the round, Meehan got going and landed at least eight left hooks to the body without a return. Only once in the fight did Dempsey throw a hard left, and that was in this round. It landed squarely in the midsection and could be heard for some distance. Still, it was Meehan's round. Dempsey later claimed to have hurt his left, which was swollen, explaining why had had not used it very often.

Bob Shand said Dempsey rushed in and landed two rights to the head, but Meehan allowed his upper body to slide back with the blows and diminish their force. Willie started a rally at ring center, scoring repeatedly with long rights and lefts to the ribs. In a neutral corner he landed twice to the head with stiff punches. Meehan was not using any of his well-known clown tactics, and also closed his hands when he hit. "It was Meehan's round all the way."

Hence, most of the reporters agreed that Meehan clearly won this round, outhustling Jack, though several questioned his effectiveness, and noted that Dempsey landed some very good stiff blows himself.

4th round

Purner said the round was the same as the prior round, with Meehan on the offensive. Jack appeared a bit tired, and was finding it difficult to deal with roly-poly Meehan's slam-bang style. One Meehan left swing to the head rocked Dempsey, who held, and Meehan pulled his hands loose and bounded away.

Al Joy said Willie went at it harder than ever. Jack kept trying for that one big blow against the ring's leading comedian, but he never landed it, and was not throwing as often, and not even trying as hard to land that one big blow. Jack even hung on, despite the fact that he did not seem tired. He merely was puzzled.

Harry Smith said Willie went at Dempsey hammer and tongs. Jack could not hold him off, and Meehan had a decided advantage.

Leon Meyer said the round was fairly even. Meehan was rushing and swinging, while Dempsey was shooting in some short jolts, with an occasional swing. Willie kept in close all through the round. With his arms working overtime, it appeared as if he was doing some great execution, but he was not, for the majority of his blows were smothered by Dempsey.

Eddie Murphy said although Meehan was fearless, and kept right after Dempsey all the time, Dempsey was able to show his skill as a boxer, and forced Meehan to miss many good swings, while Jack landed a few good ones of his own. Meehan was swinging away but mostly missing or landing on arms or anywhere, while Dempsey was landing cleanly, hardly a blow being wasted in the entire scrap. Meehan fought wildly, while Dempsey was cool. Meehan may have landed more blows than Dempsey in the round, but what Dempsey did land, were landed well, all in the place he directed them.

Bob Shand said Dempsey tried hard, but Meehan would not allow him to get set. Dempsey did land a hard right over the heart followed by a left to the head which shook up the sailor momentarily, but the left had no sting, and Willie was okay. Coming out of a clinch, Meehan landed high on the head and jumped right in again with a volley of punches to the body. Encouraged by the shouts of his friends, Meehan rooted in and Dempsey plainly was disconcerted. Jack tried repeatedly to measure him with a right, but the only time he succeeded in landing on the chin, Meehan's head went with the punch, and he came right back fighting like a tiger. Meehan had the round.

Hence, four writers gave the round to Meehan, while two scored it even.

The Decision

Fred Purner said that at the gong, Meehan raised his own right hand in the air and approached the referee, who grabbed it in token of victory. Referee Eddie Graney said, "Meehan won three of the four rounds and that was all there was to it." Wille was tendered a raucous reception in his corner.

Al Joy said Meehan outworked Dempsey and had him puzzled, so Jack lost.

Harry Smith said in a longer bout, the odds would favor Dempsey, but that is not the type of contest they fought.

Leon Meyer said Dempsey was entitled to a draw. Meehan was lucky to get the decision, for he was all but out in the $2^{nd}$ round.

Marion T. Salazar said Dempsey was entitled to no worse than a draw.

Eddie Murphy also strongly disagreed with the decision, feeling that Dempsey had earned a draw.

The *Enquirer's* Bob Shand said Referee Ed Graney hesitated, but after deliberating for about half a minute, decided that the sailor boy defeated the champion. Graney seemed anxious to get out of the ring without rendering a verdict, but Meehan ran over to him with his right arm in the air. Graney still hesitated. Dempsey then returned to ring center. It seemed as if Graney was going to call it a draw, but a few seconds later decided that Meehan had done the most work and held up his arm. Shand agreed with the decision, but with some reservations about the referee allowing Meehan to do so much clinching.

So, four local writers (two from the same paper) agreed with the decision, while three said it should have been a draw. Hence, it was three newspapers for Meehan, and three for a draw.

The *San Francisco Examiner's* Fred Purner said Referee Eddie Graney's verdict was unquestionable, for "roly-poly" Willie had three of the four rounds to his credit, and at the end had Dempsey hanging on. The fans howled with joy. Willie just waded in and battered Jack. Only in the 2nd round did Dempsey show to advantage, pounding on Meehan and scoring a knockdown. The other three rounds belonged to Meehan by unquestionable margins.

Dempsey said he had a bad left hand, and the glove was so small it did not help matters. He sacrificed his reputation for zero remuneration, which garnered him some credit and sympathy. Plus, it was only a 4-round bout, so the result would not really tarnish him much.

The *Examiner's* Al Joy said Fat Willie, the pride of the navy, in his corpulent might, had stepped into the limelight as a battler of the first rank. He might not look like a fighter, but he certainly was one. Meehan got busy fighting Dempsey all around the ring, flinging his fists into all sections of his anatomy, and putting Dempsey on the defensive.

True, the only knockdown was scored by Dempsey, in the 2nd round, with his right to the jaw which sent Willie tumbling to the mat, but Meehan was not materially harmed, and the rest of the tussle, save that one round, was his.

Jack Kearns and Spider Kelly, who were in Dempsey's corner, stood in their corner looking as if the jury had just announced a guilty verdict.

The crowd was in a frenzy, satisfied and surprised at the performance and Dempsey's defeat, but agreeing with the decision. Jack had been the 3 to 1 betting favorite. He was the most popular man before the contest, and looked the part of champion. He had broad shoulders, was tall, lithe, and brown in color. Conversely, Meehan was shorter by half a head, barrel-like in the midsection, with fat all over that wobbled jelly-like, with white skin like an infant's, looking like a big overgrown schoolboy. One lady observer said that when Meehan entered the ring, she felt sorry for him, because he had a roseate, kewpie-like form and smile, and did not look like he could last very long. But he was not at all frightened, and he could fight.

Dempsey was said to have been handicapped by an injured left hand and ill-fitting glove. However, he also hurt himself by laying back for a chance to land a knockout blow. Meehan covered his jaw very well, rolling himself up so much that he only could be hit on the top of his head, which was like hitting hard iron. The only real opening he showed was the stomach, and when he was hit in the body, it was like sinking one's glove into mush, which had little effect.

Afterward, Dempsey said,

> I had a bad left hand, which I hurt in my Dayton fight several weeks ago. I didn't say anything about it because I did not want to spoil the chance of getting the big money for the boys in the service. I knocked down Meehan in the 2nd round and I was boxing carefully. I thought I outpointed him. But I don't want to holler. What I want is a return match, and then I will show that my hand did bother me.

Meehan said, "Well, it was just as I told you. I had nothing to fear from Dempsey. I had fought him four times and it was even up with us, each having a decision and two of them being draws. I simply was determined to go after him and now I want to get the crack at Jess Willard."

Referee Ed Graney said,

> Meehan won and I was there to give the decision. One trouble with Dempsey which I noted before the fight was that the gloves were too small for him. He had a bad left hand and with the bandages used, it left the glove too small. It hurt him and prevented his punching. But the bout had to be judged on its merits and any boxer is foolish to box Meehan four rounds, for he is a bear at that distance.

Dempsey had worn a great deal of bandages and adhesive tape to protect his left hand, but there was so much of it that it made his glove so tight that it interfered with his boxing and ability to punch.

The *Chronicle's* Harry Smith said perhaps the press had not taken Meehan seriously enough, but that was as much his fault as the press's fault. Meehan had an "I told you so" spirit. He paraded down Market street receiving salutes. But Smith also said not to get carried away. Just because he beat Dempsey over a mere 4 rounds did not mean he likely ever would become champion. Furthermore, Meehan was an inconsistent trainer and performer. He had good fights and bad. In 1914, Harry Wills gave him a bad beating. Knockout Kruvosky almost stopped him, though it was more owing to lack of condition.

Willie had proven to be a master hand at stopping Dempsey's rushes. He defended in clever style, and Dempsey seemed puzzled as to how to get to and around him. Further, Meehan kept ripping in his body punches. His manner of punching was so peculiar and awkward that few had been able to solve his body punch. Dempsey was bothered by the body blows. He slowed down perceptibly in the 4th, and even winced on occasion in the 3rd. Meehan in top condition could beat most heavyweights over the 4-round distance. Even without Dempsey having a bad hand, Willie would be a problem.

Still, Smith believed that Dempsey would win in a longer battle. He carried too many guns for Meehan to win over the course of 10 rounds. Yet, Willie had proven that he could take punishment. He took enough of it in the 2nd round to demonstrate that. The audience cheered themselves hoarse when Meehan came back in the 3rd and did some lacing of his own. They loved the local underdog. Many had wagered at 10 to 8 odds that Meehan would not stay the full 4 rounds.

Kearns was upset, feeling that the bout was a draw. Some fans agreed, but Smith said local writers strongly supported the decision, which they said was popular and fair.

Graney confirmed that before the fight, Jack's seconds took a long time to get Dempsey's hands into the gloves. Kearns told him that his boy had a bad hand. Graney felt that handicapped Jack's ability to throw and land hard punches with his left. Dempsey claimed he damaged his left hand in the Kellar bout.

The chubby sailor proved to be a surprise. He fairly outboxed Dempsey, particularly in the last two rounds. He had him bewildered and unable to open up his attack. Meehan covered up in remarkably clever fashion, rendering Jack's attack ineffective. Even the sailor's swings landed more than usual. Dempsey seemed wobblier than Meehan at the end, for he did not seem able to get away from the punches of his rotund opponent.

Jack Kearns said Dempsey couldn't get full force behind his blows, and even still, with the knockdown in the 2nd round, he and Jack both thought Dempsey was leading, and Jack took his time when he might have come on faster had he realized it was close.

Graney said Meehan outboxed and outgamed him. However, perhaps significant in his ultimate decision, Graney did not call it a knockdown in the 2nd round when Meehan dropped down to the floor. Most observers agreed that it was a knockdown. So perhaps he might have called it a draw had he recognized the knockdown, but he did not.

The timekeeper also claimed that Meehan did not suffer a knockdown. "It was a case of Meehan being off balance and when Dempsey hooked him he went down for just a second." Of course, that description sounds like a knockdown.

Willie said, "That Dempsey can hit hard. He struck me one on the jaw in the 2nd [and] that hurt a lot. I didn't think he knocked me down, though most of those who saw the match thought it was a knockdown. But what if he did? Bring on Jess Willard, if you want to."

The *San Francisco Bulletin's* Leon Meyer strongly believed that Dempsey deserved a draw. Although the spectators, especially the gallery gods, cheered the decision loudly, "it did an injustice to Jack Kearns' fighter. Dempsey was at least entitled to a draw." What little damage was done belonged to Dempsey, for his punches had far more sting than Meehan's, and he came dangerously near scoring a knockout in the 2nd round, when he decked Meehan with a left hook to the jaw and pumped in pile-driving punches to the roly-poly heavyweight's head and body, rendering him wobbly. Meehan recuperated in the 3rd round, and although Dempsey momentarily staggered him with a left hook, he hurt his hand with the punch, and thereafter Meehan did better, though he did not land effectively. The 4th round was pretty even.

After the bell, Meehan walked towards Graney with his arm upward, while Dempsey started for his corner. Turning, the referee held Willie's arm, giving him the decision.

For two rounds, Dempsey looked to be a greatly improved fighter. He was fast on his feet, blocked nicely, and had a fine assortment of hooks and swings that hurt. Beginning in the 3rd round he seemed to slow up. Afterwards, he said that his hand was in pain, which affected his use of it.

Meyer conceded that Meehan fought a great fight, and deserved credit. He had his assortment of punches, including the bass-drum, and gave a wonderful exhibition of gameness under fire in the 2nd round. After the walloping he received in that round, few in attendance thought he would stick the 4 rounds, let alone win the decision.

Afterwards, Dempsey said he thought he was entitled to the decision, but would not kick about it, for "when a referee gives a decision that settles it, so what's the use of raising a howl." He said Willie was a good, game boy and could fight. Jack wished him all the luck in the world, and hoped he would make plenty of money as a result of his victory over him.

He and Kearns left on the train for Reno, where Dempsey would meet Jack Moran the following evening in a 10-round bout. Though his hand was sore and swollen, Dempsey still believed he could beat Moran.

The *San Francisco Call and Post's* Marion T. Salazar also disagreed with the decision, saying, "Why Graney gave Meehan the decision I don't know. Perhaps it was because Meehan held up his arm and it was too hard work for Eddie to reach for the arm of Dempsey." Graney seemed puzzled. At first, he started to reach for Dempsey's arm, but it was out of reach, and then he reached up with the other hand and placed it on Meehan's already upheld arm.

Meehan's corner was filled with raving, joyful, yowling maniacs, while Kearns was yelling and tearing at his well-combed hair, muttering curses and motioning Dempsey to exit the ring where he had been so unfairly treated.

Salazar said the decision should have been a draw. Many agreed with Graney, and many were against him. A draw would have obviated the arguments, and would have been the fairer result. "On punishment inflicted Dempsey had the fight away off by himself." He decked Meehan hard in the 2nd round, and nearly finished him. "Meehan never took a harder beating than he did in that second round, not even from Harry Wills. When he went to his corner it was a cinch bet that he wouldn't last out the third round." However, he recovered, and in the 3rd and 4th rounds, Dempsey fought on the inside too much, where Meehan landed loud open-handed slaps which didn't do any damage, but the sound excited the fans, which perhaps influenced Graney.

Salazar said Dempsey paid the price of Kearns' foolish overconfidence. He went up against a "ring clown," lost a decision, and was paid nothing. Kearns immediately stopped at a telegraph office and forwarded letters to every prominent Eastern sporting editor saying Graney had rendered "another of his famous Young Corbett-Jimmy Britt decisions," for Dempsey had Meehan on the floor and almost out. Salazar expected the Eastern papers to say that the "native sons" improperly awarded the local man the decision.

> Too bad. Had Graney called it a draw there would have been very little said, for Dempsey did take some wallops from Meehan that no man who is compared with Bob Fitzsimmons and John L. Sullivan should have taken.

But still Meehan didn't hurt Dempsey, and Dempsey did hurt him, and hurt him badly in that second round, and in a longer fight, say one of ten rounds, Dempsey would undoubtedly stop Meehan.

However, all this doesn't do away with the plaudits and the congratulations "Fat Willie" will be getting.

He'll be by long odds the biggest man on Powell street. When he returns to the naval training station at San Pedro the United States navy probably will give him a twenty-three gun salute.

The *Oakland Tribune's* Eddie Murphy also strongly disagreed with the decision. "There will be many arguments before the memory of last night's great battle dies. ... Hardly ten out of the hundreds of fans of Oakland who witnessed the bout could be found to admit that Meehan was entitled to the decision, and all of them were criticizing the way in which Graney gave it."

Still, he admitted that the fight had 10,000 fans wild, and they cheered and stamped at the decision. Meehan was so happy, he was like a kid, dancing and jumping and shaking hands with everyone.

This writer believed a draw would have been more appropriate. However, it appeared that Meehan convinced Graney to award him the decision by raising his own hand and walking over to the referee. Murphy said the referee did not know what he was doing, and had Dempsey raised his own hand at the end, he might have received the decision.

Eddie Graney seemed at sea when the gong rang for the end of the contest. When Meehan stepped over and raised his right hand, telling Graney that he should get the decision, Graney shoved him aside, and grabbed the hand of Dempsey only to let it drop and then do a hesitation, took several looks at each boy. Meehan again shoved up his hand and Graney grabbed it and held it in the air.

The feeling was that if Dempsey had been pushier and lobbied more for himself or held his own hand in the air before the indecisive Graney, he might have been given the decision, or it might have been ruled a draw.

It was a Meehan crowd throughout, and probably the actions of the crowd at the end of the 4th also influenced Graney to hesitate and then give Meehan the decision. The fight was close enough that it should have been a draw. But after several seconds of thinking, and the crowd yelling for Meehan, Graney went his way. Dempsey's left hand was badly swollen, and that hampered its use.

The *Oakland Enquirer's* Bob Shand verified that Dempsey had a sore, swollen, broken left hand going into the contest, which this writer noticed a couple days prior to the fight. He had a chance to make it a no decision bout, which the referee offered to him and Kearns, but they took a chance and lost, though they earned the respect of boxing fans.

Shand said the result was the biggest surprise in the history of heavyweight boxing. Meehan actually outpointed Dempsey. Had any referee other than Eddie Graney given the decision, the eastern papers would treat it as a joke, but Graney had a national reputation, and the result would be taken seriously.

Shand sympathized with Dempsey. He paid his own expenses, volunteered his services for free, and fought the best 4-round fighter in the country, because he knew Meehan would draw the most money for the cause. He risked his reputation, all to aid soldiers and sailors. Dempsey was handicapped by a broken left hand, and the referee showed Meehan favoritism by permitting him to hang on.

Shand agreed that Meehan indeed had scored the most points, landing the most punches, "so eliminating all sentiment Graney gave the decision where it belonged." Yet, if one was to evaluate Shand's round-by-round scores, 1 – even, 2 – Dempsey clear with a knockdown, 3 – Meehan, 4 – Meehan, a draw possibly could have been appropriate.

On leaving the ring, Graney said to Shand, "Well, I gave the decision to the man who won, but Dempsey should not have fought with that broken left hand." Graney said he did not score the fight by rounds, but looking at the fight as a whole, and all the way through, Meehan won. Graney said, "Dempsey had only a fraction of one round and the rest was all Meehan, but remember Dempsey had a bad hand."

Shand said that fraction was in the 2nd round, when Dempsey landed a light left immediately followed by a stiff right that set Willie down in his own corner. "It was a clean knockdown, although Meehan was up in two seconds without taking a count from the referee."

Summarizing the fight, Shand said Meehan beat Dempsey to the punch and never let Jack get set except that one time in the 2nd round. Meehan landed a dozen long lefts to the stomach in each round, and occasionally crossed with a right to the head. Dempsey gave Willie's stomach a pounding, and closed his left eye in the 2nd round, but whenever danger loomed, Meehan dropped into a clinch.

While agreeing with the decision, Shand criticized Graney for not breaking them. Shand believed that had the referee broken up the clinches more often, Dempsey probably would have landed a knockout blow, but the referee allowed Meehan to hold on throughout. Graney refused to touch the boxers or break them by force. "There was occasion to use his hands in every round last night, for Meehan refused to obey the orders to 'break,' but Eddie was more intent on saving his reputation for making the fighters break without touching them than he was on satisfying the fans." Furthermore, Meehan only half broke from each clinch and then tore right in again, whaling away to the body with both hands. He piled up many points by using this method. Long clinch, partial break, immediate charge-in with body blows, then clinch again. In open outside fighting, Meehan beat Dempsey to the punch, and then as he came to close quarters he held on, making it difficult for Dempsey to get off his punches. Allowing Meehan to clinch often, for lengthy periods of time, and not fully breaking, enabled him to use his style and tactics effectively and win the fight as it was fought.

Shand said Meehan was a tough guy to beat in only 4 rounds. "In a ten-round fight Dempsey would be a cinch." Shand advised Dempsey to heal his hand before considering fighting him again, and to insist on a longer contest. The problem though was that the local Meehan was a gate draw in San Francisco, where they only allowed 4-round contests, but was not a draw anywhere else.

Jack Kearns vehemently insisted that the decision was wrong. He thought Dempsey had won. The letter he sent out over the wires said,

> Eddie Graney rendered another of his famous Jimmy Britt-Young Corbett decisions here last night when he gave Willie Meehan a decision over Jack Dempsey. Dempsey had Meehan on the floor and almost out in the second round. He beat him badly in every round. Meehan worked a clever trick when he lifted his own hand after the last round and Graney fell for the trick. The decision was almost as unpopular as the decision Wyatt Earp rendered in the Fitzsimmons-Sharkey bout. A draw would have been giving Dempsey the worst of it.[482]

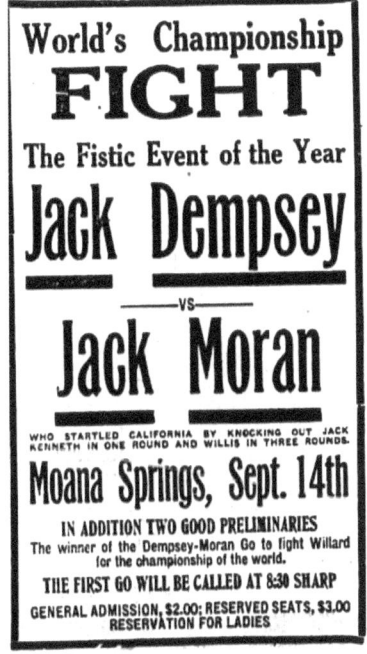

The very next evening after the Meehan war-charity contest, on Saturday September 14, 1918 in Moana Springs, in the Reno, Nevada area, in a scheduled 10-round bout sponsored by the Reno Athletic Club at the Moana pavilion, Jack Dempsey fought Jack Moran. Dem Gay, the local promoter, made the fight. Despite having a sore hand, Dempsey did not call off the contest, honoring his contract. Perhaps Jack simply was that game and willing to tough it out for the money, and/or wanted to get back to his winning ways, confident that he could beat Moran regardless of the injury.

California's Jack Moran was said to weigh 200 pounds, and had won his last six or seven fights. Moran allegedly had victories such as KO1 KO Kruvosky (who had a win over Meehan), KO2 Hendricks, KO3 Charles White, KO2 George Pappas, KO4 Russell Kane, KO4 Arthur Pelkey, and KO1 Soldier Bell. The fight poster also listed a KO1 Jack Kenneth and KO3 Willis. Secondary sources say he began boxing in 1911, and his record included: 1915 LKOby5 Fred Fulton, LND10 Bud Gorman, and LKOby7 Al Norton; 1916 KO5 Dan Ketchell; 1917 WND12 Jack Geyer, D12 Gunboat Smith, L12 Battling Levinsky, LTKOby6 Jack Dillon, WDQ7 Tony Caponi, and LKOby3 Fred Fulton.

---

[482] *Reno Evening Gazette*, September 14, 1918.

Moran was a wireless operator in the military service, and also a fancy high diver. He made a good impression on local fans who saw him spar 3 fast rounds with Wilson, a husky soldier from the university. He allegedly was about 21 years old (but likely much older), rangy in build, and "beautifully muscled." Officers and men from the detachment were impressed with his good left. Moran promised that the Dempsey bout would be no exhibition, but a real fight.

Regarding the September 14, 1918 Jack Dempsey vs. Jack Moran fight, the local *Nevada State Journal* reported that Moran was willing enough, and made a good impression in the short time he was around, for he had a peculiar crouching attitude and kept his jaw well protected, but Dempsey's short jolts soon found their mark nevertheless. Moran could do nothing with the world's championship claimant. Dempsey floored him early on for a nine-count, and when Moran came back, Dempsey sent him down and out for keeps in the 1st round. Dempsey was in a hurry to finish matters quickly, and had no trouble in doing so, finishing Moran in 1 minute 30 seconds. Others reported it lasted 70 seconds.[483]

HERE'S the roly-poly battler who created all the excitement and argument by dinting Jack Dempsey's fistic reputation.

IT'S WILLIE MEEHAN, all dolled up in one of Uncle Sam's blue uniforms. The Phat One declares that he can fight in this costume as well as in ring attire, and he's rarin' to get in some lefts and rights on the submarines that sneak under the cloak of the deep.

Kearns was trying to bolster up Dempsey, saying that the San Francisco newspapers were against the Meehan decision, but the *Chronicle* said that was not so, and his misrepresentations would backfire. The *Chronicle* noted that only two local critics said Dempsey ought to have had a draw. Both morning papers (including the *Chronicle*) and one afternoon paper gave it to Meehan. Two evening papers said it was a draw. Hence it was 3 votes for Meehan, 2 for a draw. Of the Oakland papers, there was a split, with one favoring the decision and the other holding for a draw. Even if all local and semi-local papers were counted, that would be 4 for Meehan and 3 for a draw. It was unlikely that Dempsey would get another bout, for Meehan was tied up with the military, and probably the only way they were going to allow him to box was for another West Coast 4-round patriotic show.[484]

---

[483] *Nevada State Journal*, September 11, 14, 15, 1918; *Reno Gazette-Journal*, September 10, 1918; *Reno Evening Gazette*, September 13, 1918; *San Francisco Examiner*, September 16, 1918; *San Francisco Chronicle*, September 22, 1918.
[484] *San Francisco Chronicle*, September 17, 1918.

Dempsey had his defenders. The *Oakland Enquirer* noted that the timekeeper, George Harting, said Meehan was not knocked down, but it "was a case of Meehan being knocked off balance and when Dempsey hooked him he went down for a second." The *Enquirer* responded,

> Alright, George, but supposing Dempsey had not hooked him, would Meehan have gone down? Maybe Willie might have imagined that Dempsey hooked him and thought he just had to sit down. We can't seem to get the Harting argument at all. He says that Meehan was hooked on the chin and went down, but still he was not knocked down. Maybe George will insist on a boxer being felled with an axe or a meat cleaver before he will credit the other fellow with a knock-down.

> But we're here to say that Meehan was put to the mat with a right hook to the chin, as he dropped within six feet of where the writer was sitting. Dempsey grazed the Meehan chin with a light left and brought over the right to the same place. There was considerable force behind that right hand and the fact that Meehan was off balance at the time has nothing to do with the knock-down.

> Incidentally, we know four newspaper writers who were in a better position to see the knock-down than Harting. George was on the opposite side of the ring from where Meehan fell and it is quite possible he was looking at the watch when it happened. Incidentally, the timekeeper is not an authority on knock-downs. He is there to keep time, that's all.

Graney had the same mistaken belief. So, if Dempsey held Meehan even in the relatively uneventful 1st round, clearly dominated the 2nd round and scored a knockdown, then even if he lost the 3rd and 4th rounds (some said he held Meehan even in those rounds), he should have obtained a draw.

Meehan was transferred from San Pedro to San Francisco, and currently was an orderly in the commandant's office. His victory over Dempsey had made a hit with his superior officers. Willie also was a good singer, with a strong voice, and performed in vaudeville.

Bob Shand said although Meehan won a decision over Dempsey, the heavyweight situation was not any more complicated. "In the majority of fistic experts, Dempsey is still the best heavyweight in the game today, and Meehan's win is not going to hurt Jack to any appreciable extent." If there was a rematch of more than 4 rounds, Dempsey would be the favorite. Even in a 4-round bout, if Dempsey's left hand was in better shape and a referee in the ring who would break them when Meehan held, Dempsey likely would win. Shand also said the lack of sparring partners hurt Dempsey, and his judgment of distance was off. The heavy tape he put on his broken hand did more harm than good, and he was unable to use his left except to lead and tap. Meehan noticed it too, which is why he took liberties he otherwise would not have dared taken. "And the referee played Meehan's game by refusing to step between the men and split 'em up."

Shand blamed Kearns for insisting on a decision. Kearns had said, "Meehan can't hurt Dempsey, and Jack is a cinch to win on points even though he does not knock the sailor out."

Graney scored it 3 rounds to 1, and Shand agreed. "Admitting that Dempsey did more damage to Meehan in one round than Willie did to him in three rounds that does not alter the fact that Meehan won the fight." Dempsey was unmarked, and Meehan's left eye was cut. Still, despite the fact that Dempsey landed harder and more effectively, "Meehan landed cleaner and more frequently, and that won the battle for him." Regardless, the match soon would be forgotten, and the eastern fans and writers would continue paying tribute to Dempsey.[485]

Several days after the fight, Meehan said, "Say, I'm getting tired of Kearns and Dempsey talking about sore hands and that he was entitled to a draw the other night. You notice they haven't asked for a return match, have they? Say, do you ever remember a champ getting licked that he didn't have some excuse and want a return match?"[486]

Jess Willard claimed that Meehan's victory over Dempsey put Jack out of the running. Jess was willing to fight Meehan. However, the champion absorbed criticism for such a stance.

> If Willard thinks he is going to get out of a bout with Dempsey in this manner and still hope to exist in the high esteem of the fistic fancy he is making a serious mistake. Dempsey is regarded by all fistic experts as the one heavyweight contender justly entitled to the first crack at the heavyweight crown adorning the brow of the Kansas cowboy.

This writer complimented Dempsey for boxing Meehan with a bad hand in order to raise money for soldiers and sailors. "Dempsey has done more than Willard has done in the way of boxing for patriotic purposes." Jess seemed reluctant to box for war charities for free. Hence many called him money mad, failing to keep faith with the public which had helped make him rich. The longer Jess had an "unwarranted attitude" about fighting Dempsey, the more unpopular he would become. "It is possible Jess doesn't care two shakes of a lamb's tail for the public."[487]

On September 18, 1918, while passing through Denver en route to Chicago, Dempsey, Willard, and their representatives held a meeting. Dempsey and Willard actually got along, commiserating about "Native Son" hometown decisions they lost to local fighters in San Francisco. Kearns told about how Meehan got a gift over Dempsey. Willard said he believed he beat Gunboat Smith, but lost. "You have to have a club to win out there."

Willard promised to fight Dempsey first, as soon as the war was over. He was convinced that neither the government nor the public wanted a heavyweight championship fight until then. Dempsey agreed, and seemed

---

[485] *Oakland Enquirer*, September 17, 1918.
[486] *San Francisco Examiner*, September 18, 1918.
[487] *Oakland Tribune*, September 18, 1918; *Buffalo Enquirer*, September 19, 1918.

pleased by Willard's assurances. Clearly, despite Kearns claiming that Dempsey was the champion, Dempsey recognized that Willard actually was the champion.

**Jack Kearns, Jack Dempsey, a Willard friend, Jess Willard, and Ed Sunday, brother of the famous Billy Sunday**

Despite the fact that Kearns had attacked Willard in the newspapers for a lack of patriotism and support for the war, calling him a "cheese patriot," and also attacked his manhood, calling him a "cheese champion," the meeting was cordial. Willard was unphased. The *Examiner* criticized,

> Such serious charges were figured to arouse the spirit of any red-blooded man, but it has long been evident that Willard possesses nothing but a greedy lust for money. Instead of resenting what Kearns wrote about him, Willard shakes hands and entered into a long explanation of how he will not fight anyone until the war is over. Certainly, Willard is a pitiful example of the champion pugilist of the world.[488]

Willard recently had signed an affidavit claiming that he was "just rounding" age 35, four years older than he had represented previously.

Regarding the Meehan fight, the *Examiner's* Fred Purner insisted, "Dempsey may figure to whip every heavyweight in the world with one punch, but the fact remains he was out-generaled by the famous San Francisco fat boy on this particular and auspicious occasion."[489]

Bob Shand asked why Kearns was not trying to get a return match with Meehan. Shand speculated that perhaps Kearns thought Meehan was too tough a proposition.:

---

[488] *Brooklyn Daily Times, Brooklyn Citizen*, September 19, 1918; *San Francisco Examiner*, September 23, 1918; *Oakland Enquirer*, September 24, 1918.
[489] *San Francisco Examiner*, September 20, 1918.

Personally, we think Dempsey is a better fighter than Willie Meehan and we think he would stop the sailor boy in a long fight, but it does not seem that Kearns has the confidence in his fighter that others have. Over the four-round route this Meehan boy is the toughest proposition in the world to beat, but a ten or fifteen-round fight would be something else again.[490]

The *Chicago Tribune's* Ray Pearson said that reading the reports of the Meehan bout, it appeared that the verdict favoring Meehan was out of line by a big margin, and Dempsey should have won. "That is based on the fact that Dempsey in the second round scored a clean knockdown. Meehan didn't take a count, but even if he didn't, that did not take from Dempsey the margin for which a knockdown generally counts in any ring battle." Pearson said Meehan was a tapper. Dempsey did the punching, while Meehan did the clever tapping to accumulate points. "But it is hard to see how he earned the decision on points in a four-round bout when he had a knockdown to overcome in the scale of points."[491]

Many were frustrated by Willard. "One day he is going to fight Dempsey; the next day he swears he will not don the gloves until the war is over, and now he has offered to box Willie Meehan." But then he indicated that he was willing to box Dempsey. One wondered whether he was sure himself.[492]

Dempsey was supposed to box Battling Levinsky at a patriotic benefit on September 28 in Philadelphia. However, it was called off, owing to a serious flu epidemic, but eventually re-scheduled for November.

Black fighter Harry Wills of New Orleans was after a bout with Dempsey. He had progressed sufficiently in boxing knowledge that he was able to reverse prior losses to Sam Langford. Wills was struggling to find matches, for most whites did not want to fight him. The *Chronicle* said Wills was not as good as a prime Langford was, and he might fall before Dempsey, but he could fight, and it would be a good match. "Jack will find it exceedingly difficult to avoid meting Wills, and it is certain that if he does succeed Willard, the Crescent City negro will be his most formidable and persistent challenger."[493]

26-year-old Harry Wills had fought the who's who of top elite black fighters, and even a few whites who had crossed the color line. His record included: 1912 LKOby2 George Kid Cotton (right uppercut); 1913 D10 Jeff Clark, D10 Joe Jeannette, and KO3 Kid Cotton; 1914 KO4 Kid Cotton, DND10 Sam Langford, DND10 Jeannette, W4 Willie Meehan, KO1 Charley Miller, LKOby14 Langford (Langford down in 1st and 2nd, Wills knocked out with two left hooks), and L20 Sam McVey/McVea (Wills 206, McVey 217); 1915 W20 John Lester Johnson, LND10 McVey (right

---

[490] *Oakland Enquirer*, September 21, 1918.
[491] *Oakland Enquirer*, quoting *Chicago Tribune*, September 25, 1918. Kearns claimed that while in Chicago, in sparring, Dempsey knocked out welter/middleweight Bryan Downey (56 fights) in the 2nd round.
[492] *Oakland Enquirer*, September 27, 1918.
[493] *San Francisco Chronicle*, September 27, 1918.

uppercut put Wills down in the 9th), WND10 Battling Jim Johnson, W12 McVey, and WND10 Langford; 1916 W20, LKOby19 (Wills down twice in the 19th), and WND10 Langford, WND10 John Lester Johnson, WND8 Langford (Sam down in the 2nd), W20 Jeff Clark, TKO4 (twice) Kid Cotton, WND10 Bill Tate, and KO9 and WND10 Jack Thompson; 1917 LTKOby2 Battling Jim Johnson (Wills retirement from a broken wrist), WND10 Jack Thompson, WND6 Langford, WND10 Battling Jim Johnson, WND10 and DND12 Langford, and TKO5 Jeff Clark; and 1918 KO5 McVey, KO6 and TKO7 Langford (retirement after the 7th), W20 McVey (Wills down in the 11th), TKO5 Clark, and WND6 Jack Thompson.

However, in the post-Jack Johnson era, in a world continually struggling with race issues, very few white fighters endured much criticism for not fighting top black fighters. Some white writers still argued that the color line had no place in pugilism, but not with the same vehemence and pervasiveness that was present during Jack Johnson's ascendance.

Some spoke of a potential Dempsey-Langford matchup. Edward Tranter said a Dempsey vs. Langford match was not desirable, because Langford was "too old, too fat, and too lazy for Dempsey. ... Langford has reached that decline in pugilism where he cannot possibly ever hope to come back." In his day, he was the world's most dangerous fighter, a clever boxer and a terrific hitter, but his day had passed. Still, "Even in his present condition Langford could whip half the heavies that are parading the country today as title contenders, but not Jack Dempsey."[494]

[494] *Buffalo Enquirer*, October 11, 1918.

CHAPTER 18

# Dominance Re-Affirmed

Once he traveled to Philadelphia in late September 1918, Jack Dempsey found it difficult to find sparring partners. He was sparring with veteran black fighter Jeff Clark/Clarke, who was taking plenty of punishment daily, but Clark needed someone else to help absorb the grueling. Clark tried to get Jack Thompson, another black fighter, to agree to work with Dempsey, but when he saw Clark's battered face, he declined, saying, "He hits too hard and it's not worth the chance."

Known as the Joplin Ghost, the large light-heavyweight-sized Clark, who had a 118-17-15 record, was good enough to hold wins over Battling Jim Johnson, Battling Levinsky, Joe Jeannette, Sam Langford, Kid Norfolk, and Gunboat Smith. He also had fought draws with Jeannette, Harry Wills, and Jim Johnson.[495]

Dempsey trained for a bit in Long Branch, New Jersey under veteran trainer Jimmy De Forest's tutelage.[496]

New Jersey recently had agreed to allow mixed-race bouts, lifting its prior ban on such contests. Hence, some said it was possible legally to make a Jack Dempsey vs. Harry Wills fight. Wills was said to be the best of the blacks. However, the press noted that Harry was suffering from Spanish influenza at the moment (a deadly flu strain rapidly killing many thousands, even the previously fit and healthy, including boxers Jim Stewart and Matty Baldwin), and Dempsey needed to be convinced that he had to meet the negro or abandon his pursuit for the title. It was not clear that he needed to meet Wills in order to compel a title fight. The other top blacks worth consideration were Kid Norfolk and Joe Jeannette. Norfolk was said to be overrated, while Jeannette was old. Nevertheless, Joe had a local following,

---

[495] *Philadelphia Inquirer*, October 2, 1918. Known as Jeff Clark (birth name was Clarke), his record included: 1910 WND6 Battling Jim Johnson, LTKOby2 Sam Langford, D10 Joe Jeannette, 1911 WND15 (twice) Battling Levinsky; 1912 WND6 Jeannette; 1913 LND10 Jeannette, D10 Harry Wills, KO13 Rufe Cameron, and D10 Kid Cotton; 1914 W15 Cameron and WND10 Langford; 1915 DND15, KO15, and TKO11 Rough House Ware, W20 Kid Norfolk, L10 Sam McVey, and D15 Battling Jim Johnson; 1916 LTKOby5 Langford, LKOby10 Jack Thompson, L20 Wills, and L20 Norfolk; 1917 W15 and W10 Gunboat Smith, L20 and LTKOby15 McVey, LTKOby8 Battling Jim Johnson, and LTKOby5 Wills; and 1918 LTKOby5 Wills. In late October, Clarke would fight Langford to a 12-round draw.
[496] *Daily Record*, October 10, 1918.

being a New Jersey resident, and had a long and honorable career, with vast experience. "Now that mixed matches have been officially approved in New Jersey, Jeannette intends to be more active than ever in the ring this winter."[497]

Lester Walton of the black-owned *New York Age* said opponents of mixed-race bouts had argued that such contests caused ill feeling between the races. However, he argued that color discrimination only increased rather than diminished racial ill will. Local white writers seemed to look on with favor the New Jersey commission's latest position to allow mixed-race fights. "They too, seem to have taken quite a mental somersault on the question; for it was only a few years ago when they frowned on mixed bouts." Many writers had changed their views, and now advocated for mixed-race contests. Walton still expected top white fighters to utilize the color line as a convenient barrier to hide behind when afraid of colored fighters. It certainly had served many "conscientious objectors."

Walton said the latest person to be guilty of the color line pugilistic camouflage was Dempsey's manager, Jack Kearns. There was talk of Dempsey meeting Kid Norfolk or Harry Wills, but Kearns said,

> I haven't given the matter any particular thought up to the present time. Still, I never was in favor of mixed bouts. I don't think I would make such a match for Dempsey unless I was convinced that the public desired it. There are just as good white boxers as there are colored, and if Jack licks them there will be no necessity for him meeting the black boys to prove that he is master of his class. Willard squelched the colored heavyweight division when he squelched Jack Johnson in Cuba. Why resurrect it again?

Hence, Walton said Kearns had discharged his gun charged with race prejudice. Walton said Dempsey could not truly prove himself to be the king of the heavyweights by defeating white boxers who would not stand a chance with Wills, Langford, or Norfolk.[498]

Speaking of the recent 4-round Meehan contest, in which he decked Willie in the 2nd round, Dempsey said, "They sure gave me a fine trimming on the coast. ... I have got it in for some of those referees on the coast, as I beat Meehan all the way. But of course that doesn't tell the world that I did. However, what's the use of squawking?"[499]

For the past half year or so, John Reisler had been trying to prevent Dempsey from boxing. Jack's attorney Ray Cannon had obtained a

---

[497] *New York Evening Telegram*, October 13, 1918; *Philadelphia Inquirer*, October 16, 1918.

Kid Norfolk's record included: 1915 L20 Jeff Clark; 1916 KO2 Gunboat Smith, W20 Bill Tate, W20 Clark, and KO13 Arthur Pelkey; 1917 KO13 Pelkey, WND10 (twice) and TKO8 Tom Cowler, WND10 (twice) Bert Kenny, LND10 and WND10 Gunboat Smith, W12 Billy Miske, WND12 Cowler, and LKOby2 Sam Langford; and 1918 KO3 George Christian, TKO7 Bill Tate, WND4 Battling Jim Johnson, D/LND8 and LND8 Joe Jeannette, (and eventually, November 19, 1918 L12 Clay Turner).

Joe Jeannette's recent record included: 1917 WND10 Andre Anderson, LND12 Sam Langford, and WND6 George Christian; and 1918 W/DND8 and WND8 Kid Norfolk on October 11, 1918.

[498] *New York Age*, October 5, 1918.

[499] *Chicago Tribune*, October 13, 1918; *Dayton Herald*, October 16, 1918.

temporary injunction in Milwaukee restraining Reisler from interfering with Dempsey's boxing career. Dempsey told reporters that he would quit the game before going back to John the Barber's management.

On October 17, Dempsey was in Milwaukee, Wisconsin for his court case with Reisler. Jack testified that he earned $4,200 from the Fulton fight, but only got $1,800 out of it personally.

Dempsey called Reisler "John the Barber" or "John the Razor." Hours were spent trying to get Dempsey to admit that Reisler did not owe him $900 for the John Lester Johnson contest. Jack said he was supposed to get 30% of the gross receipts. However, apparently his manager Jack Fisher had made the match and agreed to 12.5%. Yet, Dempsey insisted that he was his own manager. Jack said Reisler told him just before the contest that his end would be about $1,000, but when they settled, he only got $100. Reisler said the receipts were a little under $800, and Dempsey's share was $93, but he gave him an even $100.

Dempsey was adept at answering, "I don't remember," or "I can't think of it." Once he even said, "You know after you get a few wallops on the coco, especially from a hitter like John Lester Johnson, you can't think of all that happened the night before." Dempsey admitted that Reisler had staked him some "glad rags," or clothes, but "the whole outfit did not cost over 200 bucks." Back then, he still traveled like a hobo.[500]

Eventually, at the end of October, the circuit court judge ruled in Dempsey's favor. He upheld the injunction issued last May restraining Reisler from interfering with Dempsey's contests. The judge ruled that Reisler voided their agreement by his own actions, and a permanent injunction was granted prohibiting Reisler from interfering in any way with Dempsey's pugilistic affairs. He also awarded Kearns damages of $500 plus costs. Attorney Ray Cannon wired the results of the case to Dempsey, who had returned to Philadelphia, where he was booked to fight Battling Levinsky on November 6.

When Reisler had filed a petition for bankruptcy in New York some time ago, he failed to file or claim the Dempsey contract as an asset or liability. Judge Gregory ruled that the failure to mention said contract supported Dempsey's claim that the contract had been rescinded.

Most newsmen said the ruling essentially ended matters for Reisler, who had been defeated and would have to leave Dempsey alone.[501] However, they weren't entirely correct. Reisler would continue his pursuit with appeals and civil lawsuits in various states.

Dempsey said he was going to head to West Virginia at some point soon, "to visit some of my relatives and to look up a claim in a coal mine which my father believes belongs to him."[502]

---

[500] *Quad-City Times*, October 17, 1918; *Davenport Daily Times*, October 22, 1918; *Salt Lake Tribune*, October 27, 1918.
[501] *Pottsville Republican*, October 30, 1918; *Appleton Post-Crescent, Racine Journal Times*, October 31, 1918; *Philadelphia Public Ledger*, November 2, 1918.
[502] *New York Evening World*, October 25, 1918.

According to Kearns's posthumously published autobiography, in October 1918, a government agent asked the now-famous Dempsey to pose for photos in the Sun Shipyard in Pennsylvania for marketing/propaganda purposes, to encourage and influence more men to go into war work. The amiable Dempsey agreed to help out, and posed for some pictures, pursuant to the request. However, it backfired. He had slipped a pair of overalls over his regular clothing, and the picture clearly showed he was wearing patent leather shoes. That didn't sit well with many, who called him a slacker.

Dempsey and Kearns had been deferred from the draft, because Dempsey had a wife and also supported his parents, while Kearns supported his mother and sister.

In early October, the press reported that Dempsey would engage in work at the Sun Shipbuilding plant in Chester, near Philadelphia, Pennsylvania. Dempsey previously had worked in a Seattle shipyard in a blacksmith shop, handling a riveting machine, and was a carpenter, repairing vessels. Late October articles noted that Dempsey was said to be employed at the Sun shipbuilding yards.

The *Chicago Tribune* said that after a few days in Milwaukee for the Reisler case, Dempsey had returned to Philadelphia to work at the Sun Shipbuilding yards.

However, some noted that Dempsey had been photographed holding the tap end of a pneumatic riveting machine with inappropriate nonchalance, his overalls were painfully new, and the shoes he was wearing were new high-class leather, inappropriate for a riveter. He clearly was not one. "Jack is doing most of his shipbuilding around fight promoters' box offices." He was a fighter, not a riveter. Yet, most newspapers wisely cropped out his shoes when printing the photographs. At the time, not too many folks made a big deal about it, but a little over year later, some did.[503]

The Navy wanted Dempsey to join its ranks. The Great Lakes naval training station wanted him as a "sailor riveter." Lieutenant John F. Kennedy wired the local draft board No. 2 in San Francisco, asking for his release. "I understand Jack Dempsey is riveting in a shipyard on the Atlantic coast. ... [W]e can give him a riveting job here as an enlisted man with the colors and not for a private concern. ... Dempsey knows nothing of this. As his picture shows him riveting in a shipyard, I would announce that here is a chance to drive rivets as a sailor in Uncle Sam's shipyard." Kearns allegedly claimed that Dempsey was employed by the Moon shipyards on the Atlantic Coast as a riveter and labor recruiter. The *San Francisco Chronicle*

---

[503] *Jones County News*, October 3, 1918; *Dewar Telegram*, October 17, 1918; *Munster Times*, October 25, 1918; *Chicago Tribune*, October 24, 27, 1918.

said, "But this sort of a campaign may easily smoke out Jack and force him to get into line." Clearly, they knew or strongly suspected that Jack wasn't really a riveter.[504]

The question some later had was whether Dempsey simply was helping the government with marketing, doing his patriotic duty in that way, or trying to use the claim of working in a shipyard as a way to avoid the work or fight order, or whether it was a convenient combination of both.

Dempsey was scheduled to box Battling Levinsky on November 6 in Philadelphia for the Olympia Athletic Club. Jack was training at Long Branch, New Jersey, likely with Jimmy De Forest.[505]

An influenza epidemic had caused the postponement of their prior dates. The U.S. and the world was in the middle of a very severe deadly influenza epidemic (known as the Spanish flu) which killed an estimated 20 to 50 million people worldwide, often very rapidly. In the U.S. alone, 195,000 died just in the month of October. Eventually, this flu strain would kill around 600,000 in the U.S. within a year, killing about as many as died in four years of the Civil War (which had the most American casualties of any war), and far more than all the U.S. soldier deaths in World War I. Of the 116,516 U.S. military deaths in World War I out of the 4.7 million who served, 63,114 were killed by disease, largely due to the influenza epidemic, versus 53,402 due to combat. The flu would affect attendance at fights, because fewer folks wanted to be present in crowded public places. However, many either were indifferent to the risks, or did not comprehend them fully. Many folks wore protective masks, but still sat in crowds at sporting events and participated in patriotic

---

[504] *San Francisco Chronicle*, October 29, 1918; *Vancouver Sun*, November 2, 1918.
[505] *Philadelphia Evening Public Ledger*, October 28, 1918.

parades. The pandemic eventually would come to an end in the summer of 1919.

Black fighter Battling Jim Johnson, who had sparred with him before, declined an invitation to be Dempsey's sparring partner again, saying that Dempsey hit too hard and was the hardest hitter he ever faced. "I sure need the money, but I don't want to risk a few broken ribs for the trouble." This was coming from a man who had fought Sam Langford, Joe Jeannette, Sam McVey, Harry Wills, and Jack Johnson, some of them multiple times.[506]

Joe Jeannette had issued a defi/challenge to Dempsey or Willard, with the proceeds to go to a war charity. He was willing to fight them for free. "They cannot honestly advance the worn-out excuse of 'color line,' for the money earned by this fight will be used by these wonderful organizations to help…our gallant fighters, irrespective of race, color or creed." Jeannette said he was supremely confident of beating either Willard or Dempsey in a bout of whatever length they wanted. He said Jack Johnson refused to fight him because he wanted to be the only black champion. Joe did not think much of Willard. "As for Dempsey, he may be a great fighter. However, I have noticed in the papers where he repudiated two matches with one Kid Norfolk, whom I have twice defeated."

The *Chicago Defender* subsequently noted that most veteran black fighters had faded into obscurity. Few of the white race would fight them. "Harry Wills sizes up as one of the greatest modern human fighting machines ever put together."[507]

The local *Philadelphia Record*'s R. H. Kain said Dempsey more than likely would be the next champion. He had earned a title shot via his victory over Fulton. Willard was wealthy and fat, earning good money with oil wells, and likely not wanting to take on such a tough proposition. Willard was "one of the most unpopular fighters who ever held a title in the history of the ring. He was fortunate enough to escape the draft, and he never showed any disposition to do anything to help the cause of the 'boys over there.'" He allegedly refused to box exhibition bouts for the entertainment of soldiers or for war charity funds. He was called a grouch.

This writer also said that German fighters were not game, and tended to show the yellow. The German army was like the German fighter. "The German army is groggy and helplessly beaten. The yellow streak is again showing itself in the plaintive wailings for an armistice and peace. Nothing like the good old Anglo-Saxon wallop that has won big glove fights and victories on the battlefield." Sports like boxing had cultivated in Americans speed, activity, and accuracy. Boxing made men quick on their feet, quick of hand, and true of eye. Such made superior soldiers. Germans liked weight lifting, which made them strong, but they were slow, ponderous, and clumsy in their movements.[508]

Philadelphia was the city where major race riots recently had taken place.

---

[506] *Philadelphia Public Ledger*, October 30, 1918.
[507] *Chicago Defender* November 2, 1918; *Washington Times*, October 26, 1918.
[508] *Philadelphia Record*, November 3, 1918.

Against Battling Levinsky, Dempsey would attempt to prove to local Philadelphia fans that he was the best heavyweight in the world and the logical person to fill the championship (which Willard allegedly refused to defend). Jack would box 6 rounds or less with Levinsky.

The *Philadelphia Public Ledger* said that a year or so ago, Jack was an unknown, except for some trickling reports that were not taken seriously, given that so many alleged prospects had been thrust upon an unsuspecting public. However, walloping men like Smith and Morris made folks take notice, and especially so after his victories over Brennan and Fulton.

BATTLING LEVINSKY.

New York's Levinsky was said to be the shiftiest heavyweight ever. He had met all of the leading heavies, with the exception of Willard and Fulton, and never had been stopped or taken the count. He usually outpointed his foes, and was the hardest man in the world to hit, making him a big drawing card. Fans appreciated his speed and skill. Levinsky believed he would outpoint Dempsey.[509]

27-year-old Battling Levinsky (born Barney Lebrowitz) was a Jewish fighter, or Hebrew as they called him. His career, which began in 1910, consisted of over 200 fights, with a 145-31-29 record, including victories over Al Kubiak, Dick Gilbert, Tom McMahon, Jim Flynn, Jim Coffey, Porky Flynn, Tony Ross, Bert Kenny, Charlie Weinert, Gunboat Smith, Terry Keller, Tom McCarthy, Colin Bell, Sandy Ferguson, Jack Geyer, Al Reich, Tom Cowler, Jack Dillon, Bob Devere, Jim Barry, Bob Moha, Billy Miske, Jack Moran, Bartley Madden, Bill Brennan, and Clay Turner.[510]

---

[509] *Philadelphia Public Ledger*, November 6, 1918.
[510] Battling Levinsky's record included: 1911 DND6 Tom McMahon, WND6 Al Kubiak, DND6 Jim Barry, LND6 Jack Dillon, and LND15 Jeff Clark; 1912 WND6 Joe Grim, LND6 and WND6 Eddie McGoorty, D10 Tony Caponi, W15 (twice), W20, and W25 Dick Gilbert; 1913 WND10 Tom McMahon, DND10 Jack Dillon, LND10 and WND10 Jack Twin Sullivan, DND10 Porky Flynn, LND10 McGoorty, DND10 Charlie Weinert, WND10 Jim Flynn, and WND10 Jim Coffey; 1914 WND6 Coffey, LND10 Bob McAllister, WND10 (twice) and DND10 Porky Flynn, WND6 Tony Ross, WND10 McMahon, WND10 Coffey, L12 and LND10 Jack Dillon, WND10 Bert Kenny, WND10 Weinert, WND10 Gunboat Smith, WND10 (twice) Jim Flynn, WND10 Terry Keller, and LND10 Tom McCarthy; 1915 D12 and L20 Gunboat Smith, WND10 (twice) Tom McCarthy, WND10 (twice) and DND6 Porky Flynn, WND10 Colin Bell, W12 Sandy Ferguson, WND10 Jack Geyer, and WND10 Tom Cowler; 1916 WND10 McMahon, W12 Cowler, W12 Al Reich, LND10 (twice), WND10, DND8, and W12 Jack Dillon, WND10 Bert Kenny, WND10 Bob Devere, WND6 and W12 Gunboat Smith, D8 Porky Flynn, WND10 Jim Barry, LND10 (twice) Billy Miske, and L15 Carl Morris; 1917 WND10 Gunboat Smith, WND10 Bob Moha, WND10 Miske, W12 Jack Moran, LND10 Tommy Gibbons, DND10 Bob McAllister, WND10 Bert Kenny, WND10 Bartley Madden, LND10 Harry Greb, D12 Jim Coffey, D12, L12, and W12 Bill Brennan, W12 McMahon, and D12 Madden; 1918 D12 Brennan, WND15 and LND8 Madden, WND6 Coffey, WND8 Weinert, LND6 Harry Greb (though some said Levinsky won), and WND8 Clay Turner.

Prior to Dempsey-Fulton, Levinsky's manager predicted that Fulton would win, for Fred had the best left hand he ever saw - deadly accurate. He said he'd rather let Levinsky meet Dempsey every day of the week than spar Fulton once. He believed Levinsky could beat Dempsey, but not Fulton.

World welterweight champ Jack Britton picked Levinsky over Dempsey.

Light-heavyweight Levinsky, who at times claimed to be the world light heavyweight champion, rarely weighed more than 175-180 pounds, yet had taken on plenty of big men with power without suffering serious injury or any form of knockout. He actually did better with larger men, for he used his speed to jab and get away before they could land. He was great at the "hit and run game." Dempsey was only about 10 pounds heavier. Many believed that Levinsky was a real threat to outpoint Dempsey, given his vastly superior experience, speed, skill, footwork, and durability.[511]

The *New York Sun* said Dempsey was not so sure to beat Levinsky. The Battler was not a hard hitter, but he was clever and shifty enough to make Dempsey hustle, particularly in a short 6-round bout. He was the era's version of James J. Corbett or Philadelphia Jack O'Brien.[512]

On Wednesday November 6, 1918 at Philadelphia's Olympia Club, Jack Dempsey fought Battling Levinsky. A large crowd of 6,000 people attended. Promoter/Referee James Dougherty gave the fighters their instructions.

**Battling Levinsky, promoter and referee James F. Dougherty, Jack Dempsey**

---

[511] *Philadelphia Public Ledger*, November 6, 1918.
[512] *New York Sun*, November 6, 1918.

1st round

At the bell, a determined Dempsey went after Levinsky, who wore a worried smile. Levinsky stepped around trying to find an opening for his famous jabs. Dempsey tried time and again to land a hard body blow, but Levinsky's speed enabled him to avoid most of Dempsey's punches. Jack finally landed a good stiff left to the body. Levinsky replied with jabs, but his punches had little steam. Dempsey crowded him to the ropes. There was a lot of clinching, mostly by Levinsky, who seemed to fear the result should he take any chances. In one clinch, Levinsky left an opening and Dempsey drove his right to the stomach. One said it was when they were separating from a clinch that Dempsey landed. The Battler winced and clinched with a death grip. They had agreed to look after themselves at all times, including when coming out of clinches. Levinsky seemed troubled, and deemed it wise to keep Jack at a distance.

Levinsky jabbed away, but his punches had no noticeable effect. At times, Dempsey walked through the blows and slightly moved his head as he advanced. When Jack got close, Levinsky clinched and held. One said that at the end of the round, Dempsey cornered him and landed a shower of blows to the head and body.

Overall, the round was relatively tame. Levinsky primarily managed to keep away from Dempsey's rushes by using his jab and jumping away out of danger. He seemed able to take care of himself, and few believed he would suffer much injury in a mere 6 rounds. One said Levinsky survived because he boxed like a flash of light, and Dempsey had not fairly warmed up.

2nd round

As soon as the round started, Dempsey attacked and sent a hard left hook to the stomach that hurt, and Levinsky clinched to save himself. Bat backed away and circled the ring, jabbing continually. The Battler took a chance and came in, landing an uppercut to the body as he advanced, his best blow and only really hard punch he landed during the contest. They had a lively rally, but Levinsky got the worst of the mixing and clinched. Dempsey shook him off and went after him hard.

Levinsky would jab and back away, jab and clinch, but Dempsey was determined, and finally forced him into a corner, where he rained blows to his head and body. Levinsky covered up and clinched as best he could to protect himself from the vicious onslaught. The Battler got away and jabbed, but Jack kept coming after him as if the blows were only mosquito bites.

Finally, according to the *Philadelphia Record*, Dempsey drove in a left hook to the body that sent Levinsky to the mat. The *Philadelphia Evening Bulletin* version said that as Levinsky partly turned to step away, a right to the jaw sent him down. The *Philadelphia Public Ledger* said it was a whipping left to the jaw as they were coming out of a clinch, perfectly legal because they agreed to protect themselves at all times, and Levinsky dropped as if shot. The *Philadelphia Press* said it was a left hook to the cheek bone. Clearly,

Dempsey had been pounding away with several blows, any one of which could have caught a particular viewer's eye.

Levinsky got to one knee at about the count of three, and rose at nine, but was wobbly. He immediately clinched and held tenaciously. After breaking, Dempsey was excited and anxious to finish him, but his blows were wild and missed. Jack gathered himself for a decisive punch, and threw his right so hard that when he missed as Levinsky side-stepped, Jack threw himself to the floor. The bell rang. It had been a rough round for Levinsky, who showed a lion's heart to weather the storm.

3rd round

Dempsey never let up for a second, going after him viciously, but in a business-like manner, calm and relentless, driving Levinsky from one side of the ring to the other and back again. The weakening Levinsky was on the defensive all the time. He jabbed and ran, but his blows, even when landed, had no force at all, and Dempsey did not seem to mind them. The Battler often was on the ropes, where Dempsey drove in punishing rights and lefts to his body. Levinsky would escape, move, punch, and try to hold, but he was being pounded and weakened by hard body and head blows.

With about 25 seconds remaining in the round, Dempsey drove a terrific right to the jaw (or behind the ear), possibly followed by a short left hook, and Levinsky's legs stiffened for an instant, gave way, and he crumpled and fell back hard against and partly through the ropes and down to the floor as the rope rebounded. The lower rope mercifully prevented his head from striking the floor. One version said Levinsky hung across the rope, his body half out of the ring and teetering on the sagging rope. Those outside pushed Levinsky off the rope and into the ring, where he fell huddled into a half sitting posture against the ropes. His head fell back.

Two local versions said it was a right, one saying it was a right off a shift. Another version said it was a left hook that traveled six inches, which flashed so fast that even the keen eye of the world's cleverest big fighter could not see it coming. Possibly both landed.

Referee Jimmy Dougherty counted off the fatal ten as Levinsky shook his curly blond head as though in despair. His manager, Dan Morgan, shouted in his ear. He got to one knee by the count of nine, and tried to rise, but fell back, helpless, taking the count for the first time in his career. "He might just as well have counted to a thousand. He was totally unconscious. His head bobbed forward, and he rolled over onto the floor."

The seconds jumped into the ring, and with Dempsey's assistance, they carried the completely collapsed Levinsky to his chair in the corner. It took five minutes to revive him with restoratives. He had to be assisted from the ring to his dressing room, where he collapsed again. Later, tears could be seen flowing down Levinsky's cheeks.

All of the local reporters gave Dempsey great credit for being the first man to knock out or stop Battling Levinsky in over 200 fights. No one else had been able to do so.

The *Philadelphia Inquirer* said Dempsey proved that he was one of the best in the business by doing the major part of the forcing and stopping Battling Levinsky in the 3rd round with a right to the jaw. Prior to the knockout, it was evident that the end was near.

In the first two rounds, Dempsey followed Levinsky all over the ring, trying to connect with his sleep producers. Levinsky moved about, yet still had to take a lacing, for every time that Dempsey landed with a short right or left it shook him.

In the 2nd round, Dempsey nearly had him out from a series of hard body blows which made Levinsky close in and hold on, and he eventually went down for a nine-count.

Levinsky simply could not stop the boring-in Dempsey. His jabs had no effect and did not slow Dempsey's terrific pace, but rather only seemed to enrage Jack, who tore in. Dempsey was exceptionally clever with his left. He used it at every opportunity, and then generally followed with his right to the body with great force. The confident Dempsey had height, reach, and weight advantages.

The *Philadelphia Public Ledger's* Robert Maxwell said Levinsky merely proved that an entire 24-foot ring could be covered in 10 seconds. A wicked left to the jaw in the 2nd round started Levinsky's downfall, when he went down for a seven-count. He managed to weather the storm, but in in the 3rd round, a short right hook that traveled not more than six inches landed behind the ear and put one of the world's cleverest heavyweights on his back for the ten-count.

Dempsey was both clever and hard-hitting, and could box or slug with the best. He used a baffling shift which fooled Levinsky repeatedly, and he landed hard blows with both hands. Jack never let up in his attack, but kept boring in, head forward and arms swinging, sometimes taking a dozen jabs just to land one blow.

Many spectators remained for an hour after the fight, discussing Dempsey's wonderful work. He was called the world's greatest heavyweight.

Levinsky's manager Dan Morgan said,

> Dempsey is a wonderful fighter. He is the most dangerous man I ever have seen, because he has a knockout wallop in either hand. In the first round I thought his left was the best, but when he sent over that right in the third round I found I was mistaken. He certainly surprised me, for I believed Levinsky could stay six rounds with any man in the world.

Even when Levinsky went down in prior fights, he always rose and won the decision. Morgan concluded, "I believe Dempsey can whip Willard."

Philadelphia Jack O'Brien said, "Jack Dempsey can master Willard. Dempsey is a fighter all the way through, and I don't believe Willard could last more than eight rounds with him." He noted that Dempsey could punch hard from any angle, with either hand.

The *Philadelphia Press* said it was a stunning defeat and crushing blow to Levinsky, whose remarkable cleverness had led him to be compared with a prime Jim Corbett. Previously, in over 200 fights, he never had been knocked out, despite meeting a deep field of talent. "But neither Levinsky nor any other heavy-weight could have withstood the grueling battling of the new American heavyweight star. No blow could make the slightest impression upon him. He shook off Levinsky's hardest smashes, jabs and uppercuts as the rhinoceros would the gnats that burrow into his hide." At close quarters, he had a deadly blow, too.

Dempsey was a sensational slugger. He went up against a very clever fellow who gave the best of them a tough contest, but Jack was too much for him. Levinsky had no chance. Against Dempsey's bull-like rushes, his ability to assimilate punishment, and his terrific two-handed punches, all of Levinsky's skill availed him nothing. He was a beaten man from the start. The sporting fraternity understood why Dempsey was claiming championship honors. He was a tiger from bell to bell, a mauler, trying all the time, and could hit like a mule's kick. He convinced Philadelphia fight fans that he was of championship caliber. 6,000 fans acclaimed Dempsey, the killing puncher from California, as the real world's champion.

The press also noted that both Levinsky and Dempsey had offered their services to the National War Fund campaign.

The *Philadelphia Evening Bulletin* said Dempsey had impressed in his first appearance in Philadelphia. He furthered his titular aspirations by stopping Levinsky, "generally recognized as the world's light heavyweight champion." Dempsey's performance silenced the critics who accused him of having been fed "set ups." He outclassed the classy Levinsky throughout.

The *Philadelphia Record* said it was a fast fight all the way. Levinsky was down for the count of nine in the 2nd, and down and out in the 3rd. After Dempsey, claimant for the heavyweight championship, found that Levinsky's blows were not hurting him any, he threw science to the winds and just kept after him, hitting him any place he could, primarily to the stomach, until the Battler was too weak to offer any resistance, and the final blow laid him low.

Dempsey impressed the spectators as being a wonderfully hard hitter and aggressive boxer.

Dempsey Sent Levinsky Home With Everything But a Smile.
By Jerry Doyle.

Those who saw the contest said Willard exercised good judgment in passing him up, for Dempsey appeared to be too good for him. This writer said Dempsey looked like the best heavyweight in the country, and with a little more experience, would be equal to a bout with the world's best.

Adding to the show's drama, the government conducted a raid, looking for slackers. The big crowd was forced to show their draft cards, if they had any, as they passed through the doors. It was quite a long time before the entire audience was dismissed.[513]

A couple days after the fight, the *Philadelphia Press's* sports editor, Thomas D. Richter, said a Dempsey-Willard clash was inevitable. Willard likely received the reports of the Levinsky fight with a blend of fear and pleasure. Fear because he did not care to enter the ring with such a sturdy foe who could deal out terrific punishment. But also pleasure because he could reap a harvest of gold to fight such a man. In Dempsey, "America has found a real fighting heavyweight who will rise to great heights of popularity and so enhance the clash when it comes." Willard loved the dollar, and if offered enough money, would leave his family and farm to fight. A world championship contest against Dempsey would draw a big gate. "The time will soon be here. The war is about to an end. Spring will see sports rushing back in all their glory. The late Spring or the Fourth of July will find the country clamoring for a Willard-Dempsey bout."

Richter predicted that an open-air contest would bring Willard a fortune, a reasonable sum to Dempsey, motion picture money for each, and the title to Dempsey. Willard had been out of the ring too long to be at his best, which he needed to be in order to beat a man like Dempsey.

Ed Kane, manager of Mike and Tom Gibbons, said,

> I would pick Dempsey to beat Willard next Summer, for I do not think that Willard will ever be fast enough or conditioned enough to land effectively on Dempsey. That young man will punish him so hard in the early rounds that Willard's body will never stand the strain. I have seen some of Dempsey's other big fights, and he gets better, hits harder, and is faster every day.

The usual press mantra continued, that Willard had to fight Dempsey or retire. Dempsey's power reminded old-timers of Sullivan and Fitzsimmons.

The *Philadelphia Inquirer* said despite Levinsky's more than 200 fights of experience, he simply was overwhelmed. Dempsey was so powerful and talented, and the current crop of heavies so mediocre, that "there is hardly a white boxer who is in his class at all."[514]

It was reported that Dempsey had been paid $6,325 for the contest, while Levinsky was paid $2,875. The gross receipts amounted to $11,500, which was very good money for a 6-round no decision contest. Dempsey was paid 35% to Levinsky's 25% of the gross.[515]

Unfortunately, on the same date as Dempsey-Levinsky, Battling Jim Johnson died of the Spanish flu. He was only 31 years old. Former champ Tommy Burns was hospitalized as a result of the flu, but survived. Jim Jeffries became very ill, but recovered as well.

---

[513] *Philadelphia Inquirer, Philadelphia Evening Public Ledger, Philadelphia Press, Philadelphia Evening Bulletin, Philadelphia Record,* all November 7, 1918.
[514] *Philadelphia Inquirer,* November 9, 11, 1918.
[515] *Scranton Republican,* November 14, 1918.

CHAPTER 19

# The Color Line in a New Era

On November 11, 1918, the participants of the world war signed an armistice pausing (but essentially ending) the remaining fighting on the Western Front, while final peace settlement negotiations were ongoing. Germany agreed to withdraw its troops and surrender aircraft, warships, and military material. Two days earlier, German Kaiser Wilhelm II had abdicated. President Woodrow Wilson declared to Congress, "The war thus comes to an end, for, having accepted these terms of armistice, it will be impossible for the German command to renew it." Essentially, the war was over, though legally and formally it did not end until later.

Throughout the world, 9 million combatants and 7 million civilians had died, and 21 million were wounded. More than 70 million had participated. Some might theorize that the Spanish flu had helped bring the war to an end. The virus was killing off soldiers at a faster rate than combat did. However, the war also had helped spread the disease.

The *Philadelphia Press's* sports editor, Thomas D. Richter, wanted to see Jack Dempsey fight Harry Wills:

> But when considering an opponent for Dempsey let's inject a little of the color-line stuff into the argument. If Dempsey wants a real, stiff fight in the heavyweight class, before meeting Willard, he will have to go over into the colored division to get it.
>
> Henry [sic] Wills, a gigantic colored man from Dempsey's own State, is the only man who looks big enough, strong enough, and fast and clever enough to give the slugging white man half an argument. I have seen Wills in action three times, and he is about the smoothest-acting big piece of flesh it ever has been my fortune to look upon.
>
> Wills stands six feet four inches in height, tops Dempsey's weight by twenty pounds, is fast on his feet, keeps his head out of danger, has two mighty quick hands, and is a splendid two-handed boxer. He hits a pretty stiff punch, too, when he calls it forth. Altogether he would make Dempsey travel over any distance to finish him. Why draw the color line in a case like this?[516]

Promoters were trying to make a match between Dempsey and Wills. "If Dempsey takes that match he will not be getting in so very easy, for Wills is about the best of the big fellows, either white or black."[517]

---

[516] *Philadelphia Press*, November 8, 1918.
[517] *Philadelphia Inquirer, Philadelphia Public Ledger*, November 16, 1918.

Dempsey had fought several lesser-known blacks on the way up, but had not fought any black fighter since John Lester Johnson in 1916, and none since Kearns had taken over his management. Early on in his management of Dempsey's career, in September 1917 Kearns said they did not draw the color line, but by July 1918, that position had changed. In late September/early October 1918, Kearns confirmed that he was not keen on matching Dempsey with black fighters unless the public desired it. He did not feel it necessary to cross the line, for Dempsey was headed towards the crown without fighting black fighters.

Dempsey was scheduled to box in a War Fund show at Madison Square Garden on November 16, volunteering his services. As of the 13th, promoter Jim Coffroth had not yet found a suitable opponent. Many did not want to step into the ring with Dempsey, given his knockout power.

Initially, Dempsey allegedly had said that he would box anyone in the world, regardless of color. However, the *New York Evening World* reported,

> Joe Jeannette, the colored heavyweight, has expressed a desire to meet Jack, but Jack may be pardoned for not wanting to take him on. Like Willard, Dempsey doesn't want to create a precedent of fighting a colored man. If he did now he might later be asked to meet Harry Wills or some others of the colored fighters after he succeeds Willard as the champion. He isn't afraid of any of them and possibly would beat them as easily as he would a white contender. It is simply a matter of principle with him.[518]

The *New York Evening Telegram's* Hyatt Daab said,

> Although Dempsey in the past has asserted he did not object to boxing negro pugilists, it is understood that he has declined to meet Joe Jeannette in the Garden because such a match would establish a precedent he has no desire to set. In other words, Dempsey has drawn the color line, and at present there is a meager chance of his altering his stand.

Joe Jeannette said, "I have offered to box Dempsey any number of rounds, but he pays no attention to me. I am confident I can beat him."[519]

The *Buffalo Enquirer* said Dempsey previously had announced that he would meet anyone they cared to select for him. Jeannette declared his willingness, but "Jack thereupon immediately drew the color line."[520]

On the day of the event, the *New York Evening World* advertised that Dempsey was the headliner at the Garden's boxing show in aid of

---

[518] *New York Tribune, Brooklyn Daily Times, New York Evening World*, November 13, 1918.
[519] *New York Evening Telegram*, November 13, 1918.
[520] *Buffalo Enquirer*, November 14, 1918.

the United War Work Fund. He was scheduled to box Joe Bonds, whom Jim Coffey recently could not stop. Dempsey had won a 10-round decision over Bonds back in 1916, so he seemed to be a suitable foe.[521]

On Saturday November 16, 1918 at Madison Square Garden in New York City, Jack Dempsey was supposed to box Joe Bonds in one of the war-fund charity bouts. 6,000 or 8,000 fans contributed some $9,000 or $17,000 (depending on the source) to the war charity, United War Work Campaign Fund.

However, despite the fact that Bonds was in the arena, it was Joe Jeannette who climbed into the ring, much to the surprise of Kearns and Dempsey, who were in the ring and had expected Bonds. After some discussion, Dempsey and Kearns left.

The *Brooklyn Daily Times* said, "Dempsey promptly and positively refused to box the black. He said he had agreed to meet a white man, not a negro, against whom he is prejudiced." The crowd hooted and howled, not understanding why Bonds had not entered to box, for he was in the building. "The crowd thought double crossing had been indulged in which no doubt it was the case."

The *Brooklyn Citizen* also noted that Dempsey drew the color line and refused to box with Jeannette or Kid Norfolk. White Jack Britton, welter champ, offered to box him instead, but Jack declined that offer as well, refusing to box anyone but Bonds, and jumped out of the ring to some abuse. Kearns and Dempsey did not appreciate the shenanigans.

However, two days later, William Granger reported that Dempsey was willing and even anxious to fight Jeannette to stop the crowd's booing, but Kearns believed it was a put-up job, and refused to allow it.

"Rice," writing for the *Brooklyn Daily Eagle*, said Dempsey refused to appear against any boxer other than Bonds, which announcement received hoots and cat calls. Bonds claimed an accident, which caused a concussion, or so they said. Jack Kearns refused to allow his man to meet Jeannette.

The *New York Herald* quoted Kearns as saying, "Get him out, for we will not meet a negro." Bonds claimed illness.

The *Brooklyn Daily Standard Union* claimed that the crowd was *with* the color-line-drawing Dempsey, "and yelled for the police to throw the negroes out."

The *St. Louis Post-Dispatch* reported that Kearns said Dempsey was prepared to box any WHITE man in the world.[522]

The *New York World*'s Vincent Treanor said, "Dempsey has been on record for some time as drawing the color line, and everybody who follows sporting world doings knows this." Whether he had a right to do so was "neither here nor there." The fact remained that "Dempsey, like Willard, has said he will not fight another colored man. To have gone on with Jeannette would have created a precedent which ultimately might lead to

---

[521] *New York Evening World*, November 16, 1918.
[522] *Brooklyn Citizen, Brooklyn Daily Eagle, New York Herald, Brooklyn Standard Union, St. Louis Post-Dispatch*, November 17, 1918; *Brooklyn Citizen*, November 18, 1918.

another Jack Johnson, and everybody knows what a knock Johnson was to the gloved sport." Treanor said Bonds was the one who should be censored for running out on the match. Dempsey was ready and willing to go through with his part of the contract to box Bonds for free, and furthermore, contributed $500 of his own money to the fund, so the attempt to belittle him should not be taken seriously.

However, Dan Morgan said Dempsey showed the white feather, for it did not matter who he boxed since it was for charity, and Dempsey had fought colored men before, so there was no reason not to do so again.[523]

Morgan told the *Brooklyn Daily Standard Union* that Bonds claimed to have a bruise on his head and was in no condition to fight. Morgan suggested Jeannette as a substitute to referee Bill Brown, who agreed that Joe would make a good opponent. Morgan then told Joe to go into the ring. "In justice to Dempsey I wish to say that I believe in my heart that he would have gone on with Jeannette had not his manager, Jack Kearns, refused to permit him to do so."[524]

Jeannette told the *Hudson Dispatch*, November 19, 1918, that he had been misled into believing that the Dempsey side had agreed to the match, and did not realize Dempsey was being "framed." When Joe asked Jack whether he wanted to fight, Dempsey told him that it was up to his manager.

This newspaper's writer said Dempsey had lost a "golden opportunity" to solidify himself with the fans and show "that he feared no man."

> In view of the gallantry of the American Negroes under General Pershing in France, the sporting public no longer recognizes the drawing of the color line in pugilism. Dempsey volunteered his services for the United War Work Campaign, which doesn't discriminate between white and black fighters in our victorious Expeditionary Force. Subsequently Dempsey's refusal to box Jennette because of the latter's color didn't appeal to the crowd that went to the Garden to help the war charities.

Promoter Jim Coffroth said some folks tried to trick Dempsey into fighting Jeannette. He was supposed to box for war fund charities against Joe Bonds, but when he was in the ring ready to fight, Joe Jeannette entered instead. Dempsey was willing to fight him, but promoter Coffroth thought the trick being used was so unfair that he put it to the newsmen at ringside, and they agreed that Jeannette should not be permitted to box, because of the methods used. Jim also said that Dempsey made a $500 donation toward the fund nevertheless. Dempsey and Kearns then left for Philadelphia to box Dan Porky Flynn in two days.[525]

However, the *Philadelphia Inquirer* reported that Dempsey refused to box Jeannette when he found him in the opposite corner, and turned tail. Some saw this as Dempsey only seeking easy marks, not wanting to take any

---

[523] *New York Evening World*, November 18, 1918.
[524] *Brooklyn Daily Standard Union*, November 18, 1918.
[525] *Philadelphia Public Ledger*, November 18, 1918.

chances, and drawing the color line despite his prior claims that he did not draw the line.

The *Inquirer* said Dempsey should have met old Joe Jeannette. Kearns refused to allow his fighter to box him. True, Jeannette was substituted for Bonds maliciously as a result of a trick (Bonds was present). Still, Dempsey could have fought the 37-year-old and added to his reputation. Technically, Dempsey and Kearns were in the right, for they had agreed to fight Bonds, not Jeannette.[526]

The *New York Tribune* said Dempsey's honor should in no way be impaired though the refusal to box Jeannette. "No man of sense can impute to the refusal a grain of personal cowardice. Jeanette, a resurrected ghost of a once powerful fighting machine, hit the down grade years and years ago." This author said it would be a pity and a shame to allow a real battle between the two, given where Jeannette was in his career.

> Dempsey refused not through fear but through principle. He felt himself being imposed upon. And under the circumstances he would have shown lack of character to proceed. Dempsey made no stipulation with the promoters as to the selection of his opponent, save that he drew the color line. The promoters selected Joe Bonds, and so advertised. Bonds was on hand to fulfill his engagement – ready, in fact, when Jeanette and the manipulators behind him forestalled the white man in the ring. There are those who say that Bonds had earlier been influenced, if not bribed, to help 'frame' Dempsey. His story to writers at the ringside bore out the suggestion.

Apparently, Dan Morgan offered Bonds $100 to step aside and claim illness that evening, to allow Jeannette to step in and surprise Dempsey. This article called it a despicable act of treachery by Morgan, manager of Battling Levinsky, jealous of Dempsey's success and victory over his man, and Dan McKetrick, Jeannette's manager. As a result, the public did not get to see Dempsey box. Dempsey was a victim as well, for he had contributed $500 to the fund.

> Each follower of boxing is entitled to his personal opinion as to the sportsmanship of the color line in pugilism. But the boon has been granted to white champions of all classes in all modern times. Dempsey, it may be argued, is not a champion. But he is the logical successor to Jess Willard.

> It is not so long ago that sportdom was clamoring loudly for some white hope to remove from pugilism that abomination and disgrace, heavyweight champion Jack Johnson, whose behavior was a stench and an eyesore to whites and negroes alike. No one criticized the conqueror, Willard, for drawing the color line.

> It was not mere matter of facing Jeanette that confronted Dempsey. Had he put up his hands against the colored man he could not have

---

[526] *Philadelphia Inquirer*, November 18, 19, 1918.

refused satisfaction to Harry Wills, Sam Langford, Kid Norfolk and other colored heavyweights.[527]

The *Buffalo Evening News* wrote that there seemed to be "a dark conspiracy on the part of the white managers of black boxers to force Jack Dempsey to jump the color line which he and his manager, Jack Kearns, had clearly drawn since Dempsey loomed as a likely title holder." Dan McKetrick was behind it. Bonds must have been in on it. He did not enter the ring, but Jeannette did, who tried to taunt Dempsey into fighting him. Dempsey obeyed his manager Kearns, who refused.

> One cannot very well blame Dempsey. He had agreed to meet any white man, and had himself contributed $500 to the receipts of the show. Certainly old Joe Jeannette was no match for him anyhow, and besides that Jeannette's opponent for the evening was Kid Norfolk, who was on hand and ready, but seems to have been spirited away to help force the issue against Dempsey. If Dan McKitrick [sic] took advantage of a war work fund show to exploit a string of negro boxers he deserves to lose and ought to be ashamed of himself.

No one believed that Jim Coffroth or Charley Harvey had any inkling of what was going to happen. They both were surprised and disgusted, as was the crowd.[528]

The black-owned *Chicago Defender* offered a different perspective, saying Dempsey had shown a yellow streak in refusing to meet Jeannette, "giving the same old alibi 'Color line.'" Cat-calls and yells broke loose. Kearns announced that Dempsey would box any *white* man in the world, explicitly drawing the color line. Jeannette dared him to fight, but Jack ignored the challenge. Kearns responded, "Get him out, for we will not meet a Negro." Finally, Dempsey decided to leave.[529]

The *Brooklyn Daily Eagle's* Rice said there was some talk of Dempsey enlisting in the Navy, and then boxing in an overseas British exhibition for the government, which Rice believed was a "cheap scheme" that the government "did not for a moment fall for," given the late date. "Dempsey carefully kept out of the Navy, Army, and everything else when there was a first-class war in full blast." Rice said it would be an insult to allow him to join up at this time, only to receive a choice assignment. His case was "made all the more disgraceful by his failure to take on Joe Jeannette...when the bouts for the United War Work drive were held." Jeannette's staged entry was designed to make him look foolish, and it was successful, at least to some degree.

Yet, Rice was not in general a supporter of mixed-race bouts, and actually supported their banishment.

> Personally, we do not believe in mixed bouts. It is not a question of race prejudice against the colored friend and brother. Such bouts do

---

[527] *New York Tribune*, November 19, 1918.
[528] *Buffalo Evening News*, November 19, 1918.
[529] *Chicago Defender*, November 30, 1918.

stir up race feeling, even when the negro is such a popular and highly esteemed performer as the late George Dixon, Joe Gans or Peter Jackson, or Jeannette, who is universally liked by white men. If it were possible, and for a long time the New York State Boxing Commission made it possible, we would prevent mixed bouts as a matter of expediency – but if we had been W. H. (Jack) Dempsey on the night of November 16, 1918, we would have mingled six rounds or less with Joe Jeannette, just to show our heart was in the right place, and the place for the heart was to be behind the United War Work drive.[530]

A couple weeks later, on December 2, 1918, the *New York Evening Telegram's* Hyatt Daab opined that there was no place in boxing for the pugilist who drew the color line. Black soldiers and sailors had fought just as heroically as whites to make the world safe. No boxer, whether title holder or near champion, should employ the color line against formidable black challengers. It was problematic for Dempsey to decline to box Jeannette, potentially because he feared to meet the group of "Negro heavyweights who have been stalking his trail." Daab believed that drawing the line would cause Dempsey's popularity to wane. He had fought blacks before, and should continue to meet all comers.

> Persons who profess to know assert that personally Dempsey had no objection to boxing Negroes, and that had it not been for Jack Kearns, his manager, he would have boxed Jeannette Saturday night. All of which may be true.
>
> The public, however, is interested only in Jack Dempsey. Should he persist in observing the 'color' line the public will condemn him as he deserves. The deluge of catcalls and jeers that swept the Garden as he and his retinue slunk out of the arena last Saturday night should be sufficient warning.

Several writers wanted to see fair competition open to all, and for black fighters and their conduct to be judged on their own individual merits, particularly given that many blacks had fought valiantly for the country in the war.

However, others said drawing the color line would have no impact, or only a negligible impact on Dempsey's popularity. Baseball, the most popular American team sport, did not allow any blacks to play, and that drew little to no criticism. Those who remembered Jack Johnson and all the tumult, controversy, riots, and legal troubles and impediments associated with him were perfectly content and happy to see black fighters barred from elite competition with top whites, particularly in the heavyweight division.

There would be an ongoing tension and battle between these two perspectives, but overall, the segregationist position ultimately wound up having the edge in this era.

---

[530] *Brooklyn Daily Eagle*, November 18, 1918.

CHAPTER 20

# Rematches

On November 16, 1918 in San Francisco, Fred Fulton dominated and clearly won a 4-round decision over Willie Meehan, whose eye was closed and cut and mouth badly bleeding as a result of the awful lacing. By defeating the man who had won a 4-round decision over Dempsey, Fulton believed that put him in line for contention again, and for a potential rematch with Dempsey. Naturally, the result hurt Meehan's standing.[531]

Back again in Philadelphia, just twelve days after the Levinsky fight, and two days after the Madison Square Garden war fund benefit debacle, Dan "Porky" Flynn was given the chance to avenge his July 1918 1st round knockout loss to Dempsey. Porky Flynn had fought Fulton four times, twice going the distance. He was a willing battler with wonderful stamina. He could take punishment and deliver it. In their 20-round bout, Flynn dropped Fulton twice, but lost the decision. The local *Philadelphia Public Ledger* claimed that Flynn was even with Fulton in a 10-round bout in St. Paul. Flynn was not afraid of hard punchers. Plus, he was a very experienced veteran with 97 known fights.

The *World* reported that Flynn was guaranteed $500 for the contest, scheduled for 6 rounds.[532]

On Monday November 18, 1918 in Philadelphia, at the Olympia, Jack Dempsey fought a rematch with Dan "Porky" Flynn. Lew Grimson refereed. Flynn looked hog fat, and clearly was heavier than Dempsey.

When the fight began, Flynn found Dempsey immediately gliding and boring in, swinging both hands to the body. Jack fired a powerful straight left to the nose and followed with a stiff left hook on the chin and/or to the heart (depending on the version) that decked Dan to his knees, though he rose in an instant. One claimed that Dempsey held him up and prevented him from going down fully as he fell sideways, grabbing him under the armpits so that only Dan's glove touched the floor. "Had Dempsey shot in another punch to the stomach, as he might have done, he would have had a five-second knockout on his record." Some did not call this a knockdown.

---

[531] *San Francisco Examiner, San Francisco Chronicle*, November 17, 1918; *Philadelphia Inquirer*, November 20, 1918.
[532] *Philadelphia Public Ledger, New York Evening*, November 16, 1918.

Dempsey chased Flynn, then jostled and wrestled with him, trying to get home a punch. The *Philadelphia Public Ledger* mentioned a knockdown that several other local papers did not, saying that Dan ran into a right on his whiskers which lifted him from his feet and sent him backwards to the ground.

Later in the round, Dempsey crowded and shoved Flynn along one side of the ring, and, standing with legs wide apart and his body swinging from side to side as if on hinges at the waist line, sunk a powerful left hook into the stomach and then swish went the right in the shortest possible drive to the jaw and Flynn went flying backward through the ropes crashing onto the press stand and almost to the floor, landing on the heads of those in the press seats. "Dempsey evidently likes to knock his opponents into the laps of the newspaper men." Some claimed that Dempsey rushed and half-punched and half-shoved him either through or over the ropes and down.

Dan later complained that his back had been hurt when he struck the ropes and went through them and then landed hard. Regardless, the press agreed that it made no difference in the result.

Flynn rose and re-entered the ring. According to the *Public Ledger*, Dempsey nailed him with his mighty right, and Dan dove down. His head was resting on the lower rope while referee Lew Grimson counted to ten.

The *Philadelphia Inquirer* said Dempsey had whipped over a left to end it.

The *Philadelphia Evening Bulletin* version said that after being assisted back into the ring again, Dempsey forced Flynn along the ropes and landed a half-dozen rights and lefts to the jaw, until a short choppy left on the side of the jaw sent Porky down with his head resting on the lower rope.

The *Philadelphia Press* account by Thomas D. Richter said that when helped back into the ring, Flynn had a broad welt across his kidneys where he fell. The rough-hitting Dempsey grimly rushed him, buffeted him about for 20 seconds, and then in his corner feinted with the right, stepped in close, and ripped the finishing left to the jaw. Flynn's head traveled to the ground faster than his heels did; his head landing on the lower rope and his body crashing down with a thud. His eyes closed and his body was inert as Referee Grimson tolled off the 10 seconds.

The *Philadelphia Record* version said that after Flynn had gotten back on the platform, Dempsey forced him to the opposite corner of the ring and rained blows on his head and body. He then worked Porky over to the other side and battered him for a while on the ropes. Flynn managed to get away for a second or so, with Jack right after him. Dempsey shoved him back into a corner, where he nailed him several times on the head and jaw, sending him down.

Vincent Treanor, who was present on behalf of the *New York World*, said that after going through the ropes, Flynn looked gone, but struggled to his feet. He tried to fight back, and covered his face. Dempsey tried to pry his defense apart but couldn't, so he hooked another left into the stomach. Flynn moved away, but Dempsey glided after him with uncanny speed, maneuvered and then fired a murderous left to the stomach, followed by a right to the chin, very effectively, and Flynn went over backward. His head hit the bottom ropes and bounced off to the floor. He was out, and the count was not necessary.

The majority of accounts said it was over at 2 minutes 16 seconds of the 1st round. Newsmen described anywhere from two to four knockdowns.

Chief Bender, Flynn's second, leaped across the ring and lifted the beaten man from the floor. Dempsey helped him carry Flynn to his corner. Bender shook him and finally managed to bring Porky back from the land of dreams.

*Philadelphia Public Ledger* writer Robert Maxwell suspected that Flynn took a dive. Flynn was scared to death, and did not want to take punishment. He pawed and put up no opposition. Maxwell said Dempsey had his foes licked before he even fought them.

Some reporters occasionally believed that Dempsey's opponents were taking dives, in part because he dropped them with such ease, and his blows often did not appear to be all that powerful. However, some fighters throughout history simply had freakish power. Sullivan, Fitzsimmons, and Jeffries were like that as well, able to deck foes with short, compact, relaxed, easy blows that had a lot of deceptive power.

The *Philadelphia Inquirer* said Flynn was outclassed, and gave a sorry exhibition, hardly laying a glove on Dempsey, who started quickly in order to make an early exit. Jack was very workmanlike in his execution.

The *Philadelphia Evening Bulletin* said Flynn was very porky and soft. It appeared that there was some sort of gentleman's agreement. Flynn acted like a sacrificial lamb, and hardly could wait for Dempsey to finish the job. From the start, he left himself open to attack. Dempsey jostled him around the ring. This writer believed that Flynn was far from unconscious, and could have risen before ten had he desired.

The *Philadelphia Press*'s Thomas D. Richter said it was Dempsey's second knockout at the Olympia in two weeks. Porky Flynn once was a mighty capable heavyweight, but had grown slow of hand and foot, and was easy for Dempsey. He only was able to keep away for a couple of minutes. Flynn never had a chance from the start, and Dempsey seemed to realize it. He did not use the wild-bull rushing tactics that he did against Levinsky, though he strove with might to put over the finishing punch from the start. Flynn's efforts to box included a few futile passes, a clinch or two, and a couple of wild uppercuts that missed by a lot. The rest of the time he resorted to footwork to keep out of trouble.

To finish the fight, Dempsey caught him with the same terrible short-arm left clip to the jaw that toppled Levinsky and had sent every other contender to dreamland, "and which eventually will make him monarch and unquestioned of his class." It was a terrible punch, and a clean knockout in a workmanlike performance.

The bout not only meant another step up the championship ladder for Dempsey, but likewise marked an epoch in boxing in the country, for the sport had obtained such world-wide recognition "for its inherently good qualities since this war has engulfed the world" that it even brought into the ring that evening the president of a big college, Villanova, who also was a Catholic clergyman. He gave a speech saying that wholesome sports like boxing were the best means of keeping the mind clean and healthy. Then several women wearing the dark blue uniforms of a war relief society collected donations for the orphans of French soldiers killed in the war.[533]

The *Philadelphia Record* said the New Englander Flynn had little chance to defend himself from the savage onslaught. The Boston man was down and out in Dempsey's corner after having been battered from one side of the ring to the other and once knocked through the ropes in his own corner.

It was fast while it lasted, but it was no contest. Dempsey gave Flynn no time to rest, sailing right into him like John L. Sullivan. He slammed in left and right to the head, jaw, ribs, and stomach. Although Porky was hog fat, "the best day he ever saw he would have been no match for the powerful Dempsey, who was in fine condition and determined to end the bout as soon as possible." Flynn did not have the necessary defense. His face wore the signs of his many fistic encounters, including a flattened nose. He could take the punches of most, but not Dempsey's brand of power.

The *New York Evening World's* Vincent Treanor said that after seeing Dempsey knock out Boston's ponderous Porky Flynn in less than 1 round, one could understand why Willard was hiding away on his Kansas farm or in his Texas oil works. "Dempsey certainly proved that as a puncher and quick finisher he is one of the best men the ring ever knew. His punches, short as any one ever saw, rarely miss the mark he aims them at. He is the pugilistic sharp shooter of the age."

Flynn normally was clever, and had fought a lot of good men, once going the 20-round limit with Fulton. He also had gone the distance with men like Joe Jeannette (twice) and Kid Norfolk. In two separate fights, Flynn had been unable to get out the 1st round with Dempsey. He never had a chance. He tried to box, but it was useless, and his generalship was no good to him after the initial left hook to the chin had stung him. Without any showy footwork, Dempsey was on top of him every second.

In his free time, Dempsey liked to hang out with kids, eat pie, and drink milk.

It was announced that a mere ten days later, in Philadelphia on Thanksgiving afternoon, Dempsey and Billy Miske would be fighting a rematch.[534]

Although a slight majority of ringside reporters had said Dempsey beat Miske in their 10-round no decision contest back in May of that year, several said the contest was a draw. Miske was known as one of the toughest, gamest, most durable, quick and skillful fighters in the business.

---

[533] Charles Albert "Chief" Bender, the great Indian pitcher, who would second Flynn that evening, bid $110 for a box seat, and received applause, but was outbid by politician Tommy Sheehan, who had insisted that his son participate in amateur boxing, with a $200 bid. Bender then purchased 100 seats for $200.

[534] *Philadelphia Evening Public Ledger, Philadelphia Inquirer, Philadelphia Evening Bulletin, Philadelphia Press, Philadelphia Record*, November 19, 1918; *New York Evening World*, November 18, 1918.

One reporter said Miske was a hard man to hit solidly, and he had an iron jaw even when hit well. Dempsey too was utterly indifferent to wallops and displayed extreme coolness at all times. He was a safe bet against any man because he did not worry or hurry at any time.[535]

Since fighting Dempsey in May 1918, Miske's record included: 1918 D4 Willie Meehan, W4 KO Kruvosky, WND8 Gunboat Smith, WND8 Bartley Madden, W/DND10 Harry Greb[536], and WND6 Tom McMahon.

The 24-year-old 66-fight veteran Miske, who stood six feet tall and weighed 178 pounds, said he was not afraid of Dempsey. He beat him once before and could do it again. He feared no one, and no one could stop him. He had canceled a prior rematch with Dempsey owing to illness, and a writer had misquoted him as saying that Dempsey would knock him out. What he actually said was that given his illness, if he fought Dempsey in such poor physical condition he would be knocked out. He was feeling great now, and was ready. "I have no reason to fear him. I am just as big a man physically and believe I am just a little bit more clever. I know Dempsey hits well; in fact, I guess he can hit harder, but he has to land before he can hurt me." "I boxed Dempsey ten rounds last spring and many papers gave me the decision.

---

[535] *Kansas City Post*, May 23, 1918.
[536] The *Pittsburg Press's* Jim Jab said 159-pound Greb was beaten, and 174-pound Miske dominated the last 4 rounds, almost putting him out.

The *Pittsburgh Gazette Times'* Richard Guy said Miske outpunched Greb. The local middleweight had a lead up to the 6th, when Miske opened up an attack of solid right wallops. "So terrific was the onslaught of the big boy from the Northwest that he overcame a lead which the Pittsburgher had, mainly through superior speed, and speed alone, that he not only beat down the advantage but almost caused Greb to succumb to his hard right hand punches. Greb was well-nigh all in at the end of the fight. ... Miske was unscathed. It was the worst beating Greb has experienced..." This paper said Miske weighed around 190 pounds.

The *Pittsburgh Daily Post's* Florent Gibson said Miske opened a cut over Harry's eye, turning the tide late and giving Greb his hardest battle. Greb barely held the advantage, 5 rounds to 3, with 2 even. The sensational blows were landed by Miske, but Greb tallied up enough of a lead early on with his volume to have a slim advantage at the end.

Writing for the same newspaper, Harry Keck scored it 6 Greb, 3 Miske, and 1 even. Greb threw and landed more, but Miske landed cleaner, harder, and more effectively, giving Greb a beating in the last two rounds, cutting his eye. He came close to evening up the affair with his finish, but it was Greb's fight by a shade on his good early lead.

Make no mistake, I made Dempsey work every minute." When asked about Dempsey's impressive performance against Levinsky, Billy said Levinsky was not the same man that he was when he fought him. Miske lost a 1917 10-round no decision to Levinsky.[537]

To prepare, Miske sparred with hard-hitting burly colored fighter Jack Thompson. Dempsey sparred with black Jamaica Kid (14-4-3 record).[538]

The *Philadelphia Inquirer* said both Dempsey and Miske were contenders to the title. Miske was the toughest lad Dempsey ever had met. He was a demon for punishment and also could hand it out.[539]

BILLY MISKE

Willie Meehan, who was coming off a clear loss to Fred Fulton, and had fought Miske to a 4-round draw, said he wanted to fight the winner.

> I know I can lick either one of them. You know I fought 'em both on the coast and was the winner. You know, I think I'm too fast for them. They are good, strong fellows, but to hurt you they have to get set to punch. Now let me tell you gents right here that no guy living can beat me that can't think fast. If Miske or Dempsey ever got set and then landed it would be good-night and good-day for me. But I'm too clever for them, that's all; too clever.

When asked to scout the upcoming bout, Meehan said,

> Dempsey is the better hitter. He's a deadly puncher. He's got it all over Miske when it comes to hitting. Miske is just a little cleverer. He knows how to dodge punches. He hooks well and handles himself nicely. However, both have a similar style. It ought to be a hard fight, but you know, I can lick 'em both.

---

[537] *Philadelphia Public Ledger*, November 21, 1918.
[538] *Philadelphia Inquirer*, November 22, 1918; *Philadelphia Public Ledger*, November 25, 1918.
[539] *Philadelphia Inquirer*, November 25, 1918.

News writers were saying that no one would be surprised if the bout lasted the full 6 rounds, given Miske's skill and toughness, though Dempsey possibly could land a haymaker and stop him. His knockout record made him the most feared man in the ring. Some foes were licked even before they entered the ring with him. His scowl and reputation were enough to induce fear, let alone his punch. However, Miske gave a good account of himself over 10 rounds previously, so he wasn't afraid, and knew what to expect.

JACK DEMPSEY

WILLIE MISKE

WILLIE MEEHAN
Headliners at tomorrow's Olympia show. Meehan is here to challenge Miske-Dempsey winner

The *Philadelphia Evening Public Ledger* said Miske was the one man capable of making Dempsey fight, and would be Jack's first real test in the city. "If Miske fails, then Dempsey must be accorded the recognition he merits. He has cleaned up the heavyweight division, and the only man standing in his way for titular honors is Jess Willard."[540]

After his workout on November 27, the day before the bout, Miske stepped on the scales at 179 pounds. After Dempsey's light training at Long Branch (likely with Jimmy De Forest), he tipped the beams at 184 pounds, according to his manager.

Miske said, "I met him once before and have a very good line on his style. He is a great hitter, but it will take more than hitting to win this scrap. You know you can't win if you don't land, and I don't expect Dempsey to connect. I'm not a weakling, and you can count on me to be there at the finish."[541]

---

[540] *Philadelphia Public Ledger*, November 27, 28, 1918.
[541] *Philadelphia Inquirer*, November 28, 1918.

> **OLYMPIA A. A.** Broad and Bainbridge
> Harry Edwards, Mgr.
> **THANKSGIVING AFTERNOON. NOV. 28**
> Doors Open 1.30. First Bout 2.30
> **SIX BOUTS—WORLD'S BEST MEN**
>
> ## Jack Dempsey vs. Billy Miske
> World's Champion          St. Paul
> ## Sam Langford vs. Jeff Clark
> ## Jack Thompson vs. Jamaica Kid
> Eddie Welsh vs. Steve Morris
> Sammy Freedman vs. Eddie Denny
> Kid Porter vs. Dick Wells
> Prices—Admission $1; Reservations $2 & $3

On Thanksgiving afternoon, Thursday November 28, 1918 in Philadelphia, at the Olympia Athletic Club on South Broad Street, before a "record crowd" of 6,000, in his third fight in the month of November (Levinsky, Flynn, Miske), Jack Dempsey fought Billy Miske in a rematch, in a scheduled 6-round no decision bout. The *Philadelphia Evening Public Ledger*'s James Carolan said boxing had come back. The Olympia was jammed packed to the doors, taking up all available space. The bout generated in the neighborhood of $10,000. Hundreds were turned away from the door of the hall, once capacity was reached. Many stood outside in the rain listening to the shouts inside.

On the undercard earlier that afternoon, hulking colored heavyweight Jack Thompson fought coal-black colored light heavy Jamaica Kid (real name Bob Buckley), whom Thompson outweighed by 20 or 40 pounds (depending on the source). Especial interest was taken in the bout, for Thompson had been Miske's sparring partner, and the Jamaica Kid Dempsey's sparring partner, helping them to prepare for the main event. The Jamaica Kid was ahead on points through the first 4 rounds, outboxing and outfighting him, but in the 5th round, the much larger and very durable Thompson knocked him out cold with a single powerful right to the jaw. It took five minutes to revive the Kid with an ammonia bottle under his nose. Some took this as an ill-omen for Dempsey.

Black Jeff Clark, the Fighting Ghost, who once had been a Dempsey sparring partner, dropped Sam Langford, the Boston Tar Baby, in the 1st round with a right to the chin, and won the rest of the way, jabbing well and landing short right uppercuts, winning the 6-round no decision. Langford showed just how far he had slipped from the fighter he once was. His punching was hard, but no longer as snappy or as deadly; he was slower, and fat, carrying 30 extra pounds.

In the main event, in the 1st round, Dempsey rushed from his corner and almost toppled Miske with a quick left to the ear. Miske clinched, and on the break clipped Dempsey on the jaw with his right. Dempsey bore in, but soon found Miske's plan of campaign. Billy parried the blows and grappled. He held in such fashion that, strive as he would, Dempsey could not land a big punch. Any time he sensed danger; Billy grabbed.

After much sparring and feeling out by both, Miske swung a light left to the head, and Dempsey retaliated with a right and left to the body, his usual method of fighting. Miske fired left and right to the face, and Dempsey worked in close to a clinch. Dempsey swung a hard left to Miske's chin as the round ended.

In the 2nd round, they mostly fought up close. The aggressive Dempsey worked in and hurt Miske with a right to the body. Miske swung his right to the chin in close, but Dempsey came back with a hard right that caused Billy to rush in to clinch. There was frequent clinching in this round, and the crowd hooted a bit.

The 3rd round began with Dempsey firing a left and right to the face, forcing Billy back. Miske fired a hard right to the body that caused the fans to cheer. Most were pulling for the underdog Miske. There was more clinching in this round, and when the bell rang, the crowd hooted and hissed again.

One local writer said Miske's style of fighting produced such little action that the crowd began hooting at the round's conclusion. Miske was very defensive and cautious, only opening up in spots, then covering and clinching.

In the 4th round, Dempsey rushed from his corner and twice connected with Miske's jaw with his extended left. He also landed a hard right. He worked in close with both hands and Miske clinched. Miske came back with a right to the ear, clinched, and then on the break landed his right on the jaw. Dempsey attacked for the rest of the round, his left landing with good effect and driving Miske to the ropes. Jack landed a wicked punch to the head, but Billy came back with a straight left to the face and right to the body. Miske landed jabs to the head and rights to the body and head, but his blows were much less powerful and had no effect, whereas Dempsey's blows were hard and punishing and caused Miske to back up and/or hold.

In the 5th round, after Miske missed a right, Dempsey put him on the defensive by rushing and landing a right to the body and left to the face. He was ever aggressive and swung lefts and rights hard onto the body. Dempsey was all over him, but unable to get through his defense with the slashing blow that would end it. Miske came back with a right to the head, but Dempsey battered him with a volley of lefts and rights. Jack shot over a left to the jaw and then crossed the right with power, and, although he landed high, Miske was jarred to his toes. Dempsey followed with a storm of blows, sending his foe back to the ropes. Jack was boring in, using all of his power, and displaying his superiority as a fighter.

In the 6th and final round, Dempsey mixed his blows, alternating a left to the body and a right to the head. He continued getting them home, but as in the prior round, Miske held well in close and protected his jaw effectively at long range. The round saw plenty of action, with Dempsey as usual forcing the milling. He landed a left swing that rocked Miske's head, but Billy landed a similar blow to the face and right to the body. Dempsey tore in with both arms working, missing several wicked swings, then hooked in two quick rights to the body. The blows caused Miske to hold, but Jack worked out of the clinch and jabbed the face. Miske got in close, then landed a left to the nose. Jack punished him with a right to the body. They were punching away in a clinch at the bell.

All of the local ringside newspaper reporters unanimously agreed that Dempsey had won the 6-round no decision bout.

The *Philadelphia Press* article by Thomas D. Richter said the fighting was over in Europe, but it broke out in Philadelphia. Dempsey outfought Miske. He was the aggressor for 6 rounds, but Miske's effective grappling saved him from the crushing blows. The crowd had been spoiled by Dempsey's prior performances, recently scoring quick knockouts over men like Fulton, Levinsky, and Flynn, so they believed he would do the same with Miske. Hence, half were upset that Dempsey did not score a knockout. The other half realized that he had outfought a crafty, equally heavy fighter, who was animated with but one idea - staying the full 6 rounds. Miske never was in any real danger of going out, but it took all of his ring-craft to save his jaw from a finishing blow. The spectators were there to see Dempsey tested by a man who was as big as he, a finer boxer, a cool-headed fighter, and a fair hitter, and he was. Jack still showed his fighting ability, speed, and power.

The first three rounds furnished little real action, for Dempsey had not warmed to his task, and Miske, getting away fast, was beating him to the punch and locking him in an unbreakable grip at close quarters.

There was some hooting and jeering at the close of the 3rd round, which did not disconcert Miske, but stung Dempsey, so in the last three rounds he tore at his rival, smashing with both hands and endeavoring to finish him. The bout had little clean hitting, no knockdowns, and no gore. Dempsey tried, but Miske was in there to survive, and he did.

The *Philadelphia Inquirer* also reported that Dempsey beat Miske over 6 rounds. The St. Paul boxer was careful, usually on the defensive, and utilized frequent clinching. As a result, "Knockerout" Dempsey failed to score a knockdown. Dempsey landed several hard blows, principally a right-hand short swing when in close, but barring a few times when he seemingly was staggered, Miske never was in any danger of going out.

The bout was a bit of a disappointment, for the crowd had expected a knockout. However, Miske was far too dangerous for Dempsey to come wading in with a wide-open guard. He was the aggressor in most of the rounds, but often found Miske willing to meet him half way in the exchanges. Billy occasionally took the initiative by swinging a quick left then right to the face and body as they worked into a clinch. But primarily, Miske was careful, not so much trying to win as last. At times there was too much clinching, and some even hissed. The 2nd and 3rd rounds were tame, but overall the bout was fairly good, though not sensational.

Dempsey took the aggressive from the start, boring in continually, firing short lefts and a right, sometimes shot straight from the shoulder, varying it with a right hook. Miske often seemed bewildered. Billy used a good left at times, jabbing frequently to the face as Jack was coming in, and landed a well-placed right swing to the body, but his blows lacked the steam of Dempsey's, for the latter rarely was forced to be defensive.

The *Philadelphia Public Ledger* said Dempsey failed to score a knockout, but the verdict was all in his favor. He forced the fighting, drove home telling punches, and never was in danger. Miske was quite timid for the first three rounds, but improved in the final three and mixed it better than he had previously. He was there to stay, and watched and guarded every thrust. Still, Jack handed out a severe body lacing and was wearing him down gradually, battering the body with thudding, choppy, damaging, weakening blows. Yet, Miske was very clever, strong, willing, and game. He took the powerful right drives and left smashes without a murmur. Only once, in the 5th round, did he flinch, and then it was from a left to the stomach, which caused him to show momentary signs of crumbling. However, he managed to cover up quickly and block the extra efforts to finish him. Dempsey was good at continually jolting and bumping with his thudding blows, which would be most distressing to any foe. He crowded constantly, and never stopped shooting home the telling short shots. Miske's body was battered until it was a deep red.

Dempsey was unmarked except for a small cut over his left eye. He was strong and smiling at the end.

Dempsey said, "He was a tough boy and fought much better than he did against me in St. Paul. He has improved. They all looked for me to stop him, but it is one tough job to knock out a fellow like Miske in six rounds. He put up a good fight."

Philadelphia Jack O'Brien insisted that Dempsey was the best championship aspirant developed in the last decade. "Dempsey is an enlarged edition of Stanley Ketchel. He has that same freedom of action and the same ability to hit that characterized Ketchel's great work. ... He still has a few rough edges to be polished off, but it will not be long until he is a finished product. I consider him championship timber. He has the physique and the natural fighting qualities."

The *Philadelphia Evening Bulletin* also said that although Dempsey outpointed Miske, some were disappointed that he had not knocked him out. Dempsey said he couldn't K.O. them all. "Once you get the reputation of a knockout artist, the crowd expects you to bump 'em off every time you start." Although he beat Miske, the crowd believed he could have done it much more easily and decisively if the spirit had moved him. They believed he had carried Miske to some degree. Miske fought just to stay the full 6 rounds and justify the warm praise of a number of professional bettors who had wagered 2 to 1 and 3 to 1 that he would last the distance. In only two rounds did Dempsey show any particular animus towards his foe. In the 5th and 6th rounds, when the crowd hooted, Dempsey cut loose. Miske caught most of the punches with his gloves, ducked in close, and grabbed. Although Jack won, "The bout leaves the question of Dempsey's greatness still in dispute."

The *Philadelphia Record* said Dempsey's hard body blows wore down the Minnesotan. He rapidly was cleaning up the heavyweight division, adding Miske to his list of victims. Dempsey won by a good margin, but disappointed those who had been counting on a knockout. Miske foiled such intentions by using great boxing skill and good ring generalship. After

Dempsey's hard body blows had sapped his vitality and tired him out, Bill was forced to hold on to avoid punishment, and such tactics enabled him to be there at the final bell.

Miske showed that he could hit Dempsey almost any time he wanted, but there was not much steam behind his punches. Even when he rapped Jack full on the jaw as hard as he seemed able to hit, the most nefarious effect it had was to make Dempsey shake his head a bit and come back for more. There was a lot of clinching and wrestling, and several times when they were breaking away, Dempsey landed stiff blows to the side of the head, which on more than one occasion made Miske wobble a bit and grab and hold on all the tighter. Dempsey had only a slight weight advantage, and was a trifle taller. Miske was big enough, but Jack was the harder hitter.

From the start, Dempsey battered Billy's midsection, and he kept hammering away at his ribs and stomach throughout. Miske landed many jabs and swings to the head and face, but he did not have the knack of putting his weight behind the punches, and they did not worry Dempsey to any great extent. When the final bell rang, Miske was bleeding from the mouth and nose and evidently was weak and tired. Conversely, barring a slight trickle of blood from his mouth; Dempsey showed no evidence of the contest.[542]

Dempsey already was scheduled to battle Carl Morris for a third time; in a 20-round contest in mid-December in New Orleans.

Dan Morgan admitted that he had started all of the fuss at the United War Workers boxing show at Madison Square Garden:

> I shoved Joe Jeannette in there with Dempsey and Dempsey refused to box him, claiming he draws the color line. Bull. There isn't such a thing as the color line between real fighting men. Benny Leonard doesn't draw the color line. Neither does Jack Britton, one of the world's greatest fighters. I could name you a hundred more who don't hide behind the color line. Real fighters fight anybody. …
>
> If I wanted to do any framing I would have slipped in Mr. Harry Wills. … Dan McKettrick and Harry Pollok had nothing to do with the show on that evening. If I can be blamed for trying to give the fans a real fight, the newsies can go right on and roast till their pencils give out. Yours truly, Dan Morgan, Nov. 30, 1918.[543]

The *New York Sun's* Daniel (whose statement also was printed in the *New York Herald*) noted that drawing the color line was to be regretted in pugilism, for fighters should not draw the line. When two men fought, the question of color was not of especial value. Often it was done as a result of managerial craftiness and strategy; as a way to avoid tough challenges.

Jack Dempsey once fought John Lester Johnson, a negro, but that was before Dempsey attained any prominence. Now that he is

---

[542] *Philadelphia Press, Philadelphia Inquirer, Philadelphia Public Ledger, Philadelphia Evening Bulletin, Philadelphia Record*, all November 29, 1918.
[543] *Buffalo Commercial*, December 2, 1918.

recognized as the one challenger of Jess Willard, Dempsey has announced his unwillingness to fight a negro. The reason is one Harry Wills of ebony hue, who very likely would give Dempsey as hard a fight as Jack would want.[544]

The *New York Sun's* Cross Counter said no one believed that Dempsey was afraid of Jeannette or Kid Norfolk. However, Kearns likely felt that such a fight might open the door to a challenge from Wills, "who really is a dangerous heavyweight," and Kearns likely had some doubts as to the outcome of such a match. Dempsey was inconsistent in his drawing of the color line, but all former heavyweight champions drew it at one time or another, so he was no different. When Dempsey was a nobody, he fought black fighters, but now that he was on the cusp of the championship, things were different.[545]

Others defended Dempsey. The *Buffalo Courier* noted that some New York fight critics were saying that because of his refusal to box Jeannette, there was no place in pugilism for Dempsey, and his drawing of the color line would keep him from being a champion, for he should fight them all, white or black. The *Courier* retorted,

> If he wants to accept a challenge from a colored heavyweight, that's his business. The greatest knock the boxing game ever received was suffered because of the conduct of Jack Johnson after he became champion, and, while there are good fighters aplenty among the present-day crop of negro heavyweights whose personal conduct is all that could be desired, and whose reputations in and out of the ring are excellent, they suffer because of the prejudice which resulted from Johnson's actions.

Noted was the fact that Dempsey was about to earn $5,000 for fighting Carl Morris; very good money. Many other promoters were making Dempsey solid offers. So, clearly he was in demand, regardless of opponent. "There are scores of demands for Dempsey's services and at the end of the road there's the possibility of a match with Willard and a chance at the world's crown." Boxing fans enjoyed watching Dempsey fight. He did not stall or pull in the ring, but tried to win as quickly as possible, and the public admired him for it. "That's why he is in such big demand and at fancy prices." Hence, the feeling was that he did not need to fight a black man.[546]

Some said Dempsey should fight Meehan again. Both Fulton and Wills had beaten Meehan clearly.

Jess Willard informed Jack Kearns that he would fight Dempsey if he was guaranteed $100,000, win, lose, or draw.[547]

---

[544] *New York Sun, New York Herald*, December 5, 1918.
[545] *New York Age*, November 30, 1918, quoting *New York Sun*. In his autobiography, speaking of Wills, whom he previously managed, Kearns said, "Dempsey could have taken two of him before breakfast."
[546] *Buffalo Courier*, December 9, 1918.
[547] *La Crosse Tribune*, December 6, 1918.

Con McVey, who years ago helped train Jim Corbett, said of Dempsey, "He is the first heavyweight who looks like the old bunch. I would call him a slightly smaller edition of Jim Jeffries. He is one of the best two handed punchers I have ever seen. He is always on top of his rival. He can whip Miske any time. Miske knew this and held." McVey said Jack was the best heavyweight at present, and could whip Willard within 20 rounds.[548]

Dempsey's next contest was in in Louisiana, against Carl Morris. The last time they fought, in February of that year, Dempsey won on a foul in the 6th round, when Morris was on the verge of being knocked out.

Dempsey was to receive a guaranteed $4,000, with the privilege to take 46% of the gross receipts if such would be more substantial.[549]

The New Orleans *Times-Picayune* said Dempsey was the favorite, and appeared to be in the pink of condition. Jack said he never felt better in his whole life. He was the much smaller man in weight, but he would make up for it with his speed and terrific hitting power. The Colorado "knockout king" was the best-looking heavyweight since the days of Corbett and Fitzsimmons. He reminded one of a wild-cat, with muscles that resembled a whipcord, yet pliable and well trained. He was rangy, with thick shoulders, though when crouched, looked much shorter than he was. He was well-proportioned and carried no superfluous flesh. Most of the wagering was on the number of rounds the fight would last, for most believed that Morris had not the ghost of a chance, and the match really would be more of a Dempsey performance than a contest.

On December 14, two days before the fight, at the New Orleans Young Men's Gymnastic Club, Dempsey boxed several sensational rounds with Martin Burke, Young Denny, and a few other local boys.

Dempsey said Morris was one of the hardest men to beat, on account of his size, strength, gameness, and awkward fighting style:

> You can't get to him half as easy as you can to Fulton, Miske or any of the others. He doesn't seem to be a finished boxer, and yet he always appears to have an elbow, arm or glove in the way when you lead at him. He is awkwardly clever, you might say, but for a big fellow manages to handle himself pretty well even if he isn't graceful.

Morris was weighing 230 pounds, and said he was fit to fight the scrap of his life. Dempsey tipped the beam at exactly 190 pounds, 40 pounds less. Morris said, "All I ask is that he keep fighting and I'll guarantee there'll be plenty of milling going on."

Advance seat sales indicated that the largest crowd that ever attended a fight at the local auditorium would be on hand.[550]

The majority wagered that the "knockout king" would stop Morris within 3 rounds, despite the fact that the much larger Morris had over 60 fights of experience. They believed Dempsey simply was that good.[551]

---

[548] *New York Herald*, December 12, 1918.
[549] *Morning Tulsa Daily World*, December 12, 1918.
[550] *Times-Picayune*, December 15, 16, 1918.

LATEST PICTURE OF K. O. ARTIST

JACK DEMPSEY
Colorado heavyweight who is to meet Carl Morris Monday night in a match scheduled to go twenty rounds. This photograph was taken since Dempsey's arrival in New Orleans, and gives a fair idea of the "Knockout king's" symmetrical and well-knit physique.

On Monday December 16, 1918, in New Orleans, Louisiana, at the Louisiana Auditorium, Jack Dempsey fought a third fight against Carl Morris of Oklahoma, in a scheduled 20-round contest. Remy Dorr refereed. D. J. Tortorich promoted the show. 4,000 spectators (some said 7,000) were on hand, including former top contender Tom Sharkey.

According to the local *Times-Picayune*, at the clang of the gong, Morris tore in like a bull and flailed his powerful arms about awkwardly, rushing Dempsey to the ropes. Dempsey blocked several of the swings, though Morris managed to land one left hook to the body. Dempsey twisted out of the clinch and away from the ropes. Morris rushed in again. Dempsey stepped in and met the attack by bringing up a short half-hook half-left uppercut into the solar plexus. It did not appear to be very powerful, yet the enormous 235-pound ex-engineer flopped down onto the mat like a ton of bricks.

Wanting to give the public a run for its money, as he was counting, Referee Remy Dorr stretched out each second to about three times its normal length, hoping that Morris would rise, and yelling, "Get up!" Dorr counted him out as Morris laid there, never even making an attempt to rise. Morris simply writhed on the ground for about 20 seconds.

After the count concluded, Morris partly struggled and partly was lifted to his feet. Cries of "Fake!," "Police," "Jail the big tramp!" and the like were heard. Dempsey seemed keenly disappointed. He wanted to show his wares, and "never had dreamed the lady-like left hook with which he had met one of Morris's rushes would spell such a speedy end to the affair."

The *Times-Picayune* said Dempsey knocked out Morris in about 10 seconds (though it likely was a bit longer that that). One punch, a left hook to the solar plexus, "and a gentle left hook at that," sent Morris crumpling into a quivering heap on the floor. It was about the only blow Dempsey landed.

Whether the punch really incapacitated Morris or whether he took a dive was the debate. What caused increased bitter feeling was Morris' hold-up of the promoters, insisting that his $1,250 guarantee be paid in full up front, before he would enter the ring. Carl had counted it out carefully and handed it to his representative Ike Dorgan.

The bout was the shortest important match ever staged in a local ring. Some said it would cause a black eye to the sport. Everyone was disgusted. However, no blame was placed on Dempsey for the unsatisfactory ending.

[551] *Chattanooga News*, December 16, 1918.

There had been little or no wagering on the outcome. Dempsey was too strong a favorite at 4 to 1 and 6 to 1, with few willing to bet on Morris. Offers were made at 6 to 5 that Morris would not stay 10 rounds.[552]

Non-local sources reported that Dempsey stopped Morris in about 46 seconds, with a short left hook to the stomach during a period of hard infighting. Many fans thought Morris had slipped, and then quit. Only those near the ringside had seen the blow. It was 6 to 5 that Morris would not last 3 rounds. These reports claimed that Dempsey weighed in at 185 pounds to Morris' 220 pounds. The crowd accused Morris of faking. The police had to protect him. Dempsey earned $4,000 for very little work.

Others said it was a quick short right cross to the jaw after the body shot that actually sent him down, but it was so short and fast that few had seen it. This version said Dempsey started off with a rush and sent in a number of heavy blows to the body. Morris tried to clinch, but Dempsey tore himself away and sent in another shower of body smashes. A heavy right to the jaw made Morris groggy, and he began floundering about the ring. Dempsey tore into him, and a left to the body and right to the chin sent him down, where he remained for the full count.[553]

On the same date in Tulsa, Oklahoma, Billy Miske knocked out Fireman Jim Flynn in the 2nd round.

The *St. Louis Post-Dispatch* said Dempsey had a "remarkable punch" that only two men had been able to handle – Meehan and Miske.

The *Buffalo Enquirer*'s Edward Tranter called Dempsey the logical candidate for the title, a "wonderful bundle of fighting energy," a "veritable cyclone," "as strong as an ox," "the most wonderful heavyweight fighter of the day," a "genuine, undisputed heavyweight sensation," and the "heavyweight wonder of the present era," who had a splendid chance to dethrone Willard. Despite only weighing 185 pounds, he had the ability to deck and stop men who outweighed him by 30 and 40 pounds. "There has been no heavyweight boxer in the last ten years or more who can compare with Dempsey as a battler."[554]

The *Buffalo Times* said it was wrong to accuse Morris of faking. Dempsey had knocked out many much larger opponents early on in fights with short, snappy, powerful blows. This was nothing new for him. He could score knockouts with a single blow. He also stopped Fulton in mere seconds, the man who knocked out Sam Langford and Frank Moran. His punch was so remarkable, and he appeared to be so irresistible, that when he failed to score a knockout over Miske in 6 rounds, some quick-trigger critics accused him of pulling.[555]

The *Brooklyn Citizen* said Dempsey added to his fame as a "giant killer." There was a question as to whether Morris was knocked out or quit. Either

---

[552] *Times-Picayune*, December 17, 1918.
[553] *Brooklyn Citizen, Pittsburgh Post, El Paso Herald, Shreveport Times, Salt Lake Herald-Republican, Buffalo Evening News*, all December 17, 1918.
[554] *St. Louis Post-Dispatch, Buffalo Enquirer,* December 17, 1918.
[555] *Buffalo Times*, December 21, 1918.

way, Dempsey was the first man to make Morris take the count. Willard could not do it, nor could Fulton.[556]

On December 18, a justice of the New York Supreme Court denied Dempsey's lawyer's motion to dismiss John Reisler's lawsuit alleging a breach of a three-year contract between Dempsey and Reisler which gave the latter control of Dempsey's career until December 1919. However, the judge allowed the fighter 20 days to file an answer on the complaint.[557]

A syndicate was offering Willard $75,000 to fight Dempsey.

In his book, *Million Dollar Gate*, Kearns claimed that around this time, before the second Gunboat Smith fight, he obtained a $5,000 loan and paid off Reisler to settle matters. However, the timing appears unlikely, because the pestiferous Reisler kept popping up even after that.

Dempsey said he wanted a long bout with Meehan, one scheduled for 20 rounds instead of just 4 rounds. "I can knock him out in a long fight. Meehan is not a powerful hitter, but he can take a punch and is a very awkward and annoying opponent. However, there is no chance of a real fight with Willie unless he gets his discharge from the navy." For the time being, Meehan only could fight in San Francisco, in 4-round bouts.[558]

Dempsey was scheduled to rematch Gunboat Smith in Buffalo, New York at the end of the month, just two weeks after the Morris contest. Kearns told Smith's manager Jimmy Johnston that he was so confident that Dempsey would knock him out this time that he was willing to give a $200 gift to Smith if he was upright at the end of the 6$^{th}$ round. Smith's manager insisted that Dempsey could not knock out his man.

Smith was well respected in New York, for he had stopped the aspirations of many contenders. He even held a victory over Jess Willard. Smith and Dempsey were about the same height and weight.[559]

Since losing a 1917 4-round decision to Dempsey (a fight in which he staggered Jack in the 2$^{nd}$ round), Gunboat Smith's record included: 1917 LTKOby7 Fred Fulton; 1918 L12 Charley Weinert, LND10 Clay Turner (who in November 1918 won a 12-round decision over Kid Norfolk), L10 Billy Miske, LND6 Leo Houck, D15 Tom McMahon, and LND8 Miske. Smith had 118 fights of experience.

Fred Fulton said Dempsey was the fastest and hardest puncher in the ring at present, and likely the hardest hitter ever. Fulton claimed to have decked Willard in their 1914 4-round exhibition bout, and after that, Willard did his best to knock him out, but couldn't do it. "And Willard was a better man at that time than he is today, by a long shot." Fulton said Dempsey could hit twice as hard as Willard with either hand. His blows were paralyzing.

However, Billy Miske said he wasn't all that concerned with Dempsey's power. "Yes, Jack has a very mean left hook, which caused me much

---

[556] *Brooklyn Citizen*, December 17, 1918.
[557] *Star-Gazette* (Elmira, NY), December 19, 1918.
[558] *Buffalo Courier*, *Buffalo Express*, *Buffalo Times*, December 22, 1918.
[559] *Buffalo Commercial*, *Buffalo Evening News*, December 24, 1918.

trouble. I don't consider he's such a terrific hitter, for I fought men who can hit harder than he does. He's what I call a stinging puncher. He's easy to hit at a distance, but he's a very tough bird at close quarters."

Willie Meehan agreed with Fulton that Dempsey could clout like a mule's kick:

> It's my experience with Dempsey that his short right hand blow is the most effective. He puts a lot of weight behind it. ... He lands a little high just at the junction of the ribs. I thought he had caved in my chest and pushed his fist right through me. I was sore for a couple of days after from that very same blow. But he's got a bear of a right hand swing also. That was the blow that toppled me over in our last bout at 'Frisco. Jack is the hardest hitter I ever met, but I think I've got his number and can stand him off in a long or short bout. You'll notice he's not very anxious to meet me again. I wonder why?

So Miske thought Dempsey's best punch was his left hook, while Meehan thought it was his right.

Dan Morgan, no fan of Dempsey or Kearns, predicted that Gunboat Smith would outpoint Dempsey. Apparently, Dempsey took away Morgan's breadwinner when he knocked out Battling Levinsky. He had been bitter ever since. Morgan wrote, "If Dempsey is not allowed to wear extra heavy tape bandages, I will bet five hundred dollars Gunboat Smith outpoints him on December thirtieth. Saw Smith annihilate Jim Coffey Tuesday. Punched him so badly the big Irishman will be unable to go for some time." Smith had walloped Coffey in a gym sparring bout. Morgan said Smith was one of the most dangerous men in the game, was in perfect condition for this fight, and would win for sure.

The *Buffalo Courier* said Dempsey's knockout record might be punctured by the "Gooner," as Smith was called. Smith was tough, experienced, and could punch hard. He had the potential to hurt Dempsey, and had shown the ability to take it himself. Still, Dempsey had knocked out most of his top foes recently, except Miske, "who hugged through six rounds."[560]

An in-shape, confident Smith said, "I am not at all afraid of Dempsey. He did not do me any particular damage out in Frisco and I don't think he will here in Buffalo. ... I think I will give him a go that will surprise him on Monday night. He may get me, but if he doesn't, I'll come mighty close to getting him." The contest was arousing much local interest.[561]

Dempsey was called the "flash," "the terror," and "the new nonpareil." He enjoyed training at Long Branch, New Jersey, by the ocean. The day of the fight, Jack said, "They tell me the Gunner is all readied up. That's good. So am I. You know they all expect me to knock everybody out in a punch. That's unfair to me, because a fellow can't keep on doing it all the time, but I'll be on my toes and at him this evening. He'll know he has been to the races when we quit."

---

[560] *Buffalo Commercial, Buffalo Courier*, December 27, 1918.
[561] *Buffalo Evening News*, December 30, 1918.

JACK DEMPSEY

JACK DEMPSEY

JACK DEMPSEY

Smith claimed to have had Dempsey on the ropes in the 4th and final round of their prior fight, and would have finished him in two or three more rounds if he had the chance [a claim not supported by the primary sources]. "He isn't frightening me. I'll be with him when the tenth round closes. Punch? Sure he can punch, but you don't think I'm a cripple, do you? I'll be punching a little myself."

Smith said he was 30 years old, and still had plenty of fight left. He previously had been assigned to a gunboat in the navy, which is how he got his nickname. Regarding his fight with Georges Carpentier back in 1914, Smith said he knocked Georges down in the 6th round with a left to the chin. Carpentier got to his knees at seven, and was rising at the count of nine. Gunboat swung, thinking he was off the floor, and missed, but the referee disqualified him. He insisted that the motion pictures proved him correct, that he did not hit Carpentier when he was down. "I was disqualified for swinging and missing Carpentier." He claimed that he was cheated out of his victory.[562]

---

[562] *Buffalo Commercial*, December 30, 1918.

On Monday December 30, 1918 in Buffalo, New York, at the Broadway Auditorium, under the auspices of the Queensberry A. C., Jack Dempsey fought Gunboat Smith for the second time, in a scheduled 10-round contest. An immense throng of 5,000 or 6,000 fans were in attendance. The chatter was that Dempsey would find the Gunner to be tougher than the lumbering giants that he had been knocking over. Dempsey weighed 190 pounds even, and Smith 178 pounds.

When they met at ring center to listen to the referee's instructions, their bathrobes loosely drawn over their shoulders, they stripped magnificently, each looking well-prepared. Dempsey eyed him, but the Gunner looked down at the floor. The referee said, "I want you fellows to box a clean match. Shake hands now and come out fighting."

At the gong, Dempsey came out like a man with a mighty important piece of business on hand. He bore in with great determination. The Gunner feinted and drew back. Dempsey did not hesitate, but walked right in. Gunner backed away with his jaw protected. Dempsey jabbed and feinted Smith back to the ropes. Dempsey nailed him flush on the chin with straight left. Smith covered up, but Dempsey followed up with a snappy short five-inch left hook to the jaw and the Gunner went down as if hit by a ton of bricks. One said that after being hit with the short left jolt, Dempsey snuck in a short left uppercut to the body as the Gunboat was trying to clinch, and then he went down to the floor beneath the ropes. Only 25 seconds had elapsed. The belief that Smith would prove to be a tough test quickly changed.

Smith rose at the count of six or eight, covered, and pawed with his left. Dempsey stayed on top of him, looking for an opening. Dempsey knocked Smith's left aside and crossed his right, and even though Smith partially blocked the hooking right and it landed on the cheek bone, it was so powerful, like a sledge hammer, that Smith went down again. One writer said the punch did land on the jaw.

Smith crawled to the ropes and pulled himself up, rising at eight or nine, dazed and bewildered. Jack advanced coolly, but the Gunboat backed away as Jack followed. For the rest of the round, Smith was like a drunken man, yet tried to protect his jaw and body, back away, parry, ward and hold off the oncoming terror.

Smith went down again, the various local papers offering different versions of how it happened. The *Buffalo Commercial* said Jack brushed aside a left and hooked another right to the chin to send him down. The *Buffalo Times* said a short chop to the back of the head did it. The *Buffalo Courier* said that in a clinch, Dempsey turned Smith completely about, held one hand aloft and landed a terrific left uppercut that sent Gunboat down on his haunches, blinking.

Smith started to rise at eight, and barely got off the floor just as Referee Nugent was dropping his arm for the tenth second. Kearns claimed he was out, but the referee waived Dempsey to continue. Jack waltzed him toward the ropes. The Gunner was covering up with his arms. Dempsey belted him to the body, flooring him for the fourth time. Smith's legs bent underneath him like a jack knife.

Smith rose unsteadily, but wasn't on his feet more than 15 or 20 seconds more. Jack was on top of him, looking for an opening as the Gunner swayed about. Jack hooked another right to the body and then a left hook to the jaw, and the Gunner kissed the canvas for the fifth time.

Again Smith barely rose before ten, on unsteady legs. The *Commercial* said an overhand left hook dropped him in his own corner for the sixth time. The *Times* said Jack had measured him and then landed a finishing right which sent him down. The *Courier* version said a right to the top of the head, then left, and then another clip and Smith went down.

Unable to rise, Smith would have been counted out had the bell not saved him. Two locals said the bell rang at the count of seven or eight. Another said Smith tried to rise by using the aid of the ropes, and was on all fours when Nugent said ten at the same time the bell rang. Again Jack Kearns claimed that Smith was out, but the referee said he was saved by the bell. "I'm doing the refereeing, Jack, you attend to your champion." Smith was paralyzed. He had to be helped and dragged to his corner. There had been six knockdowns in the 1st round.

At the start the 2nd round, Smith seemed semi-recovered and in fair form, particularly given what had happened previously. He wanted to stay, but Dempsey the cyclone had his fighting blood up, and would not be denied. Dempsey got Gunboat to his corner, and a short right high on the side of the head sent him down.

Smith rose and fired a desperate right swing, but Jack stepped back out of harm's way, and the force of his own punch missing sent Smith down.

Smith rose within four seconds and clinched desperately. Jack threw him off with a blow to the head, and then a left sent him down.

He rose again. Smith's efforts to fight back were blocked, and body and head drives again brought him down.

As usual, Smith rose and tried to survive. Dempsey drew close, feinted, calmly measured him, and landed a marvelous left hook to the chin that lifted Smith clear off the floor and he came crashing down hard, with a thud. Two other versions said it was a short right hook to the jaw that sent him down for good.

Referee Dick Nugent counted to ten as Smith was lying prostrate on his back, dazed and badly defeated. Smith was groping with his hands to find some support to cling to in order to rise. During the count, Dempsey stalked about, waiting to pounce. But Smith was knocked dizzy and could not get up. The referee could have counted to forty. Smith did not fully recover until long after Dempsey was in his dressing room. The end came at 1 minute 32 seconds of the 2nd round.

Afterwards, Gunboat said, "Say, that bird is poison; just poison. He's worse than poison gas." In his dressing room, he complained that while his head was okay, there was something wrong with his legs. After receiving the first blow, he scarcely could control his limbs. He also said,

> A change has come over Dempsey. That ain't the same Dempsey I boxed on the Pacific Coast by a long shot. Man he punches like a pile driver. I don't remember a thing after getting that first clip on the chin, except when I was in my corner. I tell you he paralyzed me with the first punch. My legs felt like straws. I guess I made a bum out of myself. Well, he's a champion, that's all.

The Gunner also said Dempsey was much more confident as a result of his success. His confidence helped him fight better.

Smith subsequently went to Jack's dressing room and told him, "You'll lick 'em all, even Willard." Jack replied, "Thank you Gunner."

The *Buffalo Enquirer* reported that Dempsey badly battered Smith and stopped him in the 2nd round. Smith took the count nine times. A great crowd saw the gunner annihilated. Dempsey was far too superior for the present-day crop of heavyweights. The first knockdown took place soon after the bell. Smith was no match. He was a has-been, and it was a shame to expect him to battle a husky, healthy, snappy walloper.

Dempsey's blows were short, chopping ones, and very accurate. "Suffice to say there isn't a heavyweight contender living capable of giving Dempsey a battle." Willard was the only one who might make him work hard to win. And if they fought, the local fans would bet on Dempsey. He could hit as hard or harder than any heavyweight who ever lived. He was faster and snappier with his blows than any other heavyweight before the public. He was a great piece of fighting machinery, with a fighter's heart. Smith didn't even muss Jack's hair. At one point, Dempsey ducked a right swing, and the gunner was so weak that he toppled from his own exertion. He lasted longer than Fulton and Morris, much bigger men, but that was all.

The *Buffalo Evening News* said Dempsey's left hook settled the gunner's fate. A short crushing left hook to the jaw was the beginning of the end in the 1st round. After that, the Gunner rolled and tumbled around the ring, trying to regain his feet. He went crumbling to the floor again and again under an unrelenting Dempsey onslaught. The bell saved him only further depth charges in the 2nd round.

The gunner could not put up a fight. His famous "Mary Ann," a right arm destroyer, was in evidence only twice. Once was when he swung it wildly in the 1st, and then in the 2nd when he threw himself down with it when he hit the air. He was not aggressive at all, but covered up from the opening bell, seemingly afraid. He only raised his hands to guard his face. He hit the floor about a dozen times.

The *Buffalo Commercial* said Dempsey whipped Smith in four minutes, thirty-two seconds, or 1 minute 32 seconds of the 2nd round (not counting the minute rest between rounds). The first punch, a stiff left to the chin, robbed Smith of all his fighting equipment. He went down nine times before he took the fatal ten-count in the middle of the 2nd round. His brain was in a whirl, his legs cramped, and the control of his muscles gone. "Dempsey is the finished fighting man. He possesses that which most boxers lack – the ability to sail in and conclude matters, once he has his man groggy."

Smith had not done much boxing. He simply was too busy trying to keep Dempsey off. Other than the time he spent crouching and covering up, he was bobbing up and down. He was on the floor for more than fifty seconds of the fight. The rest of the time he was on the receiving end. He didn't land one solid blow. He once was a great fighter, but no more.

Conversely,

> Dempsey has everything. There isn't a thing lacking in his make-up. He's fast, as fast as a lightweight, he punches short and snappy. There's a world of power behind every blow he drives in. He doesn't swing and leave himself open. He just punches straight and to the point. It will take a wonderful fighter to whip Dempsey, a man as fast as lightning – and among heavies they come once in a lifetime – a stiff puncher, plus a steel-ribbed jaw and a very game and alert battler. None of the present-day heavies have a chance with Dempsey, and that goes for Mister Jest Willard.

Dempsey was the opposite of most big men. He moved with the speed of a deer, was workmanlike, beat foes to the punch, and when he landed, something was going to bend if not break. He whipped even experienced and bigger foes before they could get started.

Afterward, Jack said, "I had no wild desire to whip Smith in one round. I figured the Gunner was tough. I made it my business to sock home that first punch and get going right off the reel." After the first blow, Smith was gone. "I'd have been a sucker to let him come back." Smith doubled up in an odd way, and Jack thought perhaps he was looking for a wild haymaker, which made him cautious about stepping in to him. But soon he realized that Smith was through. "Then it was pie for me."

Dempsey later saw the Gunner at the train station with a pack of ice held to his forehead. Jack asked, "Didn't hurt you, did I?" Smith responded, "Well, I wouldn't say you hurt me, but you sure did a mighty fine job. My legs went back on me. They tell me you knocked me down nine times." "Not as many as that, Gunner." "It's all in the game, Jack. I would have treated you likewise, if I could. What's worrying me is that I must crawl into an upper. Boy! How my legs and back ache." "Here," said Dempsey, producing from his pocket a ticket for a stateroom on the train, "You take that. I like uppers. Go ahead, take it. You had a tough night." "Thanks," said the Gunner. "I'll see you on the train in the morning."

*Buffalo Commercial*, December 31, 1918

The *Buffalo Times* said Dempsey's performance made a deep impression on the fans. "Jack Dempsey is as good as they say he is, and you needn't let 'em tell you different." He stopped Smith in a very neat and workmanlike fashion, with ease. The Gunner entered the ring looking great and self-confident, but left it as a has-been. Smith was a good fighter. But he met the new nonpareil.

The *Buffalo Courier* said Dempsey never gave Smith a chance to do anything but assume the defensive, and stopped him with a volley of punches. Only the bell saved Smith at the end of the 1st round, after he had been down six times. Despite his game efforts, he could not come back. Smith was on the floor nearly half the fight. He gamely took the beating.

The marvelous Dempsey's punches counted. He had wonderful strength and hitting power. He was a young phenomenon who knew how to hit. He didn't waste punches, and could hit with power from any distance, even a few inches. Punches that that landed near the top of Smith's head had as much effect as ones that struck the chin. A snappy left half hook to the jaw started the downfall less than a minute into the 1st round.

The crowd was mesmerized, so keen on watching and following the wonderful Dempsey's every move that they didn't even shout. They were hushed and almost breathless.

Gunboat hit him only one punch, barring a few pokes to the ribs in the clinches. The one punch he landed was a light left to the side of the head, and in a counter Jack knocked him off his feet with a left. It was a clean, decisive, matter-of-fact knockout. Gunboat was paralyzed from the waist down for some time afterwards. It was several minutes before he could understand and speak again. Dempsey was as cool as ice.

The *Buffalo Express* said Dempsey won a decisive victory in a hurricane display of skill and dash. He was too fast for Smith. He scored nine knockdowns. The enthusiastic crowd marveled at his fine form. Smith's only satisfaction was lasting longer than Fulton and Morris. The first punch that Dempsey landed solidly did the business.[563]

Dempsey's performances in rematches against tough foes, improving on prior performances and results each time, further solidified his status as the top contender to the throne. Everyone was impressed.

## CHAMPION IN TRAINING

According to the *Pittsburg Press*, in 1918, Jack Dempsey had fought 22 times, won 18, lost 1, had 0 draws, 3 no decisions, and scored 17 knockouts out of his 18 victories. He even knocked out light heavyweight champion Battling Levinsky. One bout was a 4-round exhibition with his sparring partner Clay Turner at Ebbets field in Brooklyn, who later beat Kid Norfolk.[564]

Walter Monahan, a Jess Willard sparring partner, said the champion had made up his mind to give Dempsey a fight for the title. Monahan declared that Willard was keeping himself in perfect trim, and Dempsey would meet with a surprise.[565]

---

[563] *Buffalo Enquirer, Buffalo Evening News, Buffalo Commercial, Buffalo Times, Buffalo Courier, Buffalo Express*, all December 31, 1918.
[564] *Pittsburgh Press*, January 8, 1919.
[565] *Brooklyn Standard Union*, December 27, 1918.

CHAPTER 21

# Sullivan-Style Exhibitions

By 1919, it was quite clear that Jack Dempsey was the top contender to Jess Willard's crown, and it was only a matter of time before they would fight. In the meantime, Jack Kearns determined that Dempsey could capitalize on his fame with exhibitions, obtain further exposure, and also remain fight sharp, getting paid to train, which reduced expenses. As Kearns so eloquently put it, "Like a strip teaser, I always figured that you couldn't get anywhere without exposure."

The *Trenton Evening Times* said Dempsey was quiet and unassuming, and might be taken for a traveling salesman if seen in a hotel lobby.[566]

Robert Edgren said Dempsey was 23 years of age, about 190 pounds, had plenty of speed and aggressiveness, with a cool head, plenty of punch resistance, and actually compared well with past champions. He lacked nothing. Sullivan lacked condition. Corbett lacked hitting power. Fitzsimmons lacked weight. Jeffries lacked aggressiveness except when he found himself in danger of losing a decision. Burns lacked height and weight. Johnson lacked attacking ability. Willard lacked fighting spirit. Dempsey had condition, hitting power, height, reach, weight, aggressiveness, attacking ability, skill, and fighting spirit.[567]

Others, like the *Pittsburgh Gazette Times*, criticized, saying Dempsey had knocked over a bunch of has beens, and his opponents had not been of a high quality. He was barren of real potential opponents, with the possible exception of Miske, or unless he crossed the line into the territory "occupied by the dark race, where he might mingle with Harry Wills, Sam Langford, or Joe Jeannette, for instance. If Dempsey should meet Wills and defeat him in a long contest the sporting public then would accept him as a fighter of the highest quality of the time."[568]

Dempsey started appearing in a musical revue in Long Branch and Trenton, New Jersey, sparring 3 rounds with a regular sparring partner, and offering "$1,000 to any white man who can stay 3 rounds" with him, similar to what John L. Sullivan once did. Jack now was famous enough that he could make money in a theatrical career. A large company of musical and dancing

---

[566] *Trenton Evening Times* January 3, 1919.
[567] *Harrisburg Evening News*, January 4, 1919.
[568] *Pittsburgh Gazette Times*, January 5, 1919.

performers accompanied him. He normally would spar 3 rounds with a partner, "unless some reckless white man tries to earn $1,000 by staying on his feet through three rounds of hurricane action."[569] On January 13, 1919, Jack exhibited in Long Branch. On the 14th, he exhibited at Trenton.

Given that the war appeared to be over, promoters in England were angling for an international elimination bout between English champ Bombardier Billy Wells and French champion Georges Carpentier, with the winner to fight Dempsey for the right to challenge Willard.[570]

GEORGES CARPENTIER

Jimmy De Forest signed a contract to train Dempsey for the next year.[571]

On Wednesday January 15, 1919 at the Grand Theatre in Trenton, New Jersey, several thousand fans gathered to watch Dempsey start his Sullivan-style knockout tour. His opponent was a big ship-worker named Jack McGuire, also known as Curley McGuire, who allegedly had considerable experience as a boxer. He towered over Dempsey and weighed over 200 pounds. McGuire was attempting to win the $1,000 offered to anyone who could last 3 rounds. Neither man had any seconds/cornermen.

According to the local *Trenton Evening Times*, at the sound of the bell, Dempsey rushed at McGuire like a wild bull, swung his arms a couple of times, and McGuire took a dive into the ropes and down. Some

GEORGES CARPENTIER

---

[569] *Long Branch Daily Record*, January 10, 11, 13, 1919; *Trenton Evening Times*, January 14, 1919.
[570] *New Brunswick Sunday Times*, January 12, 1919.
[571] *Paterson Morning Call*, January 15, 1919.

fans hissed, feeling that Dempsey had struck him while he was down. Perhaps he had. "He didn't, however, strike him hard enough to break an egg." Jack Kearns, referee and master of ceremonies, counted to ten, for the 1st round knockout.[572]

Other reports said McGuire took one swipe at Dempsey, and then with a terrific right, Dempsey sent McGuire to the floor. It was all over in less than one minute of the 1st round of the scheduled 3-round exhibition bout. Another version said Dempsey required just two passes and one minute to end McGuire. They carried the shipbuilder out on a shutter. Dempsey was determined to outdo John L. Sullivan, who had engaged in a similar tour.[573]

The $1,000 offer to any white man who could last 3 rounds with Dempsey would continue in Pennsylvania as well.[574]

They were in Easton, Pennsylvania on January 16, 1919, where Dempsey may have stopped in 1 round a fighter named Kid Harrison.[575]

On Friday January 17, 1919 at the O'Hara theatre in Shenandoah, Pennsylvania, Dempsey sparred a few minutes with Kid Henry, and then boxed with his sparring partner. In both instances, he showed speed and cleverness. Dempsey was traveling with his company of 40 vaudeville artists and sparring partners.[576]

On Saturday January 18, 1919 at the G.A.R. Opera House in Shamokin, Pennsylvania, Dempsey knocked out brawny Kid Hogan, who was just out of the service, finishing him with one knock on the chin before he got his guard up. Another quick 1st round knockout. Hogan failed to win the $1,000 offered to anyone who could last 3 rounds.

Kearns said a bunch of Hogan's sailor friends almost choked with laughter. Whenever no local man was willing to box Dempsey at these exhibitions, he would spar 3 rounds with amateur middleweight and light heavyweight champion Martin Burke, who recently turned pro.[577]

Lightweight Johnny Ray said Dempsey was a world beater and would be the next champion:

> He is easily the best big fighter that I ever saw, and even in an exhibition bout with Clay Turner, to say nothing of his real contests in the East, his class stuck out all over him. He is as fast as a featherweight, a good boxer, keeps his feet close together and is constantly shifting from side to side, punches short and snappily with either hand and the wonderful knockout record which he is placing to his credit proves that he carries a terrific wallop.[578]

---

[572] *Trenton Evening Times*, January 16, 1919.
[573] *Philadelphia Evening Public Ledger*, January 16, 1919; *Cincinnati Enquirer*, January 17, 1919; *Long Branch Daily Record*, January 22, 1919.
[574] *Harrisburg Telegraph*, January 14, 1919.
[575] *Shenandoah Evening Herald*, January 17, 1918; *East Liverpool Review*, June 28, 1919.
[576] *Shenandoah Evening Herald*, January 15, 18, 1919.
[577] *Mount Carmel Item*, January 18, 1919; *Harrisburg Telegraph*, January 20, 1919.
[578] *New Castle News*, January 18, 1919.

Dempsey next exhibited in Harrisburg, Pennsylvania. The *Harrisburg Telegraph* said Dempsey had knocked out Jack McLinn with one blow at Trenton. At Easton he did likewise. Then at Shamokin, he took out brawny Kid Hogan, who was just out of the service, finishing him with only one knock on the chin before he got his guard up. He was doing the John L. Sullivan thing, stopping men who tried to win the $1,000 offered to any white man who could last 3 rounds with him. It appeared that he was knocking out ordinary men, not real or regular fighters. The local press advertised Dempsey as the greatest fighter since Sullivan's day.

SOME OF THE ARMY AND NAVY PLAYERS MADE UP AS MINSTREL MEN

*Harrisburg Telegraph*, January 20, 1919

A local Harrisburg black fighter who called himself Black Gunboat Smith said if Dempsey would cross the color line, he would box him. However, Kearns found a white man willing to box Dempsey.

Dempsey said that when he was young, a larger Mormon lad had started to fight him. Jack's father watched and didn't help or stop it, so he figured that he had better take care of himself, and did. "Dad was always strong for me to take care of myself, and did all he could to keep me at it."

Eventually, Jack Kearns started managing him. Dempsey was working in a shipbuilding plant at the time, as a ship carpenter. Jack also claimed that Willard had refused to fight him, even for $101,000.[579]

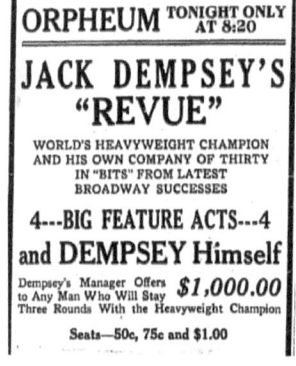

ORPHEUM TONIGHT ONLY AT 8:20
JACK DEMPSEY'S "REVUE"
WORLD'S HEAVYWEIGHT CHAMPION AND HIS OWN COMPANY OF THIRTY IN "BITS" FROM LATEST BROADWAY SUCCESSES
4---BIG FEATURE ACTS---4
and DEMPSEY Himself
Dempsey's Manager Offers $1,000.00 to Any Man Who Will Stay Three Rounds With the Heavyweight Champion
Seats—50c, 75c and $1.00

On Monday January 20, 1919 in Harrisburg, Pennsylvania, at the local Orpheum, Henry Hickey (or Hickel) took up Dempsey's offer to try to last 3 rounds to win $1,000 if he could.

According to the *Harrisburg Telegraph*, Hickey rushed in, Dempsey brushed him off a couple times, and hit him with a hook. He finally got tired of fooling around, and knocked Hickey out so flat that he had to be carried out.

A woman said, "I wouldn't be that fool for $10,000." Dempsey had knocked out his victim with the "cold abandon of a man putting coal in your cellar, and the pugilist who can floor him will indeed be a magician."

Another local paper said Jack sparred with a member of the company for a short time, and then put to sleep a man named Bill Hickey.[580]

---

[579] *Harrisburg Telegraph*, January 17, 18, 20, 1919.
[580] *Harrisburg Telegraph, Harrisburg Evening News,* January 21, 1919. That same day, January 20, 1919 in Buffalo, Clay Turner won a 10-round no decision over Kid Norfolk, avenging a LKOby4 suffered earlier that month.

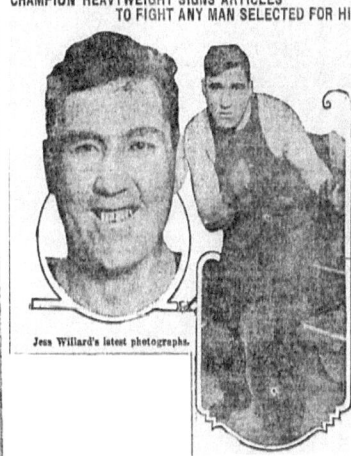

On Wednesday January 22, 1919 in Reading, Pennsylvania, at the Rajah theatre, Dempsey stopped Kid Harris of Washington in about 2 minutes of the 1st round, with a left swing to the jaw that sent him down and out like a log. But in doing so, Jack sprained his right ankle, so he didn't box the next evening.[581]

Sometime in January, (possibly January 28 or 29) in Easton, Pennsylvania, Dempsey knocked out Kid Henry. Jack said he hurt his hand slightly as a result.[582]

Jess Willard announced his concern that he might kill the much smaller and lighter Dempsey. He once had hit Bull Young with his full force and killed him. He feared a similar incident if he fought Dempsey.[583]

Tex Rickard offered Jess Willard a $100,000 guarantee, win or lose, for a fight with either Carpentier or Dempsey on July 4. However, Carpentier had a dislocated thumb, and needed time to get back into top form after his military service.

JESS WILLARD.

On January 24, Jess Willard signed an open contract with Tex Rickard to fight anyone Tex named, for a guaranteed $100,000, for any number of rounds up to 40. Willard and Rickard both had to deposit a $10,000 forfeit with a Chicago bank. Rickard also would deposit $15,000 at least 60 days before the fight, and $75,000 no later than 48 hours before the day of the fight. If Rickard failed to make any deposit on time, he would forfeit the money deposited up to that point. Jess agreed to be at the place designated for battle 60 days in advance of the

---

[581] *Reading Times*, January 23, 1919.
[582] *Harrisburg Telegraph*, *Reading Times*, January 31, 1919.
[583] *Butler Citizen*, January 21, 1919.

fight. Rickard could name the referee. Tex planned to build a special arena capable of holding 50,000 people.

Willard currently was weighing about 275 pounds. He planned to enter the ring at about 245. Jess said, "It don't matter who is selected to meet me. The purse is the thing. I am not boxing for fun. It's business with me."[584]

Willard would be fighting for the largest purse ever. Rickard allegedly had offered $1,000 less than another promoter, but Tex had a sterling reputation for coming through with full payment and being successful in big promotions, including Johnson-Jeffries, so that influenced Willard.

A few days later, in late January, Rickard said Jack Dempsey would be Willard's opponent in a fight to be held on July 4, 1919.[585]

**Jess Willard and George Lewis "Tex" Rickard**

On January 24, 1919 in San Francisco, Fred Fulton won another 4-round decision victory over Willie Meehan. Fulton was too big and clever for Meehan, using his height and reach advantages well, cutting his right eye while outboxing him with long powerful blows. In late December, Fulton had won a clear 4-round decision over Sam Langford.[586]

Fulton said if Willard was in proper condition, he would beat

---

[584] *Billings Gazette*, January 25, 1919; *Philadelphia Inquirer*, January 28, 1919.
[585] *Des Moines Tribune*, January 31, 1919. *Salt Lake Telegram*, January 29, 1919.
[586] *San Francisco Chronicle*, *San Francisco Examiner*, January 25, 1919.

Dempsey in a long fight, for Jack was not as good after the first couple of rounds. Fred also said his second victory over Meehan entitled him to a rematch with Dempsey, given that Meehan beat Jack. However, there was very little demand for a rematch, given how easily and quickly Dempsey had knocked out Fulton. Folks simply did not think Fred had the chin to withstand Dempsey's brand of ferocious speed and power. Fulton's subsequent victories only confirmed Dempsey's lofty status.[587]

On February 1, 1919 in Wells, Nevada, Jack had his wife Maxine Cates Dempsey served with divorce papers. In his filing in Salt Lake City, Utah, he charged her with infidelity. The two were said to have separated six months ago. On February 4, 1919, a divorce decree was granted by default.[588]

On February 13 in Altoona, Pennsylvania, Dempsey gave a 3-round exhibition at the Mishler theatre, demonstrating his cleverness.[589]

EDDIE SMITH,
Who Meets Dempsey Tonight.

On Friday February 14, 1919 in Altoona, Dempsey took on big local iron worker Eddie Smith, a 190-pound man who stood 6'1" and said he wanted to win the $1,000, confident that he could stay 3 rounds. He had prior boxing experience, having won a couple of bouts at Johnstown. He recently worked at the South Altoona foundries. Dempsey knocked out Smith in the 1st round, with one punch.[590]

In late February, John Reisler said his contract with Dempsey had been upheld in New York. He would start injunction suits to prevent Willard vs. Dempsey. He claimed that Dempsey owed him $36,000.[591]

On March 1, 1919 in Washington, D.C., a show was held to entertain wounded soldiers at the Walter Reed Hospital, inside the new Red Cross building. Dempsey boxed with former foe Terry Keller, now his sparring partner, in a 3-round exhibition. Dempsey exhibited his skill, outclassing Keller, demonstrating clever footwork and wonderful shifting. Still, Keller showed enough aggressiveness to force Dempsey to extend himself at times. Unlike Dempsey, Keller wore a headgear. In a letter, U.S. President Woodrow Wilson apologized that he could not attend, owing to his numerous duties and appointments.[592]

Although the President did not attend the exhibition, Dempsey subsequently met President Wilson at the White House. President Wilson

---

[587] *Salt Lake Telegram*, January 29, 1919.
[588] *Salt Lake Herald-Republican*, February 2, 5, 1919; *Deseret News*, February 3, 1919.
[589] *Altoona Times*, February 14, 1919.
[590] *Altoona Times*, February 13, 1919. No post-bout report was in the local papers. *Sayre Evening Times*, *Wilkes-Barre Evening News*, February 14, 1919; *Scranton Republican*, February 15, 1919.
[591] *Buffalo Times*, February 20, 1919.
[592] *Washington Herald*, *Washington Times*, *Evening Star*, March 1, 1919; *Washington Herald*, *Washington Evening Star*, March 2, 1919.

looked him over and said, "A lot of people think you can win the coming fight."⁵⁹³

**Dempsey and Keller**

Jim Flynn, the veteran fireman fighter, said Dempsey was too small to beat Jess Willard.

> Willard is too big for any of them to beat today. He is a real fighter, in spite of what they say of him, and I haven't any particular love for him myself. ... Jess will simply stand off and keep Dempsey, with his shorter arms, from hitting him. Willard is a good boxer, will have a good defense, and ought to be able to wear Dempsey down, even if he doesn't put him away with one punch.⁵⁹⁴

The Dempsey-Willard purse would be the largest in history, at $127,500 total to both fighters guaranteed. Hence, Dempsey would be paid $27,500, which was fantastic money for a challenger, nearly as much as Jack Johnson used to demand to *defend* his championship title against top contenders. Dempsey was not yet the champion.⁵⁹⁵

On March 4, 1919 in San Francisco, Willie Meehan won a 4-round decision over Sam Langford, fighting in his usual rough and aggressive style, winning every round.⁵⁹⁶

---

⁵⁹³ *Boston Globe*, March 10, 1919.
⁵⁹⁴ *Louisville Courier-Journal*, March 1, 1919.
⁵⁹⁵ *Pittsburgh Post-Gazette*, March 2, 1919.
⁵⁹⁶ *San Francisco Chronicle, Examiner, Brooklyn Citizen*, March 5, 1919.

JACK DEMPSEY

Dempsey soon would headline a traveling circus of boxers, wrestlers, and acrobats, who would travel around giving exhibitions in an athletic carnival. He and Kearns were capitalizing on the public's desire to see the man matched to fight for the title.[597]

On Friday March 7, 1919, at the Majestic theater in Scranton, Pennsylvania, Jack Dempsey stopped Curley McGuire in the 1st round.[598]

Starting on March 9 or 10, Dempsey was in Pittsburgh to exhibit there for several days, sparring 3 rounds with Terry Keller, who had been touring the Eastern states with Dempsey.

Herman Miller, one of Jack's sparring partners, said Dempsey would knock out Willard. "He can knock any man cold with a blow of no more than six inches. No matter how clever Willard is he cannot keep away from this fellow." Miller said that in his sparring, Jack actually held back, though you might hardly realize it, he was so powerful. "With everything in his punch nobody could stand up long."[599]

TEX RICKARD
He will handle the Willard-Dempsey fight next July 4.

From Havana, Cuba, Jack Johnson again claimed to have thrown the Willard fight. He wanted to fight Willard, Dempsey, or Fulton in Havana.[600]

Dempsey wrote that he expected to stop Willard within 10 rounds, and would weigh about 200 pounds for the fight. He planned to fight at close quarters and use inside blows to outpunch him. "I have trained myself to deliver a knockout blow that travels but a few inches." Willard was not an inside fighter. He liked to use his long left jab, fighting cautiously and defensively, playing it safe, stalling, and fighting deliberately from the outside. Dempsey's aggression and speed would keep the pace fast and make Jess fight.

Continuing, Jack said,

> Without boasting I will say that no man can go into the ring with me and stall. I always get right into the fighting from the tap of the bell and try to drop my man at the first opportunity. That is why I have always difficulty in getting sparring partners, because the better they are the more likely I am to put them down and out.

---

[597] *Chattanooga News*, March 6, 1919.
[598] *Scranton Republican*, March 7, 8, 1919. Clearly Dempsey/Kearns had no problem re-using opponents.
[599] *Pittsburg Press*, March 11, 1919; *Harrisburg Telegraph*, March 12, 1919; *Altoona Tribune*, March 15, 1919.
[600] *Buffalo Times*, March 13, 1919.

Dempsey granted that Willard was huge and strong, but "the bigger they are the harder they fall." Jack had taken out big, tall, strong men, so size did not concern him. "It has been said that I am not a clever boxer, but you don't see any marks on me. I haven't had a nosebleed or a black eye in my last six fights; there are no tin ears on my head and I haven't a scar. Which is one way of saying I don't get hit much." He expected to be the heavyweight champion of the world.[601]

Dempsey rested a bit from his touring, but would start up with his athletic carnival traveling circus after about a ten-day hiatus. Dempsey's exhibition tour was scheduled to travel to places like Syracuse, Toronto, Montreal, Toledo, Columbus, Indianapolis, Milwaukee, Minneapolis, Duluth, Des Moines, St. Louis, Omaha, Kansas City, and many others. His salary was an alleged $1,000 per day; excellent money. Kearns said Jack weighed 197 pounds, but would enter the ring between 192 and 197.[602]

There was a great deal of discussion regarding where the championship fight might be held. A lot of cities were competing to host the contest. However, some towns outright banned it from being held there.

Willard's manager said Jess already had begun training, and was weighing a little under 270 pounds.[603]

Jim Corbett said the upcoming fight was between a giant with a powerful physique and endurance, who could take a punch and box carefully, against a young, ripping, tearing fighter. Willard essentially had been outpointed in decision contests against Gunboat Smith and Tom McMahon, but he had improved since then. He proved his toughness, strength, and condition against the very skillful, experienced, and fast Johnson, but many also believed that Johnson was beaten by age, inactivity, and fatigue more than anything. Still, no ordinary fighter could beat the masterful Johnson. Willard supporters said he simply was much too big, tall, long, and strong for Dempsey. Dempsey supporters said Jack was too fast, ferocious, relentless, and powerful for Willard.[604]

Kearns said Spider Kelly would be Dempsey's trainer (or one of his trainers) for the Willard fight.

Billy Miske and Willie Meehan, the only men to go the route recently with Dempsey, gave their insights. Miske said, "Dempsey is dangerous only in close quarters. His right isn't much, but that left hander of his is a lu-lu." Meehan saw matters totally differently. "I never found that bird a bad one in close quarters and he never did me any dirt with a left hander. But, say, at long range work Jack's a regular he-man and when it comes to steam – well, that right paw of his is a Baldwin locomotive."

In late March, the *Atlanta Constitution* said neither Willard nor Dempsey would fight Jack Johnson or accept his challenge. Johnson currently was in Mexico. "Willard disposed of Johnson at Havana in 1915 and rid the ring of

---

[601] *La Crosse Tribune*, March 17, 1919.
[602] *Poughkeepsie Eagle-News*, March 18, 1919.
[603] *Richmond Times Dispatch*, March 19, 1919; *Great Bend Tribune*, March 20, 1919
[604] *Calgary Herald*, March 19, 1919.

its most objectionable character, and that he will ever get another chance is unthinkable." Besides, Johnson would be 41 years old at month's end.[605]

On Friday March 28, 1919 at the Detroit Armory in Detroit Michigan, Dempsey and Terry Kellar sparred 6 one-minute rounds. Jack just toyed with Terry, pulling his punches, but showing his speed.

Before the exhibition, Kellar informed the press that this would be the last bout between he and Dempsey, for even sparring with him was too strenuous, and he needed a rest. The first time he fought Dempsey at Ogden, he was told that Dempsey was an easy set-up. He was paid $1,600, and took the worst beating he ever endured. Kellar said he would bet everything he owned that Dempsey would beat Willard.[606]

On Monday March 31, 1919 at the Armory in Chester, Pennsylvania, Dempsey exhibited with former foe and sparring partner Andre Anderson, who recently returned from France. Anderson stood 6'5 ¼" and weighed 235 pounds. William Rocap refereed their 3-round exhibition bout, and later wrote about it. Before the exhibition, he interviewed Dempsey.

Dempsey was confident that he would beat Willard because he had strength, youth, hitting powers, and a get-there spirit. He had all the vigor and recuperative powers of youth. Willard had been absent from serious boxing for years, had accumulated a lot of fat, and at closer to age 40 than 30, would lack recuperative powers. "I weigh 195 pounds tonight, and as you know, am virtually six feet tall. I am plenty big enough for Willard. He is only human and can only stand so much. He will be like scores of others I have met. He will go down from my body blows. I will lace him about the mid-section and will soon bring him down to my size." Jack said he hit harder than Willard, and would hit him often, giving him the "greatest whaling about the body he ever received."

Regarding the Meehan fight, Dempsey said, "Meehan with his clownish antics naturally has the crowd with him, especially as they were all native sons. But I broke two of his ribs in the 4-round bout, and he knows that I can stop him any time inside of 10 rounds, hence there has never been any return match."

During the waning months of the war, Dempsey had been connected with the local Sun Shipbuilding company as a labor scout. The shipbuilders wanted him to show his stuff. Hence, in order to do so, the rounds with Anderson were cut down to 2 minutes each, so Jack could let himself out more and show them the real thing. Rocap said Dempsey proceeded to pound on Anderson.

> Dempsey gave one of the greatest exhibitions of two-handed fighting ever seen in a Chester ring. He boxed just for an instant in the first round, then he cut loose. In the third and last round he drove the big

---

[605] *Washington Herald, Muncie Star Press, Atlanta Constitution*, March 26, 1919.
[606] *Detroit Free Press*, March 28, 29, 1919; *Buffalo Times*, March 31, 1919; *Buffalo Commercial*, April 1, 1919. Jack allegedly weighed 197 pounds, though another report said Kellar weighed about 180 pounds to Dempsey's 190 pounds.
That same day, March 28, 1919 in San Francisco, Willie Meehan won a 4-round decision over Jeff Clark.

235-pound Anderson all over the ring with body blows. Dempsey sank his left and right with all of his 195 pounds back of each punch into Anderson's mid-section. His body bent, his head came over, like a flash Dempsey shot his right to the jaw, and Anderson was sent through the ropes, off the platform into the laps of the spectators. He was helped to the ring and he clinched for a moment. Dempsey shook him off and the bell rang ending the round. The timekeeper had cut it to one minute and thirty seconds.

The bout proved to Rocap that Dempsey was one of the fastest men for his size and weight ever. He was a free, hard hitter, with accurate judgment of distance. He constantly kept on top of his opponent, never allowing him to get set for a punch. Kearns had difficulty getting and keeping sparring partners for him. They did not take kindly to the going over. He was arranging for big 215-plus-pound sparring partners, including blacks Bill Tate and big Jack Thompson. Kearns told Rocap, "I have the next world's heavyweight champion."[607]

The local *Chester Times* said Dempsey boxed 4 lightning rounds and showed plainly his excellent fighting ability, showering lefts and rights on Anderson, whom he knocked out of the ring during the 2nd round, but the Chicagoan came back and continued.[608]

On Tuesday April 1, 1919 in New Haven, Connecticut, 197-pound Jack Dempsey stopped 257-pound Tony Drake in just eleven seconds.[609]

On April 2, 1919, Dempsey exhibited in Poughkeepsie, New York at the Rialto Theatre. He boxed 3 rounds with a sparring partner (who was not named, though it might have been John Lester Johnson). Although advertised to box Chicago's Andre Anderson, Andre had left the theatrical tour. Kearns said Anderson had been knocked out the very first night he was secured as a sparring partner, and that was enough for Andre, who declined to work with them further. This was after Kearns had paid for his transportation, $25 salary, plus a $25 loan/advance.[610]

Dempsey added a new sparring partner to his crew, a former opponent, black John Lester Johnson, who had been in the military overseas, and had taken a few shots at Germans in France. He recently had been discharged from the service. Some said that Johnson was a big, clever boxer, and hard hitter, who once beat a young Dempsey in a 10-rounder a few years ago, so he would be an excellent sparring partner. As a result of his military service, Johnson had not fought in over two years, since late December 1916.[611]

The *Chicago Defender* noted that Dempsey did not draw the color line when it came to sparring partners. "All Harlemites recall the bloody battle

---

[607] *Fort Wayne Gazette*, April 6, 1919, via the *Philadelphia Public Ledger*.
[608] *Chester Times*, April 1, 1919. That same day, March 31, 1919, in Pittsburgh, Harry Greb, the Pittsburgh middleweight, clearly won a 10-round no decision over Billy Miske. The *Pittsburgh Gazette Times* said Greb won 7-1-2. The *Pittsburgh Post* said middleweight Greb won 8-1-1. The *Pittsburg Press* said Greb clearly won at least 6 rounds. April 1, 1919.
[609] *Buffalo Enquirer*, *Chattanooga News*, *Wilkes-Barre Evening News*, April 2, 1919.
[610] *Poughkeepsie Eagle-News*, April 3, 1919; *Long Branch Record*, April 5, 1919.
[611] *Buffalo Commercial*, April 5, 1919; *Pittsburgh Post-Gazette*, April 9, 1919.

between Johnson and Dempsey a few years back, when Jack had a hard time staying ten rounds. It was a terrific struggle in which both men took a lot of punishment before it was over. Dempsey was a novice then and Johnson's greater experience told." John Lester had been fighting in the trenches overseas with the Hell Fighters for $30 a month, "while the money-grabbers of the game were buried in shipyards or were walking delegates for the United States employment bureau far from the roar of shot and shell."[612]

The *New York Herald's* "Cross Counter" insisted that John Lester Johnson had not beaten Dempsey. "I was present when Johnson and Dempsey met at the Harlem Sporting Club and it was a foot race, with Johnson in the lead all the way." Johnson's "claiming victories that he did not achieve will not help him very materially." The mere fact that he had served his country well in the military "does not justify him in claiming that he defeated Jack Dempsey."

*Chicago Defender*, May 17, 1919

Cross Counter wondered whether the winner of Willard-Dempsey would decline to fight Harry Wills, owing to his dark complexion. Wills said he knew that the white boxers had drawn the color line against him, and he rather expected it. In fact, no white boxer had entered the ring with Wills since 1914. The 6'3" 200-210-pound Wills had catlike speed. "As a boxer no heavyweight past or present has shown more skill or science than has Wills, and the precision and force of his punch has been demonstrated by his quick defeat of several boxers who consented to meet him other than socially." Langford had knocked him out in 19 rounds in 1916, but last year, in 1918, Wills knocked out Langford twice, in 6 and 7 rounds. He stopped Sam McVey in 6 rounds, and Jeff Clark in 5 rounds. Although all were past their primes,

---

[612] *Chicago Defender*, April 12, 1919.

they were the best he could lure into the ring. "Immediately after these performances by Wills, Willard and Dempsey reaffirmed with emphasis their repugnance to meeting a negro in the squared circle, and there the case stands." Wills would turn 27 years of age in May, and given the stances of Dempsey and Willard, he wasn't likely to get a chance at the title. However, if Dempsey temporarily became color blind, "the resultant combat would be the most exciting that ever took place in a heavyweight match." Dempsey might win with his speed and power, but he would know that he had been in a fight.[613]

The barring of blacks was something the general society and labor force was experiencing as well. The *Defender* noted that sadly, even foreign labor was given preference over American black labor.

**FAMOUS EUROPEAN BOXERS BACK IN CIVILIANS.**

Three famous European champion boxers photographed in London after discarding their military uniforms. Georges Carpentier, heavyweight champion of Europe, is shown shaking hands with Bombardier Wells, the British heavyweight. Little Jimmy Wilde, the British flyweight marvel, is shown on the extreme left. Wilde last night defeated Joe Lynch, American boxer in a fifteen-round bout.

*Buffalo Enquirer*, April 1, 1919

Jack Kearns offered the big and tall Dan Daly (a.k.a. Dailey, Daily, or Daley) $100 per week to be one of Dempsey's sparring partners in his athletic show.

Abe Attell said Dempsey was a sure winner, and he would bet on him no matter how good Willard looked in training. Willard had been too inactive and was too old, whereas Dempsey was young and could fight at a fast pace.[614]

The tour was in Schenectady, New York on April 4, 1919, at the state armory. Dempsey boxed 3 rounds with John Lester Johnson. Jack did not exert himself, but showed enough to satisfy the fans that he would give Willard a good go.[615]

---

[613] *New York Herald*, April 6, 1919; *Wilmington Evening Journal*, April 7, 1919.
[614] *New Castle Herald*, *Tulsa Daily World*, April 4, 1919.
[615] *North Adams Transcript*, April 7, 1919.

The *Cincinnati Enquirer* said Dempsey would tour the East and close the show on or about April 25 in Kansas City. He would rest for three weeks before going into training for the Willard contest.[616]

On Saturday April 5, 1919 in Syracuse, New York, before a crowd of either 2,500 or over 3,000 (depending on the source) at the local Arena, Dempsey boxed with Battling Becky, sometimes called "Fat" Becky, touted as a human punching bag. According to the local *Syracuse Post-Standard*, Becky covered up well with both hands, so Jack could not hit him effectively. However, when he received some body blows, Becky fell to the canvas. Dempsey helped him up and induced him to continue. He was down again in a few seconds, and then refused to continue.

A semi-local report said the bout was scheduled for 3 rounds, but two minutes into the 1st round, after Becky had been sent to the floor for the third time, Referee Jack Kearns waved it off. Becky was willing to continue, but the athletic club president did not want to allow it, for he might get hurt seriously. Becky did not lay a glove on Dempsey, but Jack had a hard time finding him, for he did a lot of running. However, when Dempsey did hit him, the blows could be heard for some distance.

Dempsey then boxed with Spike Sullivan, his sparring partner, but in the 2nd round, Sullivan went down for the full count, knocked out. Dempsey wound up the exhibition with some shadow boxing, which the fans enjoyed.[617]

On April 8, Dempsey and his traveling exhibition tour was at the Armory theater in Binghamton, New York. His various sparring partners and combination members included colored John Lester Johnson, colored middleweight/light heavy Lee Anderson, Martin Burke, Baltimore thunderbolt Herman Miller (a welter/middleweight with 95 fights), Italian champion wrestler Gardini, and jiu jitsu champion Oishi. Jack still was offering $1,000 to any boxer who could stay 3 rounds, but Kearns later clarified they meant any local boxer, not anyone in the world.[618]

That evening, before a crowd that taxed the Armory Theater's capacity, Dempsey boxed with his two negro heavyweight sparring partners, John Lester Johnson and Lee Anderson, 2 rounds each, for 4 total rounds. Using large gloves, Dempsey mostly chased them around the ring, showing speed, footwork, and some power, but overall it was tame and no one was hurt. Still, many suspected, based on the performance, that his hard punch was going to cause the present champion some trouble.

Dempsey was well liked, being called very amiable, and just a big, genial overgrown boy with an open mind, a strong healthy body, and a desire to have everyone for his friend. Outside the ring, the viciousness/roughness often seen in fighters was utterly lacking.[619]

---

[616] *Cincinnati Enquirer*, April 5, 1919.
[617] *Syracuse Post-Standard*, April 6, 1919; *Auburn Citizen*, April 7, 1919.
[618] *Binghamton Press*, April 7, 1919.
[619] *Binghamton Press*, April 9, 1919. Martin Burke and Herman Miller, two heavyweights accompanying the tour, also sparred. There also was a wrestling match and a jiu jitsu exhibition.

One news writer said although Dempsey generally was accredited with a victory over John Lester Johnson, "as a matter of fact, he was clearly outpointed by his dusky opponent." Still, Jack made a remarkably good showing for a green boxer, and was tabbed as a sure comer. His skills at that time were limited, but he was dead game, and never stopped hitting, no matter how hard he was stung. He took the black's best wallops and steadily came on for more. "Dempsey admits that Johnson struck him the hardest blow he ever received during his career in the ring. This was a right hander to the body that landed near the heart during one of the early rounds. The blow broke three of Dempsey's ribs, and it interfered with his breathing." Despite the pain, Dempsey fought on, continually trying to turn the tide. He never was successful at landing flush, but scored many a glancing wallop, and at the end was "almost on even terms with his dusky foe." Dempsey proved his grit and toughness back then, and had improved. Now Johnson was his sparring partner.

Under his current contract with Tex Rickard, Dempsey was forbidden from engaging in other formal contests until the Willard fight, but he could spar and exhibit.[620]

JACK DEMPSEY

Dempsey had no disfigured ears, his nose was fine, and his teeth straight and white. He was a nice, clean, big boy. He had black eyes and a nice smile and laugh. He said he was determined to win the championship. "I've just got to, you know. I feel that I'm going to, too." He appreciated other sports, like tennis and golf. He even enjoyed croquet. Neither of his parents ever had seen him box. He wanted his dad to see him, because he thought he would enjoy it. His mother lived in Salt Lake City, and liked reading about his bouts. "But she don't understand it much." Jack said he had no sweetheart, but would concern himself with that after he won the championship, if he found one that suited him. He was not much of a talker, usually allowing his manager to attend to interviews.[621]

On Wednesday April 9, 1919 in Watertown, New York, at the Armory, before a large crowd of 2,500, Dempsey first boxed 3 rounds with "rangy tar baby" John Lester Johnson. In the 1st round, Johnson exchanged evenly with Dempsey. Thereafter his wind was short and Dempsey had the best of matters. "Johnson once fought Dempsey early in his career and outpointed him, but Dempsey appears to have now developed into his superior." One said Johnson made a "feeble effort" to cope with Dempsey.

---

[620] *Wilkes-Barre Evening News*, April 7, 1919.
[621] *Binghamton Press*, April 8, 1919.

Next, Dempsey stopped a fellow named Jack Williams in the 1st round of a scheduled 3-round affair, dropping him three times. A short left hook turned the trick, decking him for the count. Some said it was a left hook followed by a right hook to the jaw. The bout lasted less than 2 minutes. Dempsey was able to fire in short hooks with ease, some so short that few could see them. Scoring knockouts did not seem to be difficult at all for Jack the Giant Killer.

The local reporter said Dempsey was a big, fast, willing boy, a great two-handed fighter with a powerful punch in either mitt. "He is not given to swings but will shoot a short right and left hook simultaneously with equal precision and weight and has a style entirely of his own. ... His short arm jolts are terrific and should raise havoc with Willard's midsection when they clash Independence Day."[622]

The next night, on April 10, 1919, Dempsey was in Ogdensburg, New York at the local opera house. He still was offering $1,000 to anyone who could stay 3 rounds with him. The "Irish-Indian" fighter drew a big audience. They wanted to see the top contender to the world championship crown. Standing-room only greeted him.

23-year-old Dempsey sparred 3 rounds with sparring partner Dan Dailey/Daly of New Castle, Pennsylvania, who had just joined the crew. Dempsey liked him because he was Willard's size, standing 6'6" and weighing 245 pounds, with an 84" reach. In 1914, Willard had stopped Daly in the 9th round.

Against Daly, Dempsey

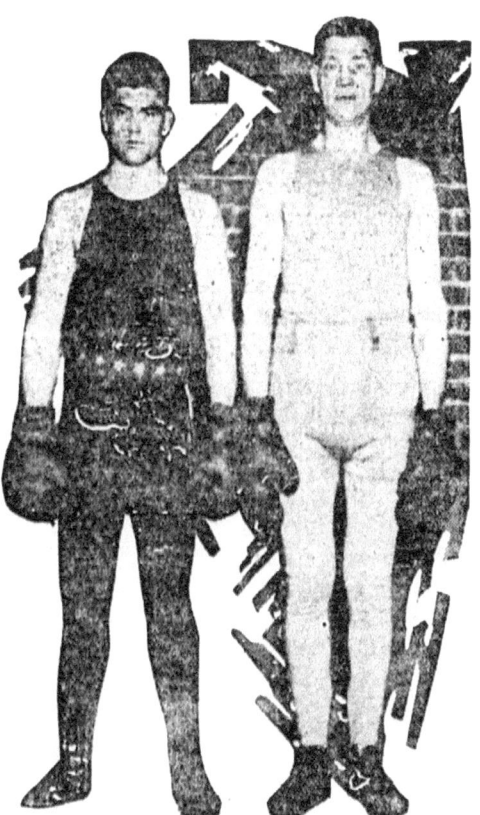

JACK DEMPSEY (LEFT) AND DAN DAILY.

showed himself to be nimble on his feet, stepping about in lively fashion. The fans enjoyed his fast footwork. He was quick and willing, with a wallop in either hand, including a clever right and left hook.[623]

---

[622] *Watertown Daily Times*, April 10, 1919. Also sparring with the Dempsey show were fighters Lee Anderson, Herman Miller, and Martin Burke, all of whom sometimes sparred with Dempsey, sometimes with each other, or sometimes with a local man.
[623] *Ogdensburg News*, April 11, 1919; *Wilkes-Barre Times Leader*, April 9, 1919. Dan Dailey's record included: 1912 WND6 Jim Coffey, WND6 Soldier Kearns, and WND10 George Davis; 1913 LND6

Damon Runyon reported that Dempsey started off as a hobo. He spent years illegally clinging to the rods or riding the baggage or decks of freight and passenger trains. He had conflicts with railroad conductors and brakemen, town hacks, constables, bulls, dicks, elbows, and other minions of the law. He fought for meager sums. Now he was going to receive $27,500 guaranteed for the Willard fight. But the title would be worth easily a quarter of a million dollars. Willard had made nearly that since the Johnson fight, and he only had one fight in the years since winning the crown in 1915. He would be earning $100,0000 more for this fight. A few years earlier in their careers, they would have fought one another for peanuts. Jack humorously said, "I've fought for a lot less."

Dempsey had an engaging frankness. He admitted being whipped several times. He even told of one no decision fight in which nearly all of the sporting writers gave him the decision, but which he candidly admitted that he got a "fine pasting" and was laid up for weeks as a result (likely the John Lester Johnson fight). Most fighters invented a bunch of bunk stories about how they beat certain opponents by using brilliant strategy, and claimed they invented certain punches. Dempsey wasn't like that. He said he was a natural fighter who fought by instinct. "How did I lick that fellow? Well I hit him in the belly and then I hit him on the chin." He also said, "Say, if some of these fighters can do all the thinking they'd have you believe they do in the ring, it's a wonder they don't out-think some of those smacks they get on the jaw." The best advice he ever got were two words from Kearns: "Move around!"

His parents were proud of him, and did not object to his profession. He drank beer on occasion, and was willing to admit it, unlike most fighters who falsely claimed they never touched a drop. But he did not smoke, for he said it made him sick. "He fights for no lofty purpose. He fights not to support an indigent family, because his family were all doing pretty well before he ever earned a nickel in the ring." (This contradicted claims that his parents were poor and Dempsey supported them.) He fought because he liked to fight, had a natural inclination for it, was good at it, and boxing earned him a good living.

Dempsey admitted to drawing the color line currently. "He draws the 'color line' at present, yet he does not lie about his reasons. He says there is no money in fighting black men. They are not good drawing cards. He has fought numerous negroes in the past and will fight them again regardless of whether he becomes champion – if there is enough money in it for him."[624]

On April 11, 1919 in Montreal, Canada, at the Theatre Francais, Dempsey sparred 6 rounds total with Spike Sullivan, Dan Daly, and John Lester Johnson. The local *Montreal Gazette* said Dempsey failed to create an impression, for his boxing lacked science, though his punching power was

---

Coffey, LND12 George Rodel, and KO2 Al Palzer; 1914 LKOby9 Jess Willard, LND10 Rodel, LND6 Coffey, and LND10 Tony Ross; and 1916 LKOby1 Carl Morris. Daily had been a sparring partner for Frank Moran prior to Moran's 1916 title challenge against Willard.

[624] *San Francisco Examiner*, April 13, 17, 1919; *Wilmington Morning News*, April 15, 1919. Runyon suspected he was older than 23, the only area he wasn't so sure about Jack's truthfulness. Jack was telling the truth.

apparent. Jack looked more like a light heavyweight than a heavyweight. He had undertaken a great task against Willard, who would have huge physical advantages. Dempsey appeared to be slow and clumsy compared to Jack Johnson and Jim Corbett in their primes, but was credited with having a harder punch than either one. Whether his punch would have the same effect on a truly large man like Willard remained to be seen. He did demonstrate remarkably good footwork and used both hands at all times. He decked Sullivan with the left in the 1st of 2 rounds, and dropped him with the right in the 2nd round. But he was forced to punch hard to make an impression.[625]

Dempsey stopped off for a rest day in Buffalo on the 13th. His athletic carnival was scheduled to show in 26 cities, a different city each day, except for Sundays, all the way until the 29th in Omaha.

Dempsey said he had been roaming the country since he was 14 years old. His father raised the devil with him for having a fight when he was a kid, and he ran away from home (changing his prior story that his parents were supportive). He came back to Montrose three years later to visit his parents, when he was 17. After embarking on his boxing career, he wound up in California broke, and eventually Kearns became his manager, and had been his pal ever since.[626]

On Tuesday April 15, 1919 in Columbus, Ohio, at the Memorial Hall, Dempsey quickly knocked out two men – Fred Wilk of Columbus and Big Harris of New York.

On April 16 in Canton, Ohio, Dempsey sparred 2 rounds with John Lester Johnson and 2 rounds with Mickey Sullivan, a light heavy from Montreal. Dempsey floored Sullivan in the 1st round, then picked him up. He had to box under wraps for the most part.[627]

The *Indianapolis Star* reported that over the past 12 days on his athletic tour, Dempsey had knocked out 12 men.[628]

Dempsey was in Muncie, Indiana on April 17 at the Wysor Grand theater. He boxed 4 friendly rounds with John Lester Johnson.[629]

On April 18 at Tomlinson Hall in Indianapolis, Indiana, Dempsey boxed 4 rounds, 2 rounds each with "Hiram" Miller of Baltimore and John Lester Johnson, a "huge colored heavyweight." At Kearns' urging, for fear that they would quit, Jack did his best not to hit his partners too hard or too often, so he stepped, dodged, and ducked. Kearns said Dempsey would weigh about 190 pounds for the Willard fight.

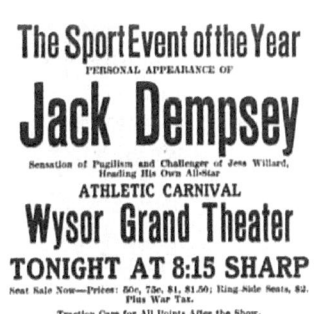

---

[625] *Montreal Gazette*, April 12, 1919.
[626] *Buffalo Commercial*, April 14, 1919; *Wilmington Evening Journal*, April 30, 1919.
[627] *St. Louis Star*, April 17, 1919.
[628] *Indianapolis Star*, April 17, 1919.
[629] *Muncie Morning Star*, April 18, 1919. *Muncie Star Press*, April 17, 1919.

WILLARD, a veritable giant, measured up as follows at the time of his last fight, in Madison Square Garden in 1916, against Moran:

Weight 259 pounds (now believed to be much heavier.)
Height 6 feet 7 inches.
Reach 83 1-2 inches.
Neck 17 1-2 inches.
Chest normal 39 inches.
Chest expanded 44 1-2 inches.
Waist 37 inches.
Thigh 25½ inches.
Calf 17 1-2 inches.
Biceps (right) 15 3-4 inches.
Biceps (left) 15 1-4 inches.
Wrist (right) 8 1-4 inches.
Wrist (left) 8 1-8 inches.

Willard has to his credit 18 knockouts.

DEMPSEY is the lightest of the heavyweight contenders who have been given a chance by ring experts to grab the title. To realize the task he has cut out for himself in beating down the mountain of muscle and bone represented by the present champion, it is only necessary to consult the following figures on the challenger's size:

Weight 197 pounds.
Height 6 feet 1 1-2 inches.
Reach 78 inches.
Chest normal 42 inches.
Chest expanded 46 inches.
Waist 32 1-2 inches.
Neck 17 inches.
Wrist 8 1-2 inches.
Thigh 23 inches.
Calf 15 inches.
Biceps 13 1-2 inches.
Ankle 9 inches.

Dempsey has twenty knockouts to his credit and has been a sensational winner of several other events. He is given more class by ring experts than any heavyweight title contender in recent years.

A lady reporter named Mary Bostwick wrote that after seeing Dempsey, she would wager on him, for she did not see how anything less than an armored tank could lick him.

Dempsey told Bostwick that fighting came natural to him, just as other things came naturally to others. As a boy in the San Luis valley in Colorado, he had gotten early fight practice with Mexicans. "Those Mexican kids were mean and we had to fight them all the time." He had a half dozen brothers, and one was a fighter. Jack could not remember when he wasn't fighting or trying to fight. He had been fighting for about six years.

Jack said it was hard getting and keeping sparring partners. He tried not to hit them too hard, "but sometimes I kind of smack 'em a little, and for some reason or other, I've lost about twelve or fifteen sparring partners since I started out." He had been exhibiting for about four months. The only regular left was a lone colored gent (likely John Lester Johnson).[630]

On Monday April 21, 1919 in Cedar Rapids, Iowa, at Greene's opera house, Dempsey boxed 3 rounds with Denver's Jack Geyer,

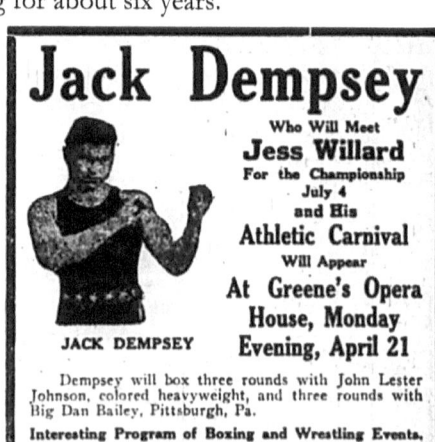

**Jack Dempsey**
Who Will Meet
**Jess Willard**
For the Championship
July 4
and His
**Athletic Carnival**
Will Appear
**At Greene's Opera House, Monday**
JACK DEMPSEY    Evening, April 21

Dempsey will box three rounds with John Lester Johnson, colored heavyweight, and three rounds with Big Dan Bailey, Pittsburgh, Pa.
Interesting Program of Boxing and Wrestling Events.
PRICES—$1, $1.50, $2, $2.50 and $3, Plus War Tax.
SEAT SALE SATURDAY MORNING.
Owing to Victory Loan Drive, Program Will Not Start Until 9:30.

---

[630] *Indianapolis Star*, April 19, 1919.

an experienced veteran who had over 50 fights (and typically weighed about 200 pounds). Dempsey was quick on his feet and landed at will on his burly opponent. "Dempsey does not favor any particular punch and has lots of steam behind any that he chooses to use." His dodging and ability to get past the guard was evident as he darted in and out and around Geyer, which he evidently intended to do against Willard. Dempsey constantly had to change and add sparring partners, for he put them out of commission quite often.[631]

In Waterloo, Iowa on the 22nd, Dempsey showed speed, hitting ability, and youth, boxing 3 short rounds with John Lester Johnson.[632]

They were at the Sioux City, Iowa Auditorium on the 23rd, performing to a crowd of 1,000. The show was said to be a thriller, though the boxing was tame. Jack sparred 2 rounds with "negro giant" John Lester Johnson, who was said to be bigger than Jack Johnson, and then 2 more rounds with Jack Geyer.

Dempsey claimed to have knocked out in 1 round several fighters who had done relatively well with Willard, including Al Williams (whom Willard stopped in 8 rounds in 1913), Tom McMahon (who won a 1914 12-round no decision over Willard), Gunboat Smith (1913 W20 Willard), and Charles Miller (1913 D4 Willard).[633] On his present tour, he had used up over 30 sparring partners, many of whom either beat Willard or gave him a hard battle. Jack claimed to have fought nine men since offering $1,000 to all comers in the towns covered. "All went over the knockout route in less than one round." Although he would earn only 1/3 of what Willard would make for their fight, "I conceded Willard the big end of the money so I could get a crack at him."[634]

On April 24 in Omaha, Nebraska, Dempsey boxed 2 rounds with John Lester Johnson and 2 rounds with Jack Geyer. "Dempsey smothered both opponents with ridiculous ease," and "generously pulled his punches and did not try for a k.o."[635]

On April 25, 1919, at the Coliseum in Des Moines, Iowa, Dempsey boxed 3 brief one-minute exhibition rounds wearing big 10-ounce gloves against Denver Jack Geyer, showing clever footwork. Dempsey made no effort to hit Geyer, for fear of hurting the aged boxer. However, it was evident that Dempsey was exceedingly fast for a heavyweight. He could step around easily enough and was able to duck and dodge and move in and out with quickness and cleverness. He did not attempt offense, so no one saw his punching power.

---

[631] *Cedar Rapids Gazette*, April 22, 1919. Jack Geyer's record included: 1910 L10 Gunboat Smith; 1911 KO9 Gunboat Smith, LTKOby9 Carl Morris, and D10 Charley Miller; 1912 W10 Gunboat Smith and W4 Frank Moran; 1913 W4 Rufe Cameron, LKOby8 Soldier Kearns, and D10 Carl Morris; 1914 L15 Dick Gilbert; 1915 LKOby3 Tom McMahon, and LND10 Battling Levinsky; 1916 LKOby5 Jim Coffey, L9 and D15 Joe Bonds; and 1917 LND12 Jack Moran.
[632] *Waterloo Courier*, April 23, 1919. Dempsey was supposed to box with Dan Dailey as well, but did not.
[633] Dempsey possibly was alluding to gym sparring bouts or exhibitions with Williams or McMahon, because no record listed any such contests. Williams was a Dempsey sparring partner in April 1918.
[634] *Sioux City Journal*, April 23, 24, 1919.
[635] *Lincoln Daily Star*, April 25, 1919.

Jack North, writing for the *Des Moines Tribune*, said the exhibition was rotten. Jack ducked and tapped over the course of a few minutes, but that was all. Fans were upset, for ringside seats cost $5.50. The show was not worth the price of the war tax. Dempsey did not demonstrate his training stunts as he was supposed to do, and did not box John Lester Johnson either, which had been advertised. Other members of the troupe exhibited with one another, but folks were there to see Dempsey do something more, and that he did not do. Likely Jack was burned out from all the daily boxing.

The *Des Moines Register*'s Sec Taylor said Dempsey appeared small in tights. He did not look like a 200-pound pugilist, nor did he look as tall as the advertised 6'1". Regardless of his real height and weight, it was certain that he would fight the champion under a much greater handicap than most fans realized.

Dempsey was not concerned by Willard's size. "I do know that I am sure he cannot hurt me and that I am the better hitter. It's true that he will have every advantage of weight, height and reach, but I have the advantage of youth, confidence and hitting power. I have met many men heavier than myself and nobody knows how much fun I have had out of my encounters with them." Kearns said Dempsey was lightning-fast at 190 pounds, his present weight, and would knock out Willard within 5 rounds.

Kearns said they would close their tour in Kansas City the following week, then head to Excelsior Springs, Missouri to rest until they knew the exact location of the big fight.[636]

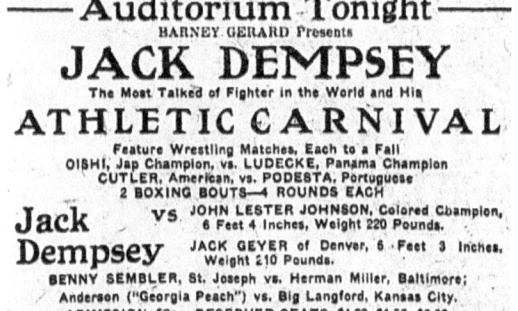

Dempsey was in St. Joseph, Missouri on Saturday April 26. He told the local reporter, "There is no doubt in my mind about the outcome of my battle with Jess Willard. I will win, and win quickly." Jack said he had youth, speed, and proven ability to hit hard enough to tumble them, regardless of size. "I expect a tough battle, but it will be short. I am going after him from the first ring of the bell, and will stay on top of him until I have won." Dempsey was a "clean-cut, gentlemanly looking fellow, wearing the latest styles and looking like a model for a brand of clothes."

The local paper said John Lester Johnson stood 6'4" and weighed 220 pounds. Jack Geyer stood 6'2" or 6'3" and weighed 210 pounds. Dempsey was scheduled/advertised to box each one 3 rounds.

1,000 fans attended the exhibition at the St. Joseph Auditorium, but were disappointed. Dempsey sparred only 3 1.5-minute rounds with John

---

[636] *Des Moines Register*, April 26, 1919; *Des Moines Tribune*, April 25, 26, 1919. Dempsey was with Kearns, John Lester Johnson, and Dan Daly, sparring partners, as well as Oishi, jiujitsu expert, and Gardini, wrestling champ.

Lester Johnson that were tame, and did not box with Geyer. Apparently, Geyer was ill from drinking some bad water, and Dempsey was said to be off form for the same reason.[637]

Dempsey's tour closed in Kansas City, Missouri on Monday April 28, 1919. He would rest for a bit before going into formal training.[638]

It was reported that Dempsey's salary had been $10,000 per month for the past three months. He had earned $32,000 from his tour, so already he was a wealthy man, at least relative to the average American.[639]

32-year-old 6'6½" 247-pound Dan Daily had been a Dempsey exhibition sparring partner. Despite his 84 ½" reach, Daily said he could not keep Dempsey off of him. Daily had fought Willard (1914 LKOby9) and Palzer (1913 KO2), and sparred with Moran, Fulton, and others. Daily predicted victory for Dempsey over Willard. "He'll knock Willard out. Nothing can stand before him."[640]

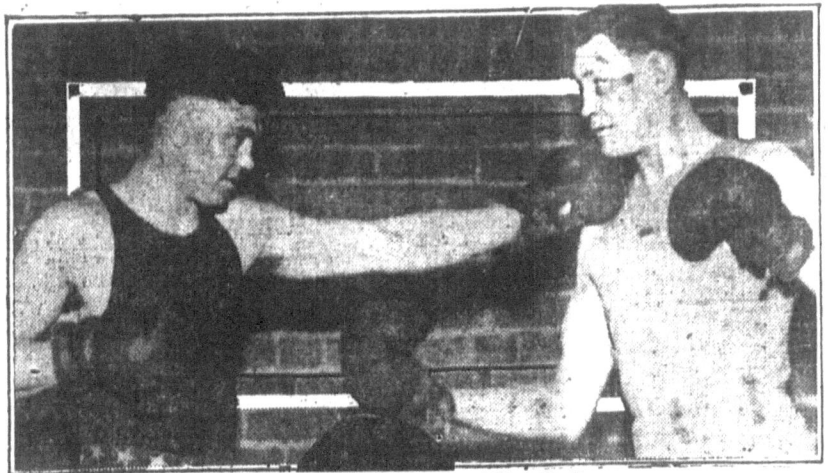

**Dempsey and 247-pound Dan Daily**

In late June, the *East Liverpool Review* claimed that during his theatrical tour through New Jersey and Pennsylvania, Dempsey dropped the following men in 1 round each: Jack McGuire, Trenton; Kid Harrison, Easton; Kid Henry, Shenandoah; Bill Hickey, Shamokin; Jim Harrison, Harrisburg; and Kid Kiofowsky, Reading.[641]

---

[637] *St. Joseph Gazette*, *St. Joseph News-Press*, April 26, 1919; *St. Joseph Gazette*, April 27, 1919.
[638] *Muncie Star Press*, April 17, 1919. The Lincoln show on the 29th was canceled.
[639] *St. Louis Star*, April 30, 1919.
[640] *Wilmington Evening Journal*, April 30, 1919. Daily claimed he floored Willard (not true), and the police stopped the mill in the 9th round (not true). Daily said he was the winner, even though the record books credited Willard with a knockout. He said he was better than Willard, and Dempsey better than he, so Jack would beat Jess. The truth is that the 236-pound Willard dominated and knocked out the then 207-pound Daly with a right uppercut in the 9th round.
[641] *East Liverpool Review*, June 28, 1919.

CHAPTER 22

# Championship Preparation

In early May 1919, Tex Rickard announced that the championship bout between Jack Dempsey and Jess Willard was scheduled for 12 rounds in Toledo, Ohio (about 58 miles southwest of Detroit), at 3 p.m. on Friday July 4, 1919. A points decision would be awarded if there was no knockout. 12 rounds to a decision was the maximum length that Ohio would allow. They also could not box for a purse under the law. Hence, Rickard was employing them each for a flat fee to give an exhibition. Both would train at the scene for five weeks prior to the contest. The press would cover their training on a daily basis for a boxing-loving public.

Rickard said $127,500 would be paid to the boxers - $100,000 to Willard and $27,500 to Dempsey. By way of comparison, in 1918 and 1919, the world's highest paid baseball player was Ty Cobb, who made $20,000 per year. Jess Willard would earn five times that amount for only one fight, as opposed to an entire season of work.

The battle would be staged at Bay View Park on Maumee Bay, which was under Toledo's jurisdiction. Tex would construct a 40,000 to 50,000 seat arena for the fight. He was co-promoting with Frank B. Flournoy, who was associated with Rickard and several others in two big cattle ranches in Paraguay, South America. One ranch had 325,000 acres and the other 90,000. They had a canning factory and packing house. Around 500 cattle out of 40,000 were killed every day.

JACK DEMPSEY

Dempsey was not at all concerned by Willard's great size, reasoning that he did very well with big men, for they just provided a bigger target. He was certain that he would win by knockout.

Although Dempsey was not yet in town, the *Toledo News-Bee* told readers that he was a good-natured, rollicking, likeable schoolboy. To meet him was to like him. He had a personality. He was not educated or polished, but neither was he a roughneck. When he spoke, he showed no traces of the hobo he formerly was. He had common sense, did not talk rough, was not a loud dresser, and was not handicapped with a look of coarseness common to many fighters. His head and face were unmarked. He had no cauliflower ears. He dressed well, with good taste. Jack was educated in the school of experience, had a big heart, and was mighty polite. He was at ease under the fire of an interviewer, and was obliging. Already he had made lots of friends among the newsmen. Dempsey attracted some attention on the street. He was not backward with strangers; with the glad hand out for all. Jack was not one to butt into the conversation much, content to let others do most of the talking, though he would "come across" if questioned. Fame had not turned his head. He led a pretty clean life, only drinking a bottle of beer occasionally, though he did not smoke. He liked lots of sleep, and was in bed by 10 or 11 p.m. every night. He did not care for the athletic circus he had been with for the past month, for it often kept him up late at night and interrupted his sleep patterns. He liked the outdoors, and enjoyed playing ball, hunting, or roaming through woods or over hills. He had played a few games of golf and liked it.[642]

Boxing since 1911, 37-year-old world heavyweight champion Jess Willard's 24-5-2 record included: 1911 LDQ10 and KO3 Lewis Fink, KO4 William Schiller, and LTKOby5 Joe Cox (Willard retired, saying, "I'm in no condition to fight."[643]); 1912 KO6 Bull Young, WND10 Arthur Pelkey (eventual white champ), D/WND10 Luther McCarty (hard-punching eventual number one contender), and KO8 Soldier Kearns; 1913 L20 Gunboat Smith (many thought it was a draw), D4 Charley Miller, KO11 Bull Young (Young died), L/DND10 and KO9 George Rodel, WND10 Carl Morris, and KO2 George Davis; 1914 LND12 Tom McMahon, KO9 Dan Dailey, and KO6 Rodel; 1915 KO26 Jack Johnson (world heavyweight championship), and 1916 WND10 Frank Moran (world title defense).

Despite the image of Willard being the older, wiser, more experienced man, Dempsey actually had double the number of bouts of experience, with over 60 fights at that point in his career. However, Willard had an aura about him as a result of being the one man who was able to knock out the seemingly invincible great Jack Johnson, who other than a very questionable 1905 decision loss and an immediately avenged 1905 disqualification, had not really lost a fight since 1901. 26 rounds of experience against Johnson was the equivalent of a graduate degree in boxing. Plus, Jess Willard was a huge and awe-inspiring mountain of a man. He made big men look small.

Tex Rickard paid Lloyd's $5,050 for a $50,000 insurance policy on the fight; should anything prevent the contest. Rickard also had a $100,000 New York accident insurance policy on himself, which cost $1,150. It would cost more to promote this fight than any other contest ever. The cost to print tickets was several thousands of dollars, in addition to the $1,500 paid for the ticket engraving. Tex already spent a good-sized sum in railroad fares, telegraph and telephone bills, and other incidentals totaling $10,000. The U.S. government would charge a 10% tax, plus Toledo had a 7% tax.

---

[642] *Toledo News-Bee*, May 5, 1919; *Sandusky Register, Dayton Herald*, May 6, 1919.
[643] *Springfield Missouri Republican*, October 10, 1911.

Ticket prices would go from $10 up to $60, an increase from prior plans, owing to the great expenses, including the very large purses.

Dempsey left Chicago by auto on May 14 to head to Maumee Bay, Toledo, along with Kearns and Billy McCarney.[644]

Dick Meade said Dempsey was dark-skinned, wearing his black hair pushed back. He was weighing 197 pounds. He wore a dark gray suit, patent leather shoes with gray uppers, supported by a bow tie and cap. He had big hands. Jack the Giant Killer said he wished the fight was taking place the next day, he was so eager.

Kearns said he was not a bit worried about the fight.

> I don't fear Willard, because he is a manufactured boxer and Dempsey is a natural fighter. Jess was simply a huge white hope, who was fistically constructed to beat Jack Johnson, an all-in champion, ready to be put away by any top-notch man. As a matter of fact, the Jack Dempsey of today could have licked Willard and Johnson in that same ring on that same April afternoon at Havana, back in 1915. ...

> [Willard will] find in Jack an elusive, fast, clever boxer, who can hit harder with both hands than any other heavyweight the ring has known. You just watch Dempsey in training, and I believe it won't be long before you have as much confidence as I have. Jack has been battling right along, and Willard is rusty. I feel as sure as I am sitting here that Jack Dempsey will be the next champion of the world.

Kearns spoke so vehemently and enthusiastically that one got the impression that he really believed what he said.[645]

**Dempsey and Kearns. Jack target shooting.**

---

[644] *Toledo News-Bee*, May 12, 14, 1919. Billy McCarney formerly managed Luther McCarty.
[645] *Toledo News-Bee*, May 17, 1919.

On May 20, 1919 in Maumee Bay, Toledo, at the Overland Club at Point Place on the bay shore, with head trainer Jimmy De Forest, Dempsey began light training. The club was a large building with plenty of rooms, a great lounging room, wide screened-in porch, a bathing beach, shade trees, and a handy tract for the erection of an arena where Dempsey would work out.[646]

### THE SHIMMY-JAZZ OF MAUMEE BAY

MAY KAPLAN    JACK DEMPSEY    JIMM DE FOREST    KING

For the first few days, Jack just did a little road work in the morning, and in the afternoon some shadow boxing and dummy punching. He was eager to start sparring. "He bubbles over with spirit and wants to do something every minute." He liked to engage in playful antics and stunts with his camp mates to take the edge off his abundant energy. He wrestled and slap sparred with Max Kaplan, camp companion and born comedian, engaged in a game of leap frog, played the harmonica, and swam. Jack's pet bulldog King was there as well.

On Thursday the 22nd, in the morning, Jack ran 4 miles along the Point Place highway, then came back and took a long hike. That afternoon, lightweight Willie Doyle boxed a little bit with Dempsey. It was fast but not rough. Dempsey also jumped into chilly Maumee Bay. Former foe Terry Keller and Big Bill Tate, a large colored fighter, both joined the camp.

Willard, who had been training in Los Angeles, just finished acting for a week in a film in nearby Riverside, which soon would show all over the country. Nevertheless, he kept training. He planned to bring with him to Toledo sparring partners Jack Hemple and Charley Miller, a 225-pounder.[647]

On Friday the 23rd, Dempsey played a game of baseball. Jack was a right-hand thrower and a left-hand hitter. He elected himself pitcher. However, soon Kearns and De Forest called him off.

Fearing injury, head trainer Jimmy De Forest allegedly banned (or tried to limit) baseball. De Forest and Rickard feared a broken finger or twisted ankle. Rickard didn't even like Jack jumping into Maumee Bay, fearing illness. He did not want anything to derail the fight.

---

[646] *Toledo News-Bee*, May 19, 1919; *Elmira Star-Gazette*, May 20, 1919.
[647] *Toledo Blade*, *Toledo News-Bee*, May 23, 1919.

The *Toledo Blade* said Dempsey was wonderfully popular with the scribes. He was obliging and likeable, willing to pose for photographs.

The fans were arguing back and forth regarding two axioms – "a good little man cannot beat a good big man," and "they never come back, once they go away."

The *Toledo News-Bee* said Dempsey was no small man. Bill Tate was 6'5" or 6'6" and around 230 or 236 pounds, yet when standing next to him, Dempsey did not appear to be a pigmy. The local press said Tate had licked Langford twice and had a draw with Harry Wills, "who today is probably the best colored heavyweight in the world." He would be an ideal man to work with, given his similarity in size to Willard.

Kearns told reporter Dick Meade that Dempsey would shoot into Willard from the start of the fight. Jess was a notoriously slow starter, and they would exploit that. Jack would fight at a rapid clip.

Willard said he was not underrating Dempsey, for there was too much at stake. "He is a wise willing strong fellow and I have no doubt he will be in there trying every minute." Jess knew that Jack was a rushing, tearing fighter with knockout power, who had earned his title shot. The champ was planning for the hardest and cleverest battle of his career. He said he was in better shape than most realized. "You see I have boxed regularly in exhibitions daily while my circus was on tour…" He already had lost 15 pounds within two months after he began work. Jess was his own trainer, doing so intelligently and scientifically, neither underworking nor overworking. He stood 6'6" in his socks, and his reach was 82 ½ inches long. He weighed 238 pounds at his best, but could weigh 20 pounds more without concern. "I know only too well that I can punch hard enough to stop Dempsey or any living man. My hitting power today is greater than it ever was. …. I can absorb punishment too. Johnson hit me some awful cracks but they didn't stop me for a second." He explained his lack of war participation, saying he was married with five children, and was over the draft age. If asked to participate, he was ready to do so.[648]

---

[648] *Toledo Blade, Toledo News-Bee*, May 24, 1919; *Chicago Defender*, May 31, 1919. Bill Tate's record included: 1914 LND10 Joe Jeannette and LND10 John Lester Johnson; 1915 DND10 John Lester Johnson and LTKOby2 Jeannette; 1916 LDQ9 John Lester Johnson, L20 Kid Norfolk, KO6 Rufe Cameron, LND10 Harry Wills (both clinched throughout), and DND10 Sam Langford; 1917 W12 and LKOby5 Langford, and LND10 Gunboat Smith; and 1918 KO1 Kid Cotton, LTKOby7 Kid Norfolk, and LND6 Jack Thompson.

On Saturday May 24, Jack was on the road again with his sparring partners, followed by a rubdown and game of kick-the-can.

In the afternoon at the Overland Club, after 3 rounds of shadow boxing, Dempsey sparred with 14-ounce gloves for his first real sparring workout of the camp, boxing 3 rounds with Sergeant Bill Tate. Tate was a giant with tremendous reach and a mighty clever left hand. They said his reach was longer than Willard's. He was good at slipping, blocking, and using his reach, reminiscent of Jack Johnson. Dempsey showed plenty of speed and bounded around the ring like a rubber ball, but didn't try to hurt Tate, boxing under wraps.

Kearns insisted that Dempsey weighed 197 pounds, while others said he really was about 185. Willard was in the 250-pound range at present.

On Sunday the 25th, Jack did road work, shadow boxed for 2 rounds of 5 minutes each with a 2-minute walking rest, hit the bag, jumped rope, and participated in a ball game between camp members and newspaper men. In his free time, Jack liked to fish, with his bulldog King by his side.[649]

On Monday May 26, Dempsey's training included boxing 4 rounds with "giant negro" Bill Tate.[650]

On Tuesday May 27, Jack started with a morning jog. When he returned at 9 a.m., he hit the punching bag. Then Dempsey sparred 1 round with Bill Tate, 1 round with Terry Keller, 2 more with Tate, 1 more with Keller, and then Tate came back for the 6th and final round.[651]

The *Toledo Blade* noted that Willard had not taken a real punch in a few years, whereas Dempsey had knocked out 27 men in the last year. Jess would need quality sparring to get him back into form.

This newspaper defended Willard, who had five kids and was over the draft age, which was a reasonable excuse to decline enlistment. Despite claims otherwise, in fact, Willard had participated in seven exhibition shows in which he donated his services for war charities. Hence, the attacks on him were unfair and based on misinformation.

On May 27 in Los Angeles, Willard boxed 11 rounds total with Jack Hempel and Charlie Miller, who once fought him to a 4-round draw. Jess knocked down Miller twice in the 1st round of their sparring, and had to go lightly with him thereafter.

---

[649] *Toledo Blade*, *Toledo News-Bee*, May 26, 1919.
[650] *Sandusky Register*, May 27, 1919.
[651] *Toledo Blade*, May 27, 1919. George Davis, who stood over 6 feet tall, arrived in camp.

Jack Hempel said, "The big fellow is wearing me out. ... It's an awful job to stand against a fellow as big and strong as he is." Hempel said Jess was rounding into Havana form, growing faster and hitting harder every day. "Dempsey will last until he puts over a punch and makes Jess mad." Estimates were that the champ was weighing in the high 250s.

Willard said he had an old score to settle with the people behind Dempsey, and would not be any too gentle with him. "I hope he's as good as they say he is. I don't take any stock in all that talk about his punch. He's had more advertising than a circus, but that doesn't worry me." Jess said he would be in first-class shape, and expected to win with ease.[652]

On Wednesday May 28, Dempsey sparred another 6 whirlwind rounds, 2 each with George "One Round" Davis, Terry Keller, and Bill Tate. Davis went reeling badly, "knocked cuckoo," and Jimmy De Forest called off Dempsey to prevent casualties. Davis took a rest and then finished his 2 rounds of sparring. Another said Tate went 4 rounds. Bill was defensive and not easy to hit, but nevertheless Jack gave all three men a severe battering.

De Forest said Jack already was near top form.[653]

---

[652] *Toledo Blade*, May 28, 1919.
[653] *Toledo News-Bee*, May 28, 1919. George Davis' record included: 1912 DND10 and TKO3 Jack Twin Sullivan, TKO7 Jim Stewart, and LKOby1 Soldier Kearns; 1913 LND10 Dan Dailey, DND10 Battling Levinsky, WND10 Tom McMahon, LKOby5 and DND10 Kearns, WND10 Jack Geyer, and LKOby2 Jess Willard; 1914 LKOby1 Geyer, KO2 Lewis Fink, LND10 George Rodel, WND10 Levinsky, and

*This Work Looks Hard, But It Is Soft For Dempsey*

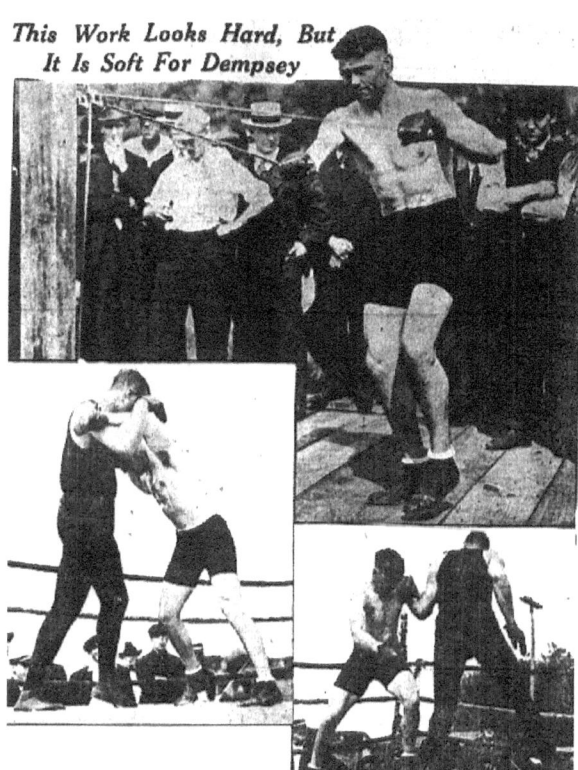

Dempsey's training included work with pulley weights

On Thursday May 29, Dempsey sparred 4 rounds with Sergeant Bill Tate, 2 with Terry Keller, and 1 round with 200-pound One-Round Davis. Dempsey put Davis down and out on his back. Unwilling to absorb the wallopings, Davis left the camp.[654]

Kearns said Dempsey had been boxing in the mornings when it was cool, but in the afternoons had been doing several rounds of training to get accustomed to the sun. Starting Friday, he would box in the afternoons for the next few days, at 2:30 or 3 p.m. Then, after three more days of sparring, he would take off from sparring for about a week so he did not go stale and overtrain. Instead, he just would do a bit of road work, bag punching, and shadow boxing.

An open-air arena at Camp Dempsey had been completed, with a canvas wall being set up, with seats all around, so the public could pay to watch him train.

---

LKOby7 Jim Flynn; 1915 LND10 Jack Twin Sullivan and LKOby3 Jim Coffey; 1916 LKOby2 Bob Devere and LKOby3 Bill Brennan; and 1919 LND10 Harry Greb and LKOby2 Tom Cowler.
[654] *Toledo Blade, Cincinnati Enquirer*, May 30, 1919; *Mansfield News-Journal*, May 29, 1919.

Willard was expected to arrive in Toledo on Saturday May 31, and would train at the Casino, within a half mile of where Dempsey was training.[655]

[655] *Toledo Blade*, May 29, 30, 1919.

Left to Right—Bill Tate, Jack Dempsey, Terry Keller, "One-Round" Davis.

Willard's business manager Ray Archer said Jess had been training since February 1, and his present weight was 258 ½ pounds, already the same weight he was for the Moran fight in 1916.[656]

On Friday May 30, Dempsey entertained a Memorial Day crowd of hundreds, including women, at the Overland Club on the shore of Maumee Bay. In fact, more women than men were present. Jack tugged the pulley weights, punched the bag until it broke from its moorings, and then boxed 4 rounds with Tate and Keller, battering them around. Kearns had him spar in the heat of the afternoon so he would be prepared for it on the day of the fight. The crowd was impressed.

Dick Meade, writing for the *Toledo News-Bee*, said Jack the Giant Killer firmly converted observers to the idea that he was the next champion. His speed was a revelation. He could hit from any angle, and could throw a blow skillfully even after taking one himself. He was like a rubber ball, with much pep. He worked smoothly and finished breathing normally. Before sparring that day, he did his customary morning stunts (running, pulling weights, punching the bag) and took a long swim in the early afternoon.

At that time, Willard was training back home in Lawrence, Kansas. He was boxing with ex-Marine Jack Hemple, who said it was a tough job to act as his sparring partner. Hemple said, "I've seen Dempsey in two fights." In his opinion, Jack would not be able to hurt Willard or knock him down. In 4 to 5 rounds, Dempsey would tire himself out trying to do so, and then Willard would beat him.

Willard said he would be in shape to go 40 rounds, though with a 12-round bout, the pace would be faster, which might prove popular with fans because it would mean plenty of fast action. He would be ready for the hardest, fastest fight of his life.[657]

---

[656] *Cincinnati Enquirer*, May 30, 1919.
[657] *Toledo News-Bee, Toledo Times, Cincinnati Enquirer*, May 31, 1919.

The *Toledo Times* said Dempsey had fared better than Willard against common opponents: Arthur Pelkey, Gunboat Smith, Charley Miller, and Carl Morris. Dempsey had stopped every one of them. Willard went the distance with all of them.[658]

Word from the West Coast, where Willard had been training prior to visiting Kansas, was that he was in great shape already. Jess had been training quietly in the Los Angeles area for several months.

**Kid McCoy, Jim Jeffries, Jess Willard**

Former Willard manager Tom Jones said Jess was a wonderful fighter, and a man of Dempsey's size simply could not whip him. "If Dempsey can stop Willard he will be a wonder among wonders."

Jim Jeffries, who had seen him in Los Angeles, declared that Willard was just as fast and strong as ever.

Dempsey was training very hard. "As a willing worker Dempsey never had an equal." Sports wondered where he got so much energy. He never tired. He was as strong as an ox and so full of fight that nothing could stop him from making a rushing, slugging battle of it.

Billy McCarney said Dempsey was the biggest lead pipe cinch to win that ever came down the pike, and he was wagering that way, expecting victory by knockout within 5 or 6 rounds.[659]

---

[658] *Toledo Times*, May 31, 1919.
[659] *Cincinnati Enquirer*, June 1, 1919. McCarney used to manage Luther McCarty, who at one time was the hottest contender in boxing before being killed in the ring by Arthur Pelkey. McCarney said Dempsey

On Sunday June 1, champion Jess Willard arrived in Toledo, two weeks after Dempsey. His good appearance exploded yarns that he was close to 300 pounds. He had been working out with Hemple and Miller for weeks, as well as climbing mountains and doing gym work.

Jack Kearns said they barred no one as a sparring partner. Anyone who wanted to spar with Dempsey was welcome to do so, including top fighters, black or white, such as Morris, Fulton, Miske, Cowler, or Wills.

Bill Tate, who worked with Dempsey nearly every day, and was the only one who had not caved thus far, was dead certain that Dempsey would beat Willard. He wanted to wager on Dempsey all of the money he was being paid to spar with him. This was coming from a man who once had defeated Sam Langford. Some, including Billy McCarney, said Tate deserved a draw against Harry Wills.

On June 1, 500 fans watched Dempsey spar 4 rounds. Cleveland light heavy Jack Lavigne or Lavin and Soldier Ely Stanton both left the ring with their knees

was the best heavyweight since McCarty, the most powerful athlete he ever knew. In 1912, Willard had boxed McCarty in a 10-round no decision win/draw when Luther was only 20 years old.

shaking after boxing only 1 round apiece. The Jamaica Kid, a 165- or 175-pound black fighter from New York, who had just arrived, gave Jack the most spirited round. He was a quick, skillful boxer and hard hitter, and reveled in exchanging blows. Terry Keller boxed Dempsey for the final round. Earlier that morning, Jack had run 7 miles, rowed a boat for 3 miles, and went swimming as well.[660]

The *Chicago Defender* noted, "Dempsey don't believe in fighting members of the Race, but evidently likes them for sparring partners."

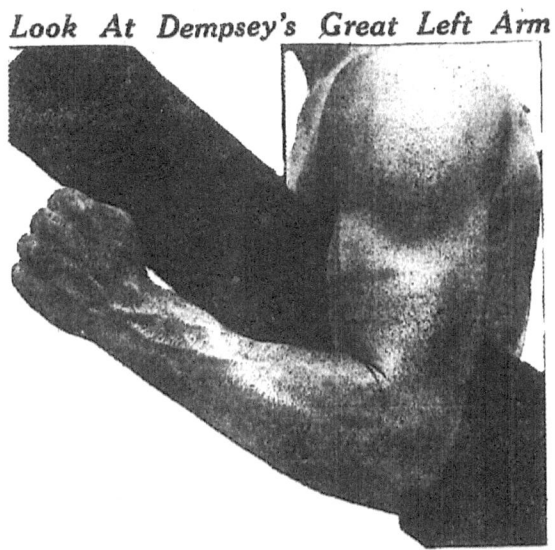

**Look At Dempsey's Great Left Arm**

The *Toledo News-Bee*'s Dick Meade said he saw Dempsey take blows on Saturday the 31st and Sunday the 1st, and was convinced that Jack had a jaw that could take it. Bill Tate clipped his jaw on Saturday, and the Jamaica Kid hit it on Sunday, neither man pulling his punches, both colored lads having mighty good kicks, and Jack took the blows very well. Meade was certain that Jack could dish it and take it, was fast on his feet, and in shape. There was no doubt that Willard would land his long left, but it was doubtful if it would stop Dempsey. The hard lefts and rights that Tate and Jamaica Kid landed didn't stop him or even make him hesitate. He kept coming with the flash and swiftness of a lightweight. It was going to take a lot to beat him back.

Jess Willard disliked his popularity and the big crowds he attracted. "I hate crowds…and I go to some lengths to avoid them. I guess the reason is that a public idol always seems sort of foolish to me; one man's just as good as another, to my way of thinking and I'd feel like a big simp with a crowd trailing after me." Jess said he weighed less than 260 pounds, and planned to take off about 10 pounds for the fight.[661]

Even though Dempsey had superior results against common opponents, some argued that he fought them when they were past their primes, whereas Willard had fought them years earlier, when they still were at their best and fresh and frisky. In 1912, Willard beat Arthur Pelkey over a dull 10 rounds. In 1918, Dempsey stopped Pelkey in less than a round. In 1913, Willard lost a 20-round decision to Gunboat Smith (though some said a

---

[660] Jamaica Kid's record included: 1916 KO15 and KO20 Gorilla Jones; 1917 LND10 Mike McTigue and LND10 Clay Turner; 1918 LKOby5 Jack Thompson; and 1919 LND6 Kid Norfolk and LND6 Panama Joe Gans.
[661] *Toledo Blade, Toledo News-Bee, Cincinnati Enquirer*, June 2, 1919; *Chicago Defender*, May 24, 1919.

draw would have been more appropriate). In 1918, Dempsey stopped Smith in the 2nd round the last time they boxed (and a 1917 W4). Willard boxed a 1913 4-round draw with Charley Miller, whereas Dempsey stopped Miller in 1 round in 1917. Willard obtained a dull 1913 10-round newspaper decision victory over Carl Morris, whereas from 1917 to 1918 Dempsey had a W4, WDQ6 (when Carl was on the verge of being stopped) and KO1 over Morris. Of course Willard, though strong, had a more cautious, careful, methodical style than Dempsey. Hence, results against common foes did not necessarily translate into how their matchup would play out.[662]

---

[662] *Dayton Daily News*, June 2, 1919.

On Monday June 2, 1919, Dempsey boxed 5 rounds with Sergeant Bill Tate, 4 with Jamaica Kid, and 3 with Terry Kellar, taking them on in rotation, for a total of 12 rounds, the scheduled length of the upcoming contest. He landed such vicious punches and set such a furious pace that they all had to try to escape punishment. Jack also ran 7 miles on the road that day. Jimmy De Forest thought Jack was quite sharp, and, fearing that he might go stale from overtraining, ordered him to rest for five days.[663]

Dempsey spars Jamaica Kid

A right decks Jamaica Kid into the corner ropes.        Attacking Bill Tate

---

[663] *Toledo Blade, Toledo Times, Cincinnati Enquirer,* June 3, 1919.

Willard was confessing to be age 35, though his former manager said he was 40 years old. The record book said he was 33 years old. He actually was 37 years of age. Jess admitted that when he started out, he claimed a younger age because he thought it would help him get more matches if promoters thought he was younger than he really was.

Most of those who saw the huge Willard asked, "How in the world can little Jack Dempsey beat that giant?" Dempsey was a great body puncher, and it seemed certain that he would attempt a whirlwind body attack. Many said Willard was invulnerable to punches, but those in the Dempsey camp said the champion never had met a puncher like Dempsey.[664]

On Tuesday June 3, in front of 2,000 spectators, Jess Willard started his local Toledo training at the Casino. He looked splendid, with just a little bit of surplus weight. He was well muscled, with powerful arms like Thor. He stepped around the ring like a man 75 pounds smaller. He slipped, side-stepped, and jumped about, turning and twisting as he shadow boxed. He was fast and limber, and his huge size and vehement aggressiveness of every movement made the crowd gasp. His left snapped like a whip. He hooked and jabbed with a vicious energy.

Willard sparred 4 rounds, decking 200-pound Jack Lavan/Lavin with a left hook. A left uppercut also sent him against the ropes. The champ shot out lightning-fast jabs. But overall, Jess was careful not to inflict injury, for every time he landed hard, he would clinch, smile/laugh, and push Lavin around until his man recovered. He also worked the weight machine, and then pulled and hauled with Lavin, no small man, although he was but a child in Willard's hands.

---

[664] *Toledo Blade, Toledo Times, Cincinnati Enquirer,* June 3, 1919.

Walter C. Kelly, who refereed Willard's bout with Bearcat Tom McMahon years ago, said Willard had improved easily 40% since then. "I am amazed at Willard. When he boxed McMahon he showed none of the stuff he is showing up there now. He simply stood up straight and used a straight left and a right cross. Now he seems to have everything." He always had a good right uppercut too.

Robert Edgren said the workout convinced everyone that Willard would be fit to defend his title. A confident Willard, who was feeling great, said, "Honestly, it may sound foolish, but I can't help thinking this is going to be the easiest contest I ever had."

Edgren said Dempsey was the most confident man in the world, with the possible exception of Willard. His face and arms were burned black from weeks in the open air. Jack was as tall as Jeffries, and in his present condition, the nearest thing to a prime Jeffries that he ever had seen.

Dick Meade said Willard appeared to be in splendid condition, and showed plenty of snap and pep. He was no decrepit old man.

Others also noted that Willard looked surprisingly good in his training, particularly given that the fight still was a month away. "Jess Willard is gaining new adherents daily since his arrival here. His condition is surprising every one. Jack Lavan, a Cleveland heavyweight who boxed three rounds with the champion yesterday was down and out following the bout."

Dempsey rested that day.[665]

It was reported that ticket sales (or reservations) already had exceeded a half-million dollars. Allegedly, 7% of the fight's gross receipts would be going to disabled soldiers.[666]

On Wednesday June 4, first Willard sparred 2 rounds with 195-pound Jack Hemple or Hempel. When Army veteran Walter Monahan/Monaghan

---

[665] *Toledo Blade, Toledo News-Bee, Mansfield News-Journal,* June 4, 1919.
[666] *East Liverpool Evening Review,* June 4, 1919.

landed a hard right, Willard landed a short snappy counter right to the jaw that sent Monahan down and out cold. After about 30 seconds of pouring water over his head, Monahan woke up and resumed sparring. Then Jess roughed and wrestled with Hempel, and followed up with shadow boxing. (Some said Jess also pounded on Jack Lavan and Joe Sullivan.) The champion's unexpected form caused many to want to wager on him.

Monaghan said, "My how Jess can hit when he is in earnest. ... Say, if he hits Dempsey on the jaw with the old right they will probably pick up Jack Kearns' hope in the $10 seats somewhere." Walter complained of a ringing in his ears for about 30 minutes afterwards.

Dempsey rested for another day. Jack Kearns was not worried at all. "The bigger they are the harder they fall."

Dempsey and Willard were different types. Dempsey loved fighting; loved to mix it. Willard took up boxing because he had the size and physique for it, but he didn't love boxing. He was more of a cautious boxer. Jack had the power and youth advantages, but Jess had height, reach, and weight advantages.[667]

On Thursday June 5, about 1,000 people watched Willard box 6 rounds – 2 with Hempel, 2 with Monaghan, 1 with Lavan, and 1 with 176-pound Joe Sullivan, who attacked, but Jess rolled away from the blows, diminishing their force. Lavan did a lot of clinching. Jess ran 5 miles that day, finishing up with a sprint.

Tom Andrews doubted whether Dempsey could get past the champ's long left, and likely would grow tired from his own efforts to penetrate the great height, reach, and jab. "Dempsey has never defeated a first-class man and doesn't know what real punishment means." Willard's heavy jolts would keep him away and nullify his rushing tactics. "Willard's coolness, strength, and experience ought to turn the trick."

Dempsey took another day of enforced rest. He only swam in the lake. Unlike Willard, Dempsey liked having crowds around him. He liked to play baseball on the beach, run races, swim, play jokes, and have visitors and exchange banter. Willard wanted to live quietly.

Willard had no black sparring partners, which was by design, for "the champion is said to have had an abhorrence for the black race." In his fight with Jack Johnson, he was "abused and ridiculed to such an extent that he can hardly be blamed for his attitude."[668]

---

[667] *Toledo Blade, Toledo News-Bee, Dayton Herald,* June 5, 1919.
[668] *Toledo Blade, Toledo News-Bee, Toledo Times,* June 6, 1919.

On June 6, 1919 in St. Paul, Billy Miske clearly won a 10-round no decision over Willie Meehan, badly beating and outclassing him, knocking Meehan down with a left hook in the 9th round, and nearly having him out at the final bell. Meehan proved that he was game and could take a punch, for he was hit with everything, and his face was a puffy bleeding mess. Miske clearly proved that he was the better fighter.[669]

---

[669] *Minneapolis Tribune*, June 7, 1919.

Meehan was coming off a 10-round no decision loss to middleweight Harry Greb (Meehan - 198 ½, Greb - 166). In 1919, Greb had beaten Bill Brennan (WND10 twice), Battling Levinsky (WND10 – Greb 164 ½, Levinsky 175[670] - and WND12), Billy Miske (WND10), Clay Turner (W12)(who was 2-1 against Kid Norfolk), and Meehan, amongst others. Although not a puncher or finisher, rarely scoring knockdowns or knockouts, and only standing 5'8", Greb was known for his punch volume and pace, fast hands, fast feet – in attacking or circling, rough and rugged style, and durability. He could outpoint nearly everyone.

On Friday June 6 at the champ's camp, in front of about 1,000 spectators, Willard boxed 6 rounds, 3 each with 195-pound Hempel and 215-pound Monahan, who was as quick as a featherweight. Monahan leapt in with sudden blows. Against both, Jess jabbed and hooked viciously, but mostly held his powerful right in abeyance. When Jess cut loose, at times it looked as if he was about to score a knockout, but then he backed off, grinned, and wrestled to allow them to recover. At short- or long-range, Willard had great strength, like a bear. He could handle them as he pleased. His short body blows made them grunt. Jess also took punches, sometimes with a smile, sometimes with a quick head movement that broke their force, and sometimes he just took them. At one point he went down against Hempel, some saying it was a knockdown, though most said his heel simply tripped on a loose spot on the mat when stepping back at the same time that he was hit by a left to the body. He quickly rose, laughed, and resumed. "Efforts to make it appear that Willard had been knocked down started immediately, but he was not and such chatter sounds like the raving of a rarebit fiend."

---

[670] The *Buffalo Times*, February 18, 1919 said, "[Greb] carried the battle to Levinsky even during the rounds the Battler went ahead, but as for showing form enough to beg a match with Jack Dempsey – well, ask somebody who was there last night. They'll tell you."

Many wondered how hard he could hit and how much damage Willard could inflict if he wanted to do so. Robert Edgren, who saw 238-pound Willard at Havana, said he had real pile-driving power. Edgren believed the 26th-round knockout over 227-pound Jack Johnson was legitimate. Jack didn't move even after the count was over, and his seconds had to drag him back to his corner. It took five minutes for him to come back to full consciousness and be able to stand up again. His legs still were shaky, and he required assistance to walk from the ring.

Willard was working out about 30 minutes each day. Some said that was not enough. They also said he was taking it too easy on his sparring partners. Others said he was working out in the morning as well, and if he went harder on his sparring partners, he would lose them.

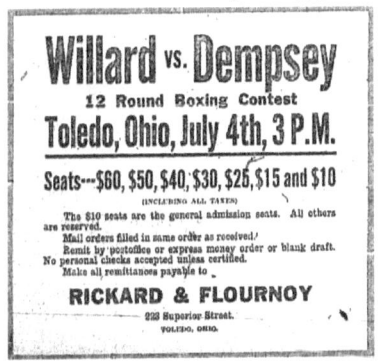

Tickets were quite expensive at $60, $50, $40, $30, $25, $20, $15, and $10. Even the cheapest seats were twice as much as ringside seats for most shows.

On Saturday June 7, Dempsey resumed training. He said he was glad to be back at it. He had a week of enforced idleness, doing no boxing and little of anything else.

Jimmy De Forest said Dempsey was the fastest, strongest, hardest-hitting fighter in the world, and "will win with a knockout as sure as there is a sun in the heavens."[671]

On Sunday June 8, before capacity crowds, both the champion and challenger worked out, the first time both sparred before the public on the same day.

Willard boxed 3 rounds each with Monahan and Hempel, and then a 7th round with Soldier Stanton. Jess worked on hooks with both hands. He rolled his head well from blows, parrying and eluding. Hempel, who was as big as Dempsey, always was

---

[671] *Toledo Blade, Toledo Times, Akron Evening Times, Mansfield News-Journal*, June 7, 1919.

pushing in and trying. He was an earnest, sturdy fellow. Nevertheless, Willard put Hempel down with a right hook, though he rose quickly. Monahan was a fast, clever boxer, and a fairly hard hitter. About 20 seconds into Willard's boxing with 6'4" Soldier Stanton, who initially appeared in Dempsey's camp about a week ago, when he lasted a round, the champ knocked Soldier Stanton so silly with a single right behind the ear that Jess had to catch him and bring him back to the corner to receive restoratives. Stanton had enough.

Dempsey sparred 4 rounds, 2 each with Bill Tate and the Jamaica Kid. Jack focused on building up his speed of attack, coming in quickly like a whirlwind, ducking and side slipping, his head shooting from side to side, offering an elusive target as he moved in, and ready to shift either way. When he got in close, he ripped body punches, making Tate grunt.

Edgren said Tate landed several left jabs that knocked Jack's head back, and he also caught him with uppercuts. Jack took it all with unaccustomed calm. Dempsey landed on Tate's chin a few times, but mostly focused on the body, bobbing and weaving, boring in, firing a volley of blows until Tate would hold. Dempsey was not putting much kick into his punches, fighting under wraps a bit.

Dick Meade said Dempsey was nearly as brown as Tate. The Jamaica Kid would have gone down at one point, but the ropes held him up.

Dempsey and cook Nick Albanese

Edgren said the general opinion was that Dempsey was faster than Willard, and perhaps in better shape, though he had some real physical handicaps to overcome. Some thought Willard was more skillful.

A photographer said Willard was faster, for he had a tougher time capturing his blows than Dempsey's. Jess fired them without any sign he was going to throw, and usually was pulling his hand back by the time the shutter went.

Although performing well in training, some said Jess did not appear as well physically as he did four years ago when he beat Jack Johnson. They wondered what impact his relative inactivity would have on him. Others said that Dempsey might run right into one of Jess's powerful rights or right uppercuts. The champ was so big; fans could not understand how such a puny-sized man by comparison had any chance with him.[672]

---

[672] *Toledo Blade, Toledo News-Bee*, June 9, 1919.

Willard had been charging 25 cents to watch him train, but he raised it to 50 cents. The paid attendance still was 2,084, which netted $1,042.

Kearns charged 25 cents to watch Dempsey train. There were 1,600 paid admissions at his camp. Fans enjoyed watching Dempsey's whirlwind style, even just for sparring bouts. Still, Willard was the champion, so that alone enabled him to draw big crowds. Some of the money was donated to churches and charitable organizations.

Rickard reported that seat sales had exceeded $800,000. The arena seated 50,000, but probably another 10,000 or so could be squeezed in. The arena was being constructed on the land overlooking Maumee bay.[673]

THE CHAMPION'S FIGHTING POSE

---

[673] *Akron Evening Times*, June 9, 1919.

On Monday June 9 at the Overland Club, Dempsey sparred 6'2" 190-pound Jack Ross of Winnipeg, introduced as the Canadian heavyweight champion. Ross started off nicely, stepping around, feinting, and popping lefts to the face like a wizard. Dempsey ignored his punches, walked in, and knocked him down with a right hook to the chin. He picked him up, walked around until Ross recovered his senses, then flattened him again with a right and left hook to the jaw, for a 1st round knockout. Bill Tate kindly reached in from outside the ring to catch Ross's head and act as a cushion as he fell.

Tate was up next. The 1st round was peppy, as usual. The 2nd round was a whizzer. Jack paid no attention to the rights and lefts poured in at him, but waded in and sent a barrage into Tate's midsection that made him gasp. Between rounds, someone shouted to Bill, "Jest like it was

in the army, eh, sergeant?" Tate replied, "Not at all. In the army we fought part of the time, but up here we fight all the time." He told the truth, for Dempsey made his sparring partners fight, never slowing the pace. Jack administered a beating, landing an especially powerful right deep into the stomach. One observer said Dempsey had a lot of speed and pep, and stepped around like a two-year-old horse just out of the barn.

Next up was the Jamaica Kid. According to the *Toledo News-Bee*'s Dick Meade, soon after starting his boxing with the Jamaica Kid, a left rubbed over Jack's right eye, the laces of the glove doing the trick, making a nasty cut in his right eyebrow and causing the gore to flow. Jack wanted to box another round, but Kearns and De Forest refused to allow it.

According to the *Toledo Blade*'s version, Dempsey emerged from his round of sparring with the Jamaica Kid with the skin scraped from his right eye, the result of being hit with the heel of a glove.

The *Toledo Times*' C. W. Howard said a blow across the right eye when they were going at it opened up an old wound, and De Forest called time. Jack wanted another round, but instead was sent to the hospital, where he received two stitches.

They really went at it at Camp Dempsey in slam-bang affairs. Although smaller, Jamaica was aggressive but elusive as an eel, with wonderful agility.

Others reported that a glancing left hook to the eye reopened a small cut that Dempsey suffered in a contest a year ago. The cut was at the edge of the eyebrow. It required two stitches to close the inch-long wound. Jack would refrain from sparring until it healed.

On the 9th at the Casino, Willard ran 4 miles and sparred 8 rounds. In the 1st round, a blow from Hempel raised a knob the size of a walnut on Willard. The champ worked 3 rounds each with Hempel and Monaghan, and then 2 more with Soldier Stanton. Jess left the ring with a shanty over his eye. Another said he emerged with a large lump under one eye. A third reporter said Jess had a small bruise just under the left eye.

Willard's wife and child had been in a car accident in Kansas recently, and that, combined with the muggy weather, was theorized to have affected his performance adversely, for he lacked vim and vigor.

Another observer said Willard went hard with Hempel, and had him wobbly several times. He smashed home his nasty, quick, short, vicious left, and Hempel's head rocked. But he was tired against Monahan, slowing up considerably and doing a lot of stalling. Monahan hit him a lot, but Jess took blows from both men like they were nothing. Jess took it easy on Stanton, whom he had stopped the other day.

Afterwards, Monahan said, "Take it from me, there isn't a man alive who can make this boy stop. I know." Most reporters agreed that it would be quite a challenge for Dempsey to make a dent in Willard, who took blows very well.

Dempsey was a human cayenne pepper box, and fought with the dash and energy of a wildcat, showing no fatigue. The difference between he and Willard, by comparison, was noticed. Another writer said he never saw a fighter bore in like Dempsey, first from one side, then the other, and then up the middle, all action, all gloves, all energy, no matter who his opponent was. Willard was more cautious and careful, paced himself more, had moments of vim followed by caution and dead spots. Still, Jess said he felt great. One reporter said the champ had a lot of new tricks, was snappy on his feet, and boxed like a bantamweight. His wind was good and he wasn't blowing at all. He had a smoothness of temper.

Willard was married with five children. He was born in Pottawatomie county, Kansas. His father, a ranchman, was an Ohio native, and his mother was from Kentucky. Jess was the youngest of three brothers (no sisters). He broke broncos until he became too heavy. He was a crack rifle and pistol shot. He could run 100 yards in 12 seconds. His estimated net worth was $500,000.

Dempsey's parents lived in Salt Lake City. He had three brothers and three sisters. He had been a hobo, miner, adventurer, and railroad section hand. He was divorced six months ago. He was knocked out only once, to Flynn, avenged. He was estimated to be worth nothing. That soon might change.

That same day, June 9, 1919 in Pittsburgh, Kid Norfolk clearly outboxed Billy Miske to win a 10-round no-decision contest.[674]

**Monaghan on the floor. Jess eludes Monaghan's right. Dempsey hits Jamaica Kid**

---

[674] *Toledo Blade, Toledo Times, Dayton Daily News*, June 10, 1919; *Toledo News-Bee*, June 9, 10, 1919; *Pittsburgh Post, Pittsburgh Gazette Times, Pittsburg Press*, June 10, 1919.

On Tuesday June 10, wearing 12-ounce gloves, Willard sparred 6 easy rounds; 3 with Hempel, 2 with Monaghan, and 1 round with Stanton, who was supposed to go another round, but one blow dazed him a bit, and that was enough for him. Jess allowed Monahan to hit his body, taking the blows with nonchalance.

Hempel said no one could prevent Willard from striking them. "I tell you that when Willard starts a blow you can't stop it. Wait 'till he gets the little gloves on – he'll drive 'em thru Dempsey."

Because of his healing cut, Dempsey did not spar, but instead shadow boxed, bag punched, hit the dummy, and worked with the weights.

C. W. Howard said Dempsey and Willard were extremely opposite types. Dempsey was ferocious, slashing and smashing away. To watch him was to come away with the opinion that no man could stand up before his attack for more than a few rounds.

Willard was the biggest gladiator in history, who towered over his foes, as broad across the shoulders as the back of an auto. He smoothly moved with sprightliness and spring. He handled his tremendous arms in a sharp, quick, alert manner, slipping, blocking, and countering.[675]

Also on June 10, 1919, in Jersey City, New Jersey, 200-pound Harry Wills won an 8-round no decision over 187-pound John Lester Johnson. In the 1st round, Johnson scored a knockdown of Wills with a right hook to the jaw. Wills retaliated by flooring Johnson in the 3rd round.[676]

On Wednesday June 11, attendance at both camps was large, and the fans seemed pleased with what the fighters displayed.

Willard boxed 6 rounds, 2 rounds each with Monaghan, Hempel, and Soldier Stanton. He did not seek to hurt hem, although he did send Hemple flopping to the floor once with a well-directed clout. Jess had eased up on Monaghan ever since the day he flattened him. As tough as he was, Hempel was beginning to show the wear and tear. Jess clearly was losing weight, his wind was improving, and he was moving faster. He also was training in private. He did not like training in front of the public, but did so because that was part of his contractual obligations to help promote the fight. He was a retiring man who did not enjoy publicity or the limelight.

Dempsey did not spar, but nevertheless the spectators enjoyed watching him shadow box and punch the various bags, working hard every second.

Jack Kearns was not at all concerned by stories about Willard's punch. He said Dempsey had the superior sparring partners.

> Say, if Willard is such a great puncher, why doesn't he get some one besides Monaghan and Hempel to train with? You don't see any tough babies like Bill Tate and the Jamaica Kid over there do you? I'd like to send Tate and Jamaica to Willard's camp and take Monaghan and Hempel on here some day, just to see what would happen. I'll bet

---

[675] *Toledo News-Bee, Toledo Times,* June 11, 1919.
[676] *Paterson Morning Call, Buffalo Times,* June 11, 1919.

Jack would stop both of them in a round. Do you think Willard can turn that trick with Tate and Jamaica? Not on your life.[677]

Allegedly, Kearns had been visiting Willard's camp incognito to scout the champion. Jess heard about it and said,

> Dempsey doesn't need to do anything like that. If he wants to see what condition I'm in he can come over himself and go in without paying a nickel. ... The only thing I have a kick about is having people here from the Dempsey camp without invitation. It isn't ethical. That's all I've got to say about it. It isn't ethical. I'm not sending anyone over to watch Dempsey for me, am I? ... I'll learn all I need to know in the first round.

Jess said he would size up Dempsey, box cautiously, avoid being hit, figure out and measure him, and then finish him off. After that he would attend to his picture business and oil fields.

Kearns had plans too. "Beat Willard? Nothing to it!" Assuming that Dempsey would win, Kearns was going to try to sign Jack to fight Georges Carpentier, for it would make a great international match.

However, despite his brash confidence, Kearns took exception to some prospective referees who issued statements saying that to win a title, a challenger had to have a clear or big lead in order to win a decision. Kearns believed that it should not matter who the fighters were, for the one who did the best work should be entitled to the decision.

There was some discussion about having two judges decide the contest, with the referee acting as a tiebreaker if there was disagreement.

Kearns said Dempsey was in shape to box all night if necessary, and *Toledo Times* writer C. W. Howard agreed. Fans liked that Jack was the type who tore in and had a kick in either hand. The public always would admire a clever man, but went wild over the aggressive puncher, which is what made Dempsey a fan favorite, even though he was spotting Willard anywhere from 50 to 75 pounds. "The public never has been very crazy over Willard. He brought back the championship to the white race, of course." But his style was not appealing, he had been inactive, and he was not a social mixer with the fans or sportswriters. He lacked charisma.[678]

On Thursday June 12, Willard again sparred 6 rounds, 3 each with Monahan and Hemple. He also did his usual shadow boxing, working the pulleys, passing the medicine ball, and stomach exercises. Jess mostly jabbed, though occasionally he fired in a vicious blow or combination, rocking heads. The champ's road work was improving as well.

Dempsey shadow boxed, punched a heavy bag, and a fast bag.

Some wondered whether 12 rounds would be enough for Dempsey to get to Willard. He stood little chance by boxing at long range, but he was a tear-in fighter, which he would need to be and do to be effective.

---

[677] *Toledo Blade*, June 12, 1919.
[678] *Toledo Blade, Toledo News-Bee, Toledo Times*, June 12, 1919.

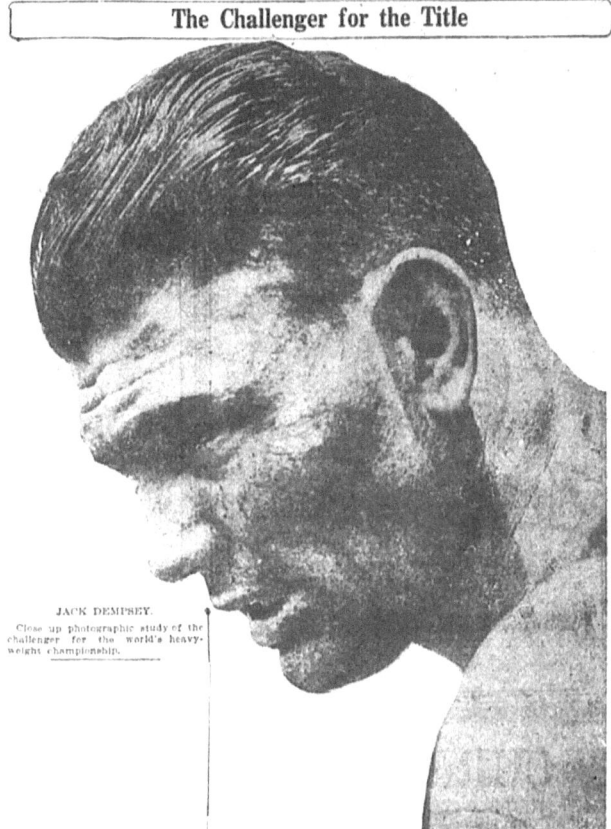

The Challenger for the Title

JACK DEMPSEY.
Close up photographic study of the challenger for the world's heavyweight championship.

C. W. Howard said, "If Dempsey wins he will be as great an idol as John L. Sullivan was in the old days, for he will have performed a wonderful feat against seemingly impossible odds, following a meteoric flight to the top that already has served to make him a popular boy." Judging by the way the fans were flocking to see them train, Toledo was more worked up over this bout than any other in over a decade or more. Hundreds of women were on hand every afternoon in addition to men.[679]

"Trouble maker" John Reisler was threatening to bring suit in Toledo to restrain Dempsey from fighting Willard unless he was paid his share.

The *Toledo Blade* said when Kearns and Dempsey first started working together, Dempsey was slow and flat-footed, with no promise beyond a wonderful punch that seldom landed. Kearns, a former clever boxer, taught Dempsey to step around and duck, and throw short punches. Dempsey's natural ability and adaptability did the rest. When they began attracting attention and large sums, John the Barber stepped in and tried to collect based on an old contract. He enjoined and sued, with mixed results. His contract had been upheld in some courts and held illegal or invalid in others. Over time, increasingly more folks felt disgust and annoyance by his constant court actions.

Reisler and his attorneys made an appointment with Rickard to try to arrange a settlement. Reisler ultimately decided to allow the fight to go forward, and seek redress in the courts for his share afterwards. He told Rickard that he was willing to settle for $10,000.[680]

Experts said Willard would be in first-class condition for the fight.

---

[679] *Toledo Times, Toledo Blade, Toledo News-Bee,* June 13, 1919.
[680] *Lancaster New Era,* June 12, 1919; *Toledo Blade,* June 13, 1919; *Buffalo Times,* June 22, 1919.

Sparring only with white boxers, Willard had drawn the color line even in training, unlike Dempsey, who at least paid black fighters to be his sparring partners. "He has refused to have negro sparring partners in camp." Willard noted that an offer had been made for Bill Tate to spar with him. "I refused flatly."

Before he fought Jack Johnson, Willard had announced that if he won, he never again would box a negro. He had seen how Johnson's reign had "lowered the game in public estimation. His scandalous conduct in private life, his reckless defiance of all speed regulations for motor vehicles, and his general insolence toward the American public, had all been most harmful." Willard recognized that there were a lot of fine colored fellows whom he respected, but "there is a race antagonism I can't help." His pledge to the American people included sparring partners. It was one thing to box blacks on the way up, but a man who held the championship was on a different plane than a fellow who just was coming along. "When I drew a color line after my contest with Johnson, I intended to observe it as long as I remained champion. I am convinced that bouts between white men and negroes have done more harm to boxing than any single factor."

Jess claimed that he did not wear hand bandages, and did not require any artificial aid whatsoever.[681]

Both camps agreed to fight in a 20-square-foot ring. Willard thought Dempsey might try the hit and get-away game. Dempsey was fine with any size ring.

On Friday June 13, Willard sparred 8 rounds, 3 with Jack Hemple, 3 with Walter Monahan, and 2 with 190-pound Bill Ketchel, also called Young Ketchel. Jess had Hempel woozy several times. Monahan spat blood from Jess' jabs. Willard landed a heavy right on Ketchel that jarred him so badly that he had enough after only 2 rounds. Jess smiled throughout and even allowed them to bang away at his body. He also wrestled for five minutes with Hempel, several times throwing him down to the canvas. Then he threw the medicine ball, worked with the elastic exerciser, and shadow boxed. He did no roadwork that morning. The champ announced that he weighed 252 pounds.

Robert Edgren said that five minutes after Willard finished his training, he stepped on the scales at 250 pounds. Jess laughed and said, "I guess that's a pretty good answer to the propaganda boys who said I'd never be in shape to box again. Here I am down to Havana form." Jess said *he* would be the one fighting Carpentier next. The champ claimed he was 35 years old.

Dempsey did his usual work without sparring, hitting a heavy bag hung high up, so he could practice hitting up at a tall man.

Jack's older brother John Dempsey, a foreman in a Salt Lake City mine, arrived on scene. Supposedly an uncle and other relatives might come from West Virginia to see Jack in action as well.

Jack Dillon arrived in town and visited Dempsey's camp.[682]

---

[681] *Akron Evening Times,* June 13, 1919; *Toledo News-Bee,* June 14, 1919.
[682] *Toledo Times, Toledo Blade,* June 14, 1919.

Willie Meehan picked Willard to defeat Dempsey. He said Jack would not be able to hit Jess, and would be lucky to go the limit with the champion. Jess had taken off a lot of weight and was looking like his old self. He naturally was a very big man. It was size vs. youth.

Willard said Dempsey could not hit hard enough to hurt him. Jack Johnson was nearly 230 pounds when he hit him many times on the jaw, but could not drop Jess even once in 26 rounds. Willard anticipated that he could go 12 rounds with the much smaller Dempsey with ease. Willard was so big and imposing that he even made 200- and 215-pound sparring partners and opponents look like middleweights by comparison.

The *Dayton News* reported that Willard was the 10 to 7 favorite in the betting odds. He still was very big at 250 ½ pounds, and likely would have more than 50 pounds of a weight advantage on the 195-pound Dempsey. Willard was five to six inches taller at 6'6" or 6'7" tall, had long arms, and was quite strong. He appeared to be rounding into form nicely, so initial wagers made him the favorite.

One proposition was a $100 wager to win $2,500 on Dempsey to knock out Willard in the 1st round. Other wagers were $100 to $2,000 that Willard did not answer the call of time for the 3rd round, $500 to $5,000 that Willard would be knocked out before the end of the 6th round, and $500 to $250 that the fight ended in a knockout.[683]

On Saturday June 14, despite the terrific heat, an afternoon crowd of 1,100 fans watched Dempsey punch the bags and go through his gymnastics. Women especially gave him a hand.

However, in private that morning, Dempsey and veteran Jack Dillon sparred 4 fast rounds. It was his first sparring since he was cut on the 9th, five days prior. Both worked hard in the 1st round, but after that, Dempsey let Dillon take the aggressive, and got a great bit of defensive practice. Dempsey did not wear a headgear, though he had some plaster over the cut.

---

[683] *Dayton Daily News*, June 15, 1919.

At the champ's camp that day, he boxed Hemple and Monahan 3 rounds each. Ketchel had left after only one day.

Ray Bronson said Willard was a master at the art of boxing. He used superior strategy to beat Johnson. Dempsey would require ring strategy and generalship to win. If he just bulled in, Willard would chop him to pieces. Jack needed both an offensive and defensive strategy.[684]

Frank Menke said Dempsey had a better record, and was powerful enough to drop any man, with any punch, and at any distance. True, Willard was known for having an iron chin, never having been down, but he never had faced a hitter like Dempsey. Others noted that Willard had absorbed the powerful 203-pound Luther  McCarty's blows when Jess was but a novice. McCarty became known as the best and most powerful white hope (until his untimely demise), and Willard had fought him on at least even terms, some feeling that Jess actually had outboxed him. He had proven that he could take hard blows.

Menke said Dempsey was game and could absorb punishment. Time after time, more experienced battlers had punished him unmercifully, but he always came back for more. "If ever a man took punches – and some awful ones – in the upward climb to pugilistic heights, that man is Dempsey."

---

[684] *Toledo Times*, June 15, 1919.

Early in his career, he was untrained in the art of defense, and knew only slugging until the other fellow dropped. Many did not realize, "Dempsey is the ultimate in taking beatings and then punching his way to victory." Hence Menke answered the question posed, whether Dempsey could take it, in the affirmative.

Menke noted the Sudenberg fight, in which Dempsey was dropped and pounded on but continued attacking no matter what. John Lester Johnson jabbed him often and broke his ribs, yet Jack kept boring in despite the pain, bringing cheers from the audience, which did not realize he was hurt. It took two months for his ribs to heal.[685]

On Sunday June 15, Willard took the scales and weighed 248 pounds. 2,500 spectators watched him in a brisk afternoon workout, sparring 8 rounds total, 3 with Hemple, 2 rounds with 229 ½-pound Jack Heinen, just discharged from the military, then 3 rounds with Monahan. Jess not only took the blows well, but showed occasional flashes of speed that were surprising. Jess rocked Heinen with rights, and a right uppercut had him out on his feet, but Jess kindly steadied him and the boxing continued.

Willard said Dempsey's injured eye would make a nice target for his jab.

1,896 spectators paid to see Dempsey train that day. Kearns allowed him to box 3 rounds with the Jamaica Kid, the light heavy who had cut him. The injured optic was covered with a piece of court plaster, and the Kid was instructed not to shoot too high. One said the session was rather tame. Robert Edgren said Dempsey pushed Jamaica hard and delivered many a blow that sounded like a brick dropping into a bucket, though he did not try to efface the Kid from the map. He wasn't trying to lose a good sparring partner. Jack beat a tattoo on his ribs, now and then shooting over a thumping left hook or lifting right. Jamaica retreated around the ring, with Dempsey high on his toes coming after him full of pep, without stopping, every step towards the Kid. Jamaica finished winded and a little groggy.

---

[685] *Toledo Times*, June 15, 1919; *Dayton Herald*, June 16, 1919.

Next, Jack worked the punching bag, pneumatic bag, and then heavy bag. He appeared to be in the pink of condition, with no fat whatsoever. Most days he spent in a bathing suit by the shore, occasionally taking a dip.

Dempsey's prize bulldog King was run over by an automobile, and his leg was injured. A vet said it merely was a sprain.[686]

On Monday June 16, Willard alternated one round with each sparring partner, giving each man plenty of rest while Jess remained in the ring with the others. That enabled Willard to open up more and fight harder. The big husky Heinen took a real thumping, getting decked by a right twice in the 1st round. Monahan ended his round dazed. Hempel took a lot of good whacks too. Despite the fact that Heinen weighed 229 pounds, his punches had no effect on Willard. Jess

hit them with ease, and showed cleverness in avoiding blows whenever he wanted. His speed was a rude jolt to those who had been picking Dempsey to win.

John M. Kelly, *Toledo Times* sports editor, after seeing Willard muss up his three sparring partners, said an army of fight experts believed it was going to be a blinger of a scrap. Dick Meade agreed that the way Willard tore into them, hitting from every angle, putting all the power in his massive frame into crushing, fast, rifling wallops and drives, changed many minds.

[686] *Toledo Times, Toledo Blade, Toledo News-Bee*, June 16, 1919.

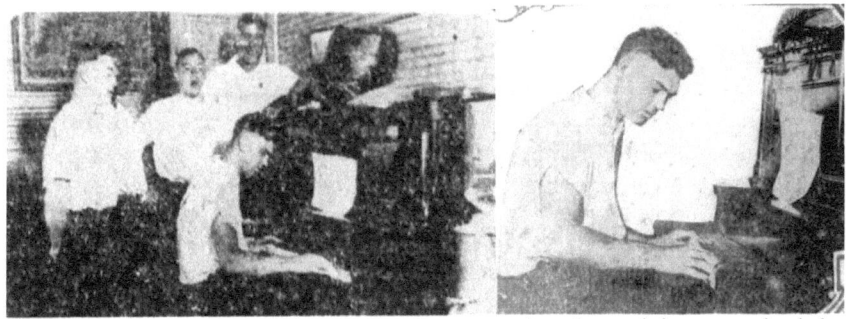

That day, Dempsey did not spar, but tugged at the weights, punched the bag, and shadow boxed. He weighed an alleged 195 pounds. Bill Tate left camp, for he was set to box Sam Langford in Minneapolis.[687]

Jack Dempsey always has time to play with the kiddies that flock to his Toledo quarters.

On Tuesday June 17, when Dempsey weighed himself on the scales in front of the reporters, wearing his regular fighting trunks and shoes, the same as he would wear for the fight, he weighed exactly 201 pounds. Most expressed surprise, believing he was even lighter than the 195 that had been reported the previous day. Most thought he was 190. Some reporters even took the scale to test it, and agreed it was accurate. Clearly Dempsey was a full-fledged heavyweight. Yet, he showed no superfluous flesh. Even though he had been training hard, he had been eating well. The Dempsey camp claimed that Willard had to watch his diet to lose weight, which would weaken him. One reporter even claimed that Dempsey had been weighing 208 pounds since he started training in Toledo.

Jack did not spar that day, but did his other usual work in front of a crowd of about 1,000.

---

[687] *Toledo Times, Toledo News-Bee*, June 17, 1919.

That same day, before a crowd of 2,000, Willard boxed 11 rounds, including with middleweight Joe Chip, brother of former middleweight champ George Chip, as well as Heinen, Hemple, and Monahan, each alternating for a round or two, in and out, while Jess remained, proving his condition to onlookers. One said that Jess was starting to get down to real work, and not taking it quite as easy on his sparring partners.

Willard said, "I am confident I will be in perfect shape for Dempsey. ... I was heavy when I started training. I took off 10 pounds before I hit Toledo. ... The fact that I cut my weight from close to 280 pounds to 248 shows that somebody had the wrong dope. ... I will reach the pink the day before the contest." Jess said the drying out process would remove another 5-6 pounds. He claimed to have an 83 ¾" reach. He said Monahan was clever at long distance, Hempel stayed in close, while 240-pound Heinen was a mixture of both, and Chip was a fast, flashy fellow. They gave him all the work he needed.[688]

The *Toledo Blade's* George R. Pulford said Dempsey was bigger, faster, and more powerful than he was when he first arrived in town. He was hitting with greater precision, like a sharpshooter, firing blows from all angles, and keeping them short. He could hit from any conceivable position, and put everything into his blows. He had been working with a 45-pound bag under Jimmy De Forest's tutelage. When he did his road work, he ran with dumb bells in his hands. He also was working in private, aside from the public training, doing 8 rounds every morning. He was so aggressive and powerful that he could win a decision even if he did not stop Willard. When shadow boxing, he was side-stepping, ducking, feinting, slipping around the ring, and punching at an imaginary opponent. He moved about like a cat, and at a fast pace. He could attack or hit and move. He could back up or off to the side, but then leap forward whaling away with both hands. He was not predictable or easily timed.

Jack Kearns said,

> Don't imagine for a minute that Dempsey will walk into Willard and take a punch in order to land one. Jack is the fastest big man in the ring today and one of the best boxers in the business. .... My opinion is that Willard will find Dempsey hard to hit with effect. Jack is always moving about, slipping his head around like a turtle and he offers a mighty poor target for any man to hit at.

---

[688] *Toledo Times, Toledo Blade, Toledo News-Bee, Sandusky Register*, June 18, 1919.

Billy McCarney had bet at 10 to 1 odds that Dempsey would beat Fulton in 1 round, and he was willing to bet real money that Jack would win in 5 or 6 rounds against Willard, and even was willing to wager something on a 1st round knockout. He was a true believer in Dempsey.[689]

A *Police Gazette* poll of experts yielded 172 votes in favor of Dempsey, 144 in favor of Willard, while 20 others were undecided.[690]

**What a Left Hook Did to Jack Heinen**

On Wednesday June 18, Willard decked Heinen with a left hook. He also boxed with Monahan, Hempel, and Chip, sparring 8 rounds total.

Walter Monahan said the champ was in even better condition than at Havana, and would startle critics. Jess was quite strong, and would land on Dempsey, who fought in an open manner with his head down, liable to be hit with Willard's very powerful uppercuts. Although Jess had not fought in a while, he had been boxing in exhibitions. His defense was very difficult to penetrate.

Dempsey again worked without sparring.[691]

On Thursday June 19, several hundred men and women saw Dempsey spar 2 rounds with Terry Keller for the moving picture men. Jack wore his nice white silk trunks, shadow boxed for a few minutes, punched the bags, and then took on Keller. Jack's tanned body appeared even browner when contrasted against his white trunks. Jack went after Terry from the start. Keller was fast and did not mind taking the hard whacks, so he gave Dempsey good work. Jack's sense of timing and distance was not affected by his layoff. He was like a tiger, whipping through his labor with grace and ease of action. Kearns and De Forest still wanted him to keep his sparring limited, cautious about the healing cut. Jack also swam, rowed a boat, played with kiddies on the beach, did road work, and punched the bags some more.

---

[689] *Toledo Blade,* June 19, 1919.
[690] *Toledo Times,* June 19, 1919.
[691] *East Liverpool Evening Review,* June 19, 1919.

Dempsey said he was hit twice on the bad eye, but it did not hurt and the eye was not injured. He was punching hard and stepping fast. He wanted to do more work, but listened to De Forest. Jack said he was not worried about Willard's long left hand. Fred Fulton had a great left, yet it didn't worry him. "I went right past it and hit Mr. Fulton on the chin." He said De Forest had built up his weight while getting him in condition, which he needed for a big fellow like Willard.

That day, Willard boxed 8 rounds with Heinen, Chip, Hempel, and Monaghan, 2 rounds each, but did not particularly extend himself. Only Heinen ran into a stiff punch. Heinen was bigger, so he could absorb more. Plus he attacked, forcing Willard to respond. In general, Willard liked to allow his foe to set the pace, and whenever one got going pretty fast, he would speed up his own work. A fast uppercut to the chin had Heinen hanging on for a few seconds in a cuckoo state. Afterwards, Jess stepped on the scales at exactly 248 pounds. He expected to weigh 245 for the fight.

The champ said he would abandon road work from this point on. Some said that was unwise, while others said he knew himself better than anyone and knew what worked best for him. The fight was about two weeks away.

**Dempsey 201, Willard 248**

For the fight, Dempsey and Willard would be allowed to wear soft bandages and tape on their hands, as per agreement. This included "soft tape over the gauze." The Boxing Commission's rule said, "All tape and bandages on hands of boxers shall be examined by referee and examining physicians." Willard insisted that just two thicknesses of tape would be allowed.

It was announced that already $352,000 in actual cash had been received from ticket sales. All of the $60 seats had been sold.

Promoter Tex Rickard said Dempsey looked like a 170-pounder, yet weighed over 200. He was the most perfect human he ever saw, a physical marvel and a man of iron. "There is a wealth of force and power buried in that lad's system."

Jimmy De Forest said Dempsey probably would enter the ring between 193 and 196 pounds.

Herbert Corey of the *Toledo News-Bee* said Willard was as big as a barn, or a pine tree. It would be size vs. speed. The crowd was puzzled by the matchup. Most favored Willard, but there was a respectable and quite argumentative minority. Corey believed Dempsey was closer to 190 pounds, for he was weighed after eating a big spaghetti and chicken dinner. Regardless, he still looked like a little boy compared to Willard. Joe Chip was a middleweight, Hemple weighed a little less than 200, Monaghan was a bit bigger, and Heinen was 220 at least. Willard dwarfed them all. He was not particularly fast, but his blows were jarring thumps. He was strong. He could lift and toss his foes away from clinches. Dempsey trained for speed and a lethal wallop. When told about Willard's great strength, Jack responded that it was not going to be a weight-lifting contest.

N. E. Brown said Dempsey was confidence personified. He was absolutely sure that he would win the championship, even though Willard was the biggest man he ever had faced. He was going to treat him simply as one more man to beat. Jack trained earnestly and slept long and hard, often not waking up until his trainer woke him. He obeyed everything De Forest said. De Forest sometimes told him to slow down his work, and at other times to speed it up.⁶⁹²

**De Forest lacing up Dempsey's gloves**     **Willard sparring Monahan**

Al Capley said Dempsey would win all the way against the money-crazed has-been. Jack would need to hit the body, given how the tall Willard was able to lean back away from blows.

George Kennedy said the fight would go the distance, and Willard's superior height and reach would enable him to win the decision.

Former champion Jim Jeffries said Willard was in good shape, having been training in Los Angeles prior to coming to Ohio. He was a big, tough, powerful man.

Middleweight champ Mike O'Dowd said Dempsey would maintain such a fast pace that he would weaken Willard in about 8 rounds, and then finish him off after that. Pal Moore said ring inactivity, balanced against Dempsey's constant activity, stopping many much bigger men, combined with his youth, led him to favor Dempsey by early knockout.

Bantam champ Pete Herman felt that a good big man beats a good little man, and he could not see how such a smaller man could beat Willard. Soldier Bartfield said Willard was too big, strong, and powerful, and would run Dempsey into his blows and win a 12-round decision.⁶⁹³

Jack Dillon was impressed by Dempsey's fast work and elusive style, combined with powerful punches, which he thought would be the champion's downfall. For his poundage and inches, Dempsey was the fastest, hardest to hit, and most terrific puncher he ever had seen. He was a ring freak and marvel.

Dillon said he had sparred Dempsey 4 rounds to see what he had, and "he lacks nothing." He thought he was easy to hit, yet, when he tried to hit him, he could land only glancing blows, despite being known for his accuracy. Dempsey was more elusive than some realized, bobbing his head from side to side, and shifting about, jerking his body in different directions, which was baffling because there was no rhythm to it to time. He never moved the same way twice, and was as full of twists and turns as a whirling

---

⁶⁹² *Toledo Blade, Toledo News-Bee, Toledo Times*, June 20, 1919.
⁶⁹³ *Dayton Herald*, June 20, 1919.

dervish. And he was fast, faster than a lightweight. Dempsey stepped in so quickly that one could not elude or duck his rushes.

Dillon and Dempsey had sparred with 12-ounce mitts, and Dempsey promised not to put his real power into his punches, yet even his taps carried more crushing force than anyone Dillon had fought, and he had been hit by Fireman Jim Flynn, Frank Moran, Charlie Weinert, Tom Cowler, Dan Porky Flynn, Billy Miske, Gunboat Smith, Jim Savage, and Al Norton. Dempsey could deck anyone, for he was a natural hitter and fast puncher. The challenger had great timing too, countering well and overcoming all defensive tricks with great accuracy. He had equal power in both hands. He could hit from any angle, and was just as powerful up close as far away. He didn't need to be set to hurt you. Dillon called Dempsey a miracle and greatest natural fighter he ever saw or boxed against. This statement was coming from a man with 230 fights of professional experience, who at one point had a claim to the world light heavyweight championship.[694]

Joe Chip said it was impossible to hurt Willard. He hit him with everything he had but could not make any impression on him. Jess was in condition, and got better the longer he went.

Tex Rickard noted that Dempsey was tireless and as fast as lightning. When boxing with Terry Kellar, no slouch, Jack rolled his head in such a way that he did not take the full force of blows. He smashed Kellar and had him groggy. Jack weighed around 200 pounds.

Robert Edgren said Dempsey had given Terry Keller a beating in their sparring. "Dempsey has a kind heart, but a wicked punch."

Also on June 19, 1919, in Minneapolis, Dempsey's 6'6" 230-pound sparring partner Bill Tate was disqualified in the 5th round against Sam Langford for excessive holding, something he had been doing in response to Dempsey's rushes. Bill would return to Dempsey's camp.

In the main event, 177-pound Billy Miske and 167-pound Tommy Gibbons fought to a 10-round no decision newspaper draw. Referee

---

[694] *Cincinnati Enquirer*, June 20, 1919. Jack Dillon's record included: 1913 TKO4 Walter Monaghan; 1914 W12 Battling Levinsky, W10 Al Norton, W10 Jim Flynn, TKO2 Charley Weinert, and W15 Dick Gilbert; 1915 WND10 Porky Flynn, WND10 and D10 Tom McCarty, WND10 Gunboat Smith, KO6 Andre Anderson, W15 Jack Lester, LND10 and DND6 Tom McMahon, WND10 Jim Savage, WND10 Weinert, WND10 Jim Flynn, WND10 Porky Flynn, and TKO4 Al Norton; 1916 W8 Porky Flynn, LND10, WND10, and LND10 Billy Miske, KO2 Tom Cowler, WND10 (twice), W15, LND10, DND8, and L12 Battling Levinsky, WND10 and KO4 Jim Flynn, WND10 Gunboat Smith, WND10 Bob Devere, WND10 Frank Moran, and LND10 Mike Gibbons; 1917 LND10 (twice) Miske, W20 Gunboat Smith, TKO6 Jack Moran, D15 Tom McMahon, WND10 George Chip, LND10 Harry Greb, LND10 Mike Gibbons, and LND6 Willie Meehan; 1918 LND10 Chip, LND12 Greb, and WND10 Bob York; and 1919 LKOby2 Phil Harrison.

George Barton said Miske was entitled to no less than a draw, and actually had a shade on points as a result of his aggressiveness. Miske was stronger, and came on better at the end. Others said the elusive/more defensive Gibbons landed the cleaner, snappier blows. Gibbons had not lost in his over 40-fight career.[695]

Jess Willard had a resting pulse of 59, and blood pressure of 124, excellent for a man of his great size.

On Friday June 20, Willard worked out in the morning, prior to the impending storm. He boxed 8 rounds with 220-pound Heinen, 187-pound Hempel, 210-pound Monaghan, and 166-pound Chip. Willard took it easy on them when they did not hit him hard, but Heinen was bigger and hit harder, so it stirred Willard's passions and he attacked, decked, and knocked out Heinen with a right uppercut. It required smelling salts and ice water to revive him. Two molars were loosened by the punch, and blood trickled from his lips. Chip had bloody lips as well. Others said all three left the ring in shaky condition.

The afternoon wind and rain interfered with Dempsey's training, so he did not do any afternoon work. His eye was healed fully, and he intended to resume his full regimen of sparring the following day.

John Reisler again popped up, saying he was seeking a settlement on his contract with Dempsey or he would seek an injunction on Dempsey's training, but not the fight itself. He wanted $10,000.

The *Toledo News-Bee*'s Herbert Corey said Dempsey would carry the fight to Willard, because he was built that way. It was his natural style. He always had been a dangerous two-handed scrapper. His only hope of winning was to outfight the champ. He likely would land, and when he did, he would awaken Willard's temper, and Jess would attack. Jess usually only liked to fight hard once hit hard himself. Otherwise, he was content to lay back and box cautiously at long range at a slow pace. Dempsey knew that Willard's bulk gave him an advantage, so Jack had been practicing backward steps on his toe tips. It appeared that his plan of attack would be to pop in, fire, then move about. Willard would try to catch him on the way in, and/or come plunging after him with his heavy hands, particularly after being struck. Jess was so big and long that he had real power when on the attack. "Dempsey's problem will be to hit him hard enough and often enough to slow him up, and yet avoid getting caught in the process."

N. E. Brown said it was evident that Dempsey would try to hit the stomach, while Willard would attack the head and jaw. Jack fought with the pronounced crouch of an infighter. His training included bending over low, jumping backward and sidewise and moving around the ring. When boxing with Bill Tate, Jack kept his low crouch and rushed Tate almost from the ground. Tate would swing at him and Jack usually stepped right under his arms. With the Jamaica Kid, Dempsey worked more on his defense.

Although Dempsey would focus on the body, Willard took his sparring partners' body blows with a smile. They also threw the medicine ball into

---

[695] *Minneapolis Tribune, New York Evening World* (Edgren), June 20, 1919; *Toledo Times*, July 1, 1919.

his body, and he seemed to enjoy it, apparently impervious to blows or pain. Their arms grew weary faster than his stomach did. So the question would be whether Dempsey could make an impression on him.[696]

Harry Wills issued a challenge to the winner of the upcoming championship fight. Kearns had tried to get Wills to be a Dempsey sparring partner, but Wills turned him down, wanting a real fight, claiming he could finish both Willard and Dempsey in short order. The *Chicago Defender* wrote,

> Dempsey and Willard have both drawn the line on Wills, due to the fact that his appearance with fighters of the topnotch class has shown him to be made of the real stuff. These white men, it is said, have been advised to do everything they can to keep the championship belt in the white man's back yard and it would be unwise to take a chance with Wills. Dempsey has shown a slight willingness to meet any man, but his manager, Jack Kearns, is afraid to trust him with a real fighter of dark skin. ... Sam Langford declared that the New Orleans lad is one of the greatest fighters in the heavyweight class and if given a chance at the Dempsey-Willard winner a new champion would be made in less than 20 rounds of fighting.[697]

The *Cincinnati Enquirer* said Jess Willard was impressing crowds, despite the fact that Dempsey looked like a winner in his workouts. Two weeks from the championship, the town was going wild over the fistic extravaganza. Everyone was talking about it.[698]

On Saturday June 21, in front of 1,000 or 3,000 people, including several hundred women, all of whom sweltered in the heat at his Maumee Bay camp, Dempsey boxed 5 rounds total. First up was 2 rounds with the Jamaica Kid, who had to duck and side-step and use all manner of tricks to keep out of danger, though it was obvious that Dempsey was not letting himself out against him. Afterwards, the Kid said, "That layoff sho done him a lot of good. He hits like a storm."

Bill Tate was next, and he employed his long left to good advantage, keeping well out of range during 1 tame round. Terry Keller went 2 rounds, and he got hit more; one of Dempsey's swings opening up an old wound on Terry's damaged right eye. Jack had been wearing a patch over his eye, but pulled it off for this sparring session.

Before a crowd of 1,000 or more, Willard boxed 8 rounds. Heinen was given the day off after being knocked out the previous day. Steamboat Bill Scott, claimant of the 6th division championship, A. E. F., just discharged from service, sparred 2 rounds and got a bloody mouth, the blood spilling down his chest. Chip, Hemple, and Monahan also swapped blows for 2 rounds each. Whenever Jess was hit with a good one, he would show some passion, but then quickly would regain his coolness and never lose his head enough to lay himself open to further blows.

---

[696] *Toledo Blade, Toledo News-Bee, Toledo Times, Cincinnati Enquirer*, June 21, 1919; *Coshocton Tribune*, June 20, 1919.
[697] *Chicago Defender*, June 21, 1919.
[698] *Cincinnati Enquirer*, June 21, 1919.

**Willard sparring Hemple**

Observers said that although Jess was 37 years old, he had lived a temperate life, and started boxing late, so his age might not be a handicap.

American soldiers in Germany might be allowed to see films of the championship fight. The Knights of Columbus had received a petition signed by more than 25,000 American soldiers asking that the organization secure the motion pictures of the fight for them. Billy Roche, who had handled hundreds of bouts among the soldiers, was commissioned to arrange the matter, if possible, and would confer with Rickard.[699]

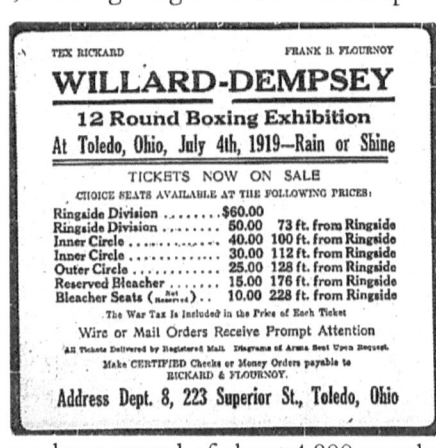

On Sunday June 22, boxing before a huge crowd of about 4,800 people, the biggest since the camps opened, Willard sparred 8 or 9 rounds with Hemple, Chip, Scott, and Monahan. He was a bit listless, slapping his sparring partners around, but rarely threw a right. Heinen had quit, for he did not like the way he had been pounded upon, and left in the interest of his own health. Willard seemed determined to take it easy on them, mostly throwing light counters, so the sparring was tame.

Some said Willard was as powerful and good as ever, and Dempsey would have a really tough time with such a mountain of a man.

---

[699] *Toledo Times, Cincinnati Enquirer, Dayton Daily News,* June 22, 1919.

Others said Willard was not what he once was. Tex O'Rourke, who had trained Willard for Jack Johnson, said it was like two different fighters, and glowing reports were false. Jess was slow, old, tired, less active, and flat-footed, with no zip, and no timing or accuracy to his punches. He only worked hard for a minute of each round, and stalled the rest of the time.

As usual, folks hiked one mile from Willard's camp to watch Dempsey, who boxed either 4 or 8 rounds (depending on the source).

Bill Tate landed a fair number of left jabs on Dempsey, as well as his hard right. Jack missed more than he had two weeks prior. The *Buffalo Enquirer's* Walter C. Kelly, who was on scene, said Dempsey had not yet recovered his form from the two-week layoff from regular sparring.

N. E. Brown said Tate was an ideal sparring partner, because he was nearly as big and tall as Willard. He was under orders to try as hard as he could to prevent Dempsey from getting in and hitting him. Jamaica Kid was shorter, broad-shouldered, and as strong as an ox. He swapped punches and attacked more, helping Jack to work on his defense.

Jimmy De Forrest.

George Pulford said one could bet the family jewels on one thing without risk; Jack Dempsey could take a punch on the jaw. He took several hard rights on his jaw from Bill Tate on Saturday and Sunday afternoon. Tate fired with the speed of a bullet and kick of a mule, and Dempsey shook off the blows, bulled in and made Bill pay. When Jack ripped in body blows, the huge Tate grunted and grabbed him. Dempsey bore in continually, seeming unaffected by blows landed on his jaw by either Tate or the Jamaica Kid, and they hit him with everything they had. Even when momentarily staggered, Dempsey only increased his speed and ripped into Tate like a cyclone on a rampage. A man who could keep boring in and shooting pile-driving blows home after stopping what he stopped was no glass-jawed doll.

Another observer said every round was a scrap. Punches flew back and forth at a fast pace, and the tireless Dempsey always looked disappointed when time was called. Dempsey avoided the majority of blows, but some landed. Tate landed one particularly solid right uppercut that knocked Jack off balance. Bill also landed some rights and jabs. Dempsey's defense and judgment of distance was a bit off, which was to be expected after his layoff from sparring. Regardless, his clever mates could not escape plenty of healthy ones. Jack attacked without let-up.

Billy Miske was supposed to spar with the champ, but sent a message saying that he was sick. It later was said that he had boils. Others said Miske had an upcoming local fight with Levinsky, and his manager did not want him taking Dempsey's hard blows before the fight.

Those who saw Willard in the film *The Challenge of Chance* were impressed with his acting. It opened for a week's engagement at the local theater, the Alhambra. The motion picture played to capacity crowds. Jess played a cowboy, who pounded on several Mexican bandits.[700]

The 23rd was a rest day for Willard. His sparring partners were thankful. Jess said he felt just as well and fit as he was four years ago. A doctor said his numbers were as good or better than most men in their 20s. He lived a temperate life, avoiding alcohol and tobacco, and slept eight hours every night.

On Monday June 23, a crowd of 2,500 witnessed Dempsey show improvement in his sparring. He boxed 6 rounds, 2 rounds each with Bill Tate, the Jamaica Kid, and Jack or Jock Malone, the St. Paul welterweight. The three alternated rounds, Tate, then Jamaica, then Tate, Malone, Jamaica, Malone, so each was fresh while Dempsey remained. On this day, Dempsey showed what he could do when he felt like it.

In the 2nd round with Tate, Dempsey worked inside Bill's long left and shot a right to the stomach followed by a lightning-fast short left hook to the point of the jaw and down went Tate. He rose and continued.

Toward the middle of the round a left hook and then right to the maxillary put Tate down and out into slumberland. Jack wanted to show what he could do, and he certainly did. Even after the application of smelling salts, Tate found it difficult to steady himself, and had to be assisted from the ring.

Jamaica Kid suffered as well. The Kid was difficult to hit solidly, constantly moving his head. However, Jack quickly took the steam out of him and rocked him several times. One of Dempsey's straight lefts caught

---

[700] *Toledo Blade, Toledo Times, Buffalo Enquirer, Cincinnati Enquirer,* June 23, 1919.

the Kid flush on the mouth and knocked him from the center of the ring all the way to the ropes, and he came back groggy. Dempsey landed a hard right that sent him half-way across the ring, and thereafter the Kid kept just as far away from him as possible for their 2 rounds. "All of Jamaica's ring stuff was needed to keep in the ring. Once Dempsey let up on him, when the black boy was at his mercy, but generally speaking he was on and over him." The Kid was considerably woozy when his 2 rounds concluded.

With the speedy and clever Malone, Dempsey boxed more cautiously, not wanting to hurt the smaller man too much. The very fast Malone had a good kick, and peppered Dempsey, who worked on his defense. Jack did not hit him hard, but nevertheless hit him with some solid blows which kept the nimble Malone on his toes all the time. Dempsey's plaster covering over his eye was rubbed off, but the skin beneath seemed sound. Malone said, "I'm watching your eye, Jack," but Dempsey replied, "Never mind the eye, it's all right."

Herbert Corey said Dempsey looked like a champion. He had speed, judgment, and "above all, oh boy! – he had the punch." For the past week, Dempsey had done little sparring, and his judgment of distance and defense had been off, although his sparring partners were very fast. The day before, Dempsey took everything his sparring partners had, and made little effort to block or retaliate beyond his usual speedy work. He did not use his wallop. That caused some to suspect that Willard might outbox him. On the 23rd though, Dempsey turned loose to show the crowd that he had been holding himself in check previously.

Each partner worked only a round at a time, rotating, so they were fresh each time they went up against Dempsey for their 2 rounds each. Nevertheless, Dempsey decked Tate with a six-inch left hook that was as destructive as an axe. Tate was very woozy and wobbly afterwards. Bill said, "I think, that Mistah Dempsey hit me once in the stomach. And then it 'pears to me that right after that he must have hit me on the chin. Seems like something hit me there. But I don't rightly know." Tate was only one inch shorter than Willard, and weighed almost the same. "For the first time since he rebegan his sparring Dempsey showed his true form."

Dempsey carried the fight to his three mates at quarter-horse speed all the time, and showed his ability to evade punishment.

For this he depends upon his odd, in and out method of attack. His head and shoulders weave to and fro like those of a fighting cock in the pit, and when he strikes it is with the same savage concentration of energy. Each of his three opponents today are faster than any man who has faced Willard in training, and he fooled 'em most of the time. But not all the time. He'll have to fool Willard almost all the time to win.

John M. Kelly said Dempsey proved he could hit and hurt a man as tall as Willard. None of the topnotch heavyweight boxers of both colors had been able to knock Tate off his feet since Langford had stopped him in 5 rounds back in 1917. Tate had boxed 32 rounds with Langford, winning one decision and earning a newspaper draw another time, and had met Wills (LND10) and plenty of others who had not been able to deck him. Dempsey knocked him out wearing big gloves.

George Pulford said form players believed that Dempsey would enter the ring in much better condition than the champion, and would win inside the limit. A visit to the two training camps would make one hesitate a long time before betting on Willard. Only Tom Jones, former Willard manager, said Jess was unbeatable. Willard was supremely confident, predicting an easy victory. However, Dempsey was sparring with real fighters who did not hesitate to wallop him at every opportunity, yet they could not stop him from boring in. He had the superior sparring.

JACK DEMPSEY
Latest picture of Jack Dempsey, taken at Toledo. Jack got on the scales last week and tipped the beam at 201 pounds.

It would be a wonderful tribute to Willard, the so-called superman, if he could take Dempsey's punches, for Jess's talk that Dempsey would not be able to hit him was "pure rot," for "Dempsey has never met a man he could not hit." He had fought speed marvels, good boxers, and big men. He not only hit all of them, he hurt, decked, and/or knocked out 90% of them. Small men of extreme speed and skill had given him more trouble than the big fellows.

Bill Tate, describing Dempsey's kick to the *Toledo Times*, said he felt like someone had tied him to a merry-go-round and kept it spinning around so fast he was awful dizzy, and couldn't get them to stop. When he woke up, he asked, "Who hit me?"

Reason dictated that Dempsey would win. However, folks then would take a look at Willard and have doubts.

Jack Heinen, speaking about Willard's power, said, "It's different than anything I have ever run into before." His blows were like a sledge hammer. When Heinen sparred with Jack Johnson, he heard a buzzing noise in his head afterwards. But with Willard, his head kept ringing, and it was worse. "I thought I could hear the bells tolling for my own funeral."

Sam Langford, who saw Jack's sparring, still was picking Willard, and said he would bet $10,000 that he could whip Dempsey himself. Langford had lost to both Fulton and Meehan in the past six months.

Dempsey said Bill Tate was almost as large as Willard, and could box with more speed, yet Jack had no trouble in reaching him, even decking and knocking him out in the 2$^{nd}$ round. The Jamaica Kid was smaller, but very fast and hit a terrific punch. They were the best sparring partners to have. Jack said his eye had healed nicely, and was absolutely healed. It would not be torn open by a punch there any sooner than any other part of his face.

For recreation, Jack walked, played cards, listened to the piano, and sang with it. He didn't really play, but several of his friends there did. He tried to pick out little tunes for his amusement. Jack was in bed by 9 p.m., and woke up at 6 a.m. or thereabouts. He wasn't worrying about the upcoming fight.

> I don't believe there is anything that really can worry me. I honestly believe there is no man in the world right now who can reach my chin with sufficient force to knock me out, and I am just as confident that I can stop any other man. I don't mean by this that I am going into battle with my chin exposed to a punch, for I believe the knockout spot is there all right if hit with sufficient force. There is a knack in keeping these things covered as well as there's a knack in hitting them. I believe I have mastered both.
>
> My sparring partners know whether or not I can take a punch. They go into the ring with me every day under instructions to let me have what they've got and hold nothing back. ... So far not a punch that has landed on me has hurt me in the least. And when I say they have not hurt me I mean just that. ...
>
> Willard is a big, strong fellow, but I am pretty tough myself and big Jess will find that he has his hands full trying to stop me. I can't remember that he ever did so much knocking out in his battles and it took him twenty-six rounds to stop poor, sick, aged Jack Johnson. What is he going to do to a man who is fifteen years younger than himself and strong and active?
>
> I am a lot faster than Jess. Anyone will grant me that. I'll hit him many a time while he is making up his mind where to hit me. And I may hit him hard enough to stop the fight before Jess expects it.
>
> Some time in every champion's life, I suppose, he begins wondering whether or not he isn't just about ready to be licked. I am wondering if big Jess Willard isn't thinking about this right now.

A motion picture outfit was offering the prospective winner $15,000 for working one week for it.

Rickard said $400,000 worth of tickets had been sold already, and there still were $600,000 more in seats left. He made arrangements to have streetcar lines running to the arena. Boats could dock there from various lake ports too. Nothing would be charged to park at the arena. Folks could drive up to the arena and park anywhere they liked, first-come first-served.

**DEMPSEY TAKING ONE ON THE JAW**

World lightweight champion Benny Leonard said Dempsey was easy to hit, for his sparring partners landed on him almost as frequently as he hit them, though he hit a lot harder. Willard too was being hit a fair amount, which was not wise against a puncher like Dempsey. But Jess didn't seem to be bothered by getting hit. Leonard said Dempsey had faster feet than Willard, and that would help him greatly.

In Toledo, the odds were even.[701]

GETTING AN EYEFUL.

[Photos by O. G. Lundberg, Tribune News Photo Service.]
WALTER MONAGHAN, JESS WILLARD.

On Tuesday June 24, 1919, Jack Dempsey celebrated his 24th birthday. He had birthday cake and fried chicken, celebrated with his camp mates, and even a number of local kids. A local writer said the sturdy youngster had won his way into the hearts of locals with his boyishness and good nature. "Today everyone who comes in contact with Dempsey likes him."

---

[701] *Toledo Blade, Toledo News-Bee, Toledo Times, Cincinnati Enquirer, Dayton Daily News,* June 24, 1919.

Robert Edgren said half the seats still were available. The hotels rapidly were filling up with newspaper writers, photographers, and sportsmen from all over the country. The scene was reminiscent of Reno, Carson, Goldfield, and the "good old days."

Willard wanted Tex Rickard to referee. However, the local boxing commission was in favor of Ollie Pecord, its chief official, who had 25 or 30 years of experience as a handler and trainer of boxers and referee of local bouts. The only objection was that he was unknown outside of Toledo. To balance that out, it was suggested that judges would be appointed to render a decision if necessary.

Edgren said none of his sparring partners could give Willard a real workout. He needed men against whom he could cut loose. "Willard is so huge, powerful and heavy, and he hits so hard and gives his men such a grueling when he works as he ought to work, that he has worn out his staff of sparring partners." Monaghan had boxed with Willard throughout his circus exhibition career. He gave him little preparation for Dempsey's rushing attack. Hempel was strong, rugged, and willing, but too slow. Willard could not cut loose with either one of them. Chip was too small. Steamboat Bill Scott could do little but pound at the body while Willard let him do it.

The champion's workout on the 24th consisted of 10 rounds of tame sparring, and some calisthenics. He threw no hard blows, stood still most of the time waiting for his sparring partners to come to him, tapped them carefully to avoid hurting them, and also allowed them to hit him with some half-hearted body blows.

That afternoon, a tremendous crowd of about 2,200 watched Dempsey train. He didn't work many rounds, but put enough steam into his work to make up for the performance's brevity. Dempsey boxed 2 rounds each with Tate and Jamaica Kid, and then danced, ducked and dodged through 2 rounds with clever Jock Malone. He gave Jamaica a rather tough session, and battered and rocked Tate. Another said Tate played a hit-and-get-away game, but still took some good blows. The Kid used a left swing to the body, but never was able to slow up Dempsey.

When asked whether Jack was a little rough with him, Tate said Dempsey was rougher than the Atlantic Ocean. "The rockin' of the transport wasn't nothin' to the rockin' he give me. Ah wasn't never seasick, but that was before I met Jack. I'll say he's rough." Jamaica Kid, considerably battered, seconded the motion.

Tate predicted that Dempsey would whip Willard in about 4 rounds. "I can't see how Willard can last any longer." He said Dempsey could knock out the champion with one blow. "Yes, indeed, yes, indeed, that boy can hit." Tate was almost as tall as Willard and only about 15 pounds lighter. "Maybe Jess Willard doesn't think so now, but before that first round is over Jess will change his mind – if he's conscious by that time. I've fought a lot of good ones in my time – most of them great hitters – but not a one that could bang like Dempsey. And no one could hit as fast, and as often. ... When they land they hurt." This was coming from someone who had fought both Sam Langford and Harry Wills. Tate said even Dempsey's lightest taps hurt. "There is crashing power in Dempsey's punches unlike anything I have ever seen. His timing is perfection itself." Jack was very accurate as well. He could hit as hard with a six-inch blow as a haymaker, and just as hard with his left as his right. Tate said he wasn't saying these things because he was Dempsey's sparring partner, but because they were true. He said every punch Jack threw had the potential to knock out any man. The Jamaica Kid agreed with everything Tate said.

William Rocap said Dempsey was closer to 190 pounds at present than 201. He took on weight the week he was not working as hard, but had been losing weight since.

Willard said he never talked boxing at home. It was a business with him. He did not want his boys to become boxers. "This seems to be the only vocation in the world where if a man strives to live straight and right he becomes a target of abuse. I want my boys to be spared that."[702]

An expert picking Willard said he had too much height, reach, and strength, and Dempsey would wear himself out trying to get inside. Willard would pick him apart from the outside, and uppercut him on the inside.

Famous respected sportswriter Tad Dorgan believed Willard was too soft. He had no trainers, but decided upon his own course of training. Tad thought that was a mistake. Jess boxed in a business-like way though.

---

[702] *Toledo Blade, Toledo Times, Cincinnati Enquirer,* June 25, 1919.

Sam Langford was picking Willard because Jess had beaten the "greatest man the ring has ever known when he beat that Jack Johnson."[703]

Willard agreed to a plan to have two judges and a referee decide the contest. Ollie Pecord, the Toledo Boxing Commission referee, was the likely referee. Pecord never refereed any contest outside of local bouts, but was well-liked and regarded as capable and cool-headed.

Heavy money was coming in to be wagered on Dempsey, and some believed he might be the slight favorite over the champ as of fight time. Never in history had a champion failed to start a fight as the favorite. Dempsey's fine appearance and recent record, combined with Willard's lengthy inactivity, made many lean towards Jack over Jess.

Benny Leonard said Dempsey had no peer in punching, and Willard was not as powerful, for he usually had to wear down a foe before scoring a knockout. Willard's best punch was his left jab, a punishing blow and one of the best seen from a heavyweight. Dempsey had knocked out Morris, Smith, and Pelkey, while Willard had not, and Jess had a loss to Smith. Dempsey practically was knocking out the much bigger Bill Tate in sparring.

On Wednesday June 25, rain left both ring floors slippery. Willard boxed 8 rounds with Hempel, Monaghan, Chip, and Scott, but did not extend himself except for one time when he badly shook Walter Monahan with rights and lefts to the chin. He mostly tapped them, and only opened up when they hit him hard or tried to mix it. He also boxed 1 additional round with *Chicago Tribune* cartoonist Pete Lianuza, who would spar a round with Dempsey that day as well.

The champ said he was entirely satisfied with his condition, and did not care to punish his sparring partners unnecessarily. He said he would taper his training until the fight, and was done with the rough stuff. He would dry out for 36 hours before the fight, taking in no water, which would bring his weight down to about 245 pounds.

The *Toledo Blade* said Willard put more zip into his work than he had for a couple of days, and seemed to pay more attention to landing his blows cleanly. He did not play defense as much as usual.

One thing few noted was that although his pace and intensity was less, Willard sparred more often and more rounds than Dempsey did.

Jack Hemple, who appeared to be worn out to a frazzle from all of the sparring, said,

---

[703] *East Liverpool Review, Dayton Herald*, June 25, 1919.

I'm played out. I have been boxing with Jess for three months and I'll be glad when it's over. It's no joke to stand up to the big fellow. He's wonderful. I know what he can do. He's better than he was in Havana. ... He can tire out any man living. Nothing can hurt him, and he hits harder than any other heavyweight that ever lived. I worked with him two weeks in Chicago, four weeks at Lawrence, and a month in Los Angeles. ... There aren't many people who know what he has done to get right. ... I don't think Dempsey or anyone else has a chance to beat him.

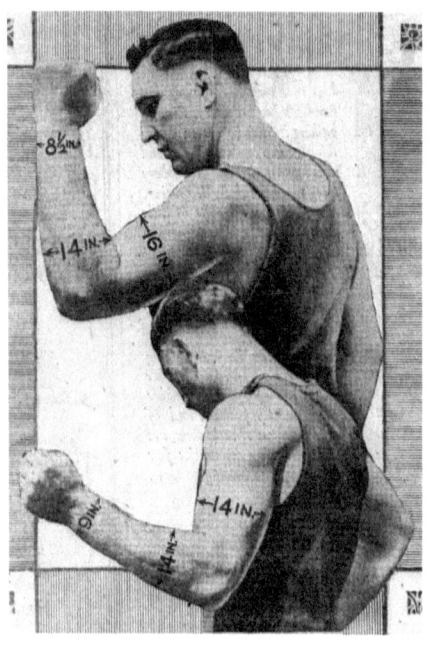

Dempsey boxed 6 rounds, rotating in Tate, Jamaica Kid, and welterweight Jack Malone (also called Jock) 1 round at a time, so each ultimately did 2 rounds while Dempsey remained in the ring the entire time. Against Tate, Dempsey was ducking, weaving, sidestepping, turning, crouching low and working in to close quarters. In the 3rd round of sparring, which was Tate's 2nd round, Bill landed one vicious right hook, but Dempsey replied by sailing in, and a couple of short right smashing jolts to the side of the head followed by a flashing short left hook to the chin sent the 236-pound "darkey" to the floor on his back. Tate wasn't out cold completely, but he was close to it.

It required the efforts of Dempsey, De Forest, and smelling salts to bring Tate back around and assist him to his feet. When he stood up again, he was wobbly. Dempsey held and waltzed him around the ring, and allowed Bill to clinch until his head cleared. Eventually Jack went after him again. When Dempsey was about to deck him again and had Tate out on his feet, trainer De Forest called time in order to save him.

The *Toledo Blade* said Dempsey actually boxed 7 rounds, 6 of which were a real workout and 1 a burlesque with a Chicago cartoonist who wanted the experience, and who also boxed a round with Willard.

The Jamaica Kid received punishment as well, despite being a very elusive target. The Kid was good at launching a rapid counterattack of his own, connecting a number of times. Despite the Kid's remarkable footwork, Dempsey's right caused him to fall groggily into a clinch. Jack allowed him to recover his wits.

Another reporter said only the smaller Malone took the offensive. Tate and the Kid mostly tried to keep away, but Dempsey was too fast for them, so they could not stay away for long.

William Rocap said Dempsey was a target for the left jab, often seeming to take the jabs intentionally with his forehead or top of his head. He also seemed vulnerable to the right uppercut, with his head bent over. These vulnerabilities were sure to be exposed by Willard.

Jim Gulder said Willard would not be able to withstand Dempsey's fast pace. Dempsey was the better trained man. Gulder believed Willard's legs were not good. He could not fight fast. He was formidable when boxing at his own pace, but if Dempsey tore into him with the speed he used in his training bouts, Jess might be at a loss as to how to keep up with him. "He certainly will not be able to deliver blows with the speed that Dempsey does." Gulder said Dempsey was the likely winner. "This youngster has nearly everything. He is a slugger, who hits hard and fast, and his judgment of distance nearly perfect." It was unclear and remained to be seen whether Jack had the same level of ring generalship or defense that Willard had. Dempsey was in great shape, and had the better sparring partners. The Jamaica Kid alone could beat all of Willard's sparring partners.

N. E. Brown wondered whether Dempsey could withstand the punishment that Willard was capable of dealing out. Dempsey was a clever boxer, fast, and had a terrific wallop. Everyone knew that. But the question was whether he could assimilate punishment. He usually dumped over his opponents before they could hammer him much. None of his prior foes hit as hard as Willard.[704]

Dempsey said that twice lately he had dropped Big Bill Tate, the best sparring partner he ever could have, "and each time I have felt sorry about it. But if I allowed myself to feel sorry enough to begin pulling my punches I would be doing myself an injustice." He could not hit Jock Malone at all, because he was too small and would hurt him. So he used him to work on his defense. He heard that Willard had to take it easy on all of his partners, for they were too fragile. The talk of Willard allowing them to hit him, doing so with a smile, was mere grandstand stuff and would be forgotten once Jack landed. "When I hit a man, big or small, he isn't going to stand up and grin about it, especially not when my hand is in a five-ounce glove instead of a big 16-ounce affair." Jack had done the hardest training of his career. "I feel great, I am boxing better than I ever did in my life and my punches carry the same old steam they always did." He would work hard until Monday, when he would taper off and then rest the final two days before the fight.[705]

---

[704] *Toledo Blade, Toledo News-Bee, Toledo Times, Cincinnati Enquirer, Dayton Daily News,* June 26, 1919.
[705] *Toledo News-Bee, San Francisco Examiner,* June 26, 1919.

**Bill Brennan and Billy Miske**

That same day, June 25, 1919, in St. Louis, Billy Miske and Bill Brennan fought to an 8-round newspaper draw, some saying Brennan had the edge and some saying Miske. One writer said he now understood why no one, including Dempsey, could stop Miske, for he had an "interlocking system of defense that as a self-protector is even more formidable than the quills upon the fretful porcupine." The *St. Louis Post-Dispatch* said both were good fighters capable of winning the title.

Al Spink of the *Cincinnati Enquirer* said never in all his years had there been such a remarkable difference of opinion regarding who would win the title fight. Half were positive that Willard would win, and the other half were just as certain that Dempsey would win. Those who supported Willard said he was a whale who could not be hurt, and too big and strong for a man of only 200 pounds or less. Even the big, strong, fast, skillful, and vastly experienced Jack Johnson could not put him down in 20-plus rounds, let alone 12. Neither could McCarty, Morris, Pelkey, Smith, or Moran.

Conversely, Larney Lichtenstein, who had managed Ad Wolgast when he was champion, said Willard would not last 4 or 5 rounds. "I have not seen a greater piece of fighting machinery than Dempsey since John L.'s time." Dempsey had marvelous strength and his blows were bone crushers. He had improved greatly over the years. He had hit and hurt the much bigger and taller Fulton, and he would hit Willard too.[706]

---

[706] *St. Louis Star, St. Louis Post-Dispatch, Cincinnati Enquirer*, June 26, 1919. Most national dispatches called Miske-Brennan a draw. The local *Star* gave Brennan the edge 4-3-1, while the local *Post-Dispatch* said Miske had the slight edge.

DEMPSEY  WILLARD

On Thursday June 26, Willard boxed 10 rounds with Hempel, Monaghan, Scott, and Chip, as well as 170-pound Fred Allen, a new man. Jess worked and moved faster than he did the day before, forcing his sparring partners more than at any time for days. Overall though, his style was similar to Jack Johnson's, making the other man come to him and then counterpunching.

Another observer said he engaged in tame mixing, pulled his punches, and did not extend himself. He liked to kid with the spectators and allow his mates to swing at him. The *Toledo Times'* John M. Kelly said Willard stepped on the scale at 243 ¼ pounds.

On the 26th, before a crowd of 2,300 or 5,000, Dempsey boxed 6 rounds total with Tate, Jamaica Kid, and Malone, working rapidly on the offensive every minute. He boxed a round with each alternately in rotation, 2 rounds apiece. He was hitting hard and fast, especially with the Jamaica Kid, who was floored once from a hard right to the jaw. The Kid remained down for a six-count, then rose and clinched to avoid further punishment. The harder the Kid worked, the better Dempsey appeared to like it, and sped up his own work more.

Once or twice it looked as if Tate was due for a nap, but at the word of Trainer De Forest, Dempsey would back off, saving him from unnecessary punishment. "Dempsey dances about all through his training. His legs are fast and tireless." He bobbed up and down continually, swaying from side to side, going around the ring in sudden, unexpected leaps. It was the method he intended to use to get past Willard's long arms and into range.

As usual with the quick St. Paul welter Malone, Jack focused more on defense, dancing and ducking under blows, swaying his head and body far to one side to avoid leads, then coming back with punches of his own, but always intentionally pulled his hand short to miss, so as not to hit or harm the smaller man. However, another report said one right uppercut to Malone's mouth brought blood and loosened two teeth.

Overhead airplane view of Dempsey's training camp on left, and Willard's on right. Barriers created an enclosure around each camp in order to prevent free views.

The *Toledo Times'* John M. Kelly said Dempsey stepped on the scales at the conclusion of his workout and weighed 197 pounds. Jack was a man who gained weight quickly but also took it off quickly as well. The A.P.'s Charles W. Dunkley said Dempsey weighed 197 before the workout.

Tate said he had taken enough punishment, and was concerned about his health. He was about to depart, but Kearns convinced him to stay, assuring him that Dempsey would take it easier on him now that the fight was so close. That day, Dempsey did not harm his jaw, but did clout him hard in the stomach.

George Pulford said if speed would win the day, Dempsey was a cinch to win. "Dempsey is as fast and as elusive as a fighting bull terrier trained to the second." If size, bulk, ability to take punishment, and a terrific kick in the right would rule the day, then Willard would retain the title. Jess was slower and more methodical in his methods.

Frank Moran, who had fought the champ, and was on scene, said Willard would win with ease. After watching Dempsey, Moran said, "If that guy's clever, I'm another Abe Attell." Moran said the champ had the strength of a horse. Frank threw his hard right at him, but Jess just blocked with his big arms, which he would do with Dempsey. He was very hard to reach, which was discouraging. "Willard leans back about a yard out of range or holds his big arms and stops your punch. Dempsey's going to get tired hitting at him."

Walter Monaghan said, "I don't care how hard Dempsey can hit. Jack will not hurt Jess by stomach punches. Dempsey will be the most surprised man in the world when he pops the champion in the belly and doesn't get results. Dempsey will also get a shock when he finds out how hard Willard is to hit. That will be very discouraging." He said Dempsey's confidence would be undermined by firing, missing, and getting hit back.

Jack Hemple said no heavyweight could stand up before Willard, and none could hurt him. He could dish out very powerful blows, and could take them without flinching. "I can't understand why there should be such a vast difference of opinion as to Willard's condition." There were great extremes – some saying he was fat, slow, and poorly conditioned, while others said he never was better.

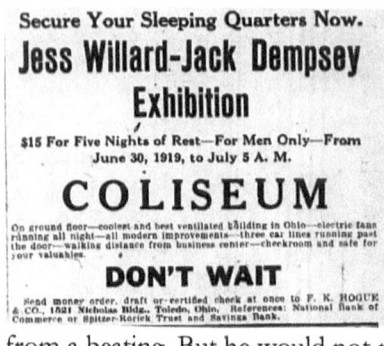

Secure Your Sleeping Quarters Now.
**Jess Willard-Jack Dempsey Exhibition**
$15 For Five Nights of Rest—For Men Only—From June 30, 1919, to July 5 A. M.
**COLISEUM**
On ground floor—coolest and best ventilated building in Ohio—electric fans running all night—all modern improvements—three car lines running past the door—walking distance from business center—checkroom and safe for your valuables.
**DON'T WAIT**
Send money order, draft or certified check at once to F. K. HOGUE & CO., 1521 Nicholas Bldg., Toledo, Ohio. References: National Bank of Commerce or Spitzer-Rorick Trust and Savings Bank.

Kearns said Dempsey was the greatest fighter who ever lived; the hardest hitting and fastest puncher. No matter how big Willard was, once Dempsey hit him clean on the jaw with his crushing blow, Jess would go down like a ton of bricks, and if he didn't stay down for the count, he would be on his way to oblivion, and try to run and attempt to save himself from a beating. But he would not run for long with Dempsey chasing him.

De Forest said Jack would weigh around 195 pounds for the fight.

Dick Meade said most experts were stringing with Dempsey, but Willard had his followers. The champ likely would enter the ring as the 10 to 9 favorite. The public liked Willard's size.

Kearns sold the Dempsey end of the moving picture rights to the Independent Sales Co. of New York. Billy Roche was planning to take a film to France to show the A. E. F. (believing such did not violate the federal law). Several newspapers planned to ship negatives of the fight to their home cities and Canada by airplane.

Oliver T. Pecord, known as Ollie, was named to referee the fight. The locals applauded the selection. The two camps, Jack Kearns and Ray Archer, agreed. Promoter Tex Rickard would be one of the judges, as well as A. J. Drexel Biddle. Pecord would be the tiebreaking vote if necessary. Jack Skelly, former featherweight, was named as the alternate referee. W. Warren Barbour of New York was named timekeeper.

REFEREE PECORD.

51-year-old Pecord, who stood 5'8" and weighed 175 pounds, was born in Troy, New York, but his parents moved to Cleveland when he was 2, then to Toledo 39 years ago, when he was 12 years old. He boxed several times in the 1890s as a welterweight/middleweight, then turned to promoting, then refereeing, having handled more than 400 contests over the course of 24 years. He was well-liked locally. He would be paid $2,500 to referee the contest.

Dempsey said his only qualifications for the referee were that he be able to count to ten (which he hoped and believed would be all he needed to do), that he be honest, and able to break big men from clinches. "There will be no work for the judges. I am confident of this."

Jack was not a big fan of judges, feeling that a referee was sufficient to decide a contest. Save for a few instances, he felt that overall, he had been treated fairly by referees in their verdicts. "Judges outside the ring are open to comment by persons in the audience, and if they have to deliberate over a decision there is a chance that they might be swayed one way or the other by the shouts of the crowd."

Some were concerned that Jack might be overtrained and would go stale. He said there was no danger of such an occurrence. He would taper off the following week, reducing a bit each day, rest the last two days, and dry out for a short time.

Willard said he spent much of his time in the ring blocking with elbows, forearms, and gloves, ducking, sidestepping, and head rolling, because defense was the essence of boxing science. "I have never been knocked down in a battle, never received a black eye or a bloody nose." He could block as fast as a lightweight. He moved faster than folks realized, but his great size and weight masked it. "I can always slip away from danger. I do this by making every motion of feet, hands and body count. There is no waste action; no useless dancing around the ring." He was efficient. He was not afraid of rushers. The fighter who combined great defense with a great offense was a sure winner over the fellow who relied altogether upon the offensive.

Those wanting to wager on Dempsey were finding it difficult to obtain odds, so they were betting on him at even odds. Few wanted to wager on Willard. They were not sure he could endure the sledgehammer attacks of the cyclonic, youthful, and superbly conditioned Dempsey.[707]

The marriage license bureau of Leavenworth, Kansas confirmed that Willard was 37 years old. On March 13, 1908, Jesse M. Willard, age 26, had married Hattie Evans, age 22, both residents of Pottawatomie County, Kansas.

The fight likely would be a big revenue generator. Willard-Moran grossed $150,608, the largest ever for a 10-round contest, and the second largest house, only behind Johnson-Jeffries (over $270,000 gate). Tickets for Willard-Moran went from $25 down to $3. Willard earned $55,100 and Moran $26,750. This fight would exceed that, and could be on the level of Johnson–Jeffries, given that the ticket prices went from $60 down to $10.

Dempsey's sparring partners said he was hard to hit cleanly, for he was quick with his feet, head movement, and hands, and had a puzzling way of weaving. Jack had been stopped only once in his career, when he was relatively young and green and still developing, to the very experienced hard-punching Flynn, which loss he avenged by knockout a year later. He had taken very hard blows from big men, and even Miske could not budge him.[708]

Films of both fighters' training and sparring would be shown in local theaters.

---

[707] *Toledo Blade, Toledo News-Bee, Toledo Times, Cincinnati Enquirer, Dayton Evening Herald,* June 27, 1919.
[708] *Cincinnati Enquirer, Akron Evening Times,* June 27, 1919.

On Friday June 27, before a large crowd of 4,800 that included men, women, boys, and girls, Willard boxed 8 rounds, 3 with Hempel, 1 with Scott, and 2 each with Monaghan and Chip. One reporter said he merely played with his "tired and punchdrunk partners." Only when he lost his temper did he cover ground with any semblance of speed or grace.

John M. Kelly said Jess had Hemple woozy and out on his feet a number of times. Steamboat Bill was shaken up by a number of heavy jolts. Joe Chip used all of his speed to keep out of the way of the piledrivers, though by no means did he escape undamaged. Walter Monahan also received a vigorous mauling.

Willard said, "I feel perfectly satisfied with my condition and will let up after Sunday's workout. I have been training for over three months and feel that I have the snap and power needed to carry me thru. Since I cut out road work I feel far better. I think I am too big and heavy to benefit by running on the road." Gym work, sparring, and shadow boxing was all he needed for his legs. He planned to fight at 245 or 246. He decided not to dry out during the final 24 hours before the contest, nor change his diet.

That day, Dempsey did not work hard, boxing only 3 rounds total with Jamaica Kid and Jock Malone. Even though he was told to go easy, and Dempsey tried to pull his punches, nevertheless, in their 2nd round, after the Kid rapped him hard on the jaw, Dempsey responded with a short left hook to the jaw that sent Jamaica Kid down to his knees. Jack lifted and held him up until his head cleared and they continued.

Dempsey said he boxed 2 rounds with Jamaica and 1 with Malone. Tate had received such a pummeling about the ribs that he asked for the day off, and Jack consented. Bill was considerably bruised as a result of the daily battering. 238-pound Tate said, "I can't stand up straight, my stomach is so sore. Mr. Jack certainly did lace 'em into me yesterday."

Jack said he heard that Willard took punches very well, but when he hit

Jack Dempsey Taking Blow on Chest from Jack Molone at Long Range.

him, he expected him to fall. "I weigh more than I ever did for a fight." Even at 187 pounds against big Fred Fulton, he quickly put him down for the count. "Weighing as much as I do now, I honestly believe it will not be a bit harder to drop big Jess Willard."

Jimmy De Forest said Dempsey actually had been taking it easy on his sparring partners. Jimmy had not turned him loose since the day he sent him 12 rounds in early June. He flashed his true form when he knocked out Bill Tate. The little he showed amazed correspondents, and gave them an inkling of what they would see on July 4. Jack would not do much work for the next week, tapering off.

Robert Edgren said both men had an easy day of training. Willard was training in the same old way, slapping and tapping, clinching and wrestling, leaning and loafing through 8 rounds with his worn-out sparring partners. "He can't hit hard because he'd knock his training staff out in four rounds – all of it." So, he was not able to show his real ability, and had to hold back.

Tommy Ryan said of Dempsey, "He has no defense at all, but he moves fast and hits hard." Ryan noted that Willard whipped Johnson, who had great defense, speed, and power, and "I can imagine what Johnson would have done to a wide open boxer like Dempsey." He was picking Willard.

However, Edgren said there was room for a difference of opinion. Many who had seen the challenger "think that Dempsey, in the ring at Havana, would have cleaned up Johnson in less than half a dozen rounds."

Tom Flanagan said Johnson was as good as ever for the first 10 rounds of the Willard contest, and tried as hard as he could to stop him, but couldn't hurt Willard at all. If the great Jack Johnson could not hurt Willard, no 200-pound man could do so in a mere 12 rounds.

Lightweight Charlie White did not see how anyone could trouble Willard. "He's too big and strong, and he hits too straight and knows too much to be beaten."

Kearns said he wanted the referee to decide the contest, not judges. However, Willard wanted Rickard to referee, and said if Tex wasn't going to referee, not being familiar with Pecord, he at least wanted Tex to be one of the judges. Kearns was confident that Dempsey was going to win by knockout, so he didn't put up much of a fuss.

Ollie Pecord said he would enforce the Toledo Boxing Commission's rules. The rules allowed them to fight in clinches, but were required to break cleanly upon the referee's command, and not punch or have to protect themselves when breaking once ordered to do so. The kidney punch (to the back) was barred. Accidental blows were allowed if one boxer turned suddenly and was hit on the kidneys. The rabbit-blow on the back of the neck was not prohibited under the rules, though Pecord was not in favor of such a blow. Hence, technically under the rules, rabbit punches were legal.

Herbert Corey said Jess Willard did not read, play games, or play the ukulele, as was the familiar custom at the Dempsey homestead. He did not write letters, was not interested in politics, or trotting horses. Dempsey was the playful one.

JACK DEMPSEY

Jack McAuliffe said battler Dempsey would slash at Willard until he fell. The difference between the two was astonishing. In the ring, Willard was easy-going and carefree, smiling and good-humored. Dempsey was a tiger, tearing and ripping. He cracked his sparring partners with a vim and vigor that paralyzed them. He tried to hold back, but it was hard for him. One right crack on the chin almost made a stiff of Jamaica Kid. "I think it would be a simple matter to drop Willard. ... Dempsey is a fighter by instinct. He likes to fight. Willard is a fighter because it makes him money. Dempsey is young and ambitious. He is in wonderful condition and expects to win the title. That is what is in his mind. Youth will carry him thru."

Former welterweight champ Ray Bronson said he did not think Dempsey could hurt or stop Willard. He noted that Miske went the distance with him twice, never being floored on either occasion. Unless he had improved wonderfully, Dempsey would not be able to play any kind of tattoo on Willard's frame, at least not one that spelled disaster. "I've seen them both fight and know what I'm talking about."[709]

Frank Moran said Willard looked great, and was even better, faster, and snappier than when they fought in 1916. He wasn't telegraphing his blows, and his defensive work was splendid. Frank said don't forget that Willard was with the circus for years, boxing twice daily in exhibitions. That practice alone kept him sharper than most imagined, and he actually had improved.

Current lightweight champ Benny Leonard was picking Dempsey.[710]

On Saturday June 28, Willard boxed 3 rounds with Monahan and 3 with Hemple, for 6 total. John Kelly said Willard knocked Hemple down with a right in the 2nd round. Tommy Ryan declared the champ to be in shape to go any distance.

Ray Bronson called Willard superhuman, the greatest heavyweight in ring history, and said Dempsey had to be an all-time marvel to win.

William Rocap said it was Willard's best performance of the week. His footwork was faster than usual and he used the ring more. In the 2nd round with Hemple, Willard decked him with a short left. In the 2nd round with Monahan, they went at it. Monahan had to clinch and grab the ropes to get his bearings, and ended his work with lips cut and mouth bleeding.

Rocap said both Dempsey and Willard had been earning very good money charging admission to their training sessions, having generated well over $25,000 total at the gate.

That day, Dempsey boxed 3 rounds, 2 with Tate and 1 with Malone. Jamaica Kid refused to box, having been decked on each of the two

---

[709] *Toledo Blade, Toledo News-Bee, Toledo Times*, June 28, 1919. Present at the workouts that day were former Jack Johnson manager Tom Flanagan, Tex O'Rourke, William Muldoon, Jack Curley, Jack McAuliffe, Benny Leonard, Pooch Donovan, and Tommy Ryan.
[710] *Cincinnati Enquirer*, June 28, 1919.

preceding days, claiming that his jaw and stomach were sore from the punishment. Jamaica said, "I'm only 24 and I have boxed with some of the best men in the world but none of them ever hit me like Mister Jack. I think I have a chance in the ring with these colored fellows, but I won't have no chance a'tall if this baby keeps on hammering me on the jaw."

It was only after Dempsey promised to box lightly with him that Tate would don the gloves. Jack worked on his head movement, eluding Tate's jabs by slipping left and right, though he received an occasional jolt. With Malone it was all speed and footwork. Dempsey moved around the ring and made little effort to counter, though he did land an occasional crack, which drew admonitions from De Forest.[711]

Also on June 28, 1919, the Treaty of Versailles was signed, formally ending the state of war, even though the fighting actually had ended on November 11, 1918. In the treaty, Germany accepted responsibility for the war, agreed to disarm, make territorial concessions, and pay damages/reparations.

One newsman said Dempsey had proven toughness. John Lester Johnson, a negro fighter, gave him the hardest battle of his career, punishing him and caving in his ribs, but Dempsey gamely took it all to the end of the 10 rounds. He had improved in the 3 years since. Bill Tate was listed as 6'5" and 230 pounds, yet even he could not hurt or deck Dempsey, while Jack could hurt him. Dempsey was younger and faster than Willard, fearless, had a sledgehammer wallop in either hand, and his activity, with plenty of bouts, kept his judgment of distance perfect. He was rugged and could set a terrific pace.

In Willard's favor was the confidence of a champion, he had fought in big battles before and won, he was bigger in every way, he was even-tempered and could not be rattled, packed a killing punch, had fought important contests under the blazing sun, while Dempsey had not, and he had been in front of enormous crowds before. Jess had the fastest left of any big man in the game, and a vicious uppercut.[712]

On Sunday June 29, only five days before the fight, in front of a crowd of nearly 5,000, after his usual pulley work and shadow boxing, first Willard boxed Hempel 3 rounds, showing flashes of speedy footwork and ducking. His jab was snappy, and he repeatedly used a right swing and right uppercut that several times had Hempel unsteady. Jess hit Hempel at will, showed plenty of snap, and defended with ease. He looked quite good.

Next Jess boxed with Monahan. In their 1st round, the top of Monahan's head collided with Willard's head and opened up a small cut over and to the side of Willard's left eye, above the eyebrow. One writer said the cut was a minor scratch. Blood trickled down the side of his face, but the injury was not serious. Another said the blood ran into his eye. Still another said the cut was superficial and the bleeding quickly stopped.

---

[711] *Toledo Times*, June 29, 1919.
[712] *East Liverpool Review, Akron Beacon Journal, Coshocton Tribune*, June 30, 1919.

In their 2nd round, a Monahan straight right to the mouth drew blood from the champ's lip, and the red stream flowed from a previously existing cold sore. The injuries nettled and annoyed Willard, who dealt out several hard blows that rocked and shook Monahan considerably. Jess fired with enough force to send him through the ropes. Walter would have fallen from the platform into the crowd if not for the assistance of spectators combined with his outstretched hands. When Walter left the ring, he was tottering and all in, and his nose, cheek bones, and lips had a carmine hue.

Overall, Willard looked good, showed pep, and performed more impressively than he had in the past, landing very effectively. Only the injuries marred the performance. Afterwards, Jess said the cut would be well-healed by Friday.

For nearly three months previously, Willard had no outward marks other than one small mouse under his eye. So both Jess and Jack had been cut, but Willard's cut was much closer to the fight. His lip also had been split. If the wounds reopened during the fight, potentially it could be a handicap.

Dempsey spent part of the morning playing billiards.

That day, Dempsey sparred 6 rounds, 2 each with Tate, Jamaica Kid, and Malone, working in rotation a round each. Jack took it relatively easy on them, primarily working for speed, true to his promise not to batter them too much. His sparring partners boxed very cautiously. Tate managed to land one good right uppercut in the 2nd round of their sparring that shook Jack a little. Rocap said it was splendidly timed and caught him as he was boring in with head down. Bill paid the price. Jack mostly hit his body, landing some hard smashes. Dempsey hit the Kid vigorously as well, and soon had him on the verge of collapse. The 4,000 spectators cheered.

Malone said, "Gee, but Jack's speeded up. I could hit him anywhere I wanted to a week ago and now it's like trying to catch a turtle's head. I don't think he will have any trouble getting away from Willard's left."

Both camps charged 50 cents admission fees, and yet great crowds showed up and paid. Crowds of 4,000 and 5,000 had been common. Many figured that Dempsey would earn almost as much money from his training sessions as he would for the fight. Each had weekly training expenses of about $1,500.

Robert Edgren said Toledo was buzzing with fight talk. Hotel lobbies were packed day and night with violently partisan visitors from all over the country. "I have never seen a match in which the people interested in sport are so positively convinced the man they favor will win." The Dempsey followers were convinced he would win by knockout within 6 rounds. The Willard advocates said he was invincible and never could be beaten by a smaller man. Willard looked very good recently, particularly on Saturday and Sunday, after which he weighed 243 ½ pounds. Jess jabbed and landed rights that drew blood from the nose and mouth and a slight cut over Monaghan's left eye. "I will say that Willard's improvement in condition the past week is startling." Edgren said that contrary to popular belief and claims, Willard was doing roadwork, but he was doing it at night.

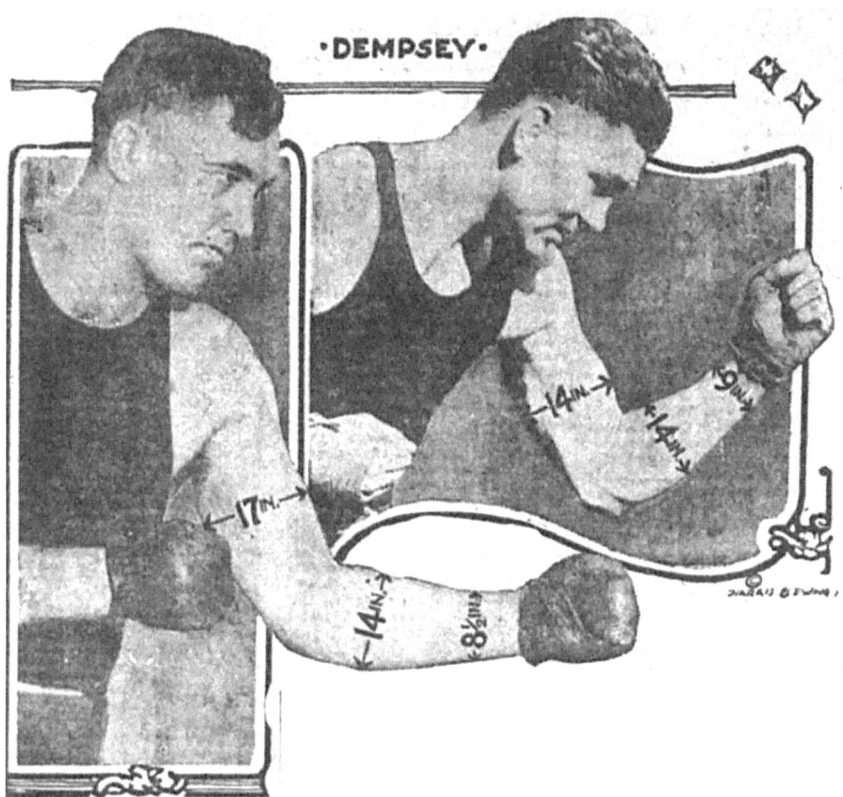

• WILLARD •

Allegedly, the fight arena was the largest ever built in modern times, its construction costing $150,000. It could seat 80,000 spectators comfortably, and another 20,000 could be squeezed in.

Frank Menke predicted that Dempsey's heavy punching would topple the champion. Dempsey likely would drive for the body, ribs, and heart until his body caved in, and then a finishing right to the jaw would end it. Willard could hit hard too, particularly with his long punches, although he also had a very powerful uppercut. Yet, Dempsey could hit harder. "Willard can take a pretty stiff punch – but he never took one like Dempsey can drive from any distance or any angle." Jack was precise with his blows, landing most of them with crushing force. Furthermore, "Dempsey is a marvel in speed. He shifts, twists and turns so rapidly that the eye hardly can follow him." He was nimble, dynamic, energetic, and lithe, like a whirling Dervish. He would tire and bewilder the larger man.

Regarding Willard's uppercut, Dempsey said, "Yep, that's a great punch – if it lands. But it don't land on me." Jack Kearns was telling everyone that they could bet their lives on Dempsey.

N. E. Brown said Dempsey in some ways was like a bull, yet that was inaccurate, because there was nothing awkward about his rushing movement. He was more like a wild-cat. "He's the fastest heavyweight I've ever seen in action." He boxed from a semi-crouch, but he also was fast on his feet as well as with his hands. He never was off balance, always set to tear in. He was splendidly built; husky but not big. His back was broad, well-shaped, and drawn taught over what seemed like a thousand muscles which rippled. His arms and shoulders were bulging and firm. He was well proportioned. His legs were well-formed, muscular but not big enough to slow him down. He worked on his toes continually, except when driving in his body blows. He stood flat-footed on the inside; feet wide apart. Even when his trainers held the heavy bag, when he hit it, they were knocked off balance. Dempsey lifted the Jamaica Kid off the canvas even when wearing big 10-ounce gloves.

De Forest told William Rocap that Dempsey hit harder and would hit more often than Willard. Jack expected to be hit as well, "but he can take it, and the man doesn't breathe whom Jack hits on the jaw squarely and can remain on his feet." Jack also could score knockouts with body blows.

Willard was a family man, devoted to his wife and kids. He preferred the quiet life. He also was a businessman, and saw boxing as a business. He wanted to make as much money as possible, and fought when a suitable opponent had been developed whom the public really wanted to see him fight. Retaining the title meant even more money for him in the future.[713]

On Monday June 30, despite the small cut he suffered the day before, Willard still sparred 6 rounds, 3 rounds each with Hempel and Monaghan. He evidently was trying to impress upon the crowd that the cut eye would not bother him, and he worked harder to prove it. Jess showed plenty of pep and aggressiveness, landing many stinging blows on both men.

Willard planned to spar up until Wednesday, two days before the fight. Some said he would dry out and not drink water for 48 hours prior to the contest. Others said he would eat and drink normally.

Jess said he never was more confident, including when he met Johnson, "the hard hitting black." Jess was stronger, hit harder, and had better defense, having improved at least 25% overall as a boxer since then. He said Johnson smashed him hard many times, but never once was he hurt. The harder he was hit, the harder he came back at him. That fight gave him confidence that he could beat anyone.

That day, the 30th, Dempsey did his final sparring, boxing 1 round each with Bill Tate, Jamaica Kid, and Jack Malone, though one said he boxed 2 rounds with Malone. Tate and Jamaica were especially pleased it was all over, for both had "stood some fierce maulings." Dempsey sparred cautiously and tamely, as did his sparring mates. He had been taking it easier on them lately, because they were badly beaten up. De Forest instructed them not to hit hard, fearing injury so close to the contest.

Afterwards, Dempsey thanked each one and gave them a friendly slap on the back. Tate said, "I certainly am glad this is over. My body certainly is sore where Jack soaked me and I'm tickled to death I'm not catching any more." 170-pound Jamaica grinned in assent. He too had been dropped and hurt several days ago.

---

[713] *Toledo Blade, Toledo Times,* June 30, 1919.

Dempsey weighed 194 pounds "au naturel" that day. William Muldoon measured Dempsey's height, and to everyone's astonishment, he was 6'2" and a shade, taller than what most said.

De Forest said Jack was done boxing until Friday.

> I am not going to have him dry out, because he's fine enough to fight any distance, and I want him to put on weight and have something to draw on. He will eat a little more the next four days and he will put on six or eight pounds. That means he will go into the ring weighing 200 pounds or more. We've taken care not to let him overtrain, and it has been hard, because he feels like working all the time. ... I never saw a boxer train better or more willingly or with a better temper. Jack is as easy in his mind as he would be if this was only an ordinary bout. ... I never saw one calmer and more easy going just before a big fight than this boy is. That's going to help him win.

Jack liked to wear an old ragged red sweater, which had been with him in training for many fights.

Kearns said Dempsey had not yet met the man he could not hit. He could land and score a knockout from any position.

Dempsey said he enjoyed every minute of his training. "I feel so good, so darned healthy, so full of pep, that I don't think I ever will let myself get out of condition, should I win and remain champion for ten years." The next few days he would shadow box, punch the sand bag, and take long walks. He said he was not peevish or crabby before the fight, like so many fighters. He had not changed a bit. "As a matter of fact, I am feeling so full of good humor that I want to play all the time." He had a happy-go-lucky disposition. "I am not worrying about Willard, for I have every confidence in the world I can beat him."

The Dempsey followers said he would score a knockout in 1 round, or within 6 rounds. The Willard advocates, mostly the experienced followers of ring affairs, said they could not imagine any man of normal size beating that giant in only 12 rounds. They said Dempsey would be hit by the sharp jabs and be a mark for Willard's powerful right uppercut.

Robert Edgren said both were clean-cut, clean-living fellows, courteous, quiet, fair and honorable, in and out of the ring. Both were in first-class condition. Normally the champion, the man who whipped Johnson, would be the favorite, but Dempsey's wonderful condition, speed, and knockout record had made a lasting impression. Willard money was growing scarce.

Herbert Corey said Willard was as perfect as a man of his age could be. He was weighing 241 pounds. Willard would refrain from liquids for about 18 hours before ring-time. He was young athletically, because he started boxing late in life, and had not suffered from beatings, wars, or too many fights, so he was not burned up. On the other hand, many said Dempsey's blows carried the voltage of a prime Fitzsimmons. He was a rushing, volleying fighter with two dangerous hands, and infinitely faster than the champion. It was fairly certain that he would land and land hard. He too likely would be hit. Willard had a fast left and homicidal right.

Jack McAuliffe was picking Dempsey. Critics were not sure where they stood. A month ago, it was all Willard, then they shifted to Dempsey after seeing him work, then they saw Willard's pep and said he could not be beaten, then saw Dempsey and said the same thing. McAuliffe said Dempsey's speed would help him hammer his way to victory.

Dempsey did not worry. "He is a big boy, happy all the time. He has the disposition of a winner." McAuliffe fully appreciated that Willard had a very fast left hand and powerful right, and probably would floor Dempsey. But Jack would get up and knock him out. "As I see it now, Dempsey cannot lose. He is too much of a fighter. He is instinctive. He will punch and punch and punch. If he goes down he will come up fighting." He had a fighting heart and spirit. Even if he was pummeled early on, it would not matter, for he would keep punching until Willard went down and out.

Battling Nelson was picking Dempsey as well.

A legion of famous fighters and boxing folks were in town to see the contest. Billy Miske and Battling Levinsky were set to fight the night before the heavyweight championship in nearby Rossford.

Grantland Rice said there were twenty times more correspondents in town than had told the story of the world war. Willard had the advantages of weight, height, reach, and physical power. Dempsey had youth, speed, condition, and stamina. Both could hit, and neither were defensive wizards, so likely someone would fall before the 12 rounds were over. It was an even fight, but Rice was slightly more inclined to pick Willard.

From their farm in Lawrence, Kansas, Hattie Willard, the champ's wife, said she was not worried at all. She looked after their five children - Zella, age 11, Frances, 8, Jess, Jr., 5, Enid, 4, and Alan, 3. Though confident in her husband, she had little to no interest in seeing boxing matches.

Willard chose a pair of gloves that would weigh six ounces, to accommodate his large hands. Dempsey would wear five-ounce gloves. Both pairs had equal thickness of padding, but Willard needed larger gloves, owing to the huge size of his hands.[714]

Jess said he would insist upon a thin layer of cotton surgical bandages, and only enough tape to hold the bandages in place.

Willard inquired about the use of grease, and Dempsey said he never greased his body at any time and had no intention of doing so for this bout. Hence, neither would use any oily matter.[715]

At the Overland Club, Dempsey met the "Mack Sennett girls" from Sennett's California studio, where they formed a part of the Sennett Bathing Beauty movie company. They were appearing at the Alhambra in Toledo that week in connection with the "Yankee Doodle in Berlin" feature. Midnight frolic performances would be given. After a few photos, Kearns swooped in and took the fighter away, spoiling the fun. He wanted no distractions. The ladies declared, "We're for you, Jack – win or lose."

---

[714] *Toledo Blade, Toledo News-Bee, Toledo Times, Dayton Herald, Buffalo Enquirer,* July 1, 1919.
[715] *Dayton Daily News,* July 1, 1919.

Toledo was dealing with a street-car crisis. The company that was running the street-car service had a monopoly and was raising their rates to intolerable levels, beyond what was charged in other cities. Mayor Cornell Schreiber and the City Council, unable to negotiate a deal, ordered the service to cease and move out of town by the end of July.

Co-promoter Frank Flournoy said a bed would be available for every visitor. The average cost of a room was $5 a night. Many enterprising men had secured vacant buildings and dance halls and installed cots, charging less. 23,000 rooms in private homes had been listed. A special train service had been obtained to bring folks to the arena.

On Tuesday July 1, before a crowd of 1,500, Willard boxed 6 rounds, 3 each with Hemple and Monahan. He looked sharp, showing speed, power, and finesse. He anticipated doing the same boxing on Wednesday, and would rest on Thursday before the Friday fight. Jess also shadow boxed, worked with the abdominal stool, and medicine ball. He weighed 245 pounds, and said he would enter the ring at that weight.

His trainer/adviser Ike O'Neil said Jess was fit to go 25 rounds, and was confident that he would win by knockout. "He is hitting faster and with more accuracy than ever before. No fighter ever had a greater left hand or used it more timely. He can stand off and jab Dempsey's head off with that left." In close, he would hook and uppercut him, for Jess had much better infighting ability than folks realized, and a very powerful right uppercut.

Monaghan said Jess would crack Jack on the way in if he was rushed. It was very hard to get past his height and reach, and even if Jack did, Jess either could tie him up or blast him with a well-timed uppercut.

Willard said the yarns spun about him were false. When he trained in California, he did mountain climbing, rope skipping, and road work. When he first came to Toledo, after 10 days of persistent road work, which included hikes, walks, and sprints, he felt that he had done enough running, and did not want to leave his fight on the road. He was preparing for a fight, not a running race. Boxing was the best preparation for boxing, which is why he sparred nearly every day. "The scratch over my eye caused by a collision with Walter Monaghan's head has healed up nicely."

"Step right up, only four bits to see the next world's champion work." That was the announcement that greeted the crowd at Dempsey's camp. Jack just shadow boxed 2 rounds, tugged at the weights and pulleys for a few minutes, and punched the inflated punching bag and stuffed bag for a round each.

Dempsey said he knew how good Willard's long left was, and how folks claimed he fought in a wide-open style. He had mapped out a plan of breezing past that left. Spectators would know what it was when they saw the 1st round. He reminded readers that folks said Fulton had the best left in the business, and he handled it just fine. "I breezed past that left so swiftly Fulton didn't know what happened. When he did realize...he was coming out of a pretty nap. And the same thing is liable to happen to Mr. Willard. I'll get by the left, all right, all right. Don't worry about that." He planned to flash in and out and from all angles, and Jess would not pop him squarely. Jack would not be tearing in wide open the way some claimed. "I'll whirl in there, you can gamble on that, but I won't be wide open."

Dempsey said he could have avoided a lot of lefts he took from Bill Tate had he wanted to do so. He intentionally took a few here and there just to get used to getting hit, in case he had to take some from Willard. He said Jess would be hitting thin air. "Watch me slide past the left on the Fourth."

Kearns said he had wagered in various cities throughout the country, about $16,000 on Dempsey to win. Some was his own money and some was Dempsey's. Bill McCarney said he had wagered every dollar he had on Dempsey. "I'm either going to go broke on this bout or have an easy summer."

All of Willard's sparring partners had wagered their savings on him. Dempsey's sparring partners were just as confident in him.

One man who claimed to have seen Dempsey fight Battling Levinsky and Billy Miske in Philadelphia said if his defense had not improved since then, he would not be able to elude Willard's blows. This fellow was picking Willard, owing to his wonderful strength, remarkable defense, and all-around physical makeup, but said Jess needed to box carefully and intelligently, for one blow from Dempsey could spell disaster.

Jack McAuliffe said each man would bring a cut into the ring. Dempsey had a cut over his right eye, and Willard over his left eye. Jess had less time to heal. "However, it is superficial and will have to be cut deeper before it really works any harm to the champion." McAuliffe was predicting Dempsey to win with relative ease after a poor start.

McAuliffe said Willard was a likeable fellow, honest and pleasant. He was straightforward. Yet, "Dempsey will prove far more popular as a champion than Willard ever has because he is a fighter. Willard's nature is retiring." Dempsey was cheerful, and folks liked him. But Willard had a lot of friends who were fond of him too.[716]

Those Predicting a Willard Victory:

Bob Maxwell, *Philadelphia Ledger* – "The big boy will win."
Bat Masterson, *New York Morning Telegraph* – "If Willard doesn't win, I sure am a poor picker."
Bob Edgren, *New York World* – "Willard's got it on Dempsey every way."
E. W. Dickerson, *Denver Rocky Mountain News* – "Jess is too big, too strong and has all around superiority over Dempsey and should be an easy winner."
Ring Lardner, Chicago sports writer – "Willard will win. He's in condition and has the punch."

Those Predicting a Dempsey Victory:

Billy Gibson, manager of Benny Leonard – "It looks to me like Dempsey will win, but I will say it will be close. Willard looks awful good."
Joe Mulvihill, *Bridgeport Herald* – "It looks to me like Dempsey will knock out the big fellow inside of five rounds."
John O'Rieley, *Bronx News* – "Dempsey will lick Jess inside of four rounds."
Battling Nelson, former lightweight champ – "Dempsey has youth and condition which will win him the fight."
Walter St. Dennis, *New York Globe* – Dempsey by decision.
Walter Kelly, *Buffalo Chronicle* – Dempsey.
W. A. Hamilton, *Boston Herald* – Dempsey.

On July 1, according to the *Buffalo Enquirer*, after shadow boxing and bag punching, Dempsey allegedly weighed 198 ½ pounds. De Forest claimed that Jack would enter the ring at about 203. Jimmy said Dempsey could set a furious pace and keep it up. He had a style that would puzzle Jess. He would land, and no man could take his punch. "Dempsey can stop any man he can hit. ... Don't let anybody tell you he's not big enough to beat Willard."

However, Benny Leonard reported that Dempsey stepped on the scales for him before lunch on July 1 and weighed 193 ½ pounds. Jack said he planned to enter the ring weighing about 195. Jack said he stood 6'1½". Others reported he weighed 194 or 196 pounds. Dempsey told Leonard,

> Why, there's only one way for me to fight him. I intend to peck at him; to dash in and out and around, jabbing and hooking. I want to tire him out. I know that he intends to box defensive, but if he thinks I am going to rush and stay inside, permitting him to rest his bulk on me, he is much mistaken. I am not going to be hit any oftener than I have to. ... I am going in there to make him miss as often as possible. I want to make him use up as much energy as possible. ... I appreciate the fact that he is big and strong...that his big bones and

---

[716] *Toledo News-Bee, Toledo Times, Buffalo Enquirer*, July 2, 1919.

big muscles should enable him to withstand a great deal more punishment than average. Therefore, I am going to fight a careful fight. I hope to wear him down and when the opportunity arrives to still have enough reserve power left myself to dash in and make the job complete and decisive.

Most said Willard was the 10 to 7 favorite. However, others reported that there was a great deal of Dempsey money to be wagered, and few takers of the bets. Many Willard backers wanted to wait until closer to the fight before they wagered. Many expected the odds to be even on fight day.[717]

William Muldoon said Dempsey was a human cyclone and tornado, and even if Willard did jab him, as Tate had done, he could not keep him off for long, and the question then would be how much punishment Jess could take, for the fierce Dempsey likely would dish it out. Jack was good-natured and smiling outside of the ring, but inside, he was a furious bulldog, seemingly unstoppable. Willard would have to hit him hard enough early on to stop or deter the onslaught.[718]

On Wednesday July 2, just two days before the fight, Willard sparred 6 rounds, 3 each with Monahan and Hemple. Monahan reopened the cut on Willard's lip. Jess also shadow boxed, did abdominal work, and a round with the medicine ball. After 35 minutes of work, the champ was done with his training. The crowd applauded him.

That day, Dempsey worked the pulley weights and did a little shadow boxing for a round, but that was all.

The arena was four miles from the heart of Toledo. Over 750,000 feet of lumber and two carloads of nails had been used to construct it. Work had started on May 17. The stands could bear a load of 80,000 people. There were four entrances to the arena. There was no stairway, but a gradual incline from the floor up to the top. Discharged soldiers would act as guards and ushers. The arena was located in Bayview park, which was surrounded by Maumee bay and the Maumee river. It was surrounded by a 12-feet-high board fence, surmounted with barbed wire. 176 press seats were available at ringside. The main event was scheduled to start around 3 p.m., rain or shine.[719]

Charlie Chrysler of Chicago brought $100,000 to wager on Dempsey, and was offering even money, but said he had been unable to place it, only wagering $2,600 of it. Hence, there was a feeling that Dempsey might actually be the favorite.

Willard said it was a big mismatch, the biggest since Corbett-Mitchell. He could not understand why he had become the underdog. "He's a good little fellow, but gosh! What chance has he with a big man like me? I'm

---

[717] *Cincinnati Enquirer,* July 2, 1919.
[718] *Buffalo Enquirer,* July 2, 1919.
[719] *Mansfield News-Journal,* July 2, 1919.

afraid I might hurt the young fellow." On July 2, Jess allegedly stepped on the scales at 239 pounds.[720]

According to Dr. J. J. Sweeney, the Toledo Boxing commission's official medical examiner, Dempsey weighed 191 pounds on Monday June 30 at noon. His pulse was only 44 beats per minute. His blood pressure was 122. His chest measured 41 3/4 and 45 7/8 inches expanded.

Dr. Sweeney said Willard was 241 pounds (50 pounds more than Dempsey), pulse 59, chest 43 and 47 3/4 inches, and blood pressure 123.

YES, GIRLS, JACK IS SINGLE, AS YOU MIGHT GATHER FROM THIS PICTURE

Photo likely taken in June 1918 in California

Dempsey often swam and bathed in Maumee Bay for recreation and fun. He hadn't been lonely, either, meeting many women on the scene.

Willard would have to pay $33,370 in taxes on his $100,000 purse.

Dempsey was the popular favorite, as three out of every five men were hoping he would win. They did not care for Willard's relative inactivity over the past four years. However, Willard money was starting to come in to match the Dempsey wagers.

Grantland Rice said there was a natural desire to see the smaller man win. Rice did not think anyone could wear down Willard in a mere 12 rounds. Even the physical wreck of Sullivan lasted 21 rounds with Corbett. Jeffries lasted 15 rounds with Johnson. Old man Johnson lasted 26 rounds before being put out by Willard.

Willard said, "I think this will be the easiest fight I ever had, because I can stop any man who comes to me, and Dempsey will come. The faster he comes, the better it will suit me. I have been panned by the propaganda boys behind Dempsey, and this is where they lose their meal ticket. I hear Dempsey is a nice fellow. I'm sorry for him, that's all."

---

[720] *East Liverpool Review, Dayton Herald, Dayton Daily News*, July 2, 1919.

Jess said he had started sparring for this fight 90 days ago with Hempel, who had lost 30 pounds owing to "strict adherence to my training rules."

Dempsey said, "I know Willard is a good fighter. If he wasn't he wouldn't be champion. Any man can be knocked out, and a man who hits as hard as Willard does might knock out anybody. I'm going to be careful that he doesn't land the right on me, and I don't think I'll need 12 rounds to show that I can beat him. I've seen other big men fall. When you sock them right they all go down."

Dempsey planned to rest entirely on the 3$^{rd}$. Kearns and De Forest barred all visitors from the camp. "I suppose they believe I might get nervous if I mixed up with the newspapermen and the crowds. That sort of thing is a joke with me. I tried to tell Kearns that, but he wouldn't listen to me." Jack was absolutely confident that he would win decisively. "I haven't the slightest feeling of nervousness." "In the last two days I've seen more newspapermen than I thought were in the world." They had treated him splendidly, and he never would forget their kindness.

Jack felt a great deal of satisfaction knowing that his own sparring partners had bet their hard-earned money on him to win. He appreciated their tribute, and said their confidence had not been misplaced. It also showed that their opinions were backed with real coin.

On Friday, he would have breakfast at 9, and possibly a light meal at noon. He would not dry out to any extent. However, he would not drink anything after noon. Three or four hours of thirst would not bother him.

Robert Edgren said he had followed every championship of importance for 25 years. "I don't remember any other bout in which public opinion has been so sharply divided." Dempsey was the sentimental favorite. The huge Willard was remarkably calm and indifferent to any criticism. He did things his own way. "I believe that when he steps into the ring at 3 o'clock Friday afternoon he will have reached the top of his form. He will be fit to defend his title. He will be 'right.' And in my judgment that means that if Dempsey wins it will be one of the most remarkable feats ever performed in a ring by a smaller man pitted against great odds." Edgren believed Dempsey might have a better chance in a longer fight. "He will have to fight better than he ever fought before." Edgren expected one of the fastest battles on record. "It is rumored that Dempsey is under instructions to move around Willard at top speed and make Willard move, to tire Willard before he risks trading punches with him." However, Willard, like Johnson, had a knack for refusing to be drawn out, and knew how to make foes come to him, which was Dempsey's natural inclination. So, fireworks were to be expected soon enough.

The *Toledo Times* said the feeling was that if Dempsey won it could be a boom for the sport. Jack Johnson "was despised because of his color and his general lack of morality." He was jolly and good-natured, but "too self-indulgent." As a boxer, he had extraordinary defensive skills and a punch, but an "instinct for self-preservation" that was "abnormally developed." Folks did not like his style in the ring or outside of it.

Jess Willard was a "money boxer. He cares nothing about the game as a sport." His style actually was very similar to Johnson's; not crowd pleasing. He was a pleasant chap, but suspicious of everyone. "In the ring he is cool and his mild manner has caused many critics to opine that he lacks the fighting spirit of a real champion. He got angry once – and his opponent died from the blow."

Dempsey was "the most agreeable chap imaginable." Despite his rough passage to the top, he maintained his even disposition and temperament, endearing him to many. "Dempsey as a boxer is a joke, but as a fighter is a wildcat. He has no particular defense, except his terrific speed of foot. He has no particular offense, except that same dazzling speed – plus the most ponderous wallop of all time, not even excepting the punch Jeffries carried."

The $127,500 purse was the largest ever for a fight. The estimated costs for staging the bout were around $400,000. Seats ranged from $10 up to $60.

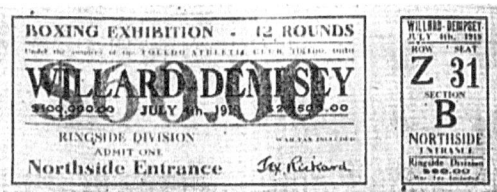

Cleveland referee and promoter Matt Hinkle, who on the evening of the 3rd would referee the Miske-Levinsky battle for the world light heavyweight championship, said Dempsey had no chance with the huge champion. Jess was as fast as a lightweight, even at 245 pounds. His jab was as quick as lightning, and Hinkle did not see how anyone could get to him, with all of his height, reach, and weight. He was not boxing like an old man in sparring.

There was a feeling that the government might lift the bars against the interstate transportation of fight films for this fight. The reason for the law, allegedly, was to eliminate the possibility of racial troubles associated with mixed contests. However, with boxing "on the present high level to which it has been raised," with official legal sanction, it was believed (or hoped) there would be little objection to showing the Dempsey-Willard pictures to the public throughout the country. Arrangements were being made to show the films to soldiers overseas.[721]

Tad Dorgan advised readers to bet on Dempsey. He said very few fighters were effective at Willard's age, and father time was undefeated. Combine that with the fact that Dempsey was a young and fast bulldog in great shape, had plenty of power to hurt anyone, loved to fight, and could not wait for the bell to ring. Willard was confident too, but it wouldn't matter, for he never had met a fighter who carried the fight to him the way Dempsey would. Tad believed Dempsey would win inside of 6 rounds.

Gunboat Smith, who had fought both, said Dempsey would win within 4 rounds. He said Willard was going into the fight for the money alone. Dempsey was the division's greatest kid. He had a terrible punch in both hands, was as shifty as a bantamweight, and had accuracy and speed.

---

[721] *Toledo Blade, Toledo News-Bee, Toledo Times, Sandusky Register*, July 3, 1919.

Frank Menke said a million dollars was in town waiting to be wagered on Dempsey at even odds, yet there were few takers.

Jimmy De Forest said, "Taking everything into consideration such as speed, strength, hitting power, gameness, endurance and the fighting spirit, Jack Dempsey is the greatest fighting machine ever turned out." Although Willard was a great man, it would not matter against Dempsey's speed, power, and rugged constitution.

Frank Moran and Tommy Ryan said Willard was a complete fighter, with offense and defense, while Dempsey was hittable.

The *Mansfield News* said never before in history had a heavyweight champion not entered the ring as the favorite, but such appeared to be the case in this instance. The preliminary bouts would start at 10 a.m., rain or shine.[722]

Frank Menke called it the most important pugilistic clash on American soil since 1910. The entire town was talking about the fight and nothing else. 40,000 to 50,000 strangers were in town.

On the 3rd, Dempsey said, "This is the lifetime opportunity for me. Ever since I was able to swing a fist I had dreams of becoming champion. Through the years I have fought to reach that pinnacle. The chance comes to me tomorrow – and I'll make good." Jack realized that Willard was 5 inches taller, had a longer reach, and would outweigh him by 45 pounds, but he was not worried. "I've always found big men easiest to whip. And I think it will be the same way with Willard. He says he can take everything in the stomach that I can send along. Well, he'll have plenty of chances – and before the first round is over. I'm going in for a knockout within the first minute of the fight – and I am going to win in quicker time than any other man that ever climbed to championship heights."

Willard said, "They've touted Dempsey as a world beater – and all along I've felt that he was overrated, even though I admit that he is a good man. ... I am his superior in every angle of the fight game – and I'll prove it without much trouble." Jess said he never felt better in his life, and was a far superior boxer to what he was in Havana.[723]

The *Toledo Blade* said Dempsey weighed 195 pounds on Thursday, the day before the fight. Willard was just over 240 pounds. Dempsey would spot Willard 45 pounds, but Jess would be spotting him 13-14 years in age.

Those who bet on which round the fight would end mostly selected the 8th round. The heaviest wagering was on the fight to last the 12-round distance. The "smart folks" thought it would go the full 12 rounds.

The arena exceeded in size anything ever built before. Hence, even if there was a huge crowd, the arena still might appear relatively empty.

Factoring in weight, reach, age, endurance, punch in either hand, overall attainments, preparedness, workouts, and credits against common opponents, mathematician Tony Waki said Dempsey had 875 points to 771

---

[722] *Mansfield News*, July 3, 1919.
[723] *East Liverpool Review, Dayton Herald, Akron Beacon Journal, Buffalo Enquirer*, July 3, 1919.

for Willard, giving him a 104 point advantage, which to his way of thinking meant that Dempsey would win by knockout.

Motion picture men took films of the scene on the 3rd, as well as various notable men.

Tex Rickard  Bat Masterson  Battling Levinsky

Benny Leonard and Battling Nelson

Patrons were warned against those trying to charge taxi rates beyond what was legal. The ordinary rate to Bayview Park, which was about 4 miles from the center of the city, was $2. Under the law, no more than 70 cents could be charged for the first mile and 10 cents for each quarter of a mile thereafter. Passengers would have to pay the war tax.

Rumors that bombs had been found planted in the arena angered Rickard, who said they were total lies without the slightest foundation. He said the arena, since its completion, had been under constant surveillance by U.S. marshals, city firemen, his own private watchman, and private detectives. No one had been allowed to approach the structure.

Damon Runyon said it was a modern-day David vs. Goliath story. Willard was insulted by the fact that the odds were even. Runyon said his loafing manner of sparring caused some to wonder about him, for he appeared just to be going through the motions to some degree. Runyon's guess was Dempsey inside of 6 rounds.

About 52,000 people in total had paid to see Willard work. Dempsey likely drew about the same number. Both had earned plenty of money just by charging admission to watch them train.

The town had a carnival atmosphere and appearance, so packed full of visitors that it was surging over with humanity. Dense crowds included many notables. Runyon knew a man with a $60 ringside seat who refused an offer of $150 for it. "There's something about the heavyweight championship, something about such names as Sullivan, Corbett, Fitzsimmons, Jeffries, that throws a mantle of romance over the sordid details incident to staging an actual bout, that appeals to everyone, in whose veins red blood courses." A huge crowd was anticipated, based on the size of the crowd in town. "The promoters will lose nothing, because the sale long ago passed the point where profit was reached." If anyone lost money, likely it would be the ticket speculators, who purchased tickets and then tried to mark them up and sell them at a profit. Supposedly, a few days ago, 28,000 such tickets still were unsold. As a result, several scalpers were selling their tickets at face value. Folks would find no trouble in obtaining seats. Hence, empty seats did not necessarily mean the seats went unsold, so the promoters would do quite well.

From Salt Lake City, Utah, Dempsey's mother Celia Dempsey said she hoped and thought her son would win, although she would not walk across the street to see it. She lived in a handsome home, a gift from her fighting son. She said William was a good boy and she wanted him to win because it meant so much to him. She thought he would win because "he goes after everything in a businesslike manner and will do the same when he fights Willard."

Writing for the *Toledo News-Bee*, Dempsey said he would be champion on Friday. People thought Fred Fulton would outbox him because of his great reach, but he reached him soon enough. He believed Willard was too old to beat him, no matter what folks said about his condition. If beaten, Jack would have no alibi. After he won, he wanted to be a fighting champion. "Folks call me a fighter. I am. I will be a fighter as a champion."

The day before the contest, both boxers were paid in full. Willard received bonds amounting to $101,000, and Dempsey $27,500. Their managers deposited their purses in the banks. It was estimated that Dempsey had earned just as much merely from his training sessions.

Estimates were that at least a quarter of a million dollars had been wagered on the fight locally. Large sums of Willard money had come in late. The night before the fight, the odds were even.

Armed men ready to shoot if necessary watched over the sleeping quarters of the fighters, determined that their rest would be undisturbed the night before the contest. Both rested on the 3rd. No one was even allowed to approach the Overland Club, where Dempsey stayed, or the Neuhausl home on Parkwood Avenue, where Willard was quartered.

On Thursday evening, July 3, 1919, in Rossford, Ohio, about four miles from Toledo, in front of a crowd of nearly 10,000, Battling Levinsky fought Billy Miske in a 12-round no decision contest that went the distance. Some said it was a slow, tame draw, while others said Levinsky won by a shade, outboxing Miske, jabbing and moving. The *Toledo Blade* said it was an uninteresting clinching match which the crowd hooted. Miske had fought Brennan just eight days ago.

The *Toledo News-Bee*'s Dick Meade favored Willard, but gave Dempsey a chance. Meade said the champ's defense was too good, and the challenger was not difficult to hit. However, Dempsey was dangerous, and the "idol of the public." As wonderful as Dempsey was, the champion had too many advantages - defense, reach, height, weight, and "one of the greatest left hands the game has ever known and a crushing right." Dempsey would be the aggressor and swing powerful blows from every angle, but the question was whether he could get to Willard or hurt him. The champ had a baffling, awkward defense. Even the lightning-fast 225-pound Jack Johnson found it challenging to penetrate Willard's defense and land cleanly very often, or to hurt him. In the meantime, Dempsey would have to deal with the long, snappy, powerful blows of the champion, who managed to hit the best defender of all time in Johnson. Jess knew how to wait and hit a man on the way in, or step in from far away to land. Meade did not think Jack could elude the champ's left. Willard was strong on Wall Street betting boards.

Jack McAuliffe said Dempsey would win by knockout, because "I think he is the greatest heavyweight of the age."[724]

The following afternoon, folks would find out who was right.

[724] *Toledo Blade, Toledo News-Bee, Toledo Times*, July 4, 1919. Celia Dempsey was 58 years old.

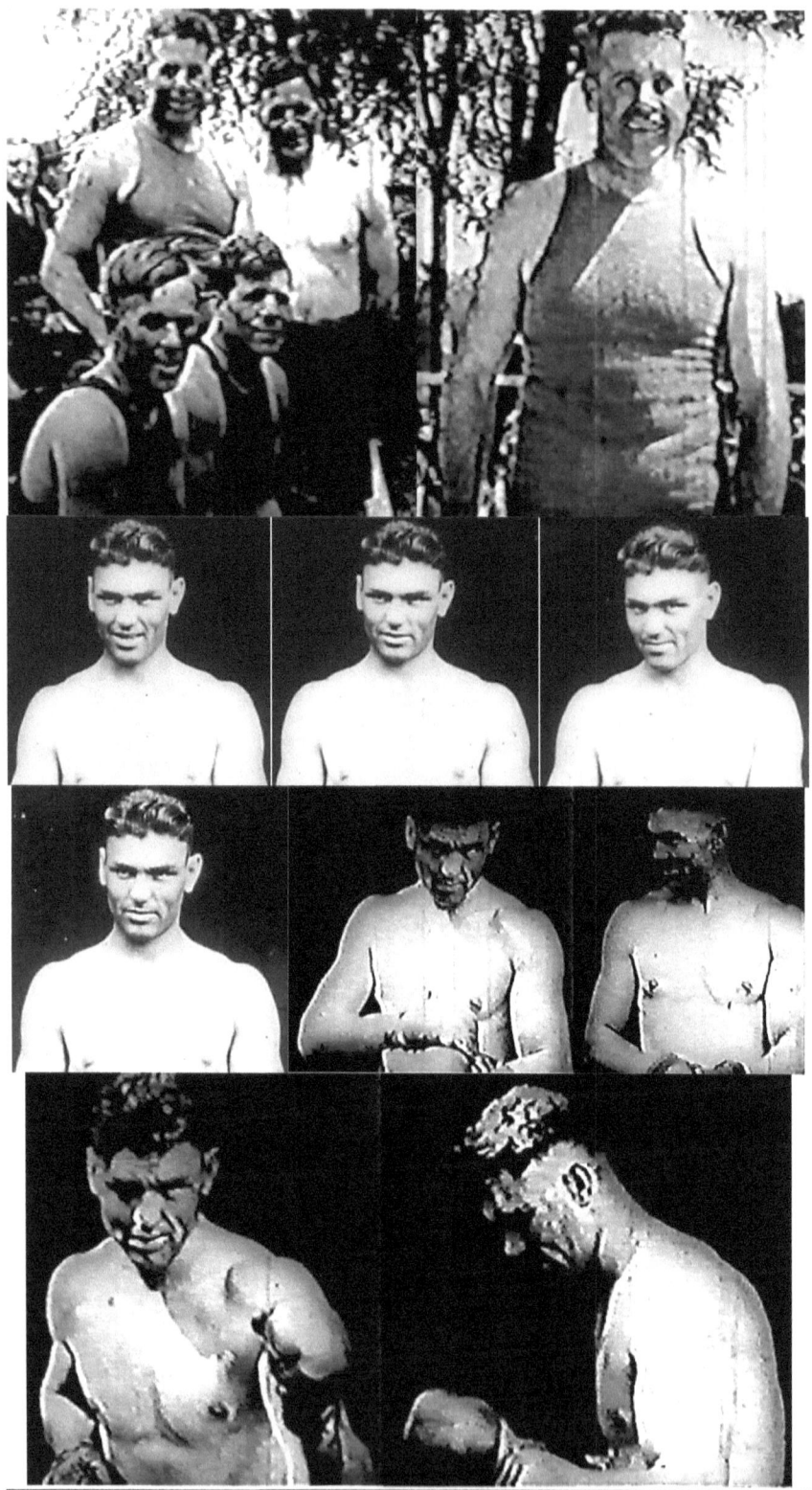

## How The Battlers Compare

| WILLARD | | DEMPSEY |
|---|---|---|
| 37 years | Age | 24 years |
| 240 pounds | Weight | 197 pounds |
| 6 feet, 6½ inches | Height | 6 feet, 1 inch |
| 83½ inches | Reach | 78 inches |
| 45 inches | Chest (Normal) | 44 inches |
| 49½ inches | Chest (Expanded) | 48 inches |
| 17½ inches | Neck | 17½ inches |
| 40 inches | Waist | 34 inches |
| 17 inches | Calf | 15 inches |
| 11 inches | Ankle | 9 inches |
| 16¼ inches | Biceps | 13½ inches |
| 10 inches | Wrist | 9 inches |

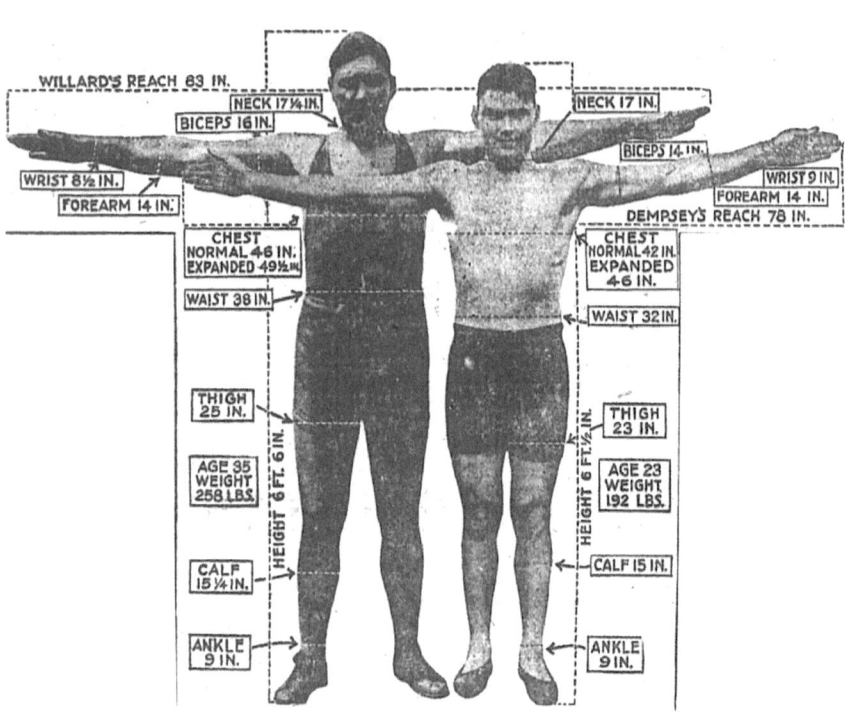

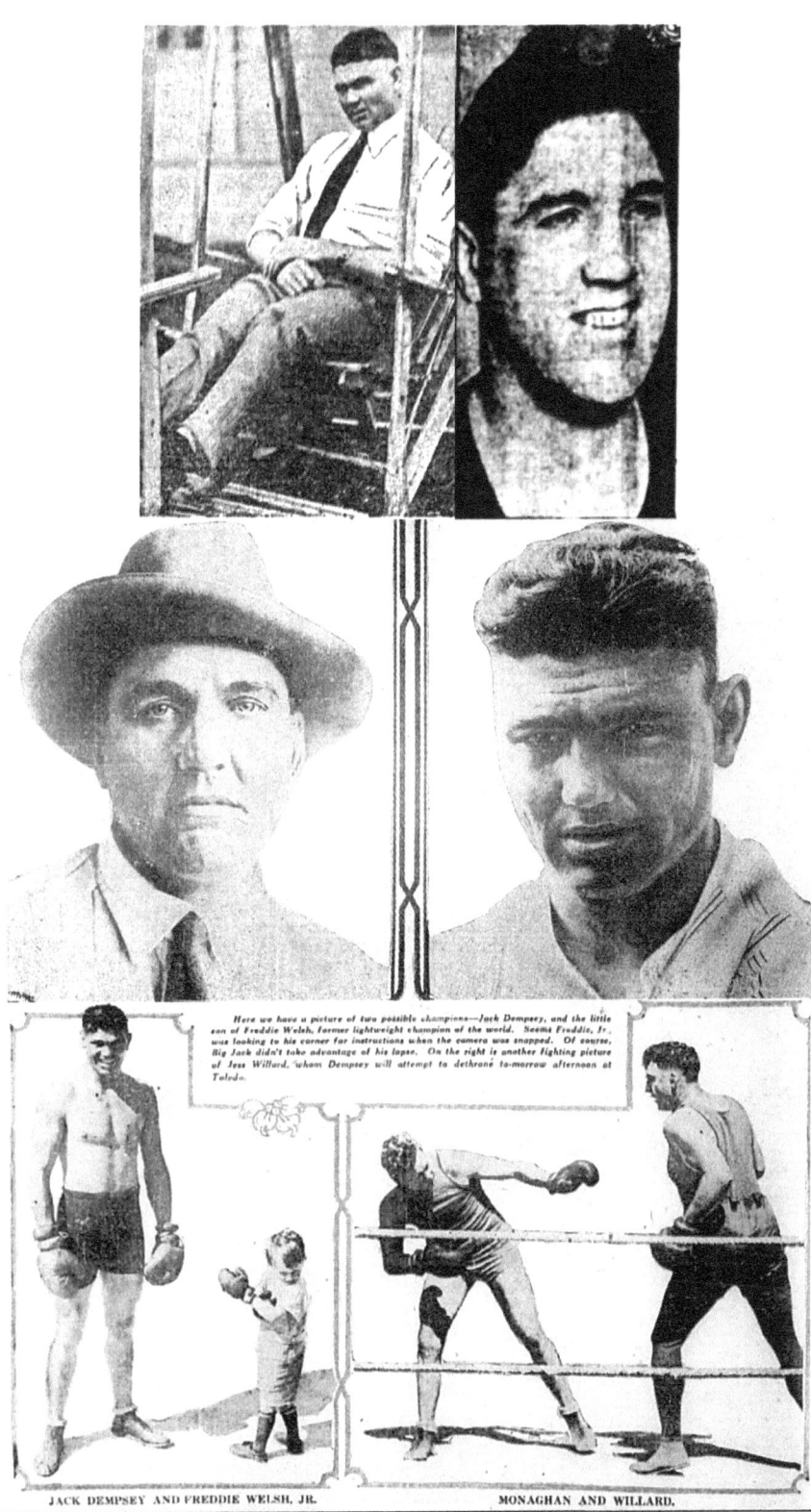

JACK DEMPSEY AND FREDDIE WELSH, JR.   MONAGHAN AND WILLARD.

# CHAMPION, CHALLENGER AND REFEREE

JESS WILLARD, OLLIE PECORD, JACK DEMPSEY.

## THE CHAMPION AND THE CHALLENGER WHO BOX TODAY FOR WORLD HEAVYWEIGHT GLOVE TITLE

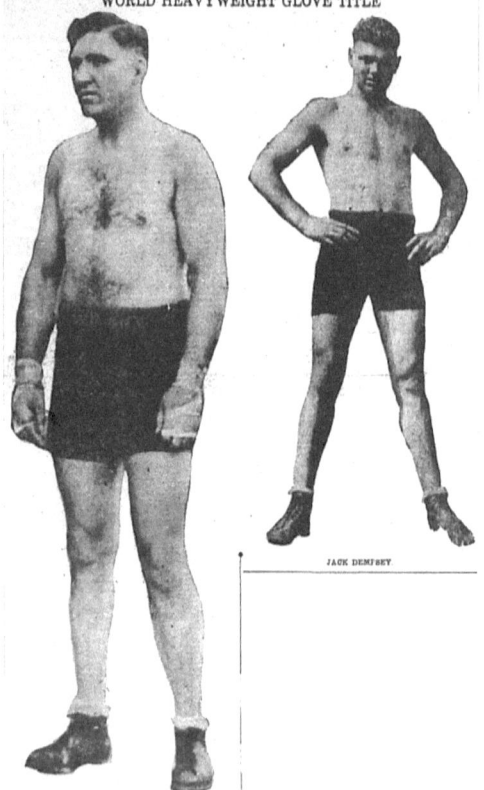

JESS WILLARD

JACK DEMPSEY

CHAPTER 23

# The Heavyweight Championship

On Independence Day, Friday July 4, 1919, at Bayview Park, by Maumee Bay, in Toledo, Ohio, 37-year-old Jess Willard defended his world heavyweight championship for the second time, against title challenger 24-year-old Jack Dempsey.

The day of the fight, the confident Willard said, "Today I am as hard as tough wire and absolutely untroubled in mind. I speculate upon the crops out on my farm in Lawrence, Kansas, upon the possibility of an oil strike on my Texas lands." Willard said he thought it would be an easy fight, for Dempsey would come to him, and that would suit him well, for he could stop anyone who came to him. He said the propaganda boys had been paid to boost Dempsey, but they couldn't fight for him. He noted that the only blow barred from the fight was the kidney punch. The neck punch behind the ear was legal. He was fine with any rules as long as they applied to both, for what was fair for one was fair for another. He was confident in his ability to win decisively.

That day, Dempsey said he eagerly was waiting for 3:30 p.m. to arrive. "I realize I have no simple task in defeating my huge opponent, but you know they say the bigger they are the harder they fall. And I think Mr. Jess is going to give the floor a solid thump." Dempsey didn't care how big Willard was. "When you sock them right, they all go down."

The *Toledo Times* said the town was throbbing with humanity. Willard was the slight favorite to retain the championship at 10 to 9, though some were betting at even odds. This paper said the arena was designed to seat 80,000 and erected at a cost of $50,000. Others said it cost $150,000.

This newspaper claimed that the boxers had agreed to bar the rabbit punch as well as the kidney punch. Dempsey would wear normal regulation 5-ounce gloves, though Willard would wear 6-ounce gloves owing to his large hands. The ring would be 20 feet square. Each would be allowed five cornermen. Soft bandages and a reasonable amount of tape would be permitted in bandaging the hands.

Others reported that Willard was the favorite at 10 to 8 odds. On the East Coast, Willard was the favorite at 5 to 4 and/or 7 to 5 odds.

In his morning-of-the-fight prediction, Ray Bronson, former world welterweight champ, was certain that Willard would retain his title. The confident Willard was in shape, a finished boxer, skillful in all of the scientific angles, with an impregnable defense, and an offense that could not be stopped.

Conversely, Bronson said Dempsey had an utter lack of defense, and a shabby offense. He might bore in at all times, and take unmerciful punishment, hoping to land a knockout punch. But he would be taking jabs and uppercuts all the time. Some said it was impossible to hit Dempsey when he tore in weaving from side to side and hitting from all angles, but Bronson disagreed, feeling that those who said such were Dempsey fans. Bronson predicted that Dempsey would get hit a lot, lose his head, and make it even easier for Willard to knock him out.

William Rocap said Dempsey had a fighting chance owing to his big punch, but criticized his defense, predicting he would get hit hard and often. Both men were in perfect condition. Rocap did not believe Dempsey had the reach or boxing ability to land well enough to hurt Willard. Many compared Dempsey with Stanley Ketchel and Terry McGovern. Rocap thought it might be like Ketchel versus the much bigger Jack Johnson. McGovern's lack of defense cost him in a fight with Young Corbett. Typically, Dempsey did not need any defense, because he simply plowed through his foes, but that would not work against Willard.

N. E. Brown predicted that Willard would knock out Dempsey within 6 rounds. Willard's victory over Johnson and Dempsey's loss to Flynn had a big impact on him. Still, he wasn't belittling Dempsey, who "is the fastest heavy I have ever seen." Yet, Willard had too much height, reach, size, weight, speed, smarts, and quality experience. He was a heavy puncher who knew how to use his physical advantages.

Philadelphia Jack O'Brien picked Dempsey. Willard seemed too slow, and the combination of age and inactivity would be his downfall.

One man wagered $40,000 on the champion to $30,000 on Dempsey.[725]

Various experts made their final selections.

Picking Willard:

Tommy Ryan: "Willard is too big and too strong for Dempsey. The champion's weight and reach will tell. He will pick off Dempsey's punches and meet him coming in with hard drives." "Dempsey has nothing. He is not a clever boxer. One of his size would need to be wonderfully clever to beat a man of Willard's size, weight, reach and boxing skill."
Fred Fulton: "Willard is a cinch. He's too big for Dempsey to hurt."
Frank Moran: "Willard should beat Dempsey in twelve rounds."
Mike Gibbons: "Willard's ring experience, his weight and reach will prove too much."
Ted Lewis: "Dempsey will not be able to overcome Willard's height, weight, and reach."
Tom O'Rourke: "Dempsey fighting Willard is like a bull trying to butt a locomotive off the track."
Tom Jones: "Willard should win. He knows more now than he did when he met Johnson."
Honest John Kelly: "Willard is altogether too big and powerful for game little Dempsey."
Sam Langford: "Willard's weight and all around ability will win."

---

[725] *Toledo Blade, Toledo News-Bee, Toledo Times, Dayton Daily News, Cincinnati Enquirer,* July 4, 1919.

Also, Joe Woodman, Jimmy Wakely, Jim Jeffries, and Charley Harvey.

Selecting Dempsey:

Gunboat Smith: "I've fought both men and it's Dempsey for mine. The big fellow will be pie for Jack."

Arnold Rothstein: "Dempsey for me. He packs the most dangerous punch of any man in the ring."

Jack Curley: "Dempsey is a wonderful fighter. He'll prove it against Willard."

Strangler Lewis: "Dempsey is one of the strongest men I ever have seen. His youth, strength and punch will topple over the champion."

Joe Mulvihill: "It looks to me like Dempsey will knock out the big fellow inside of five rounds."

Terry Keller: "There is no reason in the world why Dempsey should not win."

Otto Floto: "Dempsey will win by a knockout."

George Barton: "Dempsey will win. He is too fast and rugged for Willard."

Jack Dillon: "I have boxed both men, and take it from me Willard is going to be minus his title after July 4."

Also picking Dempsey: Young Jack Johnson, Benny Leonard, Jack Britton, Tom Andrews, Freddie Welsh, Eddie McGoorty, Billy Miske, Battling Levinsky, Battling Nelson, and Tom Sharkey.

Local Toledo rules would be in effect. They would be able to fight in clinches for a reasonable length of time provided one hand was free. Clean breaks were required at the order of the referee, without hitting on the break. Pecord said he would allow fighting in clinches as long as an arm was free, for if he were to break them as soon as they came to a clinch, the fight would be "lead, block, a clinch and a break. This would take all the life out of the contest." (More referees today should heed such wisdom.)

If the referee decided a foul had been committed or rules violated, local rules required that he should consult with the two judges to receive confirmation before issuing a disqualification.

The kidney punch (to the back) was barred under local rules. However, "Under the local rules the rabbit killer punch is not barred." Hence, punches to the back of the head were perfectly legal. Some said that would benefit Willard, who would be punching down at the crouching Dempsey.

The heat was forecasted to be at least 90 degrees. The arena was doused with water overnight in an effort to keep it cool. Jimmy De Forest said Dempsey had trained in the sun and heat, while Willard had trained in the shade, so that would help Jack.

Willard generally was estimated to weigh 240-245 pounds, and Dempsey 196-200 pounds, though some thought he might actually be lighter.[726]

Bob Edgren opined that Dempsey might be stale and overtrained. He was a sentimental favorite owing to the fact that he was the much smaller

---

[726] *New York Herald, Sandusky Star Journal, Dayton Herald,* July 4, 1919.

man. "We cheer our giant killers." Folks loved an underdog. However, the very tall and long 245-pound Willard had huge physical advantages. From what Edgren had seen of his training, he believed Willard would step into the ring at the top of his form. Bob simply did not see how Dempsey could win. "It is not at all impossible to imagine that one of Willard's tremendous blows might knock Dempsey out. And it is almost impossible to imagine Dempsey beating the huge champion down in any part of 12 rounds."[727]

The massive arena at Bay View Park, Toledo, sat along Maumee Bay. Aerial photos were taken from airplanes which circled the arena.

[727] *Detroit Free Press*, July 4, 1919.

In addition to the airplanes, a large dirigible air balloon flew overhead; with a cable holding it in place.

A huge crowd was on hand inside the humungous arena, though there were many empty seats towards the top of the bleacher stands. Attendance estimates varied widely, including 60,000, 50,000, 45,000, 40,000, 35,000, and 20,000 - 21,000. The average next-day attendance reported was between 45,000 and 50,000. On the films, the crowd appears to be quite large. (Bear in mind, the lower the attendance and gate receipts reported, the lower the taxes owed.) H. C. Hamilton said the crowd was small in the $10 seat section near the top because folks thought they would not be able to see the fight from so far away, and those tickets still were quite expensive.

Women wagered on the bout just like men did.

**Referee Ollie Pecord**

**Timekeeper W. Warren Barbour**

The heat was intense, terrific, oppressive. Ringside temperatures in the Bay View arena were reported at an insufferably hot 110, 112, 114, and 115 degrees. Associated Press writers Eddie Moss and Chris D. Hagerty said the thermometer inside the arena showed 120 degrees for the earlier bouts, but cooled off to 110 for the main event. The official temperature in Toledo was 94 degrees, but the weather bureau said the stories of much higher temperatures in the ring were to be believed, because the arena conditions made for the building up of unusual heat. Such heat could have an adverse effect on any fighter. H. C. Witwer said it was so hot it would make Hades feel like an ice plant.

The crowd suffered under the heat for hours. Many had been in the arena since 10 or 11 a.m., eating sandwiches at 25 cents each, and imitation lemonade or near-beer at 25 cents a cup. Cups of ice water sold for 5 and 10 cents, and Piel's beer for 25 cents. People even paid for little pieces of ice. Yellow eye glasses sold for $2, sunshades for $1. An occasional bay breeze gave some slight relief.

Betty Brown said there were hucksters of pillows, smoked glasses, peanuts, programs, cold beer, hot dogs, fans, newspapers, paper parasols, and sandwiches. Yellow pine planks made up the arena. The huge yellow saucer of wood was like a bowl, full of humanity. There were seven acres of seats. Thousands were white-shirted and straw-hatted. Men were everywhere. A couple hundred women were in their own section. "The heat is deadly."

The six preliminary bouts began in the late morning (between 10 and 11 a.m.), and the day only grew hotter. Dempsey sparring partner Jock Malone won an 8-round decision over Navy Rostan.

LEAPS FROM ONE PLANE TO ANOTHER

Some enjoyed the antics of aviators who circled over the arena during the morning and afternoon. With the assistance of another pilot, Daredevil birdman Lieutenant Ormer L. Locklear stood on the wings of his plane, grabbed a rope or ladder hanging down from a plane flying above him, and climbed up it to the plane above, all while over 1,000 feet in the air. Some missed the feat because they were watching a preliminary bout at the time.

Another flier, Lieutenant Blanchard, brought a roar of applause when he executed some pretty stunt flying, doing sensational tail spins, loop-the-loops, and nose dives.

At about 3 p.m., the large dirigible air balloon/ government observation blimp broke free from the cable/rope holding it in place and flew off over the lake. The men in the basket managed to let the gas out, and eventually went down into the adjacent Maumee Bay.

Ruth A. Peiter said rescue boats had reached only one of the two men carried out to sea. In the balloon at the time were Sergeant Joseph Marquette, pilot, and Fred Delevan, New York moving picture man. After the balloon went down in the lake, motor boats rushed to the rescue.

Delevan was picked up minus his camera and equipment. The search for Sergeant Marquette proved futile. Some believed he had drowned after becoming entangled in the ropes of the big gas bag. His body was thought to be lost in Lake Erie.

The impatient crowd had expected the main fight to start at around 3 p.m., but it wasn't until after 4 p.m. that it began.

At 3:30 p.m., Major Biddle appeared with his marines, who with guns and bayonets gave an exhibition of bayonet and knife fighting.

At 3:56 or 3:57 p.m., to cheers, Jack Dempsey entered the ring with only a towel draped over his shoulders and back. His trunks were white silk or satin. His socks were rolled down to the tops of his shoes. Jack was very tan, and he was unshaven. His dark body looked even darker when set off by the white trunks he wore. He walked over to his corner and sat down on his stool. Bill Tate held a huge green umbrella over him in his corner to shade him from the sun. He chose the corner with the sun at his back.

Jack Kearns was in charge. He was assisted by Jock/Jack Malone, Jamaica Kid, Denver Jack Geyer, Bill Tate, Joe Mulvihill, and Trainer Jimmy De Forest. Malone held the fan.

A minute later, Jess Willard entered, wearing an open dark green robe, smiling and circling around to display himself to the cheering crowd, with arms raised and outstretched a bit, and then he removed the robe. His silk trunks were a "perfectly lovely shade of blue" or purple, perhaps bluish-purple (Runyon said blue, Tad said purple, though most said blue). His socks were rolled down to the tops of his shoes as well. He also was tan, but not as dark as Dempsey. H. C. Witwer said Willard was nonchalant, and acted like the coolest and most self-possessed guy in the arena. Dempsey was more serious and businesslike in demeanor. Dick Meade said the smiling Willard entered with the appearance of supreme confidence and relaxation. Dempsey had a slight frown.

The films show that both Dempsey and Willard entered the ring with their hands already bandaged and taped. Jess walked over to Dempsey's corner and warmly shook his bandaged hands. Jack stood up to shake. Willard returned to his corner as Jack sat back down. Dempsey seemed relaxed and casual, his arms over the ropes.

Jess was smiling and waving to folks in the crowd. Friend Jake Lehnertz held up a large brown umbrella in his corner. Willard towered over everyone in the ring. He appeared to be in first-class condition.

Willard was seconded by Walter Monahan, Ike O'Neill, Jack Hempel, and Ray O. Archer, his business manager.

A framed championship belt was displayed to the crowd.

Their gloves were put on inside the ring. According to several newspapers, Willard's manager "Archer examined the bandages on Dempsey's hands and watched Manager Kearns tie on the gloves. Deforest went to Willard's corner to inspect the bandages and tape and watched the gloves being tied on his hands." Others said Monahan observed for Willard as well. Hempel placed on and laced up Willard's mitts. Neither camp's representatives raised any objections regarding the tape, bandages, or gloves; both sides having examined the wraps and gloves.[728]

Announcer Neecy Weinstein used a large bullhorn to announce that it was a fight for the heavyweight championship of the world, which Ring Lardner humorously said "was a big surprise to everybody." When Dempsey was introduced as the challenger, there was an outburst of applause. Jack stepped forward a foot or so and held his hands aloft to recognize the greeting. When Willard was introduced as the champion, he received more applause, and answered it with a flourish that betokened supreme confidence and appreciation for the plaudits.

Next to be introduced were the judges, Tex Rickard and Major A. J. Drexel Biddle, and timekeeper W. Warren Barbour. Jack Skelly was the alternate referee. Referee Ollie Pecord was introduced and given a hand.

At 4:07 p.m., Referee Pecord, wearing a dark beret type cap, white or light-colored short-sleeve shirt, and blue trousers with belt, nervously chewed gum and called the fighters to ring center.

At ring center, the men posed for the photographers, standing between the referee, side by side. Both fighters seemed calm. Dempsey was more serious. Each boxer wore a sash/American flag belt around his waist.

Ruth A. Peiter said the ladies felt sorry for Dempsey, for he looked like a little boy about to take on his daddy. Willard looked wonderful. He was big and confident, smiling. "The little fellow hasn't a chance. Willard will just kill him. Why, he is so big he could just step on him."

---

[728] The examination of the bandages was reported by *Coffeyville Daily Journal, Lansing State Journal, Casper Star-Tribune, Moline Dispatch, Richmond Item, Davenport Daily Times, Battle Creek Enquirer*, and many others, all on July 4 or 5, 1919.

After the photos, they faced one another at ring center. They shook/held each other's gloved hands for a while. They looked down or away, sometimes at the referee. Willard was much heavier and taller, towering over Dempsey. There was a murmur of astonishment among the crowd regarding their marked size disparity.

Kearns appeared to be wearing a white or light-colored beret/cap, colored striped shirt with white collar, with sleeves rolled up, dark-colored tie, and dark trousers. Jimmy De Forest was wearing a greyish beret, white shirt, and dark pants. Most of the cornermen were wearing white or light-colored shirts and dark trousers, some with caps/berets. Willard's chief representative was the only one wearing all dark colors, a short thin tie, long sleeve shirt, puffy pants that were curled up, and long dark socks that went up to his knees. He was the only one who came close to Willard's height. Most of the men in the crowd were wearing hats, some with berets.

Referee Ollie Pecord discussed the rules with the fighters and their representatives. "I'm the boss in the ring today. The boxing commission's rules make me the chief. And I want you to understand that while I am here I am the chief."

As they received their instructions, Dempsey rubbed/swiped his feet on the canvas, like a bull getting ready to charge, getting a feel for the gripping of the floor. One said Jack seemed a bit anxious, though not nervous, and he was serious. Jack asked questions regarding the kidney punch, rabbit punch, and the manner of breaking from clinches.

Upon returning to his corner, Jack held the ropes while facing his own corner, his back to ring center, receiving final encouraging words from Kearns and De Forest. Kearns sponged off his protégé's back. Dempsey had a scowl on his face. The fight began at around 4:09 or 4:10 p.m.

The bell rang, but it was defective and so faint that almost no one heard it. According to Robert Edgren, when Barbour pulled the bell cord, the bell only gave out a faint little tinkling sound. Neither fighter nor the referee heard it. Barbour pulled the cord again, and again it was just a little tinkle. Pecord waved his hands impatiently, and the fighters waited. Old timers shouted, "Get a hammer." For the third time, the gong tinkled, and this time the fighters heard it and started toward one another, but Pecord rushed between them and waved them back. He knew it still was too faint to be heard properly. Pulling out a whistle, Barbour tapped the tinkling gong and blew the whistle, then started his stop watch all at the same time. Others said the whistle was not used until after the 2nd round. The films show Willard standing in his corner looking bewildered, looking down to his left as if speaking to the timekeeper before the bell finally was heard.

Damon Runyon said the bell was on Willard's side of the ring, and it gave off a light tinkle. Willard twice heard it, but twice returned to his corner when he realized Dempsey did not hear the bell. Others said Pecord had directed him to return to his corner. Neither the referee nor Dempsey could hear the bell. Dempsey turned around in his corner, the bell sounded again, and the fight was on, not with a bang, but a relatively faint tinkle from a defective bell.

Dick Meade's version said Barbour pulled the cord, but there was no sound. Pecord wondered what was going on. Dempsey studied the canvas, while Willard gazed at the airplanes overhead. Lieutenant Thompson of the Marines tossed his whistle to Barbour, and he blew it, but it too was dainty, refined, and not loud, but they heard it and the bout was on.

Tad Dorgan said Dempsey, who was facing his corner rather than ring center, did not hear the bell. Willard heard it each time it went off, but Pecord and Dempsey did not, and each time that Willard left his corner, Pecord waved him back. Dempsey turned around and faced ring center. When the bell sounded for the third time, the fight was on.

In the 1st round, Dempsey came out cautiously at first, utilizing footwork to move around and circle, bouncing about with his hands low across his body, but head dipped down and slightly off to the side. Jess jabbed and Jack dipped and pulled away and circled left. Jess approached and fired a 1-2 (jab-right) and Jack simultaneously dipped, advanced, and clinched. They broke. Jack did a slight weave and stepped away. He kept lightly bouncing and moving about, off to the side. The calm Willard cautiously advanced, flatfooted, looking to get into range. He was much more aggressive than one might have anticipated. Jess jabbed, and Jack turned his head to the right, backed away, and then bounced off to his left again. He then rolled/turned right, changed directions and moved off to the right, trying to prevent Willard from getting set or a feel for his range or position. Dempsey clearly had started off as a cautious boxer, dancing and moving about, side to side, with a fair amount of careful footwork. Jack slightly approached, but dipped and circled back off to his left to elude a long Willard jab.

Dempsey suddenly started moving in but Willard sensed it and fired a 1-2 that landed high on the head as Jack advanced and dipped right. Dempsey kept advancing, and as Jess jabbed Jack dipped left and fired a quick counter left hook to the head, and Jess clinched. Dempsey dug in a couple short quick right uppercuts to the body as Jess held ineffectively. Willard landed a counter right uppercut to Jack's head and they clinched. Jess held his arms wide out to the side and Jack broke away cleanly.

Willard stepped back slightly as Dempsey advanced and fired a powerful lead left hook to the head that jolted Willard's head off to his left a bit. Jess stepped back and fired a jab as Dempsey quickly advanced with a lead left hook to the body, and Jess clinched and partially smothered Jack's follow-up rights to the body in close. Jess held and leaned in with his body weight, walking Dempsey backward. They broke away.

Dempsey walked off to the left, slightly dipped and stepped back, then a couple times dipped down and forward with weight in his front leg as if to advance, baiting Jess with this form of a feint, but then suddenly turned his torso away to the right and walked off to the right just as Willard advanced with a jab that missed. Jack was trying not to allow Willard to time him or get a sense of when he might advance. Jack turned a bit to the left but then turned and moved right again, playing with Jess's sense of position, distance, and timing. Jess stepped back slightly but then held his ground, ready to punch as the lightly bouncing and dipping Jack approached again.

As Jess jabbed, Dempsey simultaneously quickly advanced with a lead left hook to the head that partially landed and slid off the top of Willard's head as Jess slightly ducked left and blocked with his raised his right arm. Jack missed a follow-up right and Willard responded with a quick combination counter attack of left hook-right-left-right-right as Dempsey kept moving forward and bulling in. They clinched. About a minute had elapsed in the fight to that point. The pace was very fast.

While being held, Dempsey attempted a powerful left hook that missed as Jess turned off to the left and then clinched again. They broke away. Dempsey advanced with a lead right to the body under Willard's left. His lead right to the body would help him elude and get under Willard's simultaneous lead lefts to the head. Jess grabbed, and Jack snuck in a short right to the body. Jack fired a jolting left hook to the head that landed as he escaped from the clinch. Jack quickly advanced and stepped in with another lead right to the body under Willard's left. Jess immediately fired a quick counter attack of short blows, right - left hook - right uppercut that landed on the jaw but were smothered partially as Jack bulled in and clinched. They walked around holding until Referee Pecord stepped in and broke them.

Clearly, Dempsey's early strategy was to move, bounce, or walk about a bit on the outside with some head movement, suddenly shifting the range and position, forward-back or side-to-side, so Willard could not time him, and then quickly stepping in when he wanted to do so, either with a lead over or under, or with a quick counter as he was moving in. But there was no stalling by either one, for the pace was quite rapid. They were about halfway into the round.

Dempsey dipped and weaved and stepped off from his position, lightly bouncing left, as thus far in the contest he often had been doing before eventually choosing his moment to step in with an attack.

Once again, Dempsey quickly advanced as Jess jabbed, and in a ferocious rapid four-punch combination, Jack fired a right to the body-left hook-right-then final left hook that landed flush on the jaw, snapping his head, and Willard dropped down to the canvas on his rear end, with arms outstretched to catch himself. It was the final left hook that really did the trick.

What followed would be one of ring history's most horrifying yet awesome and awe-inspiring exhibitions of power and brutality on one side, and game gritty toughness on the other.

At first, Dempsey went to the closest corner near where Willard had gone down. As the count was proceeding, Dempsey walked around the referee to ring center, 3 to 5 feet away from Willard. Jess rose just after the count of five, and Dempsey immediately pounced upon him, being only about one step away.

As Jess jabbed, in combination Dempsey fired lead left hook, right to jaw, left to jaw, then set-up lead left and right to jaw as Willard fell backwards and sagged into the ropes, which stretched back from the force. But for the ropes holding him up, he would have gone down. Many referees today would call that a knockdown. Jack followed with another right, then two short left hooks to the jaw in quick succession and Willard dropped down again, to his hands and knees, near the ropes.

Dempsey stood just a couple feet away from the downed Willard. The referee got between them to start his count, and slightly pushed Jack back. Unwisely, Willard rose quickly again, at the count of three. Dempsey had stepped back away, and was eager to get around the referee and right back on the attack as soon as Jess rose.

Dempsey quickly advanced with a brutal fast overhand right over Willard's left, landing on the head, the force of which sent Jess bending over. Jack followed with a couple short left hooks as Jess outstretched his arms in an attempt to grab, but Dempsey punched himself free from the attempted clinch, firing to the head in combination, right-left-right-left-right, and then as Willard put his head down and turned away along the ropes with his hands down, Dempsey drew back and launched a big left hook that landed on the jaw, and Willard went down for the third time.

Many referees today would have jumped in and stopped it at the point in which Willard put his head down and turned away with his hands down, appearing helpless and defenseless.

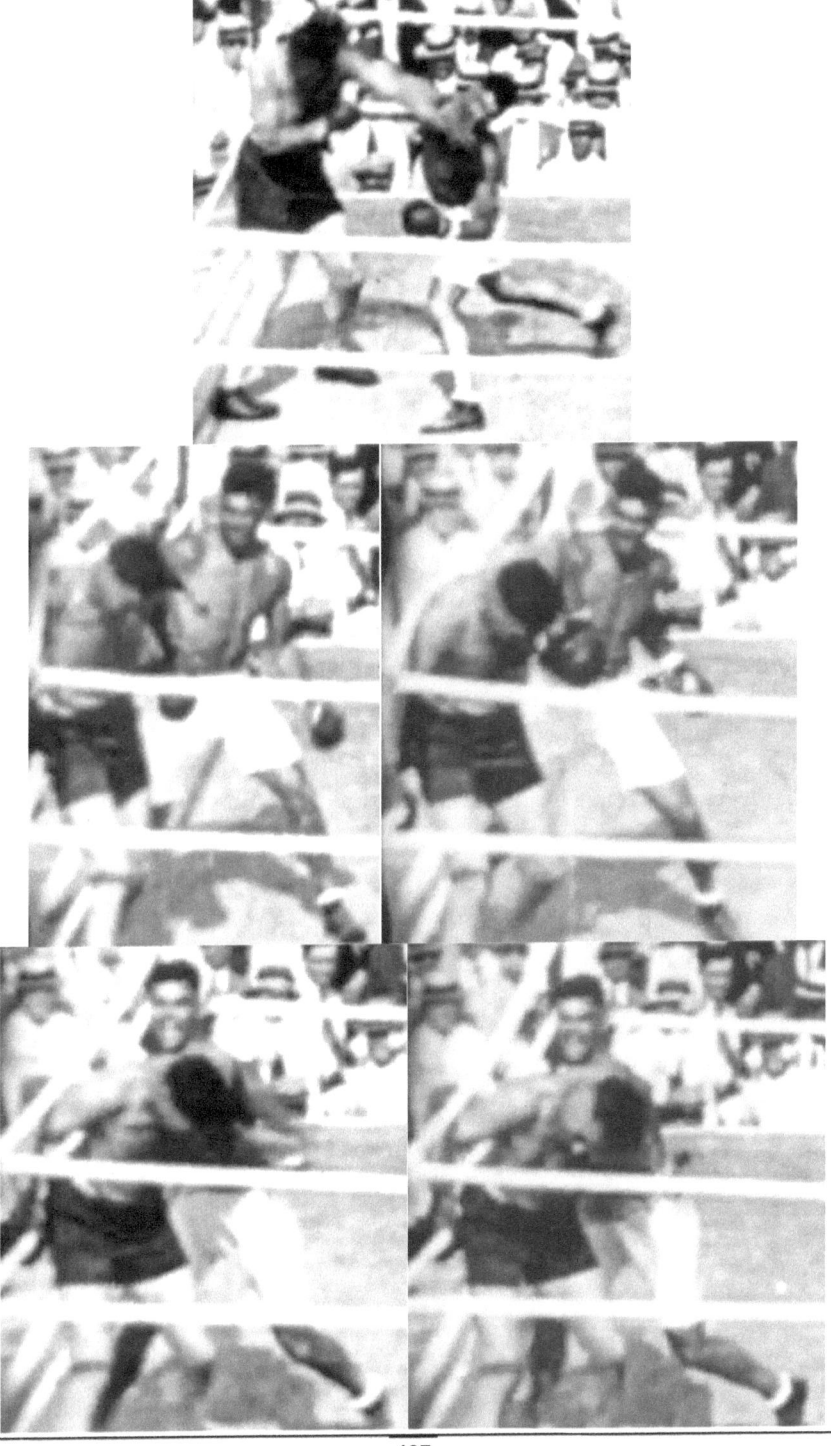

Dempsey stalked around, eagerly and excitedly ready, impatiently awaiting the ability to pounce on his wounded prey again. Eventually he went to a corner as the referee slightly pushed him back with an outstretched arm, but it was the corner closest to Willard. Also, Dempsey was standing behind Jess, who was facing the opposite direction, trying to rise from his hands and knees.

Jess partially rose, but kept his right glove on the canvas. Just as Willard's right glove slowly left the canvas at the count of six, while Jess still was stooped over, from a couple feet away, from off to his side and behind him, Dempsey immediately advanced and wound up with a pulverizing right that landed on the head before Willard even had been able to stand erect again.

Willard careened and staggered off to the left, face forward into the ropes, his head under the top rope. He rebounded off to the right with his back to Dempsey, who approached from his back side and fired another wide hooking right that appears to have landed on the back of the head, and Willard went down in a heap for the fourth time. Rabbit punches were legal.

Referee Pecord counted up to four, and again Willard rose cautiously, bending over with his glove barely grazing the canvas as Dempsey stood right next to him, off to his side, ready to strike. Pecord made little to no effort to force Dempsey to step back away from Willard. Jack was within arm's length of him, in striking range.

A bent-over Willard slowly raised his glove up from the canvas, and Dempsey actually slightly stepped back off to the side and a bit behind him, and again drew back to fire a big right that landed underneath Willard's right arm and struck him as he still was leaning over and lifting up his arm as if he thought the punch would come from over the top, but it actually snuck in from underneath.

Dempsey immediately followed with two more rights to the head, for a total of three in a row, the final right landing cleanly on the jaw and sending Jess leaning back into the ropes. Jack followed with a left hook to the jaw, right to the jaw, another hook and right to the same locations, and Jess got off the ropes moving/falling forward, grabbing Jack's left that went into his body, but Dempsey fired a powerful right over the top that landed flush on the side of the skull. The force of the blow sent Willard's torso down and off to the right. He came up again, only to be met with a huge left hook that Dempsey wound up from his knees, though it was partially blocked. Dempsey doubled it up with another shorter left hook that landed more cleanly and Willard went down for the fifth time, onto his hand and rear end in the corner.

Willard rose at the count of four along the ropes near the corner where he went down. This time Dempsey stood closer to ring center. Jack approached and ducked down low as Jess hit him with a jab and right. Dempsey struck back with a left hook high on the head, then vicious right to the jaw that turned Willard's head to the side. Jack followed with a left uppercut to the jaw, and Jess grabbed tightly. Jack pushed Willard's head back with his left to create punching room while being held, and dug a right to the body, then pulverizing right to the jaw and Jess immediately bent far over and tried to grab as best he could.

Jack pushed him off to break free from the clinch and prevent Jess from holding him, and as Jess moved and started staggering off to the right, Jack followed and landed a right, left hook, and brutal right, the force of the final blow being so tremendous, and Willard's balance being so poor, that Jess went careening off to the side, face-first into/under the top in the corner on the other side of the ring before turning and coming up.

Dempsey followed with a left hook that jolted Jess's head, then right to the jaw and another left. Jess tried to grab, and Jack followed with short body blows - right and left, then left hook to the head, and as Jess leaned over to his left in a helpless state, with his left arm over and clutching the middle rope for support, Dempsey landed two more rights to the head and Jess finally went down for the sixth time, clutching the ropes.

Referee Pecord pushed Jack back as he counted. Pecord gave Jess a four or five count. Willard did not rise under his own power, but actually required the assistance of the rope, and was bent over, clutching onto the middle rope with both hands, not fully erect, in a helpless and hopeless state. Nevertheless, sadly, the bout was allowed to proceed.

Dempsey once again approached from the side and behind Willard, and fired a right into Jess's body as he still was bent over clutching onto the rope. The force of the blow could see seen reverberating through Willard's body. Jack followed with a right to the jaw that jolted Willard's head, and then another right as Jess went down into the corner, with his left arm still draped over the middle rope, down for the seventh time in the 1st round.

The sheer brutality, fast pace, speed, kinetic ferocity, and volume of flush, clean, hard blows that Willard had absorbed in the round simply has to be seen on film to be appreciated fully. Dempsey had thrown about 65 punches in the round, nearly all very powerful blows, most of them landing.

During the count, Willard's cornerman put his stool into the ring, a sign that either the bell had rung or they thought it was going to ring, or that the fight was over. He even started to get into the ring, but then held back. Timing the films, it was just about three minutes from the start of the fight to when Jess went down for the seventh time. Dempsey stalked around.

Apparently, the bell rang sometime during the count. Most said it was at about the count of seven. At that time, a fighter could be saved by the bell (unlike today). However, very few heard the bell, owing to the crowd noise and the fact that it was defective and quite faint. The referee either kept counting, and counted Willard out, but subsequently was informed by timekeeper Barbour that the bell had saved him, or Pecord suspended the count once he realized the bell had rung and Barbour had stopped counting.

However, not hearing the bell, those in Dempsey's corner did not seem to realize that the bell had saved Willard, and seeing him sitting there and not moving at all, believed he had been counted out and the fight was over. As Jack Kearns was entering the ring, Dempsey turned to move towards Willard, as if he intended to go shake his hand, but the referee pushed him back, perhaps realizing it was not over, but not realizing that Dempsey did not understand this. He had not raised Dempsey's arm, as typically a referee would do when a fight was over. Dempsey's seconds rushed into the ring in a jubilant state, smiling and joyous. In fact, a large crowd of folks entered the ring, congratulating Dempsey, not realizing that the bell had rung. Believing that he had won, Jack went through the ropes and left the ring.

In the meantime, Willard still was down on the canvas in the corner where he had gone down. Two of his cornermen went over to attend to him, one placing smelling salts underneath his nose to revive him (something which today would not be allowed). Jess seemed to have been awoken by this, and eventually rose up with the assistance of his attendants. He staggered to the left, away from the direction of his corner, not even seeming to know where his corner was, and had to be assisted back to the right, to his corner, where he sat down. Edward Tranter said Willard was helped to his corner; shaky, weak, wobbly, and beaten. Walter Monaghan and others worked over him, "administering aromatics, smelling salts and dashing ice cold water over his head and body."

During all of this, Jack Kearns was informed that the fight was not over. He spoke with Pecord and then went over to the timekeeper. Kearns then ran back to the corner and started shouting for Jack to come back. Kearns, De Forest, and other attendants rushed out to go get him. Dempsey had to turn around and return to the ring. In the meantime, those who had entered to celebrate the victory exited the ring.

By the time Dempsey got back into the ring and sat down on his stool, there was perhaps only ten seconds or less before the bell rang. Hence, Dempsey did not really receive any rest, attendance, or instruction.

Some said the time between rounds still was one minute. Others claimed that in the confusion, a greater amount of time elapsed between rounds, including: 1 minute 20 seconds, 90 seconds, and 2 minutes 4 seconds, which helped Willard recover from his stupor and allowed Jack to return.

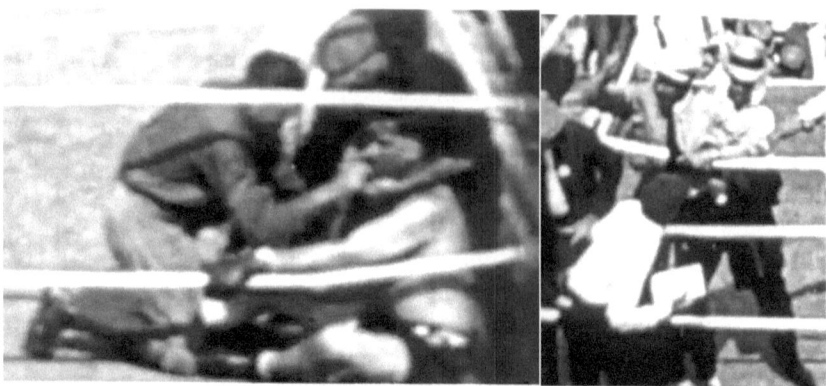

In the 2nd round, Dempsey moved in and fired a right to the body that was warded off by Willard's turning/clutching/grabbing tactics. Jack still freed himself sufficiently to land a powerful left hook to the jaw followed by a right to the jaw. Yet, Jess immediately countered with a beautifully timed powerful straight right of his own to Jack's jaw. Anyone who doesn't think Willard had one of the best chins ever should see this.

After being struck by the straight right, Dempsey covered up, leaning forward a bit, and Willard quickly followed up and nailed him with a right uppercut that jolted Jack's head up in the air. Dempsey leaned in and they clinched. Referee Pecord broke them.

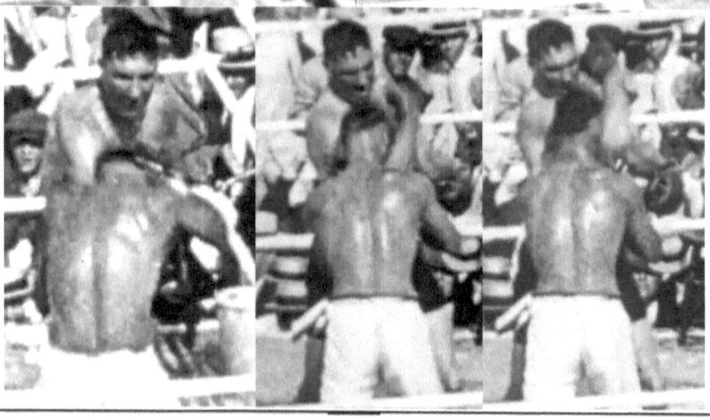

Jess jabbed the head and Dempsey fired a solid right to the body underneath it at the same time that Jess landed his left. Jess countered with a sneaky-short jolting right uppercut to the jaw, and Dempsey replied with a big left hook and right to the chin. Willard fired another short counter right that missed. Dempsey then followed with a powerful hook-right-hook-right, all landing, the final right landing quite flush and sending Jess back.

The blood on Willard's face is evident even with old black and white films, streaming down his cheek, his right eye puffy and closing. Yet, surprisingly, Jess still is frisky and sturdy given the beating he already had endured, attempting occasional single leads and counters throughout it all.

Dempsey quickly advanced, and as Jess jabbed, Jack fired a hard jolting right that landed high on the head, then he followed with a hook, right, then another pulverizing right and hooking left uppercut before being held.

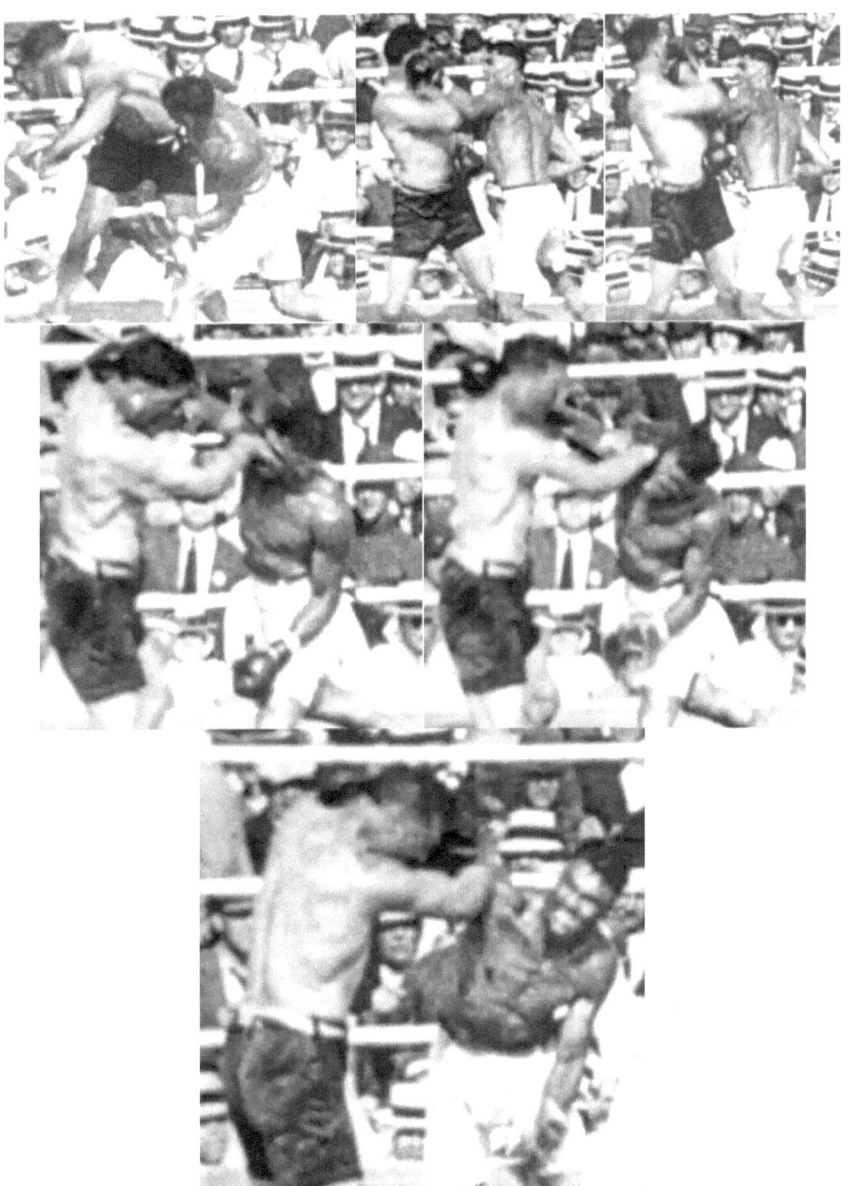

After Pecord broke them, Dempsey approached, dipped down to the right, then stepped to the left. Both jabbed at the same time but Jack's jab landed solidly and sent Jess back. Jack dipped and momentarily waited.

Dempsey advanced with a lead hook at the same time that Willard fired a right. They clinched. Pecord broke them. Jack moved left. Blood streamed down Willard's right cheek. Both jabbed at the same time and missed before Jess clinched. The referee struggled to break them.

Dempsey moved about, circling left. Jess jabbed and Jack slipped left and stepped inside, only to be held. Dempsey snuck in a snappy short right uppercut that jolted Jess's head up, then sent a lighter right hook to the head, and Willard grabbed more tightly and bulled in. Pecord broke them.

Willard fired a lead hook to the head that landed at about the same time that Dempsey fired a right to the body. Willard missed a right uppercut, and Dempsey followed with a powerful, blazing-fast, heavy, swinging left hook to the head from the southpaw stance, then two more hooks as Jess moved back to the ropes, trying to block and then firing a right that missed as the advancing Dempsey simultaneously fired a straight right and flush left hook to the jaw that badly jolted Willard's head back, sending him leaning/falling so far backwards on the ropes that it caused Jack to miss follow-up blows. But for the ropes, Willard would have gone down. Jess clinched.

While being held, Jack snuck in a couple short compact lefts to the body, then a jolting right to the jaw. Jess clinched more tightly and walked forward, leaning his weight on Dempsey. Pecord broke them. Dempsey dipped forward and then turned and walked off to the right.

Willard advanced and fired a 1-2, landing on the head of the right dipping Dempsey. They clinched, and Willard snuck in a right uppercut. Pecord broke them.

Jack landed a solid jab. They clinched, and Jess fired his right uppercut again before more clinching. Pecord broke them. Jack dipped forward and came up.

Willard stepped in with a 1-2 on the right dipping Dempsey, and followed with a left-right-left, the right landing quite solidly. Jack countered with a wild hook that missed, but he kept moving in and landed a second head-jolting left hook. Jess clinched, and Jack landed a right before Jess clinched better and bulled in. Pecord broke them.

Both jabbed at the same time, but Willard followed with a right that landed. He then fired a right uppercut, and Jack bore in and they clinched. Pecord broke them.

As Jess jabbed, Dempsey advanced with a high powerful lead right off the top of the head, and followed with a hook. Jess clinched, and Jack dug rights to the body, weaved under Jess's left arm and followed with a wide hooking right to the back of Willard's head as Jess held Jack's left. Jess clinched again and held both arms, but Jack got free with a short left hook to the head, then sneaky short but powerful right uppercut that jolted Willard's head up in the air. The bell rang ending the round, and the two separated and walked back to their corners.

Willard obviously was better off and sturdier at the end of the 2nd round than he was at the conclusion of the 1st round. He had landed some solid punches in the round, particularly rights and right uppercuts. Nevertheless, he still absorbed a lot of heavy, punishing blows throughout the 2nd round.

In the 3rd round, Dempsey fired a quick lead left hook to the jaw and Jess clinched. Inside, Jack again fired a hook that jolted Jess's head. The champ tried to clinch, but he was ineffective at it, and Dempsey snuck in a powerful right uppercut that snapped Willard's head up high in the air. Jess leaned his weight in on Jack and moved forward, trying to smother, but Dempsey landed another head-lifting right uppercut. Pecord broke them.

As Jess jabbed (and landed), Dempsey simultaneously stepped in and fired a powerful lead right that landed high on the head. Willard immediately countered with a right, short left hook as a leverage-creator, another right, and a right uppercut. Jack bulled/leaned in to smother the blows, and then planted a quick, short inside right to the side of the head. Pecord broke them from the clinch, and Jess fired a left jab on the break.

Dempsey advanced with a quick step-in and blazing-fast lead left hook to the jaw, then another flush on the jaw, followed by a left hook to the body and quickly back up to the jaw, turning Willard's head, then short right to the jaw, left hook to the body immediately followed by head-jolting left hook to the jaw, and then a backhand left to the jaw. Throughout, Willard's attempts to clinch were feeble and ineffective. He finally clinched a little better, but Jack just dug in some short body blows with his right. Pecord broke them. Willard's face clearly was quite puffy and bloody.

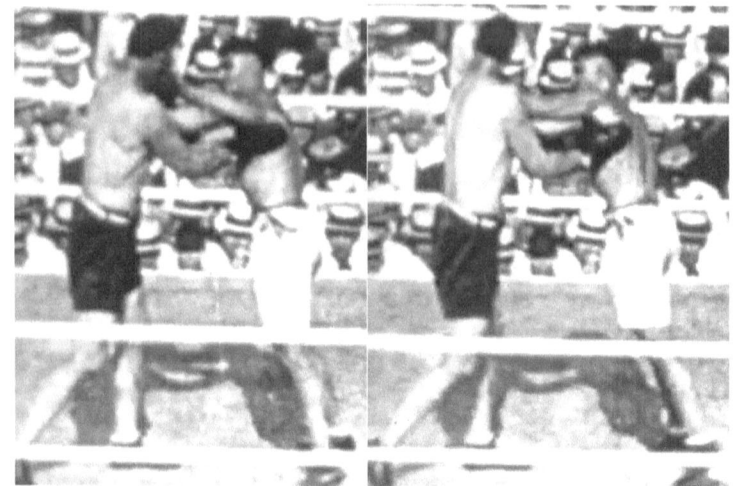

As Dempsey advanced with a right to the body, Willard landed a left hook to the head and then right or right uppercut. He held, and Jack dug in two lefts to the body. Pecord broke them. Dempsey ducked under Jess's jab as he jabbed at the same time. He followed with rights to Willard's body. Jess clinched, and Pecord broke them.

Jack advanced with a left to the body as Jess fired a left to the head. In close, Jack dug a couple rights to the body. Pecord broke them again. Jack jabbed the body, which helped him duck under Willard's right to the head. In close, Dempsey landed a left to the body, then short, snappy, head-jolting right uppercut to the jaw. Willard countered with a light right uppercut of his own, but Dempsey countered with a harder left hook to the head, then short right as Jess was leaning in to smother and hold, but Jack got in body blows with left and right. Pecord broke them.

Dempsey stepped in and landed a hard lead right to the head as Jess tried to hook. Jack followed with two quick left hooks and a right uppercut. Willard countered with a hook and right that missed as Dempsey ducked forward. Inside, Jack nailed him with a left hook to the head, then followed with a right that landed as Willard was trying to fire back but missing over the top with left-right-left-right, being forced to grab as the ducking and weaving Dempsey crowded in and tried to work the body. Dempsey still hit him with a right uppercut to the jaw. Pecord broke them.

Dempsey advanced and weaved under Jess's jab and was held, but managed to fire off a compact jolting left hook to the head, and then right uppercut to the jaw, followed by left and right to the body. Jess held, but Dempsey still managed to land another right uppercut to the head. Either Willard was not very good at holding or Jack was so strong that he was able to work himself free from his grasp and fire away anyhow. Pecord broke them.

Dempsey danced/sidestepped to the left, weaved under a Willard left hook, then swiveled his torso to the right and stepped off to the right. Willard's face was ghastly, bleeding profusely. Dempsey jabbed in and Jess held Jack's extended left arm, and tried to hold the right too, but Jack nailed him with a right uppercut. Jess held a bit better, and Pecord broke them.

As Dempsey advanced low, the game Willard nailed him with a jab and quick well-timed snappy right uppercut, then wide heavy hooking right, left hook, short right uppercut, and wide left hook as Dempsey ducked forward and bulled in close to smother. In the clinch, Jack may have dug in a right to the body. Pecord broke them.

Dempsey ducked under a left hook, countered with a left hook to the jaw, then dug the same hand into the body. Willard's pulpy, puffy, bleeding face was streaming blood all over, including down onto his chest and even all over Dempsey's body, arms, and back. He clinched, but Dempsey still nailed him with a snappy right uppercut that sent Willard's head up high again. Jess bulled in further and pushed Jack back until Pecord broke them.

Dempsey stepped off to the left, and as Jess jabbed, Jack dipped left and stepped in with a lead left hook to the jaw, followed up by a left to the body and quickly back up to the jaw with his left hook. Dempsey was very adept at working up and down and up again with the same hand, putting his punches together in bunches, in nonstop sequences.

Dempsey went back down to the body with his left and once again immediately back up to the jaw with the same hand. At the same time that Willard fired a left, Dempsey followed with a right over the top that rocked Willard's head to the side, and followed up quickly with an upward arcing left hook that rocked him back the other way, and then a right uppercut.

Despite being hit with all of those blows, after Dempsey's right uppercut, seeing an opening, Willard immediately counterattacked with a heavy right or right uppercut that landed solidly, then left, and right uppercut again. Dempsey was good at keeping his chin tucked and ducking and smothering so the follow-up blows did not land as cleanly or as obviously as the first punch (or the blows that he landed on Jess). Nevertheless, Willard still was firing back and landing some good punches.

Dempsey came back with a left hook to the jaw. Willard returned fire with a left hook but Jack ducked it. Jess followed by landing a short jolting right uppercut. Jack bulled in close. Pecord broke them and the bell rang.

Most said that sometime between the 3rd and 4th rounds, after consultation with his cornermen, Willard decided to retire. Just before the 4th round bell rang, his second threw the towel towards ring center to signify the retirement. The referee recognized the retirement just prior to the start of the round, and moved towards Dempsey's corner. Nevertheless, the 4th round bell rang.

Dempsey advanced to ring center, and the referee held aloft the new world heavyweight champion's hand. Jess rose from his stool and shook his gloved hand. The ring was flooded by cheering fans and seconds. Dempsey was mobbed, and raised up in the air on his cornerman's shoulders.

It had been one of the most brutal championship fights ever. Sometimes lost in the discussion of this fight is the punishment that Jess Willard absorbed in the subsequent two rounds after the horrific 1st round. Although he did not go down in rounds 2 and 3, nevertheless, Willard kept enduring severe punishment that would have a wearing effect on any human being. The ropes at least once saved him from going down. Yet, despite it all, Jess kept trying, landing solid blows here and there, attempting to weather the storm and find a punch that might change the tide of events. Overall though, Willard had suffered a severe battering. It actually is a wonder that he didn't die or wind up in the hospital from such a beating. It could have happened if he had kept fighting to the bitter end. From that perspective, the retirement was wise, despite the fact that Willard still was landing some good punches and technically physically could have continued.

The *Toledo Blade* said many thought it was over at the end of the 1st round, not realizing that the gong had saved Willard just as Pecord counted nine. Willard's seconds yielded the championship at the opening of the 4th round.

Aviators immediately carried photographs and motion pictures of the fight to places like Chicago, New York, and Cleveland.

Hundreds of street cars, taxis, and private cars carried the humanity away, asking $2, $3, and $5 each, which though expensive, the pleased fans cheerfully paid.

The estimated gate was $600,000, according to co-promoter Frank Flournoy; a boxing world record. The Toledo Boxing Commission got $42,000 of the proceeds (7%) for charity, and the federal government would get about $54,600 in war tax (9%).

The arena and its wood were for sale to the highest bidder. Purchasers would tear down the arena which cost the promoters $150,000 to build. The promoters' expenses, including purses, were $373,600. The promoters also had other expenses such as travel, hotel, printing, publicity, office rent, salaries of aides, ushers, etc.

Rail-Light officials estimated that approximately 300,000 passengers were carried on the city car lines in recent days.

R. L. Goldberg said Dempsey had the goods and the class, and Willard was surprised, but game to the end. Dempsey was a young, brown, sinewy, clean-muscled soldier of fortune. The crowd contained temporarily insane men and women surging and swaying amidst the excitement. At the end, Willard was seated, dejected, forlorn, and sorely wounded. The fight functionally was over at the end of the 1$^{st}$ round.

Before the fight, Willard was clear-skinned, hair neatly trimmed, and face freshly shaven. He had the same nonchalance he had in his workouts.

Dempsey showed that he was capable of systematic thought, for he did not rush at Willard as most expected. He walked and moved around carefully and cautiously. Jess jabbed away. Eventually Dempsey sailed in with his 195 pounds of fighting spirit and landed ferocious blows to the head and stomach. The blows hurt, and Willard seemed surprised, wincing. His expression grew serious. Eventually, Dempsey landed a right and Willard went down to a sitting position, astonished and dazed. Thereafter, Dempsey put him down again and again. At the end of the round, the crowd was frantic. Everyone thought it was over and Willard had been counted out. But in the confusion, it was announced that the bell had saved him. The end result was a foregone conclusion.

Jess was a sorry spectacle when he came up for the 2$^{nd}$ round. His right eye was almost closed. He was game, and tried to hit Dempsey with all the strength he could muster. Jack hit him time and again on the jaw, but Jess remained on his feet.

The 3$^{rd}$ round was terrible, for Dempsey hit him on the head and body so often that the crowd became amazed that the big champion did not go down. He displayed tremendous willpower and gameness. His face was a mass of blood, and swollen badly. It was remarkable that he lasted to the end of the round.

When the bell sounded for him to come to ring center for the 4$^{th}$ round, a towel was tossed in the ring. Willard had withstood terrible onslaughts. He knew that he was defeated and could continue no further. "He saw no reason why he should sacrifice himself for the bloodthirsty cravings of the crowd." Dempsey had youth, science, and a punch.

Frank Menke criticized that the bell was so faint that it had to be banged four times before both fighters heard it. He said Referee Pecord should have insisted on the bell being fixed before allowing the fight to progress. Robert Edgren agreed, calling the officials amateurs.

Menke said a greater champion never lived. He battered a powerful mighty human into a bleeding mass in a mere 3 rounds. The performance was the most remarkable and amazing in pugilistic annals. It wasn't a fight, but a slaughter. Willard never landed a really solid blow. Dempsey closed his right eye, smashed his nose, gashed his lips in several places, and made his body one splotch of red. Dempsey had the agility of a panther and a greater attack than any former champion.

At the end of the 1st round, with Willard down, the crowd shrieking in delirium, Ollie Pecord seemed to reach ten, pushed Dempsey back to his corner, and pandemonium broke loose. The crowd assumed Dempsey had won by knockout, and went insane. Willard's seconds assisted him and tried to bring him back, using any means they could.

Pecord and some others ordered the crowd to get out of the ring; for the fight was not over. Folks wondered what had happened. It was announced that Pecord had not completed counting him out when the bell rang. No one heard the bell, which was faulty, pronounced as such even before the fight began, it was so faint.

Menke claimed that 2 minutes 4 seconds elapsed between the 1st and 2nd rounds, which benefitted Willard.

Menke also said Pecord should have ruled a knockdown whenever Willard was hanging helpless on the ropes with his heels off the ground, a position which the rules specifically hold as a knockdown and a reason to begin a count.

Dempsey played things safely through the 2nd round, realizing that he was going to win, taking no chances, and pacing himself. Dempsey slowed up, but kept plugging away, more to reduce him a little more rather than to knock him out. He still smashed in several ripping blows to the head and body, stunning the champ some more. One drive sent Willard reeling to the ropes, and another to a corner. Jess attempted in vain to hit and clinch.

Willard came out for the 3rd round looking like a wreck. Before the round was over he was the most battered champion the ring ever had known. Dempsey landed powerful blows all over. Willard's eye closed completely. He staggered around trying to land and avoid, but it was useless. Even when he rallied and landed, Dempsey simply drove through with blows more vicious than before.

When the round concluded, Jess tottered to his corner. His head sunk upon his breast. He was nauseous and on the verge of lapsing into unconsciousness. His seconds spoke with him, and realizing that his reign was over, tossed in the towel and sponge.

For a second there was silence, but then Pecord had Dempsey come forward and raised his arm, announcing, "Jack Dempsey wins this fight on a technical knockout and so becomes heavyweight champion of the world."

Menke said Willard quit, but wasn't a quitter. No living man could have taken the beating he took in the 1st round and come back for more. His courage in rising so many times, and continuing for two more rounds, was almost beyond the fancyings of a writer of romantic fiction. He showed rare courage and gameness. Yet, surprisingly, some were questioning his gameness for not continuing until he took the full ten-count.

Grantland Rice said the one thing Willard showed was courage. Dempsey was the greatest fighting tornado the game ever had known. Never in history had any champion ever received such murderous punishment. In nine minutes, Dempsey crushed Willard into a shapeless mass of gore and battered flesh.

Dempsey gave one of the greatest exhibitions of mighty hitting ever seen. Two minutes into the fight, a left hook to the jaw decked Willard. Seven times he went down. Only six times did he rise within 10 seconds.

Willard gave one of the greatest exhibitions of raw and unadulterated gameness. He absorbed enough punishment to kill two ordinary men. Only tremendous vitality and the luck of the bell allowed him to get out of the 1st round. Nothing in the world but the bell could have saved him from being counted out, for if it had rung a few seconds later it would have been a 1st round knockout. Jess sat there dazed and helpless, bleeding, unable to rise or even move. He eventually was helped/dragged back to his corner. Everyone, including Dempsey, thought it was over and it was a 1st round knockout. Jack left the ring, but had to be called back.

The pitiless drama continued. In the 2nd round, Willard landed here and there, but had no effect on Dempsey. Jess could not check his rush. Mostly he tried to clinch. He was terrible to look at. Dempsey brutally hit his mutilated, puffy, bloody face and quivering body.

There was a question as to whether Willard would continue for the 3rd round, but he did. A fountain of gore spilled and spurted, as Willard spat out clots of blood to the canvas. It was easy to see that he would not answer the bell for the next round. His face was swollen to unbelievable proportions. His face and body were a combination of red, blue, purple, and crimson splotches. "If a six-inch shell had exploded against his right jaw it could hardly have harried his features more." As time was called for the 4th round, Monaghan's sponge was thrown up.

It was a wonder that Willard could absorb so much punishment and still remain upright. No other man could have taken that much punishment and lived, let alone stood up. It looked as if every punch would tear away his head. How Willard continued after the 1st round beating and remained on his feet in the face of the hammering thereafter was amazing, and "will ever remain one of the mysteries of the game. If Willard had not been in wonderful shape he would have been killed. He surely would never have answered the bell for the second round."

Dempsey was the most spectacular champion ever, winning the title much faster than anyone ever before. He had crushing, punishing force, and blazing speed with both hands. No wonder large men like Morris, Fulton, and others had crumpled under Dempsey's fierce blows. He hit "harder than any man that ever lived." He was a ring marvel, the "greatest hitting machine ever." He left the ring unmarked.

The interesting part of it all was that contrary to expectations, surprisingly it was Willard who assumed the aggressive from the start, not Dempsey. Jess stepped boldly and confidently in Dempsey's direction. He led and landed first. He never looked better. He was 15 pounds lighter than when he fought Moran. Dempsey was the one who started cautiously, but then, without the least indication of an impending attack, he stepped in quickly and landed his dreaded left hook, and from then on it was just a matter of time.

Still, despite all of the accolades, Rice said Dempsey was the champion boxer, but not the champion fighter, for if Dempsey were a fighter, he would have fought in the trenches overseas. Those who stood the test of cold steel and exploding shells for six cents to a dollar a day in actual war were the real fighting champions. "He missed the big chance of his life to prove his own manhood before his own soul – but beyond that he stands today as the ring marvel of the century, a puncher who will be unbeatable as long as he decides to stay off the primrose way and maintain the wonderful vitality of a wonderful human system."

Ring Lardner said the bell ending the 1st round ruined Jess; it didn't save him. It would have been more merciful for him to be counted out and not have to endure any more punishment. Anyone who branded Jess as a yellow quitter should be sued for libel. When a man is decked seven times and continues to take what he took for two more rounds, you can't call him yellow. He was out of it. If Willard had not been in condition, they would be naming his pall-bearers. "After seeing what he went through I would say Fred Fulton was lucky." Fred didn't have to absorb a brutal beating. Those who called Jess a quitter either had picked Willard, bet on him, or bet the fight to last a certain distance, so they were bitter for their own personal or financial reasons. They were not being objective. No one could have taken what he took and not retired.

After the 1st round, Dempsey climbed out of the ring. Manager Jack Kearns had to chase after him and bring him back to finish the job. Monaghan and others tried to throw water on Willard, and kept rubbing a sponge over his face, but they couldn't wipe off the punches.

No one thought Willard could last through the 2nd round, but he did. Perhaps he hoped that Dempsey had fired 12 rounds of hard punches in 1 round and would be winded. Jess was not beaten quite as badly in the next two rounds, but he still suffered. He got his eye closed tight in the 2nd. In the 3rd round, Jess didn't lose quite as much blood, but that was because he did not have as much to lose. He tried his best, but he had been subjected to an awful beating.

After the 3rd round, a few seconds after Willard sat in his chair, Monahan threw the bloody towel towards mid-ring, retiring him. "Personally I think it would have been good judgment for the boys in the big fellow's corner to of tossed in the towel a round sooner than they did and it would have been better judgment to of throwed it in right after Jess set down for the first time."

There were unconfirmed rumors that Willard's jaw was broken.

Lardner now knew that Dempsey could fight, "and if I ever get mad at him I will try and keep it to myself. Also if I was Georges Carpentier I would stay in France till the new champion dies of old age."

Lardner humorously said he did not have the opportunity to ask the judges, Rickard or Biddle, how they had it scored, "but I will take it on myself to say Dempsey had the shade."

Many had said that Dempsey was too small to reach Willard's features, but he missed none of them. Willard left his blood on Dempsey and the floor. His eye was closed early in the contest.

Supposedly, Chicago received the fight films of the slaughter by airplane in 2 hours 38 minutes (which was about 244 miles covered at 93 miles an hour). Apparently, government airplanes carried the films.

Former champion James J. Corbett said Dempsey was the greatest heavyweight since Jim Jeffries was in his prime, "and, for the good of the game; I am glad." Willard took a terrific beating. He had gameness, taking more punishment than anyone Corbett ever saw, more than many champions absorbed in a lifetime. Dempsey started off nervously, but once he got his bearings there was no lull or let up. He tore in like a wild cat, throwing and landing every punch known to pugilism, and they came so fast, every which way, from all directions, with both hands.

When Pecord was at the count of 7, the bell rang ending the 1st round. His seconds worked over Willard while he was helpless on the floor.

Willard got back to his corner just before the gong sounded for the 2nd round. Dempsey had tired himself out slugging away nonstop in the 1st round, which allowed Willard to last and recuperate a bit. Plus, Dempsey was cautious against any chance blow that might rob him of victory which so clearly was his if he bided his time.

Willard's right eye was closed, his face smeared with blood, and he was little more than a human punching bag by the end of the 2nd round.

The 3rd round was a repetition, with Jess growing more helpless. Dempsey still was tired, but kept coming in, and the champ was powerless to stop him. Willard reeled from one end of the ring to the other, helpless at close fighting. Dempsey nailed him with a number of beautiful right uppercuts, showing that he had more than one good punch.

As the gong sounded for the 4th round, Willard announced that he was through, and his second tossed in the towel.

Corbett said although Dempsey might be a bit deficient in defense, he hit hard with every punch in the book, gave a man 50+ pounds heavier "the most terrific beating ever handed a heavyweight champion, and there is no fighter in the limelight today who would stand a chance against him." He was a real champion and measured up to the champions of prior days.

Corbett told Clara Stein, "I've never seen such a terrific onslaught of blows as that young fellow handed out. They were not only swift, but scientific and sure."

The *Toledo Blade's* George Pulford said the smiling, good-natured kid had won the hearts of all who met him, and now was the biggest figure in all fistiana. There was no one in sight who could handle him.

Willard was as dead game as any fighter ever. After watching the fight, Pulford had more respect for Willard than ever before. "In one round, the first, Willard took more punishment than I ever saw handed out in 20 rounds." He was beaten from the first left hook that landed on his jaw, but never ceased trying until his bulk refused to respond. Some, like former Willard manager Tom Jones, called him a yellow dog and quitter, but they would have done the same, had they absorbed what he had, even assuming they could have risen, which most could not.

When the whistle, substituted for the bell, was blown to start the 4th round, Willard could not rise. Ray Archer threw in the towel. It was a lowdown lie and stage stuff to cast aspersions on Willard. He fought and tried as hard as he could. From the start he showed no fear. "If YOU saw the fight, you know Willard fought. If you did not see it do not let anyone tell you he dogged."

At the end of the 1st round, Pecord counted to 10, for he had not heard the tinkle-bell or the whistle which went off at the same time as the count of 7, for the timekeeper was across the ring on the other side. Harry Bullion, sporting editor for the *Detroit Free Press*, who sat within three feet of the bell, confirmed that Willard was saved by the bell and whistle.

His seconds dragged Willard to his corner to work feverishly to bring him back. They stopped the blood temporarily, but could not prevent his right eye closing. The second left hook that Dempsey delivered in the contest had closed his eye.

One moment Jack thought he was champion, and the next he was called back into the ring to continue. In the 2nd round, Dempsey lost his steam, while Willard rallied.

In the 3rd round, Dempsey was speedy and vigorous again, and gave him a terrible beating. When Willard could not rise for the 4th round, the towel was tossed in.

One *Blade* report said Willard was not seriously injured, despite the fact that his face was puffy, his right eye closed, mouth, cheek, and nose cut and bleeding. He had lost some teeth, but no facial bones were broken. A physician made that statement.

William Brady, former manager of Corbett and Jeffries, said he was the only one from New York who had picked Dempsey to win. Corbett had tried to persuade him to bet on Willard.

The *Toledo News-Bee's* Dick Meade said Willard took a bad beating. He was out on his feet, unable to start the 4th round. Monaghan had asked

Willard, "Can you go on?" Jess shook his head without looking up. Monaghan hurled the wet and bloody towel into the ring. The bell then tinkled to start the 4th round. Jess remained on his chair, but was no quitter.

Willard had taken terrific punishment from the cool, calculating, murderous-hitting Dempsey. Jess fought back as best he could in his own cumbersome, clumsy, awkward way. The left hook that decked him the first time was one of the most vicious blows that ever jolted mortal man. Then and there he was licked. By the end of the round he was a gory sight, right eye closed and bleeding, blood flowing from his nose, and he spat great gobs of gore onto the canvas. Yet, he fought on with indomitable spirit. He had unmistakable gameness.

Folks thought Dempsey would tear in at the start of the fight, but he didn't. He fiddled and defended, stepping around before moving in and punching. Perhaps his easy-going stride merely was a lure, like a pitcher who throws slowly at first. Then suddenly Dempsey attacked and landed a right and left hook flush on the jaw and Willard went down for the first time in his life.

At the seventh knockdown, Pecord counted ten and sent Dempsey to his corner. Wild yells from the timekeeper's bench attracted his attention and Ollie rushed over to find out that the bell rang at seven. The arena was in an uproar of confusion. Willard was absolutely out. Dempsey was on his way to his dressing room. He was stopped and rushed back into the ring. Dempsey briefly rested on his chair while his seconds fanned him. During this time, Willard's seconds had worked over him frantically, got him back to his corner, and worked on him some more.

The 2nd round was less eventful. Dempsey popped him several times but did not do much harm.

In the 3rd round, blood was gushing from Willard's nose, from the cut under his tightly shut right eye, and from his mouth. After that round, the towel throwing was a surprise, but it was merciful.

Referee Ollie Pecord said the first left hook had won Dempsey the championship. Soon thereafter another sent Willard to the mat. Jess was dazed. "I started to count over him while Dempsey, coolly heeding the instructions I had given him before the bout started, stepped back."[729] The champ slowly climbed to his feet at the count of six. Pecord counted five for the next knockdown. Willard's right eye was almost closed and he was bleeding from the mouth. Jess was up at four the next time. Then five. Willard was down again in a neutral corner, bleeding profusely from the mouth. His breathing was labored. "Every time Dempsey hit him on the side of his face his left eye, which was evidently badly injured, seemed to pop out and then go back again."

Pecord did not hear the bell. "I was counting over him. Suddenly I heard a shout and, glancing at the timers, I saw them shouting and waiving. The

---

[729] Pecord was wrong. Dempsey often did not step back much at all, and he did not follow the Queensberry rules, which called for a man to return to his corner following knockdowns. It seems that said rule was very loosely applied, or ignored. None of the reporters even mentioned it as an issue.

bell had rung for the end of the round, but I hadn't heard it. I was counting seven when I made out the shout that the round was over. I waved Dempsey to his corner and called for someone to help Willard."

The crowd rushed toward the ring, and some even entered, thinking the fight was over. Pecord explained things to Kearns, and the timers secured a whistle to work in conjunction with the bell which could not be heard.

Pecord said, "It was not my fault that Dempsey left the ring in the first round, because I did not hear the bell and I believe practically no one heard it. If instead of leaving the ring, Dempsey had gotten his rest between the first and second round, I feel certain he would have knocked Willard out in the second..."

In the 2nd round, Dempsey held back and was shaken by two short right crosses. However, Willard's steam was gone.

At the start of the 3rd round, Dempsey went after him again. Willard's mouth was bleeding once again. "I saw the fight couldn't go more than four rounds then. When Willard went to his corner he was all in. The tossing of the towel didn't surprise me. ... Willard was taking a lacing. ... I'm glad the towel was tossed in. It showed excellent judgment and saved the champ from making a worse spectacle of himself."

Another report claimed Pecord said the opposite, that Willard should have tried to fight in the 4th round and keep trying to win until he took a knockout punch, for although his face was bruised badly, he still had the use of his hands.

Betty Brown said it was all over in 3 lightning-fast rounds. It was "the thrill of a lifetime, a thrill well worth the price."

H. C. Witwer said the man who beats Dempsey would have to carry a pair of battle axes into the ring with him. He still was "One Round Dempsey" and the "Salt Lake City Assassin." He lived up to his reputation when he battered a reeling, blood-covered wreck all over the ring while the crowd yelled itself insane.

It was the most sensational battle for the heavyweight crown ever. It was more like an assassination. The fight essentially was over in the 1st round. Even Willard's bitterest enemies had to breathe a sigh of relief when the bloody towel was sent hurtling from his corner after the 3rd round, for otherwise it might have been fatal.

Willard suffered the most terrible beating a human being ever got and lived. "Sweet cookie, but this Dempsey guy is a killer, I'll tell the world!" No one could follow the assortment of clouts and wallops he threw from all angles. He fought like an infuriated wildcat, banging away with both hands and literally punching Willard from one side of the ring to the other. Willard went down multiple times, and the ropes saved him from going down even more.

At the end of the 1st round, when he was saved by the bell, Willard had one eye closed and blood pouring in streams from his unrecognizable face. It was a crime to send him out again for further butchering.

During the contest, Jess had fired his left but Dempsey paid no attention to it. "I doubt whether Willard landed a half dozen solid punches on the human buzzsaw before him during the entire massacre."

Dempsey handed him more punishment in 3 rounds than the average fighter absorbed in a lifetime. It was thrilling every second. Willard showed great gameness, for he endured a terrible pasting all the way.

Personally, Dempsey was "an extremely likable kid and is bound to be popular with the mob."

This writer claimed that Jim Corbett picked Dempsey. Perhaps Jim picked both.

Describing the first knockdown, Irvin S. Cobb said Dempsey landed with a thud, the sound of which was plainly audible throughout the arena. Some howled with joy, while others gasped in astonishment as Willard went down for the first time in his career.

Among the pounding, a cut was opened and widened upon Willard's brow. Blood trickled across his cheek. Willard's right eye closed and the left seemed larger than normal size.

The round ended with him sitting down, so badly battered that he was unable to lift himself up. The crowd and Dempsey thought it was over. Men leapt into the ring. They were driven out of it. The bell saved him for the moment.

In the 2nd round, Willard hung on, but it was quite unpleasant as he suffered punishment. He was stubborn and courageous. Blows rained upon him, torturing him. His face turned to a pulp, the blood streaking down. Willard's blows did no harm, for Dempsey shook them off like raindrops.

The massacre continued for one more round. The bell sounded for round 4 but Willard remained slumped on his seat.

Herbert Corey said many called Willard a coward and quitter, upset that he had retired on his stool. Tears ran down his crushed and swollen face, mingled with blood. One eye was closed entirely and the other so swollen he barely could see. His mouth hung open. His lips were cut and broken. Many seemed to feel he should die in the ring. It was a cruel drama. He had taken punishment, and was no quitter. Dempsey's fury made up for the difference in weight. He worked at Willard as savagely as a butcher poleaxing a cow. The huge crowd roared inarticulately. "Seven times he was knocked down, some say – and some say five."

On the last knockdown, Pecord counted "Ten." He turned toward Dempsey and said, "You're champion." Willard's face was streaming with blood, his teeth broken out, eyes closing, and slack jaw hanging down. The ring filled up with humanity. His seconds half dragged and half carried Willard to his corner. Dempsey leaped out of the ring and started for his dressing room. People started leaving the arena. In his corner, Willard's seconds were dousing him with water. Another sponged his face.

Then Dempsey was seen climbing back through the ropes. Pecord spoke with Dempsey. Everyone was confused, asking what was going on and what happened. Apparently the bell had tapped at the sixth count, but it was so weak no one heard it. It was not until Dempsey had left the ring that he learned about the facts and the mistake, and he was called back. "One result was that the champion had a rest of ninety seconds, instead of the sixty the rules gave him, for Dempsey could not be called back inside of the minute's rest. The other was that Dempsey had no rest at all."

Willard continued. Dempsey seemed to have lost his power. The 2nd round was in Willard's favor. But the next was his finish.

Ray Archer said there was no jaw break and no lost teeth. "Jess, I believe, never was right after that first blow on the point of the jaw. His mind was cloudy after that, and he was not his old self." Archer said Willard was confident before the fight that Dempsey would pose little trouble.

H. C. Hamilton said there were rumors that Willard had suffered a broken jaw, but Jess sent word that it was not true. Dempsey said he saw Willard spit three teeth onto the canvas.

A whistle was provided only after the wild 1st round, for the bell was defective.

Jack Kearns said Dempsey had won the fight twice. At the end of the 1st round, Pecord gave them the impression that the fight was over and Dempsey had won. He claimed Pecord raised Dempsey's arm (not true).

W. A. Gavin, president of the Civilian Boxing Board of the Army and Navy, said several aspects of the fight made it unique and challenging for the referee. The faint bell was one. At one point Willard was helpless against the ropes with his toes an inch off the floor. Under National Sporting Club rules, he was to be regarded as down, for if not for the ropes he would have fallen prostrate. However, the Toledo Commission rules did not mention this situation.

Dempsey left the ring when the fight technically still was ongoing, which some might say was a foul, but this was understandable, because he believed it was over, particularly since very few heard the bell. He might even have been misled. Ultimately, the blame fell on the bell.

Willard showed wonderful spirit, for if he had been a coward or quitter, he never would have continued after being decked so many times. He simply could not rise for the 4th round. He tried. "Dempsey displayed wonderful ability as a fighter. His coolness was marvelous."

Jack McAuliffe said Willard was through in the 1st round. Dempsey punched him so hard and fast that Willard didn't know what was happening to him. He was a beaten man when he first hit the canvas.

McAuliffe changed his opinion about Dempsey's defense, which he had criticized in previous articles. His tremendous offense overcame any defensive deficiencies. He would be champion for a long time because he worked so fast and hit so terrifically hard with both hands. He was a clean liver and masterful fighter. He was another John L. Sullivan.

Writing for the *Toledo Times*, William Rocap harshly and cruelly labeled Willard the ring's first quitter.

Willard was on the floor when the bell rang to end the 1st round. Everybody, including the referee and Dempsey, believed he had been counted out. Dempsey left. W. Warren Barbour called Pecord's attention to the fact that Willard had been saved by the bell. The referee recalled Dempsey to the ring. 1 minute 20 seconds elapsed before the bell tinkled again. Once again neither man heard the bell, and the referee had to beckon the men out of their corners.

Willard was a beaten man, and it was only a question of how much he could stand. His right eye was closed, face swollen, blood flowing from his mouth, lips, and nose. He took an awful lacing, yet stood up, took it, and fought back in both rounds 2 and 3.

Rocap believed he could have continued, yet, at Willard's request, the towel was tossed into the ring, and he sat in his chair when the bell tinkled for the 4th round to begin. "Hence Willard must be labeled a quitter. He has disgraced the sport. ... The world likes a game loser, and will applaud the man who pluckily goes down to defeat under fire." Rocap said even Willard's admirers turned from him in disgust.

Dempsey lived up to his reputation of being a terrific puncher and willing to take a few to get one in, yet he had to take very little.

Estimates were that $500,000 had been wagered in Toledo alone. Bets mostly were placed at even odds. Frank Moran lost $4,000.

John M. Kelly said Dempsey was a deadly-determined, serious-minded, rugged, slashing fighter. Willard earned the stigma of being the only heavyweight champ to surrender his crown without fighting until battered into oblivion and taking the full count. He was thoroughly beaten but not thoroughly game.

Willard had a closed right eye and bled profusely from nose and mouth, the red claret smearing his and Dempsey's body and trunks. After the 1st round, Dempsey could not deck him again, though he sent him reeling against the ropes. Willard still showed flashes of his old form.

Ike O'Neill threw in the towel just as time was about to be called for the 4th round. Both O'Neill and Monahan reached for a towel and threw one in, and the one O'Neill threw fell into the ring first. Willard presented a gory sight as he sat in his corner. His face was a battered mass. Some hooted at him as a yellow dog and quitter. Many felt he still could fight and should have fought to the bitter end.

Ray Bronson also said Willard quit, and that he never was a real champion. No other champion had quit on the stool.

Bronson said Dempsey had predicted that he would win in 1 round, and he really did. Willard was knocked out completely at the end of the 1st round. "And for Dempsey I predict a glorious career." The man who beat Dempsey would have to be a whirlwind and batter him to ribbons in order to win. "It takes heart to fight a man like Dempsey."

Associated Press writers Eddie Moss and Chris D. Hagerty claimed that Dempsey was breathing hard at the end from his own exertions. Such was understandable given the fast pace and all of the powerful blows fired.

The fight films would be shown in Toledo two days after the fight, on Sunday at the Alhambra theater. The films, taken by the Frank G. Hall company, would show for at least a week, and also would be shown immediately in Cincinnati and Cleveland.

Robert Edgren said the fight should have ended in 1 round, for Willard's corner should have stopped it. Dempsey was a bone crusher. No fighter ever was worse beaten than Willard. It was the most one-sided fight ever. Dempsey's blows were so fast and frequent that the eye hardly could follow the flying gloves. The effect was startling. Each clout changed Willard's face like a sculptor dissatisfied with a portrait in clay, and deliberately obliterating it feature by feature.

Edgren said Dempsey was one of the most remarkable fighters that ever clouted his way to a championship. "They were right when they called him a 'bone crusher.'" His training work was mere play by comparison. They weren't kidding when they claimed he actually had worked with his sparring partners and held back, even though he seemed to punish them. His speed was startling, and attack so sudden and furious that nothing could stop it. He wasn't just a plunging, battering fighter, but also was cold, calculating, and sure. He stepped in pantherlike, feinting and stepping aside.

To start the fight, Barbour tinkled the bell several times, but few heard it. He then used a bell and whistle simultaneously.

Technically, the knockout was scored at the end of the 3rd round, when Ray Archer threw the towel into the middle of the ring, with Willard terribly beaten and helpless in his corner, with one eye completely closed.

In the 1st round, over Willard's ribs, a round red-mark showed where a right had landed. Jess could not land effectively. Dempsey whipped a curving left overhand blow over Willard's arms and caught him on the right eye. It didn't put him down, but was very effective. His eyebrow was gashed, and in an instant the eye and whole side of his face puffed out of shape.

Dempsey cut loose with the full fury of his attack. He no longer turned deftly to avoid Willard's punches and draw him on. He leaned and stepped in and hit as fast as he could with both hands. The gloves crashed on the body and jaw and Willard went down time and again. The fans gasped at the sight of Willard beaten back, reeling, trying to stand up before the cyclonic furious rush. Dempsey was beating him down.

Willard's right eye was closed. His left was popped wide open. The referee counted over him, over and over again. Dempsey had grim fury on his face, scowling brows, with the power of a kicking mule in his flying fists. Blow after blow tossed Jess back. Nothing human could have stood against that storm. The blows knocked his head back until his neck nearly snapped. His huge bulk shook like an oak with the woodman's axe at its roots.

Each time that Willard went down, he rose more slowly and heavily.

At the end of the round, he was down in a corner, and the count had reached seven when timekeeper Barbour blew the whistle and tinkled the gong, and everyone near Barbour shouted to Pecord that time was up.

Pecord waved Dempsey to his corner and stopped counting. Men leaped into the ring from every side. Seconds reached Willard, helped him up and dragged him half-conscious to his chair to work on him frantically.

Pecord followed Dempsey and laid a hand on him, and Kearns exclaimed to Dempsey that it was all over. Jack stepped from the ring and started to leave. Apparently, few had heard the bell or whistle. Pecord was shoving everyone out of the way.

Confusion was everywhere except in Willard's corner. Jack Hempel and Walter Monahan were working hard to revive him. Smelling salts were shoved under Willard's nose to wake him up. Someone flagged Dempsey, who then rushed back towards the ring. Barbour tinkled the bell, blew the whistle, and waved to Pecord. Willard sat in his corner, and Dempsey finally got back into the ring. He stood there not knowing what to do. It probably had been a couple minutes since Willard was down.

Jess finally stood up and approached to fight again. Dempsey met him with furious blows, but Willard refused to fall again. His head was driven back and his face became more distorted. The champion hit with what he had. His uppercuts drove Dempsey's head back several times. Jess jabbed and hit as best he could, but the strength had gone out of him from the terrific battering of the 1st round. Still, Willard was fighting better, and it seemed he might even recover. But he was in fearful shape, his right eye closed, and the whole side of his face puffed out. His mouth opened as he gasped for breath. Dempsey sidestepped and turned away, only to flash back in with blows that shook Willard no matter where they landed. Jess still tried to land a good blow to turn the tide. He landed now and then, but he almost always was being driven back by Dempsey's faster fists. Jess was hurled onto the ropes, hanging there. But he recovered and still was fighting at the end of the round. He landed a hard left on the jaw, and Jack's knees bent. Willard landed rights and right uppercuts on Dempsey as well, and Jack was weary from trying to put that huge bulk down again.

There was one minute of rest this time. Barbour blew the whistle and Willard came on again, showing his gameness. Dempsey was deliberate, and more calculating with his blows. He landed many clean punches on the chin. Jess slowly lost his speed. Jack got him in a corner and landed a good shot, but Jess kept his feet and lunged forward trying to land a hard blow. Jack hammered him back. Willard was reeling around.

Again Jess was helped to his corner and given smelling salts. Many were shouting to Pecord to stop it. Ray Archer tossed the towel of defeat into the middle of the ring.

This time Dempsey stayed in the ring. As Jack approached him, Willard stood up, walked forward and shook his hand.

The *San Francisco Examiner's* Ashton Stevens said that when the 1st round gong saved the champion, "Willard was a dead man, who didn't know that he was dead." No other living man could have stood up to the blows rained upon him and gone on living. It was brutal and beastly.

The *Buffalo Enquirer* said Dempsey beat Willard to a pulp. Jess withstood terrific punishment, showing his gameness.

Edward Tranter said the speed with which Dempsey disposed of Willard was amazing. He tore into him like a tiger and battered him to the floor time and again, until the 1st round bell saved him.

Dempsey, not hearing the bell, believing he had won, left, and had to be called back to the ring. He received no attention or rest during the one-minute period.

In the 2nd round, Dempsey went after the champion again, but more cautiously. Willard tried hard with his left jab and right uppercut, but mostly was ineffective, though he momentarily staggered the challenger with a right uppercut. Jack swayed a trifle and stepped back, but Jess could not start a bombardment or follow up.

In the 3rd round, Dempsey again showered blow after blow upon Willard with terrific effect. Jess went reeling into the ropes. He took three uppercuts that marked him badly. Dempsey kept crowding in, his head low and body springing up and down with his attack. Willard tottered and staggered around like a man in a drunken stupor. His face was a sight to behold. His right eye was closed and blood was pouring from his mouth and nose. Some spectators shouted to Pecord to stop the fight, to save him from further punishment.

When the bell rang, Willard staggered to his corner and practically collapsed in his chair. He plainly was badly defeated. Suddenly a white towel landed in the center of the ring. Pecord grabbed Dempsey's arm, dragged him to ring center, and held it aloft. Pandemonium broke loose. Jack was hoisted up on his seconds' shoulders.

Dempsey's constant exercise and activity, coupled with bulldog courage and determination to win or die, served him well in going up against a man who had fought only once in defense of his title in four years prior. Nevertheless, Willard actually appeared to be in better shape than he was against Moran, but he went up against a much better man.

Dempsey exhibited good defense, crouching low and swaying from side to side in puzzling fashion. He ducked and dodged and stepped away, before stepping in on the attack, getting underneath Willard's long arms. Jess never had a chance to get set. Folks who had seen Dempsey in Buffalo saw the same style; a tigerish, vicious, determined, irresistible attack. He had powerful punches, well-timed and well-planted with terrific force. No man could have stood up under the fearful punishment. Willard's superhuman size and vitality were all that enabled him to last as long as he did.

The victory was popular, because fans loved Dempsey's style, which was the most ferocious since John L. Sullivan made boxing quite popular, and also because Willard had been such an inactive champion, who also had a cautious style, which never was popular with the fans. Dempsey liked to fight, and had whipped the best heavyweights en route to the crown.

Willard took a fearful beating. The next day, his face was badly bruised, his ribs and stomach ached, and he was minus a tooth or two.

The famous Tad Dorgan said Willard was a pitiable sight at the conclusion of the 3rd round. His right eye was closed, mouth torn, and legs weary. It was the first time in heavyweight history that a champ had retired in the corner, but it was understandable. He had been beaten to a frazzle, outpunched, and outfought. He almost stumbled and fell as he headed to his corner. Blood was pouring down his purple trunks. His seconds washed his puffed and bloody face, and brushed his hair back a bit. Jess asked what round it was. They told him the 4th was coming up. Just before the bell was about to ring; Willard ordered his seconds to toss in the sponge.

There never was such a one-sided fight. Jess was a punching bag. He hardly landed, and his blows had no effect.

Dempsey was cool throughout, fighting in a business-like manner. His left raised a lump like a robin's egg over Jess's right eyebrow. After the second knockdown, Willard's right eye was puffed, and blood trickled down his chin from a bust in the mouth. After the third knockdown, blood poured from his cut mouth. By the end of the round, Willard's right eye was closed, the right side of his face puffed, and there was a rip under his right eye. People were yelling to stop the fight.

W. O. McGeehan said the towel was tossed into the ring from the corner a few seconds before the bell rang for the 4th round. In 3 rounds, Willard was given the most terrible beating a champion ever received. His right eye was closed and a torrent of blood was gushing from his gaping mouth.

The bell to end the 1st round could not be heard, and the screaming spectators thought it was all over. It seemed that no human being could stand the punishment that Dempsey gave Willard in that round. In fact, the bell saved Willard at the count of seven.

Surprisingly, Willard came back and fought in the 2nd round. He tried his famous straight left and put force into his right uppercut, which he had used to kill Bull Young. But his blows did not daze or jar Dempsey. Jess kept receiving punishment. He tried to keep Dempsey away with his long left, but it was useless. It did not even jolt back Jack's head. The right uppercut was equally ineffective. Willard had tried all of his blows, mustered all of his strength, and it was useless. He had not gone down, but twice he had been hanging helpless across the ropes while Dempsey drove blow after blow into his battered and bleeding face.

In the 3rd round, Jess was half blinded. He glared out of his left eye at Dempsey, who advanced to meet him with punishing right and left hooks to the head. Jack waved aside Jess's long left and lashed mercilessly at his head again and again. Still, Willard remained on his feet with dogged courage. Dempsey lashed a terrific left hook to the jaw, and the champ rocked and swayed like a pine tree, though he kept his feet. His jaw sagged and the blood poured out of his mouth in a crimson rivulet, a ghastly sight.

When he sagged down onto his seat in his corner after the 3rd round, it was plain that the fight could not last much longer. A towel, crimson from the blood, was hurled into ring center. The next instant the ring was filled with a screaming crowd, including a number of hysterical women. They crowded around Dempsey, clawing at him.

If Willard had not been in the best of condition, he would have died from the terrific punishment. He rose again and again, but was beaten down systematically. "The tossing of the towel was wise and humane. It saved another ring tragedy, for Willard was helpless after the first round."

Dempsey punched viciously, but deliberately, with a fine sense of direction and placement. He was very accurate with his blows. He was cool and workmanlike. He had the power of a hammer, with snap and vigor. He clearly was a "great fighter, one of the greatest." He never was ruffled or marked by any blow. Conversely, Jack had knocked out several of Willard's teeth. Some even were scrambling to obtain the teeth as souvenirs, including one woman.

Damon Runyon said Dempsey had his own unique "shimmy" style, crouching with his shoulders moving. Hence, he was hard to hit cleanly, or very often.

It was a sensational battle. Dempsey had a meteoric career. He battered Willard from a powerful, mighty-looking man into a bleeding, awful mass. Willard never landed a really solid blow. Dempsey hit him with crushing, terrible force. Even before the 2$^{nd}$ round was over, some in the crowd were shrieking at the referee, "Stop it, Stop it!"

Dempsey's quick attack in the 1$^{st}$ round closed Willard's eye, smashed his nose, gashed his lips in several places, and transformed his face into a bleeding horrible mass and made his body one big red splotch. It wasn't a fight, but a slaughter. Dempsey's performance was remarkable and amazing.

The *Dayton Daily News* said never before had the title been won with such ease or so quickly. Willard led and landed first, a left jab, but that was all he did. He was made into a chopping block. Dempsey landed a three-punch combination, Willard went down, and never was the same again. He offered almost no opposition.

Dempsey was a ferocious entertaining battler, and from all appearances was going to be champion for some time, and retain his popularity given his style. He was a world beater, "possessor of one of the sweetest kicks ever packed." Jack's style was the kind that makes a hit with the fans. He had them on the edge of their seats. He was a bearcat for fighting and went at it with the love of swapping punches. The only reason Willard was able to last as long as he did was because of his bulk. Anyone else would have taken the count in the opening round after the first knockdown.

Fans debated the issue of which round the title changed hands, and there was some controversy. The payment of wagers based on the timing of the knockout hinged on the issue.

At the end of the 1$^{st}$ round, timekeeper Barbour ordered the clang when Pecord's arm was falling for the seventh time, though the sound of the gong was so weak, and so great the crowd uproar, that Pecord failed to hear the bell and kept counting over Willard as he sat on the floor near a neutral corner. Pecord counted Willard out and notified Dempsey that he had won.

Dempsey was on his way to the dressing room before his manager overtook him and told him that he was in danger of being disqualified on a technicality for leaving the ring.

The consensus of veteran ring officials and old sports was that Dempsey stopped Willard in the 3rd round, for the towel was thrown into the ring before the bell rang to start the 4th round. However, others claimed the bell for the 4th round rang and that it was over then.

It was the first time that a champion retired on the stool. It also was the shortest heavyweight championship bout in which the title changed hands.

Criticism was directed at the timer, for he did not ring the bell loudly enough. A whistle was provided to him, but this was after the wild 1st round had been fought.

Spectators were in a daze, bewildered by the dramatic and spectacular but one-sided contest. Folks were predicting that Dempsey would hold the title for a long time.

A minority criticized Willard for retiring in his corner. Tom Jones, Willard's former manager, said a real champion would have fought to the end and suffered a clean knockout. "I'm glad a chap like Dempsey is the champion. I'll be honest with you, I didn't think he could beat Jess, because Jess was so big. But he did it all right. I bet on Willard and I lost a lot of money."

Freddie Welsh, former lightweight champ, said he would rather be shot than lose his title that way, on the stool.

Jack Dillon said Willard lost in a cheap, unsatisfactory, ignominious way, on his stool sitting down, the first time in history a champion had lost in such a manner. He said there was something wrong with his heart. "It's not the kind of heart that will stay to the end, even though the first knockout blow on the jaw is inevitable. It's not the kind of a heart that a champion ought to have." Dillon said he knew this would be the result, for when he sparred with Jess, the champ was slow and soft.

In another article, Dillon said he had predicted that Dempsey would win as soon as he uncovered his tremendous left to the jaw.

Dillon said Dempsey was a lion-hearted fighter. "He'll make one of the most popular champions we have ever had. He has fought his way up from the bottom."

Addie Adams called Willard a cheese champ who showed his yellow streak. He too thought Jess should have fought to the finish, until he was down and counted out.

Adams said Dempsey swung heavy artillery; his punches having superhuman power. He drew blood from Willard's mouth until it bubbled, opened a cut under his eye, closed his right eye, and swelled up his face until it was out of shape. Ringsiders began calling for the referee to stop it. At the bell ending the 3rd round, Willard collapsed in his chair and spat out a tooth. Monahan talked to him, and Willard nodded his head. Monahan walked over and spoke to Pecord. The referee pulled Dempsey toward the center of the ring before the new champ finally realized that Willard's seconds had thrown up the sponge. Jack walked toward Jess's corner, and Willard arose, stepped forward, and they shook hands.

*Dayton Daily News*, July 5, 1919

Harvey Woodruff said never before in history had a man absorbed such a concentrated amount of punishment. "Whatever else may be said of Willard, his gameness never can be questioned." He was decked multiple times, and was out at the bell, which few heard. Not one man in twenty thought Willard could survive the 2nd round. He showed great recuperative power and ability to stand punishment.

World lightweight champion Benny Leonard said Dempsey won with a left hook accurately placed and powerfully delivered. Jack never lost his head and was the master of affairs throughout. After hurting Willard, he turned loose with a whirlwind attack.

Until 12 months ago, few had heard of Dempsey. But his rise had been meteoric. He was a real champion. He had all the attributes necessary: youth, speed, stamina, strength, and willingness. He would be champion for some time to come.

Seven times in the 1st round Willard was floored, and the seventh would have been the last had the bell not rung at nine. There was no way he could have risen.

Willard disproved any thoughts that he was not game, for never had a man taken a more awful beating. His right eye was badly cut and he was bleeding from nose and mouth. His cheek bones on both sides were swollen and red.

Dempsey showed excellent ring generalship in the 2nd round, for he did not dash madly at him, but showed some caution, keeping behind his elevated shoulders, raised to protect his jaw. He studied Willard, then took his time without overexerting himself or allowing Jess to land a lucky blow.

He knew it was only a question of time. Jess fired a left that landed, then followed with a right that landed but had no effect. Jack moved about the ring, with Jess following. Willard finally got close enough to whip up a right uppercut. Jack's head rocked backward. It was a solid blow, but Dempsey allowed his head to go with the punch to diminish its force. He did the same when boxing with the Jamaica Kid.

Willard followed with a light tap to the head with his left and hooked him several times with short rights and lefts to the head. The blows were high, Jack kept his jaw well covered, and his crouching position kept his body out of the way as well. Toward the close of the round, Jack drove in several successive rights and lefts to Willard's stomach. Each counted, and evidently hurt.

Regardless, Willard had made a surprisingly good showing and comeback in the round, given that most thought he would be put out early in the 2nd. Yet, his showing was more the result of Dempsey's cautiousness than anything, and fact that Jack was arm-weary from his efforts in the 1st round. He had thrown a lot of hard blows, and that, combined with having to punch up, had taken some effect on his arms, so he was resting a bit in the 2nd. His head movement kept him from being rattled. He showed wise ring generalship in handling matters as he did.

In the 3rd, Dempsey picked up the pace again, moving in quickly. Willard seemed weary, and his arms and legs heavy. His face was cut and swollen. His body had big red blotches. Jack hit him with a sharp right uppercut to the jaw. Jess tried a few inside rights that had no effect, for they had no power. Dempsey countered with three left hooks to the jaw and the champ swayed back and forth like a drunken man. His right eye was almost closed and his left rapidly closing. Dempsey kept working on his body in business-like fashion, with no wasted energy. Jess backed away, tried to protect himself and fight back, but it all was futile. He had no chance of lasting 12 rounds, even though Jack did nothing but walk around him until he hit him with a sharp left hook on the jaw. Jess reeled, but he caught himself on the ropes. Jack fought his way in close and Jess held. Willard tried a couple feeble right uppercuts before the bell, and Jack retaliated with a series of rights and lefts to the body and head.

At the gong, Willard staggered to his corner in a groggy state, and dropped helplessly onto his chair. He was a beaten man. His cornermen, Walter Monahan, Jack Hemple, and Little Ike O'Neill, worked on him for a full minute. When Monaghan asked him whether he wanted or was able to continue, Willard said, "No, I'm licked, throw in the towel." It was the first time that a champ had been beaten so badly that he was unable to respond to the bell and continue.

The *Akron Evening Times* reported that Willard had not been seriously injured, though he had bruises and other marks of the battle which were superficial and would yield to ordinary treatment.

The new world heavyweight champion gave several interviews. Dempsey said, "It was a whole lot easier than I thought. ... I knew I had him right off the reel in the very first round when I cracked him clean and true on the jaw with a left hook. I saw Jess shiver and stagger on his feet and I felt then and there that I was the heavyweight champion of the world."

Jack said Willard's right uppercut not only did not hurt him, it did not trouble him at all. He knew then that he could take Willard's punch, which only increased his confidence in victory. Therefore, he walked right into him, firing blows at his jaw. He felt just as easy and comfortable as when he did the same to Bill Tate. After decking Jess a couple times, Dempsey no longer was afraid of anything that Willard could throw, for he felt his blows weakening. From a crouch, Jack could see a beaten look in his eyes, but Jess would not stop.

Dempsey thought the fight was over after the final knockdown, and left the ring. Kearns called him back. "I didn't hear the bell and I couldn't hear the whistle. But I wasn't a bit flustered. I knew I had Jess and thought it was only a question of a round or two." Thereafter, "I didn't tear into the champion but contented myself by walking in slowly and aiming my blows. I didn't want to take unnecessary chances, and I made every blow count."

He slid left to get to the side of the champion's closed eye. Blood was streaming from Willard's right eye, his nose, and his mouth. Dempsey said he saw Willard spit three teeth onto the canvas. Before the 4th round, Jack Hempel flung the towel into the ring.

Another newspaper quoted Dempsey as saying,

> From the first moment I saw Willard in a gymnasium – that was two years ago – I felt that I could whip him; felt that he was just made for me. ... Willard wasn't an easy man to whip. I hit him harder in that first round than I ever had to hit any other man. But I felt that he could not stand up under long pounding – and he didn't. There's an old saying that they all go if you hit them hard enough. And Willard was no exception.

Dempsey said he wanted to be an active champion, and would take on any man who wanted to try conclusions with him. "It is a case of first come, first served. But no one will be denied a fight."

However, first Dempsey planned to tour the theaters on the vaudeville or burlesque stage, to make easy money and capitalize on his fame as champion, just as others had done, until a worthy opponent emerged for him to defend his crown. There was discussion of an eventual match with Carpentier, when Georges was ready.

Dempsey said the newsmen who accused Willard of being a quitter were wrong. Willard was no quitter, but a brave man, tough to beat, and a fine fellow. "He took a lot of punishment and stood up under it until he couldn't stand any more. He's no quitter." Dempsey said Toledo was a fine town and the people had treated him like a prince.

Dempsey told Benny Leonard,

> I expected a hard battle. I was convinced, before entering the ring, that Willard would make me travel at my fastest clip. I thought he

would sting me with his punches but he didn't. He did not seem to have anything behind them. Of course, that left hook in the first round took away much of the strength that he would have had otherwise. I was almost as much surprised as anyone in the big crowd when I floored Jess so soon after the bout started. I had intended to box him at long range as I told you I would. I did not figure the big opening until later in the bout. I had made up my mind to tire Willard as much as possible during the early rounds of the battle and then crowd him when he showed unmistakable signs of weakening. ...

I am glad I had the bag hung high so that I had to hit up at it. It helped me in reaching Willard's jaw with powerful blows. And Benny, I want to go on record as saying right now that I am going to be a real champion. I will be ready to defend the title against the first man who appears to be a logical contender. I am going to do some theatrical work, but I'll be ready to answer the call to the ring whenever it comes.

Dempsey sent a telegram to his mother, Mrs. Cecilia Dempsey, in Salt Lake City. "Your boy made good. Knocked the big fellow out in three rounds. Willard is a game fellow. I never handed out more punishment to anyone and have him come right back for more, as Willard did today." His mother was happy. "I am overjoyed."

As he rode through the downtown streets, Dempsey received cheers from the multitude that blocked traffic to see the new champ. Many women shouted, "Hello, Jack." He was accompanied by his manager Jack Kearns, his brother John Dempsey, Billy McCarney, and three other sportsmen. He wore a light suit and blue-striped silk shirt. His face was undamaged.

Ray Archer said, "Jess was licked, and we have no excuses to offer. He was game to the core. Those cries of 'yellow' were most unjust. Would you want a blind man to fight? Jess was knocked down, and got up six times. In the third round he couldn't see." Archer said Jess had not fought in three years, and did his best to get into trim, but was past his best. "I don't want to detract any from the new champion. Dempsey is a fighter from the word go."

Former champion Jess Willard gave interviews as well. There were rumors that Jess had suffered a broken jaw, but he sent word to the press that such was a mistake. He made no comment regarding the loss of teeth which Dempsey and others had observed. Willard had his battered head packed in ice bags. The local physician said he was not seriously injured, though he had many bruises that were evident even during the fight, which horrified the many lady spectators.

Frank Menke quoted Willard as saying, "A better man whipped me. It wasn't lack of condition. My system of self-training was all right for a man of my years. If I had trained otherwise I might have been beaten worse. But in defeat I have the knowledge that it took a good man – a mighty good man – to send me down."

Willard said he had no excuses to offer. He had trained well and was in top condition when he entered the ring. "The better man won in a hard, fair fight." Jess had believed that he was invincible, but learned his mistake. He was hurt badly early on, and fought in a daze and could not get his bearings.

> Once in a while I felt my head clearing and instinctively stuck out the long left that had served so well in previous fights. When I saw my opponent slipping easily past that protection and felt him pounding my body I realized for the first time that unless I landed a lucky blow I would surely lose. I did try again and again to land such a punch, putting all of my ebbing strength in right uppercuts, but the luck wasn't with me, and not one of these got home.

The blood from his wounded eye and the closing of his eye affected his vision. "I could see a dancing shape before me but it was impossible to note his movements closely."

Jess admitted that essentially the fight had ended in the 1st round. "I was knocked out before I had fairly started." "After that I was barely in there fighting on my nerve. Ray Archer and Walter Monahan wanted me to quit long before I did. After the third round, when I felt my strength slipping away swiftly and surely I gave my consent to their tossing a towel into the ring." He admitted that Dempsey fought a grand, fearless battle. Jess also said he went to the well once too often, and youth was served. He had dried out since Thursday, and did not eat since the early morning.

In his dressing room, Jess said to Benny Leonard, "Well, Jack's a better man than I am. More power to him. I hope he will go out and make even more money than I have. He's a great fighter." Leonard said that summed it up. "Dempsey is a great fighter, one of the greatest of all time."

Willard had been champion for four years, had earned plenty of money, and had invested well. "And I want to assure you that they'll never have to give a benefit for me."

Willard earned $100,000 and a 1/3 interest in the films. Dempsey received $27,000 and a 1/3 film interest as well, although there were reports that Kearns sold Dempsey's film interests to Rickard for $10,000. Hence, Rickard owned a 2/3 interest in the films.

Willard later said he did not recover from the effects of the first left hook until an hour after he left the ring. "Dempsey is a remarkable hitter. It was the first time I had ever been knocked off my feet." "It was no use to continue. My strength went from me in the 1st round." His head was not clear and his eye was closed. Jess had sent men home in the same condition, and now he knew how they felt.

Willard slept well at his temporary home at 2465 Parkwood avenue.

Some noted that Willard was the first, or one of the first, to admit his defeat by the better man. Usually fighters came up with a bunch of excuses. Willard simply said that he had been beaten by a mighty good man.

Mrs. Willard actually had traveled to see the fight, and sat in a $50 seat. Even the champ did not know she was there. She was sorry he had been beaten, but was glad he no longer was champion, for now they could live in peace and he could become a private citizen again. "This contest was the second boxing match I had ever witnessed, and I do not want to witness any more."

Folks cheered Dempsey at his local hotel for more than 15 minutes, swarming him. Crowds would not leave him in peace even to eat a meal. He received another ovation at the train station before he left town on Saturday.

That same day, on July 4, 1919 in Tulsa, Oklahoma, Harry Greb won a 15-round decision over Bill Brennan. The local *Tulsa Democrat* said although Greb's jumping-jack slapping tactics might gain him the necessary points to win decisions, his hit-and-move style failed to enthuse the spectators, for the most interesting bouts were made when both battlers were doing real hitting. There were few toe-to-toe exchanges. "He is an expert tangoist and uses up much energy without netting results. He poked Brennan continually and poked his thumb in the big fellow's eye, almost putting it out of commission. Head and elbows also were valuable aids to the Greb cause. For a victor he aroused about as little enthusiasm as any visitor ever shown here." The *Tulsa Daily World* said Greb slashed, slapped, chopped, smashed, and slammed his way to victory with his speed. He moved continually and utilized a jumping-jack attack to outbox Brennan.

Also that day, in St. Louis, Harry Wills won an 8-round newspaper decision over Sam Langford. The *St. Louis Post-Dispatch* said, "He shoved straight lefts and rights into Langford's face and also showed a good left hook. However, he did not seem to own a knockout punch." Although Wills landed many solid blows, utilizing his height and reach well, Langford shook his head and laughed at him. However, a left hook to the stomach in the 3rd round decked Langford. Yet he came up strong and fought back gamely to the end.

Georges Carpentier was matched against Joe Beckett, the British Empire titleholder, for the European title. A London promoter was offering a $125,000 purse to Dempsey for a bout with the winner, with the winner to receive 60% and the loser 40%. A Paris promoter matched that offer.[730]

The reported gate receipts for Dempsey-Willard were over $500,000, somewhere between $500,000 and $600,000.

The next day, it was said that Willard was okay, except for the swelling on the right side of his face, which was subsiding under cold applications. Jess said, "After that first hard swing to the jaw in the first round, Dempsey came in so fast that I never had a chance to clear my head and square away for a better offense or defense. I was fighting in a daze." He said Dempsey was a fast, clever, hard-hitting man. Willard insisted that he was all right and not dead or dying like some reported.

---

[730] *Toledo Blade, Toledo News-Bee, Toledo Times, Akron Evening Times, Dayton Daily News, Dayton Herald, Cincinnati Enquirer, Sandusky Star-Journal, Coshocton Tribune, East Liverpool Review, New York Evening World, San Francisco Examiner, Buffalo Enquirer, Buffalo Evening News, Buffalo Courier,* I.N.S., *Oregon Daily Journal, St. Louis Post-Dispatch, St. Louis Star, Tulsa Democrat, Tulsa Daily World,* all July 5, 1919; *Buffalo Courier,* July 5, 6, 1919; *Buffalo Times, Detroit Free Press,* July 6, 1919; *Cincinnati Enquirer,* July 9, 1919.

Many were eager to see the fight films to settle the controversy over the number of knockdowns. The referee said there were six, Dempsey said he decked him seven times (he was correct). Experts at ringside varied from five to seven knockdowns.

Some said that Willard was 56 pounds heavier than Dempsey. It was alleged that Dempsey weighed 187 pounds, while Willard weighed 243 at ring time. No one knew for certain because there was no official weigh-in.

Dempsey left Saturday for Cincinnati, where he allegedly would earn $7,000 per week in a theatrical engagement. Jack said,

> I am going to try and be a popular champion. I believe the public wants a champion who will defend his title frequently and I intend to be that kind of a champion. I believe, however, that I am entitled to take a rest and make some money out of the title doing theatrical work. I want to lay off boxing for six or eight months to do this. But I will fight just as soon as a man considered a contender is found.

Champs Who May Tackle Jack Dempsey

George Carpentier, taken while in the French aviation service, and Joe Beckett, English fighter.

Jack planned to travel around, spar 3 rounds with Bill Tate, and give a monologue explaining how he won the championship fight.

Dempsey said he had won twice. "Pecord...held up my hands [not true], saying I had won, and then pushed me back to my corner. Naturally I thought then the fight was over and I started to leave the ring, when the time keeper called me back, and we had to clear the ring of the mob of fans intent upon expressing their congratulations."

At the end of the 3rd round, Willard was groggy, reeled to his corner, and fell upon the ropes. Jack knew then that the championship was his. "He took an awful beating and certainly proved his gameness. When I shook his hand after the fight I said to him: 'Well, Jess, it's all over. I am sorry I had to cut you up so much.'"[731]

Referee Ollie Pecord's official ruling was that the technical knockout came after the close of the 3rd round. All bets would be paid based on this ruling. Some disagreed, saying the towel was not tossed into the ring from Willard's corner until the bell had sounded for the 4th round. Others said

---

[731] *Toledo Times, Sandusky Register, Cincinnati Enquirer, Coshocton Tribune,* July 6, 1919.

the towel was tossed in before the 4th round began. Rickard had requested an official ruling owing to hundreds of telegrammed requests asking if Dempsey should be credited with a victory at the end of the 3rd or at the start of the 4th. Hence, official records should list this contest as a TKO3.[732]

*Cincinnati Enquirer*, July 5, 1919

The films could be shown legally anywhere in Ohio, but nowhere else, owing to the federal law prohibiting the interstate transportation of fight films, a law passed during Jack Johnson's reign.

The films were developed and copied immediately, and exhibitions began on Sunday July 6 throughout Ohio.

There was talk of perhaps being able to show the pictures across state lines, because the fight was legal, and not a prizefight but an exhibition, for the participants were paid performers, not paid based on success. Efforts were being made to obtain permission to show the moving picture films to soldiers overseas. However, the Department of Justice said the federal law would be enforced, and it would not allow evasion of the law by the use of airplanes either.[733]

The Ohio Board of Censors eventually ruled that the fight was so brutal that women and children would be barred from seeing the films.

Dr. Starling Scott said Willard was not a quitter, but was a battered mass of bleeding flesh. He was beaten into utter helplessness, and his face a gory sight from an avalanche of blows rained upon him from all angles. Courage and instinct alone kept him going for as long as he did. Blood flowed from cuts and bruises. The sounds of sickening thuds could be heard from all over. The agony and pain were evident on his face. It was pathetic, yet satisfying to most of the crowd.

William Rocap had called Willard a quitter, but such was unjust and a slap at human intelligence. He was very game, bleeding and blind from terrific punches. He was nauseous, and his knees sagging. It was inhuman and brutal to expect him to go any further, given the record amount of concentrated punishment he had endured. Willard was done after the 1st round, and never could have beaten the count, except for the fact that he was saved by the bell.

Everyone in Dempsey's corner thought he had won, and Jack made his way through the press seats only to be called back by frenzied shouts. No one thought Willard could survive the 2nd round, but he did. He took a world of punishment in the 2nd, though not as much as in the 1st. Blood

---

[732] *Cincinnati Enquirer, Akron Beacon Journal*, July 7, 1919.
[733] *New York Herald*, July 6, 1919.

gushed from his mouth as if from a fountain. In the 3rd round, Dempsey shot in lefts and rights to the body and jaw, and Willard's defense was futile. There were several clinches, and Jess still tried to land a lucky punch. He shook Dempsey a little with a right uppercut, but Jack just came right back hooking away. At the gong, Jess was a pitiable spectacle. His face resembled a raw steak smeared with blood which ran down his breast. His right eye was closed completely, his face cut in two long strips, and a lump as large as an egg adorned his cheek bone.

It was revolting, yet, as he left, several hissed and called him quitter. One man even struck him. Willard wheeled and struck him with a back-hand punch in the face which sent that man sprawling.

It was for the good of the sport that he retired, for if he had continued and suffered even more, or perhaps been killed, it would have set the sport back and provided ammunition to those who called for its abolishment.

Harry Bullion of the *Detroit Free Press* said Willard's fatal error had been carrying the fighting to Dempsey and applying pressure upon the sturdy mauler, playing right into his hands, much to everyone's surprise. He should have utilized his usual cautious, outside, waiting policy and tried to tire out Dempsey. The new champion could not be outfought.[734]

Tex Rickard claimed that his profits would not exceed $100,000. "Poor Tex!" He said the failure of railroads to furnish special trains, and the bad impression caused by newspaper stories of crowded hotels and high prices discouraged many from coming. Rickard also said the fact that there were 20,000 men on strike in Toledo affected attendance. He was not likely to promote another contest there. It cost him $150,000 to construct the arena. Government taxes were $12,000, City taxes $42,000 ($54,000 total), plus the $127,0000 in purses for Dempsey and Willard, for a total of $373,000, plus numerous other incidental expenses. Still, despite all of the expenses, Rickard had earned a tremendous amount of money, and the fight had generated more revenue than any other prior boxing contest.

Rickard estimated the receipts at $565,000. Even after all expenses were deducted, Rickard and co-promoter Frank B. Flournoy still would earn at least $100,000 in profit, which was fantastic money.

In another interview, Rickard claimed only 19,650 paid to see the fight, and the total receipts, after $41,789.94 was deducted in taxes, were $410,732.16. The 7% charity fund for the city of Toledo was slightly under $30,000. Such numbers were far different than post-fight press reports, all of which claimed around 40,000 or 50,000 were in attendance.

A later report said only 20,000 to 21,000 were present, and the gate actually was $452,000. Government revenue agents were checking on the receipts/numbers so they could see how much was due in taxes. Mayor Schreiber said the city taxes would be used for orphans and the poor. Some wondered whether the total numbers were being deflated and reported as lower so the promoters could avoid paying full taxes. All of the $60 seats

---

[734] *Lancaster Daily Eagle*, July 7, 1919; *Detroit Free Press*, July 6, 1919.

were sold, and virtually all of the $50 seats, but the cheapest seats, which sold for $10, had disappointing sales, at only about 5,000.

There were 292 policemen in the stadium, 73 firemen, 600 ushers, 90 ticket takers, 20 ticket sellers, and 454 press representatives. Total expenses, including arena construction, purses, and taxes, were $307,500. Other miscellaneous charges would bring the expenses to about $325,000. The total proceeds after taxes had been deducted totaled $410,732.16. That would leave the promoters with a profit of less than $100,000, but still a very handsome payday and financial success by any standards.

The massive arena was sold to Chicago's American House Wrecking Co. for $25,000. Nearly two million feet of lumber had been used for one event.

NEW CHAMPION RIDES IN A HOLMES TOURING CAR

N. E. Brown said Dempsey not only had to be given credit for beating a giant, but for putting the heavyweight division back on track. His exciting, powerful, aggressive style, and the fact that he was white, would make him a popular champion. "Johnson was not of the white race and therefore could not be taken into the hearts of the fans. He was called a disgrace to his own race by the respectable colored people. What little popularity Willard claimed early in his reign as champion was due principally to the fact that he had brought the title back to the white race." But Willard was reluctant to fight, and his style was cautious too, like Johnson's. The writers also seemed to like Dempsey's personality as well.

One said Dempsey had proved the saying, "The bigger they are the harder they fall."[735]

Years later, in his 1940 autobiography, Dempsey alleged that he and Kearns had gathered up $10,000 and wagered it all on a 1st round knockout at 10-1 odds. Hence, both were upset when informed that Willard had been saved by the bell. They thought they had won big money. In his autobiography, Kearns made the same claim. However, there was no primary source support or discussion of such a wager in the newspapers prior to the fight, and Dempsey had told Benny Leonard that he had intended to box cautiously for a while. Dempsey did not exactly start off the

---

[735] *East Liverpool Review, Fremont Messenger*, July 8, 1919; *Salt Lake Tribune*, July 6, 1919; *Akron Beacon Journal, Buffalo Times*, July 9, 1919; *Cincinnati Enquirer, Dayton Daily News*, July 10, 1919.

fight as if he was trying to score a quick knockout. He had boxed fairly cautiously for the first minute of the fight. The first knockdown did not occur until the round was half-way over. Yet, Dempsey had been quoted by one newspaper as intending to win in record time, perhaps the first minute of the fight. Before the fight, Kearns had said that he and Dempsey wagered about $16,000 on Dempsey *to win*, although perhaps some of that money was on a 1st round knockout. A month after the fight, Kearns claimed to have wagered $2,000 against $20,000 on a 1st round knockout.[736]

Kearns said Dempsey weighed only 187 pounds for the fight. He said they did not want Willard to know that Jack was so small. However, most reported that he was around 195 pounds. His trainer said he would fight at about that weight. Dempsey himself claimed to be around 192-195 in various interviews. Kearns said the number was inflated. No announcement of the weights was made at ringside. No one knew for sure.

Jack Skelly said he honestly believed Dempsey was the hardest hitter ever, including John L. Sullivan.[737]

Regarding the hero worship he already was encountering, Dempsey said, "That's a part of the fight game, and I will get used to it. It's fine stuff and I must expect it. I don't mind people staring at me; though when they get rough and yank me by the arm I don't like that so very much."

Discussing the fight the next day, Dempsey said, "Some folks thought I was tiring in that second round. I was simply taking it easy. I didn't want to use myself up. You know, when you swing with all your might, as I was doing, it's bound to tire you, and I knew I was winning and played it safe." Pacing oneself was part of intelligent fighting. After it was over, he went to Jess and said, 'Well Jess, it's all over. I am sorry, but of course a fight is a fight." Willard just mumbled in response. Jack said the great heat did not bother him, for he had been training in it. He did not step on the scales before the fight, but thought he weighed about 192 pounds.[738]

William Rocap claimed the fight was fixed, but Tex Rickard vehemently denied the charges and asked for an investigation and an apology, or for him to prove his ridiculous charges.

One of the questions raised was whether Dempsey would defend his title against a black man. A *New York Times* headline stated, "Jack Dempsey, New Heavyweight Champion, Announces He Will Draw The Color Line." The column's title was "Dempsey Will Meet Only White Boxers." Jack said he would pay no attention to negro challengers, but would defend against any white man. "His statement that he has drawn the color line means that Jack will pay no attention to any challenges which might come from Harry Wills, who is just now the king-pin of the black heavyweights."

---

[736] *Round by Round* at 177. In *Dempsey* at 114, Jack claimed that Kearns told him about the bet just before the fight. *Lansing State Journal*, August 13, 1919. Kearns questioned whether the bell issues at the start of the fight caused the round to be shorter than it should have been. Perhaps the wager, if it existed, explained Dempsey's eagerness to exit the ring quickly, to "sell" that the fight was over, hoping others would acquiesce if there were doubts. This is speculation.
[737] *New York Times, San Francisco Chronicle, Salt Lake Herald-Republican*, July 6, 1919.
[738] *San Francisco Chronicle*, July 6, 1919.

Dempsey had not fought a black man since his contest with John Lester Johnson, whom Wills had beaten several times. Wills was coming off another victory over Sam Langford.

The *San Francisco Chronicle's* Harry Smith also reported, "One thing stands out, Dempsey draws the color line."

The *Salt Lake Herald-Republican* asked, "Will the league of nations permit Jack Dempsey to draw the color line?"

An Atlantic City promoter offered Dempsey a $30,000 guarantee to meet Willie Meehan 8 rounds on Labor Day. Meehan had agreed to the match. However, Kearns knew that Dempsey was worth a whole lot more than that now that he was the world champion, and they were engaging in a lucrative theatrical tour first.[739]

The *Oakland Tribune* asked who was best qualified for Dempsey to fight. "Jack has drawn the color line so there is no chance of Harry Wills becoming champion. Wills looms up as the most dangerous opponent now before the public, but there isn't a chance of the title going back to the colored people." Meehan might be able to outpoint him over 4 rounds, but he might be killed if he fought Dempsey over the long route. Billy Miske had beaten Meehan soundly recently in a 10-round contest, almost stopping him in the final two rounds.

Dempsey said he was willing to fight Carpentier whenever he was ready and wanted to do it. That appeared to be the biggest money fight.

Kearns was disappointed that Miske had lost close to Battling Levinsky. He was hoping to stage a Dempsey–Miske title bout. "We have had a tentative offer for a match with Harry Greb. I don't think Greb would have any chance with Jack, but if any promoter wants to gamble on such a proposition he can have the fight." The middleweight-sized Greb was coming off a decision victory over Bill Brennan.

Kearns said Dempsey likely would not fight again for at least seven or eight months, for he was going to make a lot of easy money in vaudeville.

Dempsey again defended Willard from attacks on his honor, character, and fighting spirit. In various interviews, he said, "He certainly was game. People that are calling him a quitter don't know what they're talking about. If he was a quitter do you suppose he would have got up so often in that first round, or would he have come out for the second round, or the third?" "Willard took the hardest beating of any man I have ever met. He's game all the way through and don't let them tell you different." "He took a lot of punishment and stood up under it until he couldn't stand any longer. He's no quitter."[740]

The *Akron Evening Times* said the fight films showed seven knockdowns, all of which took place in the 1st round. There were no knockdowns in the remaining two rounds, but Willard probably would have been floored if the

---

[739] *New York Times, San Francisco Chronicle, Salt Lake Herald-Republican,* July 6, 1919.
[740] *Oakland Tribune,* July 6, 1919.

ropes had not supported him. The first blow that decked Willard was a short right to the heart followed by a left hook to the chin.[741]

In subsequent days, Willard said the ring never knew a man who could hit like Dempsey. No one could beat him, or even had a chance to do so. Only age would topple him. "I want to say there isn't a man back as far as John L. Sullivan who hit as hard as Dempsey does now. And Jack hits with equal force in either hand." Jess said he had fought in a daze, on automatic instinct. He was glad his corner stopped the fight (with his consent), "for I might have been killed by the punches of that young and strong bull. I gave the best I had and certainly took the best Jack had."[742]

Rickard announced that Dempsey was paid $27,500 in cash, while Willard got $80,000 in Liberty bonds and the remaining $20,000 in cash.

One of the first things Dempsey did as new champion was to settle up with his former manager/financial backer/benefactor A. J. Auerbach, who allegedly discovered Dempsey and advanced/loaned him money several years ago. On Saturday, the day after the fight, Dempsey paid him $6,126.20, the original $5,340.50 debt plus interest, plus all of Auerbach's expenses for the two-week vacation he took to come out and see his former protégé win the championship. Auerbach said, "Jack Dempsey is a real man and shoots straight."

When Dempsey was matched to fight for the championship, he told Auerbach that he wanted him to come to the fight as his guest, would pay all of his expenses, and pay the debt he owed, which he did. Auerbach had held a manager's contract with him, which would not have expired until 1921, though he had released Dempsey from the contract.

Auerbach told this story:

> Jack Dempsey has a married sister by the name of Ethel Clark and who has been employed by me as a saleslady in my Salt Lake City dry goods store for four years and a half.
>
> I had noticed a rugged appearing boy who came into the store often to visit Mrs. Clark and finally I asked her who the lad was. When she told me that the boy was her younger brother and said that he had boxed a number of times at lodge entertainments I became interested and asked her to introduce me to him when he next came into the store.
>
> When we were introduced I asked Dempsey – Harry Dempsey, he called himself then – if he liked the boxing game and he was all enthusiasm. "I love it," he declared with emphasis. "Have you got any money?" I asked him and he admitted he did not have a dollar. Then I handed him $25 and told him to invest it in new clothes to improve his appearance, which he did.

---

[741] *Akron Evening Times*, July 8, 1919.
[742] *Buffalo Courier*, July 10, 1919.

We went to a gymnasium often and I put on the gloves with him and found that he was a natural fighter. I have always been a lover of boxing and immediately began making arrangements for him, not to gain any money for myself, as I did not need it, but because I knew I had a real fighter and wanted to see him succeed.

Jack was a sensation from the start. He beat Terry Kellar twice, and Kellar was considered a good man in those days. He also beat Dick Gilbert and a number of good men and I knew that my confidence in him was justified.

Remember, he was still a minor and I made no contract with him to act as his manager, accepting nothing of the money he earned, but on the contrary loaning him money.

On August 22, 1916, shortly after Dempsey became 21, we entered into a contract whereby I was to act as his manager for five years, or until August 22, 1921. I was to arrange all his matches, handle his affairs and in return receive 25 per cent of the winnings. I have a copy of that contract with me today.

Things went along well until February 13, 1917 when Dempsey was knocked out by Jim Flynn in the first round of their contest at Salt Lake City.

Dempsey was just a boy then and that sudden possession of a considerable amount of money naturally went to his head. Some of his actions did not please me and I called him into my office and had a heart-to-heart talk with him, the result of the talk being that Jack and myself parted company.

Auerbach told Dempsey if he ever needed help, he could call on him. He still liked him, even though "he did make mistakes," and A. J. never lost interest in him. Jack came upon hard times, and Auerbach frequently made him loans. Jack owed him $5,340.50 total.

Eventually Dempsey earned an international reputation, and before the Willard fight, he came into his store in Salt Lake and said, "Mr. Auerbach, I owe a lot of things to you and I've come to tell you that I'm ready to make good. My match with Willard will earn for me more than enough to pay you the money I owe you with interest and that is what I am going to do, but is not all." He didn't know where the fight would be held, but "wherever it is, I want you to come to that place a couple of weeks in advance of the fight and be my guest until it is over and you are ready to return home. I will pay your railroad fare, your hotel bills, and all your expenses and am anxious that you accept. It will make me feel a whole lot better if you do."

Auerbach accepted. He had come to Toledo two weeks ago. The day after the fight, Dempsey handed him $6,126.20, the original debt, plus interest, and the money Auerbach spent in expenses for his Toledo trip and hotel. Auerbach exhibited a copy of the 1916 contract he had. "I'm going to keep that contract as a souvenir, but I will never press any claims against

Dempsey. He proved himself a real man and one who shoots square. He is one of the greatest fighters the ring has ever known and I only hope that he amasses a great fortune, which he is almost sure to do." Auerbach had won a small fortune by betting on Dempsey to win the big fight.[743]

Mrs. Celia Dempsey sent Jack a telegram. "Dear boy. Mother is very proud of you and wishes you plenty of luck. Keep yourself clean physically, boy. Mother."[744]

George Pulford said Dempsey would spar with Bill Tate during his theatrical tour. A series of one-night stands throughout the country could earn about $120,000 for him in total, very good money for a 24-year-old, or someone of any age. He was too valuable an attraction at present to bother with title defending, as much as he liked to fight. Doc Kearns wanted them to earn, and Dempsey did as he was told. His future was in Kearns' hands, for Dempsey had implicit faith in him. Kearns had been a clever pilot.

Dempsey was pursued by women throughout his time in Toledo, and now that he was champion, he would be more attractive than ever to some women.

Despite immediate post-fight reports that the attendance was 45,000 to 50,000, those numbers had dropped severely. Six days after the fight, Dick Meade reported that although the arena could seat 97,488, the total attendance actually was only 19,552. Rickard and Flournoy paid $41,789.94 in war taxes, and $28,751.24 to the Toledo Commission for its 7% tax, although the promoters already had given the locals an advance payment of $30,000. The excess would be refunded. After those expenses, $410,732 remained. When the remaining expenses were deducted, the promoters would come out about even, or a little bit ahead. The $15 seats were the most popular. 3,000 were in the $60 division. The $10 seats had only 4,400. 206 women sat in the women's section.

Answering why the crowd was so small, some speculated that the canceling of many special trains by the government was a severe blow. Fear that accommodations were scant, the city overcrowded, and tickets scarce or in the hands of speculators who marked them up kept thousands away. Many had the erroneous idea that the bleachers were so far away from the ring that the participants only could be seen with the aid of field glasses. The bulk of the attendance did not come from locals, but those who traveled there. The locals did not turn out in sufficient force. Many were afraid of the intense heat. Others could not afford the ticket prices. Flournoy said it cost $125,000 just to erect the stadium.[745]

The *Toledo Times* said the attendance was 19,650, and the receipts, minus the war tax, were $410,732.16. Normally that was a massive, record amount, but in this instance not great given all of the expenses, which to date were

---

[743] *Toledo Times*, July 6, 1919; *New York Times*, July 7, 1919.
[744] *Toledo Times*, July 6, 1919.
[745] *Toledo News-Bee*, July 10, 1919.

$397,000, but there were additional miscellaneous expenses. It cost $1,700 just to have tickets printed.[746]

So, within a week, the claims went from the promoters would earn $100,000 to it was a break-even or only slightly profitable venture, even after the money generated from the sale of the arena and the fight films was considered. Such did not factor in what the ticket speculators paid. If they paid for seats, but had not sold them, an empty seat did not mean the promoters had not received money for the seat. On the films, the arena appeared to be pretty packed, far more than half full. Someone's numbers seem to be off.

N. E. Brown said the average fan liked Jack the Giant Killer because he fit their perception of what a heavyweight champion should be – a domineering, tearing-in fighter with a hard punch. An exciting new era had begun.[747]

Back in Long Branch, Jimmy De Forest said, "Jack is a remarkable fighter, to say the least; in fact I rate him as the best heavyweight of all times. Never before have we had a heavyweight champion who could box like he, and yet, at the same time deliver a punch which would floor an ox." De Forest said Dempsey listened to his advice and followed his instructions better than any other boxer he ever had trained. Jimmy had told anyone who would listen that Dempsey would beat Willard, so the result was no surprise to him.

De Forest said it was distasteful for anyone to call Willard a quitter, for he took a frightful beating and lost many teeth at different times.[748]

A couple days after the fight, Jack Doyle, a New York sporting man, wondered whether Dempsey had any plaster of paris concealed in his bandages. "It is possible for plaster of paris in powder form to be sprinkled within bandages. It has been done and when they are examined in merely a superficial manner, it is impossible to detect the substance. Powdered plaster of paris gets as solid as a piece of lead when it becomes moistened." He speculated, because although he acknowledged that Dempsey clearly had hitting power, "it hardly seems possible any man can hit so hard with a gloved fist as to cut Willard up in such shape as Dempsey did."[749]

Jess Willard did not agree with Jimmy De Forest, who allegedly said that Dempsey's hands were bandaged only with cotton. He used tape as well. Regardless, before the contest, Willard had shaken hands with Dempsey's wrapped hands, and shook his gloved hand, and his seconds had examined Dempsey's wraps and observed his gloves being put on inside the ring, and they lodged no objections. Both the rules and their agreement allowed for a reasonable amount of tape and bandages.[750]

---

[746] *Toledo Times*, July 10, 1919.
[747] *Toledo Times*, July 7, 1919.
[748] *Long Branch Daily Record*, July 14, 1919. Owing to other obligations, De Forest was not able to join Dempsey on his exhibition tour.
[749] *Washington Post*, July 7, 1919.
[750] *Boston Post*, July 10, 1919.

In a July 1923 interview with De Forest, who was not Dempsey's trainer at that point, when asked whether Dempsey's hands were taped differently in the Willard bout, De Forest replied, "That story is the bunk. Those accusations by the Willard crowd are false."

De Forest further said, "Champions are born, not made." "In my opinion, Champion Jack Dempsey is the greatest individual fighter this world ever saw. None of the old timers equal him." "I want to say this for Dempsey, he's very teachable and always ready to learn; probably the most apt pupil I ever handled."[751]

In November 1923, regarding the taped hands, De Forest said,

> Right here is where I have a statement to make to the public once and for all. The punching power that Dempsey had developed over all his previous battles proved so amazing to many persons when he mowed big Willard down, the crack and the kick of his blows were so forceful that after the fight many of those who had lost heavily on Willard turned detractors of Dempsey and myself. They spread stories which got wide circulation to the effect that I had 'doped' the tape on Dempsey's hands.
>
> Some of them had it that I had used plaster of paris between the gauze strips which hardened after Dempsey got his hands into the gloves. Others suspected "tea lead." This is the paper-thin lead that comes inside tea boxes and has figured in the use of bandages by unscrupulous managers, trainers, and fighters.
>
> I have never played the game that way, and for me to have done so in Dempsey's case would have been sheer idiocy. For what Dempsey most needed to beat Willard was speed. And to have weighted his hands would have defeated its own purposes. It would have made Dempsey's hands too heavy for fast use and would have slowed him up to the ponderous Willard's own gait. ... [A]ll I put on them when he went into the ring was seven wraps of soft gauze and two wraps of adhesive tape. That's everything that was in Jack's gloves, besides his hands, the day he made a quitter of big Willard.[752]

Over 40 years later, in a January 20, 1964 *Sports Illustrated* article published after Kearns' death, quoting Kearns' upcoming biography, *The Million Dollar Gate*, an estranged Kearns claimed to have loaded Dempsey's wraps with plaster of Paris, sprinkling it onto the wraps he had moistened with water, purportedly wetting them to keep Dempsey's hands cool, and then claiming to sprinkle talcum powder on his hands which really was plaster of Paris. He claimed to have done it right in front of Willard's second, Walter Monahan, who lodged no objections.

The facts surrounding the bout do not support such claims, particularly since Willard shook Dempsey's wrapped hands before the fight, and likely

---

[751] *Nashville Banner*, July 20, 1923; *Pittsburgh Daily Post*, July 22, 1923.
[752] *Philadelphia Inquirer*, November 3, 1923.

would have noticed something hard or wet. Plus, the gloves were put on under observation and examination of the opposing seconds in the ring. Furthermore, in May 1964, *Boxing Illustrated* did an experiment by duplicating step-by-step everything Kearns claimed he did, and all it did was produce a very brittle thin film that quickly and easily cracked and crumbled, and would have had zero effect.

Dempsey sued *Sports Illustrated* for defamation, it apologized, stating it did not believe Kearns, and ultimately, that part of Kearns' story never made it into the final published version of the book. No one who was there ever backed Kearns' claim - no trainer, writer, or other observer.

A July 3, 1979 *Los Angeles Times* article claimed one man believed that Dempsey held a metal bolt in his left hand and then dropped it to the canvas after the 1st round, which explained why he had less power in subsequent rounds. The claim is ridiculous, for such a bolt would have been noticed by someone at the time, or on the films. Such also would have risked immediate disqualification, which the very confident Dempsey did not need to do.

After having shot everything he had in the 1st round, a fatigued Dempsey slowed his attack just a bit in the 2nd and 3rd rounds to pace himself, but when he threw, he threw hard to the body and head, often in combination. Dempsey crouched, bobbed, weaved, and rolled his head defensively to make Willard miss or be unable to time him on the way in. Dempsey also exhibited a good ability to avoid being held for too long. Willard, who had been administered smelling salts and possibly given more time than usual to recover, took it a bit better, but still was taking a beating as Dempsey methodically pounded on him, breaking him down, and nearly decked him again, but for the ropes holding him up. Willard mostly held, though he also punched back and gamely tried, even nailing Dempsey with some good shots. It was the most brutal heavyweight championship bout anyone ever had seen since fights were filmed.

The reality is that Jack Dempsey was a very big puncher, with all-time great power. Dempsey was known as a knockout artist, having scored many 1st round knockouts. He simply did to Willard what he had been doing to a lot of fighters, including big men. Jess Willard had not fought in three years, and during the time that he was relatively inactive, young Jack Dempsey was garnering a great deal of experience, boxing all the time in real fights, not just exhibitions, and improving. From that perspective, even though Jess Willard was a big, tall, long, strong, tough champion, neither Jack Dempsey's victory nor the manner in which he accomplished it can be much of a surprise. It was no anomaly, but rather consistent with what he had been doing recently, and what many predicted he would do. Still, throughout boxing history, fans and fighters often have attempted to come up with excuses for losses, sometimes to garner momentum for a rematch. Some simply could not understand how a much smaller man could have done what Jack Dempsey did to the huge Jess Willard.

The story continues: *In the Ring With Jack Dempsey - Part II.*

Jess Willard ———— VANQUISHED and VICTOR ———— Jack Dempsey

Dempsey lands first heavy body blow after exchanging lefts and rights to the head with Willard in the first few seconds of fighting. It jarred the champion and weakened his defense.

The first clinch; it followed a fierce injury into which Dempsey forced Willard after landing that first left to the body; Willard got the worst of the infighting.

Willard recovering from the first knockdown of his career. It was after a few seconds of sparring after the first break, when Dempsey landed on Jess' chin.

Willard down for the third time; he's getting more familiar with the floor and doesn't appear as surprised as when recovering from the first tumble.

Willard down again; he's getting to feel at home on the mat; his interest in the battle appears to be waning, but he's trying to beat the count.

The sixth and last knockdown. Dempsey walking away from Willard under the impression the big Kansan is out; he failed to hear the bell and started to leave the ring.

Dempsey with Freddie Welsh, Jr., son of the former lightweight champion

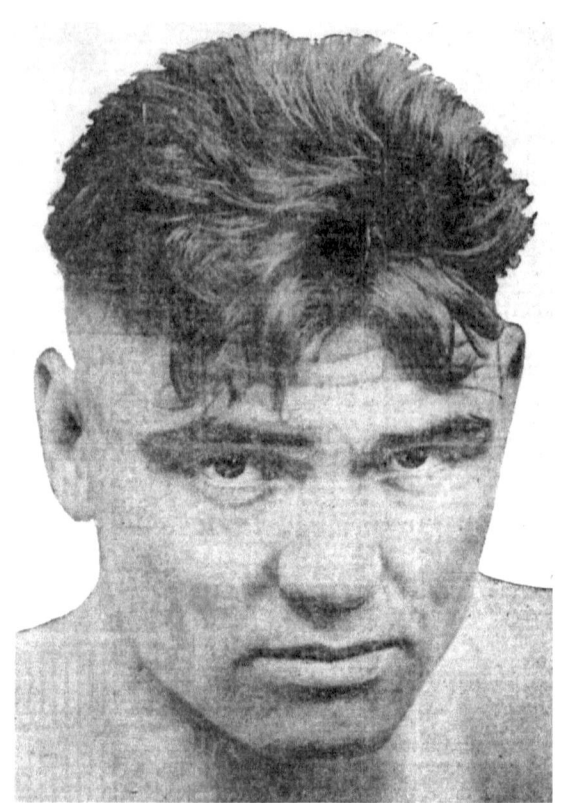

# Acknowledgments

Thank you to all who have helped me in some way with this book, whether it be donations, research, photographs, promotion, or miscellaneous other support of this book:

Evan Grant
Bob Yalen
Mike DeLisa
Clay Moyle
Gregory Speciale
Audrey Felderman
Kevin Smith
Jeremy Willett
Marilee Vannoy
Bruce Allen
Carlos Acevedo
Matt McGrain
Tom Seemuth
Thomas Hauser
Carlye Morgan
Patricia Baird, University of Iowa Interlibrary Loan
Amy Paulus, University of Iowa Interlibrary Loan
Susan Malecki, University of Iowa Interlibrary Loan
Lori Romero, White Pine County Library, Ely, NV
Lori Williams, White Pine County Library
Jaime Brunson, White Pine County Library
Raema Robertson, White Pine County Library
Michael Maher, Nevada Historical Society
Sheryln L. Hayes-Zorn, Nevada Historical Society
Nancy McInerney, Durango Public Library
Joy Jackson, Salida Regional Library
Lindsay Beckman, Montrose Regional Library
Trent Clegg, Reference Specialist, Marshall Public Library, Pocatello, ID
Michael McDonald, Franklin Ferguson Memorial Library, Cripple Creek, CO
Michelle Rozell, Franklin Ferguson Memorial Library, Cripple Creek, CO
Anne Marie Martin, Boise Public Library
Jessica Turner, Davis County Records Division
Minnesota Historical Society
Boxrec.com
Eastsideboxing.com
Trufanboxing.com
Cyberboxingzone.com

# Index

14th Amendment, 163
Adams, Addie, 528
Adams, Dick, 111, 143
Allen, Bill, 13
Allen, Fred, 440
Anderson, Andre, 63-66, 70, 71, 89, 97, 101, 108, 153, 167, 180, 181, 184, 189, 193, 195, 202, 204, 251, 259, 315, 369, 370, 423
Anderson, Lee, 373, 375
Andrews, Tom, 275, 401
Archer, Ray O., 392, 443, 516, 520, 522, 524, 531, 532
Armstrong, Bob, 67, 72
Arnold, Emory, 28, 29
Auerbach, A. J., 74-76, 86, 94, 98, 285, 541, 542
Baldwin, Matty, 14, 314
Barbour, W. Warren, 443, 477, 480-482, 496, 521-523, 527, 529
Barrieau, Frank, 44
Barry, Dave, 92
Barry, Jim, 92, 138, 146, 238, 255, 292, 320
Bartfield, Soldier, 189, 422
Barton, George, 210, 214, 226, 230, 234, 424, 475
Battling Rector, 106
Baur, George, 38
Beckett, Joe, 534
Becky, Battling, 373
Bell, Colin, 55, 147, 249, 255, 256, 320
Benefit, 3, 291
Benson, George, 106
Benz, 17
Biddle, Anthony J. Drexel, 443, 479, 480, 515
Birch, Billy, 166, 180
Blackie, Kid, 7, 11, 12, 15, 16, 18, 38
Bogan, Freddie, 106, 113
Bonds, Joe, 51, 52, 80, 99, 101, 124, 140, 153, 180, 207, 211, 249, 262, 263, 265, 270, 286, 328-331, 379
Boston Bearcat, 47, 48, 399
Bostwick, Mary, 378
Brady, William, 517
Bramer, Harry, 244
Brennan, Bill, 63, 80, 161, 165, 166, 177, 180, 183, 184, 189, 195, 202, 211, 251, 253, 260, 320, 389, 402, 439, 533, 540
Britt, Jimmy, 211, 272, 304, 307
Britton, Jack, 321, 329, 345
Bronson, Jimmy, 196, 197, 250, 252, 414, 447, 448, 473, 522
Bronson, Ray, 414, 447, 448, 473, 522
Brown, Betty, 478, 518
Brown, N. E., 421, 424, 427, 438, 451, 474, 537, 543
Brown, Warren W., 133, 135, 137, 143, 144, 150, 152, 154, 156, 158, 160
Buckley, Jim, 147, 148, 149

Bullion, Harry, 516, 536
Burke, Martin, 347, 361, 373, 375
Burke, Sailor, 255
Burns, Frankie, 27, 113
Burns, Tommy, 20, 24, 92, 236, 238, 326
Caine, Empty, 211, 212, 216, 225, 228, 229
Caldwell, Herbert, 194
Callahan, Frankie, 43
Cameron, Lucille, 15
Cameron, Rufe, 20, 108, 139, 314, 379, 386
Campbell, Emmanuel, 26, 27, 28
Cannon, Ray, 315, 316
Capley, Al, 422
Caponi, Tony, 307, 320
Carolan, James, 341
Carpentier, Georges, 55, 136, 147, 281, 283, 353, 360, 363, 372, 410, 412, 515, 530, 534, 540
Carter, Mexican Kid, 106, 108
Cates, Maxine, 62, 74, 81, 90, 97-99, 118- 121, 124, 125, 145, 200, 365
Caucasian, 122, 255
Chambers, Tom, 44, 53, 79, 80
Chip, George, 82, 83, 189, 262, 418, 423
Chip, Joe, 418, 421, 423, 445
Choynski, Joe, 280
Christian, George, 48, 49, 108, 315
Chrysler, Charlie, 464
Church of Jesus Christ of Latter-day Saints, 6
Civil War, 318
Clansman, 25
Clarke, Jeff, 20, 46, 88, 177, 189, 214, 312, 314, 315, 320, 341, 369, 541
Cobb, Irvin S., 10, 382, 519
Cobb, Ty, 10, 382
Coburn, Fred, 213, 216, 225
Cochrane, Ed W., 198, 253
Coffey, Jim, 50, 55, 90, 92, 146, 147, 153, 180, 238, 251, 260, 286, 288, 320, 328, 351, 375, 379, 389
Coffroth, James, 140, 164, 244, 263, 291, 296, 328, 330, 332
Cohan, George M., 272
Cohen, Cyril, 48
Collier, Laverne (a.k.a. Geronimo), 15, 20
Collins, Mike, 213, 245, 262, 274, 278
Color line, 4, 21, 24, 25, 88, 129, 137, 156, 161, 255, 260, 286, 313, 315, 319, 327, 328, 329, 330-333, 345, 346, 362, 370, 371, 376, 412, 539, 540
Colored, 3, 25, 26, 49, 67-70, 74, 97, 105, 155, 243, 250, 264, 315, 327-332, 339, 341, 346, 373, 377, 378, 385, 386, 395, 412, 448, 480, 481, 537, 540
Congress, 14, 327
Conrew, Young Hector, 61, 74-77, 79, 82, 87, 99
Considine, George, 275

Coplen, George, 37, 38, 39, 41
Corbett, James J., 137, 141, 142, 167, 285, 287, 321, 325, 346, 368, 377, 515, 519
Cordosh, George, 13, 14
Corey, Herbert, 421, 424, 431, 447, 453, 519
Cotton, Kid, 67, 214, 312, 386
Cowler, Tom, 89, 147, 165, 180, 183, 191-193, 195, 196, 200, 207, 212, 213, 249, 252, 255, 256, 259, 263, 266, 270, 292, 315, 320, 389, 394, 423
Cox, Joe, 99, 146, 147, 180, 238, 383
Cross Counter, 71, 261, 346, 371
Crow, Red, 15, 53, 54, 131
Curley, Jack, 91, 120, 170, 175, 177, 260, 262, 272, 273, 281, 360, 367, 447, 475
Cutler, Marty, 63, 195
Daab, Hyatt, 328, 333
Daily, Dan, 90, 372, 375, 376, 379, 380, 381, 383, 388
Daniels, Fred, 7
Darcy, Les, 51, 200, 265
Davis, George, 92, 180, 251, 375, 383, 387, 388, 389
Davis, Henry, 163
Day, Eddie, 194, 214, 234, 241
De Forest, Jimmy, 259-261, 274, 275, 314, 318, 340, 360, 385, 388, 397, 403, 406, 407, 418-422, 437, 441, 443, 446, 448, 451, 452, 463, 465, 467, 475, 479, 481, 497, 543-545
Delany, J. J., 181, 183, 184, 185, 186, 187, 189, 190
Democrat, 8, 25, 35, 87, 166, 167, 237, 246, 533, 534
Dempsey, Andrew, 5
Dempsey, Bernie, 6-13, 35, 39
Dempsey, Bruce, 125
Dempsey, Celia, 5-9, 45, 464, 470, 531, 542
Dempsey, Elsie, 6-8, 12, 45, 48
Dempsey, Florence, 6
Dempsey, Harry, 7, 10, 11, 12, 13, 15, 17, 86, 541
Dempsey, Hiram/Hyrum, 6, 125
Dempsey, John, 6, 7, 9-11, 136, 412, 531
Dempsey, Stella, 6
Devere, Bob, 63, 82, 89, 121, 147, 153, 178, 180, 251-255, 259, 266, 286, 288, 320, 389, 423
Diehl, Charley, 17
Dillon, Jack, 61, 63, 72, 82-84, 89, 92, 99, 101, 147, 176, 189, 207, 208, 211, 212, 249, 251, 255, 256, 261, 267, 282, 292, 307, 320, 412, 413, 422, 423, 475, 527
Discrimination, 315, 330
Dixon, George, 332
Dixon, Jr., Thomas, 25
Dorgan, Tad, 283, 348, 436, 467, 479, 482, 525
Dougherty, James, 321, 323
Downey, Bryan, 312
Downey, Jack, 19-23, 26, 27, 28, 35, 41-43, 45, 46, 76, 83, 84, 86, 93, 113, 237
Downing, Hardy K., 18-20, 22, 41-43, 46, 63, 77, 79, 82, 85, 86, 98, 288
Doyle, Willie, 385

Drake, Tony, 370
Dreamland Rink, 122, 135, 137, 157, 158
Dunn, Johnny, 93
Dunning, Billy, 255
Edge, Governor Walter, 272
Edgren, Robert, 178, 240, 260, 270, 276, 281, 359, 399, 402-404, 412, 415, 423, 424, 434, 446, 450, 453, 462, 465, 475, 481, 512, 522
Everett, Mexican Pete, 146
Farrell, Marty, 126, 140, 141, 144, 148, 156
Ferguson, Sandy, 165, 255, 320
Film, 9, 50, 460, 552
Fink, Lewis, 108, 383, 389
Finnegan, Jack, 279
Fisher, Liz, 89, 202, 316
Fitzsimmons, Bob, 67, 80, 137, 154, 192, 233, 241, 265, 283, 305, 307, 326, 336, 347, 359, 453, 469
Flanagan, Tom, 176, 446, 447
Floto, Otto, 65, 198, 206, 211, 214, 216-226, 233-235, 239, 240, 241, 243, 245, 247, 475
Flournoy, Frank B., 382, 460, 511, 537, 543
Fluhry, Barney, 184
Flynn, Dan Porky, 55, 65, 89, 90, 147, 193, 249, 252, 255, 256, 259, 320, 330, 334, 336, 337, 423
Flynn, Fireman Jim, 14, 35, 46, 55, 65, 75, 76, 89-100, 118-121, 125, 139, 144-147, 149, 153, 164, 167, 177-180, 183, 193, 195, 200, 202-204, 209, 215, 238, 247, 249, 251, 252, 254, 255, 256-259, 283, 286, 320, 330, 334-337, 341, 343, 349, 366, 389, 408, 423, 445, 474, 542
Flynn, Leo P., 177, 182, 184, 286
Foley, Harry, 122
Fulton, Fred, 55, 63, 65, 92, 113, 128, 129, 131, 134, 137, 153, 154, 156, 157, 161, 162, 164-167, 169, 173, 175-178, 180, 181, 183, 186-192, 195-214, 226-228, 232, 233, 235, 237, 238, 241, 245-252, 254-257, 259-262, 264-267, 270-282, 284-286, 296, 307, 316, 319, 320, 334, 337, 339, 343, 346, 347, 349-351, 356, 358, 364, 367, 381, 394, 419, 420, 432, 439, 446, 461, 470, 474, 514, 515
Gans, Joe, 27, 80, 166, 174, 332, 395
Gardini, 373, 380
Gardner, George, 92
Garrick theatre, 17, 18, 19, 20, 22
George, C. W., 59
George, Kid, 154, 156
Geyer, Jack, 20, 82, 138, 146, 307, 320, 378-381, 389, 479
Gibbons, Mike, 140, 189, 207, 261, 423, 474
Gibbons, Tommy, 189, 207, 211, 212, 262, 285, 320, 326, 423
Gibson, Billy, 63, 462
Gilbert, Dick, 55, 62, 75, 82, 84-86, 89, 146, 147, 207, 251, 320, 379, 423, 541
Gill, Jack, 13, 28
Gillian, Jack "Two-round", 42, 43
Goldberg, R. L., 511
Goldman, Lou, 196, 202
Gollop, Louis, 216, 226, 231, 232
Goodfriend, Jake, 28

555

Graney, Eddie, 136, 164, 296, 298, 300-307, 309, 310
Greb, Harry, 142, 183, 189, 207, 211, 262, 284, 286, 288, 292, 320, 338, 370, 389, 402, 423, 533, 540
Greggains, Alex/Alec, 122, 158, 161
Griffith, D. W., 25, 50
Grim, Joe, 320
Grimson, Lew, 334, 335
Gulder, Jim, 438
Hall, Frank G., 522
Hall, Sam P., 178, 179
Hamill, James, 240
Hamilton, H. C., 200, 202, 214, 239, 275, 277, 462, 477, 520
Hancock, Young, 18
Hanlon, Eddie, 143
Harris, Big, 377
Harris, Kid, 28, 361, 363, 381
Harris, Morris, 255
Harrison, Jim, 381
Harrison, Kid, 28, 361, 381
Hart, Marvin, 122, 153
Harting, George, 43, 296, 309
Hatfields, 5
Hawthorne, Fred, 263, 275, 276, 280
Heinen, Jack, 415, 416, 418-421, 424-426, 432
Hemple, Jack, 147, 385, 387, 388, 393, 399, 401, 402, 404, 407, 409, 412, 416, 418-420, 424, 434, 436, 440, 443, 445, 449, 451, 465, 480, 523, 529, 530
Hennessey, Joe, 93
Henning, Al, 214
Henry, Kid, 361, 363, 381
Herman, Pete, 422
Hickey, Henry, 362
Hill, C., 21
Hinkle, Matt, 466
Hogan, Kid, 361, 362
Holcomb, Governor Marcus, 249
Hosking, E. R., 212, 216, 226, 229, 230
Howard, C. W., 407, 409, 410, 411
Humphries, Joe, 265
Hyland, Dick, 14, 202
Irish, Kid, 76
Irwin, Toby, 137, 138, 149, 150, 151, 159, 160
Jackson, Peter, 332
Jackson, Young Peter, 17, 21, 43, 49, 93, 94, 127, 146, 292
Jamaica Kid, 262, 265, 339, 341, 395, 397, 403, 406-409, 415, 424, 425, 427, 430, 432, 435, 437, 438, 441, 445, 447-449, 451, 452, 479, 528
Jeannette, Joe, 24, 25, 48, 50, 51, 59, 67, 87, 161, 167, 177, 238, 255, 256, 263, 266, 312, 314, 315, 319, 328-333, 337, 345, 346, 359, 386
Jeffries, James J., 3, 10, 26, 67, 153, 166, 174, 203, 239, 255, 279, 280, 285, 287, 326, 336, 346, 359, 364, 393, 399, 422, 444, 465, 466, 469, 515, 517
Jemison, Dick, 257, 258
Jim Crow, 53, 54, 131

Johnson, Battling Jim, 15, 25, 37, 44, 88, 238, 255, 256, 263, 264, 265, 266, 284, 312, 314, 315, 318, 326
Johnson, Big Swede, 44, 45, 80, 86
Johnson, Clarence, 10
Johnson, Eddie, 43, 44, 59, 61
Johnson, Jack, 10, 14, 15, 17, 18, 21, 23, 24, 25, 50, 51, 68, 88, 91, 92, 101, 102, 108, 117, 122, 130, 133, 146, 148, 195, 214, 238, 243, 255, 263, 266, 271, 281, 285, 313, 315, 319, 329, 331, 346, 366, 367, 368, 377, 379, 383, 384, 387, 401, 402, 404, 412, 413, 427, 432, 433, 436, 439, 440, 446, 447, 466, 470, 474, 535
Johnson, John Lester, 66-71, 74, 88, 94, 97, 101, 164, 202, 204, 255, 256, 312, 316, 328, 346, 370-374, 376-381, 386, 409, 415, 448, 539
Johnson, Young Jack, 101, 102, 108, 133, 148, 214
Jones, Tom, 179, 393, 431, 474, 516, 527
Joy, Al, 297, 298, 299, 300, 301
Kain, R. H., 319
Kammerling, Em, 135
Kane, Ed, 326
Kanner, Jack, 240
Kaplan, Max, 385
Kaufman, Al, 92, 138, 238
Kearns, Jack, 19, 53, 113, 124-128, 131, 134, 136-141, 143-145, 148, 149, 151, 152, 154, 156, 157, 160-167, 169, 170, 178, 180, 182, 183, 193-195, 200, 202, 203, 209, 210, 213, 215, 237, 239-242, 244-250, 252, 254, 256, 258, 261-264, 274, 275, 277, 278, 281, 283, 284, 286, 287, 289, 291, 293, 295, 296, 301-305, 307, 308, 310, 311, 315-317, 328-330, 332, 333, 346, 350, 351, 354, 359, 361, 362, 367, 368, 370, 372, 373, 375-377, 379, 380, 383-389, 392, 394, 400, 404, 406, 409-411, 415, 418, 419, 425, 440, 442, 443, 446, 451, 452, 460, 461, 465, 479, 480, 481, 496, 497, 515, 518, 520, 523, 530-532, 538, 539, 540, 542, 544, 545
Keller, Terry, 54-61, 65, 79-84, 99, 101, 165, 180, 189, 192, 207, 249, 251, 256, 259, 285, 286, 288-291, 294, 303, 320, 365-367, 369, 385, 387-389, 392, 395, 397, 419, 423, 425, 475, 541
Kelly, John, 448, 474
Kelly, John M., 416, 431, 440, 442, 445, 450, 521
Kelly, Spider, 102, 135, 149, 156, 158, 164, 211, 215, 244, 301, 368
Kelly, Walter C., 399, 427, 462
Kennedy, George, 422
Kenny, Burt, 65, 66, 68, 70, 94, 101, 108, 140, 204, 207, 211, 245, 315, 320
Ketchel, Bill, 412
Ketchel, Stanley, 60, 67, 137, 175, 189, 190, 196, 211, 255, 260, 261, 280, 344, 474
Ketchell, Dan, 60, 74, 237, 307
Kid George, 154, 156
Kid Irish, 76

Kid Norfolk, 147, 161, 177, 207, 211, 212, 214, 238, 250, 254-256, 263, 286, 314, 315, 319, 329, 331, 332, 337, 350, 358, 362, 386, 395, 402, 408
Kiofowsky, 381
Kirkham, Burdette, 182, 186
Kruvosky, K.O., 127, 148, 248, 292, 302, 307, 338
Ku Klux Klan, 25, 50
Lajoie, Nap, 10
Lang, Bill, 238
Langford, Sam, 19, 24, 25, 35, 37, 39, 43, 44, 46-48, 51, 54, 59, 67, 87, 91, 92, 129, 146, 147, 165, 169, 177, 183, 189, 193, 198, 204, 214, 236, 243, 251, 253, 255, 256, 259, 260, 263, 266, 271, 281, 285, 312, 314, 315, 319, 331, 341, 349, 359, 364, 366, 386, 394, 417, 423, 425, 432, 435, 436, 474, 534, 539
Lardner, Ring, 462, 480, 514
Larue, Bill, 291
Lavan, Jack, 395, 398, 399, 400
Lavigne, Jack, 395
Law, 8, 14, 25, 36, 63, 163, 168, 200, 203, 204, 207, 260, 265, 272, 273, 274, 282, 376, 382, 443, 466, 469, 535, 536
Legality, 11, 12, 122, 185, 204, 322, 411, 447, 467, 469, 473, 475, 535
Leonard, Benny, 137, 345, 433, 436, 447, 462, 463, 468, 528, 531, 532, 538
Lester, Jack, 207, 249, 251, 423
Levinsky, Battling, 55, 60, 65, 82, 83, 89, 90, 92, 97, 140, 146, 147, 153, 176, 180, 189, 207, 208, 211, 249, 251, 255, 256, 260, 282, 285-287, 307, 312, 314, 316, 318-326, 331, 334, 336, 339, 341, 343, 351, 358, 379, 389, 402, 423, 427, 453, 462-464, 466, 468, 470, 540
Levy, Sam, 187
Lewis, Pinky, 156, 293
Lianuza, Pete, 436
Lichtenstein, Larney, 61, 440
Lincoln, President Abraham, 214, 379, 381
Litchenstein, Larney, 193, 194
Locklear, Ormer L., 478
Lyons, Ed, 20, 194
Madden, Billy, 65, 180, 258, 260, 262, 320, 338
Maher, Peter, 278, 552
Malloy, Andy, 8, 18, 21, 35, 36, 37, 92
Malone, Jack/Jock, 430, 435, 437, 438, 441, 445, 446, 448, 449, 452, 478, 479
Mantell, Frankie, 65, 289
Markham, Dale, 14
Markley, Allan, 190, 272
Marriage, 15, 81, 118, 444
Martin, Denver Ed, 146
Masterson, Bat, 8, 25, 462, 463, 468
Maxwell, Robert, 324, 336
McAdams, Verl, 13
McAllister, Bob, 99, 100, 108, 138, 140, 141-149, 152, 155, 249, 262, 320
McAuliffe, Jack, 447, 453, 462, 470, 521
McCarney, Billy, 215, 384, 393, 394, 531

McCarthy, Tom, 51, 249, 250, 252, 254, 256, 320
McCarty, Luther, 89, 92, 140, 147, 153, 158, 195, 238, 241, 383, 384, 393, 414, 423, 439
McCoy, Kid, 189, 211
McCoys, 5
McGeehan, W. O., 525
McGoorty, Eddie, 51, 183, 184, 211, 320
McGovern, Terry, 265, 278, 474
McGuire, Jack, 360, 367, 381
McKetrick, Dan, 331, 332, 345
McLaglen, Victor, 138
McLinn, Jack, 362
McMahon, Tom, 55, 77, 80, 82, 83, 90, 99, 139, 140, 145-147, 176, 178, 180, 193, 195, 255, 256, 259, 266, 285, 320, 338, 350, 368, 379, 383, 389, 399, 423
McVey, Sam, 24, 25, 35, 47, 51, 59, 87, 180, 238, 243, 251, 253, 255, 260, 263, 266, 312, 314, 319, 346, 371
Meade, Dick, 384, 386, 392, 395, 399, 403, 406, 416, 443, 470, 479, 482, 517, 543
Meehan, Willie, 20, 48, 63, 65, 99, 101, 102, 105-114, 117, 118, 120, 121, 123, 124, 126-128, 131-141, 152, 156, 165, 189, 248, 291-312, 315, 334, 338, 339, 346, 349, 350, 351, 364-366, 368, 369, 401, 402, 413, 423, 432, 539, 540
Menke, Frank, 176, 414, 415, 451, 467, 512, 513, 532
Merrill, Slick, 28
Meyer, Leon, 161, 295, 297, 298, 299, 300, 303, 304
Meyer, Reverend F. B., 295, 304
Miller, Charley, 20, 92, 99, 108, 137, 138, 139, 140, 145, 146, 151, 155, 164, 251, 312, 379, 383, 385, 387, 393, 396
Miller, Colonel J. C., 197, 198
Miller, Herman, 367, 373, 375
Miller, Hiram, 377
Mills, Dave, 67, 138, 214
Miscegenation, 131
Miske, Billy, 55, 82, 83, 89, 153, 161, 167, 176, 177, 180, 183, 189, 190, 193, 197, 207-237, 240, 242, 244, 245, 248, 251, 254, 255, 257-260, 262, 267, 271, 282, 285, 286, 288, 292, 315, 320, 337-347, 349-351, 359, 368, 370, 394, 401, 402, 408, 423, 427, 439, 445, 447, 453, 462, 464, 466, 470, 540
Mitchell, Jack, 202
Mixed-race, 25, 66, 68, 69, 70, 314, 315, 332
Moir, Gunner, 256
Monahan, Walter, 20, 146, 177, 358, 399, 400, 401, 407-409, 412, 419, 420, 421, 423, 424, 434, 436, 440, 443, 445, 450, 451, 461, 480, 497, 514, 515, 517, 523, 529, 532, 544
Moore, Billy, 214
Moore, Larry, 210, 216, 226, 230
Moore, Pal, 422
Moore, Roy, 26, 28
Moran, Frank, 17, 50, 89, 90, 137, 139, 140, 146, 147, 148, 153, 176, 181, 183, 188, 189, 193, 238, 259, 266, 271, 349, 376, 379, 383, 423, 443, 447, 467, 474, 521

Moran, Jack, 99, 147, 237, 259, 293, 304, 307, 308, 320, 379, 423
Morgan, Dan, 323, 324, 330, 331, 345, 351
Morris, Carl, 76, 90, 92, 99, 128, 134, 137, 146, 147, 152-154, 156, 158, 161-164, 166, 167, 170, 177, 193, 203, 207, 211, 212, 238, 241, 251, 255, 256, 259, 282, 320, 345-348, 376, 379, 383, 393, 396
Morris, Jackie, 265
Morris, Rex, 74, 113
Muldoon, William, 447, 452, 463
Mulvihill, J. P., 245, 247, 462, 475, 479
Murphy, Bill, 19, 21
Murphy, Eddie, 297, 298, 299, 300, 305
Murphy, Jack, 104, 111, 143
National Sporting Club, 520
Negro, 21, 24, 28, 46, 47, 48, 66, 69, 122, 130, 147, 177, 312, 314, 328, 329, 332, 333, 346, 372, 373, 379, 387, 412, 448, 539
Nelson, Battling, 14, 27, 80, 453, 462, 463, 468
Newman, Louis, 12
Norfolk, Kid, 147, 161, 177, 207, 211, 212, 214, 238, 250, 254, 255, 256, 263, 286, 314, 315, 319, 329, 331, 332, 337, 350, 358, 362, 386, 395, 402, 408
North, 48, 53, 129, 282, 372, 380
North, Jack, 380
Norton, Al, 51, 83, 89, 90, 92, 99-109, 111, 113-118, 120, 125, 127, 131-134, 139, 140, 153, 154, 156, 288, 307, 423
Nugent, Dick, 175, 355
Nuthall, Grif, 10
O'Brien, Jack, 321, 324, 344, 474
O'Neil, Ike, 461, 480, 521, 529
O'Rourke, Tex, 427, 447
O'Rourke, Tom, 474
Oishi, 373, 380
Palzer, Al, 63, 139, 238, 259, 376, 381
Papke, Billy, 283
Pearson, Ray, 178, 179, 234, 312
Pecord, Ollie, 434, 436, 443, 444, 447, 475, 477, 480-482, 484, 489, 495-498, 501, 502, 504-506, 508, 510-513, 515-518, 520, 521, 523, 524, 527-529, 535
Peiter, Ruth A., 478, 481
Pelkey, Arthur, 48, 65, 90, 146, 147, 151, 153, 177, 192, 237, 238, 239, 241, 242, 244, 245-247, 249, 254, 259, 263, 279, 307, 315, 383, 393, 395, 436, 439
Peppers, Harry, 8, 35
Pickford, Mary, 296
Pierson, Dave, 20
Pitts, Tommy, 9
Plessy, Homer, 163
Police, 12, 13, 53, 59, 124, 130, 156, 194, 195, 242, 273, 277, 282, 329, 349, 381
Pollock, Abe, 213
Pollock, John, 281
Prejudice, 25, 54, 129, 130, 210, 315, 332, 346
Price, Jack, 62, 63, 66, 69, 70, 71, 74, 86
Pulford, George R., 418, 427, 431, 442, 516, 542

Purner, Fred, 159, 297, 298, 299, 300, 301, 311
Race, 4, 10, 15, 18, 24, 25, 54, 66, 68, 69, 70, 71, 117, 122, 129, 130, 131, 243, 255, 256, 282, 313, 314, 315, 319, 332, 359, 371, 401, 410, 412, 461, 537
Race Riot, 129, 130, 282
Ray, Johnny, 361
Red Cross, 205, 235, 237, 240, 242, 244, 247, 248, 272, 365
Reddy, Jack, 197, 210, 215, 230
Reed, Henry E., 53
Reich, Al, 65, 92, 99, 147, 183, 189, 238, 259, 288, 289, 320
Reisler, John, 70, 71, 72, 73, 74, 89, 90, 92, 97, 118, 164, 194, 195, 202-204, 206, 209, 210, 215, 234-237, 239, 247, 248, 250, 252, 284, 288, 315-317, 350, 365, 411, 424
Republican, 21-23, 41-43, 45, 46, 48, 50, 55, 57-62, 74, 76, 77, 79, 82, 83, 84, 85, 86, 246, 250, 316, 326, 349, 365, 367, 383, 538, 539
Rice, 275, 277, 280, 329, 332, 453, 465, 513, 514
Rice, Grantland, 453, 465, 513
Richter, Thomas D., 326, 327, 335, 336, 343
Rickard, Tex, 10, 27, 50, 205, 363, 364, 374, 382, 383, 385, 405, 411, 421, 423, 426, 433, 434, 443, 446, 463, 468, 469, 480, 515, 532, 535, 537, 538, 540, 543
Riley, Tom, 195, 196, 197, 202, 254
Ritchie, John, 212, 216, 225, 226
Roak, Red, 292
Rocap, William, 369, 370, 435, 438, 448, 449, 451, 474, 521, 536, 538
Roche, Billy, 94, 426, 443
Rodel, George, 63, 92, 147, 180, 249, 256, 376, 383, 389
Rojas, Heriberto, 251
Roosevelt, President Franklin, 14
Ross, Jack, 406
Ross, Tony, 55, 92, 139, 146, 147, 153, 180, 320, 376
Rothstein, Arnold, 475
Rowlands, Len, 141, 148, 189
Ruhlin, Gus, 283
Runyon, Damon, 7, 44, 70, 71, 89, 97, 98, 112, 275, 277, 376, 463, 469, 479, 482, 526
Ryan, Tommy, 39, 446, 447, 448, 467, 474
Salazar, Marion T., 117, 118, 121, 124, 134, 138, 140, 144, 145, 151, 152, 155, 156, 158, 161, 162, 297, 299, 300, 304
Satty, Bull, 193, 194, 195, 196
Savage, Jim, 147, 249, 423
Schreck, Mike, 82, 83, 153, 165
Schreiber, Belle, 15, 460, 537
Scott, Bill, 425, 434, 445
Segregation, 54, 73
Sennett, Mack, 454, 455
Shand, Bob, 101, 102, 109, 114, 126, 127, 131, 132, 133, 139-141, 144, 147, 148, 150, 151, 160, 294, 297-300, 305, 309, 311
Shannon, Billy, 140, 148, 292, 295
Sharkey, Tom, 67, 211, 348

Shipbuilding, 317, 369
Simpson, Tommy, 102, 106, 109, 114, 126, 127, 132, 138, 139, 143
Sims Act, 14
Sims, Thetus, 14, 15
Slavery, 54, 73
Smith, Ed W., 166, 198, 215, 216, 226, 232
Smith, Eddie, 365
Smith, Gunboat, 63, 64, 67, 68, 70, 71, 75, 82-84, 89-92, 138-140, 142, 145-147, 149, 151-154, 157, 160, 161, 164, 167, 173, 176, 177, 183, 193, 207, 212, 213, 238, 241, 249, 251, 255, 256, 259, 262, 266, 307, 310, 314, 315, 320, 338, 350, 351, 353, 362, 368, 379, 383, 386, 393, 396, 423, 467, 475
Smith, Harry, 164, 297, 298, 299, 300, 302, 539
Smith, Homer, 108, 165, 166, 176, 180, 182, 203, 254, 288
Smith, Jack, 193, 194, 254
Smith, Matt, 38,39
Snailham, Billy, 135, 136
South, 25, 28, 53, 54, 93, 125, 129, 164, 183, 193, 194, 199, 341, 365, 382
Spanish flu, 314, 318, 326, 327
Spink, Al, 169, 195, 198, 204, 439
Squires, Bill, 92
Stanton, Ely, 395, 404, 407, 409
Stevens, Ashton, 524
Stewart, Jim, 63, 146, 147, 314, 388
Sudenberg, Johnny, 21, 27, 28, 29, 30, 31, 32, 33, 45, 262, 415
Sullivan, Jack, 65, 92, 147, 255, 256, 320, 388, 389
Sullivan, Joe, 400, 401
Sullivan, John L., 4, 6, 7, 167, 168, 177, 181, 190, 196, 279, 281, 287, 305, 337, 359, 361, 362, 411, 521, 525, 538, 540
Sullivan, Mickey, 377
Sullivan, Spike, 373, 376
Supreme Court of the United States, 163, 350
Taft, President William Howard, 10, 14
Tate, Bill, 67, 88, 92, 146, 147, 263, 312, 315, 370, 385-389, 392, 394, 395, 397, 403, 406, 409, 412, 417, 423-425, 427, 430-432, 435-438, 441, 442, 446, 448, 449, 452, 461, 463, 479, 530, 535, 542
Taussig, Moose, 101, 127, 136, 148, 292
Taylor, Sec, 380
*The Birth of a Nation*, 25, 50
*The Challenge of Chance*, 430
Thompson, Jack, 285, 313, 314, 339, 341, 370, 386, 395
Tillman, Senator Ben, 113
Tranter, Edward, 173, 204, 250, 313, 349, 497, 524
Treanor, Vincent, 329, 335, 337
Treaty of Versailles, 448

Turner, Clay, 140, 262-266, 270, 274, 284, 287, 315, 320, 350, 358, 361, 362, 395, 402
Union, 8, 15, 205, 238, 280, 281, 286, 287, 329, 330, 358
Vardaman, Governor James K., 113
Veiock, Jack, 209, 242
Walcott, Joe, 46
Walters, Alex, 69
Walton, Lester, 315
Ware, Rough House, 214, 215
Weinert, Charlie, 63, 89, 90, 147, 183, 189, 193, 207, 211, 212, 249, 256, 259, 266, 320, 350, 423
Weinstein, Neecy, 480
Welch, Jack, 136, 162, 164
Wells, Billy, 50, 146, 147, 255, 360
White, Charlie, 307, 446
Wilk, Fred, 377
Willard, Hattie Evans, 444, 459, 533
Willard, Jess, 23-25, 50-52, 55, 65, 69, 88-91, 99, 108, 113, 129, 134, 139-141, 146, 147, 149, 151-157, 160-169, 173-178, 180, 181, 183, 187, 189, 190, 192, 193, 195-200, 202-212, 214, 233-235, 237, 238, 241, 242, 247, 249, 250, 259-261, 265, 266, 270-272, 278-282, 284, 285, 288, 290, 291, 293, 295, 296, 302, 303, 310-312, 315, 319, 320, 324-329, 331, 337, 340, 346, 349, 350, 355, 356, 358-360, 362-369, 371-377, 379-390, 392-395, 398-402, 404, 407-427, 430-453, 459-470, 473-475, 479-490, 492, 494-506, 508-538, 540, 542-545
Williams, Al, 202, 379
Williams, Larry, 108, 180, 207, 251
Wills, Harry, 19, 24, 39, 43-45, 48, 54, 67, 87, 88, 99, 108, 113, 129, 139, 161, 177, 180, 204, 214, 236, 243, 255, 260, 263, 264, 266, 295, 302, 304, 312, 314, 315, 319, 327, 328, 331, 345, 346, 359, 371, 386, 394, 409, 425, 431, 435, 534, 539, 540
Wilson, President Woodrow, 25, 73, 113, 130, 327, 365
Wilson, Scotty, 202
Winsor, Fred, 74, 76, 91, 93, 95, 99, 102, 105, 111, 113, 114, 116, 118, 120-122, 124, 126, 162
Witwer, H. C., 478, 479, 518
Wixson, Cliff, 134, 140, 141, 148, 154, 292
Woodman, Joe, 88, 256, 257
Woodruff, Harvey, 528
Woods, Fred, 9, 34
World War I, 4, 5, 17, 113, 318
Wray, John E., 253, 255
Yellow streak, 319, 332, 528
York, Bob, 60, 61, 62, 75, 77, 91, 423
Young Denny, 347
Young, Bull, 363, 383, 525

Adam J. Pollack is a boxing referee and judge, attorney, author, publisher, and member of the Boxing Writers Association of America.

To learn about more boxing books by Adam J. Pollack and others published by Win By KO Publications, go to winbykopublications.com.

www.ingramcontent.com/pod-product-compliance
Lightning Source LLC
Chambersburg PA
CBHW030321020526
44117CB00030B/241